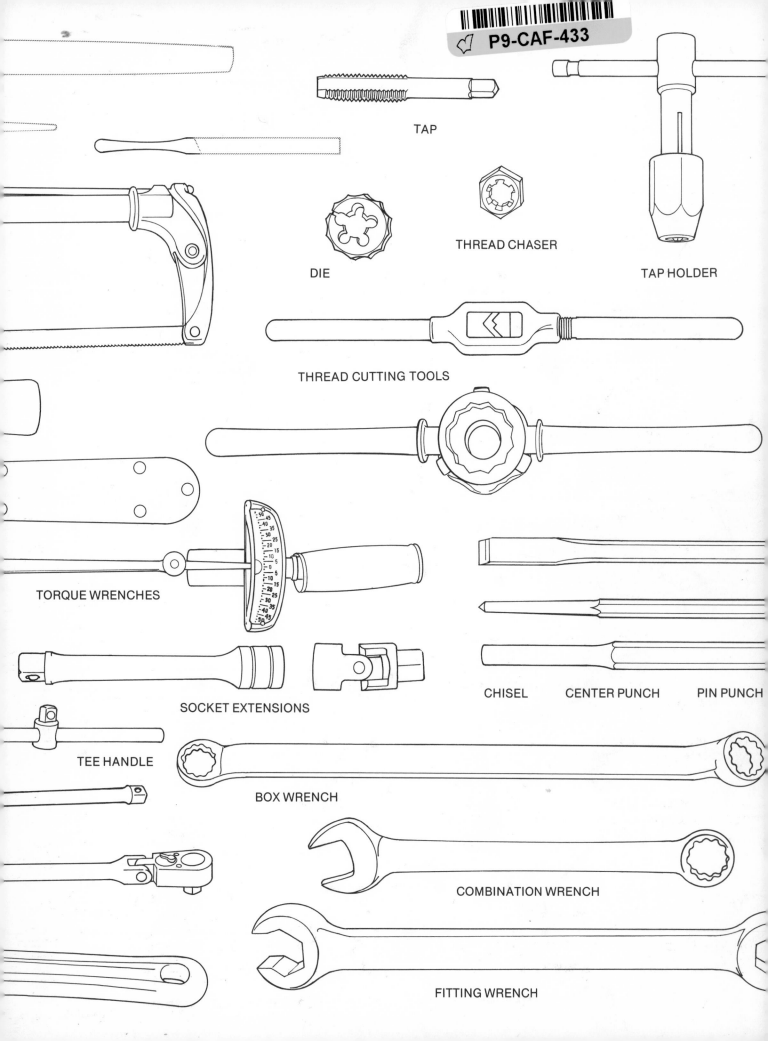

TAP

THREAD CHASER

TAP HOLDER

DIE

THREAD CUTTING TOOLS

TORQUE WRENCHES

CHISEL   CENTER PUNCH   PIN PUNCH

SOCKET EXTENSIONS

TEE HANDLE

BOX WRENCH

COMBINATION WRENCH

FITTING WRENCH

automechanics

SECOND EDITION auto

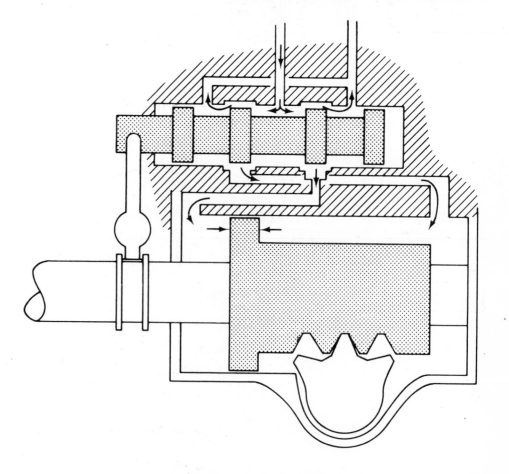

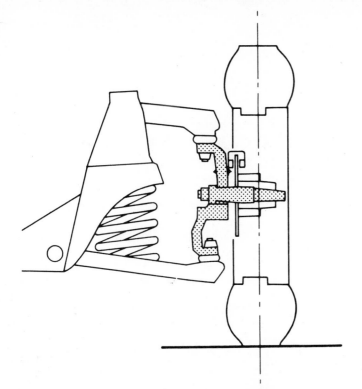

mechanics

HERBERT E. ELLINGER

Associate Professor
Transportation Technology Department
Western Michigan University

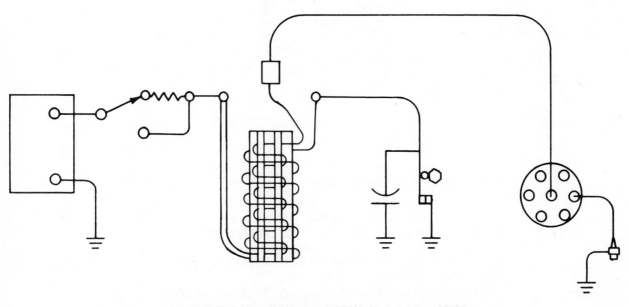

Prentice-Hall, Inc., Englewood Cliffs, New Jersey 07632

Library of Congress Cataloging in Publication Data

ELLINGER, HERBERT E
    Automechanics.

    Includes index.
    1. Automobiles—Maintenance and repair. I. Title.
TL152.E398 1977   629.28 '7 '2   76-18687
ISBN 0-13-055145-7

automechanics
second edition

Herbert E. Ellinger

© 1977 by Prentice-Hall, Inc.
Englewood Cliffs, New Jersey   07632

10 9 8 7 6 5 4 3

Printed in the United States of America

PRENTICE-HALL INTERNATIONAL, INC., *London*
PRENTICE-HALL OF AUSTRALIA PTY. LIMITED, *Sydney*
PRENTICE-HALL OF CANADA, LTD., *Toronto*
PRENTICE-HALL OF INDIA PRIVATE LIMITED, *New Delhi*
PRENTICE-HALL OF JAPAN, INC., *Tokyo*
PRENTICE-HALL OF SOUTHEAST ASIA PTE. LTD., *Singapore*
WHITEHALL BOOKS LIMITED, *Wellington, New Zealand*

To the automobile and equipment manufacturers
who have been so helpful
in supplying material used in this book

contents

Contents

Contents

x

preface

Automobile designs are rapidly changing as a result of different buyer markets, rising fuel and production costs, and the passage of new state and federal regulations. These changes continually cause an increase in the amount of knowledge required by an automechanic. To keep abreast of these changes, the automechanic student, as well as the professional, must continue to update himself. Obsolete items and methods must be given up in order to allow time for efficient work on new and revised automotive units.

This edition still has the same objectives as the first edition, but it has been revised to better meet the requirements of those who use the book. It is written for those who are interested in obtaining a thorough knowledge of automobile component operation and service. Some of the material of an engineering nature used in the first edition has been eliminated from this edition. This material is, however, still available in the specialized books that are also published by Prentice-Hall. Additional material on applied service operations and automotive components produced since the first edition was written have been put in its place. The general approach in the text is to show the operating requirements of the component being discussed and then to describe typical design features that are used to meet these requirements. This is followed by a discussion of normal service requirements and service procedures used to maintain the components. An attempt is made to use features that are common to the majority of domestic automobiles. This is followed by a discussion of variations from these basic features that are used to perform the same operation.

At many places within the text, it is useful to

place numerical values on items described to show relationships—for example, the valve and port size relationship to cylinder bore size. The numerical value and percentages given in the text are average values used in domestic passenger cars. Actual values for any specific component may be quite different from the numerical values presented because the part's design objective may have been quite different from the average part design objective. Metric units follow the customary units in parentheses. The metric values are rounded off where approximate values are used. They are carried out to more exact values only when it is required.

The author has generally avoided discussion of specific make and model automotive component disassembly and reassembly procedures. Obsolete features are purposely omitted unless they are required to show the development of a current design feature. Experimental and limited production designs have also been avoided, except where high interest level dictates a need for a short discussion. The text deals specifically with the automotive products that a student will most likely work with when he finishes his training.

The discussion in the text is directed to the reason a part must function in a particular manner and how a malfunction of that part can be recognized. This is followed by a brief discussion of procedures used to correct malfunctions. The text is intended to be used along with detailed applicable service manual instructions.

Six areas of automechanics are discussed. The first nine chapters introduce the engine, its construction, and its operation. Chapters 10 through 18 cover the operation, service, and adjustment of the engine external units and controls. Engine overhaul is given in Chapters 19 and 20. It is placed here so that the student will be able to install and connect the engine components to run after he has repaired it because he has already covered the external units and controls. The drive line is discussed in Chapters 21 through 25. This is followed by Chapters 26 through 31 on the chassis, including suspension, alignment, and brakes. Automotive accessories are briefly covered in Chapters 32 and 33. The material is presented in a manner that parallels normal procedures used in disassembly, examination, reassembly, and adjustment procedures of automotive components. This gives the student an opportunity to use the text to study the details of the automotive component as he works through his shop or laboratory project. In general, each chapter is complete so the chapters can be used in nearly any order. Where needed, references are given to preceding chapters for specific details not covered in that chapter.

The author wishes to express his sincere thanks to the large number of individuals who have provided material used in this book and those who have constructively criticized the original edition. In as much as possible, their recommendations have been incorporated in this edition. The unrestricted use of the automotive laboratories, automotive equipment, and training aids at Western Michigan University to take many photographs is especially appreciated. Again, Helen Pressey did an excellent job of typing the manuscript. The author's wife has continued to give encouragement to the writing effort that made this edition possible.

HERBERT E. ELLINGER

acknowledgments

A great number of individuals and organizations have cooperated in providing reference material and illustrations used in this text. The author wishes to express sincere thanks to the following organizations for their special contributions:

American Motors Corporation
American Society for Testing and Materials
A. P. Parts
The Association of American Battery Manufacturing, Inc.
Beckman Instruments, Incorporated
The Bendix Corporation
Bohn Aluminum and Brass Company
Borg and Beck Division, Borg Warner Corporation
Champion Spark Plug Company
Chrysler Motors Corporation
Chrysler-Plymouth Division of Chrysler Corporation
Cleveland Graphite Bronze Division,
        Clevite Corporation
Dana Corporation
The Dow Chemical Company
Eaton Valve Division,
        Eaton, Yale and Towne, Incorporated
Federal-Mogul Corporation
The Firestone Tire and Rubber Company
Ford Motor Company

Acknowledgments

Ford Division of Ford Marketing Corporation
Autolite-Ford Parts Division, Ford Motor Company
General Motors Corporation:
    AC Spark Plug Division
    Buick Motor Division
    Cadillac Motor Car Division
    Central Foundry Division
    Chevrolet Motor Division
    Delco Morane Division
    Delco-Remy Division
    Oldsmobile Division
    Saginaw Steering Gear Division
B.F. Goodrich Tire Company
The Goodyear Tire and Rubber Company
Gould-National Batteries, Inc.

Greenlee Brothers and Companay
Independent Battery Manufacturers Association, Inc.
Johnson Products, Inc.
Kelsey-Hays Company
Modine Manufacturing Company
Monroe Auto Equipment Company
Moog Industries, Inc.
Muskegon Piston Ring Company
The Prestolite Company
Raybestos-Manhattan
Sealed Power Corporation
Society of Automotive Engineers
Sunnen Products Company
TRW, Michigan Division
TRW, Replacement Division
Union Carbide Corporation
UniRoyal, Incorporated
Walker Manufacturing Company
Warner Gear Division, Borg Warner Corporation

automechanics

introduction
to the automobile

"Why did they build a car *that* way?" is a common question asked by many students.

To understand why an automobile is built in a certain way, it is necessary to know some of the questions a manufacturer must answer before he has his engineers design a car. Each major domestic automobile manufacturer produces a number of body styles, body sizes, engine sizes, transmission types, colors, optional equipment, etc. Automobiles are obviously built to meet differing owner needs. What is best for one owner may be entirely inadequate for another. For instance, the automobile requirements of a single man are quite different from the requirements of a married man with four children.

The first thing a manufacturer must consider is the specific job the automobile should be capable of doing. This is called the *design objective.* For example, is the automobile going to be required to carry a heavy load at low speeds or a light load at high speeds. Each of these operations obviously requires a different type of automobile. The design objective may be more vivid if the reader considers a race car. It is not driven to the track, but towed or transported on a trailer or truck. A race car is not designed to operate on the highway and would be very difficult to drive in city traffic. The tow car, on the other hand, will operate satisfactorily in traffic but would be a very poor race car. When discussing which car is *best,* a person must always state what type of operation the automobile is designed for.

When designing an automobile, an engineer must consider maximum required acceleration, speed, economy, load to be carried, ride and handling characteristics, size, etc., that will be expected from the vehicle. The finished automobile is a blend of these components, one feature traded off against another, to produce the final product. The maximum limits of these features are called the *design parameters.*

The next step to be considered is durability. How many miles should the vehicle operate before service is required? For example, a passenger car is designed to operate over 100,000 highway miles before major service is required. An Indianapolis race car needs to complete only 500 racing miles. A dragster can make 100 quarter mile runs in 25 miles of driving. Each part of the vehicle has a specific design life, which takes into account its operating load, speed, temperature, lubrication, etc. For example, ball bearing manufacturers provide tables which list the ball bearing life expectancy based on operating speed and load. Overloading reduces bearing life expectancy and underloading increases life expectancy.

Once the design requirements are known, the manufacturer must consider cost. With the exception of special-purpose vehicles, automobiles are designed to be sold to the general public in competition with automobiles made by other manufacturers. One of the best selling points is low price. Therefore, one of the major design objectives is to lower the price without compromising the design parameters. In some cases, a large reduction in cost can be accomplished with only a slight compromise in a design objective, and the automobile can still be kept competitive.

Sometimes, a manufacturer does not update his products as rapidly as his customers would like. This often happens with engines that are mass produced by automatic machines in a plant designed especially for that engine. Minor changes can be done by readjusting the tooling. In some cases, it is more economical to build a new plant than to revise an existing one when a completely new engine is to be built. The type of equipment used to machine engine blocks is shown in Figure 1-1.

One method of reducing cost is to change the manufacturing method. A forged part may be replaced by a cast part, and a cast part is often replaced by a stamping or sintered metal part. In

Fig. 1-1 Automatic engine production machinery (Greenlee Brothers & Company).

this way, the cost of the part is reduced by reducing the number of manufacturing operations that are required to be done on the part before it can be used in the vehicle. This type of process change is illustrated throughout this text.

In addition, plastics are replacing metal for nonstructural parts having complex shapes. In some cases, entire automobiles are made from fiberglass and plastic. Plastic parts generally reduce manufacturing costs when made in quantity and reduce weight as well.

Many product features are the result of the engineer's preference. These preferences are usually based upon previous satisfactory performance of the design. There is a tendency to continue those features until they become uneconomical or unpopular, or until new engineering management takes over. Engineering preference has generally been pushed into the background by the other design requirements that the vehicle must meet.

1-1 VEHICLE DESIGN

Vehicle design must start with occupant seating. No matter what the designer wishes, the vehicle must have room for the driver, passengers, and load. The vehicle must have enough engine power to move the load at the desired speed and enough braking power to safely stop the vehicle. While moving, the vehicle must be controllable, so that it can be driven to follow changes in the roadway and traffic conditions.

Body and Frame. The occupants should be provided with a comfortable ride to minimize fatigue. The seats must be firm with adequate support. Driver visibility must be excellent in all directions. Noise level and vibration should be as low as possible.

Different construction methods used by the manufacturers in their vehicle models are shown in Figure 1-2. Separate body and frame construction has been used for the longest time. In this type of construction, the engine, drive line, and running gear are firmly fastened to the frame; then the body is mounted to the frame with insulators to minimize noise and vibration transfer.

A second type of construction is the unitized body, in which the frame is an integral part of the body structure. Body panels add strength to the frame pieces that form part of the structure. The

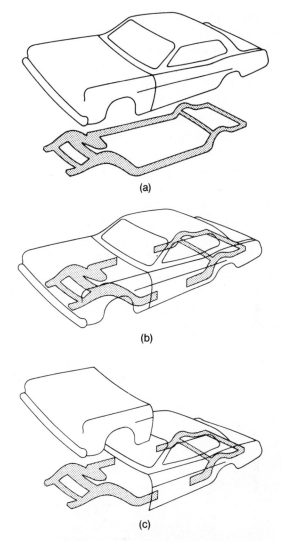

Fig. 1-2 Body and frame construction methods. (a) Separate body and frame, (b) unitized construction, (c) unitized body with stub front frame.

running gear and drive line are attached with large soft insulators to minimize noise and vibration. If the insulators are too soft they tend to give the automobile a spongy ride, and if they are too hard they do not insulate properly. Careful insulator design and location will produce an automobile that is satisfactory to drive and to ride in.

A third type of construction combines features from both of the preceding types. It uses a stub frame from the fire wall forward and a unitized body from the fire wall back. The unitized portion is very rigid, while the stub frame provides an opportunity for good insulation. This construction method is generally applied to larger body styles.

Manufacturers select their construction method by deciding which type is most economical for them to build, while still providing the noise, vibration, and ride characteristics they want to have in their automobiles. The large automobiles generally use separate body and frame construction. The majority of small automobiles use unitized construction.

Engine. Most automobiles use a gasoline-fueled reciprocating engine mounted ahead of the passengers. This location seems to provide the most room for occupants and load, as well as being a safety factor in a head-on collision. It also allows placement of the cooling radiator at the front of the car with a minimum of ducting and hoses. Engines have been placed behind the rear axle (rear engine), and between the occupants and the rear axle (midship) as illustrated in Figure 1-3. Neither has extensive application in domestic automobiles.

Some specialty automobiles use a different type of engine. The diesel engine is used in some taxicab fleets, because it uses considerably less fuel than the gasoline engine when operated at low speeds. It is quite common in Europe, where fuel costs are much greater than in the United States. The rotating combustion chamber engine is gaining popularity in small European and Japanese cars. Its use will probably increase. Turbine engines show promise, especially in commercial vehicles. They are powerful, lightweight, and low on hydrocarbon and carbon monoxide emissions. They are ideally suited to replace some diesel engines in over-the-road load carrying vehicles.

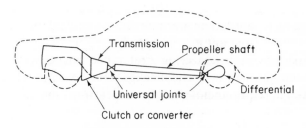

Fig. 1-4 Power drive line.

Drive Line. The drive line carries power to the drive wheels as shown in Figure 1-4. A clutch or torque converter is connected to the engine crankshaft to provide a means to effectively disconnect the engine from the drive line, so that the engine can idle while the automobile is stopped. It is engaged to drive the automobile.

A transmission is located directly behind the clutch or torque converter. Its function is to provide gear reduction which will produce high torque to start the automobile moving and drive it up steep grades. The transmission will also provide a reverse gear for backing the automobile. Gear range selection may be either manual or automatic.

In front engine, rear wheel drive, the transmission is located under the front floor pan. A propeller shaft is required to carry the engine power to the rear axle. It has universal joints on each end to provide flexibility as the suspension position changes.

A differential on the rear axle splits the incoming power to each drive wheel. This also allows the drive wheels to turn at different speeds as they go over bumps and around corners.

Automobiles with front wheel drive, or with midship or rear engines, usually combine the transmission and differential, so they do not have a

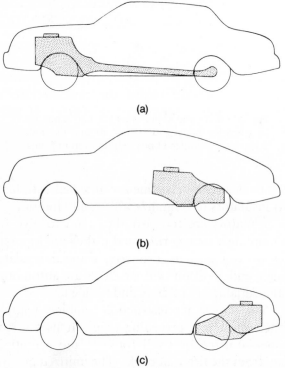

(a)

(b)

(c)

Fig. 1-3 Engine locations. (a) Front, (b) midship, (c) rear.

propeller shaft. The axle shafts between the differential and the drive wheels have universal joints on each end. Front wheel drives are the most complicated because they must steer as well as drive.

Running Gear. The four tire footprints are the only place the automobile touches the road. All of the engine power, steering, and braking forces must operate through these tire-to-road contact footprint areas. Any time the tire does not contact the road or when skidding begins, control of the automobile is reduced or lost. The suspension's job is to keep the tire in contact with the road as much of the time as possible, even on rough roads, while supporting the automobile.

The suspension consists of springs, shock absorbers, and linkages or arms. The suspension system must be strong enough to resist axle twisting from high engine power and from brake reaction.

Brakes are mounted inside the wheels. Hydraulic force from the brake pedal pushes the brake shoes against a cast iron surface with enough force to slow wheel rotation. This, of course, slows the automobile. Brake designs are either drum type or disc type. Most applications using disc brakes have disc brakes on the front and drum brakes on the rear. Four wheel disc brakes are gaining in use.

The running gear is supported with either coil, leaf, or torsion bar springs, as shown in Figure 1-5. Coil springs are most popular. They require links and arms to hold the axle in position. Leaf springs

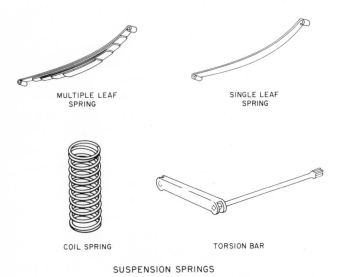

MULTIPLE LEAF
SPRING

SINGLE LEAF
SPRING

COIL SPRING

TORSION BAR

SUSPENSION SPRINGS

Fig. 1-5 Suspension spring types (Monroe Auto Equipment Company).

can hold the axle in position without an additional device. Torsion bars require the same type of support as coil springs.

1-2 AUTOMOBILE SERVICE

An automobile is serviced only when preventative maintenance is due, when the owner wants a change in performance, appearance, or comfort items, or when there is a specific problem. Preventative maintenance includes service that is done at regular intervals, so that the operator will not encounter problems on the road. This service includes oil change, lubrication, tune-up, brake adjustment, tire rotation, etc. It is routine when done according to standard operating procedures.

Changes in economy, performance, appearance, and comfort items usually involve installing a manufactured item such as power brakes, air conditioner, or radio. In most cases, these items are available in a kit with all the necessary parts and detailed installation instructions. Items may need to be replaced as well as added to give a performance change. This type of service would include changing cylinder heads, manifolds, differential gears, wheels, tires, etc. Here again, the service is routine. The technician knows exactly what the customer wants. Unfortunately technicians do not always follow the manufacturer's installation and adjustment directions. If the improperly installed part does not function correctly, the manufacturer is usually blamed and not the improper installation.

Most service work involves a repair of the part causing the customer's problem. This kind of work should start with a clear understanding of what the customer is concerned about. He wants his automobile repaired so it will operate correctly at a minimum cost to him.

In general, problems can be corrected by straightforward service procedures. These involve checking the system to identify the problem, testing to pinpoint the cause, making the required repairs, and then rechecking for proper operation. In some cases, the cause of the problem is extremely difficult to pinpoint. Under these conditions a technician's detailed knowledge of the parts' functions and their interrelationships with the other parts, along with his ability to use test equipment, allows him to rapidly and accurately correct the problem.

This book is designed to provide the technician with a background to help him or her understand why the vehicle parts are made as they are, what the parts are required to do, and how they accomplish their required task. Repair procedures are discussed for most of the automobile components.

REVIEW QUESTIONS

1. What is the difference between the design objectives and the design parameters of an automobile? [INTRODUCTION]

2. What methods are used to keep vehicle cost down? [INTRODUCTION]

3. What factors cause manufacturers to change the design features of an automobile? [INTRODUCTION]

4. Name three body and frame construction methods. What current production automobiles use each type? [1-1]

5. What are the advantages of placing the engine in the front of the automobile? [1-1]

6. What effect does the tire footprint have on the operation of the automobile? [1-1]

7. What is the suspension of the automobile designed to do? [1-1]

8. When is service required on automobiles? [1-2]

automobile engine operation

Energy is required to produce power. Natural energy, such as water power, is converted to useful rotating mechanical power through mechanical devices such as water wheels and turbines. Chemical energy in fuel is converted to heat by burning the fuel at a controlled rate. This process is called *combustion*. When combustion occurs in a space separated from the power-producing chamber, the engine is said to be an *external combustion* engine. If combustion occurs within the power chamber, the engine is called an *internal combustion* engine. Engines used in automobiles are internal combustion heat engines. They convert gasoline's chemical energy into heat within a power chamber that is called a *combustion chamber*. Heat energy released in the combustion chamber raises the temperature of the combustion gases within the

chamber. The increase in gas temperature causes the gas pressure to increase. The pressure developed is applied to a piston head or a turbine wheel to produce a usable mechanical force that is converted into useful mechanical power.

The internal combustion engine was used in some of the first self-propelled vehicles. Its development and use since that time has proven it to be a most reliable and economical engine. Recently there has been a great deal of concern over the damage being done to our environment by the emissions (exhaust gases) of automotive engines. A great amount of engineering time and money has been spent to develop an external combustion engine with a very low level of harmful vehicle emissions. There are a large number of complicated problems to be solved. They include

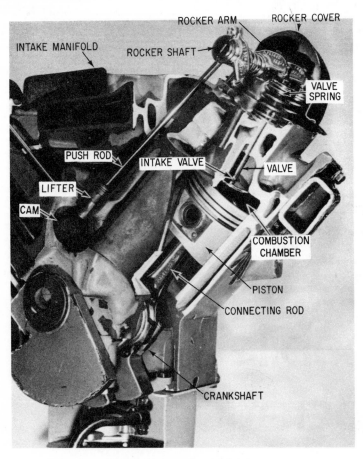

INTAKE MANIFOLD
ROCKER ARM
ROCKER COVER
ROCKER SHAFT
VALVE SPRING
PUSH ROD
INTAKE VALVE
VALVE
LIFTER
CAM
COMBUSTION CHAMBER
PISTON
CONNECTING ROD
CRANKSHAFT

Fig. 2-1 Names of major engine parts.

problems with the heat transfer medium, warm-up time, fluid sealing, boiler, condenser, transfer pumps, engine weight, and efficiency.

2-1 BASIC ENGINE CONSTRUCTION

A basic automotive engine, shown in Figure 2–1, has a *piston* that moves up and down, or reciprocates, in a *cylinder*. The piston is attached to a *crankshaft* with a *connecting rod*. This arrangement allows the piston to reciprocate in the cylinder as the crankshaft rotates. The pressure developed in the *combustion chamber* at the correct time will push the piston downward and, thereby, force the crankshaft to rotate.

The combustion chamber above the piston must be recharged with a fresh combustible mixture after each combustion. Valves are provided to do this. The *intake valve* allows a fresh charge to enter for the combustion cycle. An *exhaust valve* releases the spent gases after the piston has moved to the bottom of the stroke. Valves are opened and closed at the correct time by a *camshaft* driven from the crankshaft. The major rotating and reciprocating parts are shown in Figure 2–2.

Moving parts in contact with each other will wear rapidly unless they are lubricated. Every engine has a lubricating system that provides an oil film between the bearing surfaces to prevent contact.

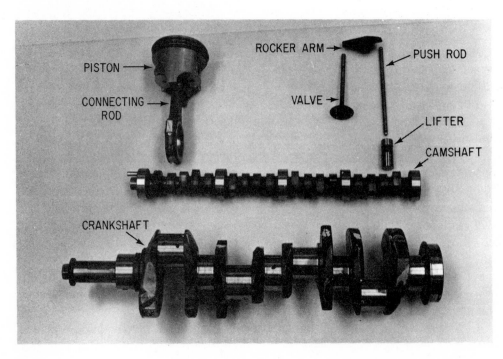

PISTON
CONNECTING ROD
ROCKER ARM
PUSH ROD
VALVE
LIFTER
CAMSHAFT
CRANKSHAFT

Fig. 2-2 Major rotating and reciprocating parts.

A cooling system is required to remove excess heat from the metal surrounding the combustion chamber. If the heat were to remain, the parts would overheat, expand, and seize.

A fuel system and an ignition system are also required to supply the correct air/fuel mixture ratio and to ignite it at the proper instant.

2-2 ENGINE CYCLES

Engine cycles are identified by the number of piston strokes required to complete the cycle. A piston stroke is a one-way piston movement between top and bottom of the cylinder. Most automobile engines use a four-stroke cycle. (See Figure 2-3.)

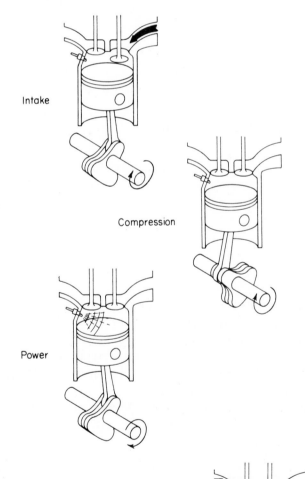

Intake

Compression

Power

Exhaust

Fig. 2-3 Typical four-stroke cycle of a spark-ignited gasoline engine.

The four-stroke cycle starts with the piston at the top of the stroke. An intake valve opens as the piston moves down on the first, or *intake stroke,* allowing the combustible charge to enter the cylinder. The intake valve closes near bottom center and the piston then moves up on the second stroke, or *compression stroke,* to squeeze the charge into a small space. Near the top of the compression stroke, the spark plug ignites the charge so the fuel will burn. The heat released raises the charge pressure and the pressure pushes the piston down on the third, or *power stroke.* Near the bottom of the stroke, the exhaust valve opens to release the spent exhaust gases as the piston moves up on the fourth, or *exhaust stroke* to complete the 720° four-stroke cycle. The piston is then in a position to start the next cycle with another intake stroke. The four-stroke cycle is repeated every other crankshaft revolution.

Some small engines use a two-stroke cycle. This cycle starts with the piston at top center on the power stroke. As the piston nears the bottom of the power stroke, the exhaust opens to release the spent gases. The intake opens very shortly after the exhaust opens and a charge is forced into the cylinder. This aids in pushing the exhaust gases from the cylinder. Both intake and exhaust valves close as the piston starts up on the compression stroke. The two-stroke cycle engine has a power stroke each crankshaft revolution.

2-3 ENGINE CLASSIFICATION

Internal combustion engines are described by referring to a number of their different design features. These can be broken down into the following, readily recognized classifications.

Operating Cycles. Four-stroke cycles and two-stroke cycles, as previously described, are the most common engine operating cycles. A third cycle, the turbine cycle used in gas turbine engines, is beginning to appear in ground vehicles. This cycle is continuous, with a constant quantity of compressed air and fuel being supplied to the combustion chamber. A constant flow of high-pressure gas from the combustion chamber is directed through a turbine to produce a usable rotating force.

Ignition Types. Engines are also classified according to their type of ignition. Most automobiles use gasoline mixed with correct proportions of air, as a fuel. This mixture is ignited with a spark plug at the correct instant in the cycle. It is, therefore, called a *spark ignited,* or *SI engine.* Heavy-duty vehicles may use less expensive distillate as a fuel. In these engines, the air is compressed considerably more than in spark ignited engines. They, therefore, become quite hot. Near the end of the compression stroke, distillate fuel is injected under high pressure into this hot compressed air. The fuel ignites spontaneously, releasing heat which further increases the combustion chamber pressure. An engine with this type of ignition is called a *compression ignition, diesel,* or *CI engine.* The four-stroke cycle is shown in Figure 2–4 and the two-stroke cycle is shown in Figure 2–5.

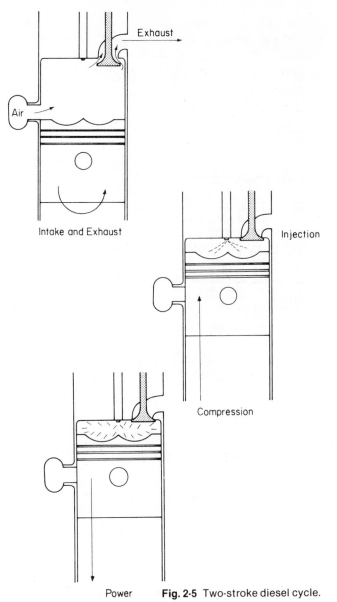

Fig. 2-5 Two-stroke diesel cycle.

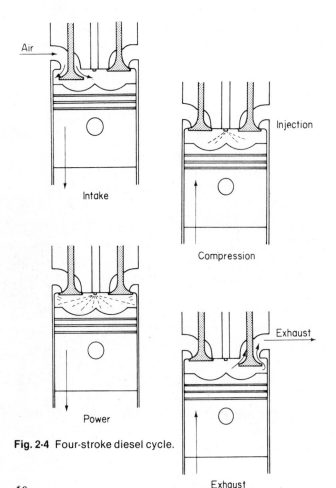

Fig. 2-4 Four-stroke diesel cycle.

Cooling Methods. Most automobile engines use a liquid, usually water plus an antifreeze, to maintain the engine at a constant operating temperature. This is done by transferring heat from the metal surrounding the combustion chamber to the liquid. The cooling liquid flows to a radiator where the heat is removed by running the liquid through thin-walled tubes that are exposed to a flow of atmospheric air. This system is called a *liquid cooling* system. The external system is shown in Figure 2–6.

Some automobile engines maintain a constant operating temperature by transferring heat from the metal around the combustion chamber directly to the air without an intermediate liquid cooling medium. This is done by ducting air across fins that surround the combustion chamber, that can be

Fig. 2-6 Liquid cooling system.

seen in Figure 2–7. Cooling the engine by this method is called *air cooling*.

Engine Configuration. The power that an engine produces is in direct proportion to the mass or weight of air that it uses. Engine designers can change this mass by altering the piston displacement in each cylinder, by changing the number of cycles per minute, by better air flow design, or by the number of cylinders used. Materials, manufacturing processes, and performance requirements are used to adjust the engine design and operating characteristics for each application requirement.

The modern automobile uses four, six, or eight cylinders. Generally speaking, as more power is required from the engine, more cylinders are used. In the evolution of the internal combustion spark ignited engine, the four- and six-cylinder engines most often use an *inline cylinder* arrangement; that is, the cylinder centerlines are parallel, one next to the other (Figure 2–8). They are usually located within a single casting, called a *block,* and the connecting rods are connected to a common crankshaft.

Eight-cylinder engines are usually made in a form that might be considered two four-cylinder

Fig. 2-7 Air cooled system (Chevrolet Motor Division, General Motors Corporation).

Fig. 2-8 Inline engine.

Fig. 2-9 V-engine.

blocks set at a 90° angle to each other, using a common crankshaft. The two blocks are in one casting in this engine, forming a *V-8* arrangement (Figure 2–9).

Several rear engine drive automobiles use a four- or six-cylinder engine with half of the cylinders at 180° to the other half. The cylinder centerlines are usually in a horizontal plane and they are, therefore, called *horizontally opposed engines.* This is shown in Figure 2–7.

Notable examples of still different combinations in production are *V-4, V-6, V-12, V-16,* and *inline straight eight.* These are usually limited production engines and are built to serve special operational requirements.

Valve Arrangement. Engines may be classified according to the location and type of the valve system employed (Figure 2–10). Valves may be placed in the block adjacent to the cylinder. This allows the inlet and outlet passages, called *ports,* to be short and surrounded by coolant. The head is a simple top for the cylinder. It includes a passage for coolant, an opening for a spark plug and a cast impression that forms the top of the combustion chamber. With both valves located on one side of the cylinder, a cross-section view would

be an L-shape. This type of valve arrangement is, therefore, called an *L-head* or *flat-head* engine.

A modification of this type of engine has one valve on each side of the cylinder. It is called a *T-head* engine because of its appearance in a cross-sectional view.

Most current automotive engines have both valves in the cylinder head. This reduces the cost of the engine block and allows better engine breathing by providing a large inlet port on one side of the head and a large exhaust port on the other side. The head is a large complex casting that provides openings for valve ports, coolant, valve actuating devices, and lubricant. The added cost and complexity of this type of cylinder head is offset by the reduced cost of the block and by the added performance produced by better engine breathing. This type of engine may either be called an *overhead-valve* engine or an *I-head* engine.

An engine combining the features of both the L-head and the I-head engines has been produced.

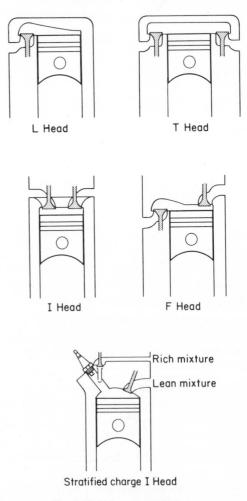

Fig. 2-10 Valve arrangements.

One valve is in the head and the other valve is in the block. This is called an *F-head* engine. It has many of the advantages of both L-head and I-head engines, but it also has many of their disadvantages as well. The F-head engine has seen limited production.

A modification of the I-head engine includes a third small valve located with the spark plug in a precombustion chamber connected by a passage to the combustion chamber. On the intake stroke a rich fuel mixture is inducted through the small valve and a lean mixture through the normal intake valve. On compression, with all valves closed, some of the mixture is pushed back into the prechamber. Ignition occurs easily in the rich charge located in the prechamber. The hot burning gases rush from the prechamber into the lean charge in the main combustion chamber, igniting it. In this way a very lean charge can be burned in the engine to minimize emissions. This method of combustion has two different combustion charges: rich and lean. Engines of this type are commonly called *stratified charge* engines.

Camshaft Location. In engines that have valves in the block, the valves are operated by a camshaft located directly below the valves. In an I-head engine, with valves in the head, the camshaft is usually located in the block. An alternate location in some engines places the camshaft above the valves on the head. This is called an *overhead-cam* engine.

When the camshaft is located in the block, the overhead valves are driven through a lifter, pushrod, and rocker arm assembly. When the camshaft is located on the head, the valves are actuated by some type of cam follower. These arrangements are shown in Figure 2–11.

Rotating Engines. Two relatively new engine types only partly fit into the preceding classifications. One is the *rotating combustion chamber* engine and the other is the *turbine.* Both have continuously rotating members, which eliminate the stop-and-start reciprocating motion of the piston engine.

The rotary combustion chamber engine operates on the four-cycle principle that can be seen in Figure 2-12. It consists of a three-lobe rotor that turns with an eccentric motion within a two-lobe epitrochoid-shaped housing. A changing volume results as the rotor turns, sweeping around inside

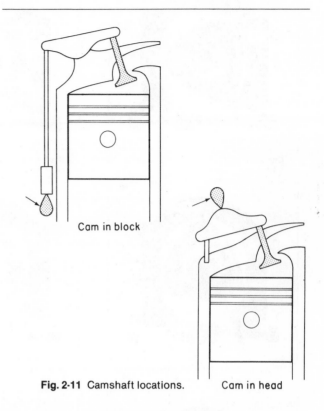

Fig. 2-11 Camshaft locations. Cam in block Cam in head

the housing. Ports are located in the housing, so that gases will be inducted and exhausted at the correct point in the cycle. One or more spark plugs are properly placed in the housing so that ignition will occur at the correct instant to produce maximum effective combustion chamber pressure, forcing the rotor to turn. The rotor uses gears to maintain the proper position in the housing as it drives an eccentric shaft.

The rotating combustion chamber engine has some definite advantages over the piston-type engine. It operates very smoothly; it produces a lot of power for its size compared to the same size reciprocating engine; it can be muffled to operate very quietly because it has no noisy valve-train operation; and it will operate on low-octane gasoline and produce small quantities of nitrogen oxides emissions. The other emissions are high and it does not operate economically compared to reciprocating engines producing similar power.

The ground turbine has five major parts: compressor, regenerator, combustor or burner, compressor-turbine, and power-turbine. The compressor and compressor-turbine are mounted on a single shaft. The compressor-turbine spins the compressor to blow air through the regenerator

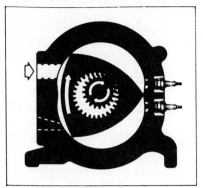

1. Chamber at minimum space volume. Intake cycle begins.

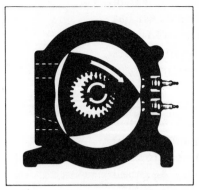

5. Start of compression cycle. (Next chamber begins intake cycle).

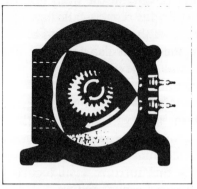

9. Power cycle continues. (Third chamber begins intake cycle).

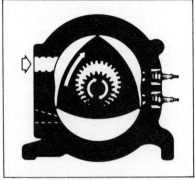

2. Rotor revolves, fuel/air mixture is drawn through carburetor (arrow).

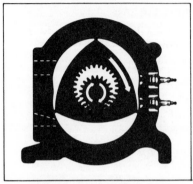

6. Fuel/air mixture is nearly compressed.

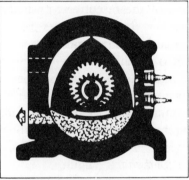

10. Expanded gases have reached maximum volume and begin exhaust.

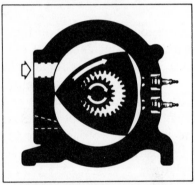

3. Chamber nearly filled with fuel/air mixture.

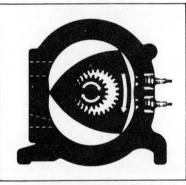

7. Charge is fully compressed. The first plug fires. Slightly later, second plug fires.

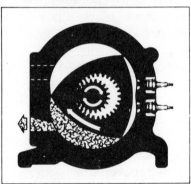

11. Burned gases discharge through port.

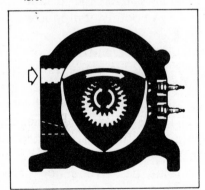

4. Chamber has reached maximum volume. Carburetor intake is almost closed and compression starts.

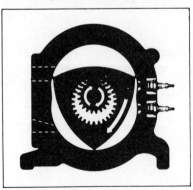

8. Gas expansion and power cycle.

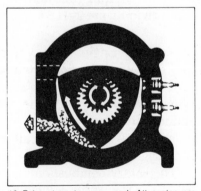

12. Exhaust cycle nears end. All cycles are then repeated on this rotor face.

Fig. 2-12 Rotating combustion chamber engine cycle (Champion Spark Plug Company).

into the combustor where the fuel is added. Once ignited, the combustion flame continues as long as the correct air/fuel mixture is present. The expanding gases flow through the compressor-turbine to supply power for the compressor, and then on to the power-turbine. The power-turbine is connected to a transmission to deliver power to the drive wheels. The hot gases flow through the regenerator before being exhausted (Figure 2–13).

The gas turbine produces high horsepower for its size and weight when compared to a reciprocating automobile engine. It requires no cooling system or torque converter on the transmission. The service life between overhauls is several times greater than the piston engine. It has low hydrocarbon and carbon monoxide emissions. The latest designs have been able to reduce nitrogen oxides emissions below the federal maximums. The turbine engine operates best at a steady speed so it is more suitable for trucks and buses than for passenger cars. It does have a potential to become an automobile powerplant to replace the piston engine in some types of passenger cars.

2-4 BASIC ENGINE SPECIFICATIONS

A number of specifications are used to describe and compare engines. It is important that a technician know and be able to use them. They include terms such as displacement, compression ratio, torque, and horsepower. A clear understanding of these terms will help the reader avoid confusion in the following chapters.

Until the last few years all measurements in the United States have been in *customary units,* such as the inch, foot, and pound. Most of the rest of the world has been using some form of the metric system. Measurements throughout the world are being standardized under an international system called *SI metrics.* To minimize confusion the following examples are given primarily in customary units. Where applicable, metric units are also shown.

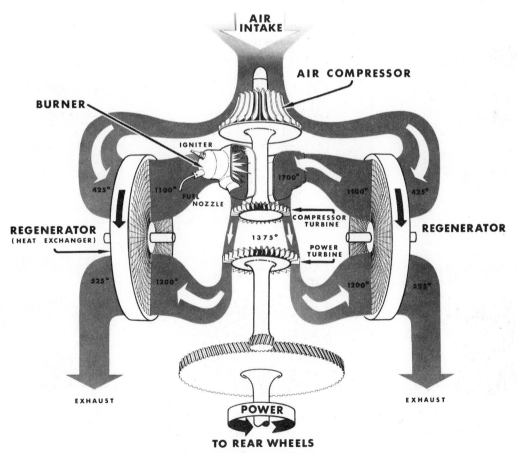

Fig. 2-13 Schematic of an automobile turbine engine (Chrysler Motors Corporation).

An engine's displacement is the volume swept or displaced by the pistons in one revolution of the crankshaft. Engine displacement is calculated by multiplying the cross-sectional area of one cylinder by the stroke, the number of cylinders, and a constant. The displacement is given in cubic inches or cubic centimeters. The following equation is used to calculate engine displacement:

Displacement = 0.785 × bore² × stroke × no. of cylinders

$$(\pi = 0.785)$$

Example (customary units):   What is the displacement of an eight-cylinder engine that has a 3.5 inch bore and a 3.75-inch stroke?

Displacement = 0.785 × 12.25 sq in. ×
3.75 in. × 8 cyl
= 288.5 cubic inches

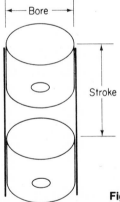

Fig. 2-14 Cylinder dimensions.

Example (metric units):   What is the displacement of a four-cylinder engine that has an 8-cm bore and a 10-cm stroke?

Displacement = 0.785 × 64 sq cm × 10 cm × 4 cyl
= 2009.6 cubic centimeters

Compression ratio is often confused with displacement because each is related to piston position and to cylinder volumes. In most engines, when the piston is at the top of its stroke, it is flush with the top of the block. The combustion chamber volume above the piston when it is at the top of the stroke is the cavity in the head modified by the shape of the piston head. This volume, added to the displacement of one cylinder, will give the volume above the piston when it is at the bottom of the stroke. The compression ratio is the ratio of the volume in the cylinder above the piston when the piston is at the bottom of the stroke to the volume in the cylinder above the piston when the piston is at the top of the stroke.

Compression ratio
$$= \frac{\text{Volume in cylinder (piston at bottom center)}}{\text{Volume in cylinder (piston at top center)}}$$

Example (customary units):   What is the compression ratio of an engine with 50.3 cubic inches displacement in one cylinder and a combustion chamber cavity of 6.7 cubic inches?

Compression ratio $= \dfrac{(50.3 + 6.7) \text{ cubic inches}}{6.7 \text{ cubic inches}}$

$$= \frac{57.0}{6.7} = 8.5$$

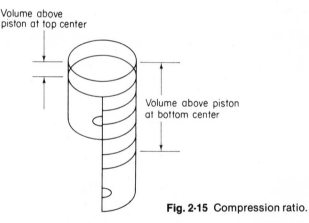

Fig. 2-15 Compression ratio.

Example (metric units):   What is the compression ratio of an engine with a 322.5 cubic centimeter displacement in one cylinder and a combustion chamber cavity of 43 cubic centimeters?

Compression ratio $= \dfrac{(322.5 + 43) \text{ cubic centimeters}}{43 \text{ cubic centimeters}}$

$$= \frac{365.5}{43} = 8.5$$

An increase in compression ratio increases the compression pressure and temperature of the compressed charge. When the charge ignites, it produces higher combustion pressure that gives the engine more turning effort or torque. High compression ratios are limited by rapid fuel decomposition (knock or detonation). High octane rating fuels are able to operate knock free, because they do not decompose at these high pressures and temperatures.

Torque is the work produced by an engine resulting from the pressure on the top of all the pistons which push on the crankshaft through their connecting rods. The actual torque of the crank- shaft varies as the cylinders move to different cycle positions. Engine torque is the average torque produced by all the cylinders throughout the cycle, and it is measured in pound-feet in the customary measuring system. It is the number of pounds at the end of a one-foot lever arm that would be required to balance the engine's twisting effort. This twisting effort goes through the vehicle drive line to turn the drive wheels. When the twisting force or torque is greater than the tire's friction on the road, the wheels will spin as the vehicle is accelerated. If the torque is not great enough to drive the vehicle up a steep incline, the transmission can be shifted into a different gear ratio to multiply torque. When torque is doubled by the transmission, the output speed is halved. To maintain constant speed, the torque must balance the load. With a constant torque, an increase in load will slow the engine, while a decrease in load will allow the engine to speed up.

Power is work done in a given period of time. The quicker a given amount of work is accom- plished, the more power is required. One *horse- power* is the amount of power required to do 33,000 foot-pounds of work in one minute. If this same work were done in fifteen seconds, it would require four horsepower.

One way to measure engine horsepower is to use electronic equipment that will indicate average combustion pressures within the cylinders, then apply these pressures to the piston on each power stroke. This is called *indicated horsepower* (IHP). It can be calculated by the following formula, using customary measuring units:

$$\text{Indicated horsepower} = \frac{\text{PLANK}}{33,000}$$

Where:
    P = Average indicated pressure
    L = Length of stroke in feet
    A = Area of cylinder cross section
    N = Number of power strokes per minute
    K = Number of cylinders

Example (customary units): If an eight-cylinder engine with a 3.5-inch bore and 3.75-inch stroke produces its maximum horsepower at 4400 rpm, what is its indicated horsepower when the average indicated pressure is 131 psi?

Indicated horsepower
$$= \frac{131 \text{ lb/in}^2 \times 0.3125 \text{ ft} \times 9.62 \text{ in}^2 \times 2200 \times 8}{33,000 \text{ ft lb/hp}}$$

$$= 210 \text{ hp}$$

The metric SI unit for power is the watt. Horsepower multiplied by 746 equals power in watts. In the above example the engine would produce 156660 watts (210 × 746) or 156.66 kw.

Engine horsepower relates output torque to engine speed. If torque were to remain constant, the power an engine produced would be directly proportional to speed. However, torque does not remain constant. The actual horsepower the en- gine produces is measured on a dynamometer and is called *brake horsepower*. Torque and speed readings obtained from the dynamometer are sub- stituted in the following formula to calculate brake horsepower (BHP).

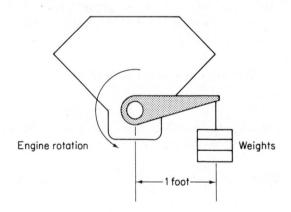

Fig. 2-16 Torque principle.

$$\text{Brake horsepower} = \frac{\text{Torque} \times \text{RPM}}{5252}$$

Example: What horsepower is an engine develop- ing when it is producing a torque of 221 pound- feet when running at 4400 rpm?

$$\text{Brake horsepower} = \frac{221 \text{ lb ft} \times 4400 \text{ rpm}}{5252}$$

$$= 185 \text{ hp}$$

The constant 5252 is developed from the angular rotation of the crankshaft and the work equivalent to one horsepower. (2π radians/33000 ft lb/hp = 5252.)

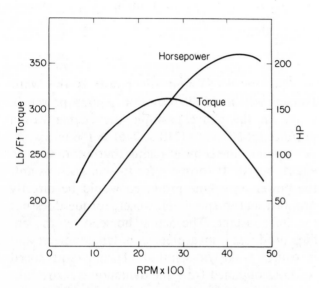

Fig. 2-17 Typical torque and horsepower curves.

Indicated horsepower is greater than brake horsepower. Their difference is considered a loss to friction and is called *friction horsepower* (FHP).

$$\text{Friction horsepower} = \text{IHP} - \text{BHP}$$

Example: What is the friction horsepower of an engine that produces 210 indicated horsepower and 185 brake horsepower?

$$\text{Friction horsepower} = 210 \text{ hp} - 185 \text{ hp} = 25 \text{ hp}$$

2-5 ENGINE EFFICIENCY

Efficiency is output divided by input. It is commonly said that one engine is more efficient than another engine. Any expression of engine efficiency must be related to some common input and output values.

Horsepower values may be used to compare engines. Brake horsepower divided by indicated horsepower gives the engine's mechanical efficiency. It is expressed as:

$$\text{Mechanical efficiency} = \frac{\text{BHP (output)}}{\text{IHP (input)}}$$

Example: What is the mechanical efficiency of an engine that produces 210 indicated horsepower and 185 brake horsepower?

$$\text{Mechanical efficiency} = \frac{185 \text{ hp}}{210 \text{ hp}} = 88\%$$

Volumetric efficiency relates the actual air consumption of an engine to the maximum possible air consumption at that speed.

Volumetric efficiency

$$= \frac{\text{Actual air consumed (output)}}{\text{Maximum possible air consumption (input)}}$$

Example: What is the volumetric efficiency of an engine that will displace 367 cubic feet per min and uses 330 cubic feet per min?

$$\text{Volumetric efficiency} = \frac{330 \text{ cfm}}{367 \text{ cfm}} = 90\%$$

Any change in throttle position, engine speed, or engine load will change volumetric efficiency. At slow speeds and full throttle there is sufficient time to fill the combustion chamber with air at atmospheric pressure. As engine speed increases, there is less time for the air to move through the intake valve so volumetric efficiency decreases. Volumetric efficiency also drops as the throttle is closed to restrict inflowing air. The speed and torque that an engine produces are controlled by changing the engine's volumetric efficiency with the throttle.

A third type of engine efficiency is thermal efficiency. This relates the maximum available heat energy in the fuel to the brake horsepower heat equivalent that the engine produces. One horsepower is equivalent to 42.4 BTU per minute in customary units. Gasoline has approximately 110,000 BTU per gallon. Using these figures, the engine thermal efficiency can be calculated by the formula:

Thermal efficiency

$$= \frac{BHP \times 42.4 \ (BTU/min)}{110,000 \ (BTU/gal) \times gal \ used/min}$$

Example: What is the thermal efficiency of an engine developing 15 horsepower at 50 mph using 2 gal of gas per hour (25 mi per gal or 1/30 gal per min)?

Thermal efficiency

$$= \frac{15 \ hp \times 42.4 \ BTU/min}{110,000 \ BTU/gal \times 1/30 \ gal/min}$$

$$= 17.3\%$$

Maximum gasoline engine thermal efficiency is approximately 25%. The rest of the heat energy is used to overcome friction or it is expelled with the exhaust or through the cooling system.

The primary value of these formulas is to help the technician understand terms used to describe engines and to understand engine operating principles. They can be of further use to compare engine operation characteristics between two engines.

REVIEW QUESTIONS

1. What is meant by internal combustion? [INTRODUCTION]

2. Name the basic parts of an automobile engine. [2-1]

3. What is a stroke? [2-2]

4. What are the strokes of a four-stroke cycle? [2-2]

5. List the design features that are used to classify internal combustion engines. [2-3]

6. How does a valve train for a cam-in-block design differ from that for a cam-in-head design? [2-3]

7. What are the advantages and disadvantages of a rotary combustion chamber engine and a turbine engine? [2-3]

8. How do displacement and compression ratio differ? [2-4]

9. Why is a high compression ratio desirable? [2-4]

10. How does the mass of air consumed affect engine power? [2-4]

11. How does power differ from torque? [2-4]

12. How does indicated horsepower differ from brake horsepower? [2-4]

intake and exhaust manifolds

Multi-cylinder engines are required to run smoothly. Smooth operation can only occur when each combustion chamber produces the same combustion chamber pressure as every other chamber in that same engine. To do this, each cylinder must receive a charge exactly like the charge going into the other cylinders in quality and quantity, with the same physical properties and the same air/fuel ratio.

The air coming into an engine will flow through the carburetor. The carburetor is the device that provides the charge quality by mixing fuel into the incoming air in the correct proportions. The intake manifold directs an equal quantity of the mixed charge to each intake valve. Each intake valve must be timed the same as the others to allow an equal quantity of the charge to enter each combustion chamber. An ignition distributor

must be timed to send a spark across the spark plug gap when each piston has compressed the charge the same amount. When all of these requirements are met the pressure in the combustion chambers will be equal.

It is unfortunate that an engine has not, as yet, been designed to meet these ideal requirements under all operating conditions. For minimum manufacturing cost, tolerances must be quite large, and so the valve and ignition timing between cylinders is not exactly the same. The charges flowing through the manifold passages encounter different passage sizes, angles, temperatures, and flow rates. All of these tend to make the quality and quantity of the charge supplied to each cylinder somewhat different, especially at low engine speeds. Intake manifolds that are carefully designed will provide more uniform charge distribution to the cylinders and, therefore, help to make the engine run smoothly, but they are costly to manufacture.

3-1 INTAKE MANIFOLD CRITERIA

The carburetor delivers finely divided droplets of liquid fuel into the incoming air in a combustible air/fuel ratio (Figure 3–1). These particles start to evaporate as they leave the carburetor. With the engine operating at the most volumetric efficiency, about 60% of the fuel will evaporate by the time the charge reaches the combustion chamber. This means that there will be some liquid droplets suspended in the charge throughout the manifold. The droplets stay in suspension as long as the mixture flows at high velocities through the manifold. At maximum horsepower, these velocities may reach 300 feet per second. Separation of the droplets from the air flowing through the manifold occurs when the mixture velocity drops below 50 feet per second. Intake velocities at idle speeds are usually below this value and, therefore, extra fuel must be supplied to the charge in order to deliver a combustible mixture to the combustion chamber at low engine speeds.

Manifold sizes are a compromise. They must be large enough to allow adequate flow for maximum power and small enough to maintain sufficient velocities to keep the fuel droplets in suspension as required for equal mixture distribu-

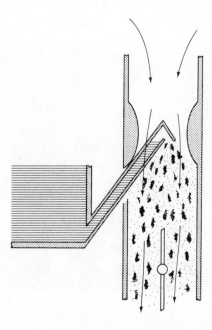

Fig. 3-1 Fuel delivered to the manifold in droplets.

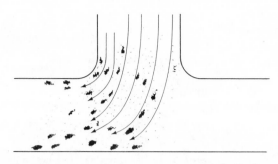

Fig. 3-2 Fuel droplets flowing around a manifold bend.

tion. Manifold size is one of the reasons that engines designed especially for racing will not run at low engine speeds. They have manifolds large enough to reach maximum horsepower, but their size allows fuel to separate from the air at low speeds. Passenger car engines are primarily designed for economy at light-load, part-throttle operation. Their manifolds, therefore, have a much smaller cross-sectional area to maintain adequate mixture velocities throughout their normal operating range.

It should be noted that fuel separation problems do not exist on engines that have fuel injected into the manifold near the inlet valve. These engines can operate satisfactorily at low speeds, even with large manifold cross sections.

In a four-stroke cycle, the inlet stroke is approximately one-fourth of the entire cycle. On a single cylinder four-cycle engine, the carburetor would be working only on the intake stroke, which is one-fourth of the time. Four cylinders are therefore, attached to the same size carburetor with cylinders timed so that each cylinder takes a different quarter of the 720° four-stroke cycle. Using this technique, one carburetor will satisfy the requirements of four cylinders just as well as it will satisfy one cylinder. This is also done in modern V-8 automotive engines. In these engines, the manifold is divided into two sections, each supplying four cylinders. When a carburetor with two large air openings, called a two-barrel carburetor, is used on a modern V-8 engine, one opening supplies each manifold passage or *runner*. The cylinders are timed so that only one cylinder draws a charge from the carburetor air opening or barrel at a time. This is illustrated in Figures 3–3 and 3–4.

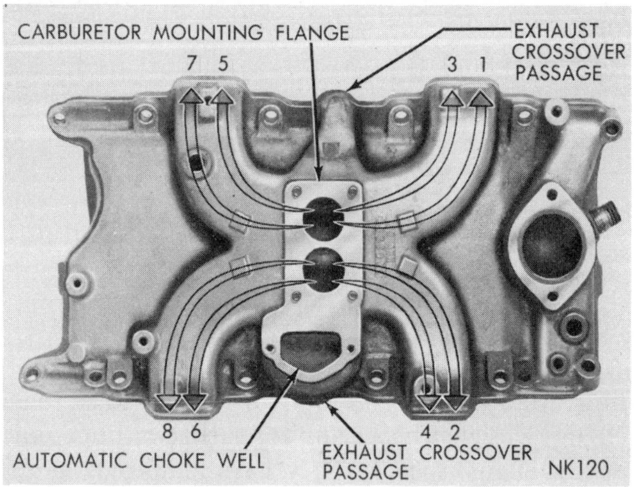

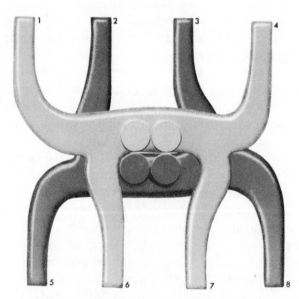

Fig. 3-3 Each side of the carburetor feeds four cylinders (Chrysler-Plymouth Division, Chrysler Corporation).

Fig. 3-4 Manifold runner core configuration (Ford Motor Company).

Six-cylinder inline engines usually have a single barrel carburetor to supply all the cylinders. In these engines, the single carburetor barrel will be supplying two cylinders at the same time. Therefore, a carburetor used on these engines usually requires a larger barrel than the carburetor barrel used on V-8 engines, where each barrel supplies four cylinders.

3-2 INTAKE MANIFOLD FEATURES

The intake manifold's primary function is to carry the air/fuel mixture from the carburetor to the intake port in the head. As it flows, the mixture picks up heat that evaporates the liquid fuel droplets, gradually changing it into a gaseous air/fuel mixture.

Runners. On some economy engines one intake passage, or runner, between the carburetor and cylinder supplies two adjacent cylinders. Most modern engines have separate runners to each intake port. This allows the designer an opportunity to make all runners in the engine an equal length and size to aid in equal air/fuel charge distribution to each cylinder.

Intake manifolds used on most V-8 engines are built with runners on two levels in order to fit them between the heads (Figure 3–4). Successive firing cylinders are fed alternately from the upper and lower runners so the runner design must match the cylinder firing sequence. One runner level is shown in Figure 3–5. The runners may be a *log type* that have the largest possible cross section for maximum air flow. Many are made in an *H* pattern that is a compromise between maximum performance and the best use of the space available. Some runners are called *tuned runners*. In the tuned runners, the length is designed to take advantage of the natural pressure wave that occurs in a gas column. The pressure wave reaches the cylinder when the intake valve is timed to open. This allows the charge to enter the cylinder with a super-charging or ram

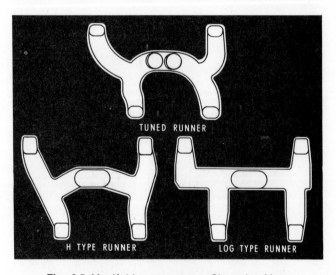

Fig. 3-5 Manifold runner type (Chevrolet Motor Division, General Motors Corporation).

effect. The ram effect is illustrated in Figure 3–6. On V-8 engines using four-barrel carburetors, the primary barrels are often centered on the runners to give good low- and mid-range performance during most operation. The secondary barrels operate only at full throttle, which occurs during a very small percentage of the operating time, so unequal charge distribution is not as critical.

The charge flow through the intake manifold is dependent upon the number of abrupt runner bends, the smoothness of the interior wall, and the cross-sectional runner shape. Sharp bends tend to

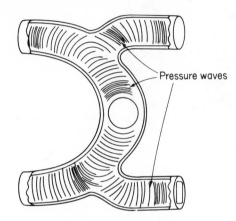

Pressure waves

Fig. 3-6 Pressure waves in the manifold runner.

increase fuel separation. The air, having less mass, is able to make turns much more quickly than the heavy fuel droplets. Rough interior runner surfaces will add a drag and turbulence to charge velocity, upsetting charge distribution. A round runner shape has the greatest cross-sectional area for its wall surface area; however, a round section is not always the most desirable. Passenger car engine manifold runner floors are flat, as shown in Figure 3–7, so that any liquid fuel that drops out of the charge will spread in a thin layer over the manifold floor and rapidly evaporate. The rear of the engine is lower than the front for better drive line positioning. Manifolds are designed so that the manifold floor is level when the engine is mounted in the chassis. The flat manifold floor keeps any liquid fuel from running to a low point. Rectangular and oval shapes are used to take advantage of the available space for more cross-section area at the expense of relatively more wall surface area when compared to round runners. The corners cause turbulence that helps evaporate

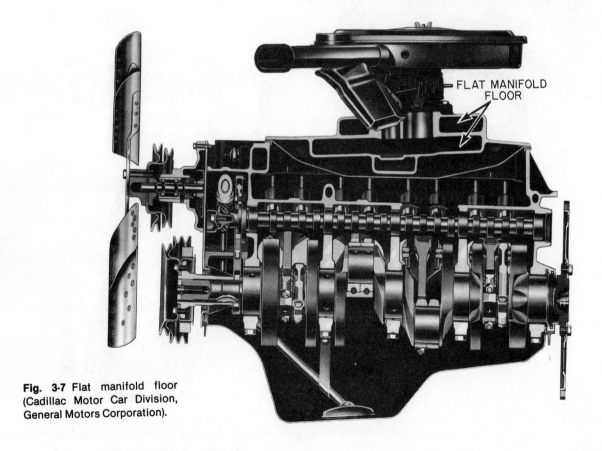

FLAT MANIFOLD FLOOR

Fig. 3-7 Flat manifold floor (Cadillac Motor Car Division, General Motors Corporation).

Fig. 3-8 Guide ribs on the manifold floor.

Fig. 3-9 Heat riser valve.

HEAT CROSSOVER

Fig. 3-10 Heat crossover in the manifold below the intake runners (Chevrolet Motor Division, General Motors Corporation).

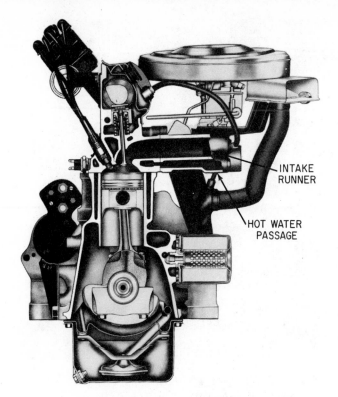

Fig. 3-11 Engine coolant used to heat the intake runners (Chevrolet Motor Division, General Motors Corporation).

liquid fuel on the surface. Main intake runners have cross-sectional areas of approximately 0.008 square inch per engine cubic inch displacement (CID), and branch runners have cross-sectional areas of approximately 0.006 square inch per CID. Ribs and guide vanes that can be seen in Figure 3-8 are often positioned in the floor of the manifold runners to aid in equal distribution of the intake gases to the cylinders, even though some of the fuel may still be in the liquid form. It is just as important for the fuel to have equal distribution as it is for the air to have equal distribution.

Manifold Heat. Heat is required to evaporate liquid fuel between the carburetor and the combustion chamber. If heat is taken from the air, the charge temperature is lowered and less heat is available for evaporation. In current production engines additional heat must be supplied to provide satisfactory fuel evaporation for smooth engine operation when the engine is cold. A mixture temperature range from about 100°F to 130°F (38°C to 55°C) will provide satisfactory fuel evaporation. Heat is supplied during low temperature operation in most current V-8 engines by using a thermostatic valve, called a *heat riser* (Figure 3-9), to route exhaust gases through a passage, called an *exhaust crossover,* positioned to heat the floor of the intake

manifold directly under the carburetor (Figure 3-10). When the engine gets to full operating temperature, the heat riser valve bypasses the exhaust gas away from the intake manifold crossover, sending the exhaust directly out through the exhaust system. Excessive heating causes the charge to expand in the manifold. This will reduce the mass of the charge that is available to the cylinder, thus reducing the engine power. An overheated charge can also lead to undesirable abnormal combustion processes, two of which are called detonation and pre-ignition. It is, therefore, important that the intake manifold is not overheated.

Some engines have used engine coolant to supply heat to the mixture by providing passages for warm coolant to flow around the intake runners as shown in Figure 3-11. This heat is not available until the engine begins to warm up. Heat from the coolant is used where mechanical design makes it difficult to use exhaust heat and where a uniform temperature is desired. Manifolds often contain a coolant passage whose function is to connect the cooling system between the V-heads to provide a common cooling outlet for the engine cooling system at the thermostat.

Choke Heat. The carburetor is designed with a choke to provide an excessively rich fuel mixture for starting. This is necessary because intake gas velocity is low during cranking and no extra heat is available for fuel evaporation before the engine starts. Most chokes are automatic and are controlled by a temperature-sensing thermostatic coil choke closing spring. In some applications, heat is delivered to the thermostatic spring through a tube from a heat chamber, called a stove, that is located in the manifold where it can sense exhaust temperatures as shown in Figure 3-12. This stove could be in the exhaust manifold or in the exhaust crossover passage of the intake manifold. An alternate method uses a pocket in the intake manifold in which the thermostatic choke coil is placed as seen in Figure 3-13. This location allows the thermostatic coil to sense exhaust temperature at the exhaust crossover in the intake manifold. A link connects the thermostatic coil with the carburetor choke plate linkage.

INTAKE RUNNER

HOT WATER PASSAGE

Fig. 3-12 Automatic choke with the heat stove in the manifold.

Fig. 3-13 Automatic choke with the heat sensing spring in the manifold stove well.

3-3 INTAKE MANIFOLD CONFIGURATION

Two general configurations appear on modern V-8 engine intake manifolds. Some engines use an *open-type* manifold. Runners go through the open-type branches. Other branches provide for exhaust crossover and coolant flow. This design allows good control of manifold runner tuning, is lightweight, and is low cost. Lifter valley covers are needed on engines using this type of manifold. In some engines, the covers are an extension of the intake manifold gasket. Figure 3–14 shows an open-type intake manifold.

A second configuration of the intake manifold, illustrated in Figure 3–15, is a *closed-type* manifold. This manifold has cast metal between the runners and is designed for use as a lifter valley cover as well as a manifold. It is heavier and more expensive to make than the open type. Because of the many joints involved, more care is required when installing it to correctly place the gaskets and seals so they will not leak. Using the closed-type mani-

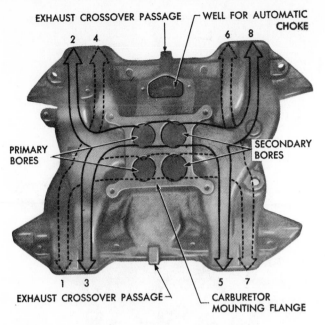

Fig. 3-14 Open-type intake manifold.

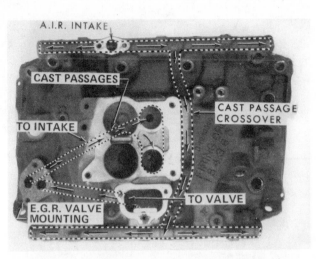

Fig. 3-15 Closed-type intake manifold (Buick Motor Division, General Motors Corporation).

fold, it is possible to lower the runners, the carburetor, and, consequently, the automobile hood line. The large mass of metal used in closed-type manifolds tends to retain engine noise and this results in quieting engine operation noise.

Closed-type manifolds have the exhaust cross-over located adjacent to the lifter valley where engine oil could contact the surface. Hot exhaust in the crossover would heat the oil that lands on its surface to cause coking and oil burning. Therefore, shields (Figure 3–16) are provided to keep the oil from contacting these hot surfaces. A sheet

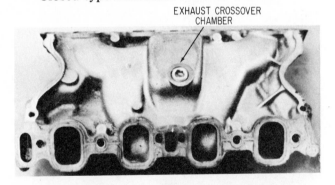

(a)

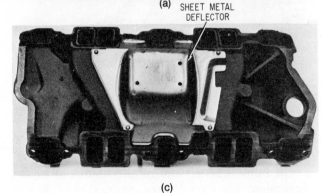

(c)

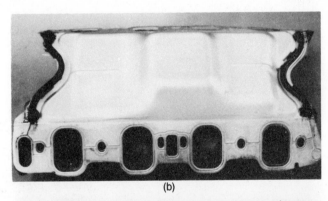

(b)

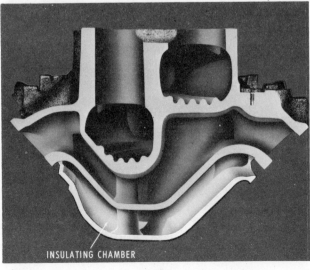

(d)

Fig. 3-16 Exhaust crossover insulation. (a) Manifold without insulation, (b) intake manifold gasket as insulation, (c) sheetmetal deflector riveted on the manifold, (d) insulating chamber cast in the intake manifold (Chevrolet Motor Division, General Motors Corporation).

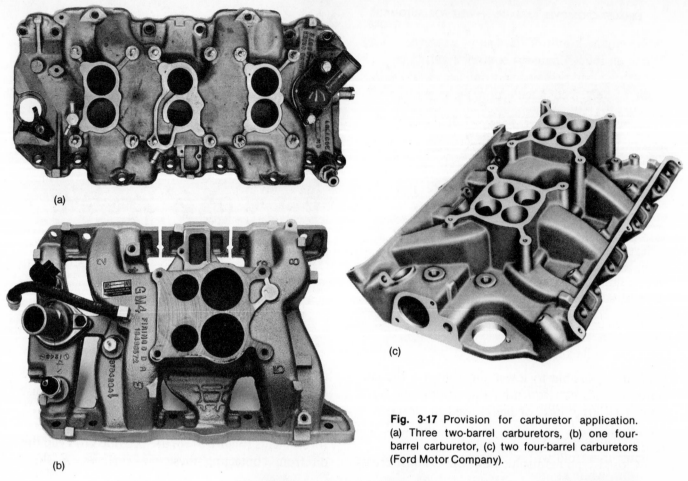

(a)

(b)

(c)

Fig. 3-17 Provision for carburetor application. (a) Three two-barrel carburetors, (b) one four-barrel carburetor, (c) two four-barrel carburetors (Ford Motor Company).

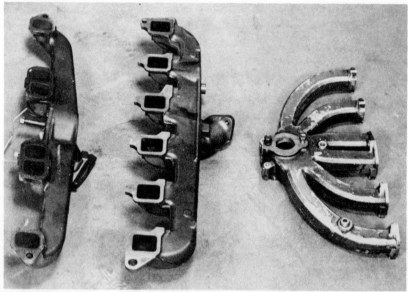

Fig. 3-18 Manifolds for inline engines. The exhaust manifold on the left has Siamese runners, the center exhaust manifold has individual runners, and the right intake manifold has tuned runners.

metal deflector may be fastened to the lifter valley side of the intake manifold or a large single-piece manifold gasket may serve this function. Some closed-type manifolds are designed with a passage that provides an air insulating space between the exhaust crossover passage and the lifter valley. This results in good insulation and noise reduction.

Intake manifolds used on V-type passenger car engines may be designed to use three two-barrel carburetors, one four-barrel carburetor, or two four-barrel carburetors (Figure 3–17).

On inline engines the intake manifold is less complicated than on V-type engines. The intake manifold can be a simple log-type that directs the charge from the carburetor to adjacent ports in the most convenient manner. Some intake manifolds are designed to minimize restrictions by using separate runners to each intake port. Typical inline engine manifolds are shown in Figure 3–18. When an inline engine is equipped with a carburetor having one primary and one secondary barrel, both barrels feed a common passage below the carburetor. When the intake manifold on an inline engine is equipped with a heat riser, the intake manifold is bolted to the exhaust manifold immediately below the carburetor. The heat riser is located at this junction.

3-4 EXHAUST MANIFOLD CRITERIA

The exhaust manifold is designed to collect high temperature spent gases from the cylinder exhaust ports and carry them to an exhaust pipe, exhaust silencer or muffler, and on to the tailpipe, where they are vented to the atmosphere. This must be done with the least possible restriction or back pressure while keeping the exhaust noise at a minimum.

Exhaust gas temperature will vary according to the power produced by the engine. The manifold must be designed to operate at engine idle and sustain full power. Under full power conditions the exhaust manifold will become red hot, causing expansion, while at idle it is just warm, causing little expansion. In passenger car operation, however, the engine will normally be run under light-load, part-throttle conditions, where the manifold temperatures will be between these extremes. Generally, the exhaust manifold is made from cast iron that can withstand extreme temperature thermal shock.

It is bolted to the head or to the block in a way to allow expansion and contraction. Some manifolds are designed so that no parting surface gasket is required, while others require a gasket.

The condition of the exhaust system is more critical now that exhaust-emission laws have been passed. The exhaust system was first used to carry smelly fumes away from the occupants. Soon mufflers were added to silence the exhaust noise. The exhaust systems have been refined to the point where the wind and tire noises are greater than the exhaust noise.

A cast iron manifold is attached to the cylinder head to collect the exhaust gases from the individual cylinders and direct them to the exhaust system. Cast iron will take the high temperatures created without burning out. On some racing engines the exhaust manifold is replaced by a welded steel tubing header. The header allows a smoother, nearly ideal design that will handle the large volumes of exhaust gas produced when the engine is operating at high speeds. Headers do not improve performance at legal road speeds, they cost more to make, and they have a relatively short useful life. Therefore they are used only where high engine speeds require their use. Sometimes owners install headers for appearance of speed and power, regardless of their cost.

Fig. 3-19 Exhaust system with a catalytic converter (General Motors Corporation).

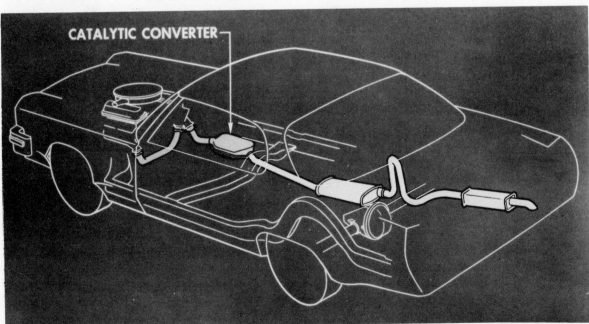

3-5 EXHAUST MANIFOLD COMPROMISES

The exhaust manifold is designed to minimize any restriction to the flow of exhaust gas. Some manifolds use cast-rib deflectors or dividers to guide the exhaust gases toward the outlet as smoothly as possible. An optimum exhaust passage cross-section must be established with well-proportioned flow areas, smooth flow paths, and maximum branch separation within the limits of the chassis environment. The chassis front suspension, steering gear box, and fender skirts limit the space that is available for the exhaust manifold. In general, the chassis and engine are designed first and then the manifold is designed to fit into the remaining space. This is shown in Figure 3-20. This is not as much of a compromise as it might seem, because severe bends have no measurable effect on the flow of exhaust gases as long as the required cross-section is maintained.

Some exhaust manifolds are designed to go above the spark plug, while others are designed to go below. The spark plug and carefully routed

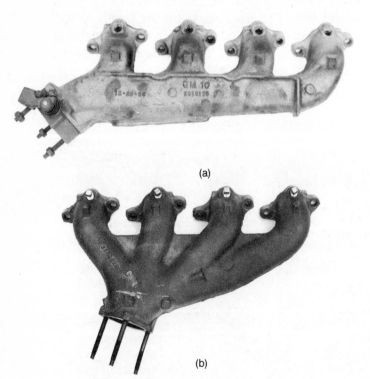

(a)

(b)

Fig. 3-20 Exhaust manifold designs. (a) Standard engine, (b) performance engine.

ignition wires are usually shielded from the exhaust heat with sheet metal deflectors.

Some exhaust manifolds have provision for a thermostatic heat riser valve built into the manifold to direct exhaust gases through the intake manifold crossover passage during warm-up. Often, a stove for the automatic choke is also incorporated in the exhaust manifold. Some manifolds are even designed with brackets on which are mounted such components as generators, and air conditioning compressors.

Exhaust systems are especially designed for the engine-chassis combination. The exhaust system length, pipe size, and silencer are designed, where possible, to make use of the tuning effect of the gas column resonating within the exhaust system similar to the tuned intake runner. However, the entire system is designed so that exhaust pulses from the cylinders are emitted to the manifold when the least pressure exists, rather than during a high-pressure wave as is done on intake manifolds. This helps scavenge the exhaust gas from the cylinder, allowing more useful space for the fresh charge and, consequently, more engine power can be produced. Tuning is most effective at one engine speed or at certain harmonics of that speed. Manifolds are, therefore, tuned to the most desirable engine rpm for the particular vehicle involved. Short pipe lengths favor high-rpm power peaks, while longer lengths tend to increase torque in the mid-range speed used in passenger car applications.

On inline engines the intake manifold is attached to the exhaust manifold. The heat riser valve is located at this attachment location. On V-eight engines the heat riser valve partially blocks one exhaust manifold exit, increasing the exhaust pressure in that manifold. This forces the exhaust gases to flow across the intake manifold exhaust heat crossover passage to the opposite exhaust manifold.

An exhaust pipe is connected to the manifold or header to carry the gases through a catalytic converter to the muffler or silencer. In single-exhaust systems used on V-engines, the exhaust pipe is designed to collect the exhaust gases from both manifolds using a Y-shaped pipe. Dual exhaust systems have a complete exhaust system coming from each of the V-engine manifolds. In some cases the exhaust pipe must be made of several parts in order to assemble it into the space available under the automobile.

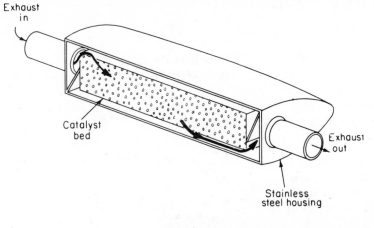

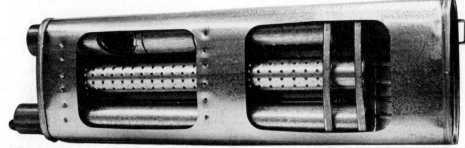

Fig. 3-21 Catalytic converter exhaust flow.

Fig. 3-22 Muffler cutaway to show the interior.

The muffler catches the high-pressure exhaust gas pulses from the cylinder, smoothing out the pressure and allowing it to be released at an even and constant rate, and minimizing the exhaust noise. It does this through the use of perforated tubes within the muffler chamber. These can be seen in Figure 3-22. The smooth flowing gases are released to the tail pipe.

The tail pipe carries the exhaust gases from the muffler to the air, away from the automobile. In most cases the tail pipe exit is at the rear of the automobile below the rear bumper. In some cases it is released at the side of the automobile just ahead of or just behind the rear wheel.

The muffler and tail pipe are supported with brackets called hangers. The hangers are rubberized fabric with metal ends that hold the muffler and tail pipe in the proper position so they do not touch any metal part. This helps to isolate the noise from the rest of the automobile.

The catalytic converter is installed between the manifold and muffler to help reduce exhaust emissions. The converter is made of a heat-resistant housing containing a bed of catalyst-coated pellets or a catalyst-coated honeycomb grid. As the exhaust gas passes through the catalyst most of the remaining hydrocarbons and carbon monoxide are oxidized. An air injection system on the engine

is generally used to supply additional air to aid in the oxidation process. Automobiles using catalytic converters require the use of unleaded gasoline. Lead in gasoline will contaminate the catalyst so that it will no longer function. Pellets can be removed and replaced using special equipment. When the honeycomb-type catalyst becomes ineffective the entire converter must be replaced.

When the exhaust valve opens, it rapidly releases a high-pressure gas. This sends a strong air wave through the atmosphere which produces a sound called an explosion. It is exactly the same sound produced when the high-pressure gases from burned gunpowder are released from a gun. In an engine, the pulses are released, one after another, and so the explosions seem to blend together in a steady roar. The muffler is designed to change this roar to a quiet hum.

Sound is air vibration. When the vibrations are large, the sound is loud. The muffler traps the large bursts of high-pressure exhaust gas in an expansion chamber and releases them gradually before the next high-pressure burst arrives. In this way, the muffler silences engine exhaust noise.

Sometimes resonators are used in the exhaust system. They provide additional expansion space at critical points in the exhaust system to smooth out the exhaust gas flow.

REVIEW QUESTIONS

1. What is the basic requirement for smooth engine operation? [INTRODUCTION]

2. Why is the air flow velocity through the intake manifold important in engines using carburetors? [3-1]

3. How does the carburetor size requirement change on a four-cylinder engine as compared to a single-cylinder engine having the same size cylinder? [3-1]

4. Why are six-cylinder engine carburetor barrels larger than carburetor barrels used on V-8 engines? [3-1]

5. Why is it desirable to have all intake runners the same size and length? [3-2]

6. What is manifold tuning? [3-2]

7. How does the finish and shape of the intake manifold affect the flow of the charge? [3-2]

8. What is the purpose of manifold heat in the intake manifold? [3-2]

9. Racing engines do not use manifold heat. Why is manifold heat used on passenger cars? [3-2]

10. What is the advantage and disadvantage of a closed-type intake manifold? [3-3]

11. When does a header have an advantage over an exhaust manifold? [3-4]

12. Under what conditions does the exhaust pipe length become critical? [3-5]

13. What is the purpose of a catalytic converter? [3-5]

14. How does a muffler silence exhaust noise? [3-5]

cylinder heads and valve trains

The passenger car engine is designed to operate smoothly at all engine loads and speeds while developing high power output and high efficiencies. *Smoothness* is defined as the lack of objectionable or disagreeable engine vibration detected inside the passenger compartment. Engine vibration can be caused by mechanical unbalance or by abnormal combustion. An unbalanced rotating crankshaft and reciprocating pistons produce undesirable vibration and roughness. Abnormal combustion produces excessive rates of pressure buildup in the combustion chamber which leads to engine roughness.

Combustion (discussed in more detail in Chapter 10) is a very complex chemical process resulting from the fuel reactions within the combustion chamber. These reactions will differ according to the fuel type, combustion chamber shape, cooling system efficiency, location of the spark plugs, and valves, compression ratio, and the quantity of the intake charge. One of the most important of these factors is the combustion chamber shape.

The combustion chamber is shaped on the bottom by the top of the piston, on the side by the cylinder wall and on the top by the cylinder head. The piston is nearly at the top of the stroke when combustion takes place so that very little of the cylinder wall is exposed to combustion. The combustion chamber shape, therefore, is primarily the result of the shape of the top of the piston and the shape of the pocket formed in the cylinder head. These shapes have a great deal to do with the control of combustion smoothness.

4-1 COMBUSTION CHAMBER TYPES

Combustion chambers of modern automotive overhead valve engines have evolved from two basic types. One is the *non-turbulent hemispherical chamber* and the other is the *turbulent wedge chamber.* Each has advantages that new combustion chamber designs attempt to combine to form the best possible compromise design.

Hemispherical Combustion Chamber. In non-turbulent hemispherical combustion chambers, the charge is inducted through widely slanted valves, compressed, and then ignited from a centrally located spark plug (Figure 4–1). The smallest possible distance exists between the spark plug and all edges of the combustion chamber so that combustion, which radiates out from the spark plug, will be completed in the least possible time. The end gases that cause abnormal combustion have little time to react and, therefore, knock is reduced to a minimum. The rapidly burning charge in the hemispherical combustion chamber causes a high rate of pressure rise. When the engine is run under medium and heavy loads at low engine speeds, it will produce some engine roughness and noise. If this type of operation is encountered in passenger cars, it may be objectionable to the passengers. However, laboratory and road tests have shown that the hemispherical combustion chamber is the best type for use in race car application where low speed conditions are seldom encountered.

Hemispherical combustion chambers are

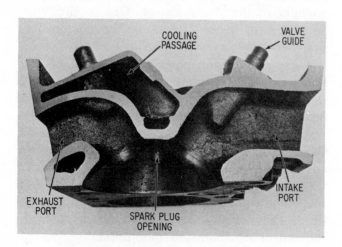

Fig. 4-1 Hemispherical combustion chamber.

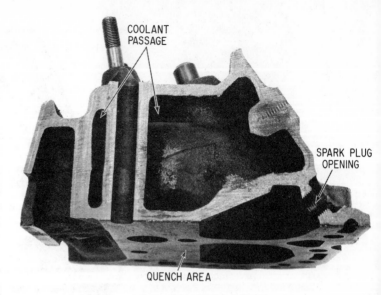

Fig. 4-2 Wedge combustion chamber.

usually fully machined to produce the required shape. This is a necessary but expensive operation that increases engine cost.

Wedge Combustion Chamber. The turbulent wedge combustion chamber is designed to produce a uniform burning rate by controlling combustion. A wedge combustion chamber is shown in Figure 4–2. This results in smooth power production. In turbulent wedge combustion chambers, the charge is inducted through parallel valves and compressed. As the piston nears the top of the compression stroke, the piston approaches a low or flat portion of the head. The gases are squeezed out of this area, called a *squish area,* into the larger portion of the combustion chamber. This produces turbulence within the charge. The spark plug, which is positioned in the highly turbulent part of the charge, ignites the charge. Ignition is followed by smooth and rapid burning. Combustion radiates out from the spark plug. The end gases remaining in the squish area would be subject to abnormal burning, but because this area is squeezed very thin, less than 0.100 in. (0.250 mm) when the piston is at the top center, the end gases are cooled and do not react. This squish area is, therefore, also called a *quench area.* Required combustion rates can be controlled by changes in the combustion chamber shape. The engine designer can make seemingly unimportant modifications in the combustion chamber shape that result in large changes in the peak pressure timing and peak pressure magnitude. He can, therefore, design the combustion chamber to specific engine and fuel requirements.

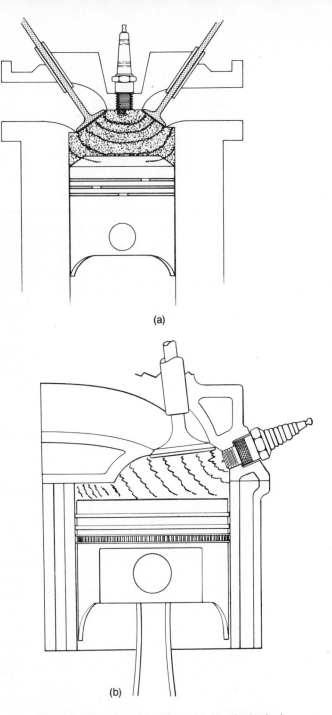

(a)

(b)

Fig. 4-3 Normal combustion. (a) Hemispherical combustion chamber, (b) wedge combustion chamber (Dana Corporation).

Turbulent combustion chambers usually remain *as cast* in the head, with no machining being done.

Unburned hydrocarbon emission from engines has become critical. The charge adjacent to the combustion chamber surface, from 0.002 in. to 0.020 in. (0.005 mm to 0.050 mm) thick, does not burn because the combustion chamber surface cools the surface charge to a temperature below its ignition temperature. These unburned surface hydrocarbons are expelled with the burned gases

on the exhaust stroke as unburned hydrocarbon emissions. Combustion chambers with low surface area for their volume, such as the hemispherical combustion chamber, emit less unburned hydrocarbons than the wedge combustion chamber which has a relatively high surface area-to-volume ratio.

The trend in combustion chamber design is to take advantage of the best features of each type and, at the same time, eliminate the less desirable features. This is done by changing the valves of the wedge head to divergent angles, repositioning the spark plug, reducing the quench area and reducing the combustion chamber surface area-to-volume ratio. The resultant combustion chamber is very efficient and smooth burning while running on available pump grades of gasoline. They are used

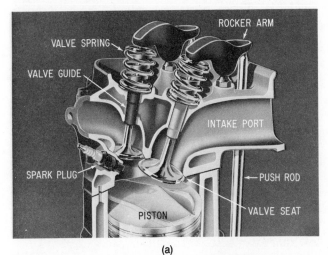

(a)

Fig. 4-4 Cylinder head parts identification. (a) Push rod engine with divergent valves, (b) overhead cam engine with an open combustion chamber having parallel valves (Chevrolet Motor Division, General Motors Corporation).

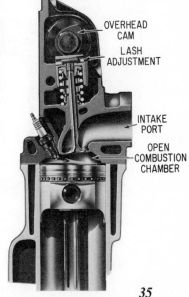

(b)

as cast rather than having expensive machined chambers. These chambers are called by names such as polyspherical, hemi-wedge and kidney shapes. Two of these shapes are illustrated in Figure 4-4.

4-2 INTAKE AND EXHAUST PORTS

Intake and exhaust system passages cast in the cylinder head are called *ports*. They lead from the manifolds to the valves. An optimum design is not always possible because of space requirements for head bolt bosses, valve guides, cooling passages, and pushrod opening clearances. Inline engines have both intake and exhaust ports located on the same side of the engine. Often, two of these cylinders share the same port because of the restricted space available. These ports are called *Siamesed ports* and are shown in Figures 4-5 and 4-6. Each cylinder uses the port at a different time. Larger ports and better breathing is possible in engines that have the intake port on one side of the head and the exhaust port on the opposite side. In these engines, a separate port is usually provided for each cylinder (Figure 4-7).

Fig. 4-5 Cylinder head with Siamesed ports.

Fig. 4-6 Close up view of a Siamesed port.

The design criteria aim is to provide an intake and exhaust system that will meet the engine's maximum power needs with the minimum restriction and, at the same time, provide satisfactory charge distribution in the induction system at part throttle and idle speeds. The engine designer will make use of air-flow measuring equipment to develop a satisfactory compromise that will meet these criteria.

The flow of gases is often different than one might think. At times, an apparent restricting hump (Figure 4-8) within a port may actually increase the air flow capacity by redirecting the flow to an area that is large enough to handle the flow. Modifications in the field, such as *porting* or *relieving,* would result in restricting the flow of such a carefully designed port.

4-3 COOLANT PASSAGES

Coolant flow within the engine is designed to flow from the coolest portion of the engine to the warmest portion. Coolant is fed into the block where it is directed all around the cylinders. It then flows upward through the gasket to the cooling passages cast into the cylinder head. The heated coolant is collected at a common point and returned to the radiator to be cooled and recycled. The typical internal coolant flow direction is shown in Figure 4-9.

Relatively large openings are provided in the gasket surface of the head into the head cooling passages. They are necessary because the cooling passage core must be supported through these openings while the head is being cast. After casting, the core is broken up and removed through these support openings. Openings to the outside of the engine are closed with expansion plugs or soft plugs, either of a convex type or a cup type. The openings between the head and the block are very often too large for the correct coolant flow. When this occurs, the head gasket performs an important

Fig. 4-7 Cylinder head with individual ports.

Fig. 4-8 Hump in the intake to increase the flow rate.

Fig. 4-9 Coolant flow in an engine (Oldsmobile Division, General Motors Corporation).

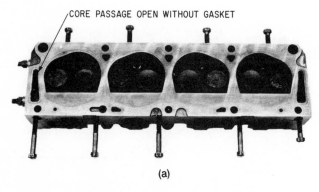

(a)

Fig. 4-10 Coolant flow control. (a) Head, (b) gasket covering the left-hand cooling passage opening.

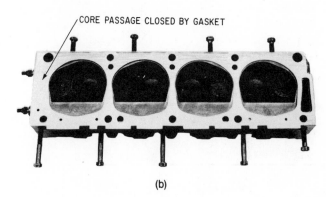

(b)

function by providing a calibrated restriction with punched holes so that the coolant will have the correct flow rate at each opening. Therefore, it is important that the head gasket is installed correctly for proper engine cooling. A restricting head gasket is shown in Figure 4-10.

Special cooling nozzles or deflectors may be designed into the head to direct the coolant toward a portion of the head where localized heat must be removed. Usually this is in the area of the exhaust valve. Some of the deflectors are cast in the cooling passages, while others are pressed-in sheet metal nozzles. Pressed-in nozzles are replaceable in some engines.

4-4 LUBRICATING PASSAGES

Lubricating oil is delivered to the overhead valve mechanism, either through the valve pushrods (Figure 4-11) or through drilled passages in the head and block casting (Figure 4-12). Special openings in the head gasket are provided to allow the oil to pass between the block and head without leaking. After the oil passes through the valve mechanism, it returns to the oil pan through oil return passages. Some engines have drilled oil return holes, but most of the engines are provided with relatively large cast holes that allow the oil to return freely to the engine oil pan. The case holes

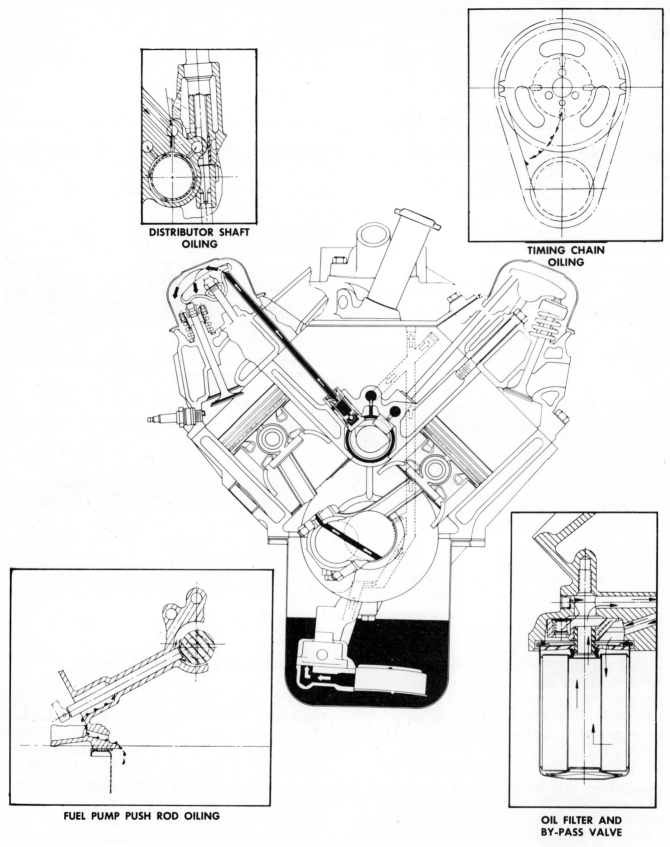

DISTRIBUTOR SHAFT OILING

TIMING CHAIN OILING

FUEL PUMP PUSH ROD OILING

OIL FILTER AND BY-PASS VALVE

Fig. 4-11 Valve gear lubricated through hollow pushrods (Chevrolet Motor Division, General Motors Corporation).

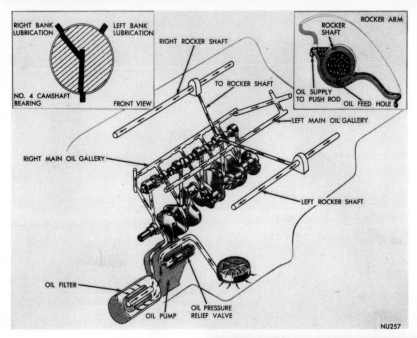

Fig. 4-12 Oil feed passages drilled through the block and head to lubricate the overhead valve assemblies (Chrysler-Plymouth Division, Chrysler Corporation).

(a)

(b)

Fig. 4-13 Camshaft drives. (a) Most popular chain drive (Chevrolet Motor Division, General Motors Corporation), (b) gear drive (Chevrolet Motor Division, General Motors Corporation), (c) overhead belt (Chevrolet Motor Division, General Motors Corporation), (d) overhead chain (Ford Motor Company).

(c)

(d)

are large and do not become easily plugged. They also tend to lighten the head casting, thus reducing cost and total engine weight.

4-5 INTAKE AND EXHAUST VALVE MECHANISMS

Automotive engine valves are a *poppet valve* design that operate in a reciprocating manner. The valve is opened by a cam that is timed to the piston position and crankshaft cycle. It is closed by one or more springs.

The cam is driven by timing gears, chains, or belts, located at the front of the engine. These are illustrated in Figure 4-13. The gear or sprocket on the camshaft has twice as many teeth as the one on the crankshaft. This results in the required two crankshaft turns for each turn of the camshaft in four-stroke cycle engines.

Most valve design features are the same for all valves; however, intake valves control the inlet of cool, low-pressure charges, while the exhaust valves must handle hot, high-pressure gases. This means that exhaust valves are exposed to more severe operating conditions and, therefore, are made from much higher quality and more expensive materials than the intake valves.

Valve Design. Extensive testing has shown that there is a definite relationship between the different dimensions of valve geometry. Engines with bores

Fig. 4-14 Identification of valve parts (Chrysler Motors Corporation).

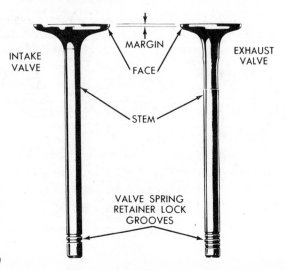

INTAKE VALVE

MARGIN

FACE

EXHAUST VALVE

STEM

VALVE SPRING RETAINER LOCK GROOVES

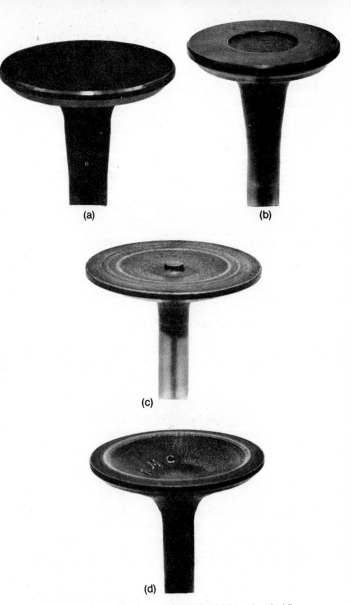

Fig. 4-15 Valve head types from rigid (a) to elastic (d).

from three to eight inches should have intake valves approximately 45% of the bore size. The exhaust valves should be approximately 38% of the bore size. The intake valve needs to be larger than the exhaust valve to enable it to handle the same gas mass because the intake valve controls low velocity, low density gases.

The exhaust valve, on the other hand, controls high velocity, high pressure, more dense gases that can be handled by a smaller valve. Exhaust valves are, therefore, approximately 85% of the intake valve size. Valve head diameter, for satisfactory operation, is nearly 115% of the port diameter and the amount the valve opens, called *valve lift,* is close to 25% of the valve diameter.

Poppet valve heads may be designed from the extremes of a rigid valve to an elastic valve as shown in Figure 4-15. The rigid valve is strong, holds its shape, and conducts heat readily, but is susceptible to valve leakage and burning, while the elastic valve is able to conform to valve seat shape so it seals easily but it runs hot and the flexing encourages breaking. The most popular shape is one with a small cup in the top of the valve head. It offers a reasonable weight, good strength, and good heat transfer at a slight cost penalty.

The valve face angles have been carefully selected to give the best compromise. With a given small valve opening distance the opening space around the valve face increases as the face angle is reduced. This value can be calculated by using the trigonometric function, the cosine, of the valve face angle. Even though a flat valve with a face angle of 0° provides maximum valve opening for a given lift, it is very difficult to seal when it is closed. Poor sealing will lead to valve burning and a short, useful valve life.

The sealing force on the valve seat is increased as the valve angle is increased. Forty-five degree face angles are used on exhaust valves and on intake valves where higher seating pressures are preferred and where deposits must be either crushed or wiped off to prevent valve leakage.

Valve Materials. Valve design and gas flow considerations have been well established to provide satisfactory performance in the modern engine. Increasing durability and cost will continue to be subjects of valve development studies. These problems are most apparent in valve metallurgy and manufacturing techniques. New manufacturing techniques must be developed as new valve materials are developed to maintain valve economy. Most of the recent valve development work has been done on exhaust valves that are subjected to an increasingly severe operational environment.

Alloys used in exhaust valve materials are chromium for oxidation resistance with small amounts of nickel, manganese, and nitrogen added. Heat treating is used whenever necessary to produce desired valve properties. Some exhaust valves are manufactured from two different materials where a one-piece design cannot meet the hardness and corrosion-resistance specifications desired. This can be seen in Figure 4-16. The valve heads are made from special alloys that can operate at high temperature, have physical strength, resist lead-oxide corrosion and have indentation resistance. These heads are welded to stems that have good wear-resistance properties. In severe applications,

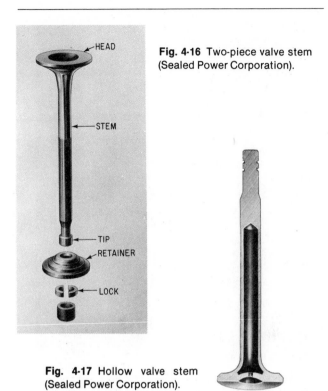

Fig. 4-16 Two-piece valve stem (Sealed Power Corporation).

Fig. 4-17 Hollow valve stem (Sealed Power Corporation).

facing alloys are welded to the valve face and valve tip.

Some heavy-duty applications use hollow stem exhaust valves that are partially filled with metallic sodium. The sodium becomes a liquid at operating temperatures. As it splashes back and forth in the valve stem, the sodium transfers heat from the valve head and dissipates it through the valve stem and guide. In general, one-piece valve design using properly selected materials will provide satisfactory service for automotive engines.

Valve Guides and Seats. The valve face closes against a valve seat to seal the combustion chamber. The seat is integrally formed in the head casting of automotive engines. Insert seats are used in some applications where corrosion and wear resistance are critical. Insert seats are also used as a salvage procedure for integral automotive engine valve seats that have been badly damaged.

Valve seat distortion is one of the major causes of valve problems. Distortion may be transient as the result of pressure and thermal stress or it may be permanent as the result of mechanical stress. Valve seat distortion must be kept at a minimum for maximum valve service life. This means that the

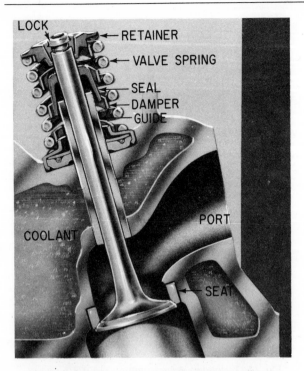

Fig. 4-18 Identification of the valve parts assembly (Chevrolet Motor Division, General Motors Corporation).

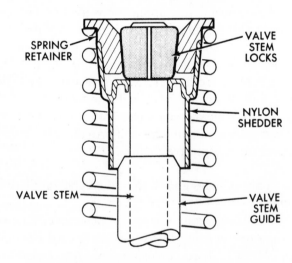

Fig. 4-19 Valve spring retaining method with nylon shredder oil deflector (Cadillac Motor Car Division, General Motors Corporation).

engine must be correctly and carefully assembled using proper parts.

A valve guide supports the valve stem so that the valve face will remain perfectly centered or concentric with the valve seat. Here again, the valve guide is generally integral with the head casting for better heat transfer and lower manufacturing costs. Insert valve guides are always used where the valve stem and head materials are not compatible. Figure 4-18 shows an insert-type valve guide and seat.

Valve Springs and Locks. A valve spring holds the valve against the seat when the valve is not being operated. One end of the valve spring is seated against the head. The other end of the spring is attached under compression to the valve through a valve spring retainer and a valve spring keeper or lock as shown in Figure 4-19.

Valves usually use a single inexpensive valve spring. When this does not provide adequate control, additional devices are added. Variable rate springs provide added spring pressure when the valve is in its open position. This is accomplished by using closely spaced coils on the cylinder head end of the spring. The closely spaced coils also tend to dampen natural frequency vibrations that may exist in a uniformly wound coil spring. Some valve springs use a flat coiled damper inside the spring. This eliminates spring surge and adds some valve spring tension. Figure 4-20 illustrates typical valve springs.

Multiple valve springs are used where large lifts are required and a single spring has insufficient strength to control the valve. Multiple valve springs generally have their coils wound in opposite directions to control surge and valve rotation.

A large number of valve locks have been used on the end of the valve stem to retain the spring. They have evolved from simple, low-cost lock pins and horseshoes to the current high-quality, split-cone lock or keeper. The inside surface of the split lock uses a variety of grooves or beads, depending upon their holding requirements. The outside of the split lock fits into a cone-shaped seat in the center of the valve spring retainer (see Figure 4-21).

One-piece valve spring retainers may be

Fig. 4-20 Valve springs. On the left the spring has equal coils. The next spring has a damper inside the coil. This is followed by a spring that has closely spaced coils and a damper. On the right the spring is taper wound.

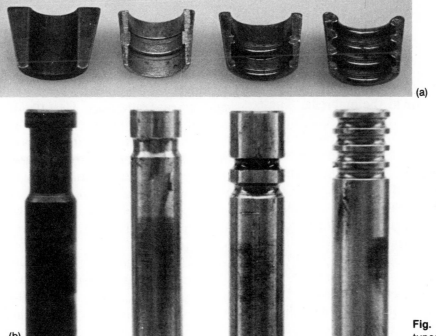

(a)

(b)

machined or forged. They are made from high quality steel so they will hold their shape under the pounding they receive in operation. Some retainers have built-in devices that cause the valve to rotate in a controlled manner. These cost more than plain retainers; therefore they are only used where it is desirable to increase valve service life. Valve rotator details can be seen in Figure 4-22.

Valve Oil Seals. Oil consumption by leakage past the valve guides is a problem in the overhead valve engine, especially around the intake valve stem where a high vacuum exists in the port as shown in Figure 4-23. A lot of design effort has gone into the development of deflectors and valve guide seals. Some early designers used umbrellas above the retainers that deflect the oil from the rocker arm to the area outside the valve spring.

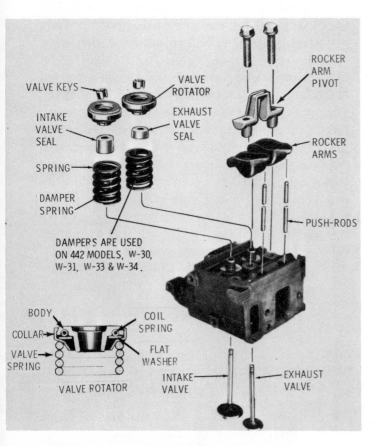

Fig. 4-22 Parts of a valve assembly showing the location of the valve rotator (Oldsmobile Division, General Motors Corporation).

Fig. 4-23 Oil pulled through a valve guide.

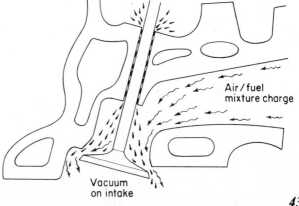

43

Later designs used synthetic rubber seals between the valve stem and retainer so that the retainer acted in the same manner as the umbrella. These can be seen in Figure 4-18. As more control was required, synthetic cups were placed on the valve stem and over the valve guide base. Some of these float and some are fastened. Plastic seals against the valve stem may be used in the synthetic cups as shown in Figure 4-25. Some advanced designs use a full plastic seal that is heat bonded to the valve retainer under the spring to deflect the oil outside of the valve guide boss (see Figure 4-19).

Care must be used when installing valve seals to be sure they are correctly installed and not damaged. Careless installation will result in oil leakage that will lead to excessive oil consumption.

Rocker Arms. Rocker arms reverse the upward movement of the pushrod to a downward movement on the tip of the valve. Engine designers make good use of the rocker arm to reduce the travel of the cam follower or lifter and pushrod while maintaining valve lift by using a rocker arm ratio of approximately 1.5:1. For a given amount of lift on the pushrod the valve will open 1.5 times the pushrod lift distance.

Rocker arm design has undergone change in new engines as a result of cost reduction programs and the need for divergent valve angles that are required in advanced combustion chamber designs. Rocker arms may be cast, forged, or stamped. Forged rocker arms are the strongest, but require expensive machining operations. They may have bushings or bearings installed to reduce friction and increase durability. Cast rocker arms cost less to make and do not usually use bushings but they do require several machining operations. They are not as strong as forged rocker arms, but are satisfactory for passenger car service. Cast rocker arms are shown in Figure 4-26.

Several types of stamped rocker arms have been developed (Figure 4-27). These are the least expensive type to manufacture. They are lightweight and very strong. Two general types are in use—those that operate on a ball stud or a pivot bar and those that operate on a shaft. The ball-stud and pivot-bar types are lubricated through hollow pushrods. The shaft type is lubricated through oil passages that come from the block, through the head and into the shaft, then to the rocker arms.

Pushrods. Pushrods are designed to be as light as possible and still maintain their strength. They may be either solid or hollow; however, they must be hollow if they are to be used as passages for oil to lubricate rocker arms. Pushrods use a convex ball end on the lower portion that seats in the lifter. The rocker arm end is also a convex ball, unless there is an adjustment screw in the pushrod end of the rocker arm. In this case, the rocker arm end of the pushrod has a concave socket and the mating adjustment screw has a convex ball end. Pushrod end types are shown in Figure 4-28.

Lifters and Tappets. Valve lifters or tappets follow the camshaft's cam contour and convert

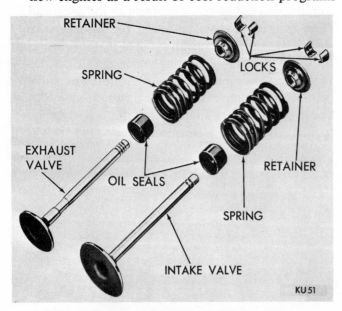

Fig. 4-24 Valve assembly parts showing the location of deflector-type oil seals (Chrysler Motors Corporation).

Fig. 4-25 Plastic insert seal held on the valve guide (Dana Corporation).

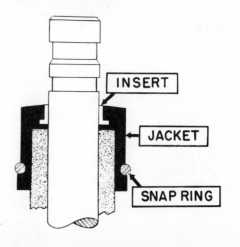

Fig. 4-26 Cast rocker arm types.

Fig. 4-27 Stamped rocker arm types.

Fig. 4-28 Types of pushrod ends.

cam geometry to a reciprocating motion in the valve train. The majority of lifters have a relatively flat surface that slides on the cam. Some lifters, however, are designed with a roller to follow the cam contour, rather than a flat surface. Because of the expense of making the roller lifters, flat lifters are used wherever possible. When the flat lifters are not able to provide satisfactory performance, roller lifters are used.

The valve train, like other manufactured parts, is made with a tolerance. This tolerance makes it necessary to have some means of clearance adjust-

ment in the valve train system, so that the valve will positively seat. Valve train clearance must not be excessive or it will cause noise or result in failure. Two methods are commonly used to make the necessary *valve clearance* or *lash* adjustments. One is a solid valve lifter with a mechanical adjustment and the other is a lifter with a hydraulic adjustment built into the lifter body.

In L-head engines, the solid valve lifter usually has an adjusting screw in the lifter. Overhead valve engines have an adjustment screw at the pushrod end of the rocker arm or a nut at the pivot point of the ball socket. Adjustable pushrods are available for some specific applications.

Valve trains using solid lifters require the valve train to run with some clearance to ensure positive valve closure, regardless of the engine temperature. This clearance is matched by a gradual rise in the cam contour, called a *ramp,* to take up the clearance before the valve is opened. This ramp ensures quiet operation. Valve trains using hydraulic lifters run with no clearance because the hydraulic unit is designed to take up any lash that may be present. Some models of engines have mechanical adjustments as well as hydraulic adjustment. The mechanical adjustments are used to place the hydraulic unit in its midrange position for normal operation. Because no clearance exists in valve trains using hydraulic lifters, no quieting ramp is provided on their cams. Typical solid lifters are shown in Figure 4-29.

The solid lifter is solid in the sense that it transfers motion axially from the cam to the pushrod or valve as a solid piece. Its physical construction is a lightweight cylinder, either hollow or with a small diameter center section and full diameter ends. In some types, the external appearance is the same as hydraulic lifters.

The major parts of a hydraulic lifter consist of a hollow cylinder body enclosing a closely fit hollow plunger, a check valve, and a pushrod cup. Engine oil pressure is fed by an engine passage to the exterior lifter body. An undercut portion allows the oil under pressure to surround the lifter body.

Holes in the undercut allow the oil under pressure to go into the center of the plunger and down through the check valve to a clearance space between the bottom of the plunger and interior bottom of the lifter body base, filling this space with oil at engine pressure. Slight leakage designed into the lifter allows the air to bleed out of the unit and allows the lifter to leak down if it should become over filled as a result of *pump up* caused by excessive engine speeds. The operating principle of a hydraulic lifter is shown in Figure 4-30.

The pushrod fits into a cup in the top open end of the lifter plunger. A hole in the pushrod cup, pushrod end, and hollow pushrod allows oil to transfer from the lifter piston center, up through the pushrod to the rocker arm, where it lubricates the rocker arm assembly.

As the cam starts to push the lifter against the valve train, the oil below the lifter plunger is squeezed and it tries to return to the lifter plunger center; however, a lifter check valve traps the oil below the lifter plunger, hydraulically locking the operating lifter length. The lifter then opens the valve as one solid unit. When the lifter returns to the flat of the cam, engine oil pressure again replaces any oil that may have leaked out.

The hydraulic lifter's job is to take up all clearance in the valve train. Occasionally, engines are run at *excessive* speeds. This tends to throw the valve open, causing *valve float.* Under these conditions, clearance exists in the valve train. The hydraulic lifter will take up this clearance as it is designed to do. When this occurs, it will prevent the valve from seating and is called *pump up.* Pump up will not occur when the engine is operated in its designed speed range.

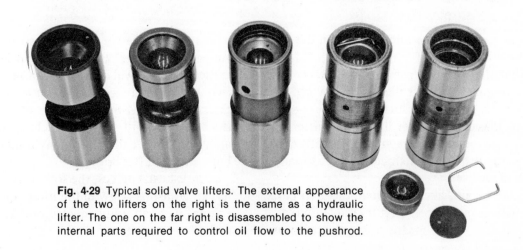

Fig. 4-29 Typical solid valve lifters. The external appearance of the two lifters on the right is the same as a hydraulic lifter. The one on the far right is disassembled to show the internal parts required to control oil flow to the pushrod.

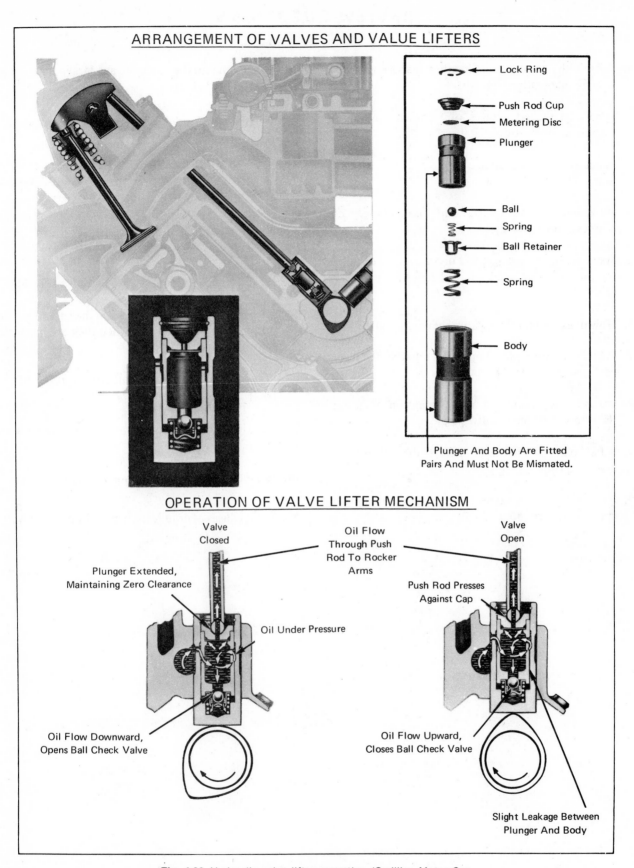

ARRANGEMENT OF VALVES AND VALUE LIFTERS

Lock Ring
Push Rod Cup
Metering Disc
Plunger

Ball
Spring
Ball Retainer

Spring

Body

Plunger And Body Are Fitted
Pairs And Must Not Be Mismated.

OPERATION OF VALVE LIFTER MECHANISM

Valve
Closed

Oil Flow
Through Push
Rod To Rocker
Arms

Valve
Open

Plunger Extended,
Maintaining Zero Clearance

Push Rod Presses
Against Cap

Oil Under Pressure

Oil Flow Downward,
Opens Ball Check Valve

Oil Flow Upward,
Closes Ball Check Valve

Slight Leakage Between
Plunger And Body

Fig. 4-30 Hydraulic valve lifter operation (Cadillac Motor Car
Division, General Motors Corporation).

REVIEW QUESTIONS

1. Why is the combustion chamber shape important to engine operation? [4–1]

2. What are the advantages of turbulent and non-turbulent combustion chambers? [4–1]

3. What is the disadvantage of excessive quenching areas in the combustion chamber? [4–1]

4. What are the advantages and disadvantages of Siamesed ports? [4–2]

5. What are the advantages and disadvantages of porting and relieving head ports of modified engines? [4–2]

6. How does coolant flow within the engine? [4–3]

7. Why are relatively large openings found in the head gasket surfaces? [4–3]

8. What is the reason for using expansion plugs on the exterior of some heads? [4–3]

9. What part of the head affects the lubrication system? [4–4]

10. How many degrees does the camshaft turn as the crankshaft turns 360°? [4–5]

11. Why is the intake valve always larger than the exhaust valve? [4–5]

12. What is the advantage and disadvantage of a rigid valve head? [4–5]

13. How do exhaust valves differ from intake valves? [4–5]

14. When are separate valve guides and seats used? [4–5]

15. Describe two types of valve stem oil seals. [4–5]

16. How do rocker arms differ when they are lubricated through the push rod and when they are lubricated through a shaft? [4–5]

17. Why are flat lifters used rather than roller lifters? [4–5]

18. Describe the operation of a hydraulic valve lifter. [4–5]

19. What is the purpose of a ramp on a cam? [4–5]

20. What causes hydraulic lifter pump-up? [4–5]

pistons, rings, and rod assemblies

All of an engine's power is developed by burning fuel in the presence of air in the combustion chamber. Combustion heat causes the combustion gas to increase its pressure. The force of this pressure is converted into useful work through the piston, connecting rod, and crankshaft.

The *piston* forms a movable bottom to the combustion chamber. It is attached to the *connecting rod,* which forms a swivel joint at each end. The connecting rod is connected to an offset portion of the crankshaft, called a crank throw, crank pin, or connecting rod bearing journal. Piston *rings* seal the small space between the piston and cylinder wall, keeping the pressure above the piston. When the combustion pressure builds up in the combustion chamber it pushes on the piston. The piston, in turn, pushes on the *piston pin* or wrist pin that connects the piston to the upper end of the connecting rod. The lower end of the connecting rod pushes on the crank throw providing the force to turn the crankshaft. This turning force, called torque, turns the drive wheels through a drive train.

As the crankshaft turns it develops inertia that causes it to continue turning to bring the piston back to its initial position where it will be ready to transfer torque from the next combustion. While the engine is running this cycle continues with the piston reciprocating and the crankshaft rotating. These motions impose mechanical forces on the parts. The combustion heat and mechanical forces are a major consideration in the part design.

5-1 PISTON CRITERIA

When the engine is running, the piston starts at the top of the cylinder, accelerates downward to a maximum velocity approximately halfway down,

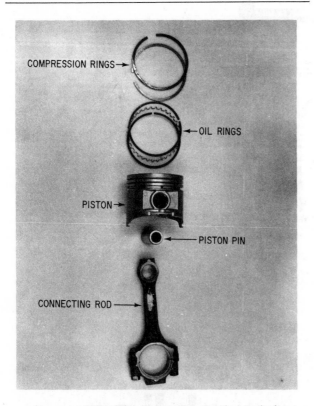

Fig. 5-1 Identification of the parts of a typical piston and rod assembly.

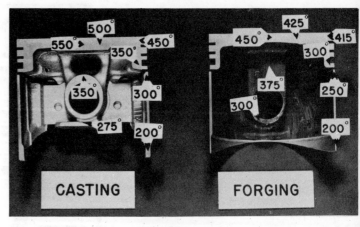

Fig. 5-2 Typical piston temperature distribution (Michigan Division of TRW).

and comes to a stop at the bottom of the cylinder during 180° of crankshaft rotation. During the next 180° of crankshaft rotation, the piston starts to move upward, accelerates to a maximum velocity, and then comes to a stop at the top of the stroke. Thus, the piston starts, accelerates, and stops twice in each crankshaft revolution. This reciprocating action of the piston produces large inertia forces. The lighter the piston can be made, the less inertia is developed. Less inertia will allow higher engine operating speeds.

The piston operates with its head exposed to the hot combustion gases while the skirt contacts the relatively cool cylinder wall. This results in a temperature gradient or temperature difference of about 275°F (147°C) from the top of the piston to the bottom, as shown in Figure 5-2.

The automotive engine piston, then, is more than a cylinder plug that converts the combustion pressure to a force on the crankshaft. It is a fine compromise between strength, weight, and thermal expansion control; at the same time, it must support piston sealing rings. The piston must have satisfactory durability to *live* under these conditions

while performing its function and while sliding against a cylinder wall.

As engine designs have developed, aluminum alloys have proved to be the best material from which to make pistons. Aluminum provides adequate strength with light weight. It does, however, increase the thermal expansion problem because the aluminum alloys have expansion rates approximately twice the rate of the cast iron used in the blocks and cylinder bores in which the pistons operate.

To further complicate piston design problems, modern automobile styling limits the space available for the engine while, at the same time, the customers demand increased engine performance. The easiest way to provide more engine power is to increase the engine displacement by enlarging the

Fig. 5-3 Piston to crankshaft clearance is minimal.

cylinder bore size and lengthening the piston stroke. Each of these require more space; however, more space isn't available. The passenger car engine designer has been able to increase engine displacement while still maintaining engine size by reducing the height of the piston to the bare minimum shown in Figure 5-3. The piston must still have enough strength to support combustion pressures and reciprocating loads, to have enough skirt to guide the piston straight in the bore, to have expansion control for quiet, long-life operation, and to be able to hold the piston rings perpendicular to the cylinder wall.

Piston Heads. Because the piston head forms a portion of the combustion chamber, its configuration is very important to the combustion process.

Generally, the low cost, low performance engines have flat-top pistons. Some of these flat-top pistons come so close to the cylinder head that recesses are cut in the piston top to provide valve head clearance. Pistons used in high powered engines may have raised domes or a *pop-up* on the piston heads, which will increase compression pressures. Pistons used in other engines may be provided with a depression or a *dish* that may be varied in depth as a means of providing different compression pressures required by engine model specifications. Piston head designs are shown in Figure 5-4.

Fig. 5-4 Piston head shapes from flat (a), to dished (e), and pop-up (f-g) on following page.

(a)

(b)

(c)

(d)

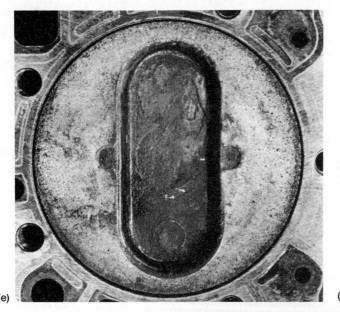
(e)

(f)

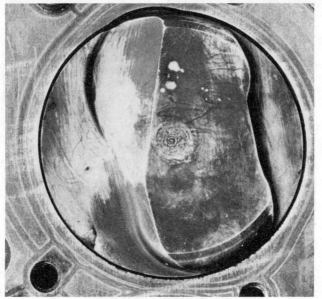
(g)

Fig. 5-4 (continued)

The piston head must have enough strength to support combustion pressures. Ribs are often used on the underside of the head to maintain strength while reducing material to lighten the piston. These ribs are also used as cooling fins to transfer some of the piston heat to the engine oil.

Piston Ring Grooves. Piston ring grooves are located between the piston head and skirt. The width of the grooves, the width of the metal between the grooves or lands, and the number of rings are critical in determining minimum piston height. Some heavy-duty pistons have oil ring grooves located on the piston skirt below the piston pin. Passenger car engines use two compression rings and one oil control ring, all located above the piston pin.

The piston ring groove depth must be deep enough to prevent the ring from bottoming in the base of the groove. Its depth becomes critical when used with some piston ring expander designs. The groove sides must be true and flat so that

Fig. 5-5 Identification of piston parts.

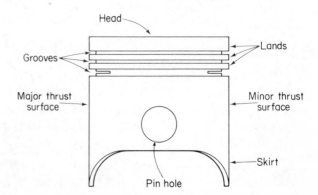

necessary sealing can occur. Oil ring grooves must be vented so that oil scraped from the cylinder wall can flow through the piston to the crankcase. This venting is done through drilled holes, saw slots, or cast slots, as shown in Figures 5-6, 5-9, and 5-10.

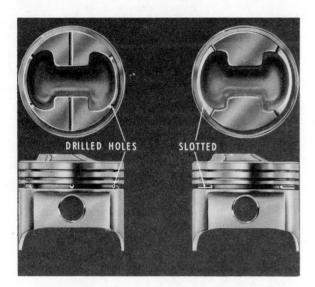

Fig. 5-6 Oil return openings in pistons (Chevrolet Motor Division, General Motors Corporation).

Piston Skirt. Piston expansion was a minor problem in older engines with cast iron pistons. Owners of these engines would tolerate piston slap noise from large piston-to-cylinder wall clearances on cold engines if the slap noise would stop when the engine warmed up. Some means of piston expansion control was required as the owner demanded quiet operation and as the engine power increased.

Piston expansion was first controlled through *slotted piston skirts* that were more closely fitted in the cylinder. The piston would expand into the slot as it was heated during operation. The most popular slot types were the U-slot and the T-slot. The U-slot design had two slots on the piston skirt that were connected together near the top of the piston skirt forming an inverted U shape. The T-slot had one slot down the piston skirt with a cross slot at the upper edge of the piston skirt to form a T-slot design. This method of expansion control carried over into the early aluminum pistons.

Aluminum pistons expand more than the cast iron pistons and the expansion slot piston skirt was too weak for the increased power demanded from the new engines. A better method of expansion control was devised using a *cam ground piston skirt* (Figure 5-7). The piston thrust surface closely fitted the cylinder, while the piston pin boss diameter fitted loosely. As the cam ground piston

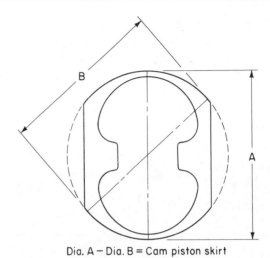

Dia. A − Dia. B = Cam piston skirt

Fig. 5-7 Piston skirt cam shape.

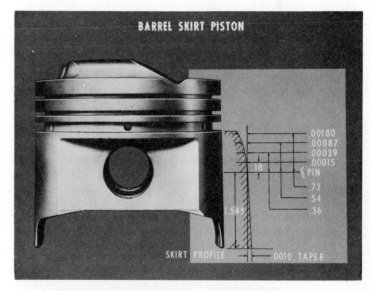

Fig. 5-8 Barrel skirt piston (Chevrolet Motor Division, General Motors Corporation).

was heated, it would expand along the piston pin, so it became nearly round at normal operating temperatures.

Later model engines have modified cam ground piston skirts by adding a progressively round skirt *cam drop* or barrel shape (Figure 5-8). The lowest portion of the piston is further from the combustion chamber and expands less than the upper portion. Therefore, the lower portion of the piston skirt may be made larger than the upper portion of the skirt at the thrust diameter. This allows the lower portion of the skirt to have a closer cold fit in the cylinder for quiet operation, while at the same time providing satisfactory service life.

Some pistons have horizontal separation slots that act as heat dams. These slots reduce heat transfer from the head to the lower skirt and, consequently, reduce the skirt temperature with an accompanying reduction in expansion. By placing the slot in the oil ring groove, some manufacturers use the slot for oil drain back as well as for heat

Fig. 5-9 Slipper skirt piston with cast oil slot heat dam.

Fig. 5-10 Trunk skirt piston with saw slot oil return and a cast heat dam opening below the pin.

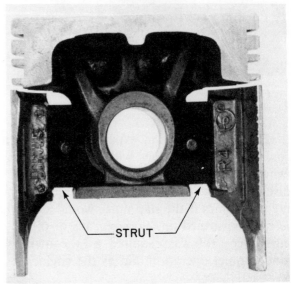

Fig. 5-11 Steel strut insert in a cast piston.

control. Placing the slot below the piston pin isolates the skirt from piston pin boss deflections that occur on the power stroke. These heat dam slots can be seen in Figures 5-9 and 5-10.

A major development in expansion control was accomplished by casting the piston aluminum around two stiff steel struts. The struts are not chemically bonded to the aluminum nor do they add any strength to the piston. There is only a mechanical bond between the steel and aluminum. The bimetallic action of this strut in the aluminum causes the piston to bow outward along the piston pin. This allows the thrust faces to expand at a slower rate than the cast iron cylinder in which they operate. Steel strut insert pistons allow good operation clearances while at the same time allowing cold clearance as small as 0.0005 in. (0.0127 mm), which will eliminate cold piston slap and noise. The strut is visible in Figure 5-11.

Fig. 5-12 Forged piston showing how the grain flow provides high strength (Michigan Division of TRW).

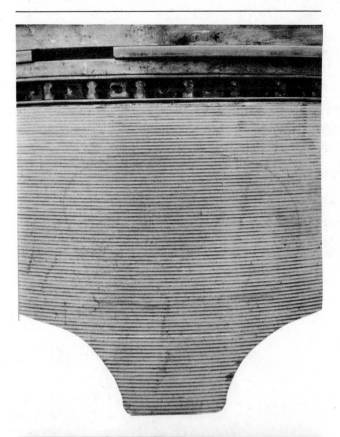

Fig. 5-13 Piston skirt surface finishes in common use.

Heavy-duty pistons are cylindrical castings with ring grooves at the top, using a trunk-type skirt. As automotive passenger car requirements have increased, the number and thickness of the piston rings have decreased and the cast aluminum piston skirt has been reduced to a minimum by using an open-type slipper skirt. High performance engines need pistons with added strength. They use impact-extruded forged pistons whose design falls between these two extremes of heavy-duty and automotive pistons.

Finish. For maximum life, piston skirt surface finish is important. Turned grooves or waves 0.0005 in. (0.0127 mm) deep on the surface of the piston skirt produce a finish that will carry oil for lubrication. Figure 5-13 shows typical surfaces of piston skirts. A thin tin-plated surface (approximately 0.00005 in. or 0.00127 mm thick) is also used on some aluminum pistons to help reduce scuffing and scoring during minimum lubrication. The piston skirt must ride on a film of lubricating oil to operate satisfactorily. Any time oil film is lacking, metal-to-metal contact will occur, and this starts scuffing. Piston scuffing leads to poor oil control, short piston life, roughened cylinder bores, and scuffed rings.

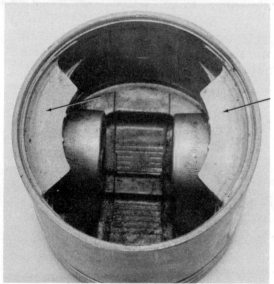

Fig. 5-14 Location of piston balance weight pads.

minimum weight. Sometimes the interior hole is tapered, large at the ends and small in the middle of the pin. This gives the pin strength that is proportional to the location of the load. Of course, a double-taper hole such as this is more expensive to manufacture and is only used where its weight advantage merits the extra cost.

Piston Pin Offset. Piston pin holes located in the piston are not centered but are located toward the major thrust surface approximately 0.062 in. (1.57 mm) from the piston center line, as shown in Figure 5-15. Pin offset is designed to reduce piston slap and noise that results from crossover action as

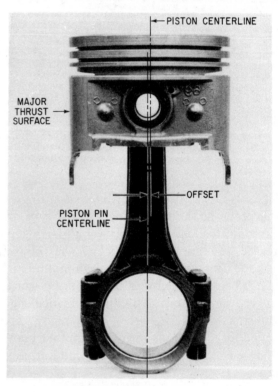

Fig. 5-15 Piston pin offset.

Fig. 5-16 Piston offset control as the crankshaft crosses over top center.

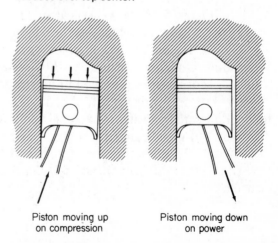

Piston moving up on compression

Piston moving down on power

Piston Balance. Pistons are provided with enlarged pads or skirt flanges (Figure 5-14) that are used for controlling piston weight. Material is removed from these pad surfaces as the last machining operation to bring the piston within weight tolerances set by the manufacturer.

5-2 PISTON PINS

Piston pins are used to attach the piston to the connecting rod, transferring the combustion chamber pressures and piston forces to the connecting rod. The piston pin is made from high quality steel in a tubular shape to provide adequate strength at a

the large end of the connecting rod swings past both upper and lower dead centers.

As the piston approaches top center in normal operation, it will be riding against the minor thrust surface as illustrated in Figure 5-16. When compression pressure becomes high enough, the greater area of the piston head on the minor thrust side resulting from pin offset causes the piston to cock slightly in the cylinder. This places the top of the piston skirt on the minor thrust surface and the bottom of the piston skirt on the major thrust surface against the cylinder wall. When the crankshaft crosses over top center, the connecting rod angularly forces the piston toward the major thrust surface. The lower skirt is already in wall contact with the major thrust surface so that the rest of the piston skirt wipes into full wall contact, thereby controlling *piston slap.*

Locating the piston offset toward the minor thrust surface will provide a better mechanical advantage. This offset direction is often used in racing engines where noise and durability are not as important as maximum performance.

Piston Pin Fits. The finish and size of piston pins are very closely controlled. Piston pins have a finish much like a mirror. Their size is held to tenths-of-thousandths of an inch so that exact fits can be maintained. If the piston pin is loose in the piston or in the connecting rod, it will cause a rattle while the engine is running. If the piston pin is too tight in the piston, it will restrict piston expansion along the pin diameter and will, therefore, produce piston scuffing. Normal piston pin clearances range from 0.0005 in. to 0.0007 in. (0.0127 mm to 0.0178 mm), which provides adequate freedom for movement between the piston and pin.

Piston Pin Retaining Methods. It is necessary to retain piston pins so that they stay centered in the piston. If piston pins were not retained, they would move endwise and gouge the cylinder wall. Piston pins are retained by one of three general methods. The piston pin may be full floating, having some type of stop located at each end; it may be fastened to the connecting rod; or it may be fastened to the piston (Figure 5-17).

Full-floating piston pins in automotive engines are retained by lock rings located in grooves in the piston pin hole at the ends of the piston pin. Some engines use aluminum or plastic plugs in both ends of the piston pin. These plugs will touch the cylinder wall without scoring, thus holding the piston pin centered in the piston.

Piston pins may be retained in the connecting rod by a clamp bolt located in the piston end of the connecting rod. The piston pin has an undercut which allows a portion of the clamp bolt side to locate the pin in the piston center. The bolt then clamps the rod around the pin, holding it securely. A newer method of retaining the pin in the connecting rod is to make the connecting rod hole slightly smaller than the piston pin. The pin is installed by pressing it into the rod so that it will be securely held by the press fit called an interference fit. With this method, care must be exercised to ensure correct hole sizes and correct centering. The press fit method is the least expensive to produce and is, therefore, found in the majority of passenger car engines.

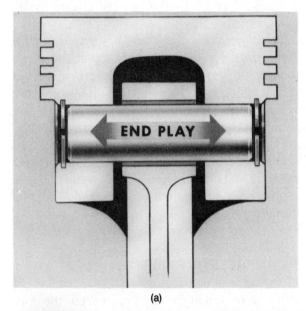

(a)

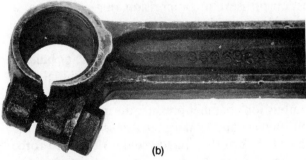

(b)

Fig. 5-17 Retaining the piston pin (a) with retaining rings (Ford Motor Company) and (b) clamping the pin.

On automobile engines, the piston is not fastened to the piston pin. On heavy duty engines where this is done, a cap screw through one side of the piston boss enters a hole or contacts a flat on the piston pin, thus retaining the pin. The cap screw is only placed on one side so that clamping does not interfere with normal piston expansion along the pin.

5-3 PISTON RINGS

Piston rings must provide two major functions; first, to form a sliding combustion chamber seal that will prevent *blow-by* of high pressure gases past the piston, and second, to keep engine oil from getting into the combustion chamber. The rings also transfer some of the piston heat to the cylinder wall where it is removed from the engine by the cooling system.

Piston rings are classified as two types—*compression rings,* located toward the top of the piston, and *oil rings,* located below the compression rings. The first piston rings were made with a simple rectangular cross section. This cross section was modified by tapers, chamfers, counterbores, slots, rails, and expanders. Piston ring materials have also changed from plain cast iron to materials such as pearlitic and nodular iron as well as steel. Piston rings may be coated with chromium or molybdenum materials.

5-4 COMPRESSION RINGS

In order to obtain maximum power from the combustion pressure a compression ring must form a seal between the moving piston and cylinder wall, at the same time keeping friction at a minimum. This is done by providing sufficient static or built-in mechanical pressure to hold the ring in initial contact with the cylinder wall during the intake stroke. Combustion chamber pressure during the compression, power, and exhaust strokes is applied to the top and back of the ring to provide the added force on the ring required for combustion chamber sealing during these strokes (Figure 5-18).

Mechanical pressure of the ring results from the

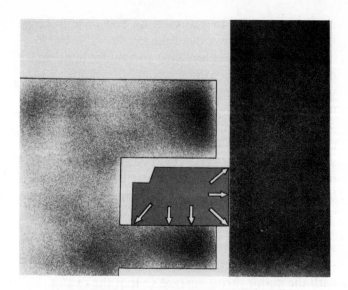

Fig. 5-18 Dynamic sealing force on the compression ring (Dana Corporation).

ring shape, material characteristics, and expanders. Rings are manufactured with a cam shape in their free state. When the piston ring is compressed to the cylinder size, it becomes round and develops the required mechanical tension. Additional piston ring control is provided by chamfers and counterbores that cause the ring to twist when it is compressed to the size of the cylinder (Figure 5-19). Twist is used to provide line contact sealing on the cylinder wall and in the piston ring groove. Line contact provides a relatively high unit pressure for sealing while, at the same time, allowing low total force which results in low friction. Expanders are sometimes used under compression rings when additional static force is required. When pressure exists in the combustion chamber, it acts on the top piston ring, forcing it to flatten on the base of the piston ring groove, sealing the ring and piston joint. For this sealing, it is important that the ring groove be flat and square. Pressure above and behind the

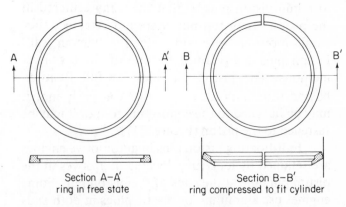

Section A–A'
ring in free state

Section B–B'
ring compressed to fit cylinder

Fig. 5-19 Ring twist resulting from ring shape.

ring will force it against the ring groove bottom and against the cylinder wall to produce an effective moving combustion chamber seal.

The piston ring gap joint will allow some leakage past the top compression ring. This leakage is useful in providing the required dynamic pressure on the second ring, so it can develop its required sealing force in the same manner as the top ring develops sealing force. Piston ring gap is critical, however. Too much gap will cause excessive blowby that will blow oil from the cylinder wall. This oil loss would be followed by piston ring scuffing. Insufficient clearance, on the other hand, would cause the piston ring ends to butt when hot. Ring end butting increases the mechanical force against the cylinder wall, causing excessive wear and possible engine failure.

A butt-type piston ring gap is the most common type used in automotive engines. This, obviously, is the least expensive to manufacture. Some low speed industrial engine manufacturers use a more expensive tapered or seal-cut ring gap to reduce losses of the high-pressure combustion gases (Figure 5-20).

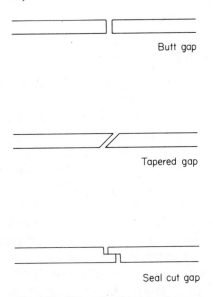

Fig. 5-20 Piston ring joint gap types.

As engine speeds have increased, inertia forces on the piston rings have also increased. Engine manufacturers have found it desirable to reduce inertia forces by reducing piston ring weight. This has been done over the years by narrowing the piston ring in fractional steps from ¼ inch to as low as ¹⁄₁₆ inch.

A discussion of piston ring cross-section, as illustrated in Figure 5-21, must start with a rec-

tangular shape. This was modified with a tapered face that would contact the cylinder wall at the lower edge of the piston ring. When a chamfer or counter bore relief is provided on the upper inside corner of the piston ring, the relief will cause the ring to twist in the groove in a positive direction, giving the same wall contact as the taper-face ring; at the same time it will provide a line contact seal in the groove. Sometimes the twist and taper face are used on the same ring.

Some second rings are notched on the outer lower corner. This, too, provides a positive ring twist. The sharp lower-outer corner becomes a scraper that helps oil control, but it has less compression control than the preceding types.

By chamfering the ring lower-inner corner, a reverse twist is provided. This seals the lower outer section of the ring and piston, thus improving oil control. Reverse twist rings require a greater taper to maintain the desired ring face to cylinder wall contact.

Fig. 5-21 Compression ring cross section as installed (condition exaggerated).

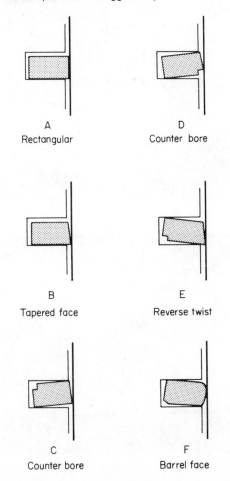

Some rings replace the outer ring taper with a barrel face. The barrel is 0.0003 in. per 0.100 in. (0.0076 mm per 0.254 mm) of piston ring width. Barrel faces may be found on rectangular rings as well as on torsionally twisted rings.

Piston ring facing materials are very important to provide maximum service life. Prior to World War II, rings were made *entirely* of cast iron. This practice was modified during the war as a result of aircraft engine piston ring development. Techniques were developed to put chromium on the piston ring face. This hard chromium surface greatly increases piston ring life, especially where abrasive materials are present in the air. During manufacture, the chromium-plated ring is slightly chamfered at the outer corners and about 0.0004 in. (0.010 mm) of chrome is plated on the passenger car engine compression ring face. These are pre-

Fig. 5-22 Compression ring facing. (a) Chromium, (b) molybdenum (Sealed Power Corporation).

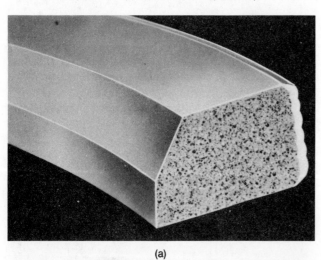

(a)

(b)

lapped or honed before being packaged and shipped to the customer.

Early in the 1960's, molybdenum piston ring faces were introduced. These rings also proved to have good service life, especially in high temperature applications and under scuffing conditions. Most molybdenum-faced piston rings have a 0.004 in. to 0.008 in. (0.1 mm to 0.2 mm) deep groove cut on the ring face that is filled with molybdenum, using a metallic spray method, so that there is a cast iron edge above and below the molybdenum. This edge may be chamfered on some applications. Piston ring facing is shown in Figure 5-22.

Molybdenum-faced piston rings will survive under heat and scuffing conditions better than chromium-faced rings. Under abrasive wear conditions, chromium-faced rings will have a better service life. There is little measurable difference between these two facing materials with respect to blow-by, oil control, break-in, and horsepower. Piston rings with either of these two types of facings are far better than plain cast iron rings. Often, a molybdenum-faced ring will be found in the top groove and a chromium-faced ring in the second groove.

5-5 OIL CONTROL RINGS

Originally, piston rings were not divided into compression and oil rings. All piston rings were plain rectangular rings. The first rings to be called oil rings were tapered rings with a scraping lower edge that removed a large part of the oil from the cylinder wall on the piston down stroke. These rings were then vented by machining slots through the ring to allow oil to return through openings in the piston. This machining, as shown in Figure 5-23, produced two scraping edges that performed better than the single edge. Steel spring expanders were added to improve radial pressure that forced the ring to conform to the cylinder wall. Many expander designs are used. They may either act as a spring between the ring groove base and the ring or their force can result from radial action when the two ends of the expander butt together under a compression force as the ring is forced into the ring groove by the cylinder.

As the oil ring requirements became greater, cast iron was no longer satisfactory. Steel rails with chromium or other types of facings replaced the cast iron scraping edges. The rails are backed with expanders and separated with a spacer. Some

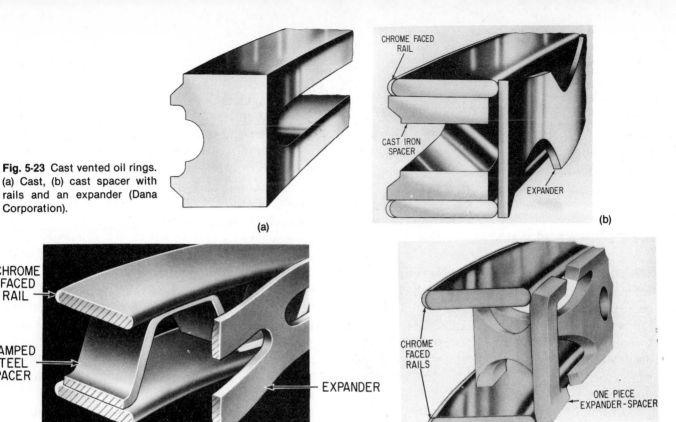

Fig. 5-23 Cast vented oil rings. (a) Cast, (b) cast spacer with rails and an expander (Dana Corporation).

(a)

CHROME FACED RAIL

CAST IRON SPACER

EXPANDER

(b)

CHROME FACED RAIL

STAMPED STEEL SPACER

EXPANDER

(a)

CHROME FACED RAILS

ONE PIECE EXPANDER-SPACER

(b)

Fig. 5-24 Steel ribbon oil rings, expanders and spacers. (a) Sealed Power Corporation and (b) Dana Corporation.

expander designs provide the spacing function as well as the expansion function. This type of oil ring is lightweight, having desirable low inertia loads, and is well ventilated so the oil can easily flow through it to the crankcase. It provides excellent oil control and has a long service life. All of this is provided at a low cost and is, therefore, used on volume-produced passenger car applications.

The piston ring cannot do its job unless it can seal against the cylinder wall through its entire normal service life. Cylinder wall finishes are critical. The cylinder wall is honed with a 60° included-angle cross hatch pattern (Figure 5-26). The coarseness of this finish must be compatible with the requirements of the piston ring facing materials.

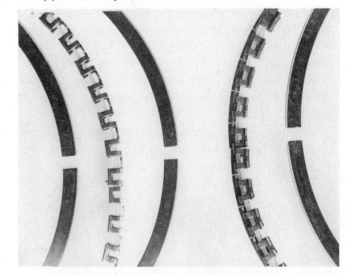

Fig. 5-25 On the left is an oil ring having a steel spacer and two steel rails. On the right is an oil ring having one rail and a combination spacer-rail.

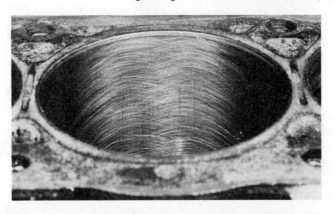

Fig. 5-26 Typical cylinder wall finish before use.

In general, the finish roughness should be a satin finish of about 25 micro-inches. Micro-inches are a measure of the average surface smoothness from the highest hump to the lowest depression.

5-6 CONNECTING RODS

The connecting rod transfers piston reciprocating force to crankshaft rotation. The small end of the connecting rod reciprocates and the large end follows the crank pin rotational pattern. These dynamic motions make it desirable to keep the connecting rod as light as possible and still have a rigid beam section. Lightweight rods also reduce the total connecting rod material cost.

Connecting rods are manufactured by both casting and forging processes. Forged connecting rods have been used for years and are always used in performance engines. Casting materials and processes have been improved so that many high production standard passenger car engines are able to replace forged connecting rods with less expensive cast connecting rods. Their cost is reduced both in the initial casting cost and in the machining cost. Generally speaking, the forging method produces lighter weight but more expensive connecting rods.

The connecting rod design, as shown in Figure 5-27, is basically two ring forms that encircle the piston pin and the crankshaft rod journal. From each of these ring forms a tangential fillet blends into a tapered I-beam section that makes up the rigid rod strut. The large split-ring form for the crankshaft end is machined after the cap is assembled on the rod so that it forms a perfect circle. Assembly bolt holes are closely reamed in both the cap and connecting rod to assure alignment. The connecting rod bolt diameters have piloting surfaces which bear in these reamed holes. The bolt heads are formed so that they have two or three sides which bear against the rod bolt bosses. The fourth side is left off so that there is sufficient cylinder skirt clearance as the crankshaft turns. Some connecting rod bolt heads are made on an angle to provide adequate clearance. These can be seen in Figure 5-29.

In some engines, offset connecting rods (Figure 5-30) provide the most economical distribution of main bearing space and crankshaft cheeks. The amount of offset of the piston pin end and the crankshaft journal end is measured in the lengthwise direction of the engine. Usually, the offset is divided equally between each end, keeping the connecting rod column perpendicular. Offset rods do not have as good a bearing endurance quality as symmetrical rods. Bearing failure occurs in the bearing edge halves nearest the shank, where the loads are greatest.

The sweep or path of the connecting rod must clear all engine parts as the crankshaft rotates. This would require minimum bolt center line distance and minimum head and nut size. The large end, however, needs to be large enough to carry a con-

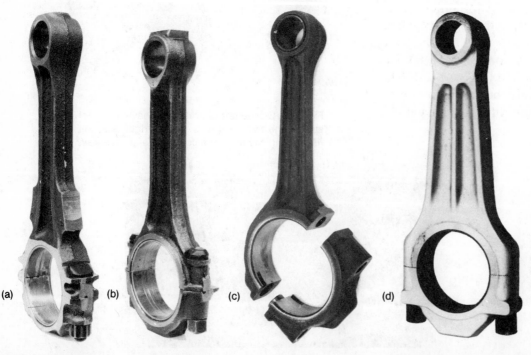

(a)   (b)   (c)   (d)

Fig. 5-27 Connecting rod types. (a) Cast iron (b) forged steel, (c) cap separated at an angle on a forged rod, (d) forged aluminum racing rod.

necting rod bearing that is designed to support the dynamic loads. The length of the bearing usually determines bearing high speed endurance capacity.

Connecting rods are made with balancing bosses, so their weight can easily be held to specifications. Some have balancing bosses only on the rod cap. Others have a balancing boss above the piston pin as well. Some manufacturers put balancing bosses on the side of the rod near the connecting rod center of gravity. Balancing is done on automatic balancing machines before the rod is installed in an engine.

Most connecting rods have *spit holes* that bleed some of the oil from the connecting rod jour-

nal. The hole may be drilled or it may be a chamfer on the cap parting surface. On inline engines oil is thrown from the spit hole into the same cylinder. It is thrown into the opposing cylinder in the opposite bank on V-engines. This oil is aimed so that it will splash into the interior of the piston and lubricate the piston pin. Occasionally, adequate lubrication is obtained without a spit hole. A hole similar to the spit holes is provided as a *bleed hole* to control oil flow through the bearing. Some heavy-duty engine connecting rods are drilled lengthwise. Oil flows through the drilled passage to the piston pin. This is an expensive process and is only used where the spit-hole method will not supply adequate lubrication.

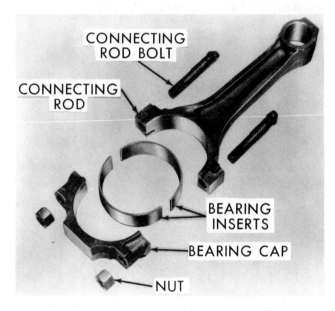

Fig. 5-28 Connecting rod assembly parts (Cadillac Motor Car Division, General Motors Corporation).

Fig. 5-29 Connecting rod balancing bosses.

Fig. 5-30 Offset connecting rod.

Fig. 5-31 Rod spit and bleed holes.

REVIEW QUESTIONS

1. Why is it necessary to make the pistons as light as possible? [5–1]

2. Why does the piston head have a pop-up or dish? [5–1]

3. Why is the piston ring groove depth important? [5–1]

4. What is done to modern pistons to control their expansion? [5–1]

5. What is the difference between cast and forged pistons? [5–1]

6. What is the purpose of specialized piston skirt surface finishes? [5–1]

7. How is a piston balanced? [5–1]

8. How does the piston pin offset control piston slap? [5–2]

9. How are pistons held in place in the majority of passenger car engines? [5–2]

10. What two functions are provided by the piston rings? [5–3]

11. How is compression ring line contact provided? [5–4]

12. Why is it important for the ring groove to be flat and square? [5–4]

13. Why does some leakage through the top ring gap have little effect on compression loss? [5–4]

14. What factors limit ring gap size? [5–4]

15. When are tapered and seal-cut ring gaps used? [5–4]

16. What is the advantage of ring twist? [5–4]

17. Describe a barrel-faced ring. [5–4]

18. What is the advantage of using facing material on compression rings? [5–4]

19. Describe the design of a modern oil control ring. [5–5]

20. What connecting rod design features help give the engine adequate cylinder skirt clearance? [5–6]

21. When are offset connecting rods used? [5–6]

22. How does an oil spit hole help the engine? [5–6]

shafts, bearings, and oil seals

Automotive engines have only two major rotating parts—the crankshaft and the camshaft. Power from expanding gases in the combustion chamber is delivered to the crankshaft through the piston, piston pin, and connecting rod. The connecting rods and their bearings are attached to a bearing journal on the crank throw that is offset from the crankshaft centerline. The combustion force is transferred to the crank throw after the crankshaft has moved past top center to produce turning effort or torque which rotates the crankshaft. The camshaft is rotated by the crankshaft through gears, with chain driven sprockets or by belt-driven sprockets. The camshaft drive is timed so the valves open in relation to the piston position.

The crankshaft rotates in main bearings. These bearings are split in half so they can be assembled around the crankshaft main bearing journals. The

camshaft, in pushrod engines, rotates in sleeve bearings that are pressed into bearing bores within the engine block. Overhead camshaft bearings may be either sleeve-type bushings or split-type bearings, depending on the design of the bearing supports.

Both shafts must be capable of supporting the intermittent variable loads impressed on them and must still have the necessary properties to function as good bearing journals.

6-1 CRANKSHAFT

All of the engine power is delivered through the crankshaft. The shaft must have the necessary shape and must be made from proper materials to meet these power demands.

65

to twist the shaft in torsion. The crankshaft must be rigid enough to keep the deflection low.

Crankshaft deflections are directly related to engine roughness. When deflections occur at the same vibrational or resonant frequency, that is, vibrations per second as another engine part, the parts will vibrate together. These vibrations may become great enough to reach the audible level, producing a "thumping" sound. If this type of vibration is allowed to continue, the part may fail.

Harmful crankshaft resonant frequencies are dampened with a torsional vibration damper. This damper usually consists of a cast iron inertia ring mounted to a cast iron hub with an elastomer sleeve. This can be seen in Figure 6-1. Elastomers are synthetic rubber-like materials. The inertia ring size is selected to control the amplitude of the crankshaft vibrations for each specific engine.

Crankshaft Material and Manufacturing. Crankshafts used in high production automotive engines may be either forged or cast. Forged crankshafts are stronger than the cast crankshafts, but they are more expensive. Casting materials and techniques have improved cast crankshaft quality so that they are being used in more and more engines. The identifying features are shown in Figures 6-2 and 6-3.

Forged crankshafts are made from SAE 1045

(a)

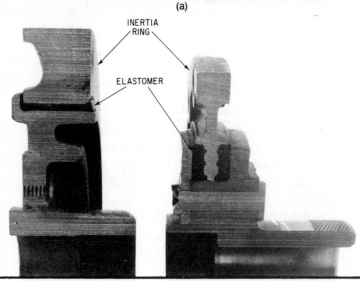

INERTIA RING

ELASTOMER

(b)

Fig. 6-1 Crankshaft torsional vibration damper. (a) Front view, (b) section view of two types.

Crankshaft Requirements. Each time combustion occurs, the force deflects the crankshaft as it transfers torque to the output shaft. This deflection occurs in two ways, to bend the shaft sidewise and

Fig. 6-2 Forged crankshaft. Forging lines indicate winding of twisting to index the crankpins.

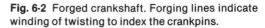

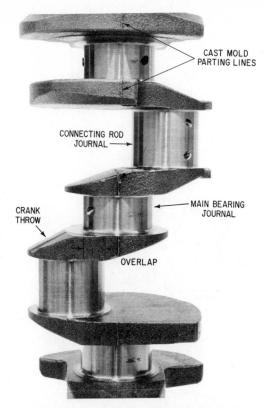

CAST MOLD
PARTING LINES

CONNECTING ROD
JOURNAL →

CRANK
THROW

← MAIN BEARING
JOURNAL

OVERLAP

Fig. 6-3 Cast crankshaft showing overlap and fillets as well as a straight casting mold parting line.

or similar type steel. The crankshaft is formed from a hot steel billet through a series of forging dies. Each die changes the shape of the billet slightly, finally forming the crankshaft blank with the last die. These blanks are then machined to finish the crankshaft. Forging makes a very dense, tough shaft with a grain running parallel to the principle stress direction.

Two methods are used to forge crankshafts. One method is to forge the crankshaft in place. This is followed by straightening. The forging in place method is usually used with forged six-cylinder crankshafts. A second method is to forge the crankshaft in a single plane, then wind it to index the throws at the desired angles. Shaft blanks are straightened as part of the winding process. Forged crankshaft design is limited by the die geometry and the forging parting lines. This means that forged crankshaft design must be a compromise between crankshaft requirements and manufacturing capabilities.

Automotive crankshafts may be cast in steel, nodular iron, or malleable iron. The major advantage of the casting process is that crankshaft material and machining cost are reduced because the crankshaft may be made close to the required

shape and size, including all complicated counterweights. The only machining required is grinding bearing journals and finishing front and rear drive ends. Metal grain structure is uniform and random throughout; thus the shaft is able to handle loads from all directions. Counterweights on cast crankshafts are slightly larger than counterweights on a forged crankshaft because the cast shaft metal is less dense and therefore somewhat lighter.

Crankshaft Design Features. The angle of the crankshaft throws in relation to each other are selected to provide a smooth power output. V-8 engines use 90° and 6-cylinder engines use 120° crank throws. The engine firing order is determined from the angles selected. Counterweights are used to balance static and dynamic forces that occur during engine operation.

Ample strength or torsional stiffness is one of the most important crankshaft design requirements. This can be provided by using materials with the correct physical properties, by having sufficient journal and crank cheek size, and by minimizing stress concentration through large fillets and properly placed lightening holes. Main- and rod-bearing journal overlap increases crankshaft strength because more of the load is carried through the overlap area rather than through the fillet and crankshaft web. This can be seen in Figure 6-3.

Stress tends to concentrate at oil holes drilled through the crankshaft journals. They are usually located where the crankshaft loads and stresses are minimal. The edges of these oil holes are carefully chamfered to relieve as much stress concentration as possible. Chamfered oil holes are shown in Figure 6-4.

Lightening holes in the crank throws do not reduce their strength if the hole size is less than half of the bearing journal diameter. These holes will often increase crankshaft strength by relieving some of the crankshaft's natural stress. In some cast crankshafts, the hole in the center of the crank throw is used for balancing, by controlling the hole depth (Figure 6-5).

Most crankshaft balancing is done during manufacture. Holes for balance are often drilled in the counterweight to lighten them. Sometimes these holes are drilled after the crankshaft is in-

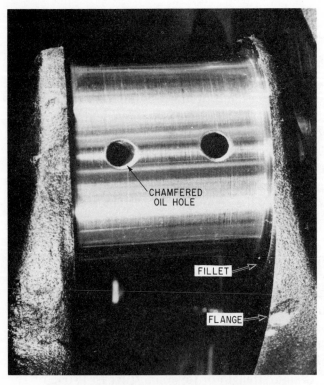

Fig. 6-4 Crankshaft rod bearing journal showing chamfered oil holes and fillet between the journal and flange.

Fig. 6-5 Balance hole drilled in crankpin.

(a)

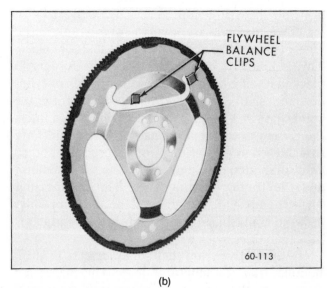

(b)

Fig. 6-6 Dynamic balancing weight shown as letter A in view (a). Torque converter drive plate weights in view (b) Buick Motor Division, General Motors Corporation).

stalled in the engine. Some manufacturers are able to control their casting quality so closely that counterweight machining for balancing is not necessary. Several engine manufacturers do final engine balancing with the engine running. Balance of these running engines is accomplished by adding weights to the damper hub and to the flywheel or automatic transmission drive plate. Typical methods of adding balance weights are shown in Figure 6-6.

Automatic transmission pressure and clutch release forces tend to push the crankshaft toward the front of the engine. Thrust bearings in the

engine will support this thrust load as well as maintain the crankshaft position. Smooth bearing journal surfaces are ground on a small boss located on the crankshaft cheek adjacent to one of the main bearing journals (Figure 6-7). The main bearing has bearing flanges that ride against these thrust bosses. Thrust bearings may be located on any one of the main bearing journals.

It has been found through experience that journal polishing direction is very important. The bearing will last much longer when the journal is polished against the direction of normal rotation than if it is polished in the direction of normal rotation. This can be illustrated by realizing that the surface finish left by grinding has slightly bent whiskers or fuzz like the teeth of a very fine file. It is smooth when the shaft turns with the direction of the teeth, but it acts like a fine milling cutter when the direction of rotation is toward the teeth. Polishing removes this fuzz.

There are many crankshaft designs. The engineer bases his selection on previous crankshaft performance and experience, modified by cost considerations. New understandings in metallurgy and manufacturing techniques along with a better understanding of the load requirements will continue to lead to crankshaft improvements.

Fig. 6-7 Thrust bearing on one crankshaft main bearing.

Fig. 6-8 Camshaft contour. Left, standard cam; right, performance cam.

6-2 CAMSHAFT

The second rotating shaft is the camshaft. Its major function is to operate the valve train. Cam shape or contour is the major factor in an engine's operating characteristics.

Camshaft Requirements. The camshaft is timed to the crankshaft so that the valves are opened and closed in relation to crankshaft angle and piston position. This allows the engine to have maximum volumetric efficiency at the engine speed selected. Cam lobe contour has more control over engine performance characteristics than any other single engine part. Engines identical in every way except cam lobe contour may have completely different operating characteristics and performance. Two cam contours are shown in Figure 6-8.

The camshaft is driven by the crankshaft through gears, sprockets and chains, or sprockets and timing belts. The gears or sprockets are keyed to their shafts so that they can be installed in only one position. The gears and sprockets are then indexed together by marks on the gear teeth or chain links. When the crankshaft and camshaft timing marks are properly lined up, the cam lobes are indexed to the crankshaft throws of each cylinder, so that the valves will open and close correctly in relation to the piston position. Typical cam timing marks are properly aligned in Figure 6-9.

As the camshaft lobe pushes the lifter upward against the valve spring force, a backward torsion force is developed in the camshaft. After the lobe goes past its high point, the lifter moves down the back side of the lobe, causing a forward torsion force. (See Figure 6-10.) This action produces an alternating torsion force at each cam lobe. These alternating torsion forces are multiplied by the number of cam lobes on the shaft. The camshaft must have sufficient strength to minimize torsion twist and must be tough enough to minimize fatigue.

Most valve trains use a spherical lifter face, 50 in. to 80 in. (1270 mm to 1432 mm) diameter, that slides against the cam lobe. It contacts the lobe off center, because the lobe has a slight taper across its face. This produces a turning effort on the lifter to cause rotation. In operation, there is a wide line contact between the lifter and the cam lobe where the highest pressure loaded surface is produced in an engine. The contact can be seen in Figure 6-11. Therefore, a great amount of design effort has gone into the metallurgy, heat treatment, design, and lubrication of the cam-to-lifter contact surface.

Camshaft Materials. Most automotive camshafts are made from hardenable alloy cast iron. It resists lifter wear and bearing wear, as well as providing the strength required. The very hardness required of camshafts makes them susceptible to chipping through edge loading or through careless handling.

Some heavy duty engine camshafts are made of steel. These must have case hardened journals and lobes to give them the required durability. Steel camshafts are also required in engines that use roller lifters.

Fig. 6-9 Camshaft timing marks. (a) Gear drive, (b) chain drive.

(a)

(b)

Fig. 6-10 Camshaft to lifter contact as the cam rotates showing the contact that tends to twist the cam.

Fig. 6-11 Cam to lifter line contact on the middle of the lifter.

Fig. 6-12 Cast iron and aluminum-nylon timing gears.

Fig. 6-13 Silent and roller timing chain.

Fig. 6-14 Oil groove around the outside of the cam bearing.

Fig. 6-15 Indexing oil holes in a cam journal.

The crankshaft gear or sprocket that drives the camshaft is made of sintered iron. The camshaft gear, when gears are used, has teeth made from a soft material to reduce noise. This whole gear is made of aluminum or fiber. When a chain and sprocket is used, the camshaft sprocket may be made of sintered iron or it may have an aluminum hub with nylon teeth for noise reduction. The timing chain is either a silent chain or roller chain. These features can be seen in Figures 6-12 and 6-13.

Camshaft Design Features. The camshaft is cast as one piece with lobes, bearing journals, drive flanges, and accessory gear blanks close to finished size. The drive end is finished first so the cam lobes will be correctly indexed to the proper angle. The accessory drive gear is finished with a gear cutter, and the lobes and journals are ground. The remaining portion of the camshaft surface is not machined.

Camshaft bearing journals must be larger than the cam lobes so that the camshaft can be installed in the engine through the cam bearings. Some engines have each cam bearing progressively smaller from the front journal to the rear, while other engines use the same size camshaft bearing journals on all journals.

Some engines make use of the camshaft journal or camshaft bearing to transfer lubrication oil from the main oil gallery to the crankshaft. One example is shown in Figure 6-14. Cam bearing clearance is critical in these engines. Other engines use drilled holes in the camshaft bearing journals to meter lubricating oil to the overhead rocker arm each time the holes index between the bearing inlet and the outlet to the rocker arm. Camshaft oil metering holes are shown in Figure 6-15. A cross section of the same metering system is shown in Figure 4-11 on page 38.

Each camshaft must have some means to control the shaft end thrust. Two methods, illustrated in Figure 6-16, are in common usage. One method is to use a thrust plate between the camshaft drive gear or sprocket and a flange on the camshaft. This thrust plate is attached to the engine block with cap screws. A second method is to allow the natural thrust developed by the oil pump turning effort to hold the camshaft into the block. A flange on the back of the camshaft drive rides against the front of the block, preventing the camshaft from moving backward into the engine. Some camshafts also add a button, spring, or retainer

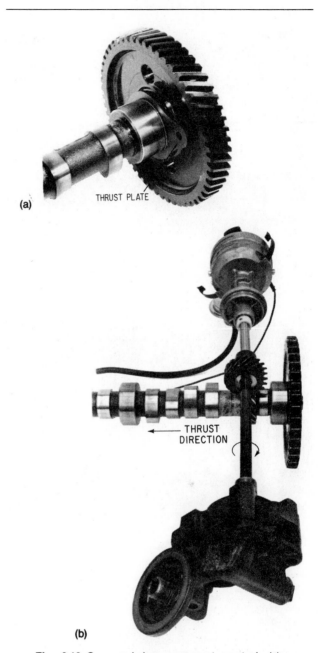

(a)

THRUST PLATE

(b)

Fig. 6-16 Cam endwise movement control. (a) Thrust plate, (b) oil pump thrust load.

on the timing cover to limit forward motion of the camshaft.

An eccentric cam lobe for the fuel pump, shown in Figure 6-17, is often cast as part of the camshaft. The pump is driven from this eccentric by a long pump linkage or pushrod. Some engines drive the fuel pump with a steel cup-type eccentric that is bolted to the front of the cam drive gear. This allows a damaged fuel pump eccentric to be

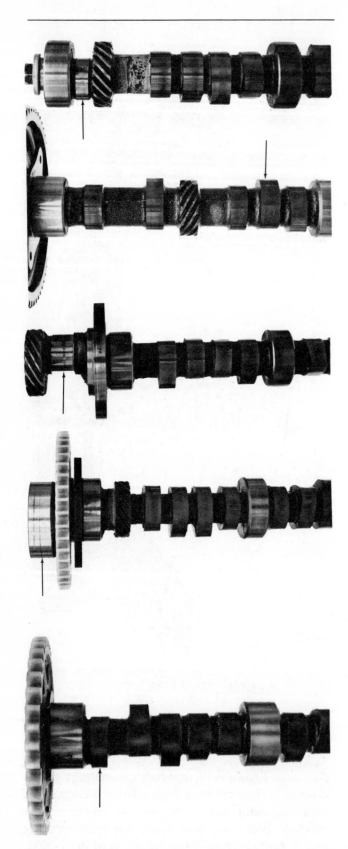

Fig. 6-17 Fuel pump eccentric locations on camshafts.

replaced without replacing an entire camshaft. It also allows the fuel pump to be mounted well forward on the engine, away from the exhaust, where it will be near the cool air coming into the front of the vehicle. This helps reduce the chance of vapor lock in the fuel pump and lines.

Camshaft materials and manufacturing methods follow standard industrial practices. Cam lobe contour features greatly affect an engine's performance. These contours are the most critical camshaft design features and require very careful machining.

6-3 DYNAMIC OIL SEALS

Dynamic oil seals are used between two surfaces that have relative motion between them, such as a shaft and a housing.

Dynamic Seal Operational Requirements. In engines, the seals keep liquids and gases in and keep contaminants out. They must do this with a minimum drag or friction. Oil seals must not press against the moving part so tightly that they wear a groove in the moving parts.

Some dynamic seals, such as piston rings, are designed to withstand a lot of pressure, while others, such as front and rear crankshaft oil seals, seal against little pressure. Seals in an engine that seal around rotating shafts are classified as radial positive-contact seals.

Seal selection is dependent upon the rubbing speed, fluid pressure, operating temperature, shaft surface requirements, and space available. When these factors are known for a specific application, the oil seal type can be selected.

Dynamic Seal Materials. Dynamic seals used in automotive engines are most frequently made from a rope packing or from synthetic rubber (see Figure 6–18).

Rope packing is the least expensive type of dynamic seal and is often used as a rear main bearing seal. It provides close contact between the seal and shaft without undue pressure. It therefore has very low friction and wear characteristics.

Lip-type dynamic oil seals are also used in engines. Some lip-type oil seals are made from leather, while others are made from synthetic rubber. Synthetic rubber is generally used for the lip-type seals in automotive engines. They can

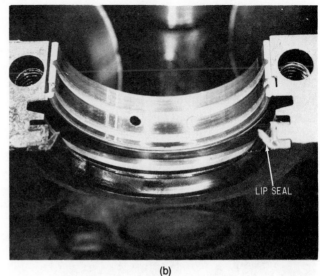

(a)

(b)

Fig. 6-18 Rear main oil seals. (a) Rope packing, (b) lip seal.

Fig. 6-19 Knurl finish on crankshaft under the rope packing-type seal.

Fig. 6-20 Timing cover lip-type oil seal with garter spring tension.

stand more shaft eccentricity and run-out than the rope-type seals. They can operate at higher shaft speeds, but they require a finer shaft finish to provide long life sealing. Lip seals place more load on the shaft than the rope-type seal, and therefore they seal better.

Dynamic Seal Design Features. Sealing is the result of an interference fit between the shaft and the seal. Rope-type seals must be packed into the seal groove, then trimmed to length. They do not function properly if they are stretched into the groove because this leaves gaps behind the seal for the oil to seep through. To help the rope packing to seal, the shaft surface under the packing may have a special finish grind or knurl that tends to pump the oil back into the engine. A knurled shaft is shown in Figure 6–19.

The lip-type seal is designed so that an increase in pressure to be sealed will increase the lip pressure against the shaft for better sealing. A spring tension element is used to help normal lip pressure in high speed applications, where excessive run-out occurs or where the fluid viscosity is low (Figure 6–20).

The seals must run with a very thin flow of lubrication. Ideal seal operation allows an oil meniscus to form on the outside of the seal with no leakage. If the seal had no lubrication, it would wear the shaft very quickly.

Lip seals are usually held in a steel case or are supported by bonding on to a steel support member. This makes the seal become a one-piece seal—for example, the seal installed on the front of the timing cover, or the split seal installed on a rear main.

Fig. 6-21 Oil slinger ring.

The oil seal is aided by an oil slinger on both front and rear ends of the crankshaft. The rear slinger may be a flange on the crankshaft. The front slinger is ususally a stamped steel ring or cup located between the damper hub and the crankshaft timing gear that is visible in Figure 6-21. The majority of oil that comes along the shaft is thrown clear of the shaft by the slinger. The seal is then able to handle any oil that remains on the shaft.

6-4 ENGINE BEARINGS

Engine durability relies on bearing life. Bearing failure usually results in immediate engine failure.

Bearing Requirements. Engine bearings are designed to support the operating loads of the engine and, with the lubricant, provide minimum friction. This must be done at all designed engine speeds. The bearings must be able to continue

to function for long periods of time, even when small foreign particles are present in the lubricant.

Most engine bearings are plain or sleeve bearing types, as contrasted to roller, ball, and needle bearings, which are called anti-friction bearings, that are used where only minimum lubrication is available. Properly lubricated plain bearings cause no more friction than the so-called anti-friction bearings because the shaft is actually rolling on a film of lubricant. In automotive engines, the lubricating system continuously supplies lubricant to each bearing. Only residual oil will be present during engine starting before the pressure builds up. During this period, the oil film will be borderline; that is, the oil film is so thin that the high spots of the shaft and bearing will actually contact each other. This will result in high friction and wear. After the oil film is established, friction drops and metal-to-metal contact is eliminated, thus stopping wear. Bearing and journal wear will only occur when the parts come in contact with each other or when foreign particles are present between them.

It is important that the engine designer provide bearings large enough so that the bearing unit load

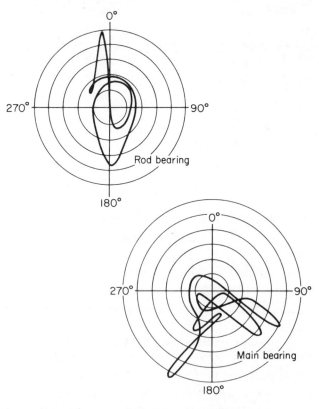

Fig. 6-22 Typical rod and main bearing load diagrams and polar diagram. Circles indicate the amount of force.

is within strength limits of the bearing. Bearing load capacity is calculated by dividing the bearing load in pounds by the bearing projected area. The projected area is the bearing length multiplied by bearing diameter. The load on engine bearings is determined by developing a polar bearing load diagram which shows the magnitude and direction of the instantaneous bearing loads. Bearing load diagrams look similar to Figure 6-22.

Here again, opposing objectives are at work. The automobile designer wants the engine to develop the greatest power and, at the same time, he wants to make the smallest engine size and the lightest engine possible. This would dictate the use of small bearings with high bearing loads. As greater bearing loads are applied, bearing life is reduced, unless a higher quality, more expensive bearing is installed. To keep costs down, one of the major design objectives of bearing engineers is to select the lowest cost bearing that will adequately meet the engine's operational requirements.

Bearing Performance Characteristics. Bearings tend to flex under intermittent loads. This is especially noticeable in reciprocating engine bearings. Bearing metals, like other metals, tend to fatigue and break after being flexed for a period of time. Flexing starts fatigue that shows up as fine cracks in the bearing surface. These cracks gradually deepen almost to the bond, then cross over and intersect with each other as illustrated in Figure 6-23. This eventually allows a piece of bearing material to fall out. The length of time before failure is called the fatigue life of the bearing. Bearings must have a long fatigue life for normal engine service. The harder the bearing material, the longer is its fatigue life. Soft bearings have a low fatigue life and low bearing load strength; however, they are generally less expensive

and are used in applications where the bearing requirements are low.

Manufacturing costs increase as the manufacturing tolerances decrease. To enable manufacturers to build engines with economical manufacturing tolerances, the bearing must have the ability to conform to small variations in the shaft position. This ability of bearing materials to creep or flow slightly to match shaft variations is called *conformability*. The bearing conforms to the shaft during the engine break-in period. In modern automobile engines, there is little need for bearing conformability or break-in, because automatic processing has held machining tolerances very close to the nominal size.

Engine manufacturers have designed engines to produce minimum crankcase deposits by providing them with oil filters, air filters, and closed crankcase ventilation systems that minimize contaminants. Still, some small foreign particles get into the bearings. The bearings must be capable of allowing these particles to embed in the bearing surface so they will not score the shaft. To embed the particle, the bearing material gradually works across the particle, completely covering it. This is illustrated in Figure 6-24. This bearing property is called *embedability*.

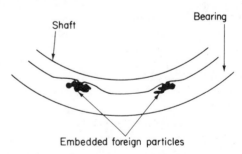

Fig. 6-24 Foreign particles embedded in a bearing.

Under some operating conditions causing temporary bearing overload, the oil film will break down, allowing the shaft to come in contact with the bearing. As the rotating crankshaft contacts bearing high spots, the spots become hot from friction. This could cause localized hot spots of bearing material that would seize or weld to the crankshaft. The crankshaft would then pull the particles around with it, scratching or scoring the bearing surface. Bearings have a characteristic called

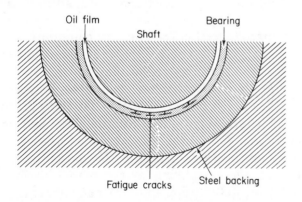

Fig. 6-23 Location of bearing fatigue cracks.

score resistance that prevents the bearing materials from seizing to the shaft during oil film break down. It is usually the result of the relatively low melting temperature of the bearing material.

Modern motor oils contain a number of additives that provide the oil with characteristics needed to satisfy engine requirements. In time, under high engine temperatures and high bearing loads, the additives break down, combine with the byproducts of combustion, and form acids. The bearing's ability to resist attack from these acids is called *corrosion resistance*. Corrosion can occur over the entire surface of the bearing. This will remove material and produce excess oil clearance. It can also leach or eat into the bearing material, dissolving some of the bearing material alloys. Either type of corrosion will reduce bearing life.

Bearing Materials. Three bearing materials are used for automobile engine bearings: babbitt, copper-lead, and aluminum. A 0.010 in. to 0.020 in. (0.25 mm to 0.50 mm) thick layer of the bearing materials is applied over a low carbon steel backing. The steel provides adequate support for the shaft load. The bearing material meets the rest of the bearing requirements.

Babbitt is the oldest automotive bearing material. Its base is either lead or tin, which is alloyed with small quantities of copper and antimony. Babbitt is still used in applications where soft material is required for soft shafts running under moderate loads and speeds. It will tolerate occasional borderline lubrication and oil starvation without failure.

Copper-lead is a stronger and more expensive bearing material than babbitt. It is used for intermediate and high speed applications. Tin, in small quantities, is often alloyed with the copper-lead bearings. This bearing material is most readily damaged by corrosion from acid accumulation in the engine oil. Corrosion results in bearing journal wear as the bearing is eroded by the acids.

Aluminum is the newest material to be used for automotive bearings. Automotive-bearing aluminum has small quantities of tin and copper alloyed with it. This makes a stronger but more expensive bearing than either babbitt or copper-lead.

Aluminum, with a small percentage of lead, is used for high quality intermediate strength bearings. Most of its bearing characteristics are equal to or surpass babbitt and copper-lead. Aluminum bearings are well suited to high speed, high load conditions.

Because of its expense, aluminum is often used along with bearings made from other bearing materials. For example, aluminum bearings may be used for the highly loaded lower main bearing shell with babbitt being used for the lightly loaded upper bearing shell on a single bearing journal.

Bearing Manufacturing. Modern automotive engines use precision insert-type bearings. The bearing is manufactured to very close tolerances so that it will fit correctly in each application. The bearing, therefore, must be made from accurate materials under closely controlled manufacturing processes.

Most of the precision insert bearings are manufactured in a continuous strip process. The low carbon steel backing is delivered to the bearing manufacturer in a roll. This steel must be within 0.001 in. (0.025 mm) of the thickness required. In processing, it is cleaned, flattened, and heated to the required bonding temperature.

The bearing material is applied to the steel strip in either of two ways, casting or sintering. In the casting process, molten bearing alloy is poured on the backing strip where it bonds as it cools. The sintering process is similar. Small particles of the bearing materials are mixed in a powdered state. The powdered bearing material is spread evenly on the continuous steel backing strip. It is then pressed and heated until it fuses together and bonds to the steel. Bonds of both processes are chemical, rather than mechanical. The finished strip is sheared into bearing blanks as it leaves this production line. The blanks are formed and coined to size in presses, then punched and machined to the final bearing configuration.

Many of the copper-lead and aluminum bearings have an overlay or third layer of metal. This overlay is usually babbitt. Babbitt overlay gives the bearing properties of high fatigue strength, good conformity, good embedability, and low corrosion. Obviously, the overplated bearing is a premium bearing. It is also the most expensive because the overplating layer, from 0.0005 in. to 0.001 in. (0.0127 mm to 0.025 mm) thick, is put on the bearing with an electroplating process.

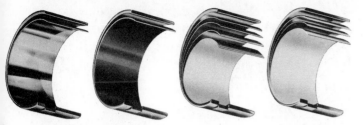

Fig. 6-25 Layers of bearing material (Sealed Power Corporation).

Overplate reduces bearing distress by cushioning the journal during the first few break-in hours of running. Once the bearing has adapted itself to the bearing journal, it will have a satisfactory life even when the overplate is gone.

Bearing Design. The physical design of the bearing must consider the loads being applied to the journal. In automotive engines, the load varies in magnitude and direction. Maximum bearing areas must be located where the forces or loads are the greatest. Oil holes and grooves are located on the lightly loaded areas of the bearing.

Oil enters the bearing through the oil holes and grooves. It spreads into a smooth wedge-shaped film that supports the bearing load by hydrodynamic action of the oil as is described in Chapter 8. Under high journal speeds, during high rpm operation, the oil film may no longer be able to maintain its laminar or smooth layer flow. When laminar flow breaks down, turbulent flow occurs and disrupts the bearing oil film. This ineffective lubrication may result in bearing failure.

Many bearings are provided with oil bleed holes so that the bearing will continue to be supplied with a fresh oil supply as described in Section 5-6. This flow keeps an adequate quantity of oil supplied to the bearing for hydrodynamic lubrication and provides a means of bearing cooling. Often, this oil bleed hole is made to aim oil at the cylinder wall for lubrication. When it does, the hole is called a *spit hole.*

A bearing design has been developed that does not require oil bleed holes. The bearing is of an eccentric design, illustrated in Figure 6-26, that has close clearances on the highly loaded bearing areas. This provides several spaces for the oil film to develop and, at the same time, provides adequate oil flow from the bearing edges for proper cooling.

The bearing-to-journal clearance may be from 0.0005 in. to 0.0025 in. (0.027 mm to 0.0625 mm), depending on the engine. Doubling the journal

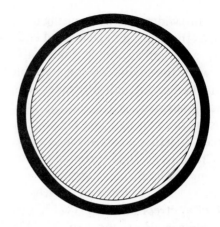

Fig. 6-26 Eccentric bearing design (exaggerated).

clearance will allow more than four times as much oil to flow from the edges of the bearing. The oil clearance must be large enough to allow an oil film to build up, but small enough to prevent excess oil flow that would cause loss of oil pressure. A large oil flow at one of the bearings would starve other bearings further along in the oil system. This would result in failure of the oil-starved bearing.

The bearing design also includes bearing spread and crush. The bearing has a slightly larger arc than the bearing housing. This is called *bearing spread* and is from 0.005 in. to 0.020 in. (0.127 mm

Fig. 6-27 Bearing spread and crush.

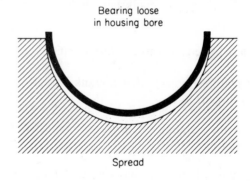

Bearing loose in housing bore

Spread

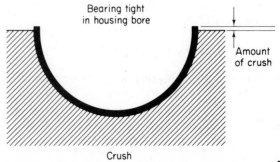

Bearing tight in housing bore

Amount of crush

Crush

Fig. 6-28 Tang on a bearing used to properly locate the bearing.

to 0.508 mm) wider than the housing bore. A lip or tang allows the bearing to be located endwise in the housing, and spread holds the bearing in the housing while the engine is being assembled. When installed, the bearing half protrudes slightly above the parting surface. When the cap is assembled, the ends of the two half bearing shells touch and are forced together. This force is called *bearing crush*. Crush holds the bearing in place and keeps the bearing from turning when the engine runs. Crush must exert a force of at least 12,000 psi (82,737 kPa) stress at 250°F (121°C) to hold the bearing in place. Forty thousand psi (275,790 kPa) stress is considered maximum without damaging the bearing or housing.

The engineer will select a bearing that is the least expensive bearing that will perform satisfactorily in operation. Replacement bearings should be at least as good a quality bearing as the original bearings, using the same oil holes and grooves. Modified engines have different bearing requirements and, therefore, they may require a higher quality bearing to provide satisfactory service.

REVIEW QUESTIONS

1. What are the major rotating engine parts? [INTRODUCTION]

2. What deflection occurs in the crankshaft? [6-1]

3. What does excessive crankshaft deflection cause? [6-1]

4. Compare forged and cast crankshafts. [6-1]

5. What features indicate that a crankshaft is either cast or forged? [6-1]

6. What is the advantage of a forged crankshaft? A cast crankshaft? [6-1]

7. What is meant by indexing a forged crankshaft? [6-1]

8. What features reduce stress concentrations in a crankshaft? [6-1]

9. How is a crankshaft balanced? [6-1]

10. Why is a thrust bearing necessary on a crankshaft? [6-1]

11. Why is the cam lobe design important? [6-2]

12. What design feature causes the valve lifter to rotate? [6-2]

13. Why do camshafts chip easily? [6-2]

14. What camshaft material is required when using roller lifters? [6-2]

15. Why are some camshaft sprockets and gears made from soft material? [6-2]

16. How do the sizes of cam lobes and cam bearing journals compare? [6-2]

17. What causes cam end thrust? [6-2]

18. How does the camshaft drive the fuel pump? [6-2]

19. What is the advantage of having the fuel pump eccentric near the front of the engine? [6-2]

20. What is the advantage of rope-type seals? lip-type dynamic seals? [6-3]

21. How does the friction of plane and anti-friction bearings compare when they have the correct lubrication? [6-4]

22. When does the most bearing wear occur in normal operation? [6-4]

23. What are the advantages of hard and soft bearing materials? [6-4]

24. When is conformability, embedability, and score resistance the most important in bearings? [6-4]

25. What are the advantages of each of the three types of bearing materials? [6-4]

26. Name two ways bearing materials are applied to the steel backing. [6-4]

27. What is the purpose of overplating on engine bearings? [6-4]

28. What causes corrosion of engine bearings that are running in motor oil? [6-4]

29. Why are bearing shells using different materials sometimes mixed on a single bearing journal in an engine? [6-4]

30. On what part of the bearing are the oil holes located? [6-4]

31. What is the purpose of oil bleed holes? [6-4]

32. How can a loose bearing cause oil starvation on other bearings? [6-4]

33. What is the purpose of the bearing tang? [6-4]

34. When is bearing spread useful? [6-4]

35. What holds the bearing securely in place as the engine runs? [6-4]

36. What is the basis for selecting bearings for engines? [6-4]

engine block and gaskets

The engine block, which is the supporting structure for the entire engine, is made of cast iron, or from cast or die-cast aluminum alloy. All other engine parts are mounted on it or in it. This large casting supports the crankshaft and camshaft, and holds all of the parts in alignment. Large diameter holes in the block casting form the cylinder bores to guide the pistons. The holes are called bores because they are made by a machining process called boring. Combustion pressure loads are carried from the head to the crankshaft bearings through the block structure. The block is provided with webs, walls, and drilled passages to contain the coolant and lubricating oil, and to keep them separated from each other. Mounting pads or lugs on the block transfer the reaction loads caused by engine torque to the vehicle frame through attached engine mounts. A large mounting surface at the rear of the engine block is used to fasten a bell housing and transmission. The modern engine block meets all of these requirements and has a longer service life than any other part of the engine.

The head, pan, and timing cover attach to the block. They need to have their attaching joint sealed so they do not leak. Gaskets are used in the joint to take up machining irregularities and changes from pressure and temperature extremes.

7-1 BLOCK DESIGN

Most domestic production automobile engines under 250 cubic inch displacement (4 liter) are inline overhead-valve six-cylinder engines. Four-cylinder inline engines have displacements of less than 150 cubic inches (about 2.457 liters). There was a time when the inline eight-cylinder engine was popular. However, as casting technology developed, production of a one-piece V-block was possible, and this design gradually replaced the inline eight for large displacement engines. A V-8 block is illustrated in Figure 7-1.

Inline engine cylinders are numbered from the front to the rear, number one being at the front. The V-engines present a different problem because, in a sense, they are two four-cylinder engines with their bases together and sharing the same crankshaft. Two approaches have been used to number the cylinders of V-engine blocks. One manufacturer (Ford) numbers the right block from one to four and the left block from five to eight. In general, the other manufacturers number their cylinders in the order in which the connecting rods are attached to the crankshaft, starting with the number one at the front of the crankshaft and going back to number eight at the rear. Some of these engines have the first cylinder at the right front. Most of the V-8 engines, however, use a numbering system having number one cylinder at the left front (Figure 7-2). As with all parts of the automobile, right and left are viewed from the driver's position.

The four-stroke cycle and crankshaft angles must be considered in the V-block design. For an

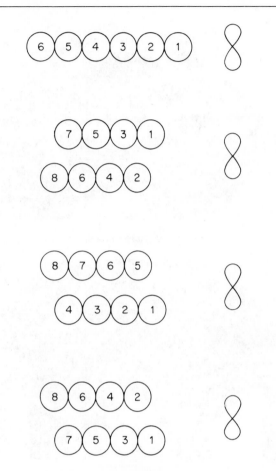

Fig. 7-2 Cylinder numbering system.

even firing engine, the V-8 must have its block at 90° (720° ÷ 8 cylinders). A V-6 or V-12 engine could use 120° or 60° blocks and have even firing impulses. One manufacturer makes a 90° V-6 engine as a production engine. This does not have even firing and requires the use of carefully tuned engine mounts for satisfactory vehicle service.

The engine block primarily consists of the cylinders with a web or bulkhead to support the crankshaft and head attachments. The rest of the block consists of a water jacket, a lifter chamber, and mounting flanges. In most engine designs, each main bearing bulkhead supports both a cam bearing and a main bearing. The bulkhead is well ribbed to support and distribute loads applied to it. This gives the block structural rigidity and beam stiffness throughout its useful life.

Two types of lower block designs are in use. One is called a V-block (Figure 7-3). The base of this block is close to the crankshaft centerline. The

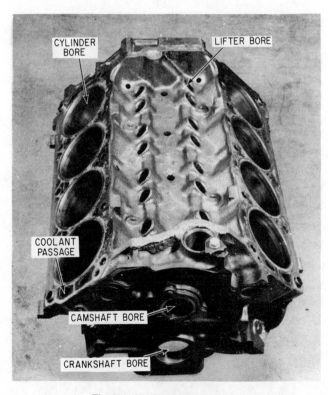

Fig. 7-1 A V-8 engine block.

Fig. 7-3 V-type engine block.

Fig. 7-4 Y-type engine block.

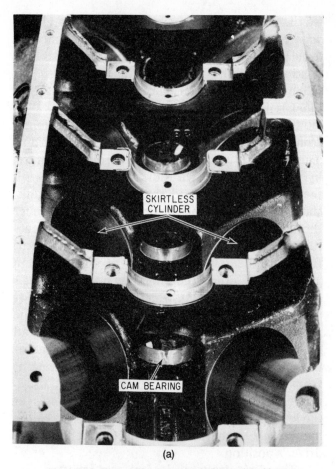

(a)

Fig. 7-5 Cylinder lower end. (a) Skirtless in a Y-type block, (b) extended skirt in a V-type block.

(b)

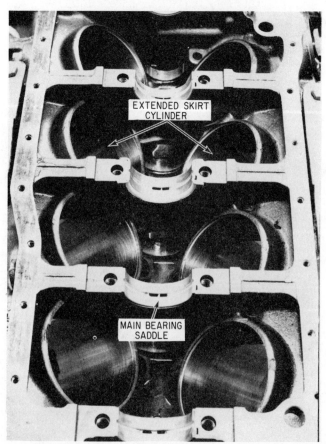

second type of block is called a Y or deep block (Figure 7-4). In this type, the deep skirt extends the oil pan rail well below the crankshaft centerline.

The V-block is the smallest and lightest of the two engine block types. The amount of cast iron used in it is kept at a minimum, making it a small, compact lightweight block. Covers, such as the oil pan and timing cover, are largely lightweight aluminum die castings or steel stampings.

The deep skirt block improves the stiffness of the entire engine. It provides a wider surface on which to attach the bell housing. This greater rigidity assures smooth, quiet engine operation and durability. The deep skirt must be wide enough to clear the connecting rods as they swing through the block and, therefore, large oil capacity is provided with its use.

The cylinder head is fastened to the top surface

of the block, called the block *deck*. The deck has a smooth surface to seal against the head gasket. Bolt holes with National Course (NC) threads are positioned around the cylinders to form an even holding pattern, using four, five, or six head bolts around each cylinder in automobile engines. These bolt holes go into reinforced areas within the block that carry the load to the main bearing bulkheads. Additional holes in the block are used to transfer coolant and oil.

The cylinders may be of a skirtless design, flush with the top of the crankcase (Figure 7–5), or they may have a skirt that extends into the crankcase. Extended skirt cylinders are used on engines with short connecting rods. In these engines, the pistons move very close to the crankshaft and require the cylinder skirt to go as low as possible to support the piston when it is at the lowest point in its stroke, as shown in Figure 7–6. This allows the engine to be designed with a low overall engine height since it has a small block size for its displacement size.

Cylinders are surrounded by cooling passages. In most skirtless cylinder designs, the cooling passages extend nearly to the bottom of the cylinder. In skirted cylinder designs, the cooling passages are limited to the upper portion of the cylinder.

During casting, the molds and cores are supported from outside. The core supports and cast-

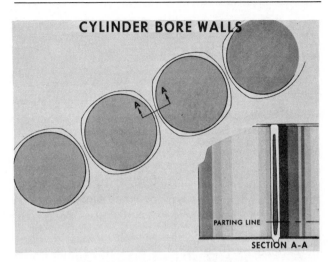
Fig. 7-7 Cylinder wall cooling passages.

ing vents will leave holes in the casting. Core holes in the block deck are closed with the gasket and head. Core holes left in the external block wall are machined to be sealed with soft plugs.

Soft plugs are of two designs. One is a convex design. For its use, the core hole is counterbored with a shoulder. The convex soft plug is placed in counterbore, convex side out. It is driven in and upset with a fitted seating tool. This causes the edge to enlarge to hold it in place. Figure 7–8 shows an installed convex soft plug. The second type of hole plug is a cup type. This type is fit into a smooth, straight hole. The cup is slightly bell mouthed, so that it tightens in place when it is

Fig. 7-6 Small clearance between the crankshaft counterweight, cylinder skirt and piston when the piston is at lower center.

Fig. 7-8 Convex-type soft plug.

driven in to the correct depth with a seating tool. An installed cup type soft plug is shown in Figure 7-9.

An engine block has many oil holes that carry lubricating oil to the required locations. During manufacture, all of the oil holes are drilled from the outside of the block. Oil holes are rarely cast in engine blocks. When a curved passage is needed, intersecting drilled holes are used. In some engines, plugs are placed in the oil holes to divert oil to another point before coming back to the original hole, on the opposite side of the plug. After oil holes are drilled, the unneeded open ends may be capped by pipe plugs, steel balls, or cup-type soft plugs. End plugs are a source of possible oil leakage in operating engines.

Fig. 7-9 Cup-type soft plug.

7-2 BLOCK MANUFACTURING

Cast iron cylinder block casting technology has come through a period of rapid development. The trend is to make blocks with larger cores, using fewer individual pieces. Oil-sand cores, shown in Figure 7-10, are forms that shape the internal

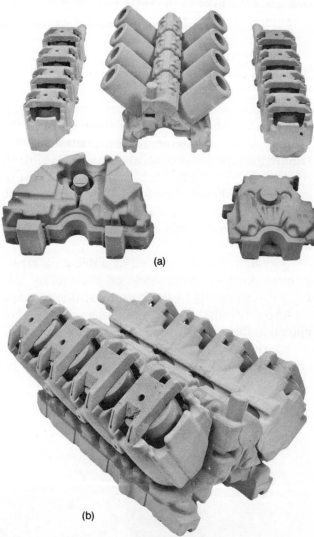

(a)

(b)

(c)

Fig. 7-10 Casting cores (Central Foundry Division, General Motors Corporation). (a) Separate cores, (b) assembled cores, (c) core box.

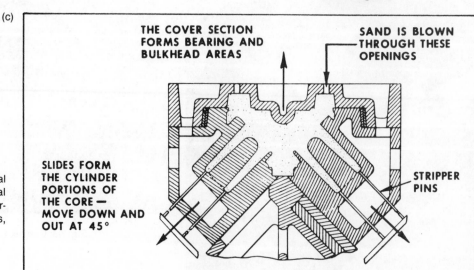

THE COVER SECTION FORMS BEARING AND BULKHEAD AREAS

SAND IS BLOWN THROUGH THESE OPENINGS

SLIDES FORM THE CYLINDER PORTIONS OF THE CORE — MOVE DOWN AND OUT AT 45°

STRIPPER PINS

openings and passages in the engine block. Prior to casting, the cores are supported within a core box. The core box also has the exterior block form liner. Special alloy cast iron is poured into the box. It flows between the cores and core box liner. As the cast iron cools, the core breaks up. When the cast iron has hardened, it is removed from the core box and the pieces of sand core are removed from the casting by vigorous shaking.

One way to keep the engine weight as low as possible is to make the block with minimum wall thickness. Engine designers and foundry techniques have made lightweight engines by making the cast iron block walls and bulkheads only as heavy as necessary to support their required loads. Much of the ability to do this is the result of cores made of a minimum number of pieces that are secured firmly in place during casting. If they should shift or float in the molten cast iron, the block wall would either be too thick or too thin in places.

Aluminum is used for some cylinder blocks. Early aluminum blocks were cast in a manner similar to cast iron blocks. They were equipped with a mechanically bonded cast iron liner for each cylinder. A more recent fabrication technique is to die cast the block from silicon-aluminum alloy without using cylinder liners (Figure 7–11). Pis-

Fig. 7-11 Die cast aluminum cylinder and crankcase (Chevrolet Motor Division, General Motors Corporation).

tons with zinc-copper-hard iron coatings are required for use in the aluminum bores.

After thorough cooling and cleaning, the block casting goes to the machining line. The top, bottom, and end surfaces are cleaned and semifinished with a broach. A broach is a large slab with a number of cutting teeth. Each tooth cuts a little more than the preceding tooth, somewhat like a large, coarse, contoured file. One pass of the broach will smooth both cylinder decks and the lifter valley cover rail. A second pass will smooth the upper main bearing bores and the oil pan rail. Some of these surfaces are completed with the broach operation, while others need to be finished with a mill, a final broach, or a boring operation. The ends of the block may be finished with a third broach.

The cylinders are bored and honed in a number of step operations until they have the required size and finish. A slight notch or scallop is cut into the edge of the cylinder on some engines using very large valves. All drilling and thread tapping is accomplished on the block line.

The main bearing caps, which are cast separately from the block, are machined and installed on the block for a final bore finishing operation. With caps installed, the main bearing bores and cam bearing bores are machined to the correct size and alignment. On some engines, these bores are honed to a very fine finish and size. Therefore, main bearing caps are not interchangeable or reversible. They may have cast numbers indicating their position.

Standard production engines use two bolts to hold the main bearing cap in place. Heavy duty and performance engines often use additional main bearing support bolts. These could be a cross bolt design in a deep skirt block or a four-bolt main cap in the V-block design. Remember that combustion chamber gases' expansion force will try to push the cylinder head off the top and the crankshaft off the bottom of the block. The engine is held together with the head bolts and main bearing cap bolts screwed into bolt bosses and ribs that are cast in the block. The extra bolt on the main bearing cap helps to support the crankshaft when high combustion pressures and mechanical load exists. Cap bolt designs are shown in Figure 7–12.

(a)

(b)

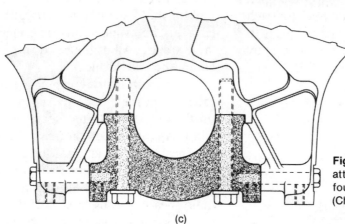

(c)

Fig. 7-12 Main bearing cap attachments. (a) Two bolt, (b) four bolt, (c) cross bolted (Chrysler Motor Corporation).

7-3 GASKETS AND STATIC SEALS

Oil, coolant, and gases flow through passages in the engine block. These are usually kept separate by cast iron walls, plugs, covers, and caps. They must not leak either internally or externally. Gaskets or static seals are used between attaching engine parts to seal the joint, thus preventing leakage.

Requirements. Gasket requirements become greater as engine pressures and temperatures become greater. Four gasket properties must be considered by the engineer when selecting gaskets for each specific application. The gasket must be impermeable, comfortable, resilient, and resistant.

Each gasket must be *impermeable* to the fluids it is designed to seal. If the fluid could penetrate the gasket, it would leak and the gasket would be of no value.

Gaskets must *conform* to any existing surface imperfections. This includes machining surface roughness and slight parting surface warpage.

A *resilient* gasket property will allow the gasket to maintain sealing pressure, even when the joint is slightly loosened as a result of temperature changes or vibration.

The environment of the gasket will change with variations in temperature, pressure, and age. The gasket must be *resistant* to all expected changes in its environment for the engine service life.

Gasket Materials. Many materials are used for gaskets, depending upon the sealing requirements and the cost. One of the oldest gasket materials is cork, a natural material from the bark of mediterranean oak and cork pine trees. For gaskets, the bark chips are held together in sheets with bonding materials, often rubber compounds. This makes a highly impermeable gasket that conforms easily. The use of cork is limited to lightly loaded joints, having uneven surfaces, such as rocker covers and oil pans. Aluminum coatings on cork gaskets help reduce heat deterioration. In some cases, the cork gaskets are rubber coated.

Cork is often replaced by gaskets made of fibers. These fibers may be cellulose, asbestos, or a mixture of the two. Gasket fibers are bonded together with a binder. The binder material used determines the gasket's properties. Some gaskets use binders that are impermeable to oil, while other gaskets swell on contact with oil. Gaskets that are designed to swell are used where the joint to be sealed cannot be tightened. The gasket's swelling will seal the joint. Gaskets that swell are not used where high pressures are present. Generally, fiber-base gaskets rather than cork are used under high pressures. Fiber gaskets require a better parting surface smoothness than is needed for cork gaskets. Gasket materials are shown in Figure 7–13.

Molded oil-resistant synthetic rubber is often used where the sealing requirements dictate special seal designs. These are often used in oil pan corner joints and on intake manifold ends. A new approach to gaskets is a plastic gasket material in a tube. It can be used in place of paper and fiber-based gaskets. It completely seals the joint as it conforms to all variations.

One of the most difficult sealing jobs in the engine is to seal the cylinder head to the block parting surface. The earliest head gaskets were copper-coated asbestos. The copper sealed into the machining marks of the head and block while the asbestos provided resilience and conformability. As engine designs were improved, copper on the gaskets was replaced by steel to withstand the higher pressures and temperatures. Steel rings, called *fire rings,* were applied to the gaskets around the cylinder openings to seal the combustion chambers. Similar rings were added around some of the other gasket holes as well (Figure 7–14).

Continued development of the engine manufacturing techniques provided smoother and flatter parting surfaces, and increased engine power brought on the embossed steel head gasket. A raised rib or embossed portion gives steel gaskets the required resiliency. A soft aluminum coating placed on steel gaskets will seal into the parting surface machining marks.

A later head gasket development uses a thin

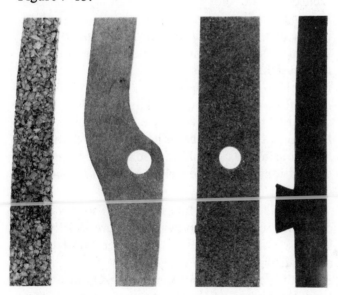

Fig. 7-13 Cork, paper, and composite gasket materials.

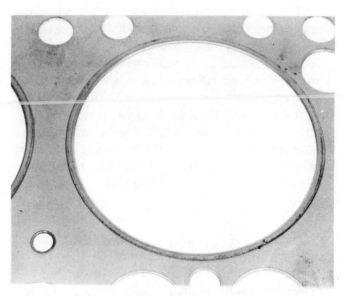

Fig. 7-14 Head gasket with a fire ring.

steel core with a thin coating of asbestos rolled on the outside to give the gasket the desirable resilient properties needed as the head and block change temperature and as the pressure varies within each cycle. Most head gaskets must be installed in a specified direction because the gasket is often used to help control engine coolant flow. When this is required, the gasket is marked *top* or *front*. When it isn't marked, the gasket should be installed with the stamped identification numbers toward the head. Head gasket types are shown in Figure 7-15.

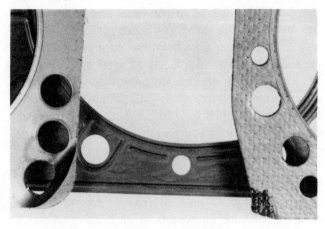

Fig. 7-15 On the left is a head gasket with metal outside the asbestos; a steel embossed head gasket is in the center; and a head gasket with a steel core and a thin asbestos outside coating is on the right.

Timing cover gaskets are usually thin fiber or paper. Cork, fiber and synthetic rubber are used in different parts of the oil pan. The intake manifold uses embossed steel or reinforced fiber gaskets. Cork or synthetic rubber sections are used on the lifter valley cover portion of the intake manifold.

It is a common practice to use a new gasket each time a part is assembled. The price of a new gasket is small compared to the labor cost of intalling it. After use, a gasket will have lost most of its sealing properties. To avoid leaks, always use new gaskets.

7-4 BLOCK ATTACHMENTS

A number of parts are attached to the engine to enclose it and to adapt it to the vehicle. These include covers, housings, and mounts.

Fig. 7-16 Alignment dowel pins for the bell housing.

Bell Housings. A bell housing enclosing the flywheel and clutch or torque converter is attached to the rear of the engine block. It is positioned with dowel pins for alignment. These can be seen in Figure 7-16. Offset dowels and shims between the block and bell housing may be used to align the bell housing in standard transmission applications, so the clutch shaft matches the pilot bearing. In original production, some bell housings are attached to the block before assembly. The bell housing's transmission hole is then machined to match the main bearing bore alignment. This minimizes driveline misalignment. Alignment of the automatic transmission is simplified by using a flex plate transmission drive. Most automatic transmission cases form the bell housing, while standard transmissions have a separate bell housing with clutch lever attachments. Aluminum bell housings are usually used in passenger car applications to keep the weight as low as possible.

Timing Covers. Manufacturers use a variety of timing covers as shown in Figure 7-17. The simplest consists of a stamped sheet metal cover attached with cap screws. Its only purpose is to cover the gears to keep foreign objects out and to keep the engine oil in. Some engines use a cast cover in the same way. A cast cover also tends to muffle the timing drive noise.

Some timing covers are die cast. These covers work in the same way as the cast covers. The die-cast process produces a finished cover with little or no additional work. Die-cast tooling is much more

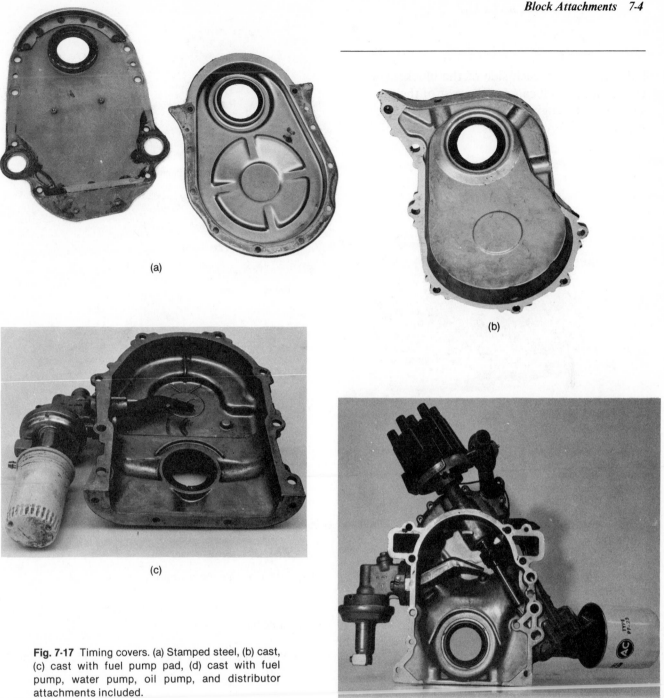

Fig. 7-17 Timing covers. (a) Stamped steel, (b) cast, (c) cast with fuel pump pad, (d) cast with fuel pump, water pump, oil pump, and distributor attachments included.

expensive than cast tooling; however, a saving is made in machining costs when using die-cast parts.

Some manufacturers have made the timing cover more complicated by including the oil pump and distributor drive along with the fuel pump and water pump. The die-cast process is used so that there is a minimum of machining operations. With these covers, the engine block contains no accessory drives.

Engine Mounts. Engines are mounted to the vehicle through rubber insulators. The engine vibrational characteristics are checked in the engineering laboratories and the engine mounts positioned close to vibration *nodes,* which are points of minimum vibration. The rubber used in engine mounts is especially compounded to absorb vibrations characteristic to each specific engine model. The mounts are usually located about halfway back on each side of the block. The rear engine mount is located at the rear of the transmission, so the engine–transmission combination is supported at three points.

(a)

(b)

Fig. 7-18 Engine mounts. (a) Old style that let the engine move when the damper rubber broke, (b) new style that is designed to hold the engine even if the damper rubber breaks.

REVIEW QUESTIONS

1. How are V-engine cylinders numbered? [7-1]

2. How are right and left banks of a V-engine identified? [7-1]

3. What are the advantages of a V-block and a Y-block? [7-1]

4. What holes are found in the block? [7-1]

5. What are the advantages of the skirtless and extended cylinder skirt designs? [7-1]

6. What is the purpose of soft plugs in engine blocks? [7-1]

7. How are oil holes made in a block? [7-1]

8. What techniques are used to keep cast iron blocks as light as possible? [7-2]

9. Describe the operation of a broach. [7-2]

10. Why must the main bearing caps be kept on the same block bulkhead? [7-2]

11. What type of block uses cross-bolted main bearings? [7-2]

12. What are four important gasket properties? [7-3]

13. What are the common gasket materials? Give an example of each. [7-3]

14. What is a fire ring? [7-3]

15. What is the most difficult sealing job in an engine? [7-3]

16. Why must a head gasket be installed in a specified direction? [7-3]

17. Why is the recommendation made to always install a new gasket? [7-3]

18. Why would a bell housing be attached to a block before final machining is completed? [7-4]

19. What do some timing covers do besides covering the timing gears or chain? [7-4]

20. What are the advantages and disadvantages of die-casting timing covers? [7-4]

21. What are vibration nodes? [7-4]

22. Where are the three engine mounts located? [7-4]

engine lubricants
and systems

Lubricating oil is often called the life blood of an engine. It circulates through passages in the engine that carry it to all the engine's rubbing surfaces. Its main job is to form a film between these surfaces and keep them from touching. This action minimizes friction and wear within the engine. The lubricant has useful secondary functions. Cool lubricant picks up heat from the hot engine parts and takes it to the oil pan where it is cooled as air moves past the pan. The oil flow also carries wear particles from the rubbing surfaces to the pan so that the particles will cause no further damage within the engine. Oil between the engine parts cushions the parts from the shock as the combustion charge forces the piston down.

The lubricant used for motor oil must have properties that will allow it to meet the engine requirements. The motor oil's most important property is its thickness at its normal operating temperature. If it is too thin the oil rapidly leaks from the clearances, thus allowing the parts to contact, resulting in scoring of the parts. When the thickness is too great the oil will require excessive power to overcome drag between the rubbing surfaces. This characteristic is noticeable when comparing the cranking speed of a cold and a warm engine.

Secondary properties, usually in the form of additives, are put in the oil by the motor oil producers to provide the oil with an ability to clean the engine, minimize scuffing, reduce rusting, resist oxidation, and maintain the oil's viscosity characteristics. The oil should be replaced when its properties no longer protect the engine.

Lubrication between two moving surfaces results from an *oil film* that builds up to separate the surfaces and support the load. To understand this principle, consider how slippery a floor seems to be when a liquid is spilled on it. The liquid, either water or oil, supports a person's weight until it is squeezed out from under his feet. If oil were put on a flat surface and a heavy block pushed across this surface, the block would slide more easily than if it were pushed across a dry surface. The reason for this is that a *wedge-shaped* oil film is built up between the moving block and the surface. This wedge-shaped film is thicker at the front or leading edge than at the rear. If the block were to be held still, the oil would be gradually squeezed out from under the block and the block would settle down on the surface. As soon as the block starts to move again, the wedge-shaped oil film will be re-established. This is illustrated in Figure 8–1.

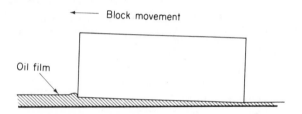

Fig. 8-1 Wedge-shaped hydrodynamic oil film.

The force required to push the block across a surface is dependent upon the block weight, how fast it moves, and the thickness or *viscosity* of the oil. If the block is heavy, it will quickly squeeze the oil from under the surface. The faster the block is moved, the less time is available for oil to be squeezed out, so a heavier load can be supported as speed is increased. This principle is used in water skiing.

The other factor in an oil film's ability to support a load is the oil's thickness. Thin oil would squeeze out faster than thick oil; therefore, the thick oil can support a much greater load. The oil can be too thick. If the oil becomes too thick it becomes sluggish, so that it will require great effort to move the block over the oil. If the oil is too thin, the block is not supported completely and the block will drag slightly on the surface. For any given block weight and moving speed, there is one oil thickness which requires the least effort to move the block. The force required to move the block

divided by the block weight is called the *coefficient of friction.*

The principle just described is called *hydrodynamic* lubrication. *Hydro* refers to liquids, as in hydraulics, and *dynamic* refers to moving materials. Hydrodynamic lubrication occurs when a wedge-shaped film develops in a liquid between two moving surfaces. When this film becomes so thin that the surface high spots touch, it is called boundary lubrication.

As the coefficient of friction increases, it takes more effort to move the block. The least effort is required when the correct wedge-shaped oil film exists. The coefficient of friction will increase during boundary lubrication or when the oil is too thick. This can be shown on the dimensionless graph in Figure 8–2, where the oil thickness or *viscosity* is expressed as Z, the speed at which the block moves across the surface is expressed as N, and the pressure caused by the block weight is expressed as P. The coefficient of friction is

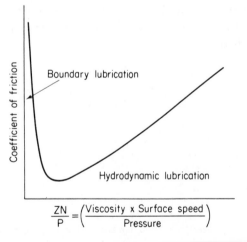

$$\frac{ZN}{P} = \left(\frac{\text{Viscosity} \times \text{Surface speed}}{\text{Pressure}} \right)$$

Fig. 8-2 ZN/P curve showing how the coefficient-of-friction changes as the oil viscosity changes.

minimum for one value of ZN/P. If the load P is increased, the value of ZN/P is reduced and the force moves left on the graph toward boundary conditions. Any increase in speed will increase ZN/P and move the expression to the right on the graph. It takes more effort to increase the speed while using the same viscosity and load. For any constant speed and load, the oil film is dependent upon the oil viscosity. Viscosity is oil's most important property.

Flat surface lubrication only exists in a few places in automotive engines. Some of these are thrust bearings, valve tips, and lifter bases on the cam. Most moving surfaces are similar to flat bearing surfaces, but they are somewhat curved. They still use the same hydrodynamic lubrication principles just described. These surfaces may be curved in one way to form a cylinder wall, lifter bore, or valve guide. When curved in the other direction, they are used as main, connecting rod, and camshaft bearings.

The engine oil pressure system delivers a continuous supply of oil to the lightly loaded portion of bearing surfaces. Hydrodynamic lubrication takes over as the shaft rotates in the bearing to produce a wedge-shaped hydrodynamic oil film that is curved around the bearing. This film supports the bearing and, when oil of the correct viscosity is used, reduces the turning effort to a minimum. Changes in viscosity, speed, or load affect the bearing lubrication in the same way they do with a block moving on a flat surface just described.

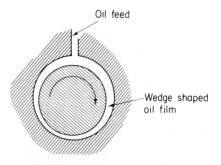

Fig. 8-3 Wedge-shaped film around a journal bearing.

A crankshaft main bearing, as shown in Figure 8-3, will be used to describe typical plane bearing lubrication. When the engine is not running, the crankshaft pushes much of the oil from around it as it settles to the bottom of the bearing. As the starter is cranked, the crankshaft tries to roll up the bearing side wall. If some surface oil remains on the bearing, the shaft will slide back to the bottom of the bearing when it hits this oil. Continued turning will repeat this sequence of climbing and sliding back. This sequence continues until the oil

pump supplies fresh oil to the bearing journal. The shaft continues to try to climb up the bearing wall; however, it now grabs oil instead of the bearing surface. This pulls oil around the shaft, forming a curved wedge-shaped oil film that supports the crankshaft in the bearing. Most bearing wear occurs during the initial start and continues until a hydrodynamic film is established.

A continuous new oil supply is required to maintain the oil film because oil will leak from the side of the bearing. This oil leakage flushes contaminants from the bearing and removes heat that is generated in the bearing.

One function of the engine lubrication system is to maintain a positive and continuous oil supply to the bearings. Engine oil pressure is high enough to get the oil to bearings with sufficient force to produce adequate oil flow for proper cooling. Normal engine oil pressure range is from 30 to 60 psi (207 to 414 kPa) while the hydrodynamic film pressures developed in the high pressure areas of the engine bearings may be over 1000 psi (6894.8 kPa). The relatively low engine oil pressures, obviously, couldn't support these engine loads without hydrodynamic lubrication.

8-2 ENGINE LUBRICATION REQUIREMENTS

The greatest lubrication demand in engines is usually considered to be the bearings. This is a misconception. Their lubrication is necessary for maximum service life of the engine; however, their lubrication is quite simple and is easily met with properly designed bearings using oil with the correct viscosity.

The highest unit pressures and the most difficult lubrication actually occur between the cam lobes and valve lifters. Much of modern motor oil formulation is based on the oil's ability to minimize lifter scuffing and wear. Cam lobes are not lubricated with positive pressure but rely on oil thrown from the connecting rods and on oil that drains back from the rocker and lifter chambers.

Valve assemblies, pistons, piston pins, oil pump-distributor drives and cam drives, require only a surface film of oil. The loads are relatively light, so that oil received from splash is usually adequate. Oil under slight pressure is usually directed to the rocker arms. The amount of pressure is not important, only that the oil is positively delivered to the moving surface needing lubrication. Some engines direct an oil flow to the cam drive. This oil helps to cushion the drive and reduce noise.

Automobile engines also use engine oil to operate hydraulic valve lifters. This places another and different kind of requirement on the engine oil. Hydraulic lifters are manufactured with extremely close fitting parts, to minimize leakage. Small foreign particles that get into these clearances could cause the lifter to malfunction. The engine oil must keep the lifter clean, limiting deposit formation that would cause lifter sticking.

8-3 PROPERTIES OF MOTOR OIL

The most important motor oil property is its thickness or viscosity. As an oil cools, it thickens and as it heats up, it gets thinner; therefore, its viscosity changes with temperature. The oil must have a low viscosity at low temperatures to allow the engine to start. Thick oil at low temperatures causes a very high coefficient of friction as can be seen on the right side of the *ZN/P* curve in Figure 8-2. If this coefficient of friction becomes too great, the cold engine will not have enough energy to carry over from one firing impulse to the next. When this happens, the engine will not start. There is a maximum oil viscosity that will allow an engine to start at any specific temperature. On the other end of the scale, with the engine hot, the oil thins and the viscosity lowers. If the viscosity becomes too low, boundary lubrication will occur and the coefficient of friction will increase, as shown on the left end of the *ZN/P* curve. Motor oil must have its viscosity between these two extremes. It must be thin enough to allow the engine to start when cold and it must still have enough body or viscosity to develop the correct hydrodynamic lubrication film when it gets to its normal operating temperature. An index of the change in viscosity between the cold and hot viscosity is called *viscosity index.* All oils thin as they get hot; however, oils with a high viscosity index thin less than oils with a low viscosity index.

The viscosity of an oil is determined by one of several types of viscosimeters. The oldest and most familiar viscosity measurement device is the Saybolt viscosimeter illustrated in Figure 8-4. It consists of an accurately machined brass tube with a calibrated opening in its bottom called a Universal

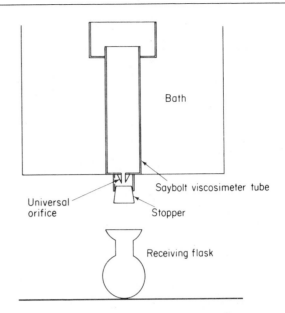

Fig. 8-4 Line drawing of a Saybolt viscosimeter.

orifice. The tube is surrounded by a bath that is maintained at the test temperature. In operation, the tube is fitted with a stopper at its lower end, then filled with the sample oil. It is given time to stabilize at the test temperature. When the test temperature is reached, the stopper is pulled from the tube, allowing the sample to flow through the Universal orifice. The viscosity from this test is reported as *Saybolt Universal Seconds* (SUS). Minimum friction occurs when the viscosity is from 30 to 40 SUS at the operating temperature.

Two test temperatures are used to classify motor oils, 0°F and 210°F (−18°C and 99°C). The 0°F (−18°C) test indicates the oil's viscosity at low temperatures and the 210°F (99°C) test indicates the oil viscosity at normal engine operating temperatures.

Viscosity testing by the Saybolt viscosimeter is quite time consuming and is being replaced by alternate viscosity test methods. The 210°F (99°C) high temperature test is done using a test procedure for opaque liquids, and the results are reported in *centistokes,* the designation for kinematic viscosity. In this test, illustrated in Figure 8-5, a measured amount of oil sample is drawn into a glass viscosimeter tube, then placed in a 210°F (99°C) bath. The top of the sample is drawn slightly above two test lines. The time it takes the sample to drain from one test line to the next is

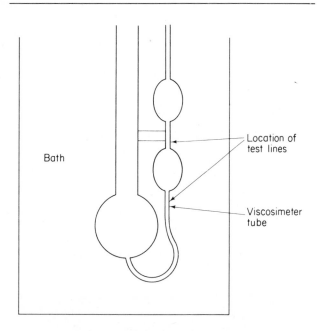

Fig. 8-5 Line drawing of a glass kinematic viscosimeter tube.

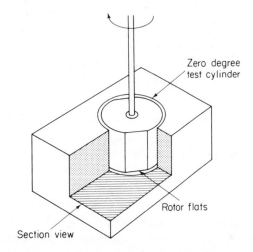

Fig. 8-6 Line drawing of a cold cranking simulator.

measured in seconds. The seconds are multiplied by the viscosimeter correction factor to get the viscosity value in centistokes. This test may be repeated a number of times for accuracy without draining the viscosimeter tube. It is easy and faster to use than a Saybolt viscosimeter.

Another test procedure uses a Cold Cranking Simulator that is replacing the Saybolt viscosimeter for 0°F (−18°C) tests. The Cold Cranking Simulator, illustrated in Figure 8-6, has a rotor, with two flats, that is placed in a cylinder. The cylinder

is then filled with the sample and the whole unit cooled to 0°F (−18°C). At this test temperature, the rotor is turned by a constant speed motor. The torque required to turn the rotor is reported in *centipoise,* a measurement of absolute viscosity. Here again, the test is quicker and simpler than the Saybolt viscosity test.

Motor oils are sold with an SAE number stamped on the top of the oil can. This number indicates the viscosity range in which the oil fits. These numbers are taken from a range of viscosities. Oils tested at 0°F (−18°C) are given an SAE number, followed by the letter "W." This "W" at one time indicated a winter grade of oil. Oils that are tested at 210°F (99°C) have a number without a following letter. For example, SAE 30 indicates that the oil has only been checked at 210°F (99°C) and falls within this grade classification *when hot.* SAE 20W-20 indicates that the oil has been tested at both 0°F (−18°C) and 210°F (99°C) and falls into the respective classifications. An SAE 10W-40 multigrade oil is one that meets the SAE 10W specification when cooled to 0°F (−18°C) and meets the SAE 40 classification when heated to 210°F (99°C). Multigrade oils must have a higher viscosity index than straight grade oils. SAE viscosity classifications are shown in Figure 8-7.

Even though viscosity is the most important oil property, motor oil has additional properties that are important. The lowest temperature at which oil will pour is called its *pour point.* Below this temperature, the oil will become plastic, so it will not produce hydrodynamic lubrication and, therefore, cannot be used below this temperature.

SAE Viscosity Number	Viscosity Units	At 0°		At 210°	
		min	max	min	max
5 W	Centipoises	—	1,200	—	—
	SUS	—	6,000	—	—
10 W	Centipoises	1,200	2,400	—	—
	SUS	6,000	12,000	—	—
20 W	Centipoises	2,400	9,600	—	—
	SUS	12,000	48,000	—	—
20	Centistokes	—	—	5.7	9.6
	SUS	—	—	45	58
30	Centistokes	—	—	9.6	12.9
	SUS	—	—	58	70
40	Centistokes	—	—	12.9	16.8
	SUS	—	—	70	85
50	Centistokes	—	—	16.8	22.7
	SUS	—	—	85	110

Fig. 8-7 Table comparing viscosity to SAE number (*Courtesy* Society of Automotive Engineers).

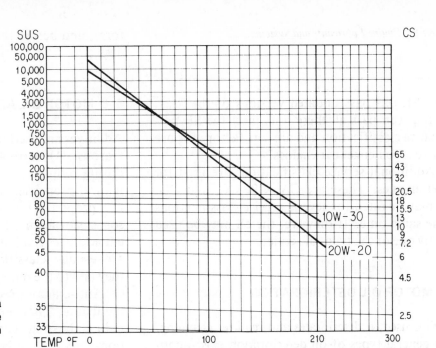

Fig. 8-8 Viscosity plotted on a standard viscosity-temperature chart (*Courtesy* American Society for Testing Materials).

As oil is heated, the volatile portions boil off. When the volatile vapors can be ignited with a small flame, the oil is at its *flash point*. The temperature at which the vapor continues to burn is called the *fire point*. Oil cannot function above the flash point temperature because of its changing characteristics at this temperature. The maximum useful range of a motor oil is between the pour point and the flash point temperatures. The flash point test is also used to determine if used motor oil contains gasoline contaminants. These are more volatile than the motor oil and will evaporate and burn at a much lower temperature than the oil itself.

Motor oil must also resist oxidation, a form of oil breakdown. It must not bubble or foam, which would upset the hydrodynamic film. Neither the oil nor the additives should break down and form acids that will corrode and cause scuffing or rusting of engine parts. They must disperse contaminants to keep the engine clean.

The American Petroleum Institute (API), working with the engine manufacturers and oil companies, has established an engine oil performance classification. Oils are tested and the oil can is marked (usually printed) with the API classification as well as the SAE viscosity number. The API classification is the only way a customer can identify the oil properties for use in his engine.

Oil classifications available in the service stations have the prefix "S." Straight mineral oil is type SA classification. It should only be used in engines that operate under mild conditions re-

quiring no additional protection. Oil for mild engine operation requiring some protection by compounding is called type SB classification. Engines requiring protection from high and low temperature deposits, wear, rust, and corrosion require oil classification SC. The SD classification was designed for the most severe type of engine service, such as low deposit build-up developed during stop and go service, as well as oxidation from high speed. It would thicken at high temperatures so SE oil was developed. Automobile manufacturers recommend only SE oil for use in automobiles built after 1971.

Oils with the SA engine oil performance classification do not have to pass any operational tests. Oils classified as SB must pass both the single-cylinder engine bearing weight loss test L-38 and the Chrysler Corporation developed cam-lifter scuffing test sequence IV. The SC oil classification uses all of the SB tests and adds the General Motors Corporation developed test sequences IIA and IIIA for scuffing, sludge, and varnish; the sequence V, developed by Ford, to measure sludge build-up, piston varnish, valve tip wear, ring sticking, and oil screen clogging; and the single-cylinder L-1 test for piston ring groove plugging. Severe tests are placed on SD classified oils. They have the same basic tests as the SC oils but they use updated sequence II B, III B, and V B tests. In addition the SD oils must pass the Falcon rust test developed by Ford that simulates the worst possible engine operating conditions with a plugged crankcase breather system running at low temperatures. SE oils pass updated versions of the tests. Oils that can pass all these tests meet the SE performance classification and are satisfactory for use in current passenger car engines.

Additional service classifications are used for diesel engines. These are CA, CB, CC, and CD. Oils may be rated for several service classifications at the same time. If they are, the oil may be used for any one of the types of service.

8-4 MOTOR OIL DETERIORATION

As oil is used, it deteriorates and requires changing. Two general types of oil deterioration exist—contamination and breakdown.

Oil may be contaminated with dirt or coolant. The most common type of contamination, however, is from the blow-by gases that work their way past the piston and rings. If crankcase ventilation is poor and the engine is cool, blow-by gases remain in the crankcase and mix with the oil. The undesirable blow-by constituents primarily consist of partially burned fuel and water vapor. Unburned fuel dilutes the oil. The highly acidic water from combustion causes rusting and corrosion. Both combine with polymerized and oxidized hydrocarbons, produced during combustion, undergoing further change in the oil to form sludge "binders" that hold organic solids, inorganic salts, wear particles, and fuel soot together. When these particles get large enough, they drop out of the oil and are deposited in the engine as a cold-engine sludge of mayonnaise consistency.

When an engine is run at normal operating temperatures for some time, the oil gets hot and breaks down. Oil breakdown is the result of hot oil combining with oxygen, and is called oxidation. This will eventually form hard carbon and varnish deposits on engine parts when it is allowed to build up over a long period of time. Two hundred and fifty degrees Fahrenheit (121 °C) is the normal maximum engine oil temperature.

Engine oil additives tend to deteriorate and be used up as the oil is used. When they can no longer do their designed job, the oil loses some of its necessary properties. Engine oils should be changed before sludge develops, before oxidized deposits

form, and before the additives lose their effectiveness.

8-5 MOTOR OIL ADDITIVES

Additives are used in motor oils for three different reasons: (1) to replace some properties removed during refining, (2) to reinforce some of the oil's natural properties, and (3) to provide the oil with new properties it did not originally have. Oils from some petroleum oil fields require more and different additives than oils from other fields. Additives are usually classified according to the property they add to the oil.

Anti-oxidants reduce the high temperature contaminants. They prevent the formation of varnish, reduce bearing corrosion, and particle formation.

Corrosion preventatives reduce acid formation that would cause bearing corrosion.

Detergents and dispersants prevent low temperature sludge binders from forming and break the sludge particles into a finely divided state. The particles will stay in suspension in the oil to be removed from the engine with the oil at the next drain period.

Extreme pressure and anti-wear additives form a chemical film that prevents metal-to-metal seizure any time boundary lubrication exists.

Viscosity index improvers are used to reduce viscosity change as the oil temperature changes.

Pour point depressants coat the wax crystals in the oil so they will not stick together and the oil will then be able to flow at lower temperatures.

A number of other oil additives may be used to modify the oil. These include rust preventatives, metal deactivators, water repellents, emulsifiers, dyes, color stabilizers, odor control agents, and foam inhibitors.

The oil producer must be careful to check the compatibility of the oil additives he uses. A number of chemicals that will help each other can be used for each of the additive requirements. However, with improper additive selection, the additives may oppose each other and lose their benefit to the oil. Each oil producer balances the additives in his oil to provide an oil with desirable properties that meet the engine's needs.

Additives available at service stations, called *proprietary* additives, generally cannot add any needed desirable property to the oil that it does not already possess. It is even possible that these additives may neutralize some of the additives already in the oil, thus degrading the oil instead of improving it. The procedure usually recommended by the engine manufacturer is to use only SE oil without additional proprietary additives. When adding oil between changes, it is a good practice to add the same brand and grade of oil that is already in the engine, thus minimizing the chance of having conflicting additives.

8-6 ENGINE LUBRICATION SYSTEM

Automobile engines use a *wet sump* in their lubrication system. The sump is the lowest part of the system and in automobile engines the sump is the oil pan. It is called a wet sump because it holds the oil supply. Some racing and industrial engines use a dry sump. A scavenger pump in these engines draws the oil out of a relatively small sump and returns it to a separate oil supply tank. The engine oil pump draws oil from the supply tank to feed the engine lubrication system.

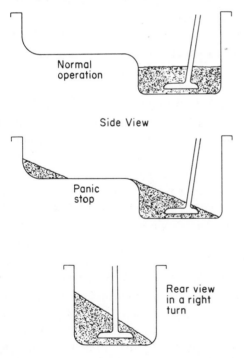

Fig. 8-9 Oil movement in the pan during vehicle maneuvers.

All production automobile engines have a *full pressure* oil system. The pressure is maintained by an oil pump that picks up the motor oil through a passage from an inlet screen in the oil pan and

forces it into the lubrication system under pressure. The inlet screen may be supplied with a *brake stop baffle* that keeps the inlet screen covered during sudden stops.

Oil Pressure. In most engines, the distributor drive gear meshes with a gear on the camshaft, shown in Figure 8-10. The oil pump is driven from the end of the distributor shaft. Some engines have a short shaft-gear that meshes with the cam gear to drive both the distributor and oil pump. Occasionally, an engine is built that uses separate gears on the distributor and on the oil pump. Both mate with the same cam gear. With these drive methods, the pump turns at one-half engine speed. In one engine type the oil pump, similar to an automatic transmission pump, is driven by the front of the crankshaft.

Automotive engine oil pumps are of two types, gear and rotor (Figure 8-11). The gear-type oil pump consists of two spur gears, in a close fitting

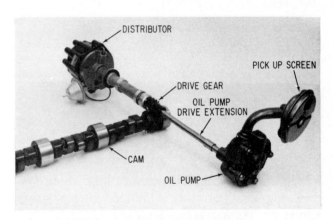

Fig. 8-10 Typical oil pump drive method.

Fig. 8-11 Rotor-type oil pump on the left and gear-type oil pump on the right.

housing. One gear is driven and the other idles. When pumping, oil is carried around the outside of each gear in the space between the gear teeth and the case. As the teeth mesh in the center, oil is forced out, thus producing oil pressure. The rotor-type oil pump is essentially a special lobe-shaped gear meshing with the inside of a lobed rotor. The center lobed section is driven and the outer section idles. As the pump rotates, it carries oil around between the lobes. As the lobes mesh, they force the oil out under pressure in the same manner as the gear-type pump. The pump is sized so that it will maintain at least 15 psi (103.4 kPa) in the oil gallery when the engine is hot and idling. Pressure will increase as the engine speed increases, because the engine driven pump also rotates faster.

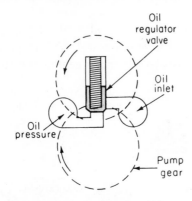

Fig. 8-12 Oil pressure regulator valve releases excess oil to the pump inlet.

In engines with full pressure lubricating systems, maximum pressure is limited with a *pressure regulator* or *relief valve* (Figure 8-12). If a pressure regulator valve was not used, the engine oil pressure would continue to increase as the engine speed increased. Maximum pressure is usually limited to the pressure that will deliver an adequate quantity of lubricating oil to engine locations. Three to six gallons per minute are required. After the oil leaves the pump, oil films are maintained by hydrodynamic forces. Excessive oil pressure requires more horsepower and provides no better lubrication. High oil pressure and resulting high rates of oil flow may, in some cases, tend to erode engine bearings.

Oil pressure is produced when the oil pump has a larger capacity than all the "leaks" in the engine.

The "leaks" are the clearances at end points of the lubrication system, such as the edges of bearings, the rocker arms, the connecting rod spit holes, etc. These clearances are designed into the engine and are necessary for its proper operation. As parts wear and clearance becomes greater, they will leak more. The oil pump's capacity results from its size, rotating speed, and physical condition. If the pump is rotating slowly as the engine is idling, oil pump capacity is low. If the "leaks" are greater than the pump capacity, engine oil pressure is low. As the engine speeds up, the pump capacity increases and tries to force more oil out of the "leaks." This causes the pressure to rise until the pressure reaches the regulated pressure.

A third consideration, engine oil viscosity, is involved in both the pump capacity and the oil leakage. Very low viscosity or thin oil slips past the edges of the pump and flows freely from the "leaks." Hot oil has a low viscosity and, therefore, is often accompanied by low oil pressure. Cold oil is more viscous and usually results in high pressures, even with the engine idling. Putting higher viscosity oil in an engine will raise the engine oil pressure to the regulated setting at a lower engine speed.

The pressure regulator is located downstream from the pressure side of the oil pump. It generally consists of a spring-loaded piston and, in a few cases, a spring-loaded ball. When oil pressure reaches the regulated pressure, it will force the regulator valve back against the calibrated spring, compressing it as the valve is forced back. This allows a controlled "leak" from the pressure system at a rate that will maintain the set regulated pressure. Any change in the regulator valve spring pressure will change the regulated oil pressure; higher spring pressures will cause higher maximum oil pressures. In most engines, the oil that is released by the regulator valve is routed to the inlet side of the oil pump to be recirculated through the pump, as shown in Figure 8-12. The regulator valve is, therefore, usually located in the oil pump housing or pump cover. This method of oil flow from the regulator valve prevents foaming and excessive oil agitation so a solid stream of lubricating oil will be delivered by the pump.

Oil Filter. Oil leaving the pump flows to the oil filter where large particles are trapped, allowing only clean oil to flow into the engine. Filters are designed to trap large particles that could damage

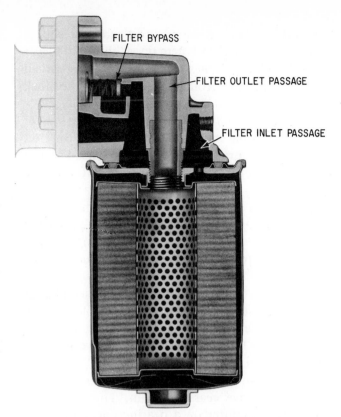

Fig. 8-13 Cross section of a typical oil filter (AC Division, General Motors Corporation).

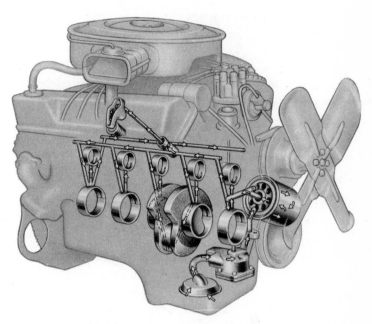

Fig. 8-14 Typical engine lubrication system (Ford Motor Company).

engine bearings. Very fine particles flow through the filter. These particles are so fine they can get between engine clearances and do no damage. As the filter traps particles, the holes in the filter become partly plugged. As they plug, the filter traps even smaller particles, thus doing a better filtering job. This better filtering, however, restricts oil flow and this could result in bearing oil starvation. All filters or filter adapters have a bypass check valve so that if the filter plugs, oil can bypass the plugged filter and go directly into the engine. The bypass valve is set at from 5 to 15 psi (34.5 to 103.4 kPa), depending on the engine and normal pressure drop across the filter element.

Filters or filter adapters are also supplied with a check valve that keeps the filter full when the engine is stopped. It keeps the oil from leaking back through the oil pump into the pan, so the oil pump remains primed and provides rapid oil pressure build-up when the engine starts.

Oil Passages. From the filter, oil goes through a drilled hole that intersects with a drilled main oil gallery or longitudinal header. Inline engines use one oil gallery. V-engines may use two main galleries or one main gallery and two hydraulic valve lifter galleries. Drilled passages through the

block bulkheads allow the oil to go from the main oil gallery to the main and cam bearings. In some engines, oil goes to the cam bearings first, then to the main bearings, while other engines direct the oil to the main bearings first, then to the cam bearings. A typical engine oil system is shown in Figure 8-14. Hydrodynamic films will build up to lubricate the bearings and journals. It is important that the bearing oil holes align with the drilled passages in the bearing saddles so that proper lubrication will be provided. Excessive bearing wear will cause excessive oil throw off from the side of the bearing and, thus, starve a bearing located further downstream in the lubricating system. This is a major cause of bearing failure. If a new bearing were installed in place of the starved bearing it, too, would fail unless the bearing with excessive throw off were also replaced. For proper operation, the lubrication system must be balanced so that each bearing uses only the designed amount of oil and leaves enough oil in the system for the remaining bearings.

The crankshaft is drilled, as shown in Figure 8-15, to allow oil from the main bearing oil groove to be directed to the connecting rod bearings. This oil forms a hydrodynamic oil film on the connecting rod bearing to support bearing loads.

Fig. 8-15 Oil cross hole drilled in a crankshaft.

From here, some of the oil may be sprayed through a spit or bleed hole. The rest of the oil leaks from the edges of the bearing and is thrown against the inside surfaces of the engine. Some of the throw-off oil lands on the camshaft to lubricate the lobes. Some of the oil splashes on the cylinder wall to lubricate the piston and rings. Some splashes onto the piston pin, illustrated in Figure 8-16. Oil that lands on the interior wall drains back into the oil pan for recirculation through the lubricating system.

The oil gallery may intersect or have drilled passages to the valve lifter bores to lubricate the lifters. When hydraulic lifters are used, the gallery oil pressure keeps refilling them. On some engines, oil from the lifters goes up the center of a hollow

Fig. 8-16 Piston pin lubricated from the spit hole.

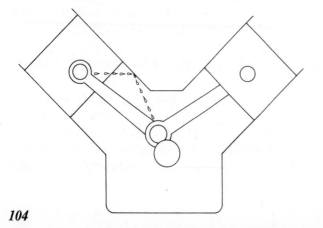

pushrod to lubricate the pushrod ends, the rocker arm pivot, and the valve stem tip, as shown in Figure 8-14. In other engines, an oil passage is drilled from the gallery or from a cam bearing to the block deck, where it matches with a gasket hole and a hole drilled in the head to carry the oil to a rocker arm shaft. Some engines use an enlarged head bolt hole to carry lubricating oil around the head bolt to the rocker arm shaft. Holes in the bottom of the rocker arm shaft lubricate the rocker arm pivot. Often holes are drilled in cast rocker arms to carry oil to the pushrod end and to the valve tip. Rocker arm assemblies need only a surface coating of oil so the oil flow to rocker assembly is reduced using restrictions or metered openings.

Oil that seeps from the rocker assemblies is returned to the oil pan through drain holes. These oil drain holes are often placed so that the oil drains on the camshaft or on cam drive gears to lubricate them.

Some engines have a positive oil flow directed to the cam drive gears or chain. This may be a nozzle or a chamfer on a bearing parting surface that allows oil to spray on the loaded portion of the cam drive.

Oil Pan. Oil in the oil pan is subjected to a number of forces. As the car accelerates, brakes, or is turned rapidly, the oil tends to slosh around in the pan. Pan baffles and oil pan shapes are often used to resist oil sloshing to keep the oil inlet under the oil at all times. As the crankshaft rotates, it acts like a fan and causes air within the crankcase to rotate with it. This can cause a strong draft on the oil, churning it to entrap air bubbles. A baffle or windage tray is sometimes installed in engines to eliminate this problem as shown in Figure 8-18. Windage trays have a good side effect by reducing the amount of air disturbed by the crankshaft so less power is robbed from the engine at high crankshaft speeds.

8-7 CRANKCASE VENTILATION

Crankcase ventilation systems are installed on all engines to remove blow-by gases from the engine. Some older engines had a screened inlet and a *draft tube* outlet that would draw vapors from the crankcase while the car was in motion. Vehicle emission studies have shown that these blow-by gases contribute to air pollution. Vehicle emission

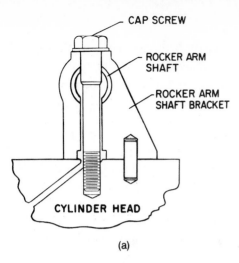

(a)

Fig. 8-17 Rocker arm lubricated from the rocker shaft (Dana Corporation) (a) Oil passage around support bolt, (b) rocker arm lubricated.

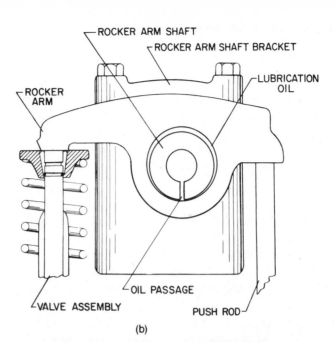

(b)

Fig. 8-18 Windage tray.

laws were passed to equip engines with positive crankcase ventilation (PCV) systems. The draft tube was replaced with a PCV valve and connecting hoses to pull the crankcase vapors into the intake manifold where they are sent to the cylinder to be burned in the combustion chamber. Under some operating conditions, the gases would be forced back through the inlet filter. A line connecting the inlet to the carburetor air filter allows back-up vapors to be inducted through the carburetor with the incoming air. This effectively eliminates all crankcase emissions and, at the same time, provides adequate crankcase ventilation that reduces oil contamination and deposit buildup.

8-8 LUBRICATION SYSTEM MAINTENANCE

During the service life of an engine, most of the lubrication system service involves oil and filter changes. Oil selection is based on the manufacturer's or petroleum companies' recommendations. These recommendations are based on extensive laboratory and fleet testing to check the compatibility of the oil to the engine. One consideration that the oil recommendation must include is the lowest expected temperature. A viscosity grade is recommended that will allow easy engine starting. A minimum starting viscosity is 5000 centipoise. Most automobile engine manufacturers recommend a multigrade oil which will allow easy cold starts and provide adequate protection when warm. A second consideration is the type of service that is to be encountered. Automobile manufacturers recommend SE service classification oil.

All automobile companies recommend using an original equipment oil filter. These are tailored to the engine requirements. High quality replacement filters are available and do an acceptable job of filtering the lubricating oil. They must, however, be designed for the specific engine application.

There is much debate about the most desirable oil change period. The automobile manufacturer's recommendations usually differ from the petroleum companies' recommendations. An oil drain period is established by considering the oil's contamination, the additive's continued effectiveness, and the original oil service classification. Running a laboratory analysis on the engine oil is the only way to determine the actual condition of the used oil. This, of course, is only possible in research and engineering laboratories. Manufacturers use this method, along with extensive service tests by both the engine manufacturers and the petroleum companies, to determine safe drain periods. The results of these tests are passed along to their respective service organizations as the recommended oil change period.

Low speed stop-and-go traffic driving causes the engine to run cool so sludge will start to build up. This type of vehicle operation puts a very few miles on the vehicle each month; however, the contamination continues to build up rapidly for each mile traveled. A time period recommendation is usually provided to take care of vehicles that are operated in this manner.

High speed, high temperature engine operation builds up varnish and carbon-type deposits. This type of operation builds mileage rapidly over a short period of time. An oil change period based on mileage is recommended to take care of this type of vehicle operation.

Most automobiles are operated with a mixture of low speed and high speed driving. The usual oil change recommendations are made on both a time and mileage basis to take care of any "normal" operation. It is further recommended that if the vehicle is operated under abnormal conditions, such as dusty roads, the oil should be changed more frequently.

If the oil change periods are extended beyond the manufacturer's recommendations, contaminants may become so large and heavy that they will fall out of the oil and deposit in the engine. When this happens, they cannot be removed from the engine when draining used oil. These deposits continue to build until the engine is disassembled and cleaned.

Engine designs have reduced contamination build-up and have increased the oil change interval. Some of these engine design features are: splash pans under the intake manifold heat riser to keep the oil away from this hot surface so the oil won't be oxidized; rocker assembly oil return passages are enlarged to allow the oil to rapidly return from hot areas to the oil pan to keep it from oxidizing; high temperature thermostats quickly warm the oil to reduce cold sludge build-up. Extended oil drain periods will not satisfactorily protect older engines that do not include the features designed for long drain periods. The drain period should not extend beyond the manufacturer's recommendation for each specific engine model.

Super premium engine oils have been developed to operate during extended oil drain periods. These oils are made from selected grades of lubricating oil stock. Improved additives are blended in to give the oil the required long life properties.

Extended oil drain periods are only recommended on engines with the proper design features when using super premium oils. Other engines and oil combinations require more frequent oil drain periods.

The difference between the automobile engine manufacturer and the petroleum company recommended oil drain period is the result of different philosophies. The automobile manufacturer's recommendations are to the original automobile owner. If these recommendations are followed, the average original owner will have minimum maintenance expense. The petroleum company recommendations, on the other hand, are based on conservative views that would provide the longest service period between overhauls. This would give minimum lifetime costs if one drove enough miles to "use up" the engine's useful life. In general, it can be stated that the petroleum companies recommend oil changes twice as often as the automobile manufacturers.

Engine oil consumption is another maintenance requirement. The average automobile owner has no idea how much oil is being consumed by the engine until he finds that it is necessary to add oil between oil changes. He seldom concerns himself about oil consumption until it becomes excessive. The only way he can tell if the consumption is excessive is by the amount of oil he adds to the engine between oil changes.

Motor oil can get out of the engine through the combustion chamber or through leaks. Leaks generally result from loose, poor fitting, or damaged gaskets, or from damaged oil seals. In some cases, leaks may result from cracked engine parts. Leaks are usually repairable without requiring an engine overhaul.

Oil can get into the combustion chamber past the piston rings, through the valve guides, through some intake gasket leaks, and through the PCV system. Of these leaks, the most expensive one to repair is the oil leak past the piston rings.

Unless excessive oil consumption affects engine operation, as evidenced by hard starting or sluggish performance, its correction will be based on economics, pride, or law. Most automobile manufacturers do not consider oil consumption to be excessive and requiring repair on new engines unless the engine uses more than one quart to each 500 to 700 miles. Fortunately the mileage is seldom this low. As the engine mileage builds up, its oil consumption will increase.

The economic consideration in oil consumption relates the cost of the oil to the cost of the repair job. If oil consumption is a result of a gasket, seal, or cracked part, the repair cost is generally low. If it requires overhaul, such as re-ringing, the repair cost will far exceed the cost of the additional oil consumed.

Many people have enough pride in their automobiles that they are willing to pay the possible high cost to have all leaks repaired, to eliminate exhaust smoke, and have minimum oil consump-tion. They will have it repaired without considering economics. Some states have pollution laws that will not allow vehicles to be operated with visible exhaust emissions. In these cases, the oil consumption will have to be maintained at a low level, regardless of cost.

Excessive oil consumption, then, is a compromise between the value of the car, the cost of repair, the cost of the extra oil, the owner's pride, and the operating laws.

In addition to motor oil, many oil and chemical companies package proprietary additives that the customer may add to his motor oil. Some of these materials are solvents that dissolve deposits, some are detergents and depressants, and others are oil thickeners. These products are similar to the products the oil manufacturers have already blended into the oil to give it the required properties at a minimum cost to the consumer. The proprietary products are high priced additives that increase the cost of the oil when they are used and they are of doubtful value in a "normal" engine that is using recommended oils. Solvents and detergents added to the oil may be useful for freeing sticking hydraulic lifters and valves. When they free up, the oil with the additive should be drained and replaced with a fresh change of the proper engine oil. If a thicker oil is desired, purchasing a heavier grade for a refill is less expensive than using a lighter grade with an oil thickener. As the engine runs, the additive thickener breaks down and the oil thins out, thus losing the desired characteristics.

When one considers the great amount of money spent by the automobile manufacturers and petroleum companies to match the engine and the oil, it seems wise to follow their recommendations. The manufacturer's warranty is based on these recommendations and, therefore, this will provide satisfactory lubrication for a normal service life of the engine.

REVIEW QUESTIONS

1. How is an oil film formed between two surfaces? [8-1]

2. How does oil thickness affect the coefficient of friction? [8-1]

3. What do the letters stand for in the expression *ZN/P*? [8-1]

4. How does the oil viscosity affect the coefficient of friction? [8-1]

5. Where does flat surface lubrication occur in an engine? [8-1]

6. Into what part of a bearing is the oil supplied? [8-1]

7. When does most bearing wear occur? [8-1]

8. What limits the high and low viscosity extremes in motor oil? [8-3]

9. At what SUS viscosity does minimum friction occur? [8-3]

10. How do multigrade oils differ from straight grade oils? [8-3]

11. What is the most important property of motor oil? [8-3]

12. What are two types of oil deterioration? What is the cause of each? [8-4]

13. What is the purpose of oil additives? [8-5]

14. Why is the oil changed? [8-5 and 8-8]

15. What is the value of proprietary additives? [8-5]

16. What is the engine sump? [8-6]

17. How is the oil pump driven? [8-6]

18. Illustrate the oil flow through a gear-type oil pump. [8-6]

19. What is the minimum oil pressure at idle? [8-6]

20. What is the oil quantity pumped by an engine oil pump? [8-6]

21. When does the pressure regulator valve operate? [8-6]

22. What happens when the oil pressure is greater than required? [8-6]

23. What causes low oil pressure? [8-6]

24. Why does low oil pressure accompany hot oil? [8-6]

25. What is the advantage of having the oil pressure regulator in the pump? [8-6]

26. What is the purpose of a bypass check valve in a filter? [8-6]

27. Where is the oil gallery? [8-6]

28. Describe the oil flow through an engine. [8-6]

29. What causes a bearing to be starved for oil? [8-6]

30. How does oil get to the overhead valves? [8-6]

31. Why is there a difference between the automobile manufacturer's and the petroleum manufacturer's oil change recommendations? [8-8]

32. What engine design features reduce oil contamination? [8-8]

33. When should an engine be overhauled to reduce oil consumption? [8-8]

cooling system operation

The primary function of the automotive engine cooling system is to maintain the normal operating temperature of the block and head. Coolant flow is held at a minimum during warm up until normal engine temperature is reached, then the coolant flow is gradually increased, as required, to maintain the normal temperature. If the engine operating temperature is too low, scuffing and wear rates will increase. If the temperature is too high, hard deposits which can cause part sticking and passage clogging will form. Operating the engine at normal temperatures will minimize these problems and provide maximum engine service life.

Two types of cooling systems are used in passenger cars, air and liquid. Some imported passenger cars use air cooling, as shown in Figure 9-1. Current domestic passenger cars use liquid cooling systems. The coolant removes the excess heat from the engine and carries it to a radiator where it releases the heat to the air.

Satisfactory cooling system operation depends upon the system's component design and the operating conditions. The design is based on the engine's heat output, radiator size, type of coolant, size of coolant pump, fan type, thermostat, and system pressure. Operating conditions change, for example, when driving in traffic, changing engine speeds and engine loads by driving up and down hills, and towing a trailer. Correct functioning of all cooling system parts is critical when the engine is operated under heavy loads in a hot climate. Unfortunately the cooling system is usually neglected until a problem occurs. Correct routine maintenance can prevent the problem as well as the cost and the inconvenience the problem causes.

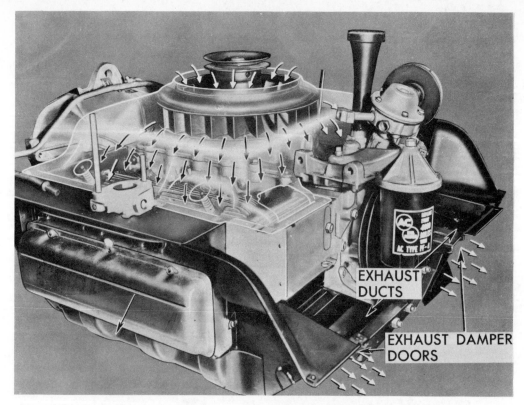

Fig. 9-1 Air flow through aircooled engine baffels and shrouds (Chevrolet Motor Division, General Motors Corporation).

9–1 COOLING SYSTEM REQUIREMENTS

The cooling system must allow the engine to warm up to the required operating temperature as rapidly as possible, then maintain that temperature. It must be able to do this when the outside air temperature is as low as —30°F(—35°C) and as high as 110°F (45°C). This will allow proper carburetion, provide satisfactory oil viscosity, and give the correct part clearances within the engine.

Peak combustion temperatures in the engine cycle run from 4000°F to 6000°F (2220°C to 3330°C). They will average from 1200°F to 1700°F (650°C to 925°C) throughout the operating cycle. Continued temperatures as high as this would weaken engine parts, so heat must be removed from the engine. The cooling system keeps the head and cylinder walls at a temperature within their physical strength limits.

Low Temperature Requirements. Minimum engine operating temperatures are critical for proper engine operation. When the temperature is too low, there is insufficient heat to properly vaporize the fuel mixture so that extra fuel is necessary to provide satisfactory engine performance. The heavy portion of the gasoline does not vaporize and remains as unburned fuel. Cool engine surfaces quench part of the combustion, leaving partially burned fuel as soot. It also cools the burned by-products, condensing moisture that is produced during combustion. The unburned fuel, soot, and moisture go past the piston rings as blow-by gases, washing oil from the cylinder wall and diluting the oil in the pan. This exposes the cylinder wall and piston rings to excessive scuffing and wear.

Gasoline is a hydrocarbon with additives to reduce detonation, surface ignition, corrosion, gum formation, and ice formation. Some of the antiknock additives contain chlorine and bromine. Gasoline combustion is a rapid oxidation process in which heat is released as the hydrocarbon fuel chemically combines with oxygen from the air. For each gallon of fuel used, a moisture equivalent of a gallon of water is produced. It is a part of this moisture that condenses and gets into the oil pan, along with unburned fuel and soot, and causes sludge formation.

The condensed moisture combines with unburned hydrocarbons and additive constituents to form carbonic acid, sulfuric acid, nitric acid, hydrobromic acid, and hydrochloric acid. These acids are chiefly responsible for engine wear by causing corrosion and rust within the engine. Rust occurs rapidly when the coolant temperature is below 130°F (55°C). Below 110°F (45°C), water from the combustion process will actually accumulate in the oil. High cylinder wall wear rates occur whenever the coolant temperature is below 150°F (65°C).

High Temperature Requirements. Maximum temperature limits are also required to protect the engine. High temperatures oxidize the engine oil. This breaks the oil down, producing hard carbon and varnish. If high temperatures are allowed to continue, they will lead to plugged piston rings and stuck hydraulic valve lifters. High temperatures reduce the oil's viscosity—that is, they thin the oil. This may allow metal-to-metal contact within the engine, which will cause high friction, loss of power, and rapid wear. Reduced oil viscosity allows the oil to get past the piston rings and through valve guides into the combustion chamber to cause excessive oil consumption.

The combustion process is very sensitive to temperature. High coolant temperatures raise the combustion temperatures to a point that detonation and pre-ignition may occur and, if allowed to continue for any period of time, will lead to engine damage.

Normal Temperatures. Between low temperature and high temperature extremes, there is a normal operating temperature range. The minimum normal temperature, controlled by a thermostat, has been gradually increased from 160°F to 180-190°F (72°C to 80-87°C). Some engines run with a minimum temperature as high as 200°F (95°C). The maximum possible temperature on liquid cooled engines is limited by the coolant's boiling point and the radiator's capacity. On air cooled engines, it is limited by the air temperature and flow rate. Engine operating temperature should be kept between these extremes, usually at the minimum temperature, for proper engine operation and maximum service life.

9-2 COOLANT

The majority of automobiles use liquid cooled systems. Coolant flows through the engine, as illustrated in Figure 9–2, where it picks up heat. It then flows to the radiator where the heat is given up to the outside air. The coolant continually recirculates, its temperature rising as much as 15°F (8.33°C) as it goes through the engine, then cooling back down as it goes through the radiator. The

Fig. 9-2 Coolant flow through a liquid cooled engine (Ford Motor Company).

coolant flow rate may be as high as 1 gallon (3.785 liters) per minute for each horsepower the engine produces.

Coolant Types. For a given volume, water is able to absorb more heat than any other liquid coolant used in automobiles. Water, however, has both a high and a low usable temperature limit. It boils at 212°F (100°C) and freezes at 32°F (0°C). There are very few places in the United States where the temperature does not at some time drop below the freezing point of water. Antifreeze protection is required when these low temperatures are anticipated. Low temperature protection is also required on some factory installed air conditioned cars to keep the heater core from freezing. All manufacturers recommend the use of *ethylene-glycol-based* antifreeze mixtures for this protection. This type of antifreeze is sometimes called *permanent* type, even though manufacturers recommend its replacement each year or two, depending on the specific vehicle manufacturer. Ethylene-glycol antifreezes have anti-corrosion additives and water pump lubricants blended into them. When antifreezes are not used, these required additives may be purchased separately and added to the cooling system water by the operator.

Only the minimum required amount of ethylene-glycol-based antifreeze should be used. It is expensive and, therefore, it is economical to use the minimum required amount. At the maximum protection, an ethylene-glycol concentration of 60% will absorb less than 90% as much heat as water. An added advantage in using ethylene-

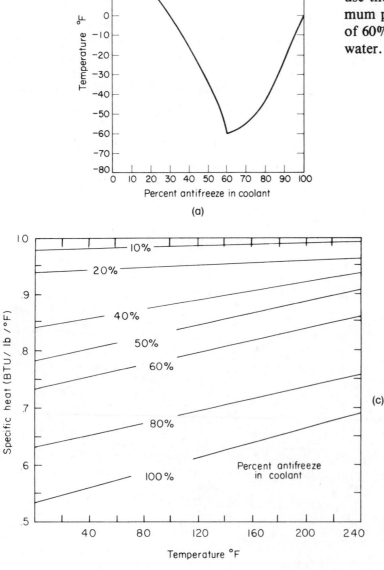

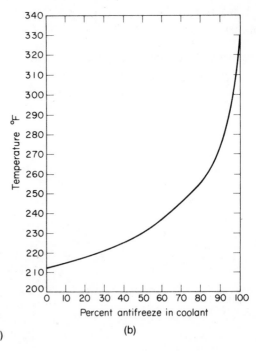

Fig. 9-3 Effect of glycol-water mixture. (a) Freezing temperature, (b) boiling temperature, (c) specific heat.

glycol-based antifreeze is the fact that its boiling point is higher than water's boiling point. Its use will allow the cooling system to run at a higher temperature level, so that a smaller radiator may be used on the vehicle. It is also helpful in transferring heat from the engine to increase the boiling point of the coolant on cars equipped with air conditioning. Graphs indicating the glycol antifreeze characteristics are shown in Figure 9-3.

9-3 LIQUID COOLING SYSTEM DESIGN

Coolant enters the engine at the center of the inlet side of the pump. The coolant pump is a centrifugal pump, pulling coolant in at the impeller center and discharging it a the impeller tips. The pump is sized and the impeller designed to absorb no more power than necessary to provide adequate coolant flow. It is driven by a belt from the crankshaft. The belt is tightened with an idler. On most engines, the alternator serves as the belt tightening idler. As engine speeds increase, more heat is developed and more cooling capacity is required. The belt-driven pump increases the impeller speed as the engine speed increases to provide extra coolant flow when it is needed.

Coolant leaving the pump impeller is fed through a *scroll*, a smoothly curved passage that changes the fluid flow direction with minimum loss in velocity shown in Figure 9-4. The scroll is connected to the front of the engine to direct the coolant into the block. On V-engines, two outlets are used, one for each cylinder bank. Occasionally, diverters are necessary in the coolant pump scroll to equalize coolant flow between the cylinder banks for equal cooling in both engine banks.

Fig. 9-4 Coolant pump with impeller and scroll.

Coolant Flow in the Engine. Coolant will flow through the engine in one of two ways, **parallel** or series. In the parallel system, coolant flows into the block under pressure, then crosses the gasket to the head through holes adjacent to each cylinder. Gasket openings are shown in Figure 9-5. In the series flow system, the coolant flows around all of the cylinder on each bank to the rear of the block where large passages allow the coolant to flow across the gasket to the rear of the heads. The series flow gasket openings can be seen in Figure 9-6. The coolant flows forward through the heads to an outlet at the highest point in the engine cooling passage located at the front of the engine. Some engines use a combination of these two systems and call it a series-parallel coolant flow.

The cooling passages inside the engine must be designed so that the whole system can be drained.

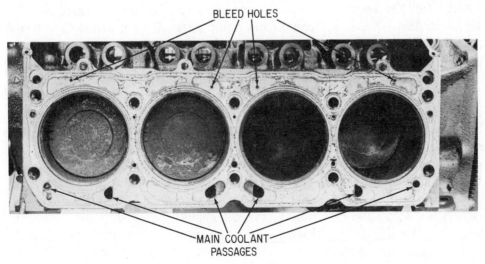

Fig. 9-5 Parallel-type coolant flow.

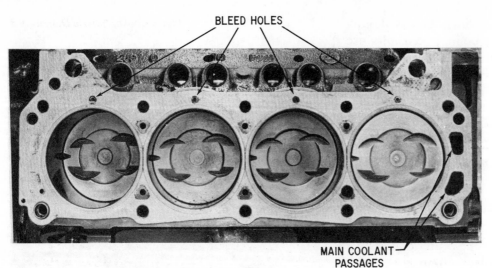

BLEED HOLES

MAIN COOLANT PASSAGES

Fig. 9-6 Series-type coolant flow.

Fig. 9-7 Internal cooling system bypass.

Fig. 9-8 External cooling system bypass.

It must also be designed so that there are no pockets in which steam can form. In series flow systems, bleed holes or steam slits in the gasket, block, and head provide this function by short circuiting a very small amount of coolant. Often, this short-circuited coolant is directed to flow coolant on hot areas in the head, such as exhaust valves, spark plugs, and the exhaust crossover.

By-pass. A thermostat is located at the engine outlet to restrict coolant flow until the engine reaches the operating temperature of the thermostat. The cooling system is provided with a *by-pass* that allows a small part of the coolant to circulate within the engine during warm up while the thermostat is closed. The by-pass is a small passage that leads from the engine side of the thermostat to the inlet side of the coolant pump. Coolant

will flow through the by-pass, short circuiting the radiator anytime there is a pressure difference on the ends of the by-pass, even if the thermostat is open. The by-pass may be cast or drilled into the engine and pump parts. This is called an internal by-pass (Figure 9–7). It may be an external by-pass visible as a hose on the front of many engines that connects the engine coolant outlet to the coolant pump (Figure 9–8). The by-pass aids in uniform warm up, eliminates hot spots, and prevents excessive coolant pressure in the engine when the thermostat is closed.

Thermostat. The thermostat is a temperature controlled valve placed at the engine coolant outlet. Typical engine thermostats are shown in Figure 9–9. An encapsulated wax-based plastic pellet positioned on the engine side of the thermostatic valve is linked to the valve. As the engine warms, heat swells the pellet, opening the thermostat through a mechanical link. As the thermostat opens, it allows some coolant to flow to the radiator to be cooled while the remaining portion of the coolant continues to go through the by-pass. This partial opening varies according to the engine cooling requirements needed to maintain normal temperatures. The coolant pump provides the force that causes coolant to flow. This flow is restricted by a closed thermostat and, therefore, the flow rate is low. The thermostat restriction causes system pressure to rise. As the thermostat gradually opens, coolant flow rate increases and pressure lowers. The thermostat will be wide open with maximum coolant flow only under extreme heating conditions, such as idling in traffic or pulling up a long steep grade in warm weather.

Radiator. The engine coolant outlet is connected to the top of the radiator by hoses and clamps. As coolant in the radiator cools, it moves from the top to the bottom of the radiator. Cool coolant leaves the lower radiator through an outlet

and hose, going into the inlet side of the pump where it is recirculated through the engine.

Much of the cooling system's capacity is based on the function of the radiator. Radiators are designed to obtain the maximum rate of heat transfer using minimum material and size to keep cost as low as possible. Vehicle designs also dictate available radiator space and, consequently, affect radiator designs.

Two types of radiator cores, shown in Figure 9–10 are in common use in domestic automobiles, the *serpentine* fin core and the *plate* fin core. In each of these types, coolant flows through oval shaped tubes. Heat transfers through the tube wall and soldered joint to fins. The fins are exposed to an air flow which removes heat and carries it away from the radiator.

Most automobile radiators are made from yellow brass or copper. These materials are corrosion resistant, have good heat transfer ability, are

Fig. **9-9** Typical automotive coolant system thermostats.

Fig. 9-10 Radiator core types (Modine Manufacturing Company). (a) Serpentine, (b) plate type.

(a)

(b)

easily formed, have the required strength characteristics, and are easily repaired by soldering. Some heavy-duty applications have used corrosion-protected steel; however, steel is seldom used in automobile radiators. Aluminum is used for radiators in special applications where weight is critical.

Core tubes are made from 0.0045 in. to 0.012 in. (0.114 mm to 0.3 mm) sheet brass, using the thinnest possible materials for each application. They are rolled into round tubes and the joints sealed with a locking seam. The tubes are then coated with solder, compressed into an oval shape and cut to length. Fins are formed from 0.003 in. to 0.005 in. (0.075 mm to 0.127 mm) copper or brass, again using the thinnest possible material to save weight and cost.

Serpentine fins are formed from solder-coated sheet, stacked between the tubes, and held in a fixture. These assemblies are heated in an oven to fuse the joints and then the assembly is submerged in liquid solder. Capillary action pulls solder into the joints, assuring a tight joint that will readily transfer heat. The serpentine type is usually used in passenger cars. It is the least expensive of the two types and cools as well as the plate type. The serpentine type is held together with the soldered joint alone, while the plate type is mechanically held by the plate fins as well as solder. Plate-type cores are, therefore, stronger than the serpentine cores.

The main limitation to heat transfer in a radiator is on the air side. Heat transfers from the water to the fins as much as seven times faster than the heat transfers from the fins to the air, assuming equal surface exposure. The radiator's heat transfer capacity is the result of the number of fins per inch, the radiator height, width, and thickness, and the number of coolant tubes. The core must be capable of dissipating heat energy approximately equal to the power produced by the engine. Each horsepower is equivalent to 42.4 BTU (10,800 calories) per minute. As the engine power is increased, the heat dissipation requirement is also increased.

Coolant tubes are straight, free flowing tubes. The fins are often given a pattern to break up any smooth laminar air flow (flow staying in layers)

that would insulate their surface. This turbulent flow will increase the heat transfer rate, but it will also add air resistance. Care is taken to design a radiator that will provide maximum cooling with minimum air resistance. With a given frontal area, radiator capacity may be increased by increasing the core thickness, packing more material into the same volume, or both. Its capacity may also be increased by placing a shroud around the fan so more air will be pulled through the radiator.

Radiator headers and tanks that close off the ends of the core are made of sheet brass 0.020 in. to 0.050 in. (0.5 mm to 1.25 mm) thick. These are fitted with tubular brass hose necks. The supporting sides are usually steel. The filler neck and the drain boss are brass. When a transmission oil cooler is used in the radiator, it is placed in the outlet tank where the coolant has the lowest temperature.

Fig. 9-11 Down flow radiator (The Dow Chemical Company).

Fig. 9-12 Cross flow radiator (Modine Manufacturing Company).

Radiators may be of the down flow (Figure 9–11) or cross flow (Figure 9–12) designs. In down flow designs, hot coolant from the engine is delivered to the top radiator tank and cool coolant removed from the bottom. In cross flow designs, hot coolant goes to a tank on one side of the radiator and flows across the radiator through the coolant tubes to the tank on the other side. In the down flow designs, the coolant reserve tank is located on the top, or inlet side. In the cross flow design, the reverse tank is placed on the outlet side. Neither type is more or less efficient than the other. Available space generally dictates the choice of the two designs. In some vehicle designs, where radiator space is small, a separate expansion or surge tank is used. This is usually positioned at the highest part of the cooling system so that it can act as a vapor separator as well as a filler neck.

Pressure Cap. The filler neck is fitted with a pressure cap. The cap has a spring-loaded valve that will allow cooling system pressure to build up to the cap pressure setting, and then will release the excess pressure to prevent system damage.

Excess pressure usually forces some coolant from the system through an overflow. The overflow is a tube leading out below the radiator where coolant is lost. Some systems connect the overflow to a platic container where excess coolant is held while the system is hot, shown in Figure 13. When the system cools, the pressure is reduced and coolant is pulled back into the cooling system, keeping the system full. The cap used on a coolant system without a coolant saver is fitted with a vacuum valve that allows air to re-enter the system as the system cools, so that the radiator parts will not collapse under a vacuum. SAE standard latching notches on the cap and neck are sized so that a high-pressure cap will not fit a low-pressure system.

Automobile engines are pressurized to raise the boiling point of the coolant. The boiling point will increase approximately 3°F (1.6°C) for each pound increase in pressure. Under standard atmospheric pressure, water will boil at 212°F (100°C). With a 15-pound (1.05 kh/cm²) pressure cap, water would boil at 257°F (125°C), which is a maximum temperature even for the lubricating system. This high pressure serves two functions. First, it allows the engine to run close to 200°F (93.3°C) with no danger of boiling coolant. Second, the higher the coolant temperature, the

Fig. 9-13 Cooling system with a plastic overflow container to conserve coolant.

Fig. 9-14 Pressure cap with the vacuum valve held open.

more heat it can transfer. The heat transferred by the cooling system is proportional to the temperature difference between the coolant and the outside air. This characteristic has led to the design of small, high-pressure radiators that are capable of handling large quantities of heat. It can be seen that for proper cooling, it is imperative to have the right pressure cap correctly installed.

A problem that sometimes occurs under these conditions involves the coolant pump. To function, the inlet side of the pump has a lower pressure than its outlet side. If inlet pressure is lowered too much, the coolant at the pump inlet could boil, producing vapor. The pump will then spin the coolant vapors and not pump coolant. This condition is called *pump cavitation.*

Fig. 9-15 Fan with a silicone drive operating within a fan shroud.

Fan. Air is forced across the radiator core by a cooling fan, usually attached to a hub on the coolant pump shaft. It is designed to do its job at the lowest fan speed with the engine at its highest coolant temperature. The fan is sometimes shrouded to increase the cooling system efficiency (Figure 0–15). The horsepower required to drive the fan increases much faster than the fan speed increases. Higher speed increases the fan noise level as well. Thermo-regulating and viscous-drive fans have been developed to drive the fan only as fast as required and to limit maximum fan speed. This reduces the fan power requirements and the fan noise. Fans with flexible plastic or flexible steel blades have also been developed. These fans have high blade angles that will pull a high air volume when turning at low speeds. As the fan speed increases, the blade angle flattens, reducing the horsepower required to drive it at high speeds.

Extra Heat Loads. Cooling systems have an added heat load when air conditioning is used. The high temperature aire conditioning condenser is usually located ahead of the radiator and this raises the incoming air temperature 10°F to 20°F (5.56 to 11.1°C). Air conditioned cars usually are equipped with a larger capacity radiator and a higher

capactiy fan than cars without air conditioning. High capacity cooling systems are also used on cars equipped for trailer towing.

Retarded spark emission controls increase heat rejection to the cooling system. There may be as much as 25% additional rejection heat at idle. In traffic, the additional heat may become critical. To help relieve this critical situation, many engines are equipped with a temperature-sensing vacuum valve similar to the one shown in Figure 9-16. When the coolant reaches a critical temperature, engine vacuum is used to advance distributor timing. This improves combustion, but reduces emission control; however, it lowers the heat rejection rate, so the engine does not overheat.

Fig. 9-16 Temperature sensing vacuum valve located in the cooling system.

Most of the heat absorbed from the engine by the cooling system is wasted. Some of this heat, however, is recovered by the vehicle heater. Heated coolant is by-passed through core tubes of a small heater. Air is passed through the heater fins, then sent to the passenger compartment. In some vehicles, the heater and air conditioner work in series to maintain vehicle compartment temperature.

9-4 COOLING SYSTEM MAINTENANCE

The cooling system is one of the most maintenance-free systems in the engine. Normal maintenance involves an occasional check on the coolant level when the engine is cool. Removing a pressure cap from a hot engine will relieve the cooling system pressure while the coolant temperature is above its atmospheric boiling point. When the cap is removed, the pressure will drop to atmospheric pressure, causing the coolant to immediately boil. Coolant will be lost and someone may be injured or burned by the high temperature coolant boiling out of the filler opening.

Manufacturers recommend that a cooling system be flushed and the antifreeze be replaced at specific time intervals. Some recommend a change each year, while others recommend a change every other year. The antifreeze should be drained to remove rust and scale from inside the engine cooling passages, as well as to remove depleted antifreeze additives. After flushing with clear water, fresh antifreeze coolant mixture with new additives should be installed.

This would also be a good time to check the condition of the coolant and heater hoses. Do not overlook the thermostat by-pass hose. Hoses should be replaced if there is any sign of deterioration. A broken hose will cause the coolant to be lost and allow the engine to overheat.

If there is no temperature gauge on the vehicle, it is desirable to remove the thermostat and check its opening temperature in a heated water bath with a thermometer, using equipment like that shown in Figure 9-17.

The pressure cap should be checked to see that it maintains the correct pressure (Figure 9-18). A low setting will reduce the cooling system efficiency and it may allow a loss of coolant.

Both the coolant pump and the fan depend upon the drive belt. This should be checked periodically to see that it is in good condition. It should be replaced if it has any indication of deterioration. Care should be exercised to see that the belt is installed on the correct pulley. Many engines use a number of belts and it is easy to mix the belts and pulley positions.

One thing that is often overlooked in cooling system maintenance is plugged radiator fins. Bugs often jam into the fins, blocking the air flow. The bugs should be blown out with high-pressure air from the back of the radiator to the front. High-pressure water may also be helpful in dislodging the bugs.

Sometimes, routine maintenance does not "cure" an overheating problem. If it is due to poor coolant circulation, the system can be *back flushed*. This procedure involves removing the hoses from the engine and radiator. A mixture of water and air is forced through the outlet side of

Fig. 9-17 Checking the thermostat opening temperature.

Fig. 9-18 Checking a pressure cap.

the radiator and through the engine outlet with the thermostat removed. If this does not provide free coolant flow, the radiator will have to be sent to a radiator shop for an acid treatment or disassembled for cleaning the tubes. If the engine block is plugged, the engine will have to be disassembled, the core plugs removed, and the cooling system scraped out.

In most cases, proper maintenance will keep the engine cooling system functioning satisfactorily for the life of the vehicle with no major repairs required.

REVIEW QUESTIONS

1. Why does an engine need a cooling system? [INTRODUCTION]

2. What happens if the engine temperature is too low? [INTRODUCTION]

3. What happens if the engine temperature is too high? [INTRODUCTION]

4. What limits the normal high and low engine operating temperature? [9-1]

5. What are the advantages and disadvantages of using glycol antifreeze? [9-2]

6. What additives are required in a cooling system? [9-2]

7. Where does the coolant enter the pump? [9-3]

8. How does the coolant flow differ in parallel and in series flow systems? [9-3]

9. Why are bleed holes used in the gasket between the head and block deck? [9-3]

10. Why is a by-pass used in the cooling system? [9-3]

11. When is the thermostat wide open during engine operation? [9-3]

12. How does the thermostat affect the pressure in the cooling system? [9-3]

13. Describe the coolant circulation in the radiator. [9-3]

14. How does the cooling ability of down flow and cross flow radiators compare? [9-3]

15. How does the strength of a serpentine-type compare to a plate-type radiator core? [9-3]

16. What is the main limitation in the heat transfer ability of the radiator? [9-3]

17. How much heat is rejected each minute on an engine developing 100 hp? [9-3]

18. How can the capacity of a radiator be increased? [9-3]

19. Where is the transmission cooler located in a radiator? [9-3]

20. How does the coolant pressure affect the boiling temperature of the coolant? [9-3]

21. What is pump cavitation? [9-3]

22. What is the purpose of a temperature-sensitive vacuum valve? [9-3]

23. What causes the coolant to blow out of a hot engine when the radiator cap is removed? [9-4]

24. What maintenance is done on a cooling system? [9-4]

gasoline and combustion

All of the energy required to operate an engine comes from the fuel. In a spark-ignited engine the fuel is gasoline. Gasoline is almost entirely composed of relatively volatile hydrocarbon molecules that have widely varying physical and chemical properties. It is designed and blended to meet the wide range of operating conditions found in spark-ignited reciprocating engines.

The hydrocarbons in gasoline vaporize and start to decompose at temperatures below 600°F (320°C) which are encountered in the combustion chamber before ignition takes place. The products of combustion are mostly gases and a large quantity of heat energy. The heat increases the gas's pressure in the combustion chamber to produce the force on the piston that is required to operate the engine.

The liquid gasoline must be changed to a vapor to burn in an engine. In engines using a carburetor to mix the correct proportions of liquid fuel and air, vaporization of the gasoline must be done in one-third of a second at idle speeds and in one-thirtieth of a second at normal operating speeds. In fuel injected engines this must occur much faster. The carburetor aids the vaporization process by breaking the liquid gasoline into a sudsy foam that rapidly mixes with the air. The correct number of molecules of fuel must combine with the correct number of molecules of oxygen in the air. At sea level the air is dense so a relatively small quantity is required for a given amount of gasoline. The air becomes less dense at high altitudes and at high atmospheric temperatures so the same volume of air contains a smaller number of oxygen molecules. This causes the charge mixture to become richer. It becomes so critical on some emission controlled engines that leaner carburetor settings are required on automobiles used in the mountains than those used at sea level. Because automobiles are frequently operated in both mountains and at sea level, some carburetors are being provided with altitude compensation devices to prevent over-rich mixtures at high elevations.

The combustion process takes place in the combustion cycle after the intake valve closes and before the exhaust valve opens. With the charge trapped in the combustion chamber, the molecules of oxygen in the air come into intimate contact with the hydrocarbon molecules of the gasoline. This enables them to burn rapidly.

When a gallon of gasoline is completely burned, it produces nearly a gallon of water as well as sulfur dioxide in an amount equivalent to the sulfur content in the gasoline. At normal operating temperatures the water is in a vapor form so it leaves the cylinder as a part of the exhaust gas. Condensed water vapor is visible in the engine exhaust when the engine is first started in cold weather. Condensed moisture with sulfur dioxide makes the water acidic and corrosive. When the engine is cold much of the moisture is condensed inside the engine, especially during low temperature operating conditions such as suburban driving. The combination of corrosion and wear under these conditions is the major reason for excessive wear of the top ring area of the cylinder wall.

10-1 NORMAL COMBUSTION

A spark plug ignites the combustion chamber charge near the end of the compression stroke. The spark produced across the spark plug electrodes at the correct instant must have sufficient energy to raise the gas temperature between the electrodes to a point at which the charge burning becomes self-sustaining. From this point, a flame front moves smoothly across the combustion chamber during normal combustion. Normal combustion is illustrated in Figure 10-1. Charge burning will take place during approximately fifty degrees of crankshaft rotation putting maximum force on the crankshaft. Actual combustion is much more complex than it first appears from this

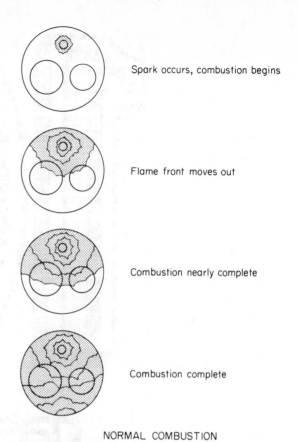

Spark occurs, combustion begins

Flame front moves out

Combustion nearly complete

Combustion complete

NORMAL COMBUSTION

Fig. 10-1 Flame front movement during normal combustion.

simplified description. In reality, the combustion gases go through many steps or phases during the combustion process. For this discussion the combustion is divided into two steps, *preflame reactions* and *combustion*.

A simple example is helpful in understanding preflame reactions. If one were to light a piece of paper with a match, the paper would first turn brown as a result of preflame chemical reactions, then it would ignite, producing a flame. The charge in the combustion chamber reacts in a similar way. As the gases are compressed and the temperature rises, preflame chemical reactions take place in the compressed charge that change the character of the charge. These preflame reactions prepare the charge for burning.

After ignition takes place, the flame front moves out in a modified spherical fashion that depends upon combustion chamber turbulence. The heat energy released behind the flame front increases combustion chamber pressure and temperature. Higher combustion chamber pressure and temperature increase the preflame reactions in a portion of the charge, called the *end gases,* that remain ahead of the flame front. Preflame reac-

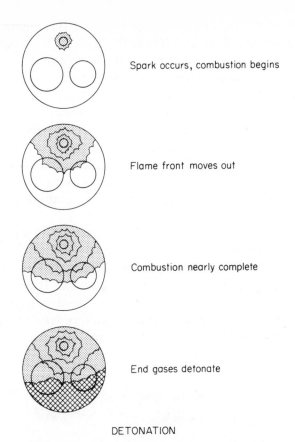

Spark occurs, combustion begins

Flame front moves out

Combustion nearly complete

End gases detonate

DETONATION

Fig. 10-2 Flame front movement during detonation.

tions become more rapid at higher engine compression ratios. When preflame reactions increase too rapidly, abnormal combustion results.

10-2 ABNORMAL COMBUSTION

Abnormal combustion may be divided into two main types—*knock* and *surface ignition*. Each of these types results in loss of power and in excessive temperature. Continued operation under either type of abnormal combustion will result in physical damage to the engine.

Detonation. Engine knock or detonation is the result of rapid preflame reactions within the highly stressed end gases. The reactions become so rapid that spontaneous ignition of the end gases occurs, as shown in Figure 10-2. This results in very rapid combustion rates within the end gases that are accompanied by high-frequency pressure waves. These waves hit against the combustion chamber walls and cause a vibration noise that is called knock or detonation.

Reducing Knock. The tendency for an engine to knock with a given fuel can be reduced by any method that will lower either combustion pressure and temperature, or both; or by any method that will reduce the time the end gases are subjected to high pressures and temperatures. In addition, a change to a fuel that is less susceptible to rapid preflame reactions will reduce the tendency to knock. Octane rating is a measure of the anti-knock properties of a fuel; a fuel that has high anti-knock characteristics has a high octane rating.

Compression ratio has a major effect on compression pressure. As the compression pressure is increased, the power that an engine is able to develop increases. This is the result of the higher combustion pressures that are produced. High combustion pressures, however, cause a greater knock tendency. Fuels with high antiknock properties are used in higher-compression-ratio engines, thus allowing the engine to run knock-free while developing increased power. Lower compression ratios are used in low-emission engines to enable them to run knock-free on low-octane unleaded gasoline.

Combustion chamber design also affects engine knock. Combustion chambers whose end gases are in a squash or quench area tend to have low knocking tendencies. This occurs because the end gases are thin and close to a cool metal surface. Cooling the gases causes a reduction and slowing of end gas preflame reactions, thus reducing the tendency of the engine to knock. This quenching of end gases is the main reason that a rotating combustion chamber engine will run knock-free on low-octane gasolines. Combustion chamber turbulence, as illustrated in Figure 10–3, is also useful in reducing knocking tendency by mixing cool and hot gases, thereby preventing a concentration of static hot end gases in which rapid preflame reactions can take place.

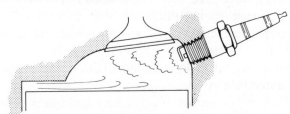

Fig. 10-3 End gases cooled in the quench area.

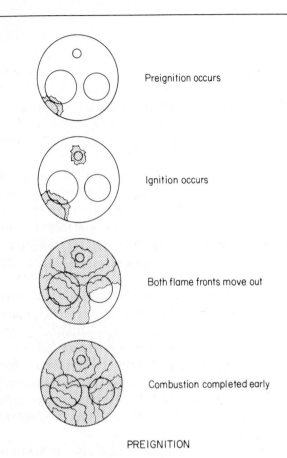

Preignition occurs

Ignition occurs

Both flame fronts move out

Combustion completed early

PREIGNITION

Fig. 10-4 Flame front movement during pre-ignition.

Surface Ignition. Surface ignition is a broad term that indicates abnormal combustion starting at any source of ignition other than the spark plug. This can be seen in Figure 10–4. The effect of surface ignition, because it produces a secondary ignition source, is to complete the combustion process sooner than normal. The result is to have maximum pressure occur at the wrong time in the engine cycle; this causes the engine to develop less power.

One source of secondary ignition is a *hot spot,* such as a spark plug electrode, a protruding gasket, a sharp valve edge, etc. These items can become so hot during engine operation that they maintain enough heat energy to form a second source of ignition. These sources seldom occur in modern engine designs as long as the engines have proper maintenance.

Another source of secondary ignition is combustion chamber deposits. These deposits result from the type of fuel and oil used in the engine and from the type of operation to which the engine is subjected. Fuel and lubricant suppliers have been doing extensive research to produce products that minimize *deposit ignition.* A deposit ignition source may be a hot loose deposit flake that ignites one charge and is then exhausted from the engine with the spent exhaust gases. This is called a *wild ping.* Sometimes, the flake will remain attached to the combustion chamber wall. When this happens, it will ignite successive charges until the deposit is consumed or the engine operating conditions are changed.

Names are given to many specific abnormal combustion conditions that are caused by surface ignition. If surface ignition occurs before the spark plug fires, it is called *pre-ignition.* It may be audible or inaudible. It may be a wild ping or it may be a continuous *runaway surface ignition.* If it occurs after the ignition is turned off, it is called *run-on* or *dieseling.*

Fig. 10-5 Piston damaged by abnormal combustion.

Continuous pre-ignition can result in rapid engine damage, usually holes through the piston, as shown in Figure 10–5. Another phenomenon resulting from pre-ignition is engine *rumble.* Rumble is a low-frequency vibration of the lower part of the engine that occurs when the maximum pressure is reached earlier than normal in the cycle. Rumble first became evident as a problem when engine manufacturers were able to greatly increase engine compression ratios as high-octane-rating fuels became available. This allowed the manufacturer to improve engine power with minor engine changes and with little thought to increasing the strength of the engine crankshaft and block. Corrective measures were taken in succeeding engine models; therefore, rumble has been nearly eliminated from modern engines.

It is interesting to note that knock-resistant fuels and antiknock additives tend to increase combustion chamber deposits and, therefore, to increase the tendency to cause surface ignition. Fuel manufacturers have had to place additional additives in their gasoline to modify combustion chamber deposits in an attempt to reduce the deposit ignition tendency resulting from the antiknock additive deposits.

Abnormal combustion seldom occurs in modern mass-produced automotive engines when the recommended grade of fuel and motor oil is used and when the engine is maintained and adjusted correctly. Some problems may exist in engines that are used exclusively for low-speed, short-trip driving. Abnormal combustion frequently occurs in engines that are modified for maximum performance and in some cases in emission-controlled engines.

10-3 GASOLINE CHARACTERISTICS

Gasoline is made from petroleum. In its natural state petroleum is made up of many different kinds of hydrocarbon molecules. The smallest hydrocarbon molecules are in a gaseous form, such as

Fig. 10-6 Apparatus used to check gasoline volatility by distillation.

natural gas and liquified petroleum gas (LPG). Next in size are gasoline molecules. Still larger molecules form diesel fuel, heating oil, and kerosene molecules. Very large molecules form the base for lubricating oil. The larger fuel molecules produce more heat energy as they are burned.

Because of the high economic value of gasoline some of the small gaseous molecules are combined in refineries to form more gasoline molecules, and some of the large molecules are split or cracked to make gasoline molecules. Modern techniques are capable of making more than one-half of each barrel of crude petroleum into gasoline.

Gasoline for automobile engines, called *motor gasoline,* must meet the needs of the engine. It must be clean and noncorrosive to the fuel-system parts. Motor gasoline must be light or sufficiently volatile to allow it to evaporate at low temperatures, so that the engine may be started, but not so volatile that it will evaporate in the fuel lines, causing vapor lock and thus preventing flow of liquid fuel. It also must not be so heavy that it will not evaporate or burn in the combustion chamber. If this happens, the unburned fuel will run down the cylinder wall, washing lubricating oil from the wall and diluting the motor oil. The volatility of the fuel is measured by a standard distillation test illustrated in Figure 10–6. In the test, a 100 milliliter (ml) sample is heated in a distillation flask. The vapors are led through a condenser and the condensate is collected in a 100 ml graduated cylinder. The temperatures of the vapors in the flask are recorded as each 10 ml is collected in the cylinder. The temperature-recovery curve is plotted on a distillation graph shown in Figure

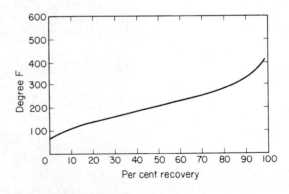

Fig. 10-7 Typical distillation graph for gasoline.

10-7. The most volatile parts of the gasoline will evaporate at the lowest temperature, while the less volatile parts evaporate at higher temperatures. The distillation range of motor gasoline falls approximately between 90 °F and 400 °F (35 °C and 205 °C). The distillation curve is nearly the same for all motor gasolines sold in a geographic area regardless of the grade or brand.

Octane Number. The primary difference between gasoline grades is their antiknock quality. Premium brands of gasoline are made from selected refinery stock and most brands contain additional antiknock additives. They have a higher octane rating than regular gasoline grades. The octane rating is a scale that indicates the resistance of the gasoline to knock or detonation.

The fuel octane number is determined in a standardized, single-cylinder, variable-compression, fuel-research engine pictured in Figure 10–8. The engine is first adjusted to standard conditions while operating on a reference fuel. Under these standard conditions, the knock meter (peak pressure measurement meter) is adjusted to mid-scale. The sample

fuel to be tested is then run in the research engine under the same standard conditions as the reference fuel. Fuel mixture is adjusted to produce maximum knock, and the compression ratio is adjusted to produce the standard knock meter reading at mid-scale. While all conditions are kept constant, the engine is then run on reference fuel blends of known octane rating, one blend with slightly higher knock and one blend with slightly lower knock than the sample being tested. The sample fuel is assigned an octane number between the two reference blends. One primary reference fuel (PRF), isooctane, has been assigned 100 as an octane number and the other primary reference fuel, *n*-heptane, has been assigned 0 as an octane number. A blend of isooctane and *n*-heptane is used to test octane numbers below 100 octane; the octane number is given as the percentage of isooctane in the blend. For example, if the PRF blend contains 95% isooctane and 5% *n*-heptane, the blend has a 95 octane rating. Octane numbers above 100 octane can be tested by adding specific amounts of tetraethyl lead to isooctane to make reference fuel blends above 100 octane. Different reference fuel blends necessary to "bracket" the sample fuel can be easily selected by referring to a table based on compression ratio that shows the approximate octane number.

Fig. 10-8 Engine and instruments used to check the octane rating of gasoline.

Two different fuel research engines and test procedures are used to test motor gasoline. One procedure is called the *Research Method* and the other is called the *Motor Method.* The Research Method engine is run at 600 rpm with the inlet air temperature adjusted to compensate for barometric pressures. The Motor Method engine is run at 900 rpm and the air/fuel mixture temperature is held at 300°F (149°C). Gasoline will produce a different octane number by each test method. The research Method usually gives a higher octane number than the Motor Method. The difference between these two octane numbers is called the fuel *sensitivity.* The sensitivity of the fuel is the result of the type of petroleum stock from which the gasoline was made. The octane number displayed on gasoline pumps is the average of the octane numbers determined by the Research and Motor Methods.

Octane Number Requirements. Gasoline has an octane number rating and each engine has a minimum octane requirement below which it will not run knock-free. The octane number requirement of the engine is the result of the engine combustion chamber design, the operating mean effective pressure, the humidity of the charge, the temperature of the compressed charge, and the deposits present in the combustion chamber.

Two types of road tests are used to measure engine octane number requirement. The Modified Uniontown procedure is a test to determine the minimum octane gasoline that is required under the most severe operating conditions of the fuel and engine combination. The Modified Borderline procedure tests the engine throughout its operating range and can be duplicated on a number of fuel samples. The Cooperative Research Council (CRC) selects a sample of automobiles each year to determine their octane requirements, and uses both test procedures to report engine octane requirements.

Details of these two tests are different; however, in both tests the engine is operated on the sample fuel at specified speeds, using specified ignition timing. The knock intensity is determined by ear and is reported as borderline, trace, moderate, or heavy knock.

In these road tests, the engine is operated on a primary reference fuel blend (isooctane and *n*-heptane) that is close to the octane number and requirement expected. If the engine knocks more than required by the test procedure, the octane number of the reference fuel blend is raised and the test rerun. If it knocks less than required, the reference fuel blend is lowered. The octane number requirement of the engine is equivalent to the primary reference fuel blend that gives the specified knock intensity required by the test procedure.

10-4 GASOLINE SELECTION

The automobile operator must select the gasoline he will use from among the available service station grades of gasoline. His choice is made between premium, leaded regular, low-lead, or no-lead gasoline. He has a further choice between major brands and the so-called independent brands. His choice is limited by the lowest gasoline grade that will start and satisfactorily operate knock-free in his engine. Automobiles with catalytic converters have the fuel tank fill opening designed so leaded gasoline cannot be used.

The main difference in gasoline grades is the octane rating; premium has the highest octane rating and the highest cost while no-lead usually has the lowest octane rating and in some cases the lowest cost. Other gasoline characteristics, such as volatility, vapor pressure, specific gravity, and cleanliness are practically equal, regardless of the gasoline grade.

Octane rating is an index of the ability of the gasoline to resist knock during combustion at high pressures and temperatures. If an engine does not knock on a low octane gasoline it serves no useful purpose to use a higher octane gasoline. The higher octane gasoline will not produce more power or run cleaner than the low octane gasoline in an engine designed to operate on low octane gasoline. If the engine knocks, a higher octane gasoline is required by the engine. A tankful or two of low octane gasoline will not damage the engine if the operator reduces the throttle opening when knock is heard. By using different gasoline grades the operator can safely determine the lowest price gasoline that will satisfy his engine. One precaution should be observed. If the automobile owner's handbook does not specify the use of no-lead gasoline the owner should *not* use no-lead gasoline. Unless the engine valves and valve seats have been specially designed for the use of no-lead gasoline, valve seat failure may occur under high power operation using no-lead gasoline. An occasional tankful of no-lead gasoline will do no harm to the valves. If no-lead gasoline is specified, leaded gasoline should not be used because it will damage the catalytic converter.

There is some difference between the minimum octane gasoline specified in the automobile owner's handbook and the gasoline octane number as posted on the pumps at the gasoline station. The reason for this is that each uses a different rating method. Traditionally, the minimum octane number requirement of an engine has been based on the Research Method octane rating of the gasoline. The recent octane number marking on the gasoline pumps is really the Antiknock Index that has been approved by a joint committee of the Society of Automotive Engineers (SAE), The American Society for Testing Materials (ASTM), and the Coordinating Research Council (CRC). It more nearly relates the fuel antiknock characteristics to the engine's response. The rating is an average of the Research and Motor Methods and this gives a lower number than the Research Number for the same gasoline.

All grades of gasoline have their volatility changed or adjusted by the oil companies throughout the year for the expected seasonal changes in temperature and geographical variations in altitude. The customer has no choice among the five volatility classes (A, B, C, D, and E) that are provided for different months of the year and for different geographical locations. For example, the D volatility grade is a summer gasoline for Alaska, a spring and fall gasoline for Michigan, Missouri, and Oregon, and a winter gasoline for Alabama and Oklahoma.

For the lowest fuel cost the operator should select the lowest price gasoline of the type specified that will run knock-free in his automobile engine. He will purchase higher price gasoline if he wishes to have added personal services, if he desires to use a particular gasoline brand when he wants to buy gasoline on credit, or if it is inconvenient to get to a service station having a low priced gasoline.

REVIEW QUESTIONS

1. Why do air/fuel mixtures that are supplied by the carburetor become richer at higher geographic elevations and temperatures? [INTRODUCTION]

2. What makes the engine exhaust acidic and corrosive when the engine is operated at low temperatures? [INTRODUCTION]

3. How many degrees of crankshaft rotation are required for typical normal combustion? [10-1]

4. What are two steps in the combustion process? [10-1]

5. What is the name given to the unburned gases present in the combustion chamber during combustion? [10-1]

6. What happens when preflame reactions occur too rapidly? [10-2]

7. How does compression ratio affect engine knock? [10-2]

8. What factors allow a rotating combustion chamber engine to run knock free on low octane gasoline? [10-2]

9. What causes dieseling after the ignition is turned off? [10-2]

10. What type of abnormal combustion is caused by combustion chamber deposits? [10-2]

11. What must happen to gasoline before it can burn in the combustion chamber? [10-3]

12. How does the volatility of regular leaded gasoline differ from unleaded gasoline in the same geographical area? [10-3]

13. Name two primary reference fuels. [10-3]

14. What limits the gasoline choice to be used in an engine? [10-4]

15. What is the value of using a higher octane gasoline than the one specified for an engine? [10-4]

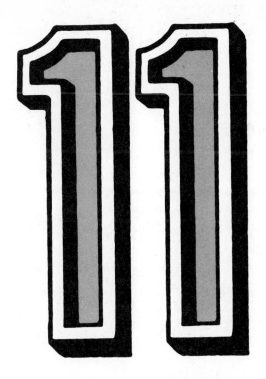

automotive fuel systems

The automotive fuel system, as discussed in this chapter, consists of the gasoline tank, fuel pump, fuel lifter, and connecting lines. Gasoline is stored in the tank that is located under the rear floor pan in front-engine automobiles. Rear-engine automobiles usually mount the fuel tank in front of the passenger compartment. The tank is vented to allow vapors and air to move in and out of the tank in order to keep pressures nearly equal as the vehicle goes up and down hills, as atmospheric pressures change, and as fuel is drawn from the tank. On emission-controlled automobiles the tank is vented through a vapor separator and a carbon canister to keep the gasoline vapors from contaminating the atmosphere. The filler neck of emission-controlled automobiles is fitted with a sealed cap. The cap has a pressure valve and a vacuum valve that allow excessive pressures to equalize.

This will prevent damage to the tank if the normal evaporative emission-control vent system fails to operate properly. The filer neck is smaller on automobiles that use no-lead gasoline exclusively.

A diaphragm-type fuel pump, usually mounted on the engine, moves the gasoline from the tank to the engine through a very fine grain filter to the carburetor or fuel injection system. Sometimes an electrically driven turbine-type pump is used in the fuel line or in the gasoline tank. To function correctly the pump must deliver liquid gasoline in sufficient volume and pressure to keep the carburetor bowl full of clean gasoline, regardless of vehicle speed or maneuvering.

When the fuel system malfunctions it is up to the technician to locate and correct the cause. The only thing the automobile operator can do is to have the proper grade of gasoline put into the tank.

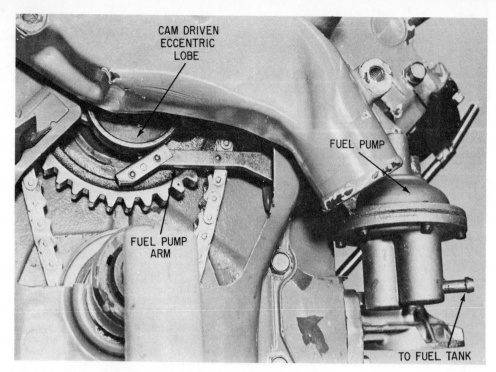

Fig. 11-1 Typical fuel pump drive method.

Three general grades of gasoline are readily available: leaded regular, leaded premium, and low-lead or no-lead. All late model engines are designed to run on no-lead gasolines.

11-1 FUEL SYSTEM OPERATION

The fuel pump moves the gasoline in the fuel system. It transfers gasoline from the tank to the carburetor or fuel injection system. Most engine-mounted diaphragm-type fuel pumps are operated by an eccentric lobe on the camshaft. This can be seen in Figure 11-1. A spring-loaded arm is held against the eccentric lobe, contacting it at all times. In some systems a short push rod is fitted between the eccentric lobe and the spring-loaded arm. The cam-actuated lever arm pulls the diaphragm from the fuel chamber side, increasing its volume and thereby drawing fuel from the gasoline tank. A spring on the lever side of the diaphragm pushes against the diaphragm as the cam eccentric lobe movement relaxes its pull on the arm lever and diaphragm. This spring pressure on the diaphragm is the force that puts pressure on the fuel. This force moves the fuel toward the carburetor or fuel injector (Figure 11-2). The fuel pump is fitted with two check valves, one on the tank side of the pump that will only allow gasoline to go into the pump (inlet check valve) and the other on the engine side of the pump that will only allow gasoline to leave the pump (outlet check valve). As the pump fuel

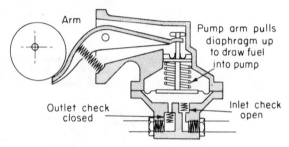

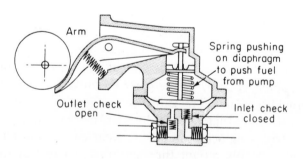

Fig. 11-2 Section view of a typical diaphragm fuel pump on the inlet and outlet strokes.

chamber is made to increase in volume by the linkage, gasoline is drawn into the pump from the tank through the inlet check. As the pump fuel chamber is made to decrease in volume by the spring, gasoline is pushed toward the engine through the outlet check.

Connecting fuel lines are made of steel or synthetic rubber hose. Steel tubing uses standard flare-type fittings to connect between the system components and beads to connect to hoses. Synthetic rubber fuel line hoses are fitted snugly over the beads on the ends of the tubing or over nipples at the system components. They are usually secured to the tubing and nipple with a hose clamp. In some cases the hose is fitted with a flare-type metal fitting end. The tubing or hose must be in good condition so that the gasoline does not leak out from or air does not leak into the system on the tank side of the pump during its intake stroke.

The gasoline tank is provided with an elaborate vapor separator that is designed to vent the tank with the automobile standing in any position. It is located within a chamber of the automobile body where it may be difficult or impossible to see without extensive work. It rarely causes a problem so it is not considered to be a part of normal vehicle service. Details of this system, the vapor separator and the vapor canister, are discussed in Chapter 17 on emission control.

11-2 FUEL SYSTEM TESTING

A most important characteristic of gasoline is that it must be able to start the engine. This sounds extremely fundamental, but its importance can best be demonstrated if one tries to start a cold automobile engine on diesel fuel. Fuel must be able to vaporize. This characteristic is called *volatility*. A basic fact that must be remembered is that the fuel must be in the vapor form to burn. It must also be mixed with air in the correct proportions, which is the function of the carburetor or fuel injector. Lastly, the fuel vapors must be intimately mixed with the air. This is accomplished in the intake manifold, head port, and combustion chamber.

All of the gasoline should be consumed in the combustion chamber. If it is not, some of the partially burned fuel can get past the piston rings and into the engine oil. The rest of it will be expelled with the exhaust gases to form unburned hydrocarbon exhaust emissions.

Fuel Filter. Correct carburetor operation requires clean gasoline. A fuel filter is placed in the gasoline supply line to trap any particle that may have been accidently put in the gasoline tank at the service station or any particle that develops within the fuel system of the vehicle.

Periodic fuel filter replacement is recommended by all automobile manufacturers. If their fuel filter replacement recommendation is followed, the operator is unlikely to have a problem from a plugged fuel filter. When the filter becomes plugged, the engine will not produce its usual power or speed. When located outside the carburetor the fuel filter can be checked by running a fuel pump capacity test on the carburetor side of the fuel filter.

Fuel Pump. The fuel pump capacity test is one of the easiest tests to perform, even when a pressure-volume fuel pump tester is not available. The fuel line is disconnected from the carburetor and directed into a measured container. If a shop towel is held around the fitting as it is loosened from the carburetor the towel will absorb any fuel leakage. The saturated towel can be removed from the engine compartment before starting to reduce the fire hazard that is always present around gasoline. An extension hose is slipped over the fuel line to make it easier to direct the flow of fuel. The engine is started and allowed to idle for 30 seconds as the fuel is being collected in a measured container.

Fig. 11-3 Running a fuel volume test. A pressure gauge is also included with this specific piece of test equipment.

The engine is then turned off. Gasoline in the carburetor is sufficient to operate the engine at idle for 30 seconds. The amount of gasoline the fuel pump delivers in one-half minute is measured. The fuel pump specifications give the amount that the fuel pump should deliver in one minute. The amount collected in the 30-second test must be doubled to determine the pump capacity per minute. For example, if 1 pint of fuel is delivered in 30 seconds the fuel pump has the capacity to deliver 2 pints in 1 minute. Fuel pumps will deliver approximately 1 pint per minute on small-displacement engines and approximately 2 pints per minute on large-displacement engines. The appropriate specifications should be checked for any specific engine being tested.

If the fuel system capacity measured on the carburetor side of the fuel filter is normal, no further test is required on the filter. If the capacity is low the test should be repeated on the fuel pump side of the filter. The filter is plugged if the test on the fuel pump side of the fuel filter is normal while the test on the carburetor side is low. If both tests are low, the problem is with the fuel pump operation or with the fuel lines.

Fig. 11-4 Making a fuel pump pressure test.

In addition to providing volume, the fuel pump is required to produce sufficient pressure to open the carburetor float valve and keep the carburetor bowl full of fuel. Fuel pump pressure is checked by placing a pressure gauge on the outlet side of the fuel pump, usually at the carburetor end of the fuel line, and measuring the fuel pressure as the engine idles. Fuel pressures will range from 5 to 10 psi, depending upon the engine. Specific applicable engine specifications should be consulted when making a fuel pressure test. A fuel pump may pass the pressure test but fail the pump capacity test. If the fuel pump eccentric is normal, low fuel pressure indicates that a new pump is needed. The pressure test is shown in Figure 11-4.

When insufficient fuel volume is produced by the capacity test with gasoline in the tank, a fuel pump vacuum test should be run. To run this test a vacuum gauge is fastened to the tank side of the fuel pump. The fuel lines from the tank will have to be plugged during the test to keep gasoline from leaking out of the line. A normal fuel pump will pull about 10 inches of vacuum (254 mm) at idle. If the vacuum is less, the pump or pump-actuating cam is faulty. A vacuum check at the tank end of the fuel line will indicate air leaks in the line that could cause low fuel-pump volume. A worn pump eccentric or plugged fuel tank filter could cause low pump capacity while still producing the required pressure and vacuum. A broken rocker arm return spring produces a tapping sound but will not affect pump operation.

Air Filter. For the engine to continue to function properly for long periods of time, the air coming into the engine must be clean. Engines are provided with air filters that trap abrasives, dirt, and other contaminants. As the particles are trapped they plug the filter pores. Excessive plugging restricts air flow into the engine and this upsets the carburetor calibration. Air filter plugging produces a fuel rich mixture which in turn reduces engine power and increases carbon monoxide and unburned hydrocarbon exhaust emissions. Badly plugged air filters will limit engine power and speed.

Some manufacturers recommend cleaning the air filter at specific mileage intervals by blowing air from the inside. Others recommend replacing it at set mileages. These schedules should be followed for maximum engine service life. Air filter changes are required more frequently when unusually dirty

Fig. 11-5 Air filter replacement.

operating conditions are encountered. Some equipment companies have developed test methods to indicate air filter plugging. These pieces of test equipment are not commonly used by the automotive service trade.

One of the more accurate air filter checks involves the use of the hydrocarbon-carbon monoxide emission tester. If the engine produces more unburned hydrocarbons and carbon monoxide with the air filter installed than it does with the filter removed, the filter is partly plugged and should be cleaned or preferably replaced. Figure 11-5 shows how an air filter is replaced.

REVIEW QUESTIONS

1. What part of a diaphragm-type fuel pump puts pressure on the fuel? [11-1]

2. What is the purpose of check valves in the fuel pump? [11-1]

3. What is the most important characteristic of gasoline? [11-2]

4. In what condition must the fuel be in order to burn? [11-2]

5. How will the operator know when the fuel filter becomes plugged? [11-2]

6. When should the fuel pressure be checked? [11-2]

7. How is the fuel pump capacity checked? [11-2]

8. Why is it important to check fuel pump capacity? [11-2]

9. What causes low fuel pump capacity? [11-2]

10. When should the fuel pump vacuum be measured? [11-2]

11. How can the technician detect an air leak in the fuel line between the tank and the fuel pump? [11-2]

12. How does a dirty air filter affect engine performance? [11-2]

automotive carburetors

A carburetor mixes the correct amount of fuel into the incoming air to give the engine a combustible charge. The charge has more fuel in proportion to the air (rich mixture) at idle speeds, during acceleration, and at full throttle than it does when operating at cruising speeds. This change in the mixture ratio is necessary to provide *drivability,* a term used to describe acceptable automobile operation.

As the engine idles, the air flow through the carburetor and manifold is slow, and so some of the fuel collects on the manifold walls. A rich idle mixture is needed to make sure that the charge reaching the leanest cylinder is still a combustible mixture. Engine modifications for emission control have improved manifold and carburetor designs so that the engine will function satisfactorily and provide drivability with much leaner mixtures than those used in pre-emission-controlled engines.

Engine power is produced by the pressure

developed as the charge expands during combustion. A rich mixture carries more fuel in proportion to the incoming air, and so it will release more energy to produce more power. This is required during acceleration and full throttle. The charge has more than enough fuel to consume all of the available oxygen contained in the charge air. If this same rich mixture were used for cruising speeds, the engine would give very poor gasoline mileage.

At cruising speeds, fuel economy is desirable. The carburetor delivers a lean mixture containing more than enough oxygen in the charge air to burn all of the fuel in the mixture. This uses all of the available fuel energy to give economical operation. Figure 12-1 shows a typical air/fuel mixture curve plotted against speed.

Excessively rich mixtures waste fuel and produce harmful exhaust emissions. Excessively lean mixtures may not ignite or may only partly burn in the combustion chamber. These unburned or partly burned combustion products go out of the tailpipe as undesirable unburned hydrocarbon emissions. Emission control carburetors are designed and manufactured to provide the correct air/fuel ratios for all engine operating conditions. It is up to the technician to correctly maintain them for continued proper operation. This is done when the engine is properly tuned up.

In most spark-ignited engines, the air and fuel are mixed and delivered to the combustion chamber as a combustible mixture. Combustible air/fuel mixtures range from an 8:1 to a 20:1 air/gasoline ratio by weight. The ideal mixture for the average gasoline is the correct amount required to burn the entire quantity of fuel. This is a *stoichiometric* mixture; that is, the substances are in the exact proportions required to complete the reaction. Internal combustion engines operate best on air/fuel ratios between 11.5:1 (rich) and 15:1 (lean), except at idle where engine mixtures may go as rich as 9.5:1 for cars built before 1968. For emission-controlled engines idle mixtures are approximately 14:1 to 16:1, with cruising mixtures as lean as 18:1 when operated near sea level.

It makes no difference if an engine is carbureted or fuel-injected, the engine still needs the same fuel mixture ratios. Fuel-injected engines that discharge their fuel close to the intake valve have more even mixture ratios between cylinders than carbureted engines because fuel injection does not depend upon air velocity and air/fuel mixing in the manifold to deliver the fuel to the cylinder.

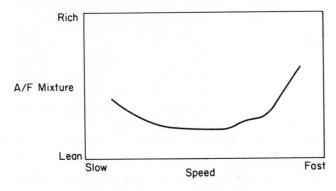

Fig. 12-1 Typical air/fuel ratio graph.

12-1 CARBURETOR SYSTEMS

Carburetor systems operate by using differences in pressure to control the flow of air and fuel through carefully sized openings called *ports* or *metering*

jets. The differences in pressure create a *signal* within the carburetor. The signal is used to control fuel flow into the air stream and this creates the air/fuel mixture needed. The openings may be designed either to be opened further or to be closed as engine operating conditions change. *Air flow* through the carburetor is controlled by engine vacuum below the *throttle plate* (manifold vacuum), by air flow through the venturi and by atmospheric pressure outside the carburetor. The greater the difference between manifold vacuum and atmospheric pressure, the more the air tries to flow past the throttle plate at part throttle openings. *Fuel flow* through the metering jets within the carburetor is controlled by the height of the fuel in the float bowl, which is exposed to the atmospheric pressure above it through the float bowl vent, and a low pressure that develops as the air flows rapidly past the discharge nozzle. The main carburetor

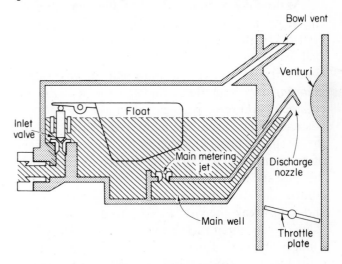

Fig. 12-2 A simple carburetor.

opening, called the *bore* or *barrel,* is partly restricted with a streamlined sleeve called a *venturi* that reduces pressure around the main fuel discharge nozzle to produce enough vacuum to pull the correct amount of fuel from the float bowl into the air stream. A simple carburetor is illustrated in Figure 12-2.

Float System. The fuel level in a carburetor is maintained by a *float* and a float valve called a *needle valve.* The float assembly has a lightweight hollow brass or a foam plastic *pontoon* with a hinge and a *tang.* As the fuel level in the bowl rises, the pontoon floats higher. It pivots on the hinge to move the tang against the needle valve. The needle valve is pushed against the seat by the float assembly tang to stop the incoming fuel flow when the float reaches a predetermined fuel level. As the fuel is used, the fuel level drops and the float lowers. This, in turn, allows the needle valve to leave the seat to refill the float bowl with fuel coming from the fuel pump. In operation, the combined action of the fuel flow, the float, and the needle valve will hold the operating *fuel level* nearly constant.

Problems occur if the fuel level is either too high or too low. High fuel level causes a rich fuel mixture with high fuel consumption and high emission levels while the low fuel level causes a lean mixture with accompanying engine surge and misfiring.

Main Fuel System. Most of the time during engine operation, fuel is used from the main fuel system. In this system illustrated in Figure 12–2, fuel leaves the float chamber through a carefully sized opening drilled in a small plug called a *main metering jet*. Fuel flows through the jet into an enlarged carburetor passage called a *main well*. A passage leading from the main well carries fuel to the discharge nozzle located in the narrow portion of the venturi. Holes that allow air to flow into this passage are called *main air bleeds*. They help control the effect of venturi vacuum on fuel flow and help break the fuel liquid into a free flowing foam of very small fuel droplets and air. The most usual problem that occurs in the main fuel system is air bleed plugging, which enriches the fuel mixture supplied to the engine. This can be seen in Figure 12–5.

Idle System. At low speeds, a very small amount of air flows through the venturi. This is not sufficient to produce fuel flow in the main system. Carburetors, therefore, are equipped with an idle system, illustrated in Figure 12–3. The idle system picks up fuel from the main well and carries it through restrictions to an elevation above the fuel level where air enters the fuel system through *idle air bleeds*. The mixture of idle fuel and air from the idle air bleed follows another passage to an

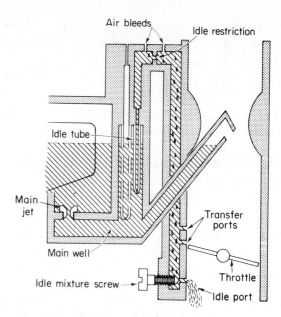

Fig. 12-3 Fuel flow in a typical idle circuit.

opening just below the throttle plate where the mixture flows past a manually adjustable needle valve to discharge the idle fuel into the air stream on the manifold side of the throttle plate. Air flows into the system around the nearly closed throttle plate. Idle speed is the result of the amount of air going through the carburetor. This is controlled by throttle position. The throttle position is set by a *throttle stop screw* or an idle air adjustment screw. The idle mixture, which provides idle smoothness, is controlled by turning a manually adjustable needle valve in the idle system. This screw is, therefore, called the *idle mixture adjuster screw*. Typical adjusters are shown in Figure 12–4.

Openings between the idle passage and carburetor barrel are located just above the throttle plate. These are called *transfer ports*. At curb idle, they are exposed to atmospheric pressure above the throttle plate, so they act as air bleeds into the idle system. As the throttle is opened slightly, the transfer ports are exposed to engine vacuum which is below the throttle plate. This causes fuel to be delivered from them, as well as from the idle port to supply the extra fuel needed as the engine speeds up and to supply the carburetor fuel needed during transfer from the idle system to the main system.

The most common idle system problem is plugged idle restrictions and air bleeds. It is most noticeable when a change in the mixture screw adjustment has no effect on engine idle. A thorough cleaning will usually correct this malfunction.

Fig. 12-4 Location of typical idle adjustment screws on a carburetor.

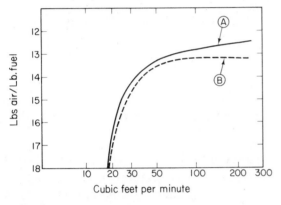

Fig. 12-5 Simple carburetor air/fuel curve A modified by a compensating air bleed to become curve B.

Power System. Lean operating mixtures produced by the main system are used for economy cruise and are not adequate for high power or for high speed operation. Carburetors are, therefore, equipped with a power system to enrich the mixture. A typical power system is illustrated in Figure 12-6. The power system will begin to operate as the engine vacuum is lowered to a specified vacuum as the throttle is opened. At idle, engine intake manifold vacuum is high, because the throttle plate is closed to restrict the air from entering the cylinder on the intake stroke. As the throttle is opened, air is allowed to enter the engine intake manifold more easily. This speeds the engine, but air can enter faster than the engine can use it and so this reduces the manifold vacuum. At wide open throttle, there is very little manifold vacuum, so manifold vacuum is a good signal to be used to operate the power system. In some carburetors, it is also necessary to use a mechanical link on the

throttle to help the vacuum operate the power system.

In the power system, manifold vacuum is applied to a spring-loaded piston or diaphragm. At high vacuum, during low speed and cruise, the spring is held compressed. At the low vacuum, during full throttle operation, the spring overcomes any remaining vacuum to move the piston or diaphragm. This opens a valve to allow additional fuel to flow from the float bowl to the main well. The additional fuel provides sufficient fuel to enrich the mixture required for full power operation.

Acceleration System. Rapid increases in speed require high engine power and high power requires a rich fuel mixture. When the throttle is quickly opened, air immediately flows into the manifold. The fuel, having greater weight, takes a longer time to start to flow than the air does, unless it is pushed. The acceleration system, consisting of a pump and valves, forces the extra fuel into the *air horn* as the throttle is opened. The acceleration system is spring loaded, so fuel will be forced out over a period of time as the spring expands. In this

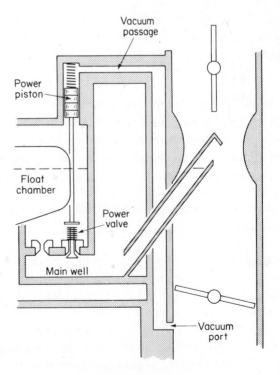

Fig. 12-6 Typical power system.

way the acceleration system delivers fuel until fuel starts to flow in the power system.

The acceleration pump may be a synthetic rubber piston seal in a cylinder or a synthetic rubber diaphragm. On the pump intake stroke that occurs as the throttle is closed fuel is brought through an acceleration pump *inlet check valve* into an expanding chamber. As the throttle is opened, the pump piston or diaphragm is moved against the trapped fuel by a spring. This forces the fuel past an *outlet check valve* and through a *pump discharge nozzle.* When the throttle is again closed, the system refills. A piston type acceleration system is shown in Figure 12–7.

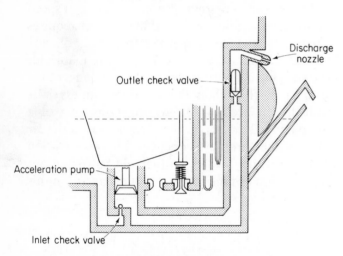

Fig. 12-7 Typical acceleration pump system.

Acceleration system problems resulting in engine stumble or hesitation are usually caused by a damaged synthetic rubber piston or diaphragm. Sometimes dirt gets on the check valve seats or plugs the discharge nozzle. Service of the acceleration system usually involves cleaning and replacement of the check valves and the pump piston or diaphragm.

Choke System. Fuel must be in a vapor form to ignite in the combustion chamber. Normal engine heat rapidly vaporizes the fuel, so no problem is encountered in a warm engine. A cold engine does not have this heat; however, the light, volatile part of the fuel will vaporize even at low temperatures. A choke system is used during cold starts to cause the carburetor to supply a large amount of

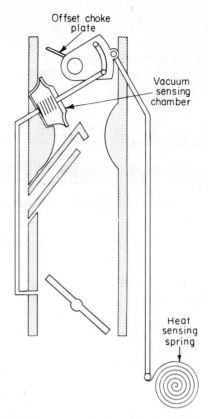

Fig. 12-8 Components of a typical automatic choke system.

fuel. The choke is located in the air horn above the main discharge nozzle as illustrated in Figure 12–8. When it is closed, engine cranking vacuum is high and so gasoline will be fed from the main nozzle and the idle system. The large amount of fuel coming from both systems produces a sufficient quantity of vapors to form a combustible mixture that will allow the engine to start. The engine quickly warms to vaporize all of the fuel. As the engine warms, the choke gradually opens. When it is fully open, the carburetor will operate normally. It stays open as long as the engine stays warm.

A heat-sensing spring holds the choke closed and a vacuum-operated diaphragm or piston and an offset choke plate try to pull the choke open. A fast idle cam is positioned by a linkage to the choke to increase throttle plate opening when the choke is closed. No heat or vacuum occurs before the engine starts so the choke will fully close and the fast idle cam will be fully positioned. When the engine is first cranked, vacuum opens the choke slightly to allow some air to mix with fuel to produce a combustible mixture. When the engine starts, manifold vacuum pulling on the diaphragm or piston increases the choke opening. As the engine warms, the choke heat-sensing spring gradually relaxes its tension, allowing vacuum to slowly open the choke. This also releases the fast idle cam, a stop at a time. When the engine is warm, the choke is fully open and the fast idle cam is fully released. The choke shaft is offset to give another opening force. If the throttle is suddenly opened on a cold engine, the offset choke plate will tip open to allow more air to enter the carburetor. The heat-sensing spring may be located in a well at the intake manifold exhaust crossover or on the exhaust manifold where it quickly senses heat. Some choke systems bring heat from a manifold stove through an insulated tube to a heat-sensing spring mounted in a choke control housing directly on the carburetor.

Choke problems usually result from a sticky choke plate shaft, a stuck vacuum piston, bent linkages, improper adjustment, and plugged or a burned choke heat tube. Damaged parts should be replaced, shaft and bushings cleaned, and adjustments correctly made.

Multiple Barrel Carburetor Systems. The foregoing discussion described basic single-barrel carburetors. When a single-barrel carburetor will not provide an adequate quantity of air/fuel mixture, a two-barrel carburetor is used. Both barrels of a two-barrel carburetor share the same float bowl, acceleration pump, choke operating mechanism, and, in some carburetors, they share the power system. Each barrel has its own main system and idle system. The remaining systems in a two-barrel carburetor are single systems to supply both barrels. The principles described for the single-barrel carburetor systems fully apply to the two-barrel carburetor systems, except that some of the parts are duplicated. The two-barrel carburetor is, therefore, no more complicated than the single-barrel carburetor.

The discussion up to this point has been limited to the primary portion of the carburetor. A secondary portion of the carburetor, including a secondary idle and main system, is built into the four-barrel carburetor and into some special two-barrel carburetors used on four cylinder engines. The secondary portion of the carburetor comes into operation under approximately the same operating conditions as the primary power system. It begins to operate when the primary throttle is opened about 60% as shown in Figures 12-9 and 12-10. After it starts to open, the secondary throttle plate opens very rapidly, so it is fully open at the same

Fig. 12-9 Secondary throttle plates beginning to open as the primary throttle plates are nearly open on a four-barrel carburetor.

Fig. 12-10 A carburetor for a four-cylinder engine with one primary and one secondary barrel.

time the primary throttle plate reaches the fully open position. The secondary system supplies large quantities of rich fuel mixture for high engine power. In moderate driving at legal speeds, the secondary system may never come into operation.

Secondary throttles on many carburetors are opened with a mechanical linkage. When this opening system is used, the secondaries usually have an air valve in the air horn that looks some-what like a choke plate. It keeps the secondary air passage closed at full throttle low rpm conditions when air flow velocity would be too low to operate the secondary fuel discharge nozzle. In other carburetors, the secondary throttle is operated through the use of a diaphragm and linkage. A spring-loaded diaphragm holds the secondary throttle closed at low speeds. A passage from the narrow portion of the primary venturi senses the venturi vacuum produced by high primary air flow velo-city. This venturi vacuum is applied to the control diaphragm to pull the diaphragm against the spring. This movement opens the secondary throt-tle plates the amount required to provide the engine with the quantity of mixture to supply the power demanded by the driver. Vacuum-operated sec-ondary throttles are illustrated in Figure 12–11.

Secondary system problems usually result from a sticking or leaking piston or diaphragm. In some cases, the power valve might leak. When problems do exist, new parts are usually installed.

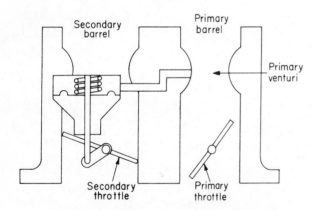

Fig. 12-11 Passages illustrating the method of using the air velocity through the primary venturi to provide the vacuum necessary to open the secondary throttle plates.

Additional Systems. Carburetors may be fit-ted with additional systems and devices to provide proper engine operation and drivability in special-ized conditions. A *hot idle compensator* (Figure 12–12) is a temperature sensing valve that opens an air passage when the engine gets unusually warm idling in traffic. The added air increases engine idle speed which, in turn, increases the coolant

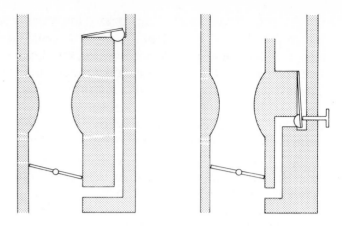

Fig. 12-12 Hot idle bypass arrangements.

pump flow and cooling fan speed. This action helps to cool the engine.

A *return check* is a dash pot-type diaphragm attached to the throttle linkage. As the throttle is closed, the return check slows the closing move-ment to prevent engine stall by gradually lowering the decelerating speed to full curb idle. Rapid throttle closing on an engine running at highway speeds will cause high intake manifold vacuum, which will draw exhaust into the intake during valve overlap. This will cause intake charge dilu-tion and misfiring. The return check prevents this.

Emission-controlled engines will usually run hotter than pre-emission-controlled engines. High temperatures will produce combustion chamber hot spots in some engines that ignite the fuel charge without a spark at the spark plug. Carburetors for these engines are equipped with an *idle stop solenoid* or anti-dieseling solenoid similar to the one illustrated in Figure 12–13. When ignition is turned off, the solenoid de-energizes. This allows the throttle plate to fully close. A fully closed throttle plate keeps air from getting into the engine so it won't afterfire or diesel.

Because some emission-controlled carburetors have very lean main metering systems, they are equipped with a separate *high speed fuelfeed* pas-sage. A pickup tube in the fuel bowl above·the main metering jets leads to a passage in the air horn with metered openings just below the choke plate. At high engine speeds, this circuit adds fuel to the incoming air to prevent over leaning.

The carburetor delivers fuel in proportion to air volume while the combustible air/fuel ratio is based on weight. Most automobile carburetors are calibrated to operate at 1000-foot (304.8 m) eleva-tion. When an automobile is driven at sea level,

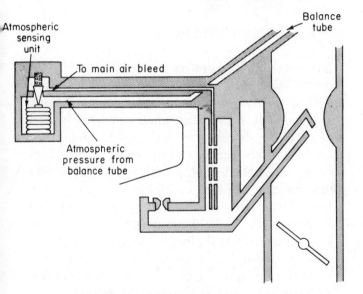

Fig. 12-13 Location of a typical idle-stop solenoid on an engine carburetor.

Fig. 12-14 Altitude compensation in the main air bleed.

there is more air mass in each cubic foot of air consumed by the engine, and so the resulting mixture is lean. This provides poor drivability. In contrast to this, automobiles operated at several thousand feet above sea level use air having less mass per cubic foot. These engines operate rich and so they produce excess hydrocarbon and carbon monoxide emissions.

To compensate for the change in the air/fuel mixture with altitude, some emission-controlled carburetors are equipped with altitude compensation. One type is shown in Figure 12–14. The altitude sensing device consists of an accordian-shaped container which is sealed so that no air can get in or out. This unit compresses as atmospheric pressure is exerted on it at sea level. It expands at lower atmospheric pressures encountered at high elevations. A valve is positioned by the movement of one end of the atmospheric pressure-sensing unit. In one type, the valve restricts the amount of air bleeding into the main well at sea level to enrich the mixture. It allows increasing quantities of air to bleed into the main well as the atmospheric pressure drops when the automobile operates at high elevations. This increase in bleed-air leans the mixture. In another type of altitude compensation, the atmospheric pressure-sensing unit moves a valve in a part throttle jet. The sensing unit expands at high elevations, pushing the valve into the jet to reduce the jet opening size. This reduces fuel flow into the main well to lean the mixture. Altitude compensation provides the automobile with low emissions and good drivability at all elevations.

Emission-control carburetors have vents connected to the evaporative emission canister. A vent valve in the carburetor opens the vent at idle and closes it at speeds above idle.

A passage located just above the high side of the closed throttle plate is connected to the distributor vacuum control. When the throttle is closed,

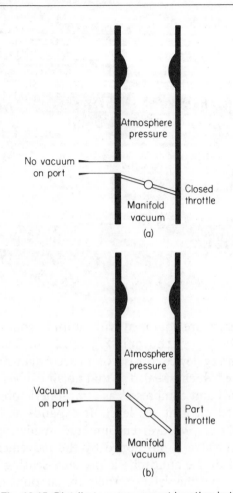

Fig. 12-15 Distributor vacuum port location in the carburetor bore.

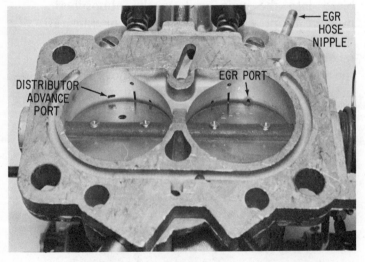

Fig. 12-16 View of the bottom of a carburetor with the throttle slightly open showing port openings.

there is no vacuum advance. When the throttle is opened, the passage is exposed to vacuum below the throttle plate. This passage is illustrated in Figure 12–15. This vacuum is used to advance the distributor ignition timing. Distributor advance is required for economy operation on lean mixtures. It takes longer for lean mixtures to burn because the molecules are farther apart. Therefore, with lean mixtures, ignition must take place early to complete combustion at the right time.

Emission-control carburetors are equipped with an exhaust gas recirculation (EGR) port. One type is shown in Figure 12–16. It does not enter into the operation of any carburetor system, but is a separate passage from a port located just above the throttle plate or at the narrowest part of the venturi. A passage connects this port to a tube on the outside of the carburetor. A hose connects the tube to the EGR system through a temperature-sensing valve.

12–2 CARBURETOR SERVICE

Carburetors should not be serviced for other than routine idle adjustments until an engine operation problem is positively identified as a carburetor problem. This means that when an engine is malfunctioning, all other engine systems should be checked for correct operation before the carburetor is condemned. Carburetor problems usually show up as a flooding condition, malfunctioning choke, severe backfiring, sticking throttle, inability to set idle, or no acceleration-pump action. On emission-controlled engines, surge-type and roughness-type drivability problems may be due to lean carburetor mixtures. Excessive carbon monoxide in the exhaust indicates a carburetor problem.

Adjusting Curb Idle. The most common carburetor adjustment is engine idle. It essentially involves setting the idle mixture screw to provide a smooth idle and setting the idle speed screw to give the specified idle speed on a warm engine. Emission-control carburetors have limiters that prevent excessively rich idle adjustments and, therefore, it may be impossible to adjust them rich enough to provide as smooth an idle as desired. Before idle adjustment is attempted, all engine systems should be functioning correctly and the engine should be operated long enough to become sufficiently warm so that the choke will fully open and release the fast idle cam.

The positive crankcase ventilation should be checked to make sure that the hoses are open and that the PCV valve moves freely. Other conditions must be met before curb idle can be correctly adjusted. Depending on the engine make and model, these conditions include having correct ignition timing; placing the transmission in neutral with the parking brake set; turning the headlights on; turning the air conditioner on; removing the vapor vent line; and removing the distributor vacuum line and then plugging it while the idle adjustment is being made. Applicable conditions are usually indicated on a sticker located on the inside fender pan, on a radiator support, or on the inside of the hood within the engine compartment. Idle is adjusted with the air cleaner installed and other vacuum hoses connected in their normal position. When the conditions that apply are met, the engine curb idle can be correctly set.

Idle settings involve two adjustments, an air adjustment that primarily controls idle speed and a mixture adjustment that controls idle smoothness. Idle *speed* is adjusted by one of two methods. The most common speed adjustment method is to limit throttle plate closing with a throttle stop screw located on the carburetor linkage. Air going around the slightly open throttle plate supplies air required for engine idle. A second method used on a few carburetor models to provide idle air is to completely close the throttle plate and to supply the air through a bypass passage in the carburetor body. The passage opening size is adjusted by a large idle-air adjusting screw protruding into the passage. Increasing air flow into the engine by either method will increase engine speed. Idle *mixture* is controlled by idle needle screws, usually located near the base of the carburetor. In some carburetor models this screw is located in the idle air-bleed passage. The screws control the amount of fuel delivered through the carburetor idle system to the incoming air. Emission-control carburetors have limiters sealed in the idle circuit that prevent excessively rich idle mixtures. The adjustable mixture screws can lean the mixture from this preset rich mixture point. In most carburetor models an idle mixture screw is provided for each carburetor primary barrel. Some carburetors, however, are designed to use a single mixture screw to control the mixture on two primary barrels.

Curb idle is adjusted by first adjusting the idle mixture screws similar to those shown in Figure 12-17, within the range of the limiter stops, to make the engine run smoothly at the highest rpm. High vacuum-gauge readings and tachometer readings help determine this point. Some manufacturers also recommend the use of an exhaust gas analyzer or hydrocarbon-carbon monoxide tester when setting idle. *Each* mixture screw should be turned 1/16 of a turn at a time, alternating between screws and allowing about 10 seconds for the engine speed to stabilize before making the next adjustment. Idle mixture is adjusted by turning the idle mixture screws clockwise to lean the mixture until the engine begins to slow down, then turning them counterclockwise to enrich the mixture. This should cause the engine to begin to speed up again. Continued turning counterclockwise will again slow the engine speed, when the screws are turned too far. Some idle screws have an internal limit-stop that will cause the screw to break if the technician tries to force it. The screws are readjusted to the point where the engine will idle smoothly at the highest speed. Idle mixture adjustment is done on each mixture screw turning them the same degree. If turning the mixture screws has no effect on engine idle, the idle system is malfunctioning. To correct this condition, the carburetor will have to be opened and the idle system cleaned to give proper operation. If the engine does not run

Fig. 12-17 Screwdriver adjusting the idle mixture.

smoothly when it is adjusted within the range of the idle mixture limiters then the external limiter stops, when used, can be removed, allowing the idle mixture to be adjusted further to give the smoothest and fastest possible idle. Some states have laws that allow only technicians with licenses for emission-control service to remove the limiter caps and make the adjustments using an exhaust-gas-analyzer or hydrocarbon-carbon monoxide tester.

With the engine running smoothly, idle speed is set by turning the throttle stop screw, similar to the one shown in Figure 12–18, to provide the specific engine idle speed. In some model emission-controlled carburetors the idle speed is set by making an adjustment on an idle-stop solenoid. This mixture screw setting should be rechecked after the idle speed has been set to make sure it is still at the best mixture setting.

Emission-controlled carburetors are adjusted lean to help keep exhaust emissions low. It is best when adjusting curb idle to use an exhaust-gas analyzer or a hydrocarbon-carbon monoxide (HC-CO) tester. The idle mixture screw is adjusted to give as smooth an idle as possible while keeping the meter reading below the maximum rich mixture specification, approximately 14:1 air/fuel ratio or less than 1% CO on emission-controlled carburetors. If the idle mixture limiter stops were removed during idle adjustment they should be replaced with colored replacement-type mixture limiter stops.

An idle adjustment procedure is given by some

Fig. 12-18 Screwdriver adjusting the idle speed.

manufacturers for use on emission-controlled engines when an exhaust-gas analyzer or HC-CO tester is not available. This method follows the normal idle adjustment procedure as previously described but also involves setting the idle speed at about 75 rpm above specified idle speed. After this adjustment is made, correct curb idle speed and emission mixture are obtained by further leaning the mixture screws equally, 1/16 turn at a time, without touching the speed screws. Alternate adjustments between mixture screws when more than one mixture screw is used until the correct idle speed is obtained. This leans the idle mixture, slowing the engine. This adjustment will cause the mixture to fall into the emission specification range. Specific idle adjustment procedures are given on the tune-up decal placed in the engine compartment.

Carburetor Overhaul. The carburetor is removed from the engine for major carburetor service. To remove the carburetor it is necessary to remove the throttle linkages, choke crossover link or heat tube, fuel line, and vacuum hoses including the PCV hose in some applications. Carburetors using coolant to heat the choke or carburetor base may need to have some of the engine coolant drained before the coolant attachments on the carburetor are disconnected. Removal of the base flange attaching nuts or cap screws will free the carburetor so it can be lifted from the engine.

For major service, the carburetor is completely disassembled except for the throttle plates, choke plate, air-valve plates, and permanently installed caps and plugs. If these items are faulty the applicable service manual procedures should be followed. The bowl cover, acceleration pump, discharge cluster, and needle valve and seat are removed. In addition, the throttle body is removed from the float bowl body on three-part carburetors. The vacuum-kick diaphragm assembly is removed along with the anti-dieseling solenoid and all other electrical or rubber parts, such as the bowl vent, air-filter gasket, and limiter caps. Some idle screws are retained with locks that prevent over-rich mixtures so these screws cannot be turned out. Idle mixture screws that turn freely by hand should be removed.

As the carburetor is disassembled the parts should be thoroughly examined to identify any abnormal wear, leakage, or cracks. It is usually advisable to make this inspection before cleaning so that the evidence is not removed from the part. The throttle and choke-plate closing should be checked to see if there is any binding or looseness and to see that they fit properly when they are closed. The technician can check throttle plate fit if he holds the plates completely closed, with the idle speed screw loosened, while he sights through them toward a light. Any alignment problems should be corrected before assembly.

Except for the float, all metal parts that can be removed from the carburetor without gaskets or rubber parts attached should be placed in a metal basket and submerged in carburetor chemical cleaner (Figure 12–19). The technician should avoid getting his hands into the chemical because it removes the natural skin oil and may cause irritation. Carburetor chemical cleaner is available in 5 gallon cans with a basket included. The cleaning time can be reduced by occasionally moving the basket up and down in the cleaner to agitate it. Fresh chemical cleaner will clean carburetor parts in about 5 minutes; used cleaner will take longer. Stubborn deposits may require loosening with a stiff bristle brush.

Fig. 12-20 Carburetor parts being rinsed with water after cleaning.

Fig. 12-19 Disassembled carburetor to be soaked in chemical cleaner.

When the parts are free of deposits they are removed from the chemical cleaner and the excess chemical is poured back into the cleaner can. The basket and parts can then be washed with water (Figure 12–20), preferably hot water so they will dry more quickly, to remove all of the chemical cleaner. Water is blown from the parts, and holes

are blown out with clean compressed air. Make sure all passages and circuits are open. This will remove any loose material and will completely dry the parts. After this type of cleaning the parts should look like new. They should be reexamined to determine if any damage is visible that was not apparent before cleaning. Wire should *never* be used to push deposits from carburetor holes or jets. The wire is very likely to damage the jet opening shape, causing it to meter improperly. Carburetor mating surfaces should be checked to see that they fit correctly. If they do not, the surfaces should be carefully filed or lapped so that they will fit to prevent leakage.

Two different types of parts kits are available for carburetor service—one for minor carburetor service, and one for a complete carburetor overhaul. The complete kit contains all of the parts in the simplified kit plus all new jets and power-system parts. It costs about three times as much as the simplified kit and so it is only used when the carburetor requires all of these new parts.

Float Level. A new float-needle valve and seat are included in carburetor repair kits and they can be installed during minor carburetor service if they are required. The old seat is removed and the new one is installed using a new seat gasket. The needle valve seat should be firmly tightened using a *properly fitting* wrench or screwdriver, as required.

One of the most important service items to be accomplished during minor carburetor service is to set the float level. Correct float level is necessary for proper fuel metering and engine performance. A number of methods are used for float level measurement. The simplest method is to measure from the top of the bowl surface to a specified place on the float, usually the top or the bottom. One method is shown in Figure 12–21. Gauges, often supplied in the repair kit, are made to the correct dimension and are much faster to use than a measuring scale. Some carburetor float levels are measured with the gasket in place, while others are set with the gasket removed.

If the float assembly is mounted in the carburetor bowl cover it can be inverted; this allows the normal weight of the float to hold the needle valve closed while the float level is measured. If the float assembly is mounted in the bowl and it is still on the engine, the float needle will have to be carefully held closed by hand. Pressure on the needle valve will distort the Viton tip of the needle so the resulting float level will be inaccurate.

If the float level is not correct it can be adjusted by bending the float arm tang that touches the needle valve. This should be done carefully so that no other part of the float arm is bent. If the float has two pontoons, both of them must be at the same height before the tang is adjusted. See the appropriate service manual or instruction sheet that comes in the repair kits for specific adjustment details for the carburetor being serviced.

The float assembly is also checked for float drop similar to the method shown in Figure 12–22. This adjustment is to make sure the float needle valve can open fully and it also makes certain that the float does not hit the bottom of the float bowl. Float drop is measured in a fashion similar to float level but it is not quite as critical.

Fuel Level. Float level is used to establish the level of the fuel in the float bowl. When the level of the fuel in the bowl is checked it is called the *wet fuel level.* If the float pontoon has been slightly distorted, such as by a partial collapse of a brass float or fuel absorption of a plastic float, the float level can be set exactly but the wet fuel level will be too high because the pontoon will sink low in the fuel. The wet fuel level can be measured on some carburetors by removing a cap or cover. On others it can be measured with the bowl cover removed. Still others have a gauge that can be mounted outside the carburetor to show the wet fuel level. The float level should be adjusted to give the correct wet fuel level for proper engine operation.

Assembly. The bowl cover should be checked with a straightedge to see that it is flat. If the cover

Fig. 12-21 Typical method of measuring float level.

Fig. 12-22 Measuring float drop.

is warped it may be possible to work down the high spots by moving the cover across abrasive paper that has been placed on a flat surface. In other cases the possible leakage across a warped cover can be sealed by using a thicker bowl cover gasket or by using two gaskets. Excessively warped covers and bowls should be replaced.

Replacement items used during minor service may consist of a gasket set only. The replacement items could also include the parts that come in a simple carburetor repair kit, which usually contain the gaskets, float-needle valve and seat, acceleration pump, check valves, and assembly clips. Some repair kits include parts that are usable for several different setting numbers on a carburetor type, so some new parts will be left over. Care is required in selecting the correct parts from those supplied in the repair kit. It is best to match them with the old parts for final identification. After the parts are installed and adjustments are made, the bowl cover can be installed. It should be lowered straight down over the bowl; the technician should be careful to guide the accelerator pump plunger and metering needles into their proper openings. Be sure that the acceleration pump rubber does not become twisted. Then install and tighten the assembly screws. If the carburetor parts are made of zinc the assembly screws should be carefully torqued. If they are made of aluminum the assembly screws may be tightened as securely as possible with a properly fitting screwdriver. The fuel line, choke linkage or heat tube, and vacuum kick are then reconnected. Where required, adjustments should be made.

If the carburetor is dry a relatively long engine cranking period will be required to fill the carburetor with sufficient gasoline to start the engine. Some technicians put gasoline in the carburetor bowl before trying to start the engine. With the parking brake set and the transmission in neutral the engine is started and warmed up. The wet fuel level may be rechecked on some carburetors as it controls the fuel in its normal operating condition. When the engine is thoroughly warm the idle speed and mixture will have to be readjusted as previously described.

REVIEW QUESTIONS

1. What does the term "driveability" mean? [INTRODUCTION]

2. Why is it necessary to have a rich mixture to produce full power? [INTRODUCTION]

3. Why is it desirable to use a lean mixture during cruising speeds? [INTRODUCTION]

4. How can the technician correctly maintain low exhaust emissions? [INTRODUCTION]

5. What is a stoichiometric mixture? [INTRODUCTION]

6. How does the mixture required on a fuel injected engine compare to a carbureted engine? [INTRODUCTION]

7. What is a "signal" within a carburetor? [12–1]

8. What controls the air flow within the carburetor? [12–1]

9. What controls the fuel flow within the carburetor? [12–1]

10. What is the purpose of the venturi? [12–1]

11. What is the purpose of the carburetor float? [12–1]

12. What is the result of an improper fuel level? [12–1]

13. Describe an idle circuit. [12–1]

14. What is the most common idle system problem? [12–1]

15. What does the power system do? [12–1]

16. How is manifold vacuum used to operate the power system? [12–1]

17. Why is a spring used in the accelerator pump operating system? [12–1]

18. What two valves are necessary in the accelerating system? [12–1]

19. What operating problems are caused by a faulty accelerating system? [12–1]

20. What systems supply fuel as the engine cranks with a closed choke? [12–1]

21. What closes the choke? [12–1]

22. What opens the choke? [12–1]

23. List the choke problems that may be encountered. [12–1]

24. How do multiple barrel carburetors differ from a single barrel carburetor? [12–1]

25. Why do some carburetors use a secondary barrel? [12–1]

26. What two methods are used to operate the secondary throttles? [12–1]

27. When does a hot idle compensator open? What does it do? [12–1]

28. What two methods are used to compensate for high altitude? [12–1]

29. Where does the distributor vacuum advance connect into the carburetor? [12–1]

30. When should the carburetor be serviced? [12–2]

31. How is the carburetor idle adjusted? [12–2]

32. In general terms, describe the carburetor overhaul procedure. [12–2]

33. How is the float level measured and adjusted? [12–2]

34. Why is it important to check the float level? [12–2]

35. What parts are replaced when the carburetor is overhauled? [12–2]

automotive batteries

The lead-acid type battery is the primary source of automotive electricity for starting today's engines. It also serves as a reserve source of electricity for the vehicle's electrical running load. The battery size that is installed in a vehicle is selected for the kind of use to which it will be subjected. Vehicles with large engines require a greater cranking force so a large battery is used. Large batteries are also used in vehicles with a number of electrically operated accessories. Small batteries are found in vehicles with small engines and light electrical loads.

A properly maintained lead-acid battery of the type used in automobiles will give from three to four years of trouble-free service. Proper maintenance involves keeping the battery clean, charged, full of water, and well supported in the battery case. When a battery fails to start the engine the technician must be able to check the battery and the rest of the electrical system to determine the cause of failure in order to properly repair the problem. It could be that the battery has failed or it could be that the other electrical system parts have failed.

13-1 NATURE OF ELECTRICITY

All matter is composed of *atoms,* which are made up of particles called *protons, electrons,* and *neutrons.* The structure of the atom is often compared to the solar system. The center of the atom, called the *nucleus,* is made of neutrons and protons. Neutrons have a *neutral* electrical charge and protons have a *positive* electrical charge. The nucleus is surrounded with rapidly spinning electrons that are *negatively* charged particles. These lightweight electrons weigh only 1/1800 as much as a proton or a neutron. An atom is represented in Figure 13–1.

It is difficult to comprehend the fact that atoms, even in solid matter, are mostly space, like the solar system. To rationalize this, it might be helpful to consider an analogy using an airplane propeller consisting of two blades. When the propeller is spinning it appears to be a flat disc, even though there is mostly space between the blades. This spinning disc would act more like a solid than empty space if one tossed a rubber ball at it. If this spinning disc could be tumbled fast enough, it would look and behave like a solid ball. The atom appears much the same. A number of electrons rapidly spinning around a nucleus at velocities as high as 4000 miles/second may produce an object that is called solid.

When the number of electrons in an atom equals the number of protons, the atom has a neutral charge. The negative charge of each electron will balance the positive charge of each proton. The electrons spinning about the nucleus revolve at different distances away from the nucleus, similar to Figure 13–2. As they revolve, they form shells at different energy levels. The electrons revolve in a fashion similar to a satellite revolving around the earth. Satellite orbits may be close to the earth

or they may extend into space, depending upon the energy or velocity of the satellite. Electrons in the lower orbits are bound tightly to the nucleus, while electrons in the outer orbits of many materials are loosely bound. Electrons may be removed from or added to the loosely bound outer orbit of these material types.

An atom is an extremely small particle. Usable matter is made up of large groups of atoms or combinations of atoms. For instance, water is made from hydrogen and oxygen atoms; petroleum is made from atoms of hydrogen and carbon; steel is made from iron, carbon, manganese, phosphorous, and sulfur atoms.

The electrons from the outer shell of the atoms in conducting matter may detach from their orbit and enter the orbit of another atom or become a free electron. The electrons move through materials in a random fashion or *drift* so that the net change is zero. That is, every electron that leaves an atom's orbit is replaced by an electron from another atom. Metals have many free drifting electrons. These materials are called *conductors*. It is interesting to note that they have three or less electrons in their outer orbits. Materials with five or more electrons in the outer orbit have a tighter bond to the nucleus with few drifting electrons. These materials are called *insulators*.

Atoms that pick up an extra electron in their outer shell have more electrons than protons, and, therefore, the atom is said to have a negative charge. If an atom were to give up one of its elec-

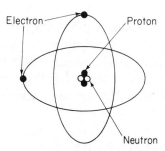

Fig. 13-1 Particles of an atom.

Fig. 13-2 Electron energy level shells.

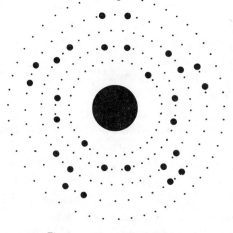

Electron energy level shells

Fig. 13-3 Electron drift.

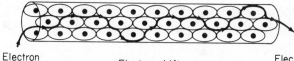

Electron in   Electron drift   Electron out

EMF forcing
electron into
conductor

Repelling force
moves electrons
along conductor

Fig. 13-4 Electron drift in one direction.

trons to a neighboring atom, it would have one more proton than electron. It would then have a positive charge. Atoms with either extra or missing electrons are called *ions*. If they have an excess of electrons, they are *negative ions*. When they are missing some electrons, they are *positive ions*.

Copper is a good conductor with many free electrons drifting within it. If a conductor has one end connected to a source of extra electrons and the other end connected to an object that lacks electrons, the general drift of electrons in the conductor will be away from the excess electrons and toward the object that lacks electrons. This drift occurs because *like charges repel* and *unlike charges attract* each other (Figure 13-4). This forced drift from the collision of the electrons will produce an *energy wave* that moves through the conductor at a speed approaching the speed of light. This wave proceeds like a series of rear end collisions on a crowded highway, where the collision rate proceeds much faster than the movement of any one of the vehicles involved in the collision.

The net drift of electrons through a conductor in one direction is *electricity*. The rate of drift is called *current* and is expressed in *amperes* (A). The electrical force that causes directional electron drift is called *electromotive force* (EMF). In automobiles, the initial EMF is produced by a battery or charging system. The EMF or amount of electrical pressure is expressed as *voltage* (V). The higher the voltage, the greater the electrical force capable of moving electrons within the conductor.

13-2 BATTERY OPERATION

A battery is made of different materials. Chemical reactions between different materials involve the movement of electrons in the outer shell of some of their atoms. Electron movement is an electrical reaction. If it results from a chemical reaction, it is called an electrochemical process. Movement of electrons resulting from a chemical reaction may be

controlled by controlling the chemical process producing the electrical current. This process can be reversed so that electrical currents cause a chemical reaction.

A lead-acid automotive battery is an *electrochemical* device. It has a voltage and can produce a current as the result of chemical reactions that deplete battery materials. A reverse current forced through the battery can cause chemical reactions that restore battery materials.

Cell Construction. A simple storage battery *element* is made of two dissimilar metal *plates* that are kept from touching each other by a *separator*. This element is submerged in a liquid sulfuric acid *electrolyte* solution. Battery parts are identified in Figure 13-5. An electrolyte is a material whose atoms become ionized in solution. These ionized atoms are free to move about in the solution. The acidity of the electrolyte weakens the electron bonds of the plate materials and so the electrons can drift, causing positive and negative ions to be formed in the plate material. The active material on one of the plates is lead dioxide, usually called

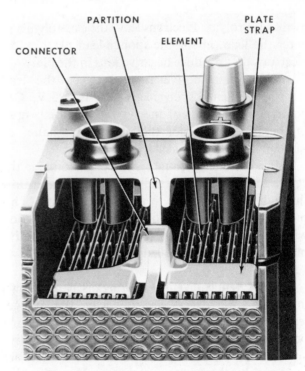

PARTITION

PLATE STRAP

ELEMENT

CONNECTOR

Fig. 13-5 Battery construction showing the connector going through the partition (Chevrolet Motor Division, General Motors Corporation).

lead peroxide (PbO₂). It is a dark brown, small-grain crystalline material. The crystalline type of structure is very porous and so the electrolyte can freely penetrate the plate. Electrons leave the lead peroxide plate and enter the electrolyte, leaving positive ions behind in the lead peroxide plate.

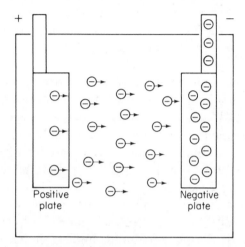

Fig. 13-6 Electron movement within a cell.

The active material on the other plate is *porous* or *sponge lead* that is also easily penetrated by the electrolyte. Electrons leave the electrolyte and enter the lead, giving the sponge-lead plate excess electrons that produce negative ions in the plate.

The electromotive force between the lead peroxide plate and sponge-lead plate is 2.13 V. Cell voltage is the result of the type of materials used in the plates and not the plate size, shape, or number of plates in a cell.

If a conductor connects the plates outside the cell, electrons can leave the negative plate and flow through the conductor to the positive plate. This process will continue as long as the chemical action within the cell transfers electrons to the negative plate. This process is called *discharging* the cell.

Cell Chemical Action. During discharge shown in Figure 13-7, excess electrons leave the sponge-lead plate through the exterior conductor, leaving positive lead ions (Pb^{++}) on the plate. Negative sulfate ions (SO_4^{--}) from the electrolyte are attracted by the positive lead ions. They combine to form neutral lead sulfate ($PbSO_4$) on the negative plate. During this time, the lead peroxide

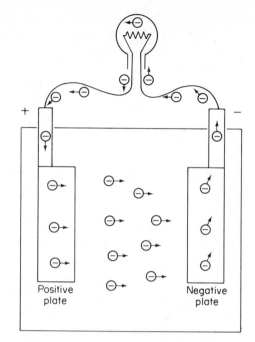

Fig. 13-7 Electron movement in a complete circuit.

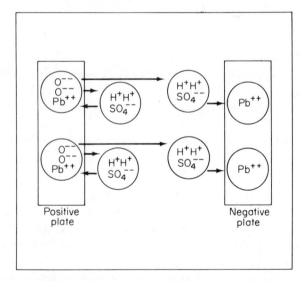

Fig. 13-8 Chemical ion movement in a cell during discharge.

(PbO_2) of the positive plate combines with hydrogen (H^+) from the electrolyte to release electrons as a positive lead ion (Pb^{++}), and water (H_2O) is formed. The positive lead ion from this reaction combines with a negative sulfate ion (SO_4) of the electrolyte to form neutral lead sulfate ($PbSO_4$) on the positive plate. Ion movement is shown in Figure 13-8.

During discharge, this reaction will continue as long as active material remains. In an ideal cell that is completely discharged, the plates will both become lead sulfate and the electrolyte will become water. A fully charged electrolyte has a specific gravity of 1.26; that is, it is 1.26 times as heavy as pure water. The specific gravity of water is 1.00. The *specific gravity* of the electrolyte indicates the amount of electrical activity remaining in the cell. A measurement of the cell's specific gravity is called the cell *state-of-charge.*

In the lead-acid battery the electrochemical process is reversible; it is reversible because the lead sulfate is only very slightly soluble and remains on the plates. If a cell is connected to a voltage higher than the cell voltage, electrons will flow backward through the cell. This reverse electrical current causes a reverse chemical action. Sulfate ions leave the plates and reenter the electrolyte. The plates again become lead and lead peroxide. The cell can only be charged or discharged as fast as the ions form and the electrons move to the negative plate. Forcing the reaction results in the formation of excess hydrogen and oxygen gases that leave the cell through the vent.

In operation, battery cells are continually being slightly charged and discharged. They are seldom fully discharged, but are usually kept near full charge.

As a cell reaches the fully charged state, hydrogen gas is formed at the negative plate and oxygen gas is formed at the positive plate. This process is called *gassing*. Because of this, care must be exercised to avoid a spark at the cell opening. In the presence of a spark, these gases combine with a sudden explosion that can ruin the cell and throw acid out of the cell. This means that all circuits, including a battery charger, should be turned off before leads are connected to or removed from the battery post to avoid sparks that could cause an explosion.

Batteries gradually wear out as they are used. This results from warping of internal parts, loosening of active plate material, hardening of plate material, and corrosive action on the separators. As the battery begins to wear out it also begins to lose its ability to form ions and thus the battery is not able to produce as much electrical power as it did when it was new. Electrical power is measured in *watts* (watts = volts × amperes). The electrical power available from an automobile battery is expressed in *ampere-hours,* the voltage being a constant 12 volts. The ampere-hour rating of the battery is based on the twenty-hour rate test described later in this chapter. The electrical power of the battery must be great enough to meet the electrical power needs of the engine. A new battery

that has only power enough to meet the engine needs will no longer provide the engine with sufficient electrical power after the battery begins to wear out. If a new battery is large enough so that it has electrical power in excess of the engine requirements, it will still be able to function after it begins to wear out, thus providing a longer battery service life.

The electrical power producing characteristic, shown in Figure 13-9, of a battery is important. An equally important battery characteristic is its reaction while being recharged, shown in Figure 13-10. A battery in a low state-of-charge has a small counter electromotive force as a result of weak chemical action within the cells. This allows the battery to accept a high amperage charging rate at a low charging voltage. As the battery state-of-

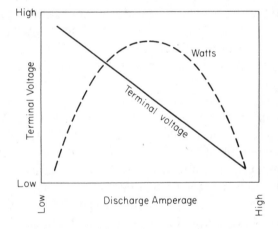

Fig. 13-9 Battery discharge characteristics.

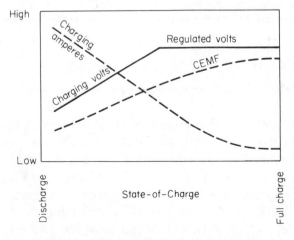

Fig. 13-10 Battery charging characteristics.

charge increases, its counter electromotive force also increases so the amperage charging rate lowers if charging voltage is held constant. Charging voltage must be increased if the charging amperage is to be kept constant. In a normal automotive charging system the charging amperage gradually decreases and voltage increases until it reaches the maximum voltage allowed by the system voltage regulator. Voltage no longer increases when it reaches regulated voltage so charging amperage will decrease as counter electromotive force increases during battery charging. This provides a desirable high charging rate for a discharged battery and a low charging rate for a fully charged battery.

Temperature affects the chemical reaction rate within the battery. Low temperature slows the chemical reaction and high temperature speeds the reaction. This is especially important during cold cranking. The chemical reaction in a cold battery produces ions at a slow rate, and so the cold battery does not produce starting current as effectively as a warm battery. If a battery has a low capacity it may fail to start a cold engine. In addition, a cold engine requires more effort to turn it over, and so it demands above-normal cranking amperage. Thus, cold-cranking problems are compounded when an under-capacity battery is used. Temperature compensating devices are used in some voltage regulators, as described in Chapter 15, to raise the charging voltage when the system is cold. This keeps the charging amperage at its normal range by forcing ions to form rapidly within the cold battery. When the battery and charging system warm up, the regulated voltage is lowered to its normal value to maintain normal charging amperage.

13-3 BATTERY FEATURES

The automotive battery is made of six *cells*. Each cell produces slightly over two volts. The cells are connected end to end, with the negative terminal of one cell attached to the positive terminal of the next cell (Figure 13-11). This type of connection is called a *series* connection. In a series circuit, the total voltage is the sum of the individual voltages, so that a six-cell battery produces twelve volts.

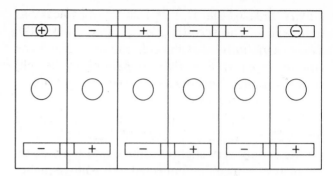

Fig. 13-11 Cell connections in a 12-volt lead acid battery.

Fig. 13-12 Cell construction with the connector going over the partition.

Within each cell there are a number of plates with separators between them. The *plates* are made from finely cast lead-antimony alloy grids that are filled with active plate material. In each cell, there is always one more negative plate than positive plate. An "eleven-plate" battery has five positive plates and six negative plates in each cell. A negative plate is placed on each side of the positive plates to allow the active positive plates to provide maximum battery performance. The plates are connected together within each cell to form a positive group and a negative group. The plate groups are interleaved with *separators* to keep them from touching. This assembly of plates and separators is called an *element*. The elements can be seen in six cells in Figure 13-12.

The separators are made from resin-impregnated cellulose fiber, microporous rubber, and plastic. They are flat on one side and ribbed on the other. The ribbed side is placed against the positive plate to allow free electrolyte flow along the positive plate. Some batteries use a fiberglas mat or specially designed separators over the positive plates to help hold the material in place on the grid, thereby reducing loss of active material into the bottom of the case, a phenomenon called *shedding*.

The element is placed in a snug-fitting case surrounded by electrolyte; this assembly is called a *cell*. Four bridges in the bottom of the case support the elements. Sub-feet on the positive plates rest on bridges 1 and 3, while sub-feet on the negative plates rest on bridges 2 and 4. This arrangement supports the plates, at the same time reducing the tendency for them to short-circuit within the cell.

Six cells are connected together to form a twelve-volt automobile battery. The battery case with six compartments is made from hard rubber, polyvinyl chloride plastic, or bituminous composition. It must withstand the acid electrolyte, shock, vibration, and temperature extremes.

The element connecting-post in older batteries came above the case cover where a connector strap was used to connect the element of one cell to the element in the next cell. Current automobile battery cell connections are below the cell cover. Two methods are used to connect the cells below the cover—over-the-partition and through-the-partition. In over-the-partition types, shown in Figure 13–13, the cell connector goes up to the underside of the cover where it crosses the cell partition. The connector extends down in the next cell to connect

Fig. 13-13 Battery with the cell connectors going over the partition.

to the plates. This type of connector keeps acid from seeping through the cover, provides a shorter electrical path than the above-the-cover connector, and uses less material. This results in increased battery efficiency at a reduced cost and lower weight. Through-the-partition-type connectors, shown in Figure 13–12, further reduce the amount of material used in the battery to further reduce the cost. It also shortens the electrical path to reduce electrical loss to a minimum. When the cell connector goes through the partition, it is critically important to seal the connector at the partition.

The cover is sealed to the case and partitions with bituminous or resin materials. These materials form an acid-tight joint that remains sealed during vibrations and temperature changes. Automotive batteries with one-piece covers are not repairable and must be replaced when they no longer function properly.

Each cell must have sufficient electrolyte to cover the plates. As the cell gasses, hydrogen and oxygen separate from the electrolyte by hydrolysis and escape from the cell. This must be replaced with water before the plates are exposed to air and dry out. Openings over the cells are usually designed to show the full electrolyte level. Vent plugs or caps designed to allow gases to escape while retaining liquid electrolyte are fitted in the openings. If the battery is overfilled with water so that the vent hole is plugged, electrolyte will be forced from the cell ahead of the gases. The loss of acid reduces the ability of the battery to function. Spilled acid will corrode parts surrounding the battery as well as provide a potential leak between the battery posts.

Some newly designed automotive batteries are considered to be sealed batteries. They have no openings through which the electrolyte can be checked, so water is never added. They do have vents through which cell gases can escape to equalize pressure and have baffles that form a liquid/gas separator. One of these is illustrated in Figure 13–14.

In the sealed battery, gassing is reduced by eliminating the antimony metal from the plate grids. Antimony tends to induce chemical reactions that cause self-discharging when the battery is not in use. Sealed batteries have replaced the antimony-lead in the plate grids with calcium-lead. Removal

Fig. 13-14 A sealed battery with side connectors.

of the antimony allows a faster charging rate until it reaches full charge. This reduces electrolyte loss while charging. When the battery reaches full charge the charge rate suddenly reduces to a very slight current. In addition the plates are enclosed in porous envelopes which keep the plates from shedding. The plates can then be placed on the bottom of the case, providing a large electrolyte reservoir above them. Most of these batteries have a state-of-charge indicator in the cover.

13-4 BATTERY TESTING

Batteries should be tested to help prevent vehicle problems that result from battery failure. The battery is tested to determine its state-of-charge and how well it either produces or accepts current. The voltage a battery produces is tested while a known current flows. If the voltage of a fully charged battery is low while discharging or if it is either too high or too low while charging, the battery is faulty.

State-of-Charge. As electricity is drawn from the battery the chemical reaction reduces the acidity of the electrolyte. This causes the electrolyte to thin and reduces its specific gravity. Specific gravity is measured with a *hydrometer,* pictured in Figure 13–15. If the specific gravity is high the electrolyte

is thick and the hydrometer will float high. If the specific gravity is low the electrolyte is thin and the hydrometer will float low. The acid concentration in the electrolyte, as indicated by the hydrometer float level, is an indication of the battery *state-of-charge.*

A fully charged battery will have a hydrometer reading of 1260 (indicating a specific gravity 1.26 times that of water). A completely discharged battery will have a hydrometer reading of 1070 (indicating a specific gravity 1.07 times that of water). The use of a hydrometer is the best means of checking a battery state-of-charge. Two precautions should be considered when using a hydrometer. If water has just been added to the cell electrolyte it will remain on top of the plates. This will produce a hydrometer reading that is lower than the actual battery state-of-charge. The second precaution has to do with battery temperature. If the battery is hot the electrolyte will be thin and the hydrometer will give a false low reading. If the

Fig. 13-15 Battery hydrometer being used to determine the battery state-of-charge.

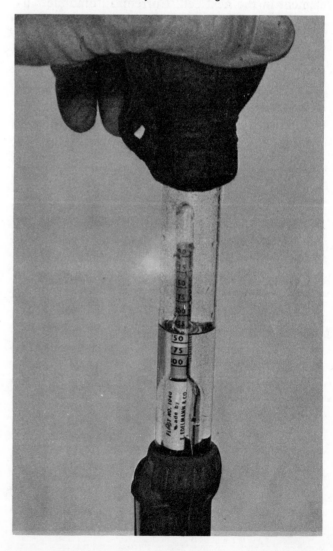

battery is cold the electrolyte will be thick and give the hydrometer a false high reading. Four points are added to the hydrometer reading for each 10°F (5.5°C) that the electrolyte temperature is above 80°F (27°C) and four points are subtracted for each 10°F (5.5°C) the electrolyte temperature is below 80°F (27°C). Good quality battery hydrometers have thermometers built into them with the correction factors indicated on the thermometer scale. Cells should be within 50 points on a good battery.

Capacity. The capacity test or load test measures the ability of the battery to rapidly convert chemical energy to electrical energy. This is done by drawing a heavy current from the battery while observing the terminal voltage at the battery posts. When current is drawn from the battery faster than the chemical action can occur within the battery, the battery terminal voltage is lowered. In the battery capacity test an *open* variable carbon pile resistor is connected in series with the fully charged battery and with an ammeter that can carry a large current, to complete an electrical circuit across the battery. The ammeter and carbon pile are usually contained within a battery-starter test unit as illustrated in Figure 13–16. A voltmeter is also connected across the battery posts or terminals. The voltmeter is also part of a battery-starter tester. Voltage is noted 15 seconds after the carbon pile is adjusted to produce a current that is three times the ampere-hour capacity of the battery. Ampere-hour capacity is a rating used to indicate the maximum electrical potential power or size of the battery and is marked either on the battery or in specification books. For a healthy full-charged battery at 80°F (27°C) or above, the battery terminal voltage should not drop below 9.5 volts at the end of 15 seconds while the current is flowing. When the battery is at 30°F (−1°C) the minimum battery voltage needed for this test is only 9.0 volts or above. If the test is performed on a battery with a hydrometer reading below 1225 the terminal voltage at the end of a capacity test will be very low, but this voltage reading serves no useful purpose in determining the battery condition, because the test is only valid when performed on a battery whose state-of-charge is above 1225. A battery with a low state-of-charge should be recharged before a capacity test is performed.

A battery with a low state-of-charge is not able to supply the amount of electrical current re-

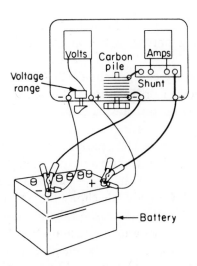

Fig. 13-16 Test connections used to measure the battery capacity.

quired for cranking the engine and still have sufficient voltage remaining to produce an adequate ignition spark. Before any electrical system checking is done the battery should be checked to be sure that it is at least three-quarters charged (1225) and that it has satisfactory capacity. If the battery meets these requirements the technician can proceed with electrical system testing. If the battery does not meet the requirements it should either be charged or temporarily replaced with a good, fully charged battery.

13-5 BATTERY CHARGING

A battery will charge when a voltage higher than the battery post terminal voltage is applied to the battery. This forces electricity through the battery in the reverse direction to produce a reverse chemical action within the battery. Charging will store energy in the battery. The higher the terminal voltage while charging, the faster the battery internal chemical action will occur. Excess charging voltage, however, will force chemical action to occur so fast that the battery will gas excessively, the plates will buckle, active material will break loose, and the battery will be destroyed. To minimize damage, battery temperature during charging should never be allowed to exceed 110°F (49°C). At higher temperatures the battery quickly loses its resistance to an external voltage, allowing the charging rate to go very high at a normal charging voltage; the battery will heat rapidly and will be ruined.

A battery charger should be turned off when it is connected or disconnected from a battery. If the charger is on, a spark may occur when the charging cable clips are attached to or removed from the battery posts. This spark can ignite the gases in the battery cell and cause an explosion. Check that the electrolyte is at the proper level, and then connect the red charger cable clip to the positive battery post. The positive post is always the larger of the two battery posts and it is usually marked with a (+) sign or red paint. The black charger cable is attached to the negative post. The charger is always turned to the lowest charging rate first, then the rate can be increased to the desired charging rate. This avoids excess voltage surges that could damage the battery.

A normal battery can be fully charged by using a charger that will force from 3 to 5 amperes through the battery. Chargers are equipped with ammeters that show the charging rate. A battery will be fully charged when three successive hydrometer readings taken at one hour intervals show no increase in readings.

A battery that has a hydrometer reading below 1225 will accept a much higher charging rate than a battery that is near full charge. A fast charger can be used for as long as 30 minutes at rates as high as 50 amperes on a partially charged twelve-volt battery. A fast charger should only be used long enough to recharge the battery sufficiently for engine starting. A normally operating vehicle charging system will finish charging the battery after the engine is running. If the vehicle charging system does not recharge the battery the charging system will have to be repaired to provide satisfactory electrical operation.

It is helpful in understanding battery operation if one connects a voltmeter across the battery to watch terminal voltage during both charging and discharging. The terminal voltage will be near 14.0 volts during slow-charging and it will be over 14.5 volts during fast-charging. After the charger is turned off the voltage will gradually drop to normal battery voltage as the high voltage surface-charge soaks into the plates. During discharge the voltage drops below normal open-circuit battery voltage. The higher the discharge rate the lower the terminal voltage. After a heavy discharge the terminal voltage will remain temporarily low. When the battery is allowed to stand, the terminal voltage will gradually increase because the surface of the plate is reactivated as the charge within the plates works to the surface to produce normal terminal voltage.

13-6 BATTERY REPLACEMENT

Failed batteries require replacement. The battery salesman must first determine the vehicle battery requirement. The original equipment battery has the lowest ampere-hour rating that will produce

Fig. 13-17 Battery being charged.

satisfactory service when all components are in excellent condition. A battery with a higher ampere-hour rating will give a longer period of useful service life. A battery with a lower ampere-hour rating will be unsatisfactory. The battery selected must have its terminals or posts located in the correct position on the cover or case to match the vehicle cables and must have dimensions that will fit in the battery carrier.

Batteries are available in two forms, wet-charged and dry-charged. Wet-charged batteries are delivered from the manufacturer to the customer filled with electrolyte and fully charged. If there is any delay in shipment or delivery the battery may have to be recharged several times during storage. Most batteries available to automobile owners after the original battery fails, called the *aftermarket,* are dry-charged batteries.

Dry-charged batteries are fully charged after manufacture, then are emptied and baked to thoroughly evaporate all moisture. The openings are sealed with a plastic seal. In this manner the battery can be stored indefinitely without deterioration. When a dry-charged battery is to be put into service the plastic seals are pushed into the battery cell space above the electrolyte where they remain and do not affect battery performance. Electrolyte, purchased in separate containers, is poured into each cell to fill it to the normal electrolyte level (Figure 13–18). Some of the electrolyte will soak into the plates so the cells will have to be topped off with electrolyte.

The battery will immediately be able to crank the engine for starting, but a 30-ampere charge for at least 10 minutes is recommended to properly condition the battery before use. A dry-charged battery properly filled and charged will have a longer service life than a wet-charged battery that has been subjected to storage.

The battery should be given a good visual inspection before the original or a replacement battery is installed. There should be no signs of cracks in the battery case or cover. The battery cover and sides should be smooth and flat. Internal damage will usually cause the battery case to bulge. The battery posts should be in good condition and secure. The battery date code should be checked to determine the battery age. Batteries seldom cause trouble in less than two years and rarely operate longer than four years. The date code is either stamped on the case or on a post, or a code

Fig. 13-18 Filling a dry-charged battery with electrolyte.

Fig. 13-19 Exterior battery features (Chevrolet Motor Division, General Motors Corporation).

is punched on a special date tag or warranty card. Date coding usually consists of a number indicating the last digit of the year the battery was put into service, for example, 5 for 1975 and 8 for 1978. This is accompanied by a letter indicating the month, with A for January, B for February, etc.

The battery carrier and clamps in the vehicle should be cleaned in the same manner used to clean the battery. Coating the clean battery carrier and clamp with acid-proof paint will help keep them in good condition.

Battery post and terminal clamps are cleaned

with a brush especially designed for this work (Figure 13-20). The brush is twisted on the post and in the terminal to form a clean, fresh surface that will have minimum electrical resistance.

The battery is mounted and clamped securely, not tightly, and the cables installed and tightened. The insulated cable is installed first, followed by the ground cable. After installation the cable clamp is often covered with grease to keep moisture from the clamp and battery post. Special materials that can be used to coat battery terminals are available in spray cans and can be purchased at automobile accessory stores. Coating the terminal will minimize corrosion that leads to resistance. The alternator belt condition and tension should be checked to ensure proper alternator driving speed.

(a)

(b)

Fig. 13-20 Cleaning battery terminals (a) and cable connections (b).

REVIEW QUESTIONS

1. What particles make up an atom? [13-1]

2. How many electrons are in the outer orbit of the atoms in a good conductor? [13-1]

3. What is an ion? [13-1]

4. How do like charges and unlike charges affect each other? [13-1]

5. What is electricity? [13-1]

6. What is the rate of electron drift called? In what units is it measured? [13-1]

7. In what units is the electromotive force measured? [13-1]

8. What is a battery element? [13-2]

9. From what material are the battery plates made? [13–2]

10. What determines the cell voltage of a battery? [13–2]

11. What is meant by the statement that the electro-chemical process of the battery is reversable? [13–2]

12. What gasses are formed on the battery plates? [13–2]

13. Why should sparks be avoided around a battery? [13–2]

14. In what terms is electrical power expressed? [13–2]

15. In what terms is the electrical power available from a battery expressed? [13–2]

16. How does the counter electromotive force of a battery affect the charging rate? [13–2]

17. What determines the voltage of a battery? [13–3]

18. What design characteristics of a battery increase its useful life? [13–3]

19. How can the technician determine the state-of-charge of a battery? [13–4]

20. Why is it important for a technician to know the state-of-charge of a battery? [13–4]

21. How can the technician determine the battery capacity? [13–4]

22. Why is it important for the technician to know the battery capacity? [13–4]

23. How can the technician fully charge a battery? [13–5]

24. When should a battery be fast charged? [13–5]

25. How is a dry-charged battery activated? [13–6]

26. What precautions should be observed when installing a battery? [13–6]

starters
and starting systems

The battery provides electrical energy to crank the engine and to fire the spark plugs. The positive terminal of the battery is connected to the starter through heavy insulated cables and switches. The negative terminal is connected to the engine block with another heavy cable or flexible strap. A heavy-duty starter switch is operated from the driver's control.

The starter switch is used to complete the battery circuit by sending current from the battery terminals through the starter, engine block, and cables. When the starter switch is open, no current will flow through the open circuit and the starter will not operate.

While cranking, the starter is mechanically connected to the engine ring gear by the starter drive mechanism. The drive mechanism engages a stationary ring gear while cranking and protects the starter from overspeed when the engine starts.

The starter cranking speed results from the starter design, the voltage supplied by the battery through cables, and the engine cranking load. The technician can do nothing about the starter design or the engine load but he can make sure the starter gets maximum possible voltage. This is done by connecting a fully charged battery to the starter with proper sized cables using clean tight junctions.

14-1 SERIES ELECTRICAL CIRCUIT

If voltage is applied to an *open* conductor, free electrons will fill the conductor, but they will *not* flow. A complete circuit is required in order to have an electron flow. With a complete circuit, electrons will flow and cause an electrical current whenever voltage is applied to the circuit. The number of electrons in a current that flow past a given point

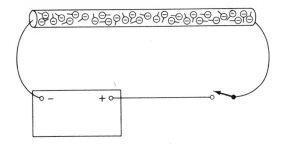

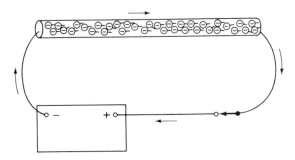

Fig. 14-1 Current will only flow in a series circuit when the switch is closed.

in one second is expressed as *amperes*. In a given sized conductor, as the voltage decreases, amperage will decrease. Current cannot flow unless there is an electromotive force or voltage to cause the electrons to move in a closed circuit. This is shown in Figure 14–1.

As the current flows in a conductor, the forced drift of the free electrons is hindered by collisions with atoms in the conductor. This produces heat which, in turn, increases free electron activity. In addition, some force is required to dislodge an electron from its shell around an atom. This force is provided by the free electrons. Dislodging the shell electron absorbs some of the free electron's energy. These two conditions are responsible for resistance to the electron drift or flow (Figure 14–2). Resistance to electron movement is measured in units called *ohms*.

There is a fixed relationship between the electrical pressure, *volts;* the electrical current, *amperes;*

and the electrical resistance, *ohms.* This relationship is expressed in an algebraic expression: ohms = volts/amperes, and is called *Ohm's Law.* If two of these values are known, the third may be calculated. If resistance in ohms is constant, the ampere flow in a conductor is directly proportional to the voltage.

The total resistance of a conductor increases as the conductor's length increases, as its cross section decreases, and as the conductor temperature increases. Wires normally used in automobile applications are selected to be as small as possible without causing excessive resistance, in order to minimize cost.

The resistance of a conductor or wire can be determined by measuring volts and amperes that it is carrying, and then using Ohm's Law (ohms = volts/amperes) to calculate resistance. In automotive service, specification for maximum resistance is usually given in terms of *voltage drop.* A known current is passed through the circuit in question. The voltage across that part of the circuit is measured. Using this method, the "voltage drop" can be used as a measure of circuit resistance any time the current passing through a conductor is known.

For example, the starter circuit resistance in Figure 14–3 is 0.0625 ohms, while the starter has a cranking voltage of 10 V and a starter draw of 160A.

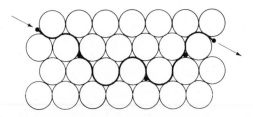

Fig. 14-2 An added electron within the conductor repels an electron.

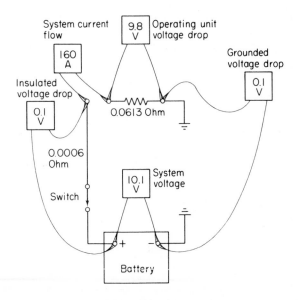

Fig. 14-3 Voltage drop in an operating circuit.

$$\text{ohms} = \frac{\text{volts}}{\text{amperes}} = \frac{10}{160} = 0.0625$$

It should be noted that battery terminal voltage in this example is only 10 V while a 160 A current is flowing. The battery is only acting fast enough to maintain 10 V at this current draw. When the circuit is opened, ion activity will immediately catch up to bring the battery EMF back to 12 V.

14-2 SERIES STARTER CIRCUIT

The *SAE Handbook* specifies that automobile batteries will have negative grounds. It further states that the maximum allowable voltage drop is 0.2 V per 100 A for cables between the battery and starter. Switches will add some circuit resistance. Resistance in most starter circuits is well below this value. Voltage drop in the starter circuit is the result of the cable terminal condition, cable length and size, and number of wire strands in the cable.

The starter circuit voltage drop can be measured

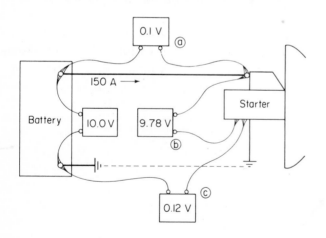

$$R_a = \frac{0.1\,V}{150\,A} = 0.00066 \text{ ohm}$$

$$R_b = \frac{9.78\,V}{150\,A} = 0.065 \text{ ohm}$$

$$R_c = \frac{0.12\,V}{150\,A} = 0.0008 \text{ ohm}$$

$$R_T = R_a + R_b + R_c$$
$$R_T = 0.00066 + 0.065 + 0.0008$$
$$R_T = 0.06646 \text{ ohm}$$

Fig. 14-4 Voltage drop in a series circuit.

by placing one of the terminals of an expanded scale (1–4 V full scale) voltmeter *at each end terminal* of the conductor being checked while the starter *is cranking.* Any voltage reading on the voltmeter indicates resistance. The greater the voltage reading, the greater the resistance, assuming constant ampere flow to the starter. This can be seen in Figure 14–4.

Each conductor, switch, and connector causes some resistance to current flow. When these current-carrying units are connected one after the other, as they are in the starter circuit, they form a *series* electrical circuit. Resistances in series add directly in ohm units. Voltage drops across the conductor, switches, and operating units in a circuit will add up to equal the measured battery voltage while current is flowing. No voltage drop exists when current does not flow. Full battery voltage will be measured across an open switch. It should be noted that the voltmeter is used without disconnecting any circuit connections.

Series resistance is similar to a line of traffic going into a raceway. The restrictions are the drive-in gate, the ticket salesman, and the ticket collector. Each car that goes through the gate also goes through each of these restrictions in series, one after the other.

It should be noted that the grounded portion of the starter circuit is just as important as the insulated side. All of the current that flows through the insulated and switch side of a series circuit also flows through the grounded side. The grounded side of the circuit is often overlooked when testing the resistance in automotive electrical circuits.

14-3 PARALLEL ELECTRICAL CIRCUITS

The remote starter switching circuit is in operation whenever the starter circuit is cranking the engine. Current that flows through the switching circuit is not the same current that flows through the starter circuit. Current from the battery splits, some going through the switching circuit and some going through the starter circuit. Systems that split the current are called *parallel* circuits. It is obvious that as more circuits are connected in parallel, more current will be able to flow. The only way more current is able to flow with a fixed battery voltage is to lower the circuit resistance. The parallel circuit does this.

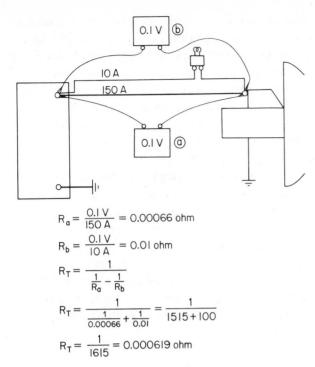

$$R_a = \frac{0.1\,V}{150\,A} = 0.00066 \text{ ohm}$$

$$R_b = \frac{0.1\,V}{10\,A} = 0.01 \text{ ohm}$$

$$R_T = \frac{1}{\dfrac{1}{R_a} - \dfrac{1}{R_b}}$$

$$R_T = \frac{1}{\dfrac{1}{0.00066} + \dfrac{1}{0.01}} = \frac{1}{1515 + 100}$$

$$R_T = \frac{1}{1615} = 0.000619 \text{ ohm}$$

Fig. 14-5 Voltage drop in a parallel circuit.

Here again, think of the raceway entrance. If a walk-in gate is opened in addition to the drive-in gate, more people can get into the raceway than by the drive-in gate alone, even though the walk-in people are restricted by ticket sales and ticket collectors.

Each restriction or resistance to current flow may be measured in ohms. Resistances added to parallel circuits make more paths for current to flow. The formula for adding these resistances is

$$R = \frac{1}{1/R_1 + 1/R_2 + 1/R_3}$$

For example in Figure 14–5 the starter circuit resistance is 0.00066 ohms and the starter switch circuit resistance is 0.01 ohms the total resistance of the parallel circuits would be:

$$R = \frac{1}{1/0.00066 + 1/0.01} = \frac{1}{1515 + 100} = \frac{1}{1615}$$

$$= 0.000619 \text{ ohms}$$

As more resistances are added, the total circuit resistance will decrease. Resistances used in parallel are called a *load*.

If a resistor is used to restrict current flow, it is called *resistance*. If it is used to allow more cur-

rent to flow by connecting in parallel, it is called a *load*.

14-4 ELECTROMAGNETISM

Each electron acts like a very small magnet, having north and south magnetic poles. Current flowing through a conductor will tend to polarize the electrons around the atoms so their magnetic poles are generally headed in the same direction. This produces a *magnetic field* that surrounds all current carrying conductors. The magnetic field is considered to be directed from the north pole toward the south pole. If one places his left thumb pointing in the direction of electron movement as in Figure 14–6, the fingers will be pointing in the direction that the magnetic field surrounds the conductor. This is called the *left hand rule*.

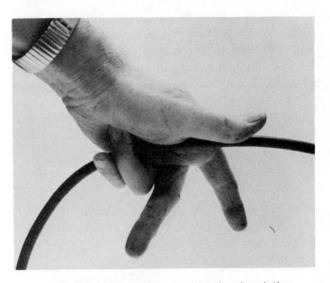

Fig. 14-6 Left-hand rule with the thumb pointing in the direction of electron flow and the fingers pointing in the direction of magnetic flow.

The strength of the magnetic field surrounding a current carrying conductor is proportional to the current strength flowing in the conductor. If more current flows, the magnetic field becomes stronger and produces more magnetic *lines of force* (Figure 14–7). Magnetic lines of force can be visualized as lines if iron filings are sprinkled on a flat surface surrounding a current carrying conductor. Lines of force actually stretch along the conductor in the third dimension to form magnetic shells.

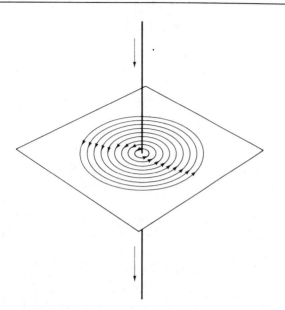

Fig. 14-7 Magnetic field around a current-carrying conductor.

Magnetic lines of force will not cross each other. When moving in the same direction, the magnetic lines of force tend to repel each other. As the magnetism becomes stronger, the lines separate. When two magnetic fields that surround

Fig. 14-8 Forces resulting from magnetic fields around adjacent current-carrying conductors.

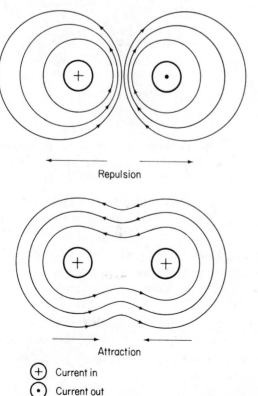

Repulsion

Attraction

⊕ Current in

⊙ Current out

adjacent conductors run in the *same* direction *between* the conductors, their fields are displaced. The force of the displaced fields tends to force the conductors to separate or repel the conductors. This occurs when current flows in opposite directions in each of the adjacent conductors.

When the magnetic lines of force that surround current carrying conductors move in *opposite* directions *between* the conductors, the lines join up. This forms a large displaced field that produces a force which will tend to pull the conductors together or *attract* the conductors. This force occurs when the current flow in the two conductors is in the same direction. All forces try to move the conductor to the center of the magnetic field.

Starter motor operation makes use of attracting and repelling magnetic forces that surround current carrying conductors, as illustrated in Figure 14-8.

14-5 STARTER MOTOR PRINCIPLES

The starter consists of two major parts—a stationary *field* and a rotating *armature* (Figure 14-9). They are often connected in series so that all the current that enters the starter will go through both field and armature.

The field is made of a number of conductor turns or windings around a soft iron core. Wrapping the conductor around the core is one method of increasing the magnetic field strength. Magnetic field strength can be measured in *ampere turns,* that is, the amperes flowing in the conductor times the number of turns the conductor makes around the core. Increasing either amperes or number of turns will increase the strength of the magnetic field. Magnetic lines of force move more easily through iron than through air. The laminated soft iron core will concentrate the magnetic field so it is more effective. Core laminations are insulated from each other to reduce the electrical eddy currents that form. Eddy currents resist current flow and produce heat.

The armature is made from a number of conductor loops or windings wrapped on a laminated soft iron core which is, in turn, mounted on a shaft and bearings that support it within the field. The conductor ends are soldered to copper *commutator bars* as shown in Figure 14-10. Carbon-copper compound *brushes* are held against the commutator bars to make electrical contact between the frame and the rotating armature.

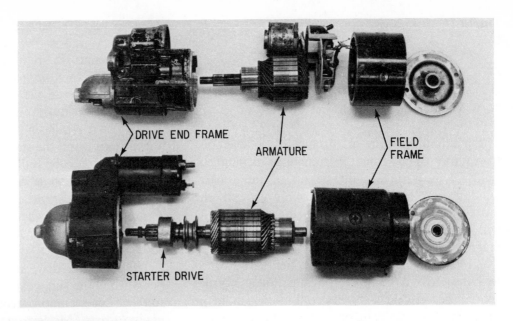

DRIVE END FRAME

ARMATURE

FIELD FRAME

STARTER DRIVE

Fig. 14-9 Starter motor parts.

Fig. 14-10 Pointer indicates the location of the soldered junction between the windings and commutator bars on a starter armature.

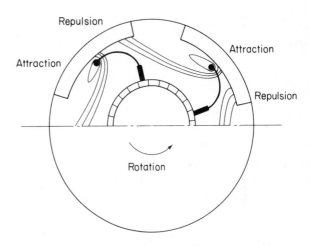

Repulsion

Attraction

Attraction

Repulsion

Rotation

Fig. 14-11 Starter winding and field attraction and repulsion.

In operation, current flows through the field and through the commutator bars into the armature windings, to develop a magnetic field around the conductors in each. The windings are designed so that the magnetic fields will attract one side of an armature winding while repelling the other side. This produces a turning effort on the armature shaft. Before the armature winding can reach its neutral point, the following set of commutator bars moves into contact with the brushes. This produces the same electromagnetic force on the following armature conductor. As the armature turns, the brushes keep changing commutator bars to keep the armature rotating. The rotating force of the armature is transferred through the starter drive mechanism to crank the engine. This principle can be seen in Figures 14-11 and 14-12.

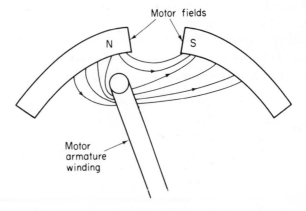

Motor fields

N

S

Motor armature winding

Fig. 14-12 Counter EMF induced in the conductor while rotating in a magnetic field.

14-6 ELECTROMAGNETIC INDUCTION

The maximum torque or turning force developed by a starter results from the strength of its magnetic fields. This is due to the design of the starter, winding size, and conductor size. In general, the more current the starter draws, the more torque will be produced by the attracting and repelling magnetic fields.

If the lines of a magnetic field are forced to cut across a conductor against their normal action, they will cause the electrons in the conductor to attempt to drift in one direction. The more magnetic lines that cut the conductor, the stronger the force to move the conductor's free electrons will become. This electromagnetic force is measured in volts, as it is in batteries. Producing an EMF by relative motion between a conductor and magnetic field is called *electromagnetic induction.* The EMF strength results from the number of magnetic lines cutting across the conductor each second.

Electromagnetic induction occurs in starter motors. As the starter operates, the armature is rotating within the magnetic field. This produces an EMF that is in a direction opposite to the EMF imposed on the starter by the battery. It is, therefore, called a *counter electromotive force* (CEMF). Counter electromotive force strength is proportional to armature speed. As starter speed increases, its CEMF increases. When the starter mechanical load plus CEMF equals battery force or voltage, the starter will not rotate any faster and its speed stabilizes. Maximum starter torque is limited by current flow and maximum speed is limited by CEMF. As a starter rotates faster, CEMF *reduces* battery amperage draw. Slowly turning starters will draw more current than rapidly turning starters because slowly turning starters develop less CEMF.

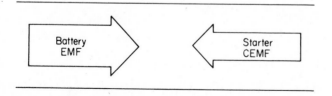

Fig. 14-13 CEMF reducing the effect of EMF.

14-7 STARTER DRIVES

Starter armatures are designed to turn at relatively high speeds to minimize amperage draw. To do this, they are geared down to the crankshaft. Starter drive ratios run from 15:1 to 20:1. Some starters have a built-in 3.5:1 reduction gear between the armature and the starter drive gear. This allows these starters to be built somewhat lighter and use a smaller crankshaft ring gear. The small starter drive pinion gear meshes with a large ring gear mounted on the flywheel or torque converter drive plate to give the required torque multiplication ratio to crank the engine.

The starter drive must be able to engage the gears while the ring gear is not turning and be able to release the armature from the ring gear when the engine starts. Modern starters use a *solenoid* to push the starter drive pinion gear into mesh with the crankshaft ring gear. An *overrunning clutch* is used to disengage the armature when the engine starts.

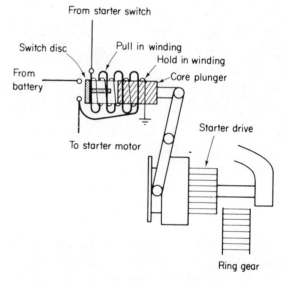

Fig. 14-14 Typical starter solenoid circuit.

The solenoid, illustrated in Figure 14–14, consists of two coils of wire around a movable core. Current flows through these coils when the driver turns the ignition switch to the crank position. Current in the solenoid coil produces a strong magnetic field that pulls the movable core toward the center of the coil. The movable core is linked to the starter drive gear, pushing it into engagement with the ring gear.

When the drive gear reaches full engagement, a set of heavy contacts on the end of the movable

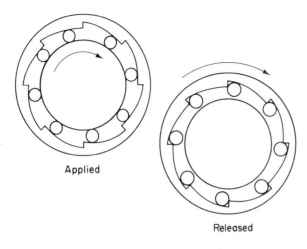

Applied

Released

Overrunning clutch

Fig. 14-15 Overrunning clutch operation.

core connects the battery to the starter motor, bypassing the heavy solenoid coil that is called a *pull-in winding.* A second winding, called the *hold-in winding,* remains energized, while starter cranking continues. When the engine starts and the driver releases the ignition switch from the crank position, current to the solenoid is cut off. A spring pushes the movable core back out of the coil. This, in turn, pulls the starter pinion gear from the ring gear.

The overrunning clutch is an assembly made of rollers or balls that wedge between a hub and outer race when turned in one direction and release when they turn in the opposite direction as illustrated in Figure 14–15. The entire overrunning clutch assembly is splined to the armature shaft. The solenoid pushes the entire overrunning clutch assembly toward the ring gear until the drive pinion gear is in full mesh with the ring gear. As the armature turns, splines on the armature shaft drive the overrunning clutch hub. Hub rotation forces the rollers up a ramp, jamming them between the hub and outer race. This pulls the outer race along, turning the starter pinion gear. When the engine starts, the ring gear spins the drive pinion gear faster than the starter will turn, the outer clutch race moves ahead of the drive rollers, rolling them down the hub ramp to release the clutch hub. The starter drive pinion gear will run with the ring gear, causing no damage to the armature. This continues until the driver releases the starter crank switch, allowing the solenoid return spring to pull the starter pinion gear from the engine ring gear. The overrunning clutch principle is illustrated in Figure 14–15.

14-8 STARTER MOTOR CONSTRUCTION

Starter fields are mounted in a starter housing called a *field frame.* Fields are held in the frame by the core that is screwed to the frame. Automotive starters have two or four field coils. Some field coils are connected in series, one after the other. Other starters use parallel windings on some of the fields to control starter motor torque and free speed characteristics.

The armature is supported in plain bearings in the *end frames.* There is a small clearance between the armature and field to maximize the effects of the magnetic forces. Bearing wear can allow the armature to rub against the field core to cause drag that will reduce armature speed, increase the amperage draw, and reduce the available starting torque.

Four brushes are held in *brush holders* in the end frame, two opposite brushes are insulated, and the remaining two are grounded. Springs and levers hold the brushes under tension against the armature's commutator. This provides good electrical contact for high starter amperage loads. If a brush spring becomes weak or the brushes wear down over half their original length, the brushes will not apply adequate pressure against the commutator. This allows the brushes to bounce, which will result in arcing and burning of the commutator bars. The starter parts are shown in Figure 14–16.

Current flows in series through the fields, insulated brushes, armature, and grounded brushes. Poor connections in any of these parts can cause high resistance and loss of cranking ability. Most of the starter resistances occur at the brush-to-commutator contacts. Armature-winding-to-commutator solder joints will give problems if the starter has been overheated, allowing the solder to melt. Figure 14–17 shows a starter that has been overheated and the solder thrown on the field frame.

14-9 STARTING SYSTEM TESTING

An improperly cranking starter can result from a defective battery, circuit resistances, malfunctioning switches, problems in the starting motor, starter drive problems, or engine resistance. The battery

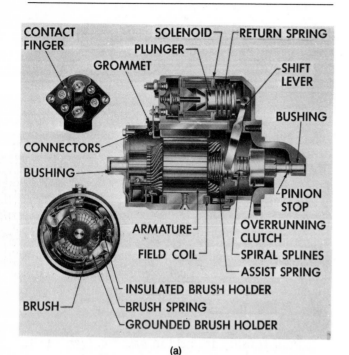

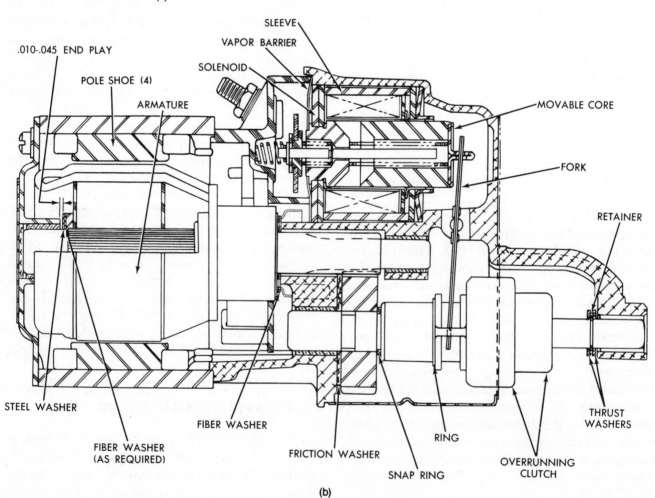

Fig. 14-16 (a) Sectioned view of a typical direct drive starter motor (Delco-Remy Division, General Motors Corporation), and (b) a reduction gear starter motor (Chrysler Motors Corporation).

(a)

(b)

Fig. 14-17 Solder thrown from an overheated starter motor armature into the field frame.

Fig. 14-18 Starter brushes on the commutator.

should always be the first item checked when any electrical problem exists. The battery must be at least 75% charged to satisfactorily perform its required function in starter system testing.

If the engine will crank, a voltage drop test of all of the starter cables, switches, and grounds should follow the battery test. If the engine does not crank, a voltage drop test across the starter switch will show if it is operating. When checking automotive switches, one voltmeter terminal is placed on each switch connection. Battery voltage will show with a switch open, and less than 0.1 V will show when the switch is closed and carrying current. If the circuit is open at some other point, the voltmeter will not register. Starter switches should be checked in this manner.

A *starter draw test* is the first test made on the starter after the battery and circuit test satisfactorily. This test can be remotely done by placing voltmeter connections across the battery terminals. The battery voltage is checked while the starter cranks the engine. A carbon-pile rheostat with an ammeter is placed across the battery and adjusted so the rheostat draws enough current to cause the voltmeter to read the same voltage that it did when the starter was cranking the engine. This test setup is illustrated in Figure 14–19. Starter amperage draw on medium-sized V-8 engines will be from 160 to 200 A.

The starter draw test will be high when the starter cranks slowly. If the amperage is too high and the battery and circuit are good, the problem is in the starter and the starter will have to be removed for further checks.

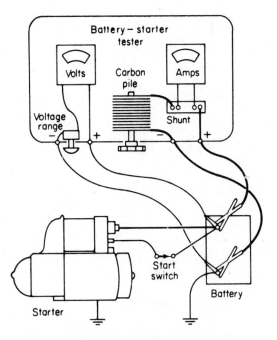

Fig. 14-19 A battery-starter tester with connections used to make the starter current draw test.

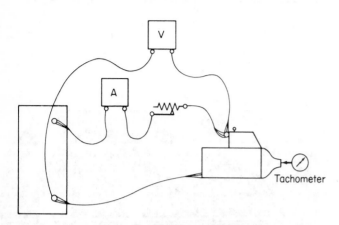

Fig. 14-20 Starter free speed test.

Two tests are run on starters that have been removed from the engine. The first measures armature free speed and amperage draw at a specified voltage (Figure 14–20). This requires the use of a tachometer that can measure armature speed. A hand-held tachometer with a friction attachment works well. Voltage is supplied by a battery through a carbon-pile rheostat which is used to control the voltage. One end of the carbon pile is attached to the positive battery post and the other end is attached to the starter post. A ground cable is attached from the battery negative post to the starter frame. Speed and amperage at the specified voltage can be compared to specifications. Low readings indicate starter problems.

The second test is a *stall test* run with the armature locked so it cannot turn. Using the same connections used in the free speed test, the voltage is adjusted to specifications and the amperage read. This value is compared to the starter specifications. Low amperage readings indicate a resistance in the starter; high readings indicate a short circuit that bypasses some of the normal circuit resistance.

If the starter is found to be faulty, it should be disassembled and each component checked for correct operation. This is called *bench checking* the starter. Many shops exchange starters for rebuilt units when tests show that malfunctions exist within the starter. It is a good practice to run the free speed and stall tests on any replacement starter to see that it functions correctly before installing it on the vehicle.

REVIEW QUESTIONS

1. What electrical property is needed to have an electrical flow in a closed circuit? [14–1]

2. What causes resistance in a conductor? [14–1]

3. What is the relationship between volts, ohms, and amperes? [14–1]

4. How is automotive wire size determined? [14–1]

5. For automotive service, what specification is given for maximum circuit resistance? [14–1]

6. Describe the way voltage drop is measured on an insulated starter circuit. [14–1]

7. What is a series circuit? [14–2]

8. How do series resistances in a circuit affect the total circuit resistance? [14–2]

9. When is a resistor a load and when is it a resistance? [14–3]

10. What magnetic properties are used in starter motor operation? [14–4]

11. What are the two major parts of a starter motor? [14–5]

12. What terms are used to describe magnetic field strength? [14–5]

13. How can a starter's magnetic field strength be increased? [14–5]

14. What does the commutator do to help turn the armature? [14–5]

15. How can voltage be induced in a coil? [14–6]

16. What values are used to indicate the strength of electromagnetic induction? [14–6]

17. What affect does counter electromotive force have on a starter? [14–6]

18. What is the gear ratio between the starter armature and the engine crankshaft? [14–7]

19. What is the purpose of an overrunning clutch in a starter drive? [14–7]

20. What does the solenoid do in a starter drive? [14–7]

21. What tests are run to determine starter circuit condition? [14–9]

22. What tests are run to determine the starter motor condition? [14–9]

charging systems and regulation

With the engine running, the charging system is designed to supply all of the electrical current required by the vehicle electrical load and to charge the battery. The battery supplies the occasional extra electrical demand that exceeds charging system capacity. This may occur at idle speed when a large number of accessories and lights are turned on.

The charging system consists of a belt-driven generator, a regulator to limit maximum voltage, and electrical wiring with switches to connect it into the automobile electrical system.

In 1960, alternators rather than generators were installed as standard equipment on some domestic automobiles. By the mid 60's all domestic automobiles were using alternators. The use of an alternator did not change the rest of the electrical system; it produced the same type of pulsing direct current that the older generator had produced.

An alternator does, however, produce current at lower engine speeds, it has lighter construction, safely operates at higher speeds, and is less expensive than a generator. All of these were good reasons to use an alternator. Figure 15–1 is a section view of an alternator.

15-1 GENERATOR PRINCIPLES

The generator makes use of electromagnetic induction principles described in Chapter 14. Relative motion between magnetic lines of force and a conductor forces the electrons to drift in one direction. This forced drift produces an EMF or voltage in the conductor. The strength of this voltage is based on the number of lines cutting the conductor each second.

More magnetic lines of force can be made to

cut a conductor in three ways. First, by increasing the *rate* at which the lines cut the conductor. Second, by increasing the *number of windings* in the conductor. Third, by increasing the *magnetic field strength*. The generator is belt-driven so its speed is dependent on the engine speed; consequently, rate has no control value. The number of generator conductor windings is part of the generator design so it cannot be used to control output.

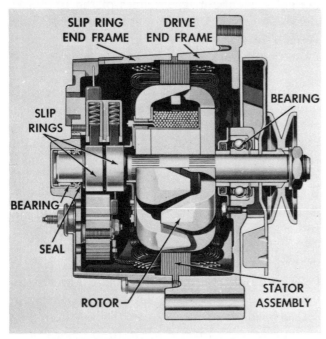

Fig. 15-1 Section view of a typical alternator (Delco-Remy Division, General Motors Corporation).

Generator output is very effectively controlled by changing the magnetic field strength of the generator field. Generators are designed so they will produce maximum output when maximum electrical system voltage is placed across the generator field. This causes maximum field current and maximum field strength. Maximum field strength will produce far more output than is normally required by the electrical system so the regulator is designed to reduce the field strength to the level that allows the generator to produce the output needed by the electrical system under each operating condition.

Modern automotive generators are rectified with a diode, an electronic device that passes current in only one direction, and are usually called *alternators*. The main conductor is wound in a frame and is called a *stator*. A field winding is wound around a hub that is supported on a shaft and bearings. Pole shoes, to concentrate the magnetic lines of force, are placed over the field wind-

ings. This field assembly is called a *rotor*. The rotor turns inside the stator, forcing the magnetic lines of force to cut the stator windings.

Each end of the rotating field coil is brought to a copper *slip ring* that is insulated from the shaft. Carbon brushes ride against and slip on these rings to connect the field windings to the regulator circuit.

In operation, the regulator controls the current flow through the field windings in the rotor. This current produces a magnetic field that will magnetize the pole shoes, half north pole and half south pole as shown in Figure 15-2. As the rotor turns, the magnetism that surrounds the pole shoes will cut the stator conducting windings. This induces voltage in the stator windings. Current will flow in the stator if it is connected into a completed electrical circuit whenever stator voltage is greater than system voltage.

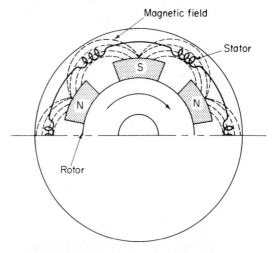

Fig. 15-2 Rotating pole shoes forcing the magnetic field through stationary conductors.

Stator. Alternator stators are made with three separate windings. Within these windings are a number of separate coils wound in series. They are spaced so the magnetic field polarity is the same on each of the winding coils at the same time. Each coil adds to the voltage of the preceding coil so that stator windings are able to produce the designed voltage.

All three windings are connected together. The most common connection used in automobile alternators is a Y connection; however, some applications use a delta connection. Both are illustrated in Figure 15-3 and they operate in a similar manner.

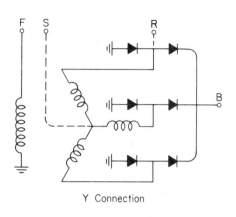

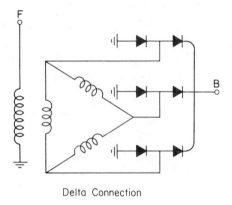

Fig. 15-3 Y and Delta alternator stator connections.

The following discussion of alternators will follow the Y connection type.

The three windings in a Y connection are connected together at the Y junction. The other end of each winding goes to a diode and then to the charging system.

Older type generators, as shown in Figure 15-4, had a stationary field and a rotating armature, similar to the starter. The conductor in the rotating armature cut the magnetic lines of the stationary field. Current from the armature flowed through commutator segments and brushes to the automotive electrical system.

Rotor. The field pole shoe fingers of the alternator rotor are alternately spaced, n-s-n-s-n-s, etc., around the rotor. Alternate magnetic fields from the rotor pole shoes cut the stator windings as the rotor turns. This causes the electrons in the stator windings to be forced one way, then back the other way as the fields alternate across the stator winding. This produces an alternating voltage in the stator as shown in Figure 15-5. If the stator were connected directly to an outside circuit, the alternating voltage would produce an *alternating current* (AC). Automotive electrical systems, however, require the voltage and current to be in one direction. This is called *direct current* (DC). Alternating current needs to be *rectified* to become direct current.

The voltage produced by each winding is proportional to the number of magnetic lines of force cutting the winding each second. The mag-

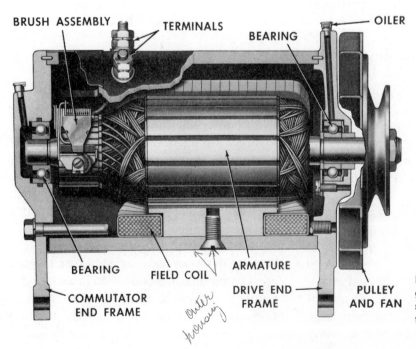

Fig. 15-4 Section view of a generator (Delco-Remy Division, General Motors Corporation).

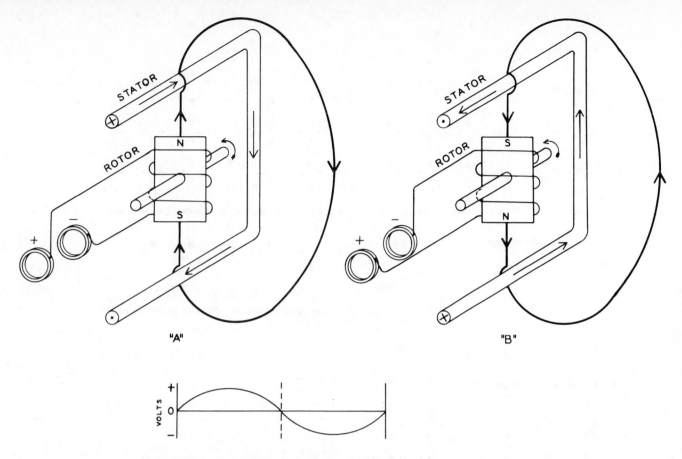

"A"   "B"

Fig. 15-5 Current reversal in the stator as the rotor turns (The Prestolite Company).

netic field starts from zero at the center of the pole shoe finger. As the rotor turns, the number of magnetic lines of force cutting the winding increases until it reaches a maximum at a point equidistant between the pole shoe fingers. It again drops to zero at the next neutral point at the center of the rotor shoe finger. The following pole shoe finger has the opposite polarity and so, in effect, the magnetic field direction changes. This changes the direction of the voltage produced in the winding. The continual buildup, first in one direction and then in another, produces a *sine wave* voltage. The name comes from the trigonometric function called *sine*. If a single conductor and a single two-pole magnet were used, the voltage would be proportional to the trigonometric sine of the angle of the magnet in relation to the conductor. Three stationary windings are equally spaced and their voltages produce three sine waves as the rotor turns. The current illustrated in Figure 15–6 produced by these voltages is called a *three-phase alternating current*.

Alternating current produced in the stator conductors is converted to direct current by a principle called rectification. Alternators are rectified using diodes, and generators are rectified with the commutator.

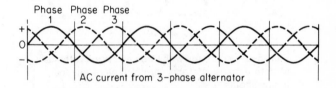

Fig. 15-6 Alternating current from three phase windings (The Prestolite Company).

15-2 SEMICONDUCTORS—DIODES

It is necessary to understand the operation of diodes if one is to understand rectification of alternator current in the automobile charging system. Diode operation is based upon semiconductor principles.

It has been previously stated that metallic atoms with less than four electrons in the outer shell are good conductors and atoms with more than four electrons are good insulators. Atoms with exactly four electrons in the outer shell are neither good conductors nor good insulators. Silicon and germanium represent materials of this type. In pure crystalline form, the electrons from adjacent atoms share the electrons of their outer shells and, in effect, they each have eight electrons

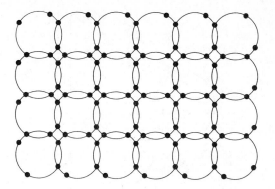

Fig. 15-7 Atoms with four electrons in a strucure.

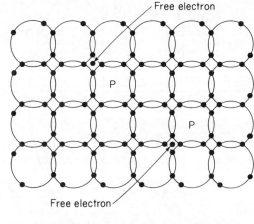

Fig. 15-8 Two atoms with five electrons within a structure made of atoms with four electrons leaving two electrons.

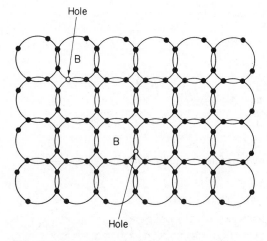

Fig. 15-9 Two atoms with three electrons within a structure made of atoms with four electrons leaving two holes.

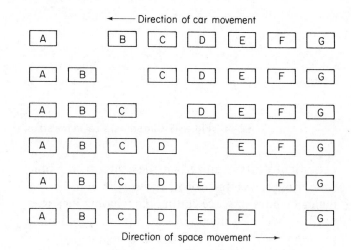

Fig. 15-10 Electrons and hole movement compared to vehicle movement in traffic.

in their outer shell. This makes them good insulators (Figure 15-7).

If silicon, for example, is slightly contaminated or "doped" at a rate of 1:10,000,000 with impurity material that has five electrons in the outer shell, such as phosphorus, arsenic, or antimony in its crystalline form, there would not be enough space in the outer shell for nine electrons. This would leave a free electron. This type of doped material would be called a negative or *N-type* material because it already has excess electrons and would *repel* a negative charge or an electron (Figure 15-8).

If, on the other hand, the silicon were contaminated or doped with impurities, such as small particles of boron or indium crystals which have only three electrons on their outer shell, a gap without an electron would remain in the outer shell. The gap, called a *hole*, would attract an elec-

tron or negative charge. Doped material with holes is called positive or *P-type* material because it would *attract* a negative charge or electrons (Figure 15-9).

Movement of electrons and holes can be compared to heavy slow-moving traffic illustrated in Figure 15-10. Assume that the cars are in a line of traffic and the first car moves up one space. As each succeeding car moves into the space ahead, the cars move forward and the space moves backward. Electrons can be compared to the car and holes can be compared to the space. Electrons and holes move in opposite directions. A hole is the absence of an electron needed to complete an atom's outer shell.

The *P*-type and *N*-type materials are called *semiconductors*. In certain combinations of materials and of circuits, semiconductors will conduct current. In other applications, they will act as insulators. In automotive applications, semiconductors are used in diodes and in transistors.

The diode semiconductor is made under very closely controlled conditions from a thin wafer of crystal silicon. Boron is painted on one side and phosphorus on the other side of the crystal to make a junction of P-type and N-type semiconductor materials (Figure 15–11). The doped wafer is put into a high temperature furnace until the doping materials are fused into the silicon. This is followed by plating the wafer for good electrical contact. It is then broken into chips 3/16 × 3/16 in. square and 0.007 in. thick, that can be encapsuled for easy assembly into electrical circuits, as shown in Figure 15–12.

Within the diode illustrated in Figure 15–13, the holes in the P-type material attract electrons toward the *junction,* that is, a thin region between the P-type and N-type materials in the crystal. As the electrons move toward the junction, they leave positive ions behind them that hold the electrons from crossing the junction into the P-type material. Some electrons do drift across the junction.

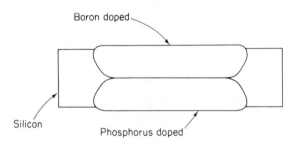

Fig. 15–11 Diode wafer.

Fig. 15–12 Encapsuled diode wafer.

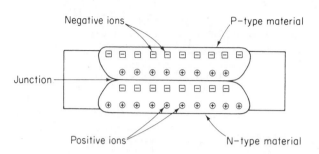

Fig. 15–13 Electron and hole movement in a diode.

However, this is an insignificant amount of electron flow and does not affect diode operation.

If the diode is connected into a circuit with the negative side of the circuit connected to the N-type material and the positive side of the circuit connected to the P-type material, a current will flow across the diode. This is called a *forward bias.* Electrons from the circuit put additional electrons on the N-type material. These electrons will satisfy the positive ions that had been holding electrons from crossing the junction. With this restraining force satisfied by new electrons, the electrons at the junction move across the junction and on through the circuit, resulting in a current flow.

If the polarity of the diode is reversed, forming a *reverse bias,* the electrons in the negative side of the circuit are attracted by the holes in the P-type material. The N-type material's electrons are attracted to the positive side of the circuit. This results in moving both the electrons of the N-type material and the holes of the P-type material away from the junction. The tendency to move in opposing directions allows an insignificant current flow across the junction. In effect, there is no reverse current flow through a diode.

The diode is used as a one-way electrical check. It will allow current to flow in one direction (forward bias) by acting as a conductor and will stop the current back flow (reverse bias) by acting as an insulator. This is illustrated in Figure 15–14.

Excessive reverse voltage will force a current to flow across the diode junction, rapidly heating the diode. If the reverse voltage forces a sufficiently large current across the junction, the diode will be damaged by overheating. Some special diodes are heavily doped so they will withstand relatively large reverse currents without damage. When made in this way, they are called *Zener diodes* and are used

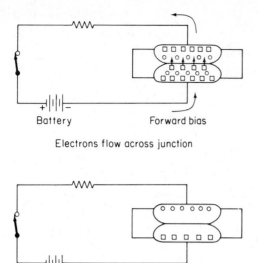

Battery   Forward bias

Electrons flow across junction

Battery   Reverse bias

No electrons flow across junction

Fig. 15-14 Electron and hole movement with a forward bias and a reverse bias.

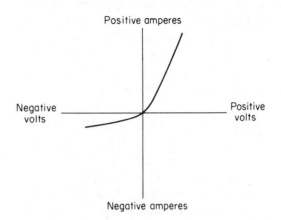

Fig. 15-15 Curve showing how a diode conducts current with voltage.

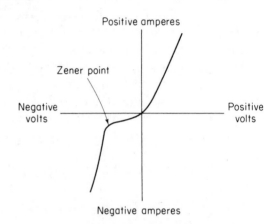

Fig. 15-16 Curve showing how a Zener diode conducts current with voltage.

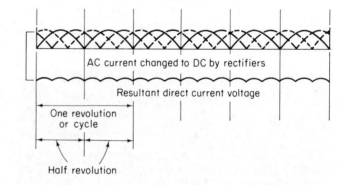

Fig. 15-17 Full wave rectification (The Prestolite Company).

in systems where voltage control is required. At less than the designed reverse bias voltage, they act as a normal diode. Above this designed voltage, they will conduct a reverse bias current. Current flow that results from voltage change is illustrated in Figures 15–15 and 15–16.

Diodes used in alternators are designated as positive or as negative diodes. Their exterior case looks similar; only the actual diode chip is reversed within the case. In the negative diode, the *P*-type material is connected to the case and the *N*-type material to the diode lead. In the positive diode, the *N*-type material is connected to the case and the *P*-type material is connected to the diode lead. Positive diodes have their part number printed in red and the negative diodes have their part number printed in black.

15-3 ALTERNATOR RECTIFICATION

If the current from each of the three-phase alternating voltages produced by the stator were fed through one-way electrical check valves or diodes, it would stop the reverse half of the current, while leaving the forward half to flow in the circuit. This is called *half-wave rectification.* In alternators, this would reduce the electrical output by half, so full-wave rectification is used. Full-wave rectification reverses the effective polarity of one-half of the sine wave, so that the whole wave is in one direction,

as shown in Figure 15–17. The electrical circuit only senses maximum voltage which is a direct current ripple. The alternating current in a generator armature is rectified by commutator bars, while the alternator current produced in the alternator stator is rectified by diodes.

In operation, the voltage in each coil builds in

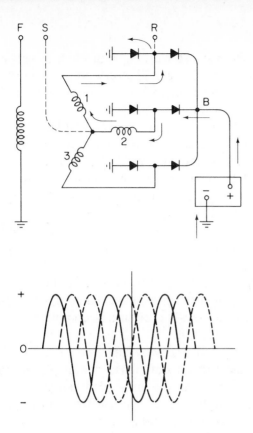

Fig. 15-18 Phase 1 to Phase 2 rectification.

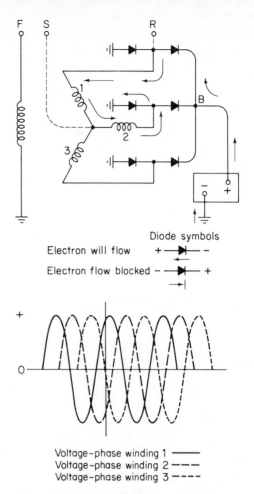

Diode symbols

Electron will flow $\quad +$ ▶️ $-$

Electron flow blocked $-$ ▶️ $+$

Voltage-phase winding 1 ———
Voltage-phase winding 2 – – –
Voltage-phase winding 3 - - -

Fig. 15-19 Phase 2 to Phase 1 rectification.

the positive direction, then collapses. This is immediately followed by building in the negative direction and again collapsing, operating in a continuous cycle. The phase windings are equally spaced and take turns building and collapsing. To help understand diode rectification in each of the following illustrations, the action will be stopped instantaneously when one of the phases is at zero as it is reversing its polarity.

Figure 15-18 shows the first rectifying stage as current flows from phase winding 1 to phase winding 2 (phase winding 3 is momentarily at zero). Electrons flow from phase winding 1, out the grounded diode and into the grounded side of the battery. This reserves the electron flow through the battery to cause the battery to charge. Electrons then flow to phase winding 2 through its positive diode, through the Y connections, and on to the phase winding 1 to complete the circuit.

The second rectifying stage is shown in Figure 15-19. With phase winding 3 neutral, the electrons flow from phase winding 2 through the grounded diode, then on the negative battery post. Electrons move from the positive battery post through the positive diode of the phase winding 1. The circuit is completed through the Y connection.

Phase winding 2 is momentarily at zero during the rectifying stage three in Figure 15-20. Electrons

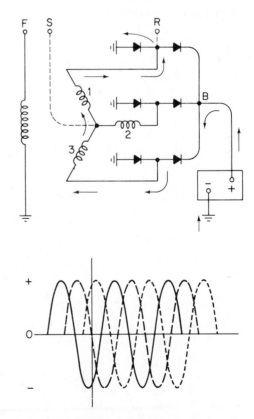

Fig. 15-20 Phase 1 to Phase 3 rectification.

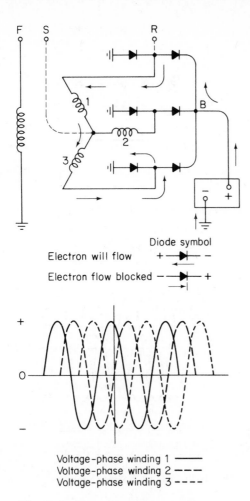

Fig. 15-21 Phase 3 to Phase 1 rectification.

Diode symbol

Electron will flow $\quad + \blacktriangleright\!\!-\ -$

Electron flow blocked $\quad - \blacktriangleright\!\!|\ +$

Voltage-phase winding 1 ———
Voltage-phase winding 2 – – –
Voltage-phase winding 3 – – – –

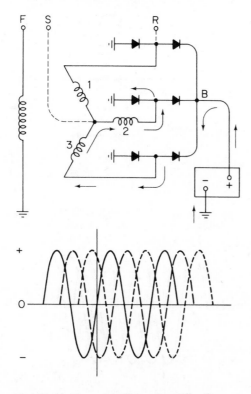

Fig. 15-22 Phase 2 to Phase 3 rectification.

flow from phase winding 1 through the grounded diode to the grounded battery post. The flow continues to the positive diode of phase winding 3 and the Y connection to complete the circuit.

During rectifying stage four, phase winding 2 is neutral. Electrons leave phase winding 3 through its negative diode to flow to the battery. The phase winding 1 positive diode carries the electrons from the positive battery post through the winding and Y connection.

Rectifying stage five is timed to show the electron flow while phase winding 1 is at zero as it is changing polarity. Electrons flow from phase winding 2 through the grounded diode and the battery, then on into phase winding 3 through its positive diode. The circuit is completed through the Y connection.

The sixth rectifying stage is the reverse of stage five. Electrons from phase winding 3 go to the battery through the grounded diode. From the positive battery post, the electrons flow through the positive diode and into phase winding 2. The

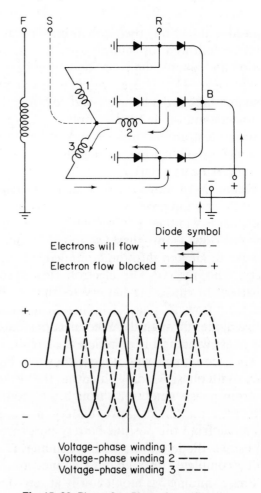

Diode symbol

Electrons will flow $\quad + \blacktriangleright\!\!-\ -$

Electron flow blocked $\quad - \blacktriangleright\!\!|\ +$

Voltage-phase winding 1 ———
Voltage-phase winding 2 – – –
Voltage-phase winding 3 – – – –

Fig. 15-23 Phase 3 to Phase 2 rectification.

Y connection completes the circuit to phase winding 3.

It should be noted that as the electron flow reverses within the phase windings, the outside circuit from the alternator ground and from the alternator battery (BAT) terminal is always in the same direction. The entire external voltage of an alternator is a pulsating voltage in one direction, just as the voltage from the generator is pulsating in one direction. This one-way voltage is the force that moves a direct current when the circuit is completed.

Each free end of the three stator windings is connected to the leads of one negative diode and one positive diode. The three negative diodes are pressed into the alternator case or into a diode plate where they can make a good electrical connection through the engine and ground wire to the battery. The three positive diodes are pressed or molded in a block of aluminum or heavy sheet metal called a *heat sink*. It is insulated from the alternator frame and is exposed to an air flow to keep the diodes cool. The insulated heat sink is connected to the insulated or positive side of the battery. Typical diode locations are shown in Figure 15-24.

Battery current will not flow through the diodes because they are connected in a manner in which the battery put a reverse bias voltage on each of the diodes. When the operating alternator voltage increases above battery voltage, a forward bias is placed on the diodes and they conduct current to charge the battery and to supply current to operate accessories.

15-4 TESTING CHARGING CIRCUITS

Many service technicians do not understand charging systems; when they have a charging system problem, they will most likely change parts until the system operates. This method is time consuming

and the parts are expensive for the customer. Modern test equipment allows charging system testing to be quick and simple. Test equipment used along with a thorough understanding of charging system operating principles will lead to quick, accurate diagnosis. Only the malfunctioning part will need to be repaired, thus saving time, parts cost, and come-back.

As in any electrical test work, the first thing to check is the battery. It should be tested to see that it is healthy and charged. If it is faulty, it should be replaced with a good battery before any further tests are run.

Alternator Tests. The battery test is followed by an alternator *output test*. In this test, as illustrated in Figure 15-25, a test ammeter is connected in the charging circuit, either at the alternator or at the battery. The alternator field wire is removed and a jumper wire connected between the field terminal and battery terminal on mechanically regulated internally grounded types or between the

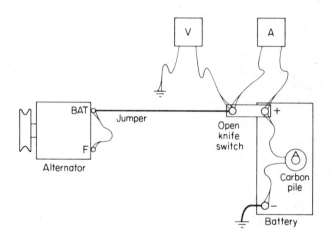

Fig. 15-25 Alternator output test connections on an internally grounded field alternator.

Fig. 15-24 Typical diode installations in alternators.

(a)   (b)

Fig. 15-26 Tab in an alternator with an internal regulator. The tab is used to by-pass the regulator for full field current by inserting a screwdriver and touching the tab while holding the screwdriver against the edge of the hole. (a) External view, (b) internal view.

field and ground on externally grounded types. A heavy carbon-pile rheostat is placed across the battery and adjusted as necessary to hold the system voltage at the voltage given in the applicable specification, approximately 14 to 15 V. The engine is started, and adjusted to the required speed, about 1500 rpm. The carbon-pile rheostat is tightened to reduce charging voltage or loosened to raise voltage to specifications. Alternator output is read on the ammeter while the engine speed and voltage are operating at specification settings.

Alternators with regulators built inside the alternator case have their fields connected like an externally grounded system. The technician can by-pass the regulator by inserting a screwdriver through a hole in the alternator case, as shown in Figure 15-26, so that the screwdriver blade touches a tab on the internal regulator at the same time that it touches the edge of the hole. This completes the field circuit to ground to give maximum field current.

Some service manuals do not recommend the use of an ammeter to check alternator output; they recommend instead that the charging system be checked while it is fully connected in its normal manner. If the ammeter connection should separate during an output test it would send a high voltage surge through the electrical system that could damage solid-state control units used in other systems. When an ammeter is not used, alternator

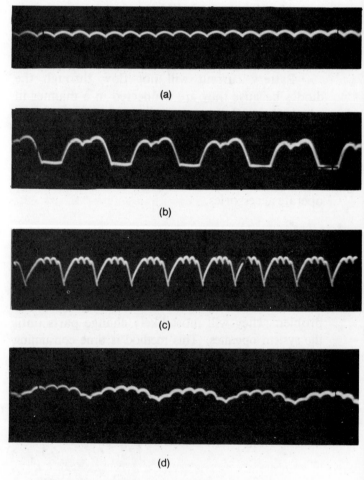

(a)

(b)

(c)

(d)

Fig. 15-27 Alternator scope patterns. (a) Normal, (b) shorted diode or shorted stator, (c) open diode, (d) partly shorted diode or stator.

output is checked by measuring the system voltage while all electrical accessories are turned on and the engine is run at a specified speed. Applicable service manuals should be consulted for details of the recommended output test procedures.

If the alternator output is low, further alternator tests are required. One of the best test instruments for alternator problem analysis is the oscilloscope. Many engine scopes have connections and circuits so that they can be used for alternator testing. The pattern displayed on the scope, similar to Figure 15-27, will show a normal pattern, open diode, shorted diode, open stator, or shorted stator. If several of these malfunctions occur at the same time, they will produce an unusual abnormal pattern. Serious malfunctions will show up

on meters. Another means to trouble shoot the alternator is to disassemble it and check each part for a malfunction so that it can be repaired. Figure 15-28 pictures disassembled alternators.

Failure of electrical components may be classified under three causes: *shorts, grounds,* and *opens,* as illustrated in Figure 15-29. Any one of these will result in a malfunctioning electrical unit.

Shorts occur when two adjacent conductors make an electrical contact. The electrical current can go from one conductor to the next, bypassing

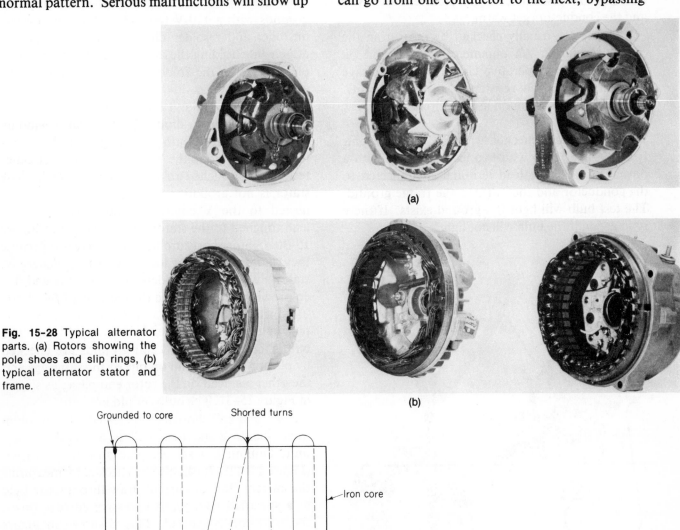

Fig. 15-28 Typical alternator parts. (a) Rotors showing the pole shoes and slip rings, (b) typical alternator stator and frame.

(a)

(b)

Fig. 15-29 Shorts, opens, and grounds on an electrical coil (The Prestolite Company).

a portion of the circuit. This part of the circuit gets no current. The short reduces circuit resistance so the conductors can carry more current and, therefore, become warmer.

Grounds are a special form of a short in which the insulated conductor makes electrical contact with the frame metal. In automotive applications, the frame is connected to the negative battery post so current follows the conductor to the ground point, completing the circuit in the shortest possible way, bypassing the rest of the circuit. This failure also has low resistance so more current will flow and the conductors get warm.

Shorts are usually checked by measuring the circuit resistance. An ohmmeter can be used on high-resistance inoperative circuits and a voltage drop method on low-resistance operating circuits. No method is in common use for circuits with very low resistance.

Grounds are checked with a continuity light. It uses a light bulb with two leads in series with a power source. One lead terminal is connected to the conductor and the other to the frame ground. The test bulb will light if a ground exists. If there is no ground, the bulb will not light.

Fig. 15-30 Testing a stator for grounding (The Prestolite Company).

Opens may also be checked with a continuity light. The test lead terminals are placed at each end of the conductor suspected to be faulty. An open exists if the bulb does not light. There is a complete circuit if the bulb lights. Another means of checking an open is to use a voltmeter. One voltmeter lead is attached to the ground and the other lead is touched to junctions along the conductor circuit while the battery is connected into the circuit. An open exists when the voltmeter no longer indicates battery voltage as the leads are moved from junction to junction.

The same methods used to find shorts, grounds, and opens can be used to check individual alternator components. Stators are disconnected from the diodes for checking both continuity and grounds with a 110-V test light. When necessary, unsolder and resolder diode connections. This is done while holding the diode lead with a long nose pliers between the soldered joint and diode. The pliers act as a heat sink to draw the soldering heat into the pliers so that it does not go into the diode. Heat can damage a diode. To test stator winding continuity, the test bulb should light when one test lead is connected to the Y connection and the other test lead is touched to the stator free ends. The stator is not grounded when one test lead is connected to the Y connection and the other test lead touched to the stator core as shown in Figure 15-30. Stator shorts are not easily detected because they normally have low resistance. Generally, stator shorts will be evident by an overheated discolored insulation around the location of the short.

Field coil continuity in the rotor is checked by placing one 110-V test lead on each slip ring. The bulb should light. Field coil grounds are checked by placing one test lead on one of the slip rings and the other test lead on the rotor end piece, as shown in Figure 15-31. The bulb should not light.

A field coil short may be tested with an ohmmeter because the field coil is a high-resistance unit. Ohmmeter leads are placed on the slip rings (Figure 15-32). It can also be checked by measuring the current flow or current draw through the field at a specified voltage. If excessive current flows, the field coil is shorted. This is shown in Figure 15-33.

Any stators or field coils that are shorted, grounded, or open will have to be replaced. They are normally repaired only in specialized rebuilding facilities.

A disconnected diode can be checked with a

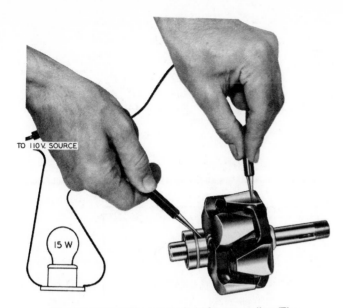

Fig. 15-31 Testing a rotor field for grounding (The Prestolite Company).

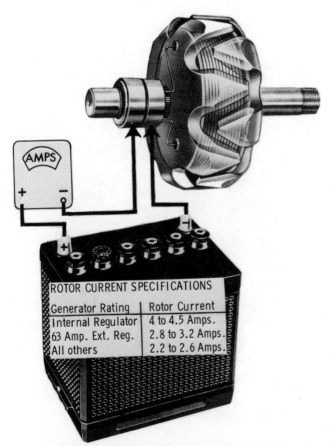

Fig. 15-33 Testing the rotor field for current draw (Oldsmobile Division, General Motors Corporation).

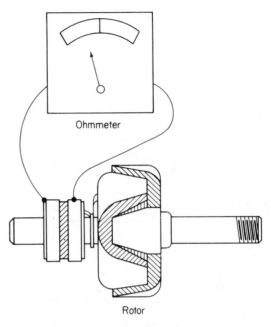

Fig. 15-32 Testing a rotor field for continuity (The Prestolite Company).

12-V DC test light. The test bulb should light when one test lead is connected to the diode case and the other test lead is connected to the diode lead wire. The bulb should not light when the test leads are reversed. The diode is faulty if the bulb remains on or off with each connection. Diode tests are illustrated in Figure 15–34. Faulty diodes are not repairable and must be replaced.

Some diodes can be replaced individually using the correct removing and installing tools. In other alternators, a positive or negative diode plate containing three diodes is replaced if any one of the diodes is faulty. Still other alternators are designed so the entire diode rectifier bridge is replaced when one diode is faulty. Detailed replacement procedures may be found in the applicable vehicle service manual.

Occasionally, the brush holders become grounded. These are checked with a 110-V test light from the brush to the alternator frame. Most brush holders are provided with a cross hole. A pin is inserted in the hole to hold the brush after the brush is compressed against its spring, so the

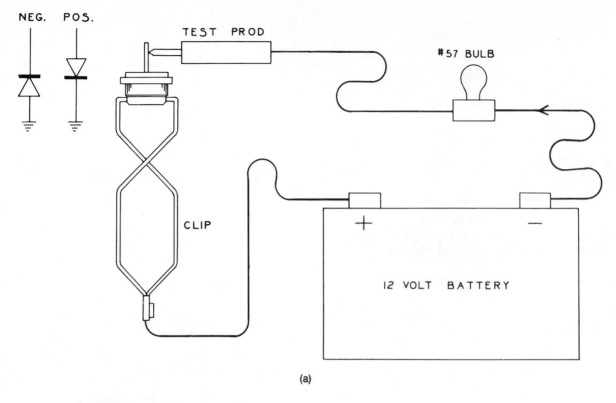

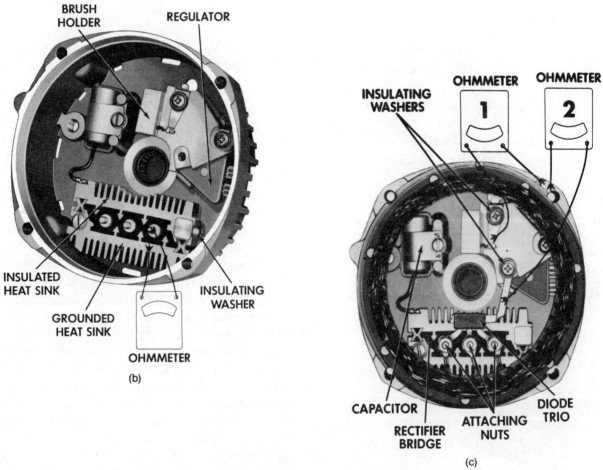

Fig. 15-34 Testing a diode. (a) Out of the alternator (The Prestolite Company), (b) and (c) in the alternator frame (Oldsmobile Division, General Motors Corporation).

Fig. 15-35 Holding the brushes with a wire for easy alternator assembly.

alternator may be easily assembled (Figure 15–35). After assembly, the pin is removed to allow the brushes to contact the slip rings.

Voltage Drop Tests. All conductors must be free of abnormal resistances if the charging system is to function correctly. Voltage drops throughout the charging circuit are checked while the alternator is producing 20 A in the circuit, using the same test connections as used to check alternator output as illustrated in Figure 15–36. The insulated charging circuit should have a voltage drop of less than 0.7 V on systems with an ammeter, or 0.3 V on systems with a charge indicator lamp. The grounded side of the circuit should have a voltage drop of less than 0.1 V.

When the alternator functions properly and no excess resistance is found in the charging circuit the jumper wire can be removed and the regulator connected so that the regulator operation can be checked.

Checking the Regulator Setting. The voltage regulator limits maximum voltage in the charging system. If the regulator setting is too low, the battery will not fully charge. A setting too high will shorten the service life of the ignition points, battery, electric motors, radio, lights, etc., by forcing excessive current through them. High voltage regulator settings may be first recognized as an unusual amount of headlight flare when the

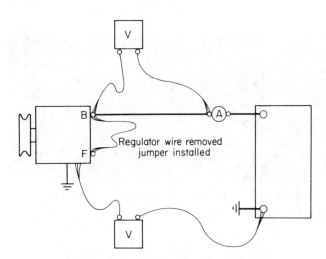

Fig. 15-36 Connections for testing an internally grounded field alternator for measuring the charging system voltage drop.

engine accelerates from idle. The battery will also use excessive water as a result of excessive gassing.

Charging system *voltage* increases when there is no place for the current to flow and decreases when there is a demand for electrical current. A regulator being tested must have the system placed under loads that will produce a system voltage that is in the regulator controlling range. Some manufacturers do this by using engine speed, lights, and a carbon-pile rheostat across a fully charged battery. Other manufacturers install a 1/4-ohm series resistor in the charging circuit to add sufficient circuit resistance to increase system voltage into the regulating range. The test set-up is shown in

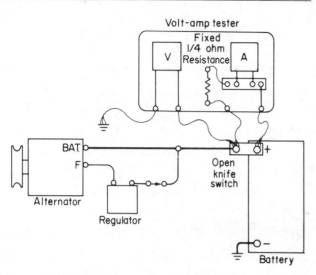

Fig. 15-37 Measuring charging system voltage regulator setting with a ¼-ohm resistance to restrict current flow in the charging system.

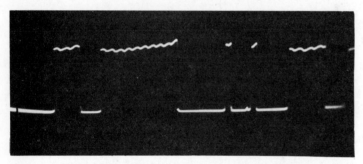

Fig. 15-38 Scope pattern of a mechanical regulator's field voltage while regulating.

Figure 15–37. Specific test settings and specification procedures are provided by each vehicle manufacturer. These should be followed to obtain correct voltage regulator settings. Usually, the specified range is between 14 and 15 V. Test procedures vary from manufacturer to manufacturer, from model to model, and from year to year. Generally, speaking, mechanical regulators have internal field grounds, while solid-state regulators have external field grounds. It is important to use the correct applicable procedure and test specifications for the vehicle and for the test equipment being used to obtain satisfactory regulator settings.

Mechanical voltage regulators have two sets of points, normally-closed and normally-open. The normally-closed points regulate at approximately 0.5 V lower than the normally-open points. At set engine speeds and charging current flow (see specific applicable procedures) the regulated voltage can be read with a voltmeter. It is helpful if an oscilloscope or engine scope is connected to the regulator field while making this check. A typical scope pattern is shown in Figure 15–38.

A scope shows that regulation is accomplished by controlling the length of time a voltage surge takes place in the field coil. As the voltage increases, the full voltage surges are shorter and shorter until the normally-closed points float. As alternator speed increases, the normally-open field-shorting points make contact, reducing the voltage surges to the field coil.

Mechanical regulator voltage settings are made by adjusting the spring hanger position (Figure 15–39) to increase spring pressure as higher voltage

Fig. 15-39 Typical mechanical voltage regulator adjustment methods.

Fig. 15-40 Mechanical voltage regulators. The regulator on the right also has a field relay on the same frame.

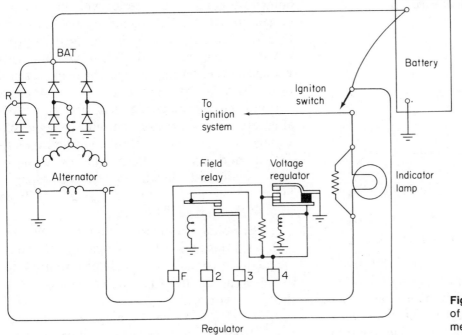

Fig. 15-41 Schematic diagram of a charging circuit using a mechanical regulator.

is needed. Solid-state regulators are adjusted by changing the setting of a variable resistor, if they are adjustable. If the regulator cannot be adjusted when required, it is replaced.

Field Relays. Field relays are often placed in the voltage regulator box (Figure 15–40). Their purpose is to supply current to the alternator field through the voltage regulator points when the relay points are closed. The field relay will close at approximately 8 V, fully energizing the alternator field.

Charging systems use ammeters and indicating lights to show if the battery is being charged or discharged. The indicator lights parallel a resistance. Field current is fed through the resistor and light until the field relay closes. When the relay

closes, battery voltage is impressed across the regulator end of the light. With battery voltage on both sides of the light, no current will flow and the light will go out. A typical schematic wiring diagram is given in Figure 15–41.

Many other variations are used in the charging circuit. Each should be checked with manufacturer's tests and procedures using the correct specifications.

15-5 CHARGING SYSTEM REGULATION

The battery regulates voltage in the charging system up to a maximum voltage that is limited by the voltage regulator. The maximum amount of current produced by the alternator is limited by the alternator design. Maximum current in a commutator-rectified generator is limited by a current regulator.

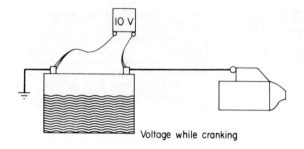

Voltage while cranking

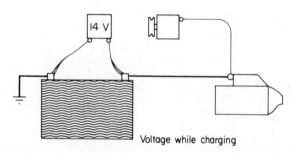

Voltage while charging

Fig. 15-42 Voltage while cranking and while charging.

Battery Regulation. The battery supplies electrical power to crank and start the engine. If the start is slow, quite a bit of electrical energy is withdrawn from the battery and this results in a slightly lower battery voltage. As soon as the engine starts, the charging system comes into operation to supply the vehicle electrical load and recharge the battery. The charging system voltage increases as the battery CEMF voltage increases. While the battery CEMF is low, the charging system supplies high current to the battery. As the battery becomes charged, battery CEMF increases, decreasing the charging amperage rate. This change is accompanied by an increase in the voltage of the entire charging system. When battery CEMF reaches the regulator voltage setting, the regulator begins to take control to limit the voltage level. This is illustrated in Figure 15–42.

Mechanical Voltage Regulator Operation. The voltage regulator consists of breaker points mounted on an armature above a voltage-sensitive coil with

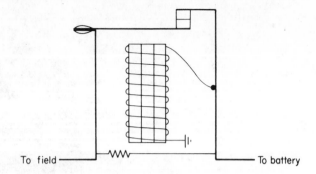

To field   To battery

Fig. 15-43 Circuit of a typical single point mechanical voltage regulator.

associated supporting mechanical and electrical components (Figure 15–43). The voltage regulator points are connected in series with the alternator or generator field. The points are *normally-closed* to allow full current flow in the field to provide maximum magnetic field. When charging system voltage reaches setting voltage, the regulator points open, breaking the field circuit. This stops field current and the magnetic field decays, reducing alternator or generator output voltage. When voltage drops, the points close, re-establishing field current and magnetic field. This cycle happens very rapidly, as shown on the oscilloscope in Figure 15–38, keeping the voltage essentially constant as shown on a voltmeter.

The voltage regulator points are held closed with an adjustable calibrated spring. An electromagnetic force pulls the regulator armature down to open the points when system voltage reaches the setting voltage.

The electromagnet of a voltage regulator is made from a great number of fine wire turns wrapped around a soft iron core. This wire has high resistance because it is long and has a small diameter. Its high resistance will only allow a very small current to flow when charging because it is connected across the charging system from the insulated side to ground. The amount of current flowing in the regulator coil is determined by charging system voltage. As the charging system voltage increases, the current flow through the coil increases which, in turn, increases the coil's magnetic field strength.

The magnetic strength of a coil is measured in *ampere turns*. The voltage regulator coil has a low amperage and a high number of turns. When amperage or current flow in the coil circuit is strong at a high charging system voltage, the magnetism of the coil pulls on the spring-held armature with the movable contact point attached. This separates the points to break field current flow, reducing the system voltage. The reduced voltage weakens the coil's magnetism so the armature spring closes the points. This cycle continues all the time the regulator is controlling system voltage.

A resistor is used across the regulator points to form a by-pass so that some field current will flow. This keeps the field from decaying completely when the points are open, but will weaken it to a voltage level close to nominal battery voltage. This results in a rapid field response that provides smooth voltage control. Other resistors may be used in the voltage regulator to reduce point burning and to aid in maintaining smooth voltage control.

In most charging systems, the resistor across the points allows somewhat more current to flow through the field while the points are open. With field current being fed through the resistor and the charging system running under light electrical loads at moderate speeds, the generator voltage matches the electrical load. When this happens, the points float and do not touch. Any increase in speed or any reduction in electrical load results in excess system voltage.

To prevent excessive voltage at higher speeds on alternators and on some high output generators, a second *normally-open* contact point is added to their voltage regulators (Figure 15–44). This second point is grounded. As system voltage increases, more current flows through the voltage regulator coil winding, pulling the armature further and causing the second set of voltage regulator points to contact the grounded point. All of the current flowing through the resistor is then directed to ground so no current flows through the field. This causes the alternator magnetic field to decay,

dropping system voltage which, in turn, reduces the voltage regulator coil magnetic field strength. When the system voltage lowers, the spring opens the normally-open grounding points, allowing current to again flow through the resistor to the field coil, building up the magnetic field in the alternator rotor and increasing system voltage. This action recycles, causing the points to vibrate on the normally-open grounded point.

Magnetism attracts the regulator armature through an air gap shown in Figure 15–45. The effectiveness of a magnet reduces as the square of the distance through which it must act. The magnetism would be only one-quarter effective at twice the air gap. The air gaps between the coil core and armature are critical for correct regulator operation and must be within specifications. Mechanical regulator voltage settings are adjusted by changing the armature return spring tension. Increasing spring tension increases the regulator coil strength required to move the armature. The coil magnetic strength increases as system voltage increases.

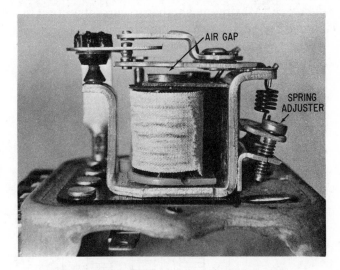

Fig. 15-45 Location of the air gap and spring adjuster for setting the operating voltage of a mechanical regulator.

Current Regulation. The current flowing in the alternator reverses itself, increasing and decreasing as it alternates in the same manner as the voltage. As the current flow increases in a stator, it forms a magnetic field around the winding. This newly formed field cuts across adjacent conductors

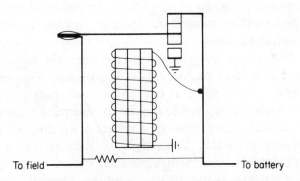

Fig. 15-44 Circuit of a typical dual point mechanical voltage regulator.

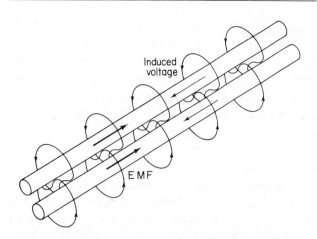

Fig. 15-46 Inductance by voltage induced from the magnetic field surrounding the adjacent current-carrying conductor in a coil.

within the stator coil winding (Figure 15-46). This produces a counter voltage in the adjacent conductors which opposes the initial voltage induced by the rotor field. This principle of inducing a counter voltage in a coil wire that is carrying an increasing or a decreasing current is called *inductance*. Maximum alternator current output is limited by the induced counter voltage. As counter voltage approaches the output voltage, amperage output stabilizes at a maximum safe value.

Current regulation of commutator rectified generators is similar to voltage regulation except that the current regulator coil design is different, as shown in Figure 15-47. Normally-closed single contact current regulator points are connected in

Fig. 15-47 Circuit of a typical generator regulator.

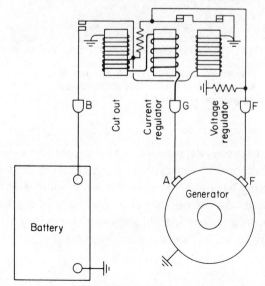

series with the voltage regulator points and field. Whenever the current regulator points open, field current is lowered to the amount of current that will flow through a resistor. The current regulator coil is made of a few turns of heavy wire that carry all of the current produced by the generator. When the generator is producing maximum regulated current, the current regulator coil has enough ampere-turns to open the current regulator points. This drops field current, reducing field strength which, in turn, lowers generator output. The current regulator coil strength decreases as generator output current drops and this allows the armature spring to close the points, re-establishing field current in the generator. The current regulator points vibrate to limit current output.

The voltage regulator and current regulator do not control the generator output at the same time. When there is a large amperage flow, electrical pressure cannot build up. When current flow is restricted, voltage will increase.

Voltage limitation is required to protect the battery and accessories. If too much voltage were to be impressed on them, it would force them to carry excess current. This, in turn, would result in overheating and short service life. Current limitation protects the alternator or generator. If they were allowed to produce more than their design current, they, too, would overheat and fail.

Reverse Current. Commutator rectified generators are provided with a *cut-out* that disconnects the battery from the charging system when the generator is not charging. The cut-out is located in the same box with the voltage and current regulators. When the engine starts, generator voltage builds up and current flows through the cut-out coil's series and shunt windings. When the ampere-turns of this circuit become strong enough, coil magnetism will pull the *normally-open* points into closed position, completing the battery-to-generator connection to put current in the electrical system.

Current flows backward between the battery and generator as the engine is stopped. This reverse current splits at the cut-out coil, part going through the shunt winding in its normal direction and part going through the series winding in a reverse direction. The magnetic fields of the two cut-out windings neutralize each other, releasing the cut-out armature so the points open to disconnect the battery from the generator.

Reverse current requires no switching in diode-rectified generators (alternators). It was shown in Section 15-3 how diodes prevent battery current from leaking through the alternator.

Solid-State Regulation. Mechanical regulators are being replaced by solid-state regulators. Typical solid-state regulators are shown in Figure 15-48. They are constructed with no moving parts, making use of semiconductors, resistors, capacitors, and conductors. In some regulators, these parts are assembled from individual parts. This fabrication technique is called *discrete.* Some of the units may be encapsuled into groups. These groups are assembled into an operating unit and the fabricating method is called *hybrid.* A more advanced fabrication method used to produce a single integrated circuit is called *monolithic.* Discrete and hybrid fabricating techniques are used in applications where the regulator is separate from the alternator. Monolithic techniques are used in applications that have the regulator built into the alternator case. The solid-state regulator parts work in the same manner regardless of the fabricating technique that is used.

The advantage of the solid-state regulator over the mechanical regulator is its ability to control higher field currents with improved durability and reliability. It is almost a foolproof regulator system; it has a smaller size; and, when manufactured at high production rates, it costs less than a mechanical regulator.

The solid-state regulator must control the alternator field current just as the mechanical regulator does. On-off switching is done with a solid-state semiconductor switch called a *transistor,* rather than with breaker points that are used on the mechanical regulators.

15-6 SEMICONDUCTORS—TRANSISTORS

The transistor is another of the many uses for semiconductor material. Diodes used in automotive applications are usually made of doped silicon crystals. Transistors are usually made from germanium crystals using indium to dope *P*-type material and antimony to dope *N*-type material. A diode is made of two materials, *P*-type junctioned to *N*-type. Transistors add another junction to the diode, forming either *PNP* or *NPN* transistors with two junctions. Most automobile applications use *PNP*-type transistors in discrete and hybrid construction. The *NPN*-type is used in monolithic regulators.

Transistor Construction. The manufacture of a transistor, for example, a *PNP*-type transistor, starts with a germanium crystal that has been doped with antimony. It is cut into thin slices to make a wafer of *N*-type material. Pure germanium crystals are applied to each side of the *N*-type wafer.

Fig. 15-48 Typical solid-state semi-conductor regulators.

Indium is then placed on each side of this wafer and it is heated to fuse the indium into the surface germanium crystals that are on each side of the *N*-type wafer. When this is complete, it forms a single crystal wafer consisting of three regions, *N*-type material in the center and *P*-type material on each side, forming a *PNP* transistor. The *P*-type materials are close together with a very thin layer of *N*-type material between them.

The outer edge of the *N*-type material of the thin wafer is attached to a metal ring with the wafer fitting in the hole of the ring, as illustrated in Figure 15–49. An extension from the ring is used to attach the electrical conductor. This center *N*-type material of the transistor is called the *base*. The transistor with its base connection is placed in

PNP transistor schematic

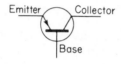

PNP power transistor construction

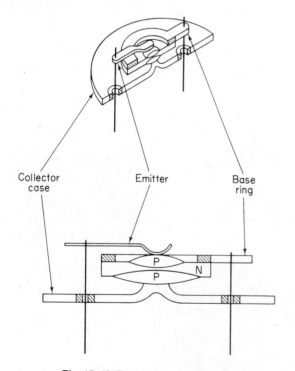

Fig. 15-49 Transistor construction.

a copper container with the larger *P*-type area against the container inner surface. The container serves as an electrical connection called the *collector* as well as a heat sink to keep the transistor cool. A strip of metal connected to the smaller *P*-type material area serves as an electrical connection called an *emitter*. This unit is brazed together and sealed into a case. The wire from the emitter is run through the insulator from the transistor case for an electrical connection. Some transistors also use a wire-type connector for the collector. The actual transistor is only the small wafer crystal. Connections and case make up the bulk of the transistor assembly.

Some transistors are *integrated* in a complete monolithic circuit. These circuits start with a silicon wafer. The wafer is coated with a ceramic insulation and an emulsion that masks some of the insulation material. Where it is not masked, the ceramic insulation is removed by etching to expose silicon. Doping material is fused into the silicon, the wafer again is ceramic coated, masked and etched in other places, and then another doping agent is used (Figure 15–50). In some places conductors are developed, other places resistors. This process gradually builds up a complete circuit with transistors, conductors, and resistors within the wafer. The wafer is scribed and broken into chips. Each chip is a complete circuit with all operating parts required for alternator regulation. These complete circuit chips are encapsuled with electrical leads for charging circuit connections.

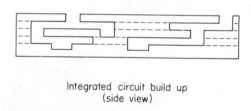

Integrated circuit build up
(side view)

Fig. 15-50 Typical integrated circuit buildup.

Transistor Operation. A *PNP*-type transistor will be used to describe transistor operation. The *N*-type material in the central region is the base. It is made as thin as possible. The *P*-type material in the outer regions forms the emitter and collector. The emitter is connected through the operating unit to the positive or insulated side of the battery. The collector is connected to the grounded or negative side of the battery. The transistor base circuit is used to control transistor operation.

Electricity is movement of electrons. It has been previously shown that as the electrons move in one direction, holes will move in the opposite direction, holes being the lack of electrons. It is easier to understand *PNP*-type transistor operation if a simplified explanation is given in terms of hole movement rather than electron movement.

Assume that the emitter is connected through the operating unit to the positive battery terminal. The collector is connected through ground to the negative battery post, with the base circuit switch open, as shown in Figure 15-51. Whenever possible, electrons fill holes to make neutral atoms. Excess holes supplied by the battery collect along the junction between the emitter and base. Holes in the collector are attracted toward the negative side of the battery. As the holes move toward the battery, free electrons are left behind and these hold the holes in position.

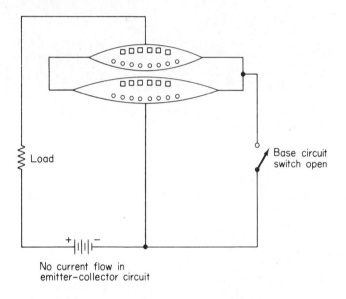

Fig. 15-51 Transistor circuit with open base circuit.

When the base circuit switch is closed, as illustrated in Figure 15-52 (having the same polarity as the collector), holes will move from the emitter to the base and back to the battery ground. As the holes from the emitter cross the base junction, their energy carries most of them across the second junction into the collector. This produces a current in the operating circuit. The base current is about 2.0% of the total emitter current. When the base circuit is reopened, hole movement stops, the transistor charges become neutralized, and hole movement to the collector stops, stopping the current flow from the emitter to the collector.

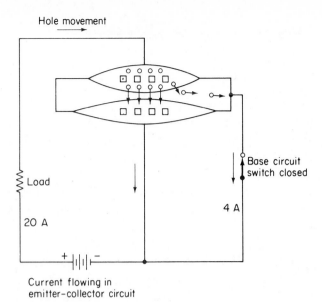

Fig. 15-52 Transistor circuit with a conducting base circuit.

Transistor Regulation. Transistor regulators are based on the same basic principle as mechanical regulators. They control alternator voltage by controlling the alternator field strength. Instead of breaker points, the transistor regulator uses a power transistor to do the required field circuit switching. The power transistor's operation is controlled by other transistors, diodes, and resistors. Regulators built in a discrete or hybrid form can be repaired in some cases, but monolithic regulators cannot be repaired. It is important to understand the operation of transistor regulation in order to understand proper transistor regulator testing.

A simplified transistor regulator circuit is shown in Figure 15-53. Using the hole movement explanation method, holes come from the battery to transistor T_1 emitter. The base is connected to

Fig. 15-53 Basic transistor regulator circuit.

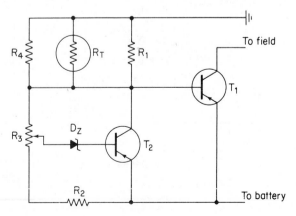

the ground through R_1 so it conducts. With the base conducting, current can go from the emitter to the collector and on to the alternator field to supply full alternator field current.

Battery voltage is also impressed on the emitter of transistor T_2. The base of T_2 is connected to the Zener diode D_z which is reverse biased so no base current will flow and transistor T_2 is turned off so it will not conduct. Voltage also is impressed on resistors R_2, variable resistor R_3, R_4, and thermal resistor R_t, allowing a very small current to flow to ground. A voltage drop exists across each resistor as current flows.

The Zener diode is the voltage sensing device in the solid-state regulator. It is used to control maximum circuit voltage. When the reverse bias voltage across the Zener diode reaches its breakdown point, it will conduct current in the reverse direction. The reverse bias voltage is equal to the voltage drop across R_2 and part of R_3. Changing the connection point of the Zener diode on variable resistance R_3 is used to adjust regulator settings, when solid-state regulators are adjustable.

When the Zener diode conducts, the base of transistor T_2 is turned on and T_2 conducts from the collector to ground through R_4. The collector of T_2 then places the same voltage on the T_1 base as the emitter of T_1. With the voltage the same on the emitter and on the base, transistor T_1 is effectively turned off, stopping field current to the alternator. The alternator voltage falls off when the field current stops, and the Zener diode stops conduction in reverse bias which, in turn, stops the base current of T_2, turning it off. This allows the base current of T_1 to restart conduction through R_1 and begin to supply field current to the alternator. This cycle is repeated at a very high rate, controlling the alternator voltage. Figure 15–54 shows a

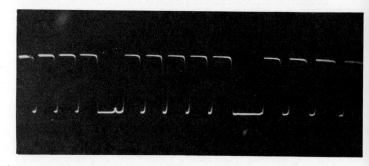

Fig. 15-54 Scope pattern of a transistor regulator's field voltage while regulating.

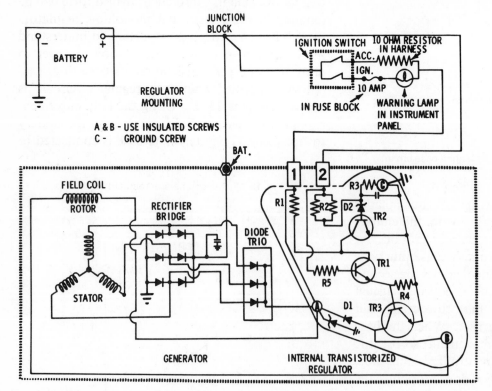

Fig. 15-55 Complete alternator-transistor regulator circuit (Oldsmobile Division, General Motors Corporation).

scope pattern of the rapid field voltage control with a solid-state regulator.

The resistor R_t is sensitive to temperature. At low temperatures, it has high resistance. This reduces current flow through the series resistances. A higher circuit voltage is required at low temperatures to force the Zener diode to conduct in a reverse bias. This causes the charging system to operate at higher voltages when cold and at lower voltages when warm to be compatible with battery operation characteristics.

The basic transistor operating circuit is smoothed out and speeded up using resistors and capacitors as shown in Figure 15–55. Transient voltages and leakage are controlled with additional diodes, resistors, and capacitors.

Summary. A few automobiles still in operation use generators. Many automobiles use mechanically regulated alternators. In the late 1960's some automobiles were supplied with solid-state regulators, but by 1975 nearly all automobiles were produced with solid-state regulators. Most of the General Motors and some Ford products use integrated regulators built inside the alternator.

Solid-state regulators are replaced when they no longer function properly. Their service is limited to testing for proper operation.

REVIEW QUESTIONS

1. What three ways can be used to increase the number of magnetic lines of force cutting a conductor per second? [15–1]

2. What method is used to control alternator output? [15–1]

3. Name the two major electrical components of an alternator. [15–1]

4. What is the function of the alternator brushes? [15–1]

5. What is meant by the term *rectification?* [15–1]

6. How are the coils spaced in the stator? [15–1]

7. What is a three-phase current? [15–1]

8. In what part of an operating alternator does AC current exist? [15–1]

9. Make a line drawing to show how the field of a two-pole magnet cuts a loop conductor. [15–1]

10. What atomic structure makes a good conductor? [15–2]

11. How do *N*-type and *P*-type materials differ? [15–2]

12. What is a diode junction? [15–2]

13. What is meant by forward and reverse bias? [15–2]

14. How does a Zener diode differ from other diodes? [15–2]

15. How does half-wave rectification differ from full-wave rectification? [15–3]

16. What is the purpose of a heat sink? [15–3]

17. What is the first thing to check when testing the charging circuit? [15–4]

18. What must be done to an alternator to force it to deliver its maximum output? [15–4]

19. What are three electrical failures that can occur in a coil? How can each be checked? [15–4]

20. Why is it important to use a pliers to hold the diode lead between the diode and the joint being soldered? [15–4]

21. What is the purpose of a voltage regulator in the charging system? [15–4]

22. When does the charging system voltage increase? [15–4]

23. How is the charging system resistance measured? [15–4]

24. How is the charging system voltage regulator setting measured? [15-4]

25. How does the battery CEMF affect the charging system voltage? [15-5]

26. When does the battery regulate voltage? When does the regulator control voltage? [15-5]

27. How are the voltage regulator points connected to the alternator? [15-5]

28. What happens to the alternator field current while the mechanical regulator's normally-closed points are closed? When both points are open? When the normally-open points are closed? [15-5]

29. How does the control of maximum current by an alternator differ from control by a commutator-rectified generator? [15-5]

30. Why is it necessary to control voltage and current? [15-5]

31. How does inductance affect the current flow in a coil? [15-5]

32. What keeps the battery from discharging through an alternator and through a generator when the engine is not running? [15-5]

33. What is the advantage of solid-state regulation? [15-6]

34. How does a transistor differ from a diode? [15-6]

35. What are the names given to the three major parts of a transistor? What is connected to each? [15-6]

36. Which two transistor circuits have the same polarity? [15-6]

37. What is the voltage sensing device in a solid-state regulator? [15-6]

38. What is the value of having a temperature-compensated voltage regulator? [15-6]

ignition system operation

The ignition system forces an electrical arc across the spark plug electrodes to ignite the combustion chamber charge. This arc must have enough energy to increase the temperature of the surrounding charge to the kindling point at which combustion becomes self-sustaining. The voltage necessary to overcome the resistance of the spark plug gap and cause the spark to reach the charge kindling temperature is called *required voltage.*

It makes no difference what type of ignition system is used. It may be a conventional design, it may use high-energy transistor switching, or it may use a capacitive discharge system. The spark must be delivered to the spark plug with enough energy to ignite the charge.

It is not only important for the charge to ignite, but it must ignite at the correct instant so that the charge will produce maximum useful energy

as the hot gases expand within the combustion chamber. The spark arc is timed so that maximum combustion chamber pressure occurs when the crank pin is 5 to 10° after top center. The ignition firing or timing point needs to be adjusted for changes in the quality of the charge that affect burning rates so that maximum pressure will always occur at 5 to 10° after top center under all operating conditions requiring power.

16-1 IGNITION TIMING AND ENGINE SPEED

In a typical engine, the first 10% of the combustion charge burns at a constant rate, that is, it takes a specific length of time to burn, no matter what the engine speed happens to be. To compensate for this, a *centrifugal mechanical timing advance mechanism* is used to advance the ignition firing point as engine speed increases. This is shown as a graph in Figure 16-1.

From 10% on, combustion rate increase is proportional to engine speed, primarily because of increased turbulence created by a high velocity intake charge, combustion chamber squash area, and flame turbulence. At some high rpm, depending on the engine design, the first 10% becomes insignificant so that no further advance is required. Without this characteristic, engines could not run at high speeds.

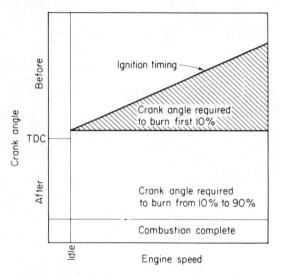

Fig. 16-1 Combustion burning rate in terms of engine speed and degrees of crankshaft rotation.

16-2 IGNITION TIMING AND ENGINE LOAD

The mass of the charge that is taken into the combustion chamber as the result of throttle position and engine load also affects timing requirements. Under light throttle conditions, high manifold vacuum occurs and a small quantity of charge is drawn into the combustion chamber from the manifold. Pressure resulting from compression of this thin charge is low and its burning rate is slow. This low-pressure type of charge requires high advance to be able to complete combustion at 5 to 10° after top center. At these low compression pressures, the spark plug will arc at a low *required voltage.*

At low speed and full throttle, a large charge enters the combustion chamber because the open throttle provides minimum intake restriction. When compressed, this charge is dense and has high pressure. More gas molecules are present between the electrodes. Once kindled, combustion occurs quite rapidly so timing is retarded to have combustion complete at 5 to 10° after top center.

This could be compared to going to a drag race. If the race began at six o'clock, one would plan to start early enough to arrive on time. His starting time would depend on the road type, the traffic anticipated, and the weather. The ignition system anticipates the expected length of time to complete combustion, then it must start early enough in the cycle so that combustion is completed at the correct time. The advance can be mechanical or electronic.

A *mechanical vacuum timing advance mechanism* is used to change ignition timing to compensate for throttle position and engine load. Timing is advanced under high vacuum, light-load operation when the burning rate is slow. It is retarded under low vacuum, heavy-load operation when fast burning rates occur. The vacuum advance fully retards at full throttle because it is not required for maximum engine power. Its primary function is to provide fuel economy during part throttle operation by igniting the charge at an advance which will give maximum mean effective pressure at the operating conditions. Many of the controls on the engine modify the vacuum advance operation.

16-3 REQUIRED VOLTAGE

Required voltage is the actual voltage produced in the secondary ignition circuit to overcome ignition resistance and fire the spark plug. If required voltage exceeds the maximum voltage available, misfiring will occur. Voltage required to arc across the spark plug is based upon a number of operating variables and physical conditions existing in the ignition system.

Operating variables that affect required voltage are based on the compression pressure and the air/fuel mixture ratio of the charge in the cylinder. Compression pressure changes as the throttle is opened and closed, being highest when the throttle is wide open at low engine speeds and lowest when the throttle is closed during deceleration. When engine speeds increase, compression pressure lowers as a result of lower volumetric efficiency. Figure 16–2 shows that required voltage is low when the compression pressure is low and high when the compression pressure is high.

The air/fuel ratio effect on required voltage is lowest when the ratio is adjusted to produce best power, approximately 12:1. Any change from this air/fuel ratio, either rich or lean, will increase required voltage, as illustrated in Figure 16–2. Emission-controlled engines operate with lean mixtures. To ignite, the charge must be between the spark plug electrodes, and the spark arc must have enough thermal energy to start a self-propagating flame in the mixture. (Figure 16–3).

The spark plug gap is the "voltage regulator" that controls required voltage. It is located in the combustion chamber so its gap senses compression pressure and charge air/fuel mixture. Required voltage is sensitive to the gap spacing between the spark plug electrodes. A larger gap requires increased voltage. Too small a gap reduces the required voltage but also reduces the opportunity for a combustible mixture to get into the electrode gap. Small gaps also reduce the air/fuel mixture igniting range. The largest spark plug gap is re-

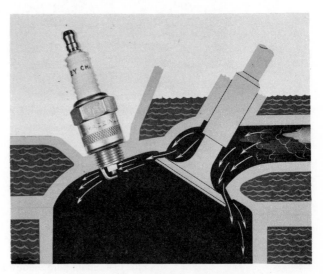

Fig. 16-3 Induced charge gases reaching the spark plug electrodes (Champion Spark Plug Company).

quired at idle speeds when the least amount of turbulence exists in the combustion chamber.

At idle speeds, the charge turbulence is low and, therefore, the chance of having the correct mixture move into the spark plug electrode gap is also low. The minimum spark plug gap that will produce satisfactory engine idle is 0.025 in. (0.625 mm). Most ignition systems use gap specification over 0.030 in. (0.75 mm). As engine speed increases, combustion chamber turbulence will also increase and this reduces the gap requirement. In engines operating above half-load, a gap of 0.005 in. (0.127 mm) would actually provide satisfactory operation. Combustion chamber turbulence must not, however, be so great as to blow the initial flame from between the spark plug electrodes until it becomes hot enough to maintain combustion.

The shape of spark plug electrodes (Figure 16–4, as well as the gap, affects required voltage. New spark plug electrodes have the lowest required voltage. The electrode becomes eroded after a number of arcs, rounding off the original sharp edges. This erosion increases the voltage requirement.

Any increase in secondary circuit resistance increases the voltage requirement. Secondary wiring with loose connections increases resistance. Wide rotor gap to cap electrodes will increase resistance. Damaged secondary wires increase resistance. The difference between the voltage available from the ignition system and the required

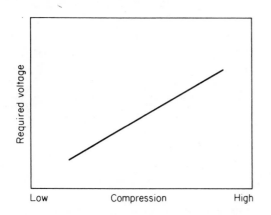

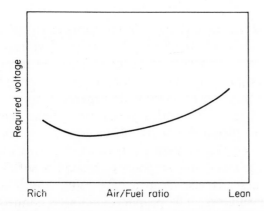

Fig. 16-2 Required voltage modified by compression and air/fuel ratio.

Fig. 16-4 Spark plug electrode shape (AC Spark Plug Division, General Motors Corporation) (a) Normal, (b) badly worn.

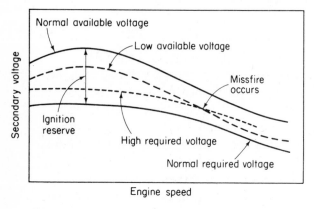

Fig. 16-5 Available and required voltage compared to engine speed.

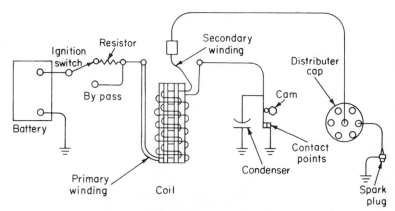

Fig. 16-6 Typical ignition system circuit.

voltage is called *ignition reserve*. Misfiring occurs when no ignition reserve remains. This can be seen in Figure 16-5.

16-4 IGNITION SYSTEM OPERATION

The ignition system, illustrated in Figure 16-6, uses the battery as a primary source of electrical energy until the engine is started. After the engine is running, the charging system provides the primary electrical energy. Electrical power is carried through wires, switches, and resistors to an ignition coil. The coil transforms low primary voltage to high secondary voltage which is delivered through a distributor to the spark plug in the cylinder, where it ignites the combustion charge.

The *ignition coil* is the *source* of the energy used to produce a spark or an electric arc across the spark plug electrodes. It consists of two windings, primary and secondary, around a soft iron core and placed within a case using connections and insulators. The primary winding is connected in series with the battery breaker points, resistor, and ignition switch. The secondary is connected in series with the distributor rotor, distributor cap, and spark plug.

In operation, battery voltage pushes current through the coil primary. This current flow builds up a magnetic field around the primary winding and in the soft iron core (Figure 16-7). When the breaker points open, the circuit's current flow stops, causing the magnetic field to collapse. During collapse, the magnetic lines of force rapidly cut through the secondary windings as they collapse (Figure 16-8). This rapid relative motion between the magnetic lines of force and conductor induces a high voltage in the secondary with sufficient energy to force an arc to flash across the spark plug electrodes. This entire sequence of events must occur each time a spark plug fires. In an eight-cylinder engine running at 4000 rpm, there are 266 spark plug firings each second. It is impossible to follow this action with a meter because the meter cannot move fast enough, so a cathode ray oscilloscope is used to show this constantly changing voltage.

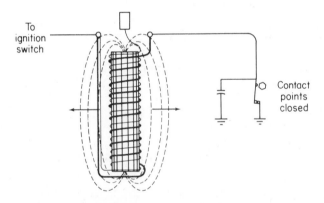

Fig. 16-7 Magnetism built up in the coil while the breaker contact points are closed.

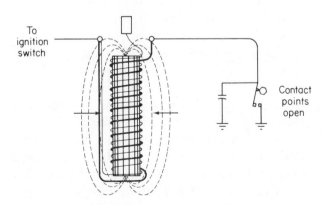

Fig. 16-8 Voltage built up in the secondary windings when the points open and the magnetic field collapses.

16-5 OSCILLOSCOPE MEASURING INSTRUMENT

A cathode ray oscilloscope display appears on the face of an electron tube that is similar to a television picture tube. The oscilloscope, illustrated in Figure 16-9, is powered by electrical and electronic circuits sensitive to voltage and time. The gun in the base of the picture tube emits a stream of electrons, called a *beam,* that is directed toward the face of the tube between electrically charged plates.

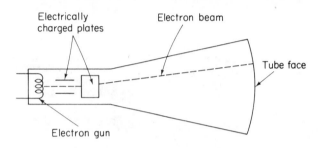

Fig. 16-9 Simplified cross section of an oscilloscope display tube.

The electric charge on these plates deflects or sweeps the beam up and down or sideways. The sideways or horizontal sweep of an oscilloscope is based on time. Sweep speeds are based on centimeters per decimal part of a second, such as: 0.1, 0.01, 0.001, etc., of a second.

The electron beam is focused to hit the tube screen. The screen has a coating so that it momentarily holds the light, allowing slow decay. As the beam sweeps, it leaves a light beam line on the scope face. The start of the beam movement must be initiated or triggered. When an electrical signal triggers the start of the horizontal beam sweep (X-axis), it will sweep the entire screen, then stop until it is triggered again. Each trigger impulse restarts the beam on the left side of the scope pattern, even if the beam has not completed its sweep across the screen.

Scope controls are provided to adjust voltage sensing (Y-axis) and sweep rate (X-axis) as well as vertical and horizontal positioning of the sweep pattern. Using these controls, the operator can measure or look at the characteristics of any portion of the oscilloscope pattern displayed.

The ignition system has its own characteristic

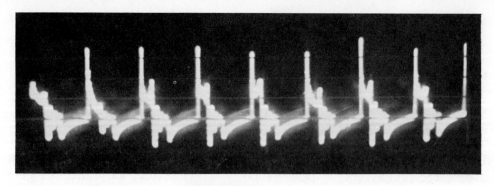

Fig. 16-10 Typical ignition scope pattern with some malfunctions.

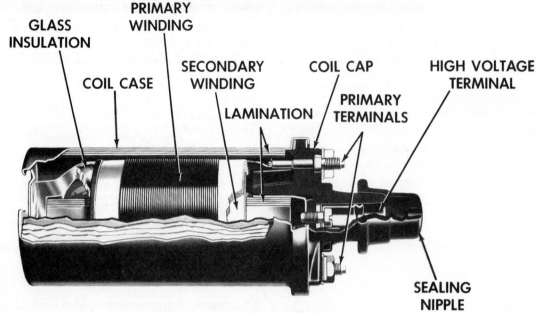

GLASS
INSULATION

PRIMARY
WINDING

COIL CASE

SECONDARY
WINDING

COIL CAP

HIGH VOLTAGE
TERMINAL

LAMINATION

PRIMARY
TERMINALS

SEALING
NIPPLE

Fig. 16-11 Ignition coil nomenclature (Delco-Remy Division, General Motors Corporation).

oscilloscope pattern as shown in Figure 16-10. It will be used to describe the details of the ignition system operation. When the details of this pattern are known, they can be applied to ignition scopes as an aid to engine analysis and diagnosis.

16-6 COIL OPERATION

The typical standard automotive ignition coil, shown as a cutaway in Figure 16-11, has from 100 to 180 primary windings using #20 copper wire. The primary winding carries a high current so it becomes warm. It is, therefore, wrapped on the outside of the secondary winding to aid in its cooling. The secondary coil has 18,000 winding turns of #38 wire. Both wires are coated with insulating varnish and the winding layers are separated with oiled paper. A laminated soft iron core is placed in the center of the coils and a laminated soft

iron shield is wrapped around the outside. The laminations of the core and shield limit magnetic eddy currents that would reduce coil efficiency. This assembly is placed in a can with a ceramic insulator, filled with insulating transformer oil, then sealed. Coils are not repairable. If tests show them to be faulty, they must be replaced.

Battery voltage forces a current to flow through the primary coil when the breaker points are closed. The amount of current that flows through the primary circuit is limited by the resistance of the long copper primary wire and by other resistances in the circuit. As current flow increases, the magnetic field around the primary coil wire expands across adjacent wires, which induces a counter voltage that opposes the input current flow. The counter voltage slows full current build-up causing it to occur over a period of time. This is shown in Figure 16-12. This characteristic is called *inductance,* as previously described in Section 15-5.

The primary magnetic field build-up induces a voltage in the secondary, but it is not strong enough to form an arc across the spark plug electrodes.

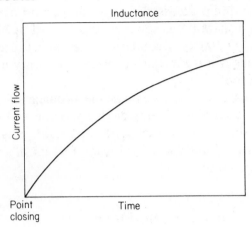

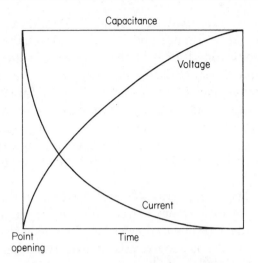

Fig. 16-13 Current and voltage in relation to time as the system capacitance becomes charged.

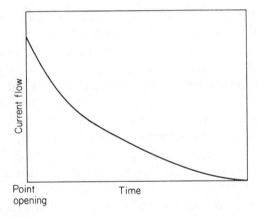

Fig. 16-12 Primary current flow in relation to time as the points close and open to induce a secondary voltage.

Capacitance is another electrical property that affects the ignition system. When two conductors are close together but insulated from each other, the negative charges in one conductor will attract the positive charges in the adjacent conductor somewhat like electron attraction in diodes. These charges will remain as long as the conductors remain insulated from each other. In this way, they are able to store electrical energy. The capacity of the secondary ignition circuit is based on the design of the secondary coil and on the length and routing of the secondary wiring. (Figure 16-13).

As current flows through the primary coil, its magnetic field builds up until full current flows, at which time the coil has reached magnetic saturation. This stores electrical energy in the coil by induction.

When the breaker points open, primary current flow stops with the aid of the primary condenser.

As the primary current stops, the magnetic field quickly collapses, cutting the coil windings.

Rapid collapse of the coil magnetic field produces voltage in the primary and secondary windings, charging their capacitances. The capacitive portion of the electrical energy builds up in the secondary coil until it has sufficient voltage to ionize gases between the spark plug electrodes. This voltage produces the familiar spike on ignition scope patterns. This can be seen in Figure 16-14. The time that it takes to reach required voltage

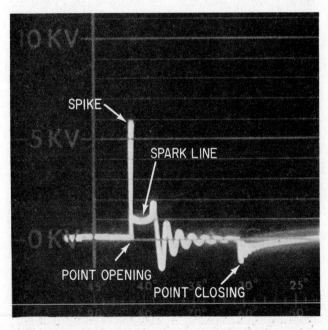

Fig. 16-14 Typical single-cylinder scope pattern.

is called *rise time.* Ionization breaks down spark plug gap resistance and the required voltage falls to about one-fourth of the spike-peak voltage as the arc is established. Duration of the arc is fed by inductance as the magnetic lines of force continue to collapse through the secondary windings. This portion of the ignition scope pattern is called the *spark line.* Ignition takes place during capacitive discharge and during the first part of inductive discharge.

The total energy that can be stored in the coil is based on primary current and on the length of time the current can flow before the breaker points reopen. Primary current is limited by the current carrying ability of the breaker points. Normally, the primary current is limited to a 4.2 A flow, which allows the breaker points to last thousands of miles. If primary current flow were increased to 5.4 A, the breaker points would burn in a very few miles. The ability to operate with high primary currents is one of the main advantages of transistor and electronic ignition systems. A power transistor can carry twice as much current as breaker points without being damaged. The length of time the primary current can flow to build up the magnetic field is limited by the number of degrees the crankshaft turns while the breaker points are closed and by the engine's speed. The longer the current can flow through the coil the more energy will be stored in the coil until the coil is saturated. At low engine speeds, more energy can be stored in the coil than at high engine speeds, as a result of greater coil saturation by the primary current. The primary circuit is responsible for producing *available voltage* in the secondary circuit.

The total stored coil energy is dissipated as voltage and current in the arc that forms across the spark plug electrodes. This energy can be released in a very short period of time with high voltage and high current flow or it can be released slowly at a low voltage and low current flow. Energy release from the coil could be compared to electrical energy release through light bulbs. A given amount of electrical energy from a battery could be released through an instantaneous brilliant flash of a flash bulb or through a sustained dim light of a flashlight. For ignition systems, a fast energy release across the spark plug electrodes

provides the best ignition of the charge. It is called a *fast rise time* because the capacitive portion of the energy releases rapidly, producing the ignition scope pattern spike. Fast rise time will force the arc to jump across the electrode gap on a partly fouled spark plug; however, this type of operation is demanding on secondary insulation because high voltage will try to flash over the secondary insulation, too.

Fast rise time reduces the problem of slight electrical drains. Energy discharge occurs so rapidly that slight drains, such as fouled spark plugs, do not allow time for a significant amount of energy to leak away.

16-7 PRIMARY CONDENSER

A condenser is installed electrically across the breaker points in the ignition system. It is made from two long strips of electrical conductor foil *plates* separated by insulating paper. The number of electrons that can accumulate on one side of a plate is limited by the plate's size and the distance between plates. The larger and closer together the plates are, the more electrons they can store. This electron storage ability is called *capacity.* The measurement of condenser capacity is a farad. It is a very large unit, so the smaller unit, *microfarad* (mfd = 10^{-6} farad) is used to describe the capacity of automotive ignition system condensers.

The condenser foil strip plates and insulation are rolled together, then placed in a container and sealed. A lead wire contacts one foil strip and the container case contacts the other. A disassembled condenser is shown in Figure 16–15. The strips of foil are close together so there is electrical attraction between electrons and electrical holes across the insulation paper. The insulation paper keeps the circuit open so the electrons cannot cross to the other plate.

When the breaker points are closed, the primary circuit is complete and a current flows through the primary coil windings. When the breaker points open, the primary current is interrupted causing the coil magnetic field to start to collapse. This collapse produces an induced voltage in the primary winding that tends to keep the primary current flowing. This induced voltage may reach 250 V which is high enough to force electrons across the breaker point gap as they are beginning to open. An arc across the breaker point gap would absorb

PAPER
CAN
LEAD WIRE

Fig. 16-15 Condenser construction.

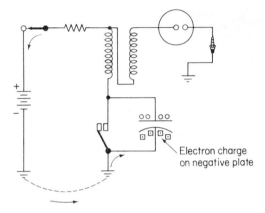

Electron charge on negative plate

Fig. 16-16 Positive and negative charges on the condenser plates when the breaker points open.

electrical energy. The condenser provides a place for the electrons in the primary current to go during initial breaker point opening. The attraction of the positive condenser plate is so great that the electrons move freely into the negative plate, producing a high voltage charge on the negative plate, as illustrated in Figure 16–16. As the electrons pack into the condenser, they bring the primary current to a quick controlled stop which, in turn, causes a rapid collapse of the primary field. During this time, the breaker points have opened far enough so the voltage will not cause flashover across the breaker point gap.

The high electron charge on the negative plate attempts to fill the holes in the positive plate. With the breaker points open, the only way for the electrons to get to the positive plate is back through the battery and primary circuit. As they flow, they cause a reverse current flow through the coil primary that forces a complete magnetic field collapse from its original direction and produces a build-up in the opposite direction. Electrons flow in this direction until they pack into the other side of the condenser plate, leaving holes behind them. This high charge in the reverse direction causes a second reversal and a current again flows forward through the primary circuit producing an

oscillation of the primary current. Each cycle has less intensity until the electrical energy is expended. The entire cycle is repeated when the breaker points close to again store energy in the coil by allowing a current to flow from the battery.

This rapid collapse of the primary magnetic field produces the high voltage (up to 25,000 V) required to ionize the spark plug electrode gap and force the electrical arc across. The primary current flow, the rate of collapse of the coil primary magnetic field, and the coil winding ratio between the primary and secondary windings are responsible for the maximum available voltage in the ignition system. The system seldom operates at this maximum voltage. It will only produce the amount of voltage that is required to fire the spark plug at the operating conditions.

16-8 LEAKAGE

Available voltage is produced from the total energy stored in the coil by the primary current. This energy can be reduced by secondary leakage. Leakage erodes useful available voltage by shunting some of the energy around the spark plug electrodes. This can be seen in the scope pattern of Figure 16–17. One of the main causes of ignition leakage is spark plug fouling. Spark plug fouling occurs when conducting deposits build up on the nose of the spark plug insulator within the combustion chamber. If this leakage is small, the spark plug will fire. As the leakage increases, it drains away electrical energy, so that there is not enough energy remaining to produce the required arc across the spark plug gap.

The ignition system is designed for a very rapid energy release, or high rise time, so the energy is released faster than it can leak away and, therefore, will be able to flash across the spark plug electrode gap before appreciable leakage occurs.

Secondary leakage also occurs through weak

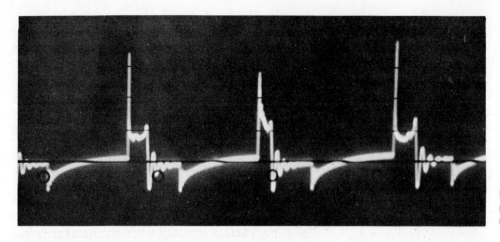

or cracked secondary insulation, especially at wire supporting brackets, across dirty coil tops, across dirty spark plug insulators, and across dirty distributor caps. Moisture and carbon tracks inside the distributor may be other paths for electrical leakage.

Corona accompanies high secondary voltages. It is an external leakage along ignition wires that is sometimes visible in the dark. Corona increases as the conductor becomes wet and dirty. Eventually, corona will lead to insulation failure and secondary leakage.

From the foregoing discussion, it would seem desirable to increase ignition system energy to overcome all required voltage and leakage. An over-capacity ignition system, however, rapidly erodes the spark plug electrodes and insulators to give short spark plug life. It also overloads the secondary insulation so that it would fail prematurely. High-energy ignition systems require special insulation.

In summary, ignition systems are designed to supply enough energy to the spark plug electrode arc to raise the charge located between the electrodes to the kindling temperature. This must be hot enough that the small flame is not quenched by the cool spark plug parts and the cool cylinder head. The ignition system energy must be large enough to meet ignition requirements and still be able to give maximum service life without overloading the ignition system.

16-9 IGNITION RESISTOR

Twelve-volt automotive ignition systems (Figure 16–18) use a resistor or ballast in the primary circuit to control available voltage and total energy stored in the coil. This may be a separate resistor or a resistor wire between the ignition switch and coil. With current flow, the resistance increases as its temperature increases. During low speed operation, the ignition breaker points are closed for a longer period of time than at high speeds, so more current will flow. The current reduction resulting from increased resistor temperature reduces breaker point burning during low speed operation. At high engine speeds the points are closed for shorter periods of time and so the resistor cools and its resistance drops. This allows higher voltage to reach the coil for more rapid coil saturation. This change can be observed on a voltmeter with the positive lead on the resistor side of the coil and negative lead on ground. When the ignition is first turned on with closed points, voltage will be high. As the resistor heats, the voltage drops.

The ballast type of resistor is designed to maintain constant resistance regardless of its temperature. It limits primary current at low temperature while still providing an adequate primary current at high temperatures.

The ignition resistor provides about one-half of the total resistance in the primary circuit and is the only part of the ignition system that is temperature-compensated.

During cranking, the ignition resistor is by-passed so that the entire electrical system voltage is placed across the coil, as shown in the accompanying illustration. This provides a momentary overload for a few cycles until the engine starts. The voltage in the electrical system during cranking is lowered to about 10 V by the heavy starter current draw and therefore the voltage is not excessive for the coil. When the engine starts, the electrical system voltage increases to the regulator voltage setting, about 14 V. The resistor then becomes effective to limit the running voltage of the coil to approximately 7 to 8 V when the breaker contact points are momentarily closed as the engine operates.

Fig. 16-18 Typical ignition system parts.

16-10 SEMICONDUCTOR IGNITION

The conventional breaker point ignition system just described, invented by Charles Kittering, is the most economical type of ignition system to produce. It has some shortcomings that can be overcome by using one of the ignition systems incorporating semiconductor electronics that were first introduced commercially in 1962.

Secondary available voltage is limited by a 5-ampere maximum current flow which the breaker points can handle. Electronic ignition systems remove the breaker points from the coil primary circuit. A primary current as high as 10 amperes is carried by a power transistor to increase coil saturation and this, in turn, increases available voltage. One type of system uses breaker points without a condenser to send an electrical pulse which will trigger a transistor. The transistor will transmit electrical energy from the battery to the coil in a more efficient manner than the breaker points alone can do. When used as a pulse trigger, the breaker points are required to carry only 1.0 ampere so they will not burn as rapidly as conventional points. This gives the breaker point contact surfaces an extended service life.

Breaker points have further limitations even when they are used with transistors. The low current flow across the contact surfaces allows the points to become dirty and so they will not conduct electricity. Breaker points still have rubbing block wear and therefore require periodic replacement, even when the contact surface is excellent. At high engine speeds, above 6000 rpm, breaker points tend to float or bounce, causing ignition to

become erratic. This limits high speed engine operation.

A second type of semiconductor ignition system replaces the breaker points and cam with a rotating *pole piece, armature,* or *reluctor* and a pickup coil to form a *breakerless* ignition system shown in Figure 16-19. In normal operation the

Fig. 16-19 Breakerless distributors. (a) Armature, (b) reluctor.

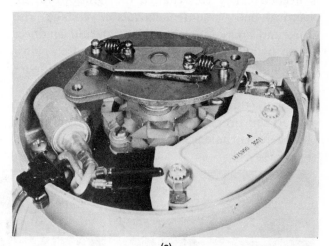

(a)

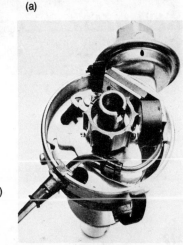

(b)

transistor circuit conducts primary current through the coil. As the pole piece, armature, or reluctor turns, the magnetic field across the pick-up coil reverses. This momentarily stops current flow through the switching transistor. This turns the power transistor off, which abruptly stops primary current flow as effectively as opening the breaker points. Electronic circuitry delays the power transistor from turning back on until the spark plugs have fired; then it immediately turns back on. This effectively provides a dwell over 40 degrees on 8-cylinder engines. This can be seen in Figure 16–20.

The conventional inductive Kittering ignition system can be replaced by a capacitive-discharge (C-D) system. A third type of ignition system uses breaker points to trigger a C-D system, while a fourth type is a breakerless C-D ignition system triggered by a rotating pole piece similar to the second type of ignition system previously described.

Modern semiconductor technology and devices make it possible for automotive electronic engineers to produce any desired type of ignition pulse that is needed. They can change the ignition system electrical energy content, available voltage, rise time, and spark duration. The ignition engineer has to balance the required ignition pulse against the complexity and cost of the system (Figure 16–21).

Spark duration must be long enough to form a good self-propagating flame in the combustion chamber. Turbulence in the combustion chamber that is produced as the charge is compressed may blow the initial flame from the spark plug before a good flame-front is established. If the spark duration is too short the charge will not reignite and the cylinder will misfire. Lean mixtures, especially at part-throttle cruising speeds, require more heat to ignite than do rich mixtures, and so increased spark duration is helpful. More of the ignition electrical energy will be available for spark duration if the rise time is kept short.

Semiconductor ignition has been an available option on some automobiles since 1962. A number of after-market kits and system diagrams are available. Generally speaking, the semiconductor ignition systems are sophisticated and complex. This increases their cost. They have no advantage for emission control, performance, or economy as long as the engine can continue to fire each cylinder and each power stroke at the correct instant. They require special radio-frequency suppression when the automobile is using UHF radio equipment. In operation the conventional ignition system deteriorates and no longer correctly fires the charge, or the timing changes as a result of point and distributor wear. The breakerless semiconductor ignition system, on the other hand, will continue to function properly. The main advantage to a breakerless semiconductor ignition system in a passenger car is that it minimizes the need for ignition system maintenance, except for spark plugs, spark plug cables, rotors, and distributor caps. This has become sufficiently important on emission-controlled engines that Chrysler Corporation made breakerless transistor ignition standard on certain engines in 1972 and on all engines in 1973. Other manu-

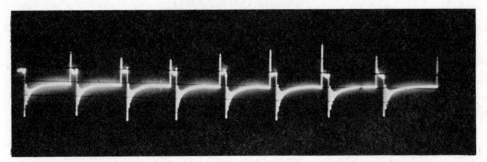

Fig. 16-20 Ignition scope pattern of an electronic ignition system.

Fig. 16-21 Available voltage as compared between standard and transistor ignition.

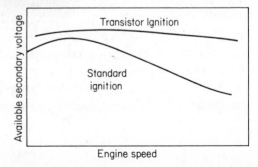

212

facturers soon followed, and in 1975 all engines were equiped with these systems. Many owners neglect and fail to properly maintain the standard ignition system and so their engines operate poorly and produce an abnormal quantity of hydrocarbon emissions. The breakerless transistor ignition system will remain at peak efficiency. If it fails, the engine usually stops and the faulty component has to be replaced. The electronic components cannot be repaired. If the system is going to fail, about one-third of the failures will occur in the first 100 miles (160 km) and two-thirds will occur in the first 2000 miles (3200 km), well within the warranty period. After 2000 miles (3200 km), the chances of system failure are extremely low.

In the breakerless semiconductor ignition, the pulse is created as a rotating pole piece, armature, or reluctor, and is turned past a magnet. The magnet in the distributor is made from powdered metallic barium-ferrite bonded with phenolic resin. When protrusions or projections line up, the magnetic lines of force are free to concentrate through the pole pieces, armature, or reluctor. This reduces the system *reluctance,* which is the resistance to magnetic lines of force. An instant after this alignment occurs the magnetic lines of force reverse through the pickup coil to produce a voltage pulse signal which is sensed by the ignition amplifier. The amplifier produces the current required to trigger the ignition coil. Typical amplifiers are shown in Figure 16-22.

The distributor used in the semiconductor ignition system is similar to the distributor used with the conventional ignition system. It uses the same mechanical advance and vacuum curves be-

cause these are made to match the ignition timing requirements of the engine. The mechanical characteristics of the distributor are more critical if the system is to be service-free while it maintains accurate timing. Distributor bearings must be accurately aligned and sized, permanently lubricated, and rigidly supported to provide required rotor shaft alignment for a long service life.

A trend toward maintenance-free electronic controls in automobile components has been firmly established. This trend has been rapidly increasing as technology, manufacturing capacity, and reliability increase and as cost is reduced. The trend is also apparent in the use of electronic components to control no-skid braking and no-spin acceleration systems. Electronic fuel injection is within the capability of manufacturing but the need for it at this time is not as great as its higher cost. It is becoming more and more important for the automotive technician to have a good understanding of operating procedures and testing principles used in semiconductor controlled systems.

16-11 DISTRIBUTOR OPERATION

The ignition distributor is driven from the engine camshaft at one-half crankshaft speed. The breaker points, condenser, rotor, cap, and timing advance mechanisms are located in the distributor. This arrangement, as shown in Figure 16-23, puts all of the ignition system's moving parts into a single unit.

The distributor gets its name from the portion that directs the secondary output to the spark plugs in the correct sequence to match the engine firing order. Coil secondary electrical output is fed to the center distributor cap tower. It flows through the tower to a button inside the cap. A spring clip on the rotor contacts the center button. The rotor has a conductor plate from the spring clip to an extended tip that comes close to the distributor cap electrodes as the rotor turns. This can be seen in Figure 16-24. It lines up with each distributor cap electrode in sequence as the breaker points open. This allows the secondary impulse to be directed through each spark plug lead to the spark plug in the correct firing order.

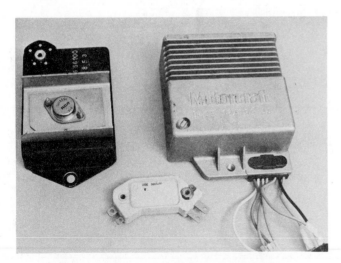

Fig. 16-22 Electronic ignition system amplifiers.

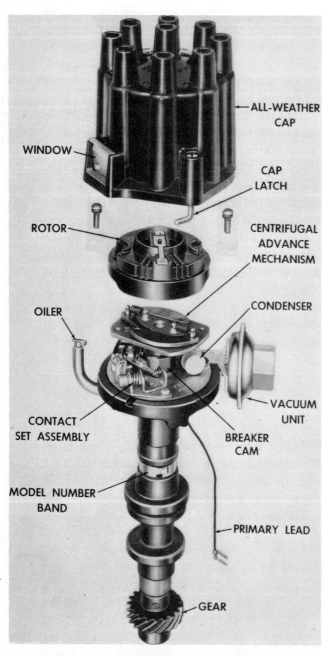

Fig. 16-23 Exploded view of a typical distributor (Delco-Remy Division, General Motors Corporation).

- ALL-WEATHER CAP
- WINDOW
- CAP LATCH
- ROTOR
- CENTRIFUGAL ADVANCE MECHANISM
- OILER
- CONDENSER
- VACUUM UNIT
- CONTACT SET ASSEMBLY
- BREAKER CAM
- MODEL NUMBER BAND
- PRIMARY LEAD
- GEAR

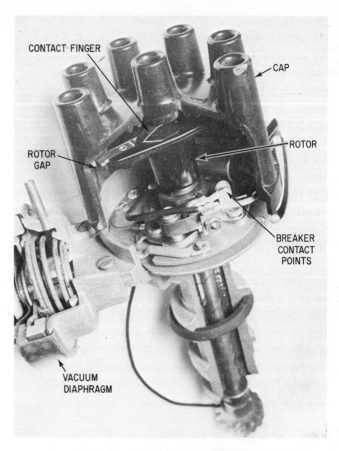

Fig. 16-24 Typical parts in a distributor.

- CONTACT FINGER
- CAP
- ROTOR GAP
- ROTOR
- BREAKER CONTACT POINTS
- VACUUM DIAPHRAGM

Fig. 16-25 Typical distributor drive train.

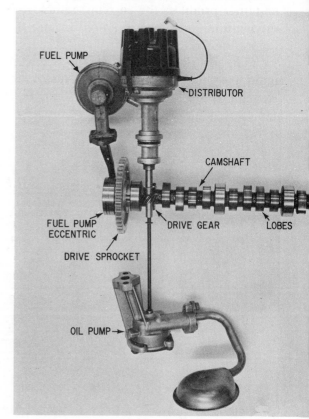

- FUEL PUMP
- DISTRIBUTOR
- CAMSHAFT
- FUEL PUMP ECCENTRIC
- DRIVE GEAR
- LOBES
- DRIVE SPROCKET
- OIL PUMP

It is convenient to locate the breaker point cam on the same shaft as the rotor because these two parts must always maintain their relative position for rotor and electrode alignment. A breaker point contact set is attached to the breaker plate within the distributor. Adjustments are provided to allow the points to be positioned closer to the cam for a larger point gap or away from the cam for a smaller point gap.

One cam lobe is provided for each cylinder. Four-cylinder cam lobes are spaced at 90°; 6-cylinder cam lobes are spaced at 60°; and 8-cylinder cam lobes are spaced at 45°. Within each of these cam angles, the points must be closed long enough to store electrical energy in the coil and must open far enough to minimize point arcing. The points are normally closed from 65 to 70% of the cam angle to provide coil saturation. This is known as the *dwell angle*. Any change in the breaker point gap will change the dwell approximately one degree for each 0.001 in. (0.025 mm) change in point gap.

The distributor cam opens the breaker points and a breaker point spring closes the points. A weak breaker point spring will allow the points to be thrown clear of the cam and so they will float and bounce when they close. When this happens, the points will not be able to close fast enough, the dwell period with the points closed will be shortened, and consequently the available voltage will be reduced. Excessively high breaker point spring tension will cause rapid rubbing-block wear and the point gap will reduce. This will also reduce available voltage.

Original-equipment distributor points are designed to maintain constant breaker point gap and dwell. Normal breaker points gradually burn, which tends to enlarge the gap. This is countered as the breaker point rubbing block wears on the cam, which tends to close the gap. These two service wear conditions counteract each other to keep the breaker point gap nearly constant. If wear caused the breaker point gap to decrease, the engine's basic timing angle would be retarded. If wear caused the gap to increase, the timing would advance.

The breaker point cam is driven by the distributor shaft through a mechanical advance mechanism (Figure 16–25). The advance mechanism consists of centrifugal flyweights that are retained by springs. As the distributor shaft rotates faster, the flyweights swing outward against spring pressure. Cam surfaces on the flyweights will advance or move the breaker point cam position forward in the direction of cam rotation in relation to the distributor shaft position. The distributor shaft drive is timed to a specific crankshaft angle with the distributor advance mechanisms in full retard. The distributor shaft always maintains this position in relation to the crankshaft while the distributor advance mechanism moves from this timing base that is called *basic timing*. The mechanical centrifugal advance is sensitive to engine speed, advancing the ignition timing as engine speed increases to compensate for the constant combustion rate that occurs while the first 10% of the combustion chamber charge burns. Flyweights and springs control the amount of timing change at any specific engine speed by turning the cam in the direction of shaft rotation so that the contact points open sooner. In service, the amount of advance is checked on a distributor machine or advance controls on a timing light. The actual advance is compared against advance specifications. Corrections in advance rate are usually made by changing the counterweight springs or by adjusting the spring hanger position (Figure 16–26).

The breaker plate, upon which the breaker points mount, is movable within the distributor housing and is held in position by a link from a vacuum diaphragm. The outside portion of the vacuum diaphragm is connected by tubing to sense vacuum at a port within the carburetor. High ported-vacuum pulls the diaphragm which, in turn, pulls the breaker plate in an advance

Fig. 16-26 Typical mechanical advance mechanism.

direction against the direction of rotation; this opens the contact points sooner. During high ported-vacuum operation, the engine runs with a less dense lean mixture that burns slowly and, therefore, requires a high advance to complete combustion at the correct 5-10° after top center. As the throttle is opened, manifold vacuum is reduced. This lowers ported vacuum causing the vacuum advance mechanism to retard the breaker points. The combustion charge mixture is more dense and usually richer as the manifold vacuum

drops. This requires less advance to complete combustion at 5-10° after top center. The vacuum advance mechanism is sensitive to manifold vacuum which, in turn, is sensitive to engine load and throttle position.

In most carburetors, the vacuum-sensing port is located just above the high portion of a closed throttle plate. At full idle, with the throttle closed, no vacuum is applied to the distributor vacuum diaphragm, because the port opens into atmospheric pressure above the throttle plate. As the throttle is opened, the port is exposed to manifold vacuum so it will sense engine vacuum to advance the distributor.

The breakerless pulse generator located in the distributor (Figure 16–27) uses the same mechanical centrifugal advance mechanism to provide the engine with the advance required by engine speed. The pick-up coil is mounted on a movable plate just as breaker points are so it will be moved to provide advance that is sensitive to engine load and throttle position.

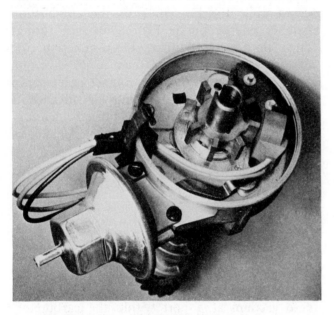

Fig. 16-27 Pulse generator located on the movable plate connected to the vacuum advance unit.

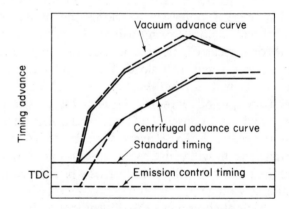

Fig. 16–28 Distributor advance curves.

Fig. 16-29 Parts of a unitized high energy ignition system with the coil located in the distributor cap.

Mechanical and vacuum advance mechanisms work together to provide the engine with the advance required to give the most efficient combustion and lowest practical emission level at each operating condition (Figure 16-28). A change in the basic timing or advance mechanisms will cause normal performance to deteriorate. If, on the other hand, the engine is modified from the original manufacturer's configuration, timing and advance curves would also have to be modified to produce the most efficient performance. References on emission controls should be consulted for control devices used to modify the vacuum advance for minimum exhaust emissions.

16-12 DISTRIBUTOR TESTING

Distributors may be tested in or out of the engine, depending upon the equipment available. Distributor advance may be checked by using a timing light that has a built-in time delay, while the engine is operated at a predetermined rpm or degree per second. This type of timing light has an electronic circuit that will sense the signal from number one

Fig. 16-31 Timing pointer used when checking a distributor on a distributor machine.

spark plug wire, then delay a known period of time before flashing the light. Time, then, is used to measure degrees of distributor advance. Engine timing advance is checked by first setting the basic timing with the delay switch turned off. Engine speed is increased to the specified test speed which will advance the timing. The timing light flash is then electronically retarded until the apparent timing mark is in its original position. The amount of timing delay is read on the instrument scale in degrees of advance, as shown in Figure 16-30.

The distributor may be removed from the engine and checked on a distributor machine. A machine electrical lead is connected to the distributor primary lead to sense point opening. A second lead may be used for a ground connection. The distributor machine has a typical ignition system built in so the distributor breaker points energize a coil in the normal manner. The coil secondary flashes a neon light.

The distributor shaft is clamped to a variable speed drive mechanism. A degree wheel is a part of the drive mechanism. Secondary voltage flashes the neon light each time the breaker points are opened. This light reflects on a pointer which, in turn, lines up with the degree wheel pictured in Figure 16-31.

Fig. 16-30 Checking the engine timing with a timing light.

The distributor is driven at speeds listed in the specifications and the actual advance is observed on the degree wheel. If the distributor is out of the specification range, it will need further service, such as cleaning flyweight bearings, replacing flyweight springs, adjusting flyweight spring hangers, cleaning movable breaker plates, or replacing the vacuum diaphragm unit.

Variations in spark timing degree and in dwell variations may indicate worn parts. See the applicable shop manual or equipment manufacturer's manual for the specific test and repair procedures.

Condensers are checked for opens, leakage, and capacity. They are so well built that they seldom fail. When failures do occur, most are the result of vibration or careless handling that breaks the leads or the ground connection.

Breaker points are checked for gap and/or dwell as well as point resistance. The breaker cam is ground with a set amount of lift. As the breaker point gap is adjusted wider, the rubbing block must start to open the breaker points sooner in order to be wide open at the cam high point. Gap changes will, therefore, affect dwell and engine timing. If the breaker cam is not worn, point gap will be correct if dwell is correct. Breaker cams seldom wear and when they do, the wear is visible.

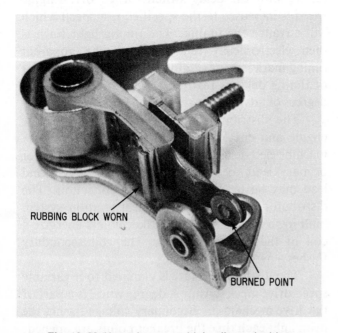

RUBBING BLOCK WORN

BURNED POINT

Fig. 16-32 Normal wear on high mileage ignition contact points.

As breaker points operate, they develop a frosty appearance on their contact surfaces. This type of surface makes a good electrical contact. The breaker points should be checked for resistance to make sure the electrical contact is good. Excessively worn points are pictured in Figure 16-32. Resistance is checked by allowing primary current to flow with a sensitive voltmeter connected from the primary distributor lead at the coil to the distributor ground. There should be less than 0.1 V drop. The test connections are illustrated in Figure 16-33.

To check resistance in the ignition circuit between the battery and the coil, the voltmeter should be connected between the ignition resistor switch terminal and the positive battery terminal post with the ignition switch turned on and the distributor breaker points closed. Voltage drop reading should be a maximum of 0.6 V. Specifications should be checked for exact values that apply to each engine or vehicle model.

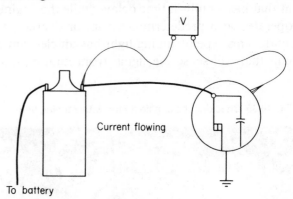

Current flowing

To battery

Fig. 16-33 Test connection for measuring voltage drop across the ignition points.

Points and Condenser. Two methods can be used to replace the points and condenser. The amateur mechanic will usually change them while the distributor is installed in the engine, because he does not want to disturb the basic engine timing. The professional technician will usually remove the distributor from the engine because he can usually do a better and faster job of replacing the breaker points and condenser. It also gives him a chance to examine the rest of the distributor for potential problems.

Breaker point replacement starts with removal of the distributor cap. It is fastened with spring clips, screw driver lock clips, or screws. The cap is loosened and placed at the side of the distributor with all of the ignition cables remaining in the cap. If the distributor is to be removed from the

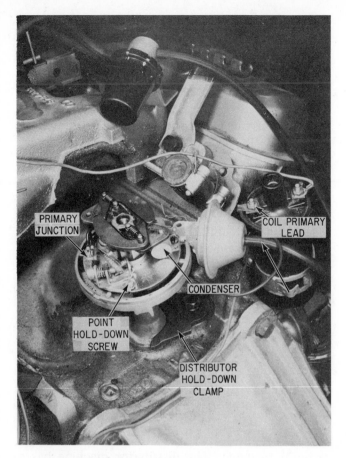

Fig. 16-34 Location of parts that are used when replacing the points and condenser.

engine, the vacuum advance unit and rotor positions should be noted and marked on the distributor housing so that the distributor can be replaced in the same position after the points and condenser are installed. Typical distributor attachments are shown in Figure 16-34. The primary lead is removed from the coil and the vacuum hose from the vacuum advance unit nipple; then the distributor hold-down clamp is removed so that the distributor can be pulled straight out of its engine opening. Heavy internal engine deposits will sometimes make distributor removal difficult. Careless prying can break the housing and bend the shaft. As some distributor models are removed the distributor shaft will turn a small amount, as a result of their angled-drive gear teeth. This rotation should be noted to ease reinstalling the distributor. The following breaker point changing procedure will be the same if the distributor is in the engine or if it is on the bench.

The distributor rotor is removed. On distributors having the centrifugal mechanical advance below the breaker points, the rotor is merely pulled off from the shaft. Two screws will have to be removed from the rotor to free the rotor from distributors having the mechanical advance mechanism above the breaker points. If the rotor tip or distributor cap electrodes show excessive burning, they should be replaced with new parts, especially if the engine has been misfiring prior to the distributor service. Contact breaker points are exposed when the rotor is removed on most distributors. Some distributors require the removal of a metal shield dust cover to expose the points.

The primary wire and condenser are attached to the breaker points at a single junction. The junction may have a screw or a bolt and nut, or it may be held by a spring pressure fit. The junction is separated and the single hold-down screw is removed so the points can be lifted from the distributor. If the condenser is to be replaced it can also be removed by taking out one hold-down screw. After wiping the cam a new condenser and breaker point set can be installed in reverse of the order used to remove them. If a screw is dropped into the distributor the screw must be retrieved because it will break the distributor or distributor drive when it jams within the distributor. Cam lubricant should be wiped smoothly over the cam surface and a drop of oil should be put on the felt plug inside the cam. Excessive lubrication will get on the points and cause them to burn. The distributor bearings should be oiled if an oiler is used on the distributor. Most modern distributor bearings have permanent lubrication or are lubricated with motor oil from within the engine.

When a distributor is in good mechanical condition the ignition point dwell will be correct if the breaker point gap is correct. A breaker point gap between 0.016 in. (0.04 mm) and 0.018 in. (0.045 mm) will allow the engine to start and will usually place the dwell within the correct range. Some 4-cylinder engines require a breaker point gap of 0.025 in. (0.055 mm). The gap is adjusted while the breaker point rubbing block is on the highest part of one of the breaker cam lobes as, shown in Figure 16-35. Some technicians adjust the points to the correct dwell, rather than putting a thickness gauge between the points, since a gauge may accidently put dirt between the points.

Breaker point sets must be adjusted properly for maximum service. They should be checked for

Fig. 16-35 Point gap adjustment when the rubbing block is on the high point of the cam.

Fig. 16-36 Measuring the breaker point spring tension.

contact point alignment and for spring tension. Contacts can be aligned by carefully bending the stationary contact to align it with the movable contact. Point spring tension of 19 to 23 oz is checked with a spring scale similar to the one shown in Figure 16-36. Tension can be increased by pushing the point spring into the holding screw, and it can be reduced by sliding the spring from the holding screw. After any point adjustment the gap or dwell should be rechecked. In a professional shop the centrifugal and vacuum advance mechanisms would be checked at this time.

Specifications for distributor advance are given in the service manual and on special specification sheets. The distributor is rotated at very slow speeds and the degree wheel is lined up so that one of the illuminated pointers is at 0°, as shown in Figure 16-31. The distributor speed is slowly increased until the pointer begins to advance. This is the first specification checkpoint for the mechanical centrifugal advance. Two or more additional specification checkpoints are given. They specify a certain degree advance at a given rpm, one at medium speeds and one at high speeds.

If the distributor centrifugal mechanical advance is incorrect some distributors are designed so that the spring hangers on the centrifugal weights can be adjusted. Other types will require new springs. Sometimes the weight, cam pivot points, or breaker cam pivot gets sticky and restricts movement. Whenever the centrifugal mechanical advance does not meet specifications it is a good plan to disassemble, clean, and relubricate the weight cam pivots. This is most easily accomplished on a distributor that has the mechanism directly under the rotor.

Vacuum advance is also checked on the distributor machine. The distributor machine has a vacuum pump with a vacuum gauge and control. The distributor is rotated at approximately 1000 rpm and vacuum is gradually applied to the vacuum-control unit. Advance should start at a given vacuum. Several other checkpoints are specified to determine the correct rate of advance. It is a good practice to remove the vacuum hose and block it with a finger, then adjust the machine to 15 in. (383 mm) Hg of vacuum. Without changing the settings, reconnect the vacuum line to the distributor. If the vacuum diaphragm does not leak the gauge will go right back up to 15 in. (383 mm) Hg. If a leak exists the vacuum will be lower. This condition can only be corrected by replacing the vacuum-control unit.

16-13 TIMING

Assume that the engine has not been cranked and the distributor is positioned and reinstalled correctly. A quick check of the distributor timing can be made without special timing tools. The engine should be turned with the starter, a little at a time, until the damper timing marks line up (Figure 16-37). This procedure is called *bumping* the starter. If the rotor is not pointing toward the number one ignition-cable terminal, turn the engine one additional revolution. By turning the crankshaft either with the starter or with a wrench on the front crankshaft nut, adjust the timing mark at the specified basic engine timing degree. This may be found in the owner's handbook, service manual, or specification sheets. With the distributor hold-down clamp loose, move the distributor housing in the direction opposite to the normal rotation of the rotor until the points just start to open with the rotor pointing to the ignition cable terminal that leads to number one cylinder. The control arm of the vacuum unit points in the direction of distributor rotation. This will be as close to the correct timing as it is possible to get without the use of a timing light. Tighten the hold-down clamp and re-install the distributor cap, being careful to fit the cap into the aligning notch. Replace any of the spark plug cables that have come out of the distributor cap while the cap was off the distributor. With the vacuum hose attached the engine should run.

The amateur mechanic is often completely confused if he has forgotten which way the rotor pointed or if the engine has been inadvertently cranked while the distributor was out of the engine. The key to retiming the ignition is to set the engine crankshaft to the position that number one cylinder *should* fire. The distributor is turned to the position that *will* fire number one cylinder. With both positioned, the distributor can be installed on the engine. The resulting timing will be close enough to start the engine.

Fig. 16-37 Ignition timing marks on the engine vibration damper.

Finding the crankshaft angle needed to fire number one cylinder is the most confusing part of basic timing for one who has never done it. Either of two methods will assure satisfactory results. Number one spark plug must fire as the piston moves up on the *compression* stroke with both valves closed. The number one piston top center position is marked as zero on the crankshaft damper timing mark. Automotive engines have a four-stroke cycle so the timing mark passes the zero mark at the end of the exhaust stroke (as the intake stroke begins) and at the end of the compression stroke. The correct piston position can be found by holding a finger over number one spark plug hole to feel pressure as the piston comes up on the compression stroke while the engine is being cranked. When pressure is felt in number one spark plug hole bump the starter switch enough so that the timing marks align. This is the correct crankshaft position to fire number one spark plug. Correct crankshaft position can also be found by watching the valves of number one cylinder if the rocker cover is off. If the number one exhaust valve is closing and the intake valve is opening as the marks line up, the crankshaft must be turned one complete revolution and the timing marks realigned. This sets the correct crankshaft position for timing.

The first consideration when the distributor is to be timed to the engine is to make sure the housing will be correctly aligned on the engine so that the vacuum advance unit will be positioned properly. The second consideration is the location of the cap tower in which the number one ignition cable is located. The rotor is turned in the normal direction of rotation until the rotor approaches the number one electrode and the breaker points are just ready to open. This is the position the distributor rotor should have when the distributor is installed in an engine that has had its crankshaft positioned correctly. Be sure the distributor vacuum advance unit is aligned properly as the distributor is installed. The distributor with a tang drive will fit directly in the drive slot if the drive has not been rotated. Distributors with a gear drive will turn a few degrees as the gear is engaged with the engine gear and so the shaft must be positioned to compensate for the gear angle. This might require lifting the distributor and engaging the next tooth if it does not line up correctly the first time it is installed. A little practice will enable the technician to quickly estimate the amount of turn.

Sometimes the distributor does not go all the way down into the engine because the oil pump drive does not mesh. A simple method to get the distributor to line up with the oil pump drive is to crank the engine with the distributor installed in the engine as far as possible. As the engine is cranked the oil pump drive will line up and the distributor will fully seat. The engine will have to be cranked through two full revolutions to correctly realign the timing marks on the compression stroke. With the distributor hold-down clamp loose, the distributor housing can be rotated slightly in a direction opposite to a rotor rotation to visually set the breaker points in a position so that they are just ready to be opened by the distributor cam. This position is close enough to start the engine. Final timing should be done with a timing light as the engine runs.

If the ignition cables have been removed from the distributor cap they can be easily reinstalled in the correct cap tower. Number one cable goes into the tower toward which the rotor points when the timing marks line up as number one cylinder is on its compression stroke. Following around the cap in the direction the rotor turns, the ignition cables are installed according to the engine firing order. The cylinder firing order is usually shown in raised cast numbers on the manifold. If it is not, it will have to be found in a specification book. Crank the starter slightly to positively identify the direction of the rotor rotation. The vacuum advance unit control arm points in the direction of rotation. Place the spark plug cable leading to the next cylinder in the firing order into the next distributor tower. Follow this by inserting each succeeding cable into the cap towers in the proper firing-order sequence. If the engine is not going to be timed with a timing light reinstall the vacuum hose. With the parking brake set and the transmission in neutral, start the engine.

If a dwell meter is available, it should be attached and the ignition point dwell checked. Dwell and point gap are shown in Figure 16–38. Dwell can be easily adjusted on an external-adjustment distributor with the engine idling. If dwell is incorrect on the other types of distributors the engine will have to be stopped, the distributor cap removed, and the gap changed sufficiently to bring the dwell into specification. Some dwell meters can be used to check dwell while the engine is being cranked. If one of these meters is used the rotor will have to be removed and the dwell adjusted as the engine is cranked. Timing should *always* be reset after adjusting dwell.

If a timing light is available connect the pick-up cable to the number one ignition cable and connect the light to its proper power source, either the vehicle battery or the shop 110-volt line. It is critical on most emission controlled engines to attach this timing light pick-up to number one spark plug cable even if it is not as accessible as one of the other spark plugs. Set the parking brake and place the transmission in neutral; then start the engine. Let it run slowly at curb idle speed with the vacuum line to the distributor removed and plugged so air does not go into the carburetor. With the timing light aimed at the timing marks and the hold-down clamp slightly loose, adjust the distributor until ignition occurs at the specified degree. Tighten the hold-down clamp and recheck the timing. Readjust the timing as necessary; then reconnect the distributor vacuum line.

In addition to basic timing the timing light can be used to determine if the distributor mechanical centrifugal advance and vacuum advance mechanisms are operating. Remove and plug the distributor vacuum line so air does not enter the carburetor port. With the timing light aimed at the timing marks, gradually increase the engine speed. The timing marks should appear to move in the

Fig. 16-38 Breaker point dwell change as the gap is changed.

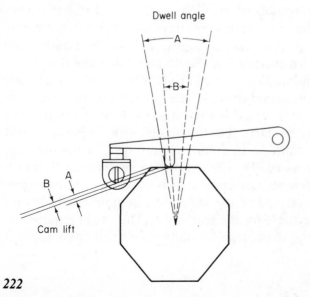

Dwell angle

Cam lift

advance direction when the mechanical centrifugal advance is operating. With the engine running and held at approximately 1200 rpm, watch the timing marks with the timing light as the vacuum line is reconnected. The timing mark will again move in the advance direction if the vacuum advance mechanism operates. This test will indicate that the distributor advance mechanisms are operating, but it does not indicate that the advance mechanisms are operating correctly.

Some timing lights are made with built-in advance meters. When doing basic timing the technician must be sure to have the meter turned off so that it will operate as a simple timing light. After basic timing is set, the engine is brought up to a specified speed. At this speed the advance meter control is adjusted so that the timing light makes the timing mark appear to be in the same position as it was while the basic timing was set. The meter reading indicates the number of degrees the distributor has advanced. This advance check can be done with the vacuum line off to measure mechanical centrifugal advance and the vacuum line reconnected to measure the additional advance produced by the vacuum advance mechanism. The distributor vacuum advance line must be connected at the end of this test. If the timing advance is not correct the distributor will have to be tested on a distributor machine.

16-14 SPARK PLUGS

The entire ignition system culminates in an arc between the spark plug electrodes. If the correct spark plug is not used, ignition will malfunction, resulting in a misfire or in damaged pistons. The spark plug must concentrate the conversion of the electrical energy to thermal energy at a location in the combustion chamber which will ignite enough of the charge so that combustion of the remaining charge will proceed in a normal manner.

The spark plug consists of three major parts, the shell, the insulator, and the electrodes. These can be identified in Figure 16-39. The shell supports the insulator and has threads that screw into the head. The thread portion must be long enough to allow the electrodes to enter the combustion chamber. This length is called the spark plug *reach*. If the reach were too long, it could damage the valves or piston. Threads on the spark plug are metric 14 and 18 mm threads. The shell seals the

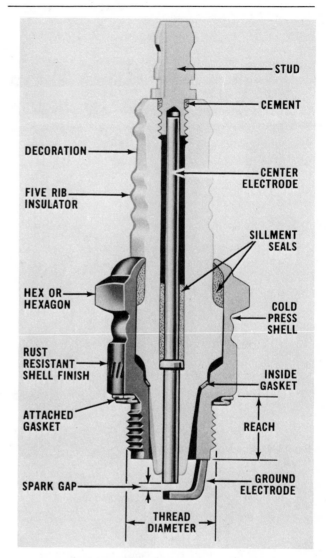

Fig. 16-39 Spark plug nomenclature (Champion Spark Plug Company).

combustion chamber spark plug hole. Some shells seal with a tapered spark plug seat. Others seal with a metal spark plug gasket (Figure 16-40).

The ceramic spark plug insulator is sealed inside the shell, so that it makes a pressure and thermal seal. Much of the spark plug development work has been concentrated on the insulator. It must withstand high thermal and mechanical stress as well as insulate the high secondary voltage. During manufacturing, the insulator ingredients are formed to a putty-like consistency. The putty is formed in the insulator shape, then fired in a furnace. The finished insulator is close to diamond hardness. It is placed in the shell with sealing material, then the shell is crimped around the insulator to produce

Fig. 16-40 Typical spark plugs used in modern automotive engines. The four on the left use gaskets. The two on the right have conical seats.

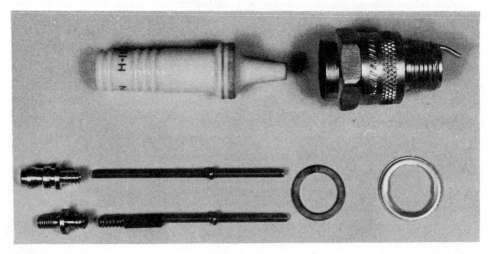

Fig. 16-41 Spark plug parts before assembly.

Fig. 16-42 Resistance-type spark plug (AC Spark Plug Division, General Motors Corporation).

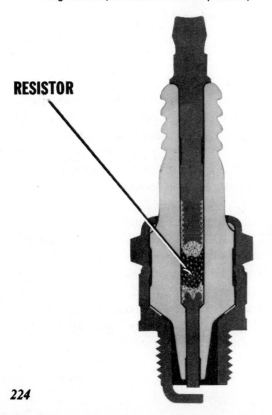

RESISTOR

a gas-tight seal. Spark plug parts are shown in Figure 16–41.

The center electrode is placed in a hole down through the center of the insulator. Modern electrodes are made from two pieces, one to attach to the spark plug cable and the other to extend into the hot combustion chamber. Using two pieces allows the spark plug manufacturer to select the type of metal that will best meet the requirements under which it must operate. The electrode is sealed with a gas-tight electrical conducting seal material.

Some spark plug types, as shown in Figure 16–42, have a resistor installed between the two sections of the electrode. Its 10,000-ohm resistance changes the ignition secondary oscillating frequency at the instant the arc is established across the electrodes. This change in frequency moves the electrical radiation out of the television and radio frequencies to suppress interference. The resistor also provides long spark plug electrode life by cutting down peak current that flows in the arc across the electrode gap.

Spark plugs must operate within a specified temperature range. If the spark plug operates too cold, it will foul with deposits. These deposits will leak off coil electrical energy, so the spark plug will not fire. If the spark plug operates too hot, it will erode rapidly and will cause pre-ignition. Pre-ignition will lead to physical engine damage. The minimum spark plug temperature for nonfouling operation is 650°F (343°C). Above 1500°F (816°C), pre-ignition will occur. Spark plugs must operate within these temperatures under all normal operating conditions.

When an engine is running under heavy loads, such as sustained high speed driving, the combustion chambers become hot. During high temperature operating conditions, a cold spark plug is required to prevent spark plug overheating. Engines that have a tendency to run cold and foul from oil or from light duty operation require hot spark plugs to keep the plug temperature high enough to eliminate fouling. Drag racing operation is such a short-time operation on each run that cold spark plugs are seldom necessary.

A cold spark plug transfers heat from the spark plug nose through the shell faster than a hot spark plug, as illustrated in Figures 16-43 and 16-45. The spark plug heat range selected for replacement spark plugs should match the manufacturer's specifications. Modified engines may require a different heat range spark plug than those specified for the

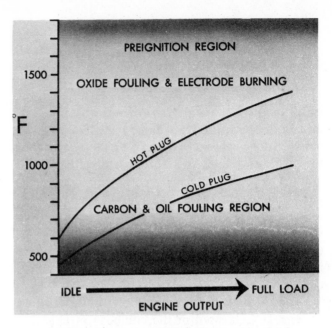

Fig. 16-44 Spark plug operating temperature heat limits controlled by the spark plug's heat range (Champion Spark Plug Company).

original engine. Spark plugs for modified engines should be selected by working up from cold spark plugs. If fouling occurs, the next hotter heat range that does not foul should be used. In this way, it is possible to avoid pre-ignition. The pre-ignition region can be seen in Figure 16-44.

Fig. 16-45 Heat flow through a spark plug (Champion Spark Plug Company).

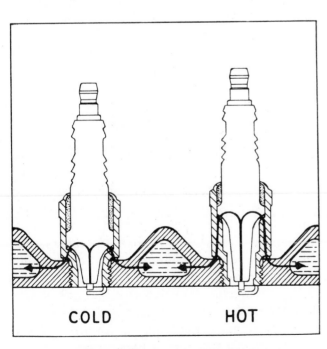

Fig. 16-43 The spark plug's cooling path controls its heat range (Champion Spark Plug Company).

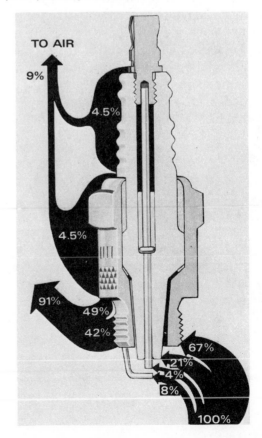

It is interesting to note that the center electrode of automotive spark plugs is of negative polarity. Hot bodies are known to have increased electron activity. The center electrode is the hottest part of the spark plug and, therefore, requires the lowest voltage to force free electrons to form an arc. The hot negative center electrode helps to keep required voltage low. If the polarity is reversed, required voltage will increase. Secondary polarity can be changed by reversing the primary coil leads, so care is required to see that coil connections are made correctly.

The spark plug is the end point in the ignition system. It is located in the combustion chamber where it is subjected to combustion deposits, erosion, and corrosion. Spark plugs require periodic service regardless of the type of ignition system used.

Spark plugs are removed by first removing the spark plug cable. This is done by carefully twisting and pulling the boot that fits over the spark plug to remove it without damaging or stretching the cable. Blow air around the spark plug to remove any loose material. Use a good spark plug socket, with an internal cushion, to remove the spark plug without damage. Generally the spark plugs are removed and laid out for inspection. A better practice to follow when a compression test is to be run while the spark plugs are out of the engine is to loosen the spark plugs about one-quarter turn, and reattach the spark plug cables; then start the engine and speed it up two or three times. Any carbon chips that have broken loose from the combustion

Fig. 16-46 Typical spark plug conditions (The Prestolite Company).

chamber surface as the spark plugs were turned will be blown from the engine and will not get under a valve and cause erroneous compression test readings.

When the spark plugs are removed they should be examined critically. This examination is often called *reading the plugs*. The condition of the electrodes and the type of carbon on the spark plug nose give a good indication of how that particular cylinder has been operating.

The most obvious spark plug condition is the type of carbon on the spark plug nose, as shown in Figure 16-46. Normal spark plugs will have a light tan to gray deposit, depending on the additives in the gasoline that has been used in the engine. If the deposits are slight and white with badly eroded electrodes the spark plug has been running very hot. Heavy sooty deposits indicate rich air/fuel mixtures, and heavy wet deposits indicate high oil consumption. Dry fluffy carbon deposits indicate incomplete combustion. Some engines, especially ones with high mileage, tend to develop heavy white deposits that bridge the gap. This results from oil consumption which forms the deposits. Spark plug manufacturers supply full color pictures of these conditions so that the technician can compare the spark plug appearance and diagnose the problem.

Spark plugs can be cleaned and serviced; however it is the general practice to install new spark plugs when a tune-up is done on a customer's engine. The customer usually plans to get over 10,000 miles (18,537 km) before the next tune-up and so new spark plugs are expected. Maintenance on automobiles equipped with a catalytic converter specify new spark plugs at specific service intervals.

16-15 SPARK PLUG CABLES

Modern engines use nonmetallic resistance-type conductor secondary cables. As with spark plug resistors, these cables provide ignition radiation suppression (IRS cable) or television and radio noise suppression (TVRS cable) of radio-frequency emissions from the ignition system. Aluminum distributor cap electrode inserts are used with suppression-type ignition cables. Old model engines used metal conductor secondary cables with copper distributor cap inserts. Mixing distributor caps and cable types will produce corrosion which will add resistance to the secondary circuit.

Suppression-type ignition cable should not be

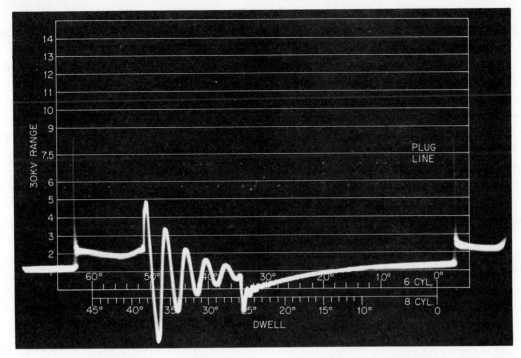

Figure 16-47 A normal secondary ignition pattern of one cylinder.

replaced with metal conductor cable. Ignition systems are designed to satisfactorily handle the resistance built into the cable. The use of metal conductor cables on these systems will lead to rapid spark plug-electrode erosion and to radio-frequency emission that causes interference in nearby radios and television sets. Federal Communication Commission laws prohibit the use of metal conductor secondary cables.

Emission-controlled engines run much hotter than non-emission controlled engines. Old style ignition cables will not last in these high underhood temperatures. Care must be exercised to make sure that the proper high-temperature secondary cables are used for replacement in emission-controlled engines. High temperature cable insulation is made from either hyplon or silicone materials.

16-16 IGNITION SYSTEM TESTING

The ignition system is one of the interrelated engine systems. Input voltage to the coil primary is determined by the battery or by the voltage regulator. Ignition system output is the required voltage at the spark plug. Any change in combustion chamber conditions such as compression pressure, temperature, and air/fuel mixture ratios will affect required voltage; therefore, these must be considered when testing ignition systems.

A cathode ray oscilloscope is one of the best instruments to observe overall characteristics of the complete operating ignition system. Normal or abnormal operating conditions are indicated by the scope when using information in this chapter along with applicable engine specifications.

The ignition oscilloscope displays secondary voltage on a time base. The scope sweep is usually triggered by number one spark plug cable; however, any secondary cable could be used. As the voltage increases in number one spark plug wire, a spike is produced at the right edge of the pattern. This is the trigger that immediately shifts the sweep to the left edge to begin a new pattern trace.

Anything in the primary that has an effect on available voltage is reflected in the secondary pattern. Parts which the scope pattern indication shows to be faulty are usually rechecked with a specialized tester to verify the malfunction.

Scope Patterns. The oscilloscope is useful in ignition system testing to give an overall view of the engine condition as it operates. The ignition scope has a voltage pickup on the coil-to-distributor secondary cable to measure secondary voltage. A second scope lead is connected to the number one spark plug cable as a trigger. Each time the number one spark plug fires, the scope is triggered and the pattern starts on the left side of the scope screen. A typical scope secondary pattern is shown in Figure 16-47.

227

The ignition system must build up a sufficient voltage to force its way across the largest gap in the secondary circuit. This gap normally is the spark plug electrode gap. It requires about 7 to 8 kV as indicated by the top of the pattern spike. This is required voltage. As soon as the electricity arcs across the gap it ionizes the charge gases between the gap to allow a small milliamp current to flow; this reduces the voltage needed to maintain the arc. The lower arc voltage is indicated by the spark line that results from the immediate fall of secondary voltage to about 25% of the original required voltage, or to about 2 kV, as the coil dissipates its energy while it is providing current for the spark plug arc. This can be seen in Figure 16–48. After the arc is formed a small milliamp current flows in the secondary circuit. Because current is flowing, any resistances that are in the secondary system will affect the voltage level of the spark line portion of the scope pattern. Factors that produce secondary circuit resistance normally cause the spark line to slope downward toward the right. Factors that increase secondary circuit resistance in a spark plug cable or spark plug will cause the spark line voltage to be higher and shorter than normal, while factors

that lower the resistance produce a spark line that is lower and longer than normal.

When the coil energy is no longer sufficient to maintain an arc across the spark plug the spark line stops. This is followed by a series of five or more oscillations as the ignition system energy dissipates. Abnormal operation of the coil or condenser will reduce the number of these oscillations.

Breaker point closing causes a momentary reverse voltage signal that produces a sharp dip in the pattern line. The pattern line comes up to normal as the coil saturates before the points open to produce a spike for the next cylinder firing. The horizontal line from the point closing signal to the next firing is the total time the points are closed and it is called *dwell*. Dwell is from 65-70% of the total distance between firing spikes. Most scopes are designed to allow a single pattern to be positioned over a scale that can be used to read dwell directly without the aid of a separate dwell meter. Figure 16–49 shows all eight cylinders in a raster pattern.

It is not only important to know the required voltage but it is also important to know the available voltage to be sure sufficient *ignition reserve* is present. This is measured by removing one of the spark plug leads while the engine is running at approximately 1500 rpm. Available voltage should be between 20 and 30 kV, as shown in Figure 16–50.

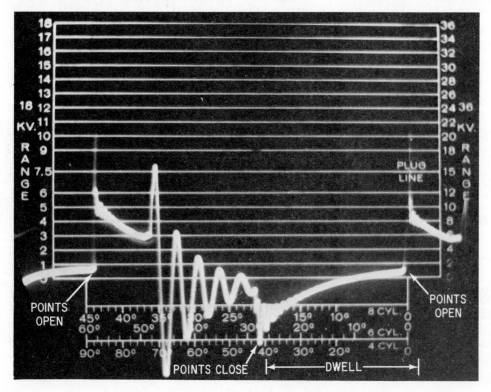

Fig. 16-48 Oscilloscope pattern of the ignition secondary voltage as the contact points open and close and as an arc forms across the spark plug electrodes.

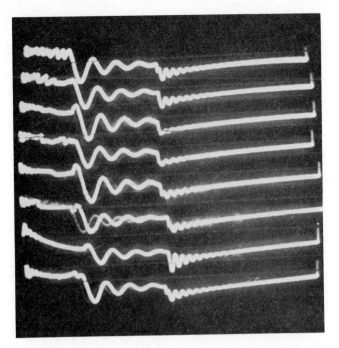

Fig. 16-49 Oscilloscope raster pattern of the secondary ignition voltage.

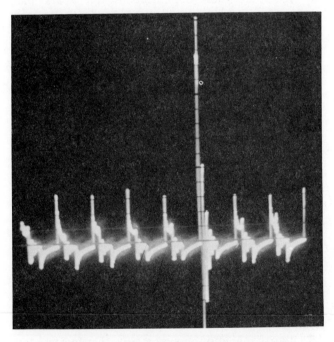

Fig. 16-50 A parade display of eight cylinders with one spark plug cable removed to indicate available voltage. Notice that the tail of the high available voltage spike is about one-half its height. Moving from left to right, the first cylinder pattern has a rising firing line indicating turbulence in the cylinder; the second pattern shows a fouled spark plug; and the third indicates high resistance; the fourth, low resistance; the fifth, normal. Available voltage is shown on plug six, and the last two are normal.

Readings below 20 kV indicate problems in the primary ignition circuit. Damage can occur to the secondary insulation from the high voltage produced if the test is extended over a considerable length of time. The spark plug cable should, therefore, only be removed long enough to recognize the pattern.

The scope pattern in the available voltage test normally has a tail half as long as the spike. If this tail is short or missing, it indicates secondary leakage.

Ignition Primary Pattern. Some ignition scopes also display a primary voltage pattern (Figure 16–51). This is useful in examining the breaker point opening and closing signal as well as checking dwell and dwell variations.

Many other items and variations may be determined with ignition scopes. Manufacturer's instructions on the scope being used should be consulted for details of the particular scope pattern indications.

Semiconductor ignition systems can be checked using standard ignition test equipment found in service shops. Specialized testers are manufactured for specific ignition systems for rapid tests of the components. These units use switches and lights to indicate the component condition. When a fault occurs in the ignition circuit it can be traced in the same manner as in the standard Kittering ignition system.

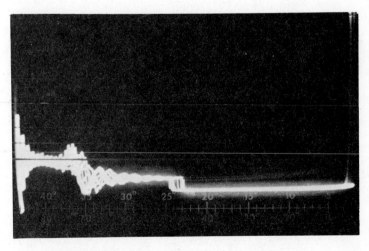

Fig. 16-51 Typical superimposed primary scope pattern of all cylinders.

REVIEW QUESTIONS

1. What is required voltage? [INTRODUCTION]

2. When should maximum pressure occur in the combustion chamber? [INTRODUCTION]

3. What is the purpose of the centrifugal mechanical timing advance? [16–1]

4. What is the purpose of the vacuum advance timing mechanism? [16–2]

5. What controls the required voltage in the ignition system on a running engine? [16–2]

6. What engine operating condition requires the largest spark plug gap? [16–3]

7. What breaker point action causes the arc to flash across the spark plug electrodes? [16–4]

8. Why is an oscilloscope used to measure ignition voltage? [16–4]

9. What is measured on the scope X-axis and Y-axis? [16–5]

10. Why is the primary winding wrapped outside the secondary winding in an ignition coil? [16–6]

11. What is the purpose of the coil laminations? [16–6]

12. What slows full current build-up in a primary coil? [16–6]

13. What portion of the ignition scope pattern is produced by the capacitive and inductive portions of the coil energy? [16–6]

14. What is the advantage of fast rise time? [16–6]

15. Where is the ignition condenser fastened electrically? [16–7]

16. What is the purpose of the ignition condenser? [16–7]

17. How does leakage affect the energy stored in a coil? [16–8]

18. What happens when excess energy is stored in the coil? [16–8]

19. Why is a resistor used in the ignition system? [16–9]

20. What is the advantage of semiconductor ignition over the conventional breaker point system? [16–10]

21. What are two types of semiconductor ignition systems? [16–10]

22. What is the main advantage of a breakerless semiconductor ignition system in a passenger car? [16–10]

23. Compare the distributor advance mechanisms of a breakerless distributor and a distributor with breaker points. [16–11]

24. What happens to ignition timing if the breaker point gap decreases, due to rubbing block wear? [16–11]

25. What parts of a breaker point distributor are checked with the distributor in a distributor machine? [16–12]

26. How is basic timing set when reinstalling a distributor after servicing it on a distributor machine? [16–13]

27. What are the requirements of the spark plug insulator? [16–14]

28. What is the purpose of the built-in spark plug resistor? [16–14]

29. Why do spark plugs require a heat range? [16–14]

30. Why is the spark plug center electrode negative? [16–14]

31. How does the spark plug condition indicate combustion chamber condition? [16–14]

32. What is the purpose of nonmetallic conductor secondary cables? [16–15]

33. How is the correct distributor cap to be used with TVRS cables identified? [16–15]

34. Describe the important parts of the ignition scope pattern. [16–16]

35. Illustrate ignition scope patterns that indicate low compression, high resistance, and spark plug fouling. [16–16]

36. Why are speed and vacuum important when setting basic timing? [16–16]

37. How is the distributor advance tested on an operating engine? [16–16]

38. Discuss ignition system service. [16–16]

emission controls

Pollution has become a major problem throughout the world. This has led to a great deal of research in an attempt to stop additional pollution and to clean up presently polluted areas. Antipollution research indicates that the automobile is a major contributor to air pollution in the United States.

Air pollution is evident in a number of ways. It may be unsightly, as smoke, soot, or dust. It may be foul-smelling, as diesel odor or sewage treatment gases. The most serious type of air pollutants are those that present health hazards. Automobile emissions are considered to contribute to this last type of air pollution.

During the 1950's emission from automobiles was identified as a contributor to smog in the Los Angeles basin. The Los Angeles basin is a valley with the Pacific Ocean on the west and mountains surrounding the other three sides. Prevailing west

winds from the Pacific blowing against mountains tend to hold the air particles within the basin area. The usual shining California sun causes a photochemical reaction among the particles in the air that converts them to a yellow-brown haze called *smog,* as illustrated in Figure 17–1. It irritates the eyes, causes breathing problems, deteriorates some materials, and damages plant life.

Since the phenomena that produced smog were first identified in California, other cities have had large increases in the number of automobiles. When weather conditions are favorable the automobile emissions may be sufficient to form smog in any metropolitan area.

The principal products that are involved in photochemical smog formation are the hydrocarbons, usually the types called olefins and aromatics, and the oxides of nitrogen. Olefins are especially reactive in smog formation. They are straight-chain unsaturated hydrocarbon molecules with a double bond. The double bond is easily broken when other atoms are present to combine with the hydrocarbon molecule. In the presence of sunlight, these hydrocarbons and oxides of nitrogen are changed in a series of chemical reactions to produce smog components. The principal components of smog are: ozone, which is a powerful oxidizer that hardens rubber and is a health hazard in high concentrations; aldehydes, which are eye irritants; and a compound called peroxyacylnitrate (PAN), which terminates the photochemical reaction chain.

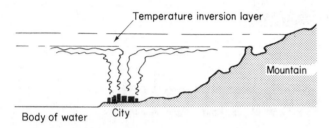

Fig. 17-1 Conditions conducive to smog formation.

In a non-emission-controlled vehicle, crankcase vapors account for 25% of the total vehicle emission, the exhaust 60%. The remaining emissions evaporate from fuel tank and carburetor vents.

17-1 HARMFUL EMISSIONS

Harmful exhaust emissions consist of carbon monoxide (CO), hydrocarbons (HC), and oxides of nitrogen (NO_x). Emission-control devices on modern automotive engines are designed to keep them at a minimum.

The amount of carbon monoxide produced during combustion has been used for years as a measure of efficient combustion. A rich air/fuel mixture produces a large amount of carbon monoxide. As the mixture is leaned carbon monoxide is reduced until almost none is produced at an ideal cruising air/fuel mixture. Carbon monoxide does not contribute to the formation of smog but its emission is regulated by federal standards as a means of controlling efficient combustion and maintaining a healthy atmosphere. Carbon mon-

oxide is harmful because it forms stable compounds in the bloodstream that will block oxygen from acting with the hemoglobin in the blood. In low concentrations, it causes headache. In higher concentrations it leads to coma and death by asphyxiation.

Lowering the carbon monoxide level is accomplished by operating the engine as lean as possible while still preventing misfiring. Heating the lean mixture enables it to ignite more readily, thereby reducing the tendency to misfire at lean air/fuel mixtures. Most of the carbon monoxide forms during idling and during deceleration when rich mixtures are used to compensate for poor fuel distribution within the manifold. They also form when a cold engine is being choked.

One of the vehicle emissions that contributes to smog is unburned and partly burned hydrocarbons. Unburned hydrocarbons drift into the atmosphere as gasoline vapors while the gasoline tank is being filled. They leak out of the gasoline tank vents and from the carburetor float bowl vent when the engine is not operating. Some hydrocarbons also come from the combustion chamber when a cylinder misfires, when the carburetor mixture is too rich, or when the combustion chamber is cool.

Hydrocarbons, especially the olefins and aromatic types, contribute to the formation of photochemical smog. In the amounts in which they are normally present in the atmosphere, they have no direct harmful effect on a person's health. Unburned hydrocarbons in the exhaust are reduced by leaning the mixture, just as CO is reduced. If the mixture becomes so lean that the engine misfires the unburned hydrocarbons *increase* greatly while CO remains low.

Most of the unburned hydrocarbons are produced by the surface quenching action of the combustion charge caused by the cooling effect of the metal surface of the combustion chamber. This is impossible to avoid. The quenching effect is reduced by redesigning the engine to reduce the combustion chamber surface-to-volume ratio. To do this the engine bore is reduced and the stroke increased. The rotary combustion chamber engine has a very high combustion chamber surface area compared to its volume and it therefore produces large amounts of unburned hydrocarbons.

The second smog-producing constituent produced in the combustion chamber is oxides of nitrogen (NO_x). They form when air, which consists of approximately 80% nitrogen and 20% oxygen, chemically reacts to combine these elements in a high-temperature environment. The engine combustion chamber provides this high-temperature environment. Engine thermal efficiency and power will increase as engine temperature increases. This also increases the production of oxides of nitrogen. The higher the peak cycle temperature, the greater the production of NO_X. The production of NO_X also increases as the mixture is leaned until an excessively lean mixture occurs. This, of course, causes misfiring, which results in an increase in unburned HC. The exhaust emission products created by a piston engine are graphed in Figure 17-2. Because the rotary combustion chamber engine operates at low thermal efficiencies it produces small amounts of NO_X. Diesels and turbines operate at high temperatures with large quantities of air and so they produce large amounts of NO_X.

Lead in the quantities that are present in gasoline produces no identifiable health hazard in itself. Lead is being eliminated from gasoline to minimize contamination of the catalyst in converters that are used on most 1975 and later model automobiles using spark-ignited internal combustion engines. These converters will help to oxidize the HC and CO, and to reduce NO_X to harmless products. It is easier to oxidize the HC and CO products than it is to reduce NO_X. This makes it easier to lower the

amount of controlled emissions in the exhaust from a rotating combustion engine than it is to lower the amount of those emissions in the exhaust from piston engines.

17-2 EMISSION REDUCTION

California leads the nation in passing laws that require new automobiles to produce less emissions of the type that lead to the development of smog. Federal emission-control regulations for new automobiles are now in effect for the whole country. Automobile manufacturers have met the requirements of the first emission laws by providing the engine with positive crankcase ventilation. Additional laws followed and the automobile manufacturers have met their requirements. Carburetor and intake systems have been modified to provide each combustion chamber with a mixture that more nearly meets ideal combustion requirements. The ignition system is designed to provide ignition at a time in the combustion cycle that results in lower smog-producing emissions. Combustion chamber designs and coolant temperatures have been changed to reduce harmful emissions. The exhaust system has been modified to aid in the combustion of products not fully burned within the combustion chamber. Vapors from the fuel tank and carburetor are vented to an activated carbon charcoal canister where they are trapped and stored to keep them from drifting into the atmosphere. A typical 1971 emission-control system is shown in Figure 17-3.

Vehicle emissions come from the engine crankcase, gasoline tank, carburetor, and exhaust. The crankcase vapors from engines built since 1968 are completely controlled. Evaporative vapors from the gasoline tank and carburetor are controlled under almost every condition in automobiles built since 1971. In order to run, the engine will use large amounts of air and expel a large quantity of exhaust, and so engine exhaust cannot be eliminated. Federal standards require the exhaust gases to be modified so that they contain only a very small percentage of harmful exhaust components.

This section describes the most common emission-control systems in use at the time this chapter was written. Variations of these systems

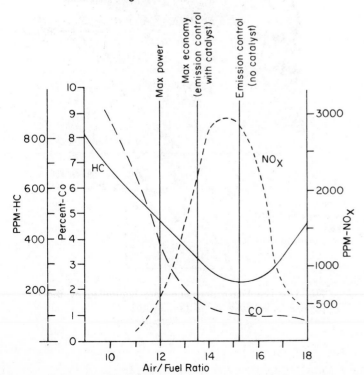

Fig. 17-2 Exhaust gas contaminant changes as the air/fuel ratio changes on a non-emission-controlled engine.

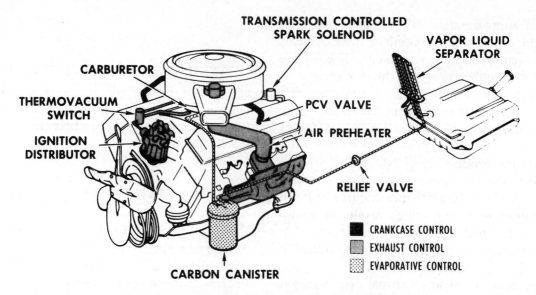

Fig. 17-3 Typical emission controls used on modern engines (GM Research Laboratories, General Motors Corporation).

are used for special applications. Later designs will, no doubt, be on the market by the time this book is published. It is therefore important to follow current specifications and procedure manuals when working on emission-controlled vehicles.

Crankcase Emission Control. Crankcase vapors are a combination of light hydrocarbons, crankcase oil vapors, and combustion chamber gases that have been blown past the pistons and rings during the compression and power strokes. Crankcase oil vapors are the light volatile portions of the motor oil that evaporate at engine operating temperatures. Combustion chamber gases that find their way into the crankcase are blow-by gases, primarily made up of gases that come from the quench area within 0.002 in. to 0.020 in. (0.05 mm to 0.5 mm) of the combustion chamber wall surface. These gases are cooled by the relatively low-temperature combustion chamber wall surface until they are too cool to burn. This explanation is supported by tests which show that blow-by gases have the same olefinic content as the gasoline being used, which indicates that these blow-by gases are unburned. Every time a driver opens the throttle, the blow-by rate increases, even though the throttle is not held open long enough to increase vehicle speed.

A hose between the air cleaner and rocker cover allows filtered air to enter the engine to ventilate the crankcase. The air circulates through the engine, picking up blow-by gases and oil vapors.

Blow-by gases combine with oil vapors and fresh air to form crankcase vapors. Crankcase vapors are drawn from the crankcase through a *positive crankcase ventilation* (PCV) valve and a hose leading to the engine manifold where vacuum will draw the gases to be burned in the combustion chamber, as shown in Figure 17–4.

The PCV valve controls the crankcase emission system operation. At high manifold vacuum a spring-loaded plunger in the PCV valve is pulled against an opening to form a restriction in the valve. At idle and low speed when manifold vacuum is high very few crankcase vapors are produced and

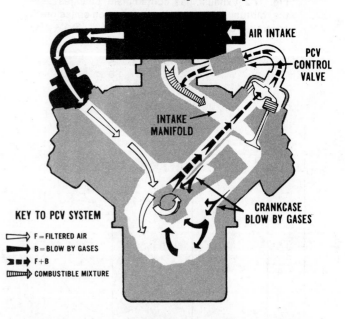

Fig. 17-4 Crankcase emissions are controlled by the positive crankcase ventilation system (GM Research Laboratories, General Motors Corporation).

so a low flow through the PCV valve is sufficient to keep the crankcase clean. High air flow through the PCV system at idle and at low speed would severely lean the air/fuel mixture delivered to the engine, causing poor drivability. The operation of the PCV valve is illustrated in Figure 17–5.

As the throttle is opened engine speed increases, blow-by increases, and the manifold vacuum decreases. With this change in pressure the spring opens the PCV plunger to allow increased crankcase ventilation. With a large volume of air/fuel mixture flowing through the carburetor and manifold at high engine speeds, the increased volume of crankcase vapors allowed to enter the manifold through the PCV valve is insignificant. The PCV valve plunger balances between engine vacuum and spring pressure to provide proper ventilation at all normal speeds and all normal power settings. Full power at low speed may produce more blow-by than the PCV valve can handle. The vapors will then vent through the inlet hose and carburetor.

In operation the PCV valve and hoses may become filled with gummy deposits that restrict their action. It is recommended that they be replaced at regular intervals, such as 12 months or 12,000 miles (19,320 km), to keep the system operating properly. When the PCV system is operating properly it completely controls all emissions from the engine crankcase.

Evaporative Emission Control. The last vehicle emission to be controlled was evaporative loss from the fuel tank and from the carburetor vents. California started controls of evaporative losses in 1970. The controls were extended to apply to the entire United States in 1971. Evaporative losses are the result of the evaporation of highly volatile portions of the gasoline. They are entirely unburned hydrocarbons. These volatile portions of the gasoline provide vapors necessary for starting a cold engine. Their use in gasoline also allows the petroleum refiners to use a large portion of the crude petroleum stock to make gasoline and thus keep the gasoline price as low as possible. Petroleum producers and vehicle manufacturers work together to provide gasoline that will function satisfactorily in the engine at a reasonable cost to the consumer.

Gasoline evaporation is no longer allowed to vent into the atmosphere but the vapors are directed through tubing to a canister filled with activated carbon or charcoal. A typical evaporation control

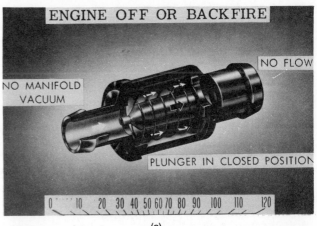

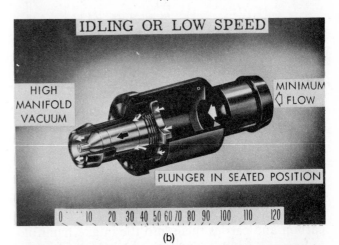

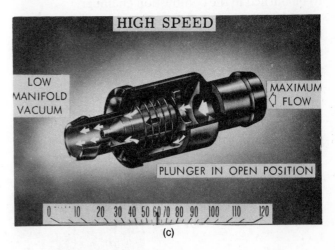

Fig. 17-5 Positive crankcase ventilation valve operation (a) Valve position with plunger closed, (b) valve position with plunger seated, (c) valve position with plunger open (AC Spark Plug Division, General Motors Corporation).

system is shown in Figure 17–6. Vapors given off by the gasoline in the tank and in the carburetor when the engine is not running are piped to the activated-carbon canister where they are absorbed. Two types of canisters are pictured in Figure 17–7.

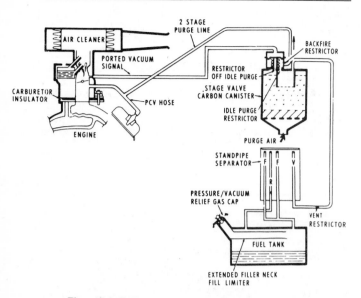

Fig. 17-6 Typical evaporative emission control system (AC Spark Plug Division, General Motors Corporation).

When the engine is restarted fresh air is drawn through the activated carbon. The incoming fresh air purges or removes the vapors from the activated carbon and carries them into the intake manifold to be burned in the combustion chamber.

Many carburetors used on evaporative systems have a vent that opens any time the throttle is fully closed to allow carburetor bowl vapors to flow through tubing to the canister. Some carburetors vent into the air cleaner and have no external vents. The gasoline tank vent system is more complicated. It has baffles that maintain an air space above the gasoline even when the tank is completely filled.

Vents are led from each corner of the tank and from the air space above the gasoline to a *vapor separator*. This arrangement allows the vapors to leave the tank when the vehicle is parked in any position and at the same time retains the liquid gasoline in the tank. The vapor separator is usually a chamber positioned in a body panel, in a rear quarter panel, above the gasoline tank, or in the trunk directly behind the rear seat. One type of vapor separator is shown in Figure 17–7. Vapors go to the top of the separator while the accumulated gasoline liquid is returned to the tank. Vapors from the top of the separator are led through a tube to the carbon canister where they are absorbed. The tank is equipped with a pressure/vacuum fill cap that completely closes the filler opening. Pressure will build up in the tank from the gasoline vapor pressure that is normally produced as the gasoline evaporates. Vacuum may occur at times as the engine draws gasoline from the tank if air is not allowed to enter the tank to take the place of the gasoline withdrawn. All air or vapors entering or leaving the gasoline tank go through the activated carbon canister. The pressure/vacuum valve in the tank filler cap will open if either tank pressure or vacuum becomes excessive.

Exhaust Emission Control. Exhaust emission control is accomplished by carefully controlling the air/fuel mixture being sent to the combustion chamber, by controlling the combustion process, and by eliminating any harmful emission products still remaining in the exhaust gases.

Unburned hydrocarbons and carbon monoxide emissions are most critical at idle and during acceleration and deceleration when the engine runs

Fig. 17-7 Parts of the evaporative emission system. (a) Canisters, (b) separator.

with a rich mixture. Oxides of nitrogen are produced at cruising speeds when the engine runs with lean air/fuel mixtures and high thermal efficiencies that are accompanied by high peak combustion temperatures.

Emission control starts with the carburetor. Emission-control carburetors are very carefully calibrated and adjusted to operate as lean as possible while they still provide each cylinder with a combustible mixture. With mixtures on the lean side of their design range the engine may tend to idle rough and may surge during cruising operation. Careful carburetor adjustment will minimize this tendency.

When the engine is cold it must be partially choked to operate. This provides the engine with a rich air/fuel mixture that produces a large amount of unburned hydrocarbons and carbon monoxide. Emission-controlled engines have their chokes calibrated to open as rapidly as possible and still maintain drivability. This is done by heating the thermostatic choke-spring more rapidly or by using a more sensitive thermostatic choke-spring and vacuum break assembly. Some model engines use an electric heater to open the choke more rapidly than is possible using engine heat alone. Emission products that are produced by the engine will reduce as the choke opens.

Lean air/fuel mixtures ignite more readily if they are preheated. Emission-controlled engines are provided with an intake air preheater similar to the one pictured in Figure 17-8. When the engine is cold, air is drawn through a shield placed around one exhaust manifold. As soon as the engine starts

Fig. 17-8 Parts of an inlet air preheat mechanism (AC Spark Plug Division, General Motors Corporation).

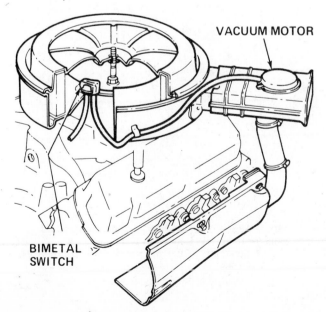

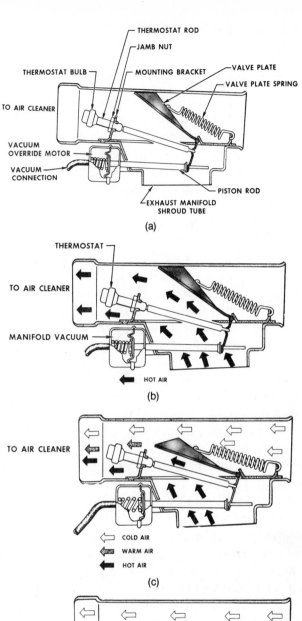

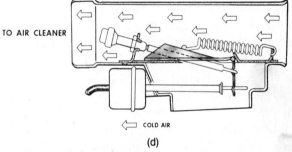

Fig. 17-9 Air preheater with thermostatic pellet control and vacuum override (a) Part identification, (b) warm air supplied to a cold engine, (c) warm–cold air mix supplied to a partly warm engine, (d) cold air supplied to a warm engine (AC Spark Plug Division, General Motors Corporation).

and the manifold becomes warm, manifold heat begins to warm this incoming air. The warmed air is ducted to an air cleaner inlet that is provided with a damper to allow only heated air to enter the engine. Heating continues until the temperature of the incoming air rises over 100°F (38°C). At this temperature the damper in the air cleaner begins to open to mix underhood or outside air with heated air coming from around the exhaust manifold as shown in Figures 17–9 and 17–10. Mixing continues until the incoming air reaches 135°F (57°C) at which time the damper has moved to the position that allows only underhood or outside air to enter the air cleaner. The outside air duct is pictured in Figure 17–11. The air damper may be controlled by a temperature-sensitive plastic pellet balanced against a spring force in a manner similar to a cooling system thermostat. It may also have a vacuum override that tends to increase the flow of heated air during acceleration. An alternate operating method is to use a temperature-sensitive spring to open a vacuum valve which in turn will control a vacuum diaphragm, sometimes called a vacuum motor, to properly position the air-control damper. The most usual cause of damper malfunctioning is cracked or incorrectly attached vacuum hoses.

Many factors affect combustion of the charge once it gets into the combustion chamber. The combustion chamber shape greatly affects the amount of unburned hydrocarbons remaining in the exhaust. The charge that is close to the combustion chamber surface is kept so cool that it does not burn, and these unburned gases form much of the unburned hydrocarbons in the exhaust. The areas of the combustion chamber that quench the charge have been kept to a minimum in emission-control engines. This can be seen in Figure 17–12.

To help burn lean mixtures, the combustion chamber temperature must be high. Increasing the operating temperatures of the cooling system thermostat helps to provide high combustion chamber temperatures. Temperatures are also kept high by restricting distributor vacuum advance that normally occurs on non-emission-controlled engines. High engine temperatures cause more rapid HC oxidation in the combustion chamber to lower the amount of HC remaining in the exhaust. While the engine is idling in traffic, coolant flow through the engine is low because the coolant pump is turned slowly and the fan is driven slowly. This condition may lead to excessive engine temperature. The distributor vacuum advance system is provided with a temperature-operated by-pass valve illustrated in Figure 17–13. At an engine temperature

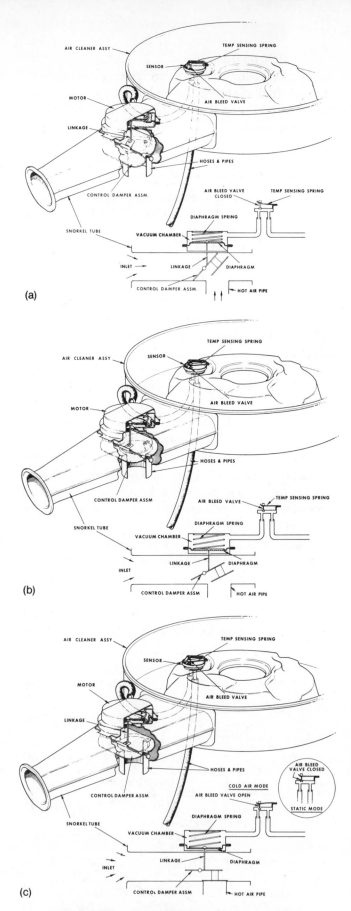

(a)

(b)

(c)

Fig. 17-10 Air preheater with a sensor controlled vacuum motor (a) Supplying warm air to a cold engine, (b) supplying warm–cold air mix to a partly warm engine, (c) supplying cold air to a warm engine (AC Spark Plug Division, General Motors Corporation).

Fig. 17-11 Cold air supplied through a conduit from air outside the automobile.

(a)   (b)

Fig. 17-12 Combustion chamber modified to reduce wall quenching. (a) High quench wedge head, (b) modified low quench head.

of approximately 220°F (104°C) the by-pass opens to provide distributor vacuum advance. This causes the engine to run more efficiently and this in turn increases the engine speed. Higher engine speed increases cooling-pump fan speed to cool the coolant faster and to pass more air across the radiator; this results in a lower engine operating temperature.

Engine emission-control systems using the features just described to clean up the exhaust are given a number of different names by the automobile manufacturers. They have essentially the same operating units and have names such as IMCO (Improved Combustion), CAP (Clean Air Package), CAS (Clean Air System), CCS (Controlled Combustion System), and Engine Modification. The essential parts of these systems are shown in Figure 17–14.

Fig. 17-13 Temperature operated by-pass valve showing internal parts.

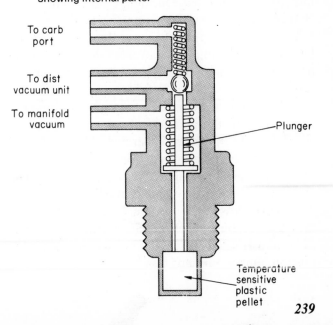

To carb port

To dist vacuum unit

To manifold vacuum

Plunger

Temperature sensitive plastic pellet

239

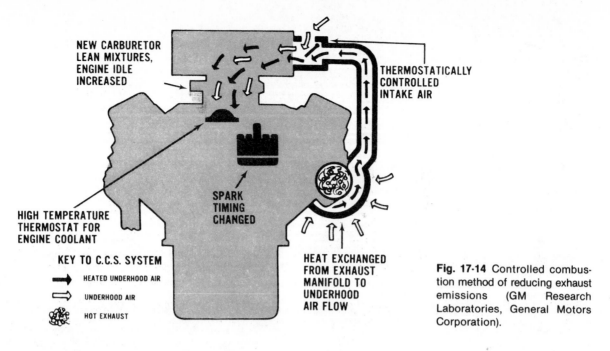

NEW CARBURETOR LEAN MIXTURES, ENGINE IDLE INCREASED

THERMOSTATICALLY CONTROLLED INTAKE AIR

HIGH TEMPERATURE THERMOSTAT FOR ENGINE COOLANT

SPARK TIMING CHANGED

KEY TO C.C.S. SYSTEM

→ HEATED UNDERHOOD AIR

⇨ UNDERHOOD AIR

HOT EXHAUST

HEAT EXCHANGED FROM EXHAUST MANIFOLD TO UNDERHOOD AIR FLOW

Fig. 17-14 Controlled combustion method of reducing exhaust emissions (GM Research Laboratories, General Motors Corporation).

Valve timing has a great effect on combustion. In non-emission-controlled engines the valves were timed to give the engine efficient operation at its design speed. Low speed engines had a short valve opening duration and very little valve overlap. Overlap occurs when both valves are partly open between the exhaust and intake strokes. High speed engines have a long duration and a large valve overlap. Most emission-controlled engines have a short valve opening duration with a large valve overlap. The relatively short valve opening is normal for the low speed automobile engine. The large valve overlap allows some of the exhaust gas to return to the engine with the fresh intake charge. In some cases the exhaust manifold is restricted to increase back pressure. This dilutes the charge with the inert exhaust gas to minimize the amount of mixture used, thereby reducing the peak combustion charge temperature. Lowering the peak combustion temperature results in a reduction of NO_x. Unfortunately, long valve overlap does contribute to a rough engine idle and poor low speed operation.

A second, more positive means of diluting the charge is with the addition of an exhaust gas recirculation (EGR) system illustrated in Figure 17–15. The system recirculates a portion of the exhaust gas back through the engine intake manifold. The exhaust gas takes up volume and will not burn. This leaves less space for the fresh charge to get into the combustion chamber. A smaller amount of combustible charge results in a lower peak combustion temperature and less NO_x production. The

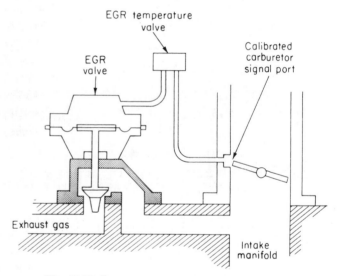

EGR temperature valve

EGR valve

Calibrated carburetor signal port

Exhaust gas

Intake manifold

Fig. 17-15 Operating principle of the exhaust gas recirculation valve.

intake manifold exhaust crossover is a convenient place to interconnect the intake and exhaust systems. The EGR system in some engines consists of metered holes between the exhaust crossover and the intake manifold floor. Most EGR systems are equipped with a recirculating valve which limits exhaust gas recirculation so that it only occurs when the engine operating conditions tend to promote the formation of NO_x. These conditions are light acceleration and cruising speeds when the air/fuel mixture is lean. The exhaust gas recirculating valve is closed at idle and at low speeds, and gradually opens as the throttle is opened and manifold air velocity increases. It closes again at full throttle. The EGR valve is shown in Figure 17–16.

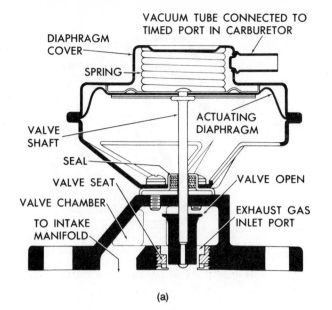

DIAPHRAGM COVER

VACUUM TUBE CONNECTED TO TIMED PORT IN CARBURETOR

SPRING

VALVE SHAFT

SEAL

VALVE SEAT

VALVE CHAMBER

TO INTAKE MANIFOLD

ACTUATING DIAPHRAGM

VALVE OPEN

EXHAUST GAS INLET PORT

(a)

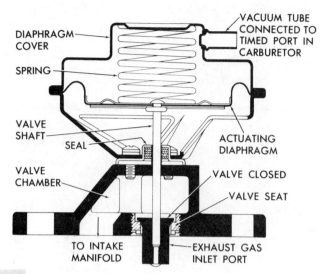

DIAPHRAGM COVER

SPRING

VALVE SHAFT

SEAL

VALVE CHAMBER

TO INTAKE MANIFOLD

VACUUM TUBE CONNECTED TO TIMED PORT IN CARBURETOR

ACTUATING DIAPHRAGM

VALVE CLOSED

VALVE SEAT

EXHAUST GAS INLET PORT

(b)

(c)

Fig. 17-16 Parts of the exhaust gas recirculation system. (a) EGR open, (b) EGR closed, (c) back pressure modulated EGR (Cadillac Motor Car Division, General Motors Corporation).

Fig. 17-17 Speed sensor to limit emission control operation.

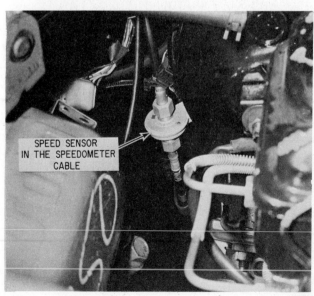

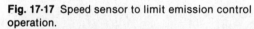

SPEED SENSOR IN THE SPEEDOMETER CABLE

The EGR system may also be equipped with a valve that blocks EGR operation at low engine temperatures and low vehicle speeds. This is accomplished by a speed sensing unit in the speedometer cable and a temperature sensing unit in the engine cooling system. Some EGR valves are modulated by a backpressure transducer that senses pressure in the exhaust manifold. The EGR is turned off at full throttle. EGR valve controls are shown in Figures 17–17 and 17–18.

After the exhaust gas leaves the combustion chamber it can be cleaned up using several different methods. The first method used was to pump fresh air into the exhaust manifold. This system is shown in Figure 17–19. The fresh air supplied

Fig. 17-18 Temperature controls to limit emission control operation.

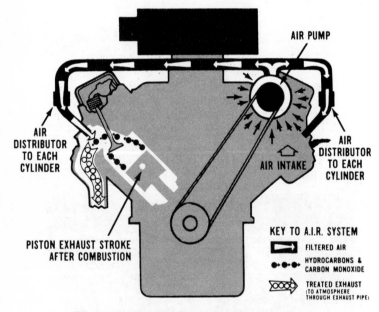

Fig. 17-19 System used to pump fresh air into the hot exhaust gases (GM Research Laboratories, General Motors Corporation).

KEY TO A.I.R. SYSTEM

FILTERED AIR

HYDROCARBONS & CARBON MONOXIDE

TREATED EXHAUST (TO ATMOSPHERE THROUGH EXHAUST PIPE)

The vane is travelling from a small area into a larger area—consequently a vacuum is formed that draws fresh air into the pump.

As the vane continues to rotate, the other vane has rotated past the inlet opening. Now the air that has just been drawn in is entrapped between the vanes. This entrapped air is then transferred into a smaller area and thus compressed.

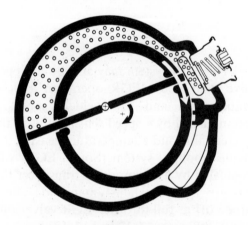

As the vane continues to rotate it passes the outlet cavity in the pump housing bore and exhausts the compressed air into the remainder of the system.

Fig. 17-20 Operation of the air pump (Chevrolet Motor Division, General Motors Corporation).

additional oxygen that helped burn the HC and CO still remaining in the exhaust gases. This method does not affect engine efficiency, except for the small amount of power required to operate the air injection pump.

The vane-type air injection pump, illustrated in Figure 17-20, belt driven from the crankshaft, takes air in through a filter and pumps it through a diverter valve, check valve, and injection tubes placed in the cylinder-head exhaust port or exhaust manifold. A *check valve* prevents back flow if exhaust pressure momentarily exceeds the air pump pressure. The *diverter valve* (Figure 17-21) will bypass pump-air to the atmosphere or to the intake manifold when the throttle is quickly closed.

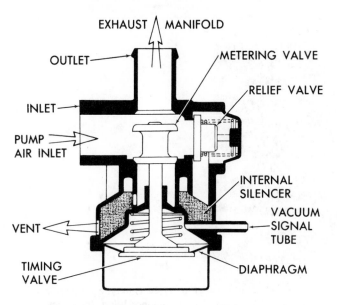

Fig. 17-21 Diverter valve operation (Cadillac Motor Car Division, General Motors Corporation).

Quick throttle closure creates a high intake manifold vacuum that will draw a rich fuel mixture from the carburetor. This is too rich to ignite in the combustion chamber so it goes out the exhaust valve into the exhaust manifold. If fresh pump-air were forced into these rich exhaust gases the mixture would lean sufficiently to ignite when the next cylinder released hot exhaust gases into the exhaust system. This would result in an explosion in the exhaust system that could rip the muffler open. The diverter valve is therefore sometimes called a *backfire valve*.

The air pump emission-control systems have a number of different names depending on the manufacturer. They are called AG (Air Guard), AIR (Air Injection Reactor), Thermactor, and Air Injection System. All operate in a similar manner

and several use identical parts. Figure 17-22 is a schematic drawing of this system.

The air pump system is usually used with other exhaust emission-control devices to reduce exhaust emission products to acceptable levels.

Exhaust gas that cannot meet the federal standards using the above systems requires further modification. A thermal reactor (Figure 17-23) can be installed in place of the exhaust manifold. It is an enclosed insulated series of chambers that maintains high exhaust gas temperatures for a longer period of time than is available during the power stroke. This gives time to more completely oxidize HC and CO products remaining in the

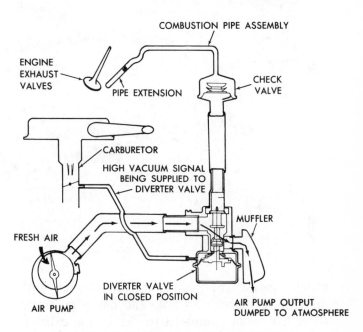

Fig. 17-22 Details of the air injection system (AC Spark Plug Division, General Motors Corporation).

Fig. 17-23 Principles of a thermal reactor.

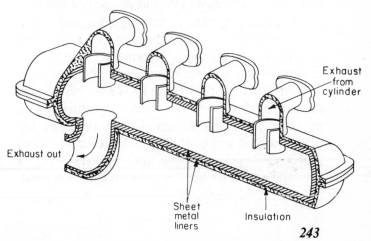

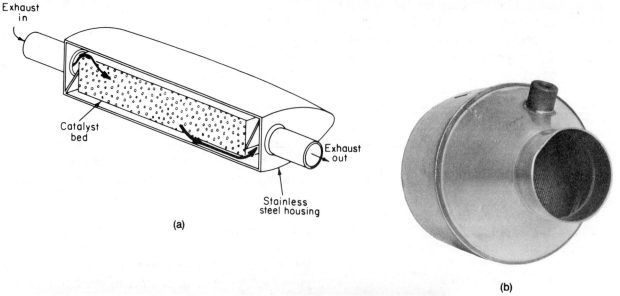

(a)

(b)

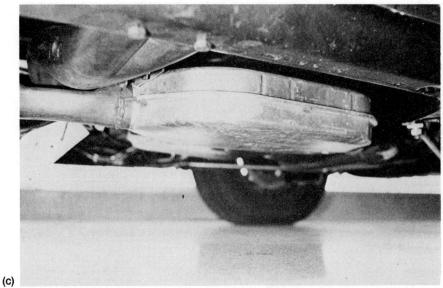

(c)

Fig. 17-24 Catalytic converter.
(a) Pellet bed type, (b) honeycomb, (c) typical instillation.

exhaust gases. The thermal reactor takes a lot of underhood space, runs hot, and has a relatively short life when compared to the simple exhaust manifold.

A more common device is a catalytic converter (Figure 17-24) made of a bed of catalyst pellets or of a honeycomb grid of catalyst installed in the exhaust system of late model automobiles. As the exhaust gas passes through the catalyst bed or grid, the remaining objectionable exhaust contaminants are consumed at a much lower temperature than in the thermal reactor, because of the action of the catalyst. An air injection system provides additional air that is required. The life of the catalyst will be shortened by contamination, especially lead contamination. Vehicles using a catalytic converter must be run on lead-free gasoline for the maximum life of the catalyst.

17-3 MEASUREMENT OF EMISSIONS

A major problem in the control of vehicle emission is the measurement of these emissions. It is a time-consuming process that involves expensive laboratory equipment. Basic gas analysis is done using a chemical absorption process. In this process, a sample of a mixture of gases is run through a series of chemicals, one at a time. Each chemical absorbs one of the gases from the exhaust sample, which reduces the sample volume. The gas component removed is reported as a percentage of the entire sample.

Obtaining a good sample for chemical absorption is an associated problem. Exhaust samples may be trapped in a plastic bag and transferred to the laboratory for analysis. Evaporative vehicle emissions are taken from a sealed room or shed in which a vehicle has been placed. During a soak period, the vehicle and the room are kept at a specified temperature for a standard period of time prior to taking the evaporative emission sample.

A faster means of determining the exhaust emission is through the use of a nondispersive infrared analyzer (NDIR). This method has become an industry standard for measuring emissions. It is calibrated with specially prepared standard gas samples. The standard gas sample quality is checked by chemical absorption.

The infrared analyzer passes a pulsating infrared beam through each of two tubes or cells. The reference cell is filled with a nonabsorbing reference gas. The gas sample to be analyzed flows through the sample cell. Gases in the sample cell will absorb some of the energy of the infrared beam. After passing through the gases, each of the infrared beams hits a chamber adjacent to a balanced diaphragm detector. Both sides of the

detector are filled with the gas type being examined. The amount of energy remaining in each beam increases the pressure in its side of the detector diaphragm. Unequal energy passing through the reference and sample gases will cause a difference in pressure in the detector chambers that deflects the diaphragm. Diaphragm deflection is proportional to the concentration of the gas sample being analyzed.

A separate analyzer is required for each gas component. Exhaust emissions are checked at the customer service level with nondispersive infrared analyzers for hydrocarbons (usually normal hexane) and carbon monoxide. Exhaust gas analyzers are shown in Figure 17–25.

Hydrocarbon emissions are a combination of

Fig. 17-25 Sensor used in an infrared tester. (a) Assembled unit, (b) principles (Beck Instruments Incorporated), (c) FID sensing unit (Beckman Instrument Incorporated).

(a)

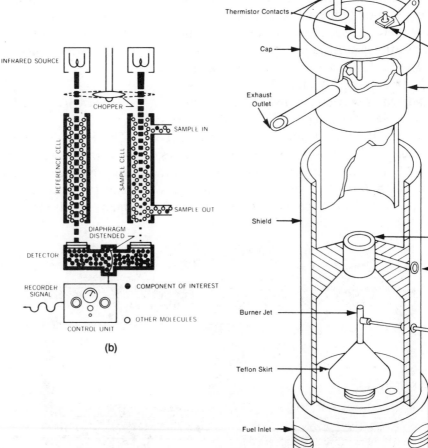

(b)

(c)

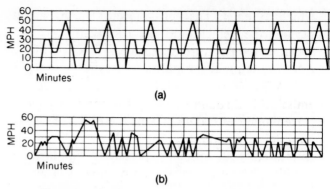

Fig. 17-26 Emission test cycles. (a) California cycle, (b) mass cycle.

a number of different hydrocarbon gases. In early tests, automobile manufacturers measured only for hexane, using a nondispersive infrared analyzer. This was inadequate for mass sampling. A flame ionization detector (FID) will indicate the amount of all unburned hydrocarbons in the exhaust sample quickly and accurately.

The heart of the FID tester is a hydrogen burner that produces a negligible number of ions. An ion is an atom with excess or missing electrons that makes the atom have an electrical charge. Introducing a sample of the exhaust gas containing unburned hydrocarbons produces a large number of ions proportional to the amount of hydrocarbon. A voltage difference between the burner jet and collector ring attracts the ions and thus produces a small current. The current is proportional to the number of ions produced. Electronic equipment amplifies the current flow signal and displays the results on a meter.

Exhaust-emissions testing to meet federal standards requires the use of a $14,000 dynamometer and a minimum $25,000 instrument console in a room that has adequate ventilation and exhaust. These are usually backed up with a $75,000 computer. The California cycle sequence based on selected vehicle speeds under 30 mph is run seven times and requires approximately fifteen minutes. The mass cycle, consisting of a nonrepetitive series of idle, acceleration to 50 mph, cruise, and deceleration modes, takes nearly twenty-three minutes after a 12-hour soak period at room temperature. Exhaust-emission analysis of this type is very expensive and is limited to vehicle development work

and to quality control checks. It is not done as a part of tune-up procedure. A number of service-level instruments that measure hydrocarbons and carbon monoxide are available to help the technician do emission-control maintenance. Exhaust emission test cycles are shown in Figure 17–26.

No federal standards have been set for HC or CO emissions at the customer service level. Several states have passed laws and cities have passed ordinances regulating maximum allowable exhaust emissions as measured with automotive service-type test equipment. These laws are not uniform but they are quite liberal so that any automobile having reasonable maintenance will pass. The maximum limits of the test will pick out vehicles that produce an abnormal amount of polluting emissions.

17-4 EXHAUST EMISSION TESTING

The HC-CO tester, illustrated in Figure 17–27, is one of the newest service instruments available to the technician. It was designed for checking exhaust emissions of automobiles in service, but many additional uses have been found that make it

Fig. 17-27 An infrared tester used to measure hydrocarbons and carbon monoxide exhaust emissions.

a useful, versatile tester for diagnosing engine problems.

The probe of the HC-CO tester is inserted in the exhaust pipe to sample the exhaust emissions. The amount of carbon monoxide in the exhaust is directly related to the air/fuel mixture delivered to the engine by the carburetor and manifold. Hydrocarbons in the exhaust are directly related to unburned or partly burned fuel. An emission-controlled automobile running normally will have HC emissions below 100 ppm (parts per million) and CO emissions between 0.5 and 1.0%. Non-emission-controlled engines will have higher normal emission levels of about 400 ppm HC and 3.0% CO. HC-CO tester readings above these ranges usually indicate some depreciation in the engine emission-control system or a fault in either the mechanical or electrical portion of the engine. The other exhaust pollutant, NO_X, is not measured at the service garage level. Almost no NO_X is produced by the engine running with no load. Most service organizations do not have dynamometers for loading the engine and so they would have no means to test the engine for NO_X emissions. In addition, state and local regulations do not specify NO_X standards. The most a service technician can do to maintain a low NO_X level is to make sure that all of the emission-control devices are functioning properly.

Federal emission standards that apply to the automobile manufacturer have been set by the national government. Standards that must be followed by the consumer and technician are set by state and local governments. These standards differ from each other. If engine emissions are less than the following maximum levels, they will pass any of the state and local standards that applied at the time of this writing.

Model Year	HC Maximum	CO Maximum
----65	1000 ppm	6.0%
66—69	400 ppm	4.0%
70—74	300 ppm	3.0%
75----	250 ppm	1.5%

It can be seen when comparing these maximums with the normal HC and CO levels previously discussed that any automobile operating correctly will fall below these maximum standards.

Tests for HC and CO are run at idle and higher speeds. Some test equipment manufacturers give specific test speeds while others are more indefinite. Emission levels should not increase when speeds are held above idle. Generally they will decrease at higher engine speeds. Any increase in emission at higher speeds indicates that a problem exists.

If the exhaust emissions are normal no further checking of the emission controls is necessary. A problem exists when either HC or CO or both exceed the limits.

Hydrocarbons in the exhaust may become very low but they never reach zero because some combustion chamber surface quenching always exists. The amount of hydrocarbons in the exhaust gas increases when the combustion charge does not completely burn. This can happen when the cylinder does not fire or when there is only partial combustion. It can also happen when the mixture is so rich that there is more fuel than oxygen available for combustion. In any case high HC emission indicates a waste of power-producing fuel.

Carbon monoxide in the exhaust is high when there is a rich mixture. The level of carbon monoxide lowers as the mixture is leaned. When the mixture becomes too lean, as indicated by a very low CO reading, the charge will not sustain combustion and so high levels of hydrocarbons are exhausted. The emission-control carburetor is designed to run at the leanest point possible to keep HC at its lowest level. In most emission-controlled engines this occurs when the CO in the exhaust is about 0.75% and the HC is near 100 ppm.

By interrelating the amount of HC and CO in the exhaust with readings obtained with other tune-up test equipment, and with his knowledge of how the systems operate, the technician can rapidly diagnose and correct engine problems. If the CO level is normal and the HC level is high, the problem is either electrical or mechanical. An engine scope can be used to quickly verify the condition of the ignition system (except timing). If the ignition system is normal the high HC with normal CO indicates mechanical problems. These problems can be caused by items like improperly operating valves, low compression, incorrect timing, faulty air injector system, and unequal fuel distribution in the intake manifold. The air injection pump should be made inoperative when checking engine problems.

A check to see which cylinder is at fault can be done by shorting out one cylinder at a time. A normally operating cylinder that is shorted will cause the HC meter to swing to the high side. A faulty cylinder that is shorted will cause only a slight increase in HC level. Cylinder shorting should be avoided on engines equipped with a catalytic converter. If it becomes necessary, shorting should be done only long enough to get the required instrument reading. Cylinder shorting allows excessive unburned hydrocarbons to reach the converter where they will burn. This produces excess heat that can ruin the catalyst.

If the HC level is high with CO abnormally low the problem is the result of a very lean fuel mixture. This can be verified by holding a shop cloth over the carburetor intake to partially restrict the air flow when the engine is running at approximately 2000 rpm. If the engine is running too lean the engine will increase its speed, the CO level will come up, and the HC level will go down. Lean mixtures can be corrected by rechecking and resetting all carburetor adjustments, especially the float level and the idle mixture screws. Intake manifold leaks can also cause the lean mixture. They can usually be found by putting oil around the manifold joints or by removing vacuum hoses to identify the system in which the air leak occurs while using the HC-CO tester. Extended operation at very lean mixtures leads to valve burning.

High CO is always accompanied by a high HC level. This results from a rich mixture being delivered to the engine. The rich mixture may be caused by a dirty carburetor air filter, stuck choke, faulty PCV system operation, inoperative heat riser valve, or a carburetor that needs service. Each of these items, except the carburetor, can be removed from operation or bypassed to see how the change affects the emissions. The faulty item can be serviced or replaced. If none of these corrects the problem, the carburetor will have to be serviced.

The HC-CO tester can be used for a number of other auxiliary tests. While running the exhaust-emission test, remove the PCV valve from the engine. If the valve has been functioning properly the CO level will become lower than when the valve was installed. If the technician places a thumb over the valve, this will stop air flow through the PCV system and cause a higher level of CO than when the valve was installed in the engine. If this does not occur, the valve or hoses are faulty and should be replaced.

Rapid throttle opening will produce an increase in CO and HC as the accelerating pump operates. If the CO drops slightly before increasing, there is a delay in accelerator pump operation. The pump should be adjusted or repaired as required.

The carburetor power valve operation can be checked with the HC-CO tester. To make this test, disconnect the accelerator pump linkage and adjust the idle speed to approximately 1000 rpm. After noting the CO level, snap open the accelerator to a specific manifold vacuum starting at 12 in. Hg (30 cm). Then allow the engine to return to the 1000 rpm setting. Repeat this by snapping the throttle to obtain 10 in., 8 in., 6 in., and 4 in. Hg (25 cm, 20 cm, 15 cm, and 10 cm) vacuum readings while observing the CO meter each time. When the power system operating vacuum is reached, there will be a noticeable increase in CO. If this does not occur the power valve in the carburetor is malfunctioning and should be serviced.

All of the preceding tests are run with the HC-CO tester probe in the exhaust pipe. The probe can be used to check for unburned hydrocarbons at other locations. If the probe is passed slowly below the fuel line, any gasoline leakage will be indicated by an increase in HC. If the probe is held over the radiator fill opening (not touching the coolant) any leakage of combustion gases into the coolant will show as an increase in HC. A thinking technician will develop other uses for this versatile test instrument.

REVIEW QUESTIONS

1. What method is used to lower the carbon monoxide level in the engine exhaust? [17–1]

2. What engine operating conditions produce the most carbon monoxide? [17–1]

3. What causes most of the unburned hydrocarbons in the exhaust? [17–1]

4. What increases the production of oxides of nitrogen in the combustion chamber? [17–1]

5. What makes up crankcase vapors? [17–2]

6. Does the PCV system reduce the engine power or efficiency? [17–2]

7. Does the evaporative control system reduce the engine power or efficiency? [17–2]

8. During what operating conditions are oxides of nitrogen produced? [17–2]

9. During what operating conditions are unburned hydrocarbons and carbon monoxide exhaust emissions most critical? [17–2]

10. How does carburetor calibration help minimize emissions? [17–2]

11. What device helps drivability of a cold engine? [17–2]

12. How does temperature affect ignition of lean air/ fuel mixtures? [17–2]

13. What two methods are used to dilute the inlet charge with an inert gas? [17–2]

14. What was the first device used to clean the exhaust after it leaves the combustion chamber? [17–2]

15. What is the purpose of the catalytic converter? [17–2]

automotive engine testing

Only three things are needed for an engine to run: compression, fuel, and ignition occurring at the right time in the cycle. This is basic and must be the underlying consideration in all engine troubleshooting problems. Proper engine operation goes a step further; the engine must have sufficient compression and must have the correct air/fuel mixture charge continually being delivered to the combustion chambers. A tune-up essentially involves preventive maintenance operations, exact carburetor adjustments, and correct ignition timing for all operating conditions.

Compression is developed as the piston squeezes the charge on the compression stroke of the engine cycle. The amount of compression pressure developed in the combustion chamber depends upon a full intake charge and minimum leakage as the charge is compressed. The intake and exhaust valve timing must be correct in relation to the engine cycle in order to pull a full charge into the cylinder. The valves are required to seal tightly, the piston rings must seal the small space between the pistons and the cylinder wall, and the gaskets must be tight to prevent leakage during compression.

The engine needs fuel to start. Most readers who have had some experience with trying to start a balky engine have poured a small quantity of raw gasoline down the carburetor barrel. The vapors from the gasoline mix with the incoming air to produce a combustible mixture, even if there is no fuel in the carburetor. The function of the carburetor is to supply the correct air/fuel mixture for continued running after the engine first starts.

Ignition is more critical than either compression or carburetion for engine starting. The ignition must be intense enough to jump the spark plug gap and it must occur in the engine cycle just as the piston approaches top center on the *compression stroke*. This allows the charge to push the piston down as it burns and builds up pressure. Ignition timing has to be changed for efficient engine operation and to maintain low exhaust emissions as the engine speed changes and as the engine produces power to move the vehicle.

18-1 TUNE-UP REQUIREMENTS

The routine minor tune-up is usually done to restore engine economy and performance after a number of miles of operation. A minor tune-up can be done using common hand tools and a limited amount of test equipment. The minor tune-up is the type of tune-up usually done by service stations and by individuals who maintain their own automobiles. When a minor tune-up does not correct a problem, more extensive use of test equipment will be required to pinpoint the cause of a problem. Most problems can be found during a major tune-up or by specialized tests made on the specific system that is malfunctioning.

An engine tune-up is a procedure performed on an engine to make it develop its best performance while it produces the lowest emissions possible. It is usually run at periodic intervals when engine performance has deteriorated or when the operator wants to be sure that he will have dependable service on a trip or in winter weather. A tune-up may also be run as a troubleshooting sequence when there is some abnormal engine condition.

The minor tune-up consists of a visual inspection, routine mechanical service, and instrument tests. The visual inspection includes checking the engine mounting and attachments for abnormal conditions, such as checking the condition of all wires, hoses, belts, and carburetor linkages. The engine should be examined for coolant, fuel, oil, and exhaust leaks. Any defects that could affect engine operation or vehicle safety should be repaired. This might include mechanical service such as freeing the heat riser, retorquing bolts, and adjusting belts. Mechanical service also includes servicing the spark plugs and ignition points. It usually includes cleaning or replacing air and fuel filters and making sure that the vehicle has an adequate supply of oil, coolant, and brake fluid. Instrument checks include engine basic timing,

operation of timing advance mechanisms, and setting engine idle. The minor tune-up might also include the cylinder balance test and a check of the emission-control component operation.

Mechanical Condition. A tune-up cannot produce satisfactory engine operation if the combustion chamber doesn't hold compression. Most tune-up technicians follow a battery check by removing the spark plugs and checking each combustion chamber for its ability to compress the gases. This can be done by two methods: a compression test or a cylinder leakage test.

A *compression test* is run with the throttle blocked wide open and all the spark plugs removed. A compression gauge, similar to the one shown in Figure 18–1, is installed in the spark plug holes, one cylinder at a time. The engine is cranked through the same number of compressions on each cylinder so cylinder pressures can be compared.

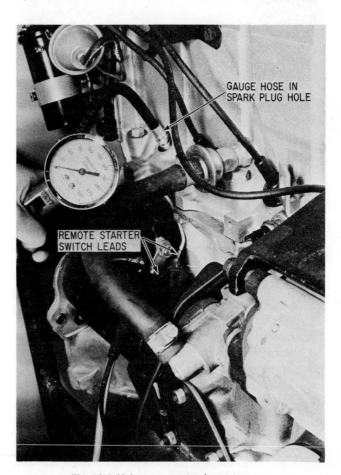

Fig. 18-1 Using a compression gauge.

Pressure in all cylinders should be within 10% of each other for standard operation. Compression pressure developed in this test is dependent upon cranking speed, and the amount and condition of lubricant on the cylinder wall. If this test shows excessive compression variation, a small quantity of oil is squirted into each cylinder through the spark plug opening and the engine cranked several revolutions. This oil will seal piston ring leakage. The compression test is again run. It is now called a *wet compression test*. Normal and nearly equal compression on all cylinders on this second test indicates leaking piston rings. If low or unequal compression still exists, it indicates valve leakage.

A *cylinder leakage test* is another method that can be used to determine combustion chamber sealing. The cylinder is turned to top center, and

controlled air pressure is forced into the cylinder through a regulator. Pressure drop on the instrument shown in Figure 18–2 indicates cylinder leakage. Normal leakage may be up to 10%. When excessive leakage does exist, the exact source can be determined by listening through the carburetor for intake valve leakage, through the oil fill opening for piston ring leakage, and through the tail pipe for exhaust valve leakage.

If satisfactory combustion chamber sealing exists, it is worthwhile to proceed with the rest of the tune-up. Spark plug service is an obvious next step because the spark plugs are out of the engine for the compression test. They should be serviced or replaced with the correct spark plug. Spark plug service was described in Chapter 16. It is the usual practice on each periodic tune-up to change the breaker points and condenser without testing them. The condenser rarely causes trouble and seldom needs to be replaced but the customer has had both points and condenser changed on tune-ups over the years so he usually expects to have a new condenser installed as part of the periodic tune-up. Breaker points do wear. Their contact surface becomes pitted and the rubbing block wears. In breakerless electronic ignition systems this step is not required when doing a tune-up.

Breaker points are provided as an assembly set. Sometimes a cam lubricant is packaged with them so the cam will receive the correct type of lubricant (Figure 18–3). Some part suppliers selling to do-it-yourself consumers put all of the normally replaced ignition components in a single package. These would include points, condenser, spark plugs, rotor, and sometimes a distributor cap. A description of the procedures used to replace points and condensers is given in Chapter 16.

Carburetor service is one of the mechanical checks done during a *major* tune-up. The carburetor is disassembled, cleaned, and reassembled using new parts from a repair kit. Carburetor repair kits are available from a simple gasket set to a complete rebuilding kit that includes almost all new jetting and calibrating components. The most popular carburetor repair kits used for tune-up have new gaskets, an inlet float valve, an acceleration pump, check valves, and assembly clips. The carburetor choke should be checked while the carburetor is cold to see that it is fully closed and that the linkages operate freely before the engine is started. After the carburetor is serviced the engine can be started and the timing set.

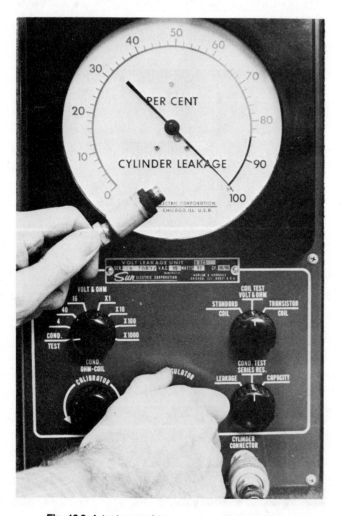

Fig. 18-2 A tester used to measure cylinder leakage.

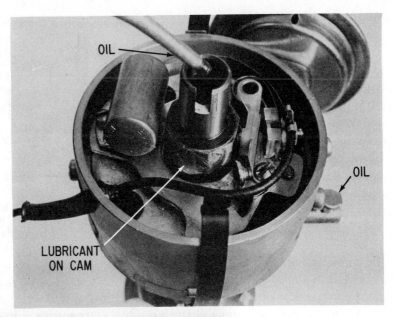

OIL

OIL

LUBRICANT
ON CAM

Fig. 18-3 Lubricating points on a distributor.

Fig. 18-4 Setting the basic ignition timing.

Tune-Up Test Sequence. Several tests are run before the engine is started. In addition to the battery check, the breaker point resistance, the cranking voltage, cranking vacuum, and cranking coil output may be checked. Instruments are attached, the engine is started and run at idle while dwell, idle speed, and basic engine timing are checked.

When using a timing light, connect the pick-up cable to number one ignition cable and connect the light to its proper power source, either the vehicle battery or the shop 110-volt line. It is critical on most emission-controlled engines to attach this timing light pickup to number one spark plug cable even if it is not as accessible as one of the other spark plugs. Set the parking brake and place the transmission in neutral, then start the engine. Let it run slowly at curb idle with the vacuum line to the distributor removed and plugged so air does not go into the carburetor. With the timing light aimed at the timing marks, and the hold-down clamp slightly loose, adjust the distributor until ignition occurs at the specified degree as pictured in Figure 18-4. Tighten the hold-down clamp and recheck the timing. Readjust the timing as necessary, then reconnect the distributor vacuum line.

Two modern instruments are used to make overall operating system tests. The ignition scope shows voltage being developed in the ignition system and the hydrocarbon-carbon monoxide (HC-CO) tester shows the relative amount of these gases being produced by the engine. When the technician learns to recognize scope patterns and HC-CO values, a quick but detailed look at the patterns and instrument readings as the engine speeds are changed will give an overall indication of engine operation. Properly using these testers, the technician can show that the entire system is functioning well, or he can pinpoint the cause of a problem.

Required voltage is considered to be the voltage reached by the top of the spike on a scope pattern. The engine will run as long as the ignition system has more voltage available than that required by the engine. The ignition system available voltage can be measured on the scope by setting the scope pattern dwell line on the zero volt line and then removing one of the spark plug cables to force a voltage increase on that cable, causing the ignition system to develop full voltage. For normal operation the ignition system should be able to produce more than 20,000 volts available to fire the spark plug. High-energy systems produce over 30,000 volts.

The HC-CO tester, described in Chapter 17, is a useful tool for checking the overall operation of the engine. The amount of carbon monoxide coming from the exhaust pipe is affected by the carburetor operation; high carbon monoxide results from rich mixtures and low carbon monoxide from lean mixtures. When the engine is operating normally it will produce low hydrocarbon emissions. Whenever combustion is not complete, the hydrocarbons in the exhaust will be excessive. High hydrocarbon readings result from rich or excessively lean mixtures, and from engine misfiring. It also is high if the ignition timing is not correct. This could be the result of an inoperative emission-control unit. In general terms, the engine idle should be adjusted to operate with the lowest hydrocarbon reading possible, and this requires lean carburetor mixtures. Emissions should decrease as the engine speed is increased above idle.

The engine is brought up to a specified test speed, between 1500 and 2000 rpm (see equipment manufacturer's specifications for the specific test speed). The engine scope will indicate coil polarity,

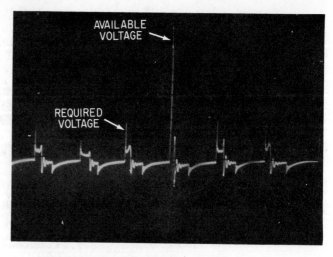

Fig. 18-5 Secondary leakage indicated by the tail missing from the available voltage spike.

required voltage, available voltage, breaker point action, ignition system leakage (shown as the tail missing on the available voltage spike in Figure 18-5), and ignition system resistance. The HC-CO tester will indicate the engine operating condition. Interpretation of these readings will direct the technician to problems that exist in the engine systems.

The engine is returned to idle to check idle speed, manifold vacuum, and HC-CO if the tester is used. Quick accelerations from idle will put a load on the spark plugs and the engine scope will indicate if the spark plugs are firing normally. The HC-CO tester will indicate momentary high readings as the acceleration pump operates.

The instrument test may precede or follow standard tune-up service operations, such as distributor service, carburetion service, air and fuel filter service, and valve lash adjustment on solid lifter engines. Tests may show that additional tests or adjustments are necessary. These would include battery circuit voltage drop, starter amperage draw, generator output, charging circuit voltage drop, regulator setting, ignition primary circuit voltage drop, fuel pump tests, carburetor rebuilding, and cooling system tests of the filler cap and thermostat.

The tune-up sequence may be used before or after routine service. Running the tune-up test sequence before performing routine service will point to items that require special service. This limits the servicing time to those items actually needing service. Running a tune-up test sequence after servicing insures satisfactory workmanship and customer satisfaction.

Tune-up test sequences differ for each make of test equipment. Each manufacturer provides a test sequence to be used with his equipment, and will usually supply specifications. Automotive shop manuals also show tune-up test sequences. These are often keyed to one type of test equipment, either commercial types or a type manufactured especially for the vehicle manufacturer.

Basically, all shop test equipment is a special application of voltmeters, oscilloscopes, ohmmeters, tachometers, dwell meters, vacuum gauges, and exhaust gas analyzers. Individual test units are packaged in cases and cabinets with interconnecting switches, shunts, rheostats, and electronic controls so that many tests can be made with few engine connections. The greatest difference in test procedures results from the different methods used to interconnect the basic test instruments. It is important to follow the procedures provided with the test equipment being used to get meaningful results.

18-2 SERVICE REQUIREMENTS

Customers require service for routine maintenance, when they have a problem, or when appearance, comfort, and performance items are needed. Tune-ups are usually classed as a routine maintenance procedure in which the preceding items are checked, tested, and serviced. Some engine problems may also be corrected by routine tune-up procedures. In this case, it would be advisable to pre-test the engine to identify the problem so that it can be definitely corrected.

Engine problems may be classified as problems that affect engine operation, such as loss of power, rough running, overheating, excessive fuel consumption; or as problems indicated by improper vehicle instrument readings. These problems are usually identified by the tune-up sequence procedure. Problems may involve leaks from the oil, fuel, or coolant systems. These are usually located visually and repaired by replacing gaskets or seals. Broken parts are located visually and repaired or replaced. Squeaking belts, seals, or bearings are located by sound and sight. Some excessive emissions may be seen or smelled. These can be corrected by repairing the engine if it is causing these excess emissions.

Appearance and performance items are routine in nature, often requiring installation of a parts kit. These items, in turn, become problems if they do not operate correctly or if they do not satisfy the customer.

18-3 TROUBLESHOOTING

Troubleshooting a customer's problem requires an understanding of how the parts of a vehicle operate, how they should normally appear, and how to use proper test equipment and procedures. The greatest difficulty in troubleshooting is identifying the specific cause of the problem. After it has been identified, any qualified mechanic can repair it.

Troubleshooting charts are often presented to help identify the cause of problems. The best of these charts are presented in the shop manuals for each vehicle. They are more specific than a general troubleshooting chart that is designed to apply to any vehicle. In addition, most manufacturers publish service bulletins for their service technicians. These bulletins point out problems which frequently occur in their product line and give details on correction procedures. Keeping up-to-date on service bulletins is one of the best methods for a dealer mechanic to make quick problem diagnoses and repairs to automobiles in the product line.

An important point in troubleshooting that is frequently overlooked by the service writer or mechanic is that he does not carefully listen to the customer's complaint. The customer's description, aided by a few leading questions, will be of great help in identifying the customer's problem. Once the problem is identified, tests and inspections can be made to determine the cause of the complaint. When the cause is identified, it can be easily corrected and rechecked.

18-4 DYNAMOMETERS

An engine must function correctly while it moves an automobile. This requires a greater load on the engine than the loads that are applied while the engine is running in neutral gear. An engine or drive wheels may be connected to a dynamometer which can control and measure a simulated road load on the engine.

Dynamometers have begun to find their place as useful tools for diagnosis and testing in the customer service market, especially in test lanes and for testing emissions.

Dynamometers are used in testing many rotating components, especially the engine, its accessories, and the chassis drive line. Many people have the misconception that a dynamometer does all the testing. In reality, a dynamometer can put a controlled load on the operating system and can measure that load. Other test equipment, such as temperature indicators, pressure indicators, accelerometers, exhaust-gas analyzers, etc., are installed on the unit being tested to give readout information while the unit is operating on the dynamometer.

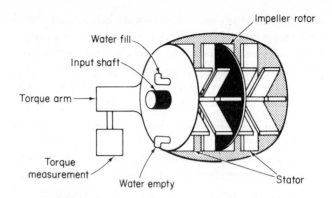

Fig. 18-7 Cutaway drawing of a water-brake dynamometer.

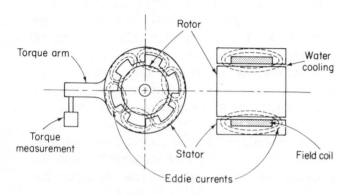

Fig. 18-6 Drawing of an eddy-current dynamometer.

Dynamometers can be made in a great many ways. The most common types are electric dynamometers and water-brake dynamometers. Sometimes, friction brakes and fans are used to absorb known loads and are, therefore, used as dynamometers.

Two types of absorption dynamometers are used as diagnostic tools for chassis dynamometer applications; the eddy-current absorption unit and the water-brake absorption unit. The eddy-current dynamometer (Figure 18–6) is designed so that eddy currents will develop within the dynamometer metal as the dynamometer field current is increased. Eddy currents resist rotation, absorb power, and convert the power to heat. The eddy-current dynamometer is cooled with water or air. It provides good load control but it is quite expensive.

Water-brake dynamometers are basically a fluid coupling (Figure 18–7). A finned rotor turns within a stationary finned housing. The coupling is partly filled with water. The more water that is in the coupling, the more power that is required to spin the rotor within the housing. An arm keeps the

housing from spinning. A scale on the end of the arm measures the force in pounds. Water within the coupling absorbs power by converting it into heat, so the coupling water must be continually cooled. This is done by passing the water through a heat exchanger or by continually replacing part of the coupling water with fresh cool water.

Most dynamometers are used by engine and equipment manufacturers. Some are used by the large engine remanufacturers to check their rebuilt units. Engineering schools often have dynamom-

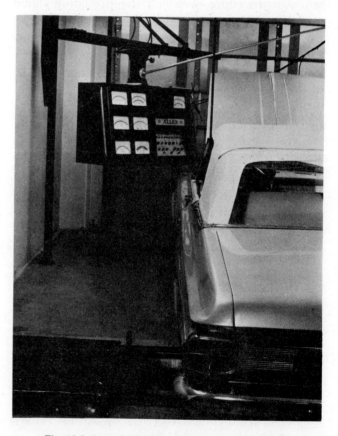

Fig. 18-8 An automobile on a chassis dynamometer.

eters as tools for research projects. Some industrial arts and vocational schools have obtained relatively inexpensive water-brake engine dynamometers for use with small engines to demonstrate internal combustion principles.

The use of dynamometers in the automotive service market is usually limited to high-volume operators such as fleet operators, test lane facilities, inspection lanes, and large dealers. The chassis dynamometer (Figure 18–8) is used to put a measured load on the engine. This gives the operator an opportunity to check the engine with tune-up and emission test equipment connected as the engine runs under a controlled load. The dynamometer instrumentation indicates total power being delivered by the rear wheels while the tune-up and emission test equipment indicates the engine operating condition. The readings developed during a dynamometer run will have to be interpreted to determine the engine conditions.

Normal engine power on a dynamometer indicates satisfactory engine condition and no further detailed testing is required. Low power or rough operation indicates an abnormal condition. The cause of these conditions while running may be indicated by the tune-up instruments used with the dynamometer; if not, further detailed checks are necessary. The important point to remember is that the only function of the dynamometer is to put a controlled load on the engine so that the engine performance can be tested with test instruments while running under simulated road conditions.

A dynamometer test of a vehicle may be used to check an engine to see if it needs service, or it may be used to check the engine after service to see that the engine is functioning correctly.

It should be noted that engine performance is checked as the engine is operating at that instant. It does not indicate that the engine will function as well in the future. This is like a race car that is functioning perfectly during one lap, but may not function as well on the next lap. Some part may be just about to fail, but this will not be indicated by the dynamometer or by tune-up instrumentation. The best method to ensure continued satisfactory operation is to give the engine a good hands-on visual inspection.

An engine that has been given a thorough visual, mechanical, and instrument inspection will provide dependable service when all detected faults have been corrected. With study and practice the technician will be able to rapidly service an engine to provide it with standard levels of performance, economy, and emissions.

REVIEW QUESTIONS

1. What three things are needed for an engine to run? [INTRODUCTION]

2. What is a tune-up? [18–1]

3. What is the first thing to check on a tune-up? [18–1]

4. What methods are used to determine if the engine is developing satisfactory compression? [18–1]

5. What mechanical checks are done on the ignition system during a tune-up? [18–1]

6. What mechanical carburetor checks are done during a tune-up? [18–1]

7. What safety precautions should be observed when checking the engine operation? [18–1]

8. What two modern test instruments are designed to make overall operating system tests? [18–1]

9. What information can be obtained from an ignition scope pattern? [18–1]

10. What operating conditions produce high CO emissions? Low CO emissions? [18–1]

11. What operating conditions produce high HC emissions? Low HC emissions? [18–1]

12. Why should an instrument check of the engine operating conditions be made before service? Why should it be made after service? [18–1]

13. In what way are brands of test equipment similar? In what way are they different? [18–1]

14. When does an automobile require service? [18–2]

15. How does a tune-up differ from troubleshooting? [18–3]

16. What does a dynamometer do? [18–4]

17. What two absorption methods are used on service-type dynamometers? [18–4]

18. What is the best test method to ensure continued satisfactory engine operation? [18–4]

upper-engine service

The engine will require disassembly for internal service when adjustment and repair of the engine accessories do not correct the engine problem. Engine problems requiring upper-engine service are primarily limited to the valve train (except for the cam), gaskets, and cracks that develop in the manifolds and heads. Valve-train problems are usually evident as noise. The sounds produced by the valve train occur at one-half the engine speed. Valve problems lead to loss of compression. Gasket problems and cracks can cause loss of compression and vacuum, or loss of oil and coolant. Often, these problems are identified during a tune-up. One of the first mechanical checks to be done during a tune-up is to check engine compression. A low compression reading is an indication that further checks should be made to positively identify the cause. The compression loss could be the

result of leaks in the valves, head gasket, or piston rings. The head will have to be removed to correct any of these compression problems. This chapter will be limited to the service of the head, manifold, and valve train. Piston ring service is covered in Chapter 20.

19-1 COMPRESSION TEST

There are a number of ways to check the engine compression. One of the newest methods uses a piece of test equipment to kill one cylinder at a time and measure the loss in engine speed. Little loss indicates a weak cylinder. Another method is to put air into the cylinder at a specified rate and measure the leakage rate while the piston is at top center. Using this method, the technician can listen at the exhaust, carburetor, and oil fill opening to identify the source of leakage.

The most common method of measuring compression is with the use of an especially designed pressure gauge. A fitting attached to the gauge is put in place of the spark plug of the cylinder being tested (all spark plugs removed). The engine is cranked over five compressions on that cylinder. The pressure developed on the first and on the fifth compression is noted. The pressure obtained on the first compression indicates the severity of the leak. The pressure on the fifth compression indicates the amount of leak. The normal pressure developed on the compression test is proportional to the engine compression ratio. Compression pressures will run from 100 to 140 psi (689.5 to 965.3 kPa).

Low compression should be rechecked after putting a small quantity of oil in the cylinder through the spark plug opening. The oil will temporarily seal the piston rings. If the pressure comes up close to normal when the compression test is rerun (wet compression test), the compression loss is produced by the piston rings. If the pressure only comes up slightly, the compression loss is caused by a valve or gasket. These can be corrected by upper-engine service. It is always advisable to verify any low reading by rechecking with one of the other test methods. Once the compression leak is positively verified, the engine can be disassembled for service.

19-2 HEAD REMOVAL

The normal procedure when doing upper-engine service is to leave the engine in the chassis, removing only the components that are required to perform the service that is needed. It is advisable to clean the engine exterior and the engine compartment before work is begun. A clean engine is easier to work on, it helps keep dirt out of the engine, and it minimizes accidental damage from slipping tools.

Working on top of the engine is made easier if the hood is removed. With fender covers in place, the hood is loosened from the hinges by removing two or three cap screws on each side.

Fig. 19-1 Connecting hoses and wires marked before removing them from the engine.

With a person on each side of the hood to support it, the hood is lifted off as the cap screws are removed. The hood is usually stored on fender covers placed on the top of the automobile, where it is least likely to be damaged.

The coolant is drained from the radiator and engine block to minimize the chance of getting coolant into the cylinders when the head is removed. The exhaust is disconnected from the exhaust pipe and muffler. On some engines, it is easier to remove the exhaust pipe from the manifold. On others, it is easier to separate the manifold from the head and leave it attached to the exhaust pipe. On V-type engines, the intake manifold must be removed before the heads can be taken off. In most cases, a number of wires, accessories, hoses, and tubing must be removed before the manifold and head can be removed. If the engine is not familiar, it is a good practice to put tape on each of these items removed, as shown in Figure 19–1. The tape can be marked to identify the location so that each item can be easily replaced during engine assembly.

The following disassembly procedure applies primarily to push rod engines. The procedure will have to be modified somewhat when working on overhead cam engines.

Removal of the rocker covers gives the technician the first opportunity to see inside a portion of the engine. A good visual examination of this area should be made to identify and determine the cause of any abnormal condition. Pay special attention to the type and quantity of deposits. Examine the rocker arms, valve springs, and valve tips for obvious defects.

Remove the manifold hold-down cap screws

and nuts. If the gaskets are stuck, a flat blade, such as a putty knife, can be worked beside the gasket to loosen it. Care must be taken to avoid damaging the parting surface as the gasket is loosened. When the manifold and lifter valley cover are off V-type engines, the technician has another opportunity to examine the interior of the engine. Here again, check the deposits. The push rods and lifters are exposed for a visual inspection. On some V-type engines, it is possible to see the condition of the cam at the bottom of the lifter valley, as pictured in Figure 19-2.

Fig. 19-2 Camshaft visible after the intake manifold is removed.

It is a good practice to keep all of the engine parts in order so that their exact location in the engine is known. This serves two purposes. First, it gives the technician an opportunity to trace abnormal conditions to their sources. It also gives the technician an opportunity to put normally operating parts back together in the same way they were operating before service.

There are two theories that apply to cleaning an engine while servicing only a part of the engine. One theory says the deposits should not be disturbed on any part of the engine not directly involved in the repair. The thinking is that it is difficult to remove the deposits that are loosened and it takes additional time that is not directly involved with the repair being accomplished. The other theory recommends thorough cleaning of all accessible deposits to make the engine last as long as possible after the repair. This would in-

crease the cost of repair to the customer. The deposits found in the lifter valley fall into this cleaning discussion.

With the manifold off the V-type engine, any obvious abnormal conditions are noted, then the rocker arms are loosened and the push rods removed. The usual practice when reconditioning the valves is to leave the lifters in place. They can be removed at this time, however, if they are causing the problem or if the entire valve train is to be serviced.

The final major disassembly is the removal of the head. The head cap screws are removed and the head is lifted from the block deck. If the head gasket is stuck, careful prying on the head will loosen the gasket. Special precautions should be taken to pry on edges of the head that will not break. Parting surfaces should not be scratched. Scratched or burred surfaces will lead to leaks on the repaired engine.

The combustion chamber is exposed when the head is removed. The combustion chamber pocket in the head and the top of the piston should be given a thorough visual examination. The most obvious condition is the deposits such as those in Figure 19-3. A normal combustion chamber is coated with a layer of hard, light-colored deposits. If the combustion chamber has been running too hot, the deposits will be thin and light colored. If the combustion chamber has been running too cold, the deposits will be thick, dry, and black. Heavy wet deposits result from oil that is entering the combustion chamber. If oil comsumption is excessive, the large quantity of oil going into the combustion chamber will wash the carbon deposit from the entry location.

With the heads removed and placed on the bench, the valves are removed. A C-type valve spring compressor, similar to the one being used in Figure 19-4, is used to free the valve locks or keepers. The valve spring compressor is air-powered in production shops where valve jobs are being done on a regular basis. Mechanical valve spring compressors are used where valve work is only occasionally done. After the valve lock is removed, the compressor is released to free the valve retainer and spring. These are lifted from the head along with any spacers being used under the valve

Fig. 19-3 Normal combustion chamber deposits.

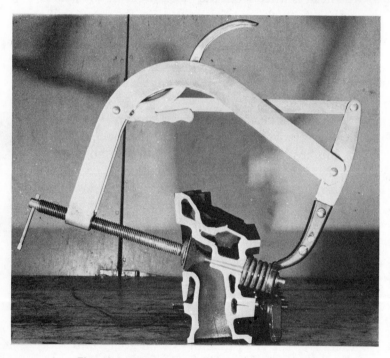

Fig. 19-4 Valve spring compressed so the valve locks can be removed.

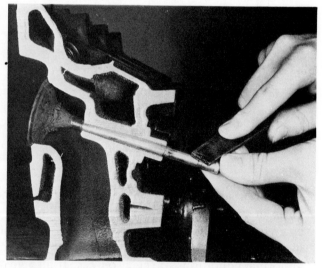

Fig. 19-5 Removing burrs at the valve lock grooves before removing the valve from the guide.

spring. Here again, the arrangement of the parts should be kept in order to aid in diagnosing the exact cause of any malfunction that shows up. The valve tip edge and lock area should be lightly filed or stoned, as shown in Figure 19–5, to remove any burrs before sliding the valve from the head. Burrs will scratch the valve guide.

When all valves are removed following the same procedure, the valves, springs, retainers, locks, guides, and seats should be given another visual examination. Any obvious faults should be noted. Parts that are obviously not repairable should be marked and set aside for later reference and fault diagnosis. No further labor time should be expended on them.

19–3 CLEANING

Parts that are not obviously damaged or worn beyond repairable limits should be cleaned. Cleaning parts is usually relegated to an assistant. However, if the technician cleans the parts, he will be able to make a detailed observation of each part's condition that indicates the kind of service and operation the engine has had. This type of detailed observation is useful in analyzing malfunctions noted during parts inspection.

Two basic types of cleaning are done on an engine, degreasing and decarbonizing. Degreasing is usually done with petroleum spirits that only remove grease and oil. Some degreasing cleaners can be mixed with petroleum spirits or kerosene, sprayed on the parts to be cleaned, then hosed off with water. This will remove dirt as well as grease and oil.

Decarbonizing chemicals are available as a bath in which the parts to be cleaned are submerged. Heating the decarbonizing bath will speed cleaning action. After a soak period, parts are removed and hosed off with water. Decarbonizing materials are very irritating. They should be immediately rinsed off if they contact the skin.

Vapor degreasers do a very effective job of cleaning parts. Parts come from the vapor tank with a powdery surface that is easily brushed off. The parts are so dry that they will rust easily. After inspection, they should be lightly oiled.

Heavy deposits can be removed by scraping, wire brushing, or blasting. Eye protection is especially necessary when using any of these cleaning methods. It is also important to avoid damaging the part as it is cleaned. Care is critical when clean-

ing soft metals such as aluminum and bronze. Scraping is usually done with a blade, such as a putty knife. Wire brushing may be done with a hand brush or with a power brush, either in a hand drill shown in Figure 19-6 or as a wire wheel. Abrasive blasting is done with a special nozzle using air pressure blowing glass or plastic beads. These beads have a tendency to lodge in the corners of the part being cleaned. The beads must be thoroughly cleaned from the part before the engine is reassembled.

The valves are usually cleaned on a wire brush (Figure 19-8). The rocker assemblies, push rods, springs, and retainers are cleaned with solvents

Fig. 19-7 Chipping the hard carbon from the intake valve with a discarded valve.

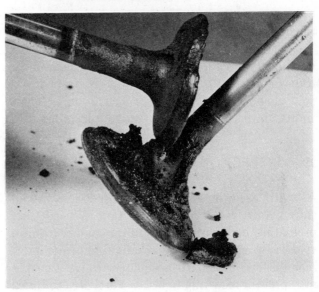

Fig. 19-8 Removing carbon from a valve with a bench wire wheel.

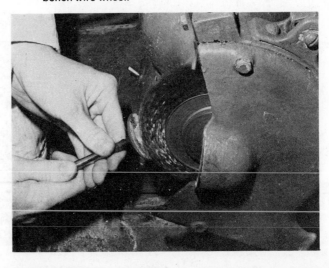

Fig. 19-6 Cleaning the carbon from the head with a wire brush on a drill motor.

Fig. 19-9 Removing carbon from a valve guide with a valve guide cleaner.

or a vapor degreaser. The hard carbon deposits on the head are removed by scraping or wire brushing. Valve guides are cleaned with a valve guide cleaner having either scraping blades or wire brush on the tool (Figure 19-9). The head is finally cleaned with solvents or vapor degreasing. When all the parts are thoroughly cleaned, they are ready for inspection.

19-4 INSPECTION

As with each preceding step, inspection should start with a good visual inspection. When either premature or high-mileage failure has occurred, a visual inspection will aid in evaluation of the interrelationship of the parts, so that corrective measures may prevent recurring failures. Parts are examined for wear patterns, scoring and pitting, foreign materials, and contamination. When abnormalties

are found, the mating parts should be thoroughly examined to determine the specific cause of failure.

The visual inspection is followed by a dimensional inspection. All parts are measured and their dimensions compared to the manufacturer's specifications for the engine being worked on. Specifications give sizes and clearances. Parts either must be within specification tolerances or must be reconditioned to fall within the specification tolerance before they are used again. Parts that cannot be made to meet the specifications will have to be replaced.

19-5 VALVE CONDITION

A careful examination of the valves removed from the engine will indicate causes of valve failure. Valves fail because their operating limits have been exceeded. The cause of the failure must be corrected to enable new or reconditioned valves to perform satisfactorily. Valve failure results from misaligned valve seating, excessive temperature, high velocity seating, and high mileage. These conditions are usually interrelated.

Valve Seating. Valve burning (Figure 19-10) and valve guttering (Figure 19-11) are common types of valve failure. They result from poor seating that allows the high-temperature and high-pressure gases to leak between the valve and seat. Poor seating results from insufficient valve lash, hard carbon deposits, valve stem deposits, excessive valve stem-to-guide clearances, or out-of-squareness between the valve guide and seat.

Insufficient valve lash may result from improper valve lash adjustment on solid lifter systems and from collapsed hydraulic lifters. The clearance will also be reduced from valve head cupping shown in Figure 19-12, or valve face seating wear.

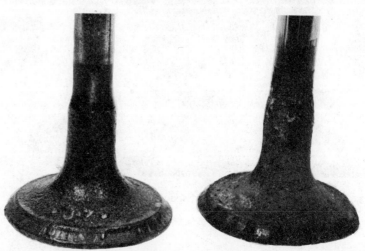

Fig. 19-10 Stages of valve face burning.

Fig. 19-11 Stages of valve face guttering.

Fig. 19-12 Cupped valves. Right valve is severely cupped.

Fig. 19-13 Valve face peening.

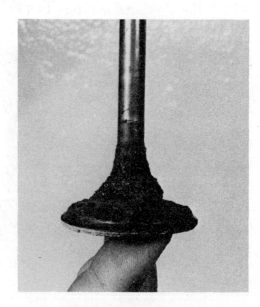

Fig. 19-14 Heavy carbon build-up on an intake valve.

Hard carbon deposits that loosen from the combustion chamber and stick between the valve face and seat can hold the valve slightly off its seat. This reduces valve cooling through the seat and allows some of the combustion gases to escape. Continued pounding on hard carbon particles gives the valve face a peened appearance, pictured in Figure 19-13. Positive valve rotors help to combat the effects of deposits and thereby prevent valve burning.

Fuel and oil on the hot valve will break down to become hard carbon and varnish deposits that build up on the valve stem. Heavy deposits are shown in Figure 19-14. These deposits cause the valve to stick in the guide so the valve does not seat completely and the valve face burns.

If the valve stem has excess clearance, too much oil will go down the stem to increase deposits. This is especially critical on intake valves. In addition, wide valve guide clearance will allow the valve to cock, especially with rocker arm action. Continued cocking keeps the valve from seating properly and leakage occurs, burning the valve face.

Sometimes, the cylinder head will warp as the head is tightened to the block deck during assembly. Other times, heating and cooling will cause warpage. When head warpage causes valve guide and seat misalignment, the valve cannot seat properly.

Excessive Temperatures. High valve temperature occurs when the valve does not seat properly; however, it can occur even when the valve is seating properly. Cooling system passages in the head may be partially blocked by casting imperfections or by deposits built up from the coolant. Extremely high temperatures are also produced by pre-ignition and by detonation, forms of abnormal combustion. Both of these cause a very rapid increase in temperature that can cause uneven heating, giving a thermal shock to the valve. The shock will frequently cause radial cracks in the valve which, in turn, will allow the combustion gases to escape and gutter the valve face. If the radial cracks intersect, a pie-shaped piece will break from the valve head, such as those pictured in Figure 19–15. A thermal

Fig. 19-15 Valves broken by thermal shock.

shock can also be produced by rapid cycling from full throttle to closed throttle and back again.

High engine speeds require high gas velocities. The high velocity exhaust gas impinges on the valve stem and tends to erode the metal. The gases are also corrosive so the valve stem will tend to corrode. The corrosion rate doubles for each 25 °F increase in temperature. Erosion and corrosion of the valve stem cause *necking* that weakens the stem and leads to breakage. Necking is shown in Figure 19–16.

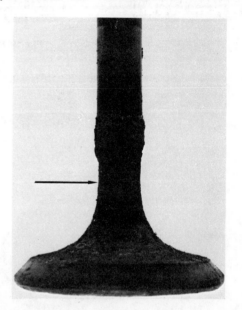

Fig. 19-16 Valve stem necking.

Misaligned Valve Seats. Each time the valve closes when the valve-to-seat alignment is improper, the valve head must twist to seat. If twisting or bending becomes excessive, it fatigues the stem and the valve head will break from the stem. The break appears as lines arcing around a starting point.

High Velocity Seating. High velocity seating is indicated by excessive valve face wear, valve seat recessing, and impact failure, as shown in Figure 19–17. It can be caused by excessive lash in mechanical lifters and by collapsed hydraulic lifters so the valve hits the seat without the effect of the cam ramp to ease it onto its seat. Excessive lash may also be caused by wear of parts such as the cam, lifter base, pushrod ends, rocker arms, and valve tip. Weak or broken valve springs allow the valves to float away from the cam lobes so the valves are uncontrolled as they hit the seat. The normal tendency of hydraulic lifters is to pump up

Fig. 19-17 Valve stem breakage from misalignment.

under these float conditions and this reduces valve impact damage.

Impact breakage may occur under the valve head or at the valve lock grooves. The break lines radiate from the starting point. The valve head usually falls into the combustion chamber and is jammed between the piston and head. In most cases, it will ruin the piston before the engine can be stopped, as pictured in Figure 19–18.

High Mileage. High mileage indications show excessive wear of the valve stem (Figure 19–19), guide, valve face, and seat. They are usually accompanied by considerable deposits. The valves will, however, still be seating and will show no indication of cracks or burning.

19-6 VALVE-TRAIN CONDITION

Valve failure may be the result of the valve-train condition. This is usually evident as wear. Valve-train wear can result from exceeding operating limits and from loss of lubrication.

Camshaft. Camshaft failure shows up as cam lobe failure. Lobe failure starts as small pits caused by heavy edge wear, illustrated in Figure 19–20.

Fig. 19-18 Valve broken from high velocity seating that broke the piston.

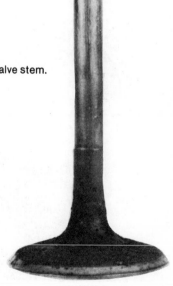

Fig. 19-19 Badly worn valve stem.

Fig. 19-20 Edge wear on a cam.

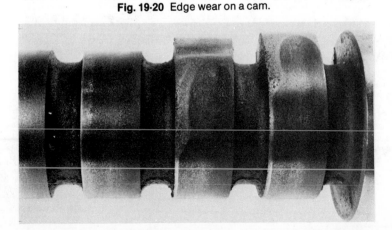

The lobe will gradually break down as the engine is operated until it looks like a round journal. A badly worn cam will cause badly worn lifters. Occasionally, the lobe will chip as the result of impact damage, usually from careless handling. The camshaft will be discussed in more detail in Chapter 20.

Lifters. Camshaft lobe failure will damage the lifter face. Face failure may start with pits or with smooth wear. The face gradually becomes concave (Figures 19–21 and 19–22). This will also wear the cam. Pitted or concave lifter faces are not repairable, but the lifter should be replaced. For maximum service life, install new lifters with a new cam. A worn

Fig. 19-21 Lifter face worn concave causing cam edge wear.

cam may rapidly damage new lifter faces and thus give a short lifter service life. Worn lifters always damage the cam.

Hydraulic lifter parts are selective fit and cannot be interchanged between lifters. Lifters that show no abnormal wear should be disassembled and cleaned, one at a time, to avoid intermixing parts. After reassembly, they should be checked for leak-down rate. If the rate is excessive, the lifter should be replaced. In practice, the labor to clean a lifter is more expensive than the price of a new lifter.

Rocker Arms. When worn, rocker shafts and matching rocker arms should be replaced. A worn face on a stamped rocker arm requires replacement of the rocker arm. Some of the older cast rocker arms could have their faces ground, but this practice has been discontinued. Replace worn stamped rocker arms, pivot balls, or shafts. Worn rocker arms are pictured in Figure 19–23.

Pushrods. Pushrod failure results from lack of lubrication or from overstressing. Lack of lubrication results in excessive pushrod end wear. Overstressing will cause bent pushrods. Rod bend can be detected by rolling the pushrod across a flat surface. Any wobble indicates a bent rod. Pushrods that are bent or worn must be replaced.

Valve Springs. Valve springs may rotate in use and become shiny on the end, as shown in Figure 19–24. They may develop pits or take a set. Wear

Fig. 19-22 Excessively worn lifter faces.

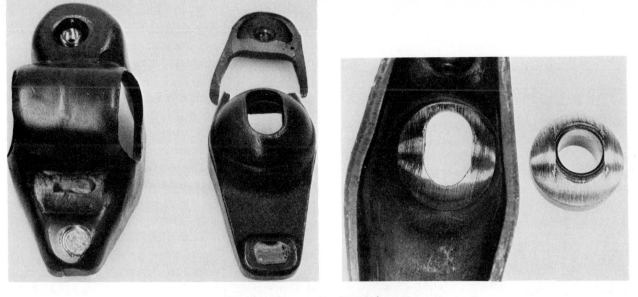

Fig. 19-23 Worn and broken rocker arms.

and pits are checked visually. Valve spring set may result in warping the spring or in loss of tension. Valve spring warpage is checked with a square on a surface plate, maximum out of square is 1/16 in. (1.5 mm), as shown in Figure 19–25. Spring tension is checked in a valve spring gauge (Figure 19–26). The spring tension is checked at the installed length and at the valve open length. Pressure loss up to 10% is serviceable. Any valve

Fig. 19-26 Checking valve spring tension.

Fig. 19-24 Spring end wear from excessive rotation.

Fig. 19-25 A square being used to check valve spring squareness.

Fig. 19-27 Drawfiling the head parting surface.

Fig. 19-28 Checking the head flatness with a straightedge.

spring abnormality is cause for replacement. Because valve springs are inexpensive, they are often replaced each time the valve system is reconditioned.

Valve Retainers and Locks. Inspection of valve retainers and locks is limited to a visual inspection. Cracks and wear or questionable serviceability are reasons for replacement. If the lock or retainer should fail, the valve could fall into the combustion chamber and do extensive damage.

19-7 VALVE SYSTEM SERVICE

The following procedure describes the service steps that are used when doing a valve job on an automobile engine used in street operation. There are many special modifications and procedures used for racing and for blueprinted engines. These are interesting, but they are beyond the scope of this book.

Cylinder Head. Most of the service work on a cylinder head involves work on the valve guides and seats. The clean head gasket surface is drawfiled flat to remove any raised portions (Figure 19–27) and then checked for bend and warpage with a straightedge (Figure 19–28). The head surface must be ground or milled flat if a thickness gauge more than 0.006 in. (0.15 mm) will fit between the straightedge and head (Figure 19–29). If warpage is not corrected, it will misalign the seats and guides when the head is installed and torqued on the block deck. Equal amounts should be removed from both heads on V-engines to maintain the

Fig. 19-29 Grinding the head parting surface to flatten it.

(a)

(b)

Fig. 19-30 Measuring valve stem to guide clearance. (a) Using a small hole gauge and outside micrometer (Dana Corporation), (b) using a dial gauge (American Motors Corporation).

guide is checked on each end and in the middle with a small hole gauge and micrometer (Figure 19-30). Some manufacturers space the head off the seat, then measure the looseness with a dial gauge against the side of the tip. Guides with excess clearance may be reamed to take an oversize valve stem or they may be knurled or bushed.

Knurling provides a satisfactory valve guide repair when correctly done. The knurling process produces a spiral groove on the interior of the guide with a sharp edged wheel supported by a special tool. Metal is displaced inward adjacent to the groove, making the hole smaller. Successively larger wheels are used until the valve will no longer enter the guide. The guide is then reamed to provide the correct valve stem-to-guide clearance. Measuring tool details are given in Section 20-4.

Another valve guide repair method is to tap a thread in the valve guide, then insert a special spiral brass spring in these threads. This is followed by a burnishing tool that firmly presses the brass into the threads. The final step is to ream the brass insert to the correct size. Valve guide repairs are pictured in Figure 19-31. The manufacturers of engines having integral valve guides recommend hand reaming valve guides to accept a valve with an oversized stem. This, of course, means that

Fig. 19-31 Valve guide repair. (a) Knurled valve guide, (b) brass spring valve guide insert.

(a)   (b)

equal match between the intake manifold and head. Additional material will have to be removed from both intake manifold gasket surfaces of the heads to keep the manifold and head openings aligned. Tables are available in automotive machine shops where the work will be done to calculate the required amount.

After the head surfaces have been conditioned, the diameter of the valve guide is checked. Normal service limit is 50% greater than new limits. The new valves must be used. It is most likely that the valves which had been operating in the loose guides have excessive stem and face wear and so they would have to be replaced in any case.

The valve seat must be concentric with the valve guide. Seat faces are ground with a stone driven through a holder that is supported by a pilot placed in the guide (Figure 19–33). The stone must be dressed or cleaned with a diamond tool on

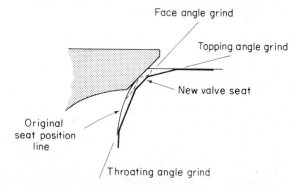

Fig. 19-32 Method of adjusting the valve seating position by grinding throating and topping angles.

Fig. 19-33 Grinding the valve seat.

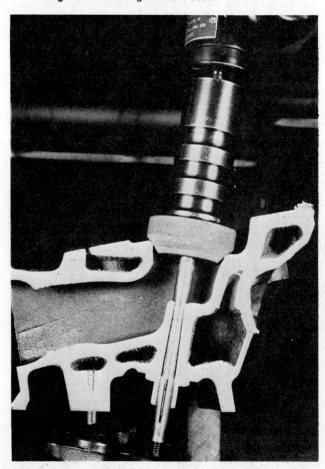

a dressing fixture to correctly align the stone face with the holder center to ensure the correct seat face angle and to clean the stone grinding surface. Light grinding cuts are made to clean and align the seat surface while removing minimum material. If excessive valve seat wear exists, the old seat can be cut out and a new seat installed. This is an automotive machine shop job.

The valve and seat are ground at an *interference angle* with the valve 1/2 to 2° less than the seat. This produces high contact pressure at the combustion chamber edge of the seat which seals the valves and prevents leakage (Figure 19–34). Seat run-out must not exceed 0.002 in. (0.05 mm). If the seat has excess run-out it must be lightly reground, and then the run-out should be rechecked.

Valve seat grinding widens the valve seat. Normal seat widths range from 1/16 in. to 3/32 in., depending on the engine. The top of the seat can be adjusted downward by *topping* the seat with a 15° grinding stone. The lower edge can be raised by throating with a 70° grinding stone (Figure 19–32). Seat location on the valve face must be checked with a new or reconditioned valve. This can be seen in the section view in Figure 19–35. The valve is coated with *prussian blue* or *mechanic's blue*,

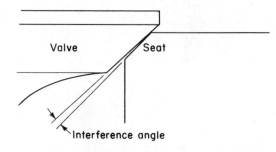

Fig. 19-34 Valve seat interference angle (exaggerated).

Fig. 19-35 Marking the finished valve seat position with mechanics blue.

Fig. 19-36 Grinding the valve face.

valve will not close if the valve tip extends too far from the valve guide on engines with hydraulic lifters and nonadjustable rocker arms. If the valve is too long, the tip may be ground as much as 0.020 in. (0.5 mm) to reduce its length. If it is too short, the valve face or seat may be reground, within limits, to allow the valve to seat deeper. Where excessive grinding has been done, shims can be placed under the rocker shaft on some engines

Fig. 19-37 Refinishing the valve tip with a grinder.

Fig. 19-38 Measuring the valve stem length as installed after grinding.

then inserted in the guide and lightly bounced on the seat to transfer the blue to the seat. The valve is removed, wiped clean, and reinstalled. A second light bouncing should transfer the blue back onto the valve to show a full circle contact pattern at the position about 1/4 of the valve face below the valve margin.

Valve Service. Valve faces are ground on a valve grinder (Figure 19-36). The grinder head is set at the correct valve angle to provide the recommended interference fit and the grinding stone is dressed to remove any roughness. The valve is clamped in the work head as close to the valve head as possible to prevent vibrations. The rotating grinding wheel is fed slowly to the rotating valve face. Light grinding is done as the valve is moved back and forth across the grinding wheel face, keeping the valve from going off the edge of the wheel. The valve is ground only enough to clean the face. The margin should be over 0.060 in. (1.5 mm). Aluminized valves will lose their corrosion resistance properties when ground, so for satisfactory service, they must always be replaced if they need refacing.

Slight imperfections on valve tips can be removed by grinding in a special fixture (Figure 19-37). A maximum of 0.020 in. (0.5 mm) may be ground from the tip. If more grinding is required, the valve must be replaced.

Reconditioned valves are installed in reconditioned guides to check the final valve length. The length is measured as shown in Figure 19-38. The

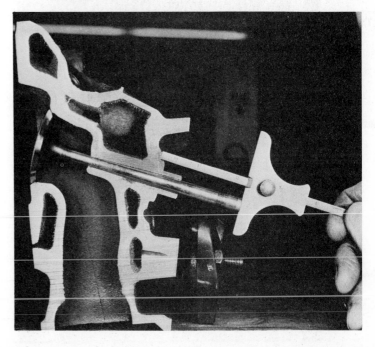

to provide correct hydraulic lifter plunger centering. These shims must have the required lubrication holes to allow oil to enter the shaft.

Valve retainers and locks are installed on valves without the spring. The distance from the retainer to the head is measured to check the installed spring length as shown in Figure 19-39. If it is too long, shims up to 1/16 in. should be installed at the head end of the spring to shorten the spring length within limits. The shim location is pictured in Figure 19-40. If the valve requires more than 1/16 in. shim, the valve and possibly the seat will have to be replaced.

Any sharp edge produced during valve servicing should be removed with a hand stone. This reduces the chance of damaging seals or wear on the sharp edges.

Head Assembly. The head and valve parts should be thoroughly cleaned to remove all traces of grinding grit and dirt that may have accumulated while the parts were disassembled. This is best done with a brush and soapy water. Each valve is lubricated with clean motor oil as it is installed. New valve seals are used. Springs, shims, and valve locks must seat squarely and securely. The

Fig. 19-39 Measuring the installed valve spring length.

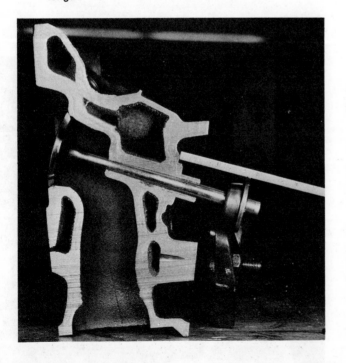

Fig. 19-40 Shim under the valve spring to correct valve spring tension.

valve tip should never be struck in an attempt to seat the valve or lock. Striking won't help valve seating, but it may initiate a fracture that would break the valve. If only a valve job is being done, the engine can be reassembled.

19-8 ENGINE ASSEMBLY

The parting surfaces of the head and block should be recleaned. The new head gasket is checked for proper fit. Unless otherwise marked as *top* or *front*, the gasket identification numbers go against the head (Figure 19-41). There are two schools of thought regarding the use of sealers on head gaskets. One says that the gasket is designed to properly seal when installed dry. This allows easy removal when the head must be serviced again. The other says that it is good insurance to prevent leakage by using a sealer. If the head and valve train are properly serviced, it is unlikely that the job will have to be done again within the useful life of the automobile. If sealer is to be used, it should be spread or sprayed evenly over both sides of the head gasket. The head gasket is then properly positioned on the block deck.

Fig. 19-41 Head gasket position marking.

The head is carefully lowered on the block deck and the dowels seated to correctly align the head. All of the head cap screws are installed finger tight. Torquing the head cap screws must follow an exact sequence, so as to form a good seal and eliminate warpage. The torquing sequence is given in the applicable service manual. In general, the center cap screws are torqued first. Cap screws adjacent to the center are tightened next. This procedure is followed until the end cap screws are tightened. It is the usual practice to go through the torquing sequence twice. The first time, the cap screws are torqued to half the specified torque and the second time to full torque. Some technicians go through the sequence a third time to ensure proper torque. Head cap screw torquing is shown in Figure 19–42.

The valve train should be assembled and adjusted before the manifold is installed so that the entire valve system can be observed for correct assembly. Special care should be taken to get the push rods positioned correctly. Some push rods have hardened ends that are put at the rocker arm end. Some engines have different length push rods on the intake and exhaust valve trains.

If the valve train is adjustable, the adjustment can best be made before the manifold is installed. It is necessary to position the hydraulic lifters in the middle of their travel. It helps to observe the lifter as the adjustment is being made. Engines having no valve train adjustment are set during the valve job by correctly positioning the valve tip height. Valve trains must be adjusted before the engine is started.

Some service manuals give a specific sequence to be used to adjust the valve train. The following procedure can be used on any engine having valve lash adjustment. The engine is turned in the normal direction of rotation until both valves on number one cylinder are closed and the top center timing mark aligns. At this crankshaft position, the valves are adjusted. Hydraulic valve lifters are adjusted until the clearance is gone. This can be observed by looking at the lifters with the manifold

Fig. 19-42 Torquing the head cap screws during assembly.

still off the engine. The adjustment is tightened the specified amount to center the plunger in the lifter bore (from one-half to one-and-a-half turns more). Solid lifter systems are adjusted 0.002 in. (0.05 mm) greater than the specified hot clearance (Figure 19–3). This will be very close to the correct valve lash on the warmed-up engine.

The engine is turned in the normal direction of rotation to the next cylinder in the firing order (90° on eight-cylinder engines, 120° on six-cylinder engines, and 180° on four-cylinder engines), and the valves on this cylinder are adjusted. This procedure is repeated in the firing order until all the valves have been adjusted. The technician will usually go through the valve lash check on solid lifter engines a second time just to make sure that the preliminary lash has been adjusted correctly. When the valves are adjusted, the manifold can be installed.

The manifold parting surfaces are wiped clean, and the gasket (coated with sealer if sealer is to be used) is placed on the head and block parting surfaces. Special care must be taken to properly position the intake manifold gasket lap on V-

(a)

Fig. 19-43 Adjusting valve lash. (a) At the pushrod end, (b) pivot ball, (c) on overhead cam follower.

(b)

(c)

engines in the corner of the head and lifter valley. The manifold is carefully lowered into position, care being taken to avoid moving the gaskets as the manifold seats.

The manifold cap screw threads are coated with sealer to help prevent coolant leaks and put in place. In some manifolds, the screws must be a specified length to hold securely and still not bottom. As with heads, the manifold's cap screws are torqued in a specified sequence to form a secure seal.

Some exhaust manifolds use gaskets while others do not. Exhaust gaskets are always put on dry. The exhaust manifolds are torqued from the center outward. Exhaust leaks produce unnecessary noise and, in some engines, upset the correct operation of the emission controls.

It is a generally accepted practice to include new belts, hoses, a tune-up, oil change, and antifreeze with the valve job. These are accomplished as the engine is reassembled. Details of these procedures are given in the related chapters of this book.

The valve train does not require a break-in. When the engine is running and warmed up, the solid lifter valve lash is checked and adjusted, then the rocker arm covers are secured. With the engine completely assembled, it is checked for leaks. If the engine exterior is dry, the automobile can be delivered to the customer.

REVIEW QUESTIONS

1. Why is a compression check important in upper-engine service? [19–1]

2. What is the advantage of cleaning the exterior of the engine before the heads are removed? [19–2]

3. Why are wires and hoses marked with tape as they are removed? [19–2]

4. What is the purpose of a visual inspection during disassembly? [19–2]

5. How are stuck head and manifold gaskets loosened during disassembly? [19–2]

6. Why is it important to know the exact location of each part? [19–2]

7. What internal cleaning should be done during upper-engine service? [19–2]

8. What should be observed when the heads are removed? [19–2]

9. What are the two basic types of parts cleaning done on engines? [19–3]

10. Describe the cleaning methods. What upper-engine parts are cleaned by each method? [19–3]

11. Name two inspection procedures used in upper-engine service. [19–4]

12. Why do valves fail? [19–5]

13. What valve problem is caused by poor valve seating? [19–5]

14. What valve problems will lead to premature valve failure? [19–5]

15. What type of valve failure results from abnormal combustion? [19–5]

16. What causes valve necking? [19–5]

17. What conditions cause a valve stem to break? [19–5]

18. What wear is likely to occur between the cam and lifter? [19–6]

19. Why does excessive wear occur when old lifters are used on a new cam? [19–6]

20. Why should lifters be cleaned and reassembled one at a time? [19–6]

21. How is pushrod straightness checked? [19–6]

22. How are valve springs checked? [19–6]

23. Why is it very important to check the head alignment? [19–7]

24. When is valve guide service required? [19–7]

25. What is the advantage of an interference angle between the valve face and seat? [19–7]

26. How is valve seat position adjusted to properly contact the valve face? [19–7]

27. How can the technician determine that the valve face is properly ground? [19–7]

28. Why is the valve tip ground? [19–7]

29. Why are shims used under valve springs? [19–7]

30. How are cylinder heads properly aligned on the block deck? [19–8]

31. What is the general head torquing sequence? [19–8]

32. Why is it desirable to adjust the valve lash before the intake manifold is installed on V-type engines? [19–8]

33. What precautions should be taken when installing the intake manifold? [19–8]

34. Why is it desirable to coat the intake manifold cap screws with sealer? [19–8]

35. Why is it not necessary to break in a valve job? [19–8]

20
lower-engine service

The most common reason for servicing the lower end of the engine is to replace the rings and recondition the pistons. This is usually accompanied by replacement of the connecting rod bearings. It is customary to service the valve train whenever the head is removed, and this is usually done at the same time. Head and valve train service are discussed in Chapter 19 and so they will not be repeated in this chapter. Servicing the rings and doing a valve job will reseal the combustion chamber so that the engine will have high compression once again. This will allow the engine to produce its normal power. The ring and valve job will generally reduce oil consumption.

There are other reasons for servicing the lower end of the engine. These include loss of oil pressure, abnormal sound, bearing knock, and parts breakage. In some cases, the engine is disassembled and serviced as a high-mileage routine maintenance job to head off any serious damage.

Lower-engine service can be classified as an overhaul or a rebuild. In this discussion, an overhaul will be considered as correcting a problem within the limits of service specifications. An engine will be considered rebuilt when it has been completely disassembled and all parts are brought back to the specifications of a new engine. Most rebuilding for domestic passenger cars in street use are done at shops specializing in rebuilding. The old engine is often exchanged for a rebuilt engine to minimize the time the automobile is tied up in the repair shop. When rebuilding is done on an assembly line and the parts of one engine are not necessarily kept together, the assembled engine is said to be remanufactured. Engines are carefully rebuilt by hobbyist-owners and by racing mechanics. If the labor cost is considered, this type of custom rebuilding is more expensive than a remanufactured engine.

This chapter on lower-engine service will be aimed at the engine overhaul approach rather than at rebuilding. Engine rebuilding requires an automotive machine shop. An overhaul can often be done with typical shop tools. If specialized work is required, only those pieces that require this service are taken to the automotive machine shop.

The technician must first decide whether the lower end of the engine must be opened up for service. A run-through of the checks listed at the beginning of Chapter 19 for upper-engine service will help determine if the lower end requires service.

20-1 ENGINE REMOVAL

The engine heads and manifolds can be removed with the engine in the chassis. In some model automobiles, the oil pan can also be removed with the engine in the chassis. The engine has to be removed from the chassis of most domestic automobiles for lower-engine service. When this is required, the manifolds and heads are not removed until the engine is out of the chassis. This makes disassembly much easier.

There are two ways to remove the engine. The engine can be lifted out of the chassis with the transmission attached or the transmission can be separated from the engine and left in the chassis. The method to be used must be determined before the engine is disconnected and pulled. In the following discussion, it is assumed that the engine is removed for overhaul with the transmission attached.

First, the battery is removed to avoid sparks and acid. If the engine compartment is steam cleaned, it will be much easier to work on the engine. The engine oil and coolants are drained. They should be examined for condition before they are discarded. With fender covers in place, the hood is removed as described in Chapter 19. All coolant hoses are removed and the transmission oil cooler lines disconnected from the radiator. The radiator mounting bolts are removed and the radiator is lifted from the engine compartment.

This is a good time to have the radiator cleaned while it is out of the chassis during engine overhaul. If it does not require cleaning, it is placed where it will not be damaged as the overhaul progresses. The automobile trunk makes a good storage place for the radiator.

If the engine is air conditioned, the compressor can usually be separated from the engine, leaving all air conditioning hoses securely connected to the compressor and lines. The compressor can be fastened to the side of the engine compartment where it will not interfere with engine removal. It may also be necessary to loosen the condenser and fasten it aside. If it is necessary to disconnect the air conditioning lines the system will have to be bled down, as described in Chapter 33, before opening the system. All openings should be securely plugged immediately after opening to keep dirt and moisture from the system. They should remain plugged until immediately before reassembly. The air conditioning system will have to be evacuated and recharged after the overhaul is finished and the system assembled.

All wires, hoses, tubing, and controls that connect from the automobile to the engine are tagged for location and then disconnected. This aids in reassembly after overhaul. It is a good practice to remove the distributor, carburetor, alternator, and fan to avoid accidental damage during engine removal. It is also a good practice to recondition these units while the engine is being overhauled so that the finished engine will operate trouble free for a long time.

Under the car, the propeller shaft is removed and the exhaust pipes disconnected. It may be necessary to loosen the steering linkage idler arm to give clearance in some installations. The transmission controls, speedometer cable, and clutch linkages are disconnected and tagged. These are fastened so they will be out of the way and not bent as the engine is removed. The automatic transmission cooling lines and the starter wires are removed.

The engine has three mounts, one on each side and one at the back of the transmission. The mount bolts are removed. This leaves the engine resting on the mounts. A sling, either a chain or lift cable, is attached to manifold or head cap screws on top of the engine. A hoist is attached to the sling and snugged to take up most of the weight. The rear cross member is removed and the transmission is lowered. The hoist is tightened to

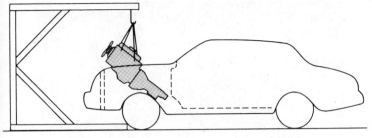

Fig. 20-1 Engine with the transmission attached being lifted from the chassis.

lift the engine. The engine will nose up as it is removed with the front of the engine coming almost straight up as the transmission slides from under the floor pan as illustrated in Figure 20-1. The engine and transmission are hoisted free of the automobile, swung clear and lowered on an open floor area. Blocks are placed under the engine to steady it. The hoist is loosened, but kept attached to the engine as a safety measure until the transmission is removed.

The exterior of the engine should be given a thorough visual examination before any other work is done. After noting any fluid leaks and obvious faults, the exterior of the engine should be thoroughly cleaned. Steam cleaning is a good way to clean the exterior of the engine.

20-2 ENGINE DISASSEMBLY

The transmission and clutch are removed. The procedure for removing a standard transmission and clutch is given in Chapter 21. The procedure for removing an automatic transmission is given in Chapter 24. All remaining accessories are removed from the engine and stored where they will not be damaged. Engine disassembly is best done on an engine stand but it can be done on blocks on a clean floor. The manifolds and heads are removed as described in Chapter 19.

The obvious condition of the combustion chambers and lifter chamber, and any head gasket leakage, can be observed with the heads off (Figure 20-2). These conditions should be noted. At this point, the cylinder taper and out-of-round should be checked just below the ridge and just above the piston when it is at the bottom of the stroke as shown in Figures 20-3 and 20-4. These measurements will indicate the extent of cylinder wall work required. If the cylinders are worn beyond limits, they will have to be rebored to return them to a satisfactory condition.

The engine is turned upside down and the oil pan is removed. This is the first opportunity to see the working parts in the bottom end of the engine. Deposits are again a good indication of the engine condition and the care it has had. Heavy sludge indicates infrequent oil changes. Hard carbon indicates overheating. The oil pump pick-up screen should be checked to see how much plugging exists. The connecting rods, caps, and main bear-

Fig. 20-2 Normal carbon deposits on the pistons.

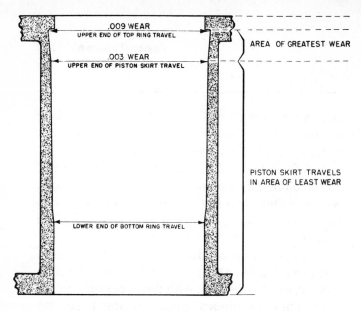

Fig. 20-3 Location of the cylinder bore wear (Dana Corporation).

Fig. 20-4 Measuring the cylinder bore wear immediately after the head is removed.

ing caps should be checked to make sure they are numbered. If not, they should be numbered with number stamps or prick punch. The parts are marked so they can be reassembled in exactly the same position. The identification punch marks should be made on the mating line as shown in Figure 20–5.

Piston and Rod Removal. The ridge above the top ring travel must be removed *before* the piston and connecting rod assembly is removed.

This is necessary to avoid catching a ring on the ridge and breaking the piston. Failure to remove the ridge will probably result in breaking the second piston land when the engine is run after reassembly with new rings as pictured in Figure 20–6. The ridge is removed with a cutting tool that is fed into the metal ridge. A guide on the tool prevents accidental cutting below the ridge. The

Fig. 20-5 Rod and main bearing caps identified to show their position. (a) Numbers, (b) punch marks.

(a)

(b)

ridge reaming job should be done carefully with frequent checks of the work so that no more material than necessary is removed. One type of ridge reamer is shown in Figure 20–7.

Connecting rod nuts are taken off the rod to be removed so the rod cap with its bearing half can be removed. The rod bolts are fitted with protectors made of aluminum or short pieces of rubber hose (Figure 20–8). These keep the rod bolts from touching the bearing journal surfaces on the crankshaft. If they did touch, the sharp

threads of the bolts could easily nick the surface, as pictured in Figure 20–9, so that a new bearing would be damaged. The connecting rod is carefully pushed up until the piston rings are free of the block deck. This must be done carefully because the piston ring drag stops when the rings are free of the cylinder bore. Excessive force on the rod

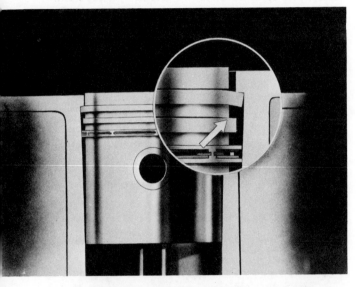

Fig. 20-6 Usual failure of the second land if the cylinder ridge is not removed before removing the pistons (Sealed Power Corporation).

Fig. 20-7 Ridge removal.

Fig. 20-8 Crankshaft protectors on rod bolts.

Fig. 20-9 Crankshaft journal nicked by a rod bolt.

Fig. 20-10 Connecting rod hitting the cylinder skirt bottom as it is removed carelessly.

will allow the piston to jump out of the bore when the ring moves out past the block deck. If the piston is not caught, it will fall to the floor and be damaged. Care should also be exercised to avoid hitting the bottom edge of the cylinder as illustrated in Figure 20-10. A burr here will scratch the piston skirt. When removed, the rod cap and bearing should be placed back on the rod to keep them together. This procedure should be followed with all the other pistons. No further parts need to be removed from the block when the so-called "ring-and-valve-job" is to be done.

Shaft Removal. The camshaft can be removed with the engine in the chassis on most automobiles. It is necessary to remove the radiator and grill to do this. The engine must be out of the chassis if the crankshaft is to be removed.

The next step in disassembly is to remove the water pump and crankshaft damper. The damper should be removed only with a threaded puller similar to the one in Figure 20-11. If a hook-type puller is used around the edge of the damper, it will probably pull the damper ring from the hub. If this happens, the damper assembly will have to

be replaced with a new unit. With the damper off, the timing cover can be removed, exposing the timing gear or timing chain. Examine these parts for excessive wear and looseness. Bolted cam sprockets can be loosened and removed to free the timing chain. Pressed-on sprockets are removed only when they are faulty. They are removed from the camshaft after pulling the camshaft from the block. This may require removal of the crankshaft gear at the same time. It is necessary to remove thrust-plate retaining screws when they are used. Camshaft drive details are covered in Chapter 6.

Fig. 20-11 Pulling the crankshaft damper.

Fig. 20-12 Lifting the camshaft from the block.

The camshaft can be removed at this time or it can be removed after the crankshaft is out. It must be carefully eased from the engine to avoid damaging the cam bearing or cam lobes. This is done most easily with the front of the engine pointing up as shown in Figure 20-12. Bearing surfaces are soft and scratch easily, and the cam lobes are hard and chip easily.

The main bearing caps should be checked for position markings before removal. They have been machined in place and will not perfectly fit in any other location. After marking, they can be removed to free the crankshaft. When the crankshaft is removed, the main bearing caps and bearings are reinstalled to reduce the chance of damage.

20-3 CLEANING

Cleaning the lower-engine is similar to cleaning the upper-engine as described in Chapter 19. During the cleaning process, parts should be rechecked for condition. Only parts that are not obviously damaged or worn beyond useful limits should be cleaned.

In some cases, the piston rings are removed before cleaning. In other cases, the pistons are given a preliminary degreasing before the rings are removed. Piston rings should be removed with a piston ring expander. The best type is shown in Figure 20-13. Care should be taken to prevent

Fig. 20-13 Removing the piston rings with a ring expander.

damage to the piston as the rings are removed. As they are taken off, they should be checked for unusual conditions. If the interference-fit piston pin is to be replaced, it is pressed from the rod using a correctly sized removing arbor and support plate to prevent piston damage as illustrated in Figure 20-14. Free-floating piston rings are pushed out of the piston after removing the retaining rings. Putting the piston under hot water will help expand the piston to allow easier pin removal.

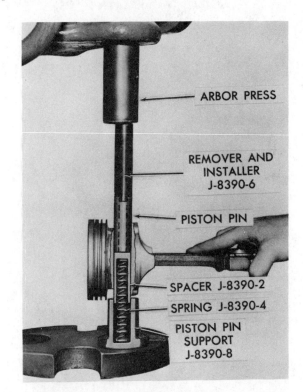

ARBOR PRESS

REMOVER AND INSTALLER J-8390-6

PISTON PIN

SPACER J-8390-2

SPRING J-8390-4

PISTON PIN SUPPORT J-8390-8

Fig. 20-14 Pressing a piston pin from a piston and rod (Cadillac Motor Car Division, General Motors Corporation).

The carbon on the head of the piston is removed by scraping with a blade, such as a putty knife (Figure 20-15). Special care should be taken to avoid rounding any of the sharp edges on the piston or removing any piston metal. A wire buffing wheel should *not* be used on aluminum pistons because it usually rounds the edges. Production shops may clean pistons with a glass or plastic bead blast. Piston ring grooves are scraped clean with a ring groove cleaning tool similar to the one shown in Figure 20-16. Grooves can also be cleaned by carefully using a broken ring filed

Fig. 20-15 Cleaning the piston head by scraping the carbon.

Fig. 20-16 Cleaning the piston ring grooves with a special ring groove cleaner.

to a sharp edge. The sides of the ring groove should have all of the carbon removed. Piston cleaning can be finished in a decarbonizing bath or vapor degreaser.

All of the disassembled parts are cleaned with a decarbonizer. This can be a hot chemical or vapor tank. After the parts are removed from the chemical decarbonizer, they are washed with hot water and dried with compressed air. Parts removed from the vapor tank may only require blowing and wiping to remove the dust that remains on the surface.

Iron and steel parts that are completely free of oil will usually rust rapidly. It is a good practice to wipe all machined surfaces with an oily rag. This will put a very light oil film on the surface and prevent rust.

When all of the parts have been thoroughly cleaned, they are ready for inspection.

20-4 INSPECTION PROCEDURES

Each part is given two types of inspection. First, the parts are given a good visual inspection. If no obvious faults exist, the parts that need it are given a dimensional inspection.

During the visual inspection, the parts are examined for wear patterns, scoring, pitting, and foreign materials. When an abnormal condition is found, the mating part should be examined for unusual conditions. This technique is followed part-to-part until the specific cause of the failure is identified. Parts that pass the visual inspection are given a dimensional inspection.

All parts for which specifications are given are measured. The sizes and clearances must be within the specification tolerance or the part must be reconditioned so it will fall within the dimensions given.

Measuring Tools. The automotive technician's basic measuring tool is the *micrometer*. It is based on decimal divisions of an inch or decimal divisions of a centimeter. The technician's type of inch micrometer is used to measure sizes to the nearest 0.001 in. and the metric micrometer will measure to the 0.01 mm. Specifications for automobile part sizes and clearances are given in these units.

Micrometers are usually used to measure external sizes. However, some micrometers are designed to measure inside and depth dimensions. These are not regularly used in engine service. Two common measurements made with an outside micrometer are piston diameter and bearing journal diameter.

The micrometer is based on divisions of the inch or millimeter. The thread pitch in the micrometer determines the amount of movement of the spindle for each thimble revolution. In inch micrometers, one revolution of the thimble moves the spindle 0.025 in. As the thimble is rotated one revolution, the edge of the thimble moves from one of the 0.025 in. subdivisions to the next. The edge of the thimble has 25 divisions, each representing a spindle movement of one thousandth of an inch. To read a micrometer, the technician places the size of the micrometer at the left of the decimal point (zero in Figure 20–17). At the right of the decimal point, he places the largest visible number on the barrel which represents tenths of an inch (0.3). He then adds 0.025 in for each visible subdivision past the last visible number (0.025 × 2 = 0.050). Finally, he adds the number of divisions shown on the thimble as it lines up on the barrel scale (0.022). The reading technique is shown in Figure 20–17 (0.372 in). The micrometer reading method is similar when a metric micrometer is used.

To assure accuracy, micrometers should be checked with a reference gauge before using. Another basic gauge for the technician is the *feeler* or *thickness gauge.* It is a flat, accurately sized strip of metal. Feeler gauges are available in 0.001 in. (0.025 mm) thickness steps up to 0.025 in. (0.625 mm) or in gauge sets of popular sizes. Larger gauges are sometimes required. They may be flat metal strips, blocks, or wire. Some are for general purpose use, while others have very specific uses. Several types are shown in Figure 20–18.

Thickness or feeler gauges are used to measure

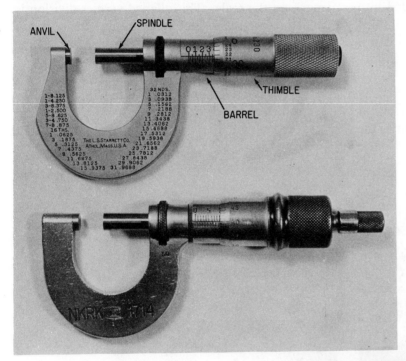

Fig. 20-17 Typical outside micrometers used to measure engine parts.

Fig. 20-18 Typical thickness gauges used in engine service.

the clearance between two flat surfaces, such as crankshaft thrust clearance, gear backlash clearance, piston ring side clearance, and gap clearance. Examples of these are shown in Figure 20–19.

A *square* is used to check the squareness of parts. Parting surface flatness can be checked with a straightedge placed across a part in several directions. The amount of warpage or bend can be determined by trying to slide gauges of various thickness under the straightedge.

A *dial gauge* is a useful measuring tool, especially for determining differences or amounts of movement. The dial gauge face is divided into 0.001 in. (0.025 mm) divisions, with full dial rotation indicating spindle travel of 0.100 in. (2.5 mm). A dial gauge is especially useful to measure endplay and out-of-round and shaft run-out.

A bend in a cylindrical object is checked by supporting the object in vee blocks or bearings at each end with a dial gauge tip placed against the center. Bend is indicated by the dial gauge movement as the object is turned. This type of bend measurement is called *run-out*.

Dial gauges on a special fixture are used to measure cylinder bore out-of-round and taper. A standard dial gauge with a support may be used to measure shaft end play, gear backlash, valve-in-guide looseness, valve-opening travel, and flange run-out.

A *vernier* is another tool that can be used to measure sizes within 0.001 in. (0.025 mm) for either outside or inside measurements. The jaws are placed across the item to be measured. The size is shown on the scale similar to the scale on the micrometer barrel. Vernier divisions are shown on the slide, one of which lines up with a division mark on the scale. This aligned vernier division is added to the scale value to determine the part size to the nearest 0.001 in. (0.025 mm). A dial gauge and vernier are shown in Figure 20–20.

Accurate hole sizes are determined with a *small hole gauge* or *telescopic gauge* used with an outside micrometer illustrated in Figure 20–21. The largest gauge that will fit is placed in the opening and

Fig. 20-19 Thickness gauges in typical measuring locations.

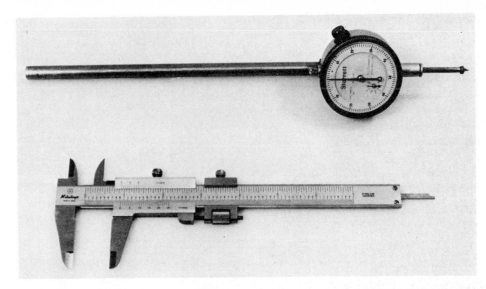

Fig. 20-20 A dial gauge (*above*) and a verner caliper (*below*).

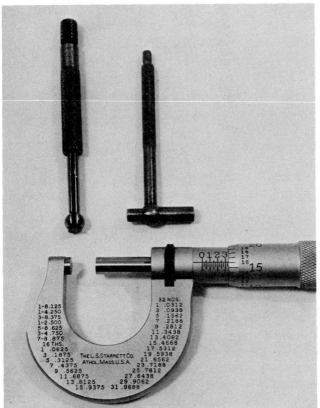

Fig. 20-21 Inside measurements are checked with a small hole gauge or telescopic gauge. The gauge is then measured with an outside micrometer.

correct torque, and then disassembled. The width of the Plastigauge crush indicates the amount of clearance, as shown in Figure 20–22. The smaller the clearance, the more crush exists, making the Plastigauge pattern wider.

Highly stressed parts used in performance engines are checked for cracks with specialized nondestructive testing procedures. A magnetic particle inspection called *Magnaflux* is used to check iron and steel parts. In this process, the part is magnetized and covered with iron particles. These particles are attracted to any magnetic pole

Fig. 20-22 Typical use of Plastigauge crush to measure clearance (Dana Corporation).

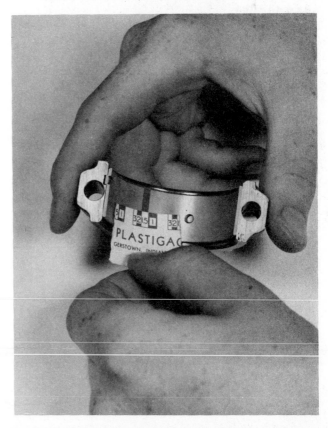

expanded to the opening size. It is then removed from the opening and the gauge is measured with the micrometer to determine the opening size.

Clearances between closely fitting assembled parts, such as bearing clearances, can be accurately measured with Plastigauge strips. A strip of Plastigauge is laid across the area being measured. The parts are assembled correctly, tightened to the

Fig. 20-23 Magnetic particle inspection showing a crack in a gear.

Fig. 20-24 Normal piston skirt wear.

that forms adjacent to a weak area or on cracks. A crack made visible by Magniflux is pictured in Figure 20–23.

Parts made from nonmagnetic materials are checked with a fluorescent penetrant called *Zyglo*. The clean part is dipped in the penetrant, rinsed, and dipped into a developer. The part then is inspected under an ultraviolet light. Any place that penetrant soaks into a surface crack will show up as a white line.

20–5 PISTON CONDITION

Normal piston wear shows up as even vertical wear on the thrust surfaces and slight looseness of the top ring in the groove as shown in Figure 20–24. This type of piston can usually be reconditioned for additional useful service.

Heat Damage. Holes in pistons, burned areas, severely damaged ring lands, and scoring are obviously abnormal conditions. The exact nature of the abnormalities should be determined so that the cause can be corrected and the driver given advice that will minimize the possibility of the damage recurring.

Combustion knock or detonation will burn the edge of the piston from the head down in behind the rings as pictured in Figure 20–25. This

Fig. 20-25 Heat damaged piston.

burning usually occurs at a point furthest from the spark plug where the hot end gases rapidly release their heat energy through detonation. In some cases, it breaks through the piston head. Pre-ignition results from multiple flame fronts that build temperature and pressure early in the combustion cycle. High temperature softens the piston, allowing combustion pressure to burn through, usually near the middle of the piston head, as shown in Figure 20–26.

Another form of heat damage is scuffing similar

Fig. 20-26 Hole in piston head.

Fig. 20-27 Scuffed piston skirt.

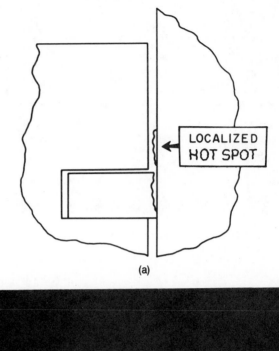

(a)

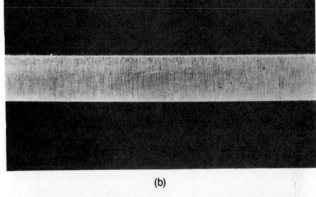

(b)

(c)

to that pictured in Figure 20–27. This occurs when excessive heat causes the piston to expand until it becomes tight in the cylinder bore. The lubricant is squeezed from the cylinder wall and allows metal-to-metal contact. Excessive heat can come from a malfunctioning cooling system as well as from abnormal combustion.

Piston rings may get hot spots from a lack of lubrication, from high combustion temperatures, or from ineffective cooling systems. Metal from the ring hot spots will transfer to the cylinder wall, scuffing the ring and piston (Figure 20–28).

Worn piston rings allow hot combustion gases to blow by the piston and so allow oil to come up from the crankcase to the combustion chamber. Hot combustion gases meet the oil in the area of

Fig. 20-28 Piston ring scuffing. (a) Exaggerated drawing of ring metal transfer to the cylinder wall, (b) scuffed piston ring face, (c) scuffed cylinder wall (Dana Corporation).

Fig. 20-29 Piston rings stuck in their grooves (Dana Corporation).

Fig. 20-30 Skirt wear caused by a misaligned connecting rod.

the rings where the heat partially burns the oil. This produces hard carbon around the rings, causing them to stick in the grooves as shown in Figure 20–29. If this is the only piston problem, it can be corrected by a thorough cleaning and by installing new piston rings.

Corrosion Damage. Lowering operating temperatures will produce a corrosive mixture in the oil. This will be aggravated by coolant leakage into the combustion chamber. Corrosion will produce mottled gray pits on the aluminum piston.

Mechanical Damage. Piston damage can result from mechanical problems. Connecting rod misalignment will show up as a diagonal thrust surface wear pattern across the piston skirt, which indicates that the piston is not operating straight in the cylinder (Figure 20–30). This, in turn, means that the rings are not running perpendicular to the walls so they cannot seal properly.

Piston damage can come from the loss of a piston pin lock ring. The lock will come out if the lock grooves are damaged, if the lock ring is weak, or if the rod is bent so that a side load is placed on the piston pin forcing it against the lock ring. The piston and possibly the cylinder will be badly damaged as the lock ring slides between them. A new piston is required when this type of damage occurs as can be seen in Figure 20–31.

Pistons crack, usually on the skirt or near the piston pin boss. Cracks generally occur at high mileage, because of overloading, or because of improperly designed pistons. Any crack in a piston is cause for rejection. Typical piston skirt cracks are shown in Figure 20–32.

Fig. 20-31 Damage caused by a loose piston pin lock ring (Sealed Power Corporation).

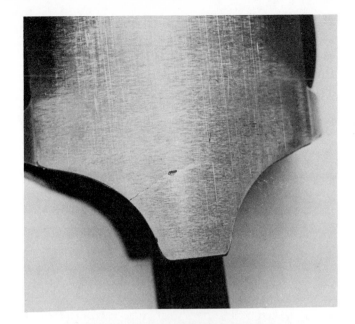

Fig. 20-32 Cracked skirts on two pistons.

the ring to only hit the high spots and results in high localized side loads on the ring when the ring inertia is greatest. These loads may break the ring which, in turn, generally cause excessive piston damage similar to that shown in Figure 20–34. Worn piston skirts cause excess clearance, which allows the piston to slap.

20-6 PISTON SERVICE

Pistons may be reconditioned if they have no obvious defect that would be cause for rejection. Piston reconditioning is usually done with specialized

(a)

(b)

Fig. 20-33 Piston groove wear. (Dana Corporation). (a) Cross section of a worn groove, (b) side view of a worn upper ring groove.

Dirt entering the engine greatly increases the wear rate. Dirt will scratch and wear the face of the piston rings and wear the side of the ring and groove. The top piston ring side clearance must not exceed 0.006 in. (0.15 mm). Dirt may be airborn and come in through an ineffective air filter element or through an air leak between the filter and the carburetor air horn. Dirt in the oil will cause abnormal wear on the piston skirts, sides of the ring groove, and the oil ring. Worn piston rings must be replaced. Piston ring groove side wear is usually uneven, as shown in Figure 20–33. This causes

293

Fig. 20-34 Damage caused by a broken ring (Dana Corporation).

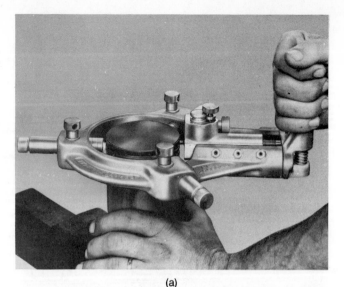

(a)

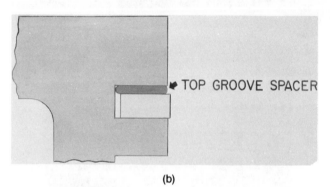

(b)

Fig. 20-35 Piston groove reconditioning. (Dana Corporation). (a) Groove machining, (b) groove spacer in place.

Fig. 20-36 Measuring piston side clearance with a thickness gauge.

service equipment in an automotive machine shop. The operations are listed here to help provide an understanding of the reasons for each operation.

Ring Grooves. The top ring grooves with excessive side clearance are machined about 0.025 in. (0.625 mm) wider than the standard groove. One type of tool used for this is pictured in Figure 20–35. A steel groove spacer is placed above the new ring in the machined groove to return the side clearance to standard dimensions.

Skirt. Piston fit in the bore is checked by placing the piston in the cylinder, together with a long strip feeler gauge on the piston thrust side, as done in Figure 20–36. A force of five to ten pounds on the feeler gauge indicates correct clearance. A pull of less than five pounds requires the use of a thicker gauge strip. A pull of more than ten pounds requires the use of a thinner gauge. If the piston-to-cylinder clearance is greater than is specified, the piston will have to be expanded, or the cylinder will have to be rebored and fitted with a larger piston.

(a)

(b)

Fig. 20-37 Piston resizing. (a) Knurling tool, (b) appearance of a knurled piston skirt (Dana Corporation).

(a)

Fig. 20-38 Piston pin fitting. (a) Honing a piston pin hole, (b) and (c) checking a piston pin hole size (Sunnen Products Company).

In operation, the piston skirt will wear or collapse. Wear also occurs on the cylinder wall. The combination of wear and collapse will produce excess piston-to-cylinder clearance. Piston skirts are expanded by producing an interrupted surface on them that displaces metal upward between the teeth of the knurling tool, as illustrated in Figure 20–37. This effectively increases piston skirt size. Skirt size can be controlled by the amount of pressure placed on the knurling tool. The knurled piston surface carries lubricating oil to help maintain an oil film while providing a close fitting clearance to reduce noise.

Pins. Piston pins may be replaced with new oversize pins. The holes in the piston and connecting rod are accurately sized with a pin hone similar to the one pictured in Figure 20–38. Tight fitting

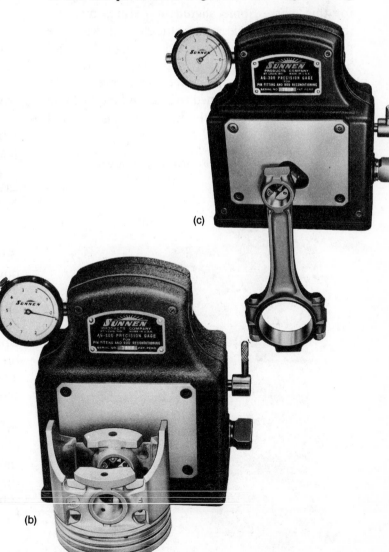

(c)

(b)

piston pins may cause the piston to seize on the pin in its expanded position, producing piston skirt scuff near the piston pin boss. If the pin is too loose, it will produce a knock or rattle when the engine is in operation.

The automobile machine shop usually services the connecting rod and piston as an assembly. A new piston pin is fitted, and, in addition, the connecting rod is checked for alignment. It will be straightened as part of normal piston assembly service.

Connecting Rods. The connecting rods can stretch, bend, or twist. In operation, their small and large eyes can enlarge. The rod stretch is measured between the eye centers. The rod eyes are checked for size and eccentricity. The bend and alignment are checked on a fixture designed for this work. Some alignment fixtures measure the bare rod, while others measure it with the piston installed, as illusrated in Figure 20–39. Stretched rods are usually replaced. An oversize piston pin is put in an enlarged small eye. To do this, the small eye is honed to size. When the large eye is enlarged, about 0.015 in. (0.4 mm) is removed

Fig. 20-39 Checking the connecting rod alignment.

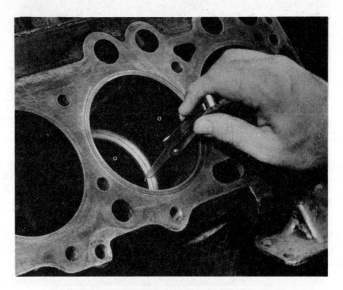

Fig. 20-40 Measuring piston ring gap in the lower part of the cylinder (Dana Corporation).

from the cap parting surface. It is reassembled and the hole is machined to the proper size. Connecting rods are usually reconditioned in an automotive machine shop.

Cylinder Wall Service. When only a ring and valve job is to be done and no service done on the shafts, the cylinder wall is reconditioned and the pistons and rods are assembled and installed in the block. The cylinder wall is usually serviced before the pistons are replaced. The upper cylinder ridge was removed as the engine was disassembled. Smooth glazed cylinder walls provide good anti-scuff surfaces and need no further service. Cylinder walls that are wavy or scuffed should be smoothed by honing as described in Section 20–10.

Fitting Piston Rings. The new piston rings are fitted into the lower portion of the cylinder, pressed down with a piston head, and the end gap measured with a feeler gauge as shown in Figure 20–40. Minimum gap should never be less than specified. If it is, the ends could touch during operation. This would cause severe ring scuffing and possibly ring breakage. Excess clearance is not critical unless it is more than 0.040 in. (1.0 mm) greater than specifications.

The side clearance should be checked on each ring *before* the rings are installed on the piston, as illustrated in Figure 20–41. If any clearance is too small, the ring groove should be checked to correct the fault. Small clearance is most likely caused by some hard carbon overlooked during cleaning or by handling damage that has nicked the ring land.

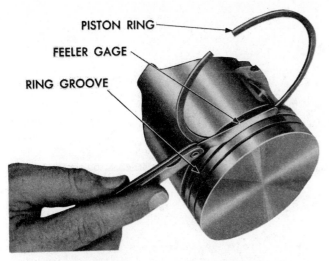

Fig. 20-41 Measuring piston ring side clearance (Chrysler Motor Corporation).

All rings must move freely all the way around the ring grooves.

Piston Assembly. All of the required reconditioning of shafts, bearings, and block should have been completed and reassembled before the pistons are reassembled. The piston is installed on the rod, making sure it is turned correctly. This can be checked by the position of the rod location number and piston head notch. Rings are carefully installed on the piston. This can best be done by using the same tool that was used to remove the ring, as was shown in Figure 20–13. Cast iron rings break easily if twisted or stretched too much. Extreme care must be exercised if installing rings when special tools are not available.

Before the pistons are installed in the cylinder, the piston and cylinder wall are given one last cleaning and then heavily coated with fresh motor oil. Protectors are put over the rod bolts to avoid crankshaft journal damage. A ring compressor, as shown in Figure 20–42, is used to hold the piston rings all the way into their grooves as the piston is eased into the cylinder. Piston binding as it is pushed into the bore is usually caused by a ring slipping from the compressor and catching on the block deck. Forcing the piston into the cylinder will break the ring and possibly the piston land. Pistons must go into their original cylinder and they must face in the correct direction to avoid valve interference.

New connecting rod bearings are usually installed at the same time that new rings are being installed. The crankshaft is usually in serviceable condition if the only problem was a "ring job."

Standard or undersize bearings that will produce rod bearing clearances within specifications must be used. Bearing backs must be clean and dry. The bearing surface should be lubricated with fresh motor oil. Bearing caps should be tightened to the correct torque using the correct size socket that won't cause the cap to shift as it is tightened.

Fig. 20-42 Installing pistons. (a) Using an adjustable steel ring compressor, (b) using a cast iron ring compressor.

(a)

(b)

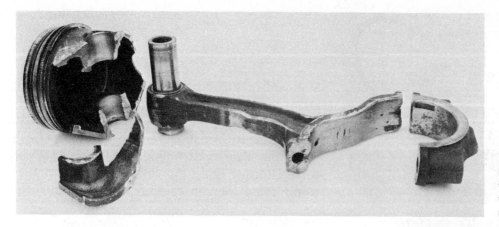

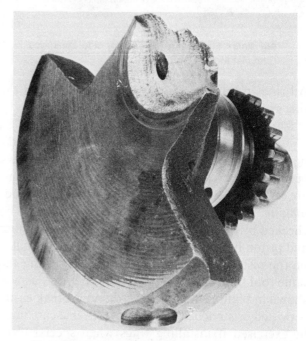

Fig. 20-43 A rod assembly that was completely destroyed when one of the connecting rod bolts failed.

Figure 20–43 shows the result of an improperly torqued connecting rod bolt. Standard engine assembly procedures are followed, using new gaskets and seals.

20-7 SHAFT AND BEARING CONDITION

Shaft damage includes damaged bearing journals, bends or warpage, and cracks. Shafts with abnormalities must be reconditioned or replaced.

Crankshaft. The crankshaft is one of the most highly stressed engine parts. The stress increases four times every time the engine speed doubles. Any sign of a crack is a cause to reject the crankshaft. If a cracked crankshaft continues in service, it will break as did the shaft in Figure 20–44. Cracks in high production passenger car engines can be detected with a close visual inspection. High-rpm racing crankshafts should be checked with Magnaflux to show up any minute crack that would lead to failure.

Bearing journal scoring is one of the most common crankshaft defects. Scoring appears as scratches around the journal circumference, generally near the center of the journal, as shown in Figure 20–45. Dirt and grit carried in the oil enter between the journal and bearing. If the particles are too large to get through the oil clearance, they will partially embed in the bearing and scratch the journal. Dirt can also be left on the journal during assembly. Maximum journal life depends upon the continuous supply of clean lubricating oil.

Crankshaft journals can have nicks or pits in them. Nicks are caused by carelessness when the journal is bumped with another part while exposed or while being assembled (Figure 20–46). Pits can be caused by corrosion.

Fig. 20-44 A crankshaft that was broken at the front of the number one crank pin.

Fig. 20-45 A scored crankshaft bearing journal.

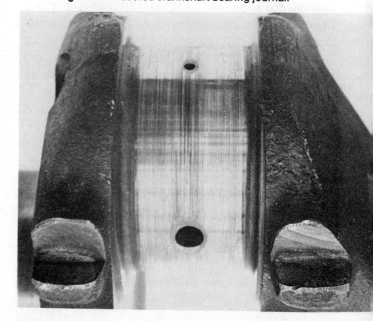

298

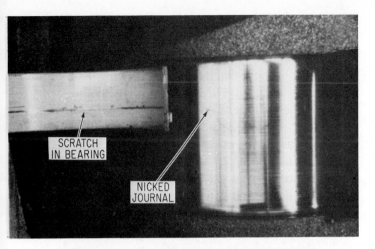

Fig. 20-46 Careless handling caused the crankshaft nick on the crankshaft journal on the right. This in turn scored the bearing on the left of the illustration. These marks were present on a brand new engine.

SCRATCH IN BEARING

NICKED JOURNAL

Rough journals and slight bends can be corrected by grinding the journals on true centers. Forged shafts with excess bend should be straightened before grinding. A typical crankshaft grinder is shown in Figure 20–48.

If the relatively inexpensive standard production crankshaft is damaged beyond grinding limits, it should be replaced. Excessive damage is pictured in Figure 20–49. More expensive racing crankshafts, or crankshafts that are to be modified, can have the journals built up by welding or by special metal spray techniques. They are then straightened and reground. This process is expensive and,

Fig. 20-47 Checking crankshaft runout with a dial gauge with only the end main bearing shells installed.

Fig. 20-48 Grinding a crankshaft.

A bent crankshaft can be detected by supporting the end main bearing journals in vee blocks. A dial gauge on the middle bearing journal will show run-out as the crankshaft is turned. If vee blocks are not available, the crankshaft can be supported by the two upper half end bearings in the block as shown in Figure 20–47. The other bearing shells must be removed. A dial gauge is used in the same manner to indicate the shaft bend or run-out.

Journals will wear out-of-round and become tapered. Out-of-round and taper are measured with a micrometer, taking measurements at a number of different locations on each journal.

Fig. 20-49 A badly damaged crankshaft caused by a broken connecting rod as shown in Figure 20-43.

Fig. 20-50 A badly worn camshaft.

therefore, is done only when it is less costly than purchasing a new special crankshaft.

Camshaft. Cam lobe damage is the most usual type of camshaft failure. Lobe surface breakdown usually starts at the highly loaded cam nose or at the edge of the lobe where extreme pressures exist. Wear becomes rapid once the damage breaks through the cam's hard surface, causing pitting, grooves, scoring, or flaking. This type of wear is illustrated in Figure 20-50. The most critical period for cam wear is the first fifteen minutes of operation after the engine is assembled. Cam lubrication is critical during this time when engine lubrication is marginal. Manufacturers

recommend specific cam surface lubricants, to be used during assembly. They run all the way from SE motor oil to especially prepared lubricants available at their own dealer parts department.

Cam lobes are designed with a slight taper across the surface, and the tappet or lifter has a slight crown. This positions the contact point slightly away from the geometrical center. The offset causes lifter rotation that produces a nearly even wear pattern. A flat based lifter or a used lifter on a new camshaft will contact the high edge of the cam lobe, producing edge wear that will lead to surface breakdown.

Passenger car camshafts having abnormal wear, like crankshafts, are replaced. Camshafts can be reground on special profile cam grinders. This can be done as a repair procedure or as a means of modifying the cam contour. It is generally more expensive to grind a camshaft than to purchase a new standard production camshaft. Grinding is, therefore, only done on special camshafts and on some low production heavy-duty camshafts.

Grinding a camshaft increases the distance between the top of the lifter and the rocker arm. Adjustable rocker arms can be changed to compensate for this distance. Nonadjustable rocker arms with hydraulic lifters would require a longer push rod. The new push rod adds to the expense of camshaft grinding.

Bearings. Bearing distress or failure will result from foreign particles, from lubrication breakdown, from overloading, and from corrision. Any bearing failure is cause for replacement; however, a close visual examination of bearing distress will indicate the cause of failure. The cause must be corrected before the engine is reassembled, to prevent recurring failure.

The best procedure for examining bearings is to remove the bearing shells from the block, rods, and caps. They should be placed on a table in the same order as their location in the engine, bearing face up as pictured in Figure 20-51. Abnormalties can then be related to the other bearings and to the shaft journals.

Foreign particles are dirt, metal chips, or abrasives. Dirt may have been left in the engine when it was assembled, even between the bearing and cap. It may enter through breather openings or through faulty filters. The dirt is carried in the oil to the bearings. Metal chips may have lodged in the engine during machining operations. They

Fig. 20-51 Bearings laid out for inspection.

are also produced as internal parts wear. Normally, the small metal particles from wear will settle to the bottom of the oil pan, get trapped in the oil filter or be drained from the engine with the used oil. When rapid breakdown and wear occurs, as shown in many illustrations in this book, the particles may move through the lubrication system to the bearing. The most likely causes of small metal particles are oil pump gear wear, cam and lifter wear, rocker arm wear, and timing gear wear. Aluminum particles come from piston skirt wear. Abrasives are left in the engine after reconditioning whenever the parts are not thoroughly cleaned using proper cleaning methods. Abrasives tend to

embed in soft bearing metals, like aluminum, brass, copper, and babbitt. When this happens, the abrasives rapidly cut into the hard bearing journal that is running against them. Soft metals should never be reconditioned by using an abrasive.

Foreign particles embedded in bearings, pictured in Figure 20–52, should be checked to determine their source. Bearing materials tend to cover them so they will not damage the shaft. Large particles will not embed, but will score the bearing and shaft. Badly scored bearings are shown in Figure 20–53. The specific type of embedded particle can be determined by scraping some of the embedded material from the bearing surface near the parting surface where most material will collect. Steel particles can be picked up with a magnet. Aluminum particles will dissolve in a drop of 10% solution of sodium hydroxide, producing bubbles. Other particles, such as dirt, brass, and copper, can best be identified by their color.

Lubrication breakdown may result from the motor oil not getting to the bearing, from heat that excessively thins the motor oil, and from overloading the bearing so oil is squeezed from the bearing surface. These problems are inter-related and may occur at the same time. Oil starvation wipes or extrudes low-melting-temperature bearing material from the steel backing. Tem-

Fig. 20-52 Foreign particles embedded in a bearing.

Fig. 20-53 Badly scored bearings.

peratures may increase enough to cause even the steel bearing backing to turn to a blue color from overheating. This can be seen in Figure 20–54.

The main reason oil does not get to a bearing is excessive oil leakage or throwoff from other bearings that are closer to the oil pump. When leakage from bearing clearances becomes greater than the oil pump's capacity, at the speed the pump is running, oil starvation will occur. Worn cam bearings often cause this oil leakage. The valve train holds the camshaft down on the bottom of the bearing all of the time so that the wear occurs only on the lower side of the bearing. The excess bearing clearance above the cam does not produce a knock because the load is always in the downward direction. Oil delivery to the upper side of the worn cam bearing can freely escape to the pan, thus reducing the amount of oil available to the main and rod bearings where oil starvation may occur. Blocked oil passages are usually the result of misaligned oil holes in a bearing shell. The mismatch is readily visible on the outer surface of the bearing shell.

Oil starvation may occur at very high engine speeds in some engine designs. High crankshaft rotational speed may cause centrifugal forces in the oil holes that are greater than oil pump pressure.

The oil must have a laminar or smooth flow to provide a hydrodynamic oil film. At excessive speeds the film can no longer flow smoothly, and turbulence will develop. This causes voids in the oil surface and oil starvation occurs in these voids.

As the lubrication film breaks down, friction and heat increase. Heat thins the oil which, in turn, reduces the lubrication film. This process is unstable and increases rapidly until bearing failure occurs.

Full throttle low-speed operation, or *lugging,* puts very high loads on the bearings. High loads tend to squeeze oil from the bearing. Thin oil will squeeze out faster than a more viscous oil. Engine and engine parts manufacturers caution against lugging because it causes rapid damage to engine parts. Lugging can only occur with vehicles equipped with a solid drive line. Automatic transmissions allow enough slippage at full throttle low-speed operation so that lugging cannot occur.

Each time a load is applied on a bearing, the bearing surface flexes slightly. Flexing occurs during all engine operation. The effect increases as the engine loads increase. Gradually, the flexing will cause bearing fatigue, which will be indicated by fine cracks in the bearing surface. In time, the cracks will join at the backing bond to loosen pieces of the bearing material from their backing. The loosened piece overheats, then melts, which increases the rate of bearing failure. Fatigue failure results in bearings appearing as in Figure 20–55.

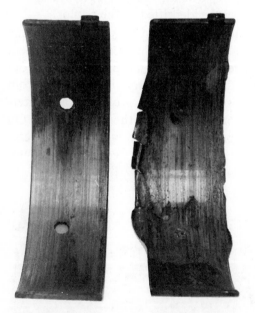

Fig. 20-54 Bearing damage resulting from lack of lubrication. On the left is a partially damaged bearing and on the right is an excessively damaged bearing.

Fig. 20-55 Bearing fatigue failure.

Bearing overloading may occur on a part of a misaligned bearing. This may be the result of a bent rod or shaft, or a warped engine block. Journal taper usually results from journal wear; however, it is always possible to have faulty grinding. It results in bearing wear as in Figure 20-56.

Fig. 20-56 Bearing wear from a tapered journal.

Lightly loaded short trip driving does not produce sufficient heat to drive off condensed water and gases. These collect in the oil, causing acid and sludge. The acid attacks the bearings and the bearings corrode.

Faulty bearing installation can lead to premature failure. Bearings that fit too tightly will not leave enough oil clearance so oil starvation occurs. Bearing shells with insufficient crush may rotate with the shaft. Dirt that becomes trapped behind the bearing shell causes a tight spot in the bearing, which will fail.

Careful interpretation of bearing distress will pinpoint the cause of the distress. The cause must be corrected so that the reconditioned engine will have a normal service life.

20-8 SHAFT AND BEARING SERVICE

Inspection of the crankshaft will indicate any abnormalities (Figure 20-57). A shaft in good condition only needs to have the bearing journals polished with fine polishing cloth. The polishing abrasive should be moved in the direction opposite that of rotation to minimize the effects of microscopic "teeth" that result from polishing.

If crankshaft wear, bend, or scoring is beyond limits, it should be reground to a standard under-

size. Crankshaft grinding is done on special grinding equipment by a highly skilled operator.

Camshaft repair is limited to regrinding when it is more economical or expedient than purchasing a new camshaft.

Bearings are replaced as a normal reconditioning procedure. The correct size bearing should be selected to provide proper bearing clearances. When shafts are ground, undersize bearings are used.

Dynamic oil seals are replaced each time the engine is disassembled to the point where the seals are accessible. Seals are inexpensive, compared to the work required to get at them if they leak later on. Replacement is a good preventative maintenance procedure.

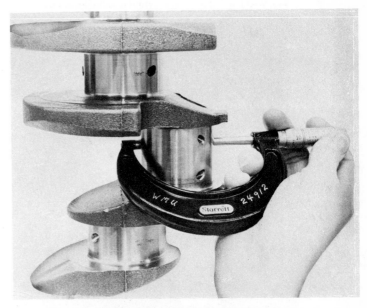

Fig. 20-57 Measuring the size of the connecting rod journal of a crankshaft.

20-9 BLOCK CONDITION

Block abnormalities occur in the cylinder wall, cooling system, and shaft bore alignment, and as broken parts. All of the other engine parts depend upon the block for support, alignment, and operating climate.

Cylinder wall wear, as visible in Figure 20-58, is one of the most noticeable block conditions. Cylinder walls, in normal use, have a smooth glaze from the burnishing effects of the piston and rings

Fig. 20-58 A badly scored cylinder wall caused by an improperly installed oil control ring.

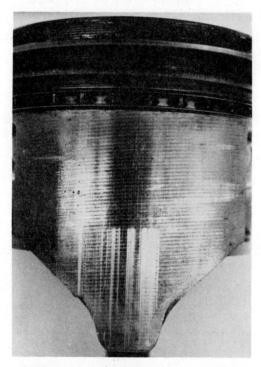

Fig. 20-59 A damaged piston skirt scored by a burr on the bottom of the cylinder that was put there when the connecting rod hit the cylinder skirt as the rod was removed during disassembly, as shown in Figure 20-10.

during operation even when taper, out-of-round, and wavy wall conditions exist. Dirt and broken rings will cause scratches on the wall. If the scratches are allowed to remain, they will allow oil

to go into the combustion chamber on the intake stroke and combustion gases to blow into the crankcase during the power stroke.

Occasionally, the connecting rod is allowed to strike the bottom edge of the cylinder wall as the piston and rod assembly are removed or installed. This will nick the bottom edge of the cylinder and raise sharp points. If these points are not removed, they will scratch the piston skirt as shown in Figure 20-59.

Piston pin locks that come out of the piston will usually score the cylinder wall. If the piston pin drifts out of its bore, it, too, will score the wall. If the oil ring spacer is overlapped, it will score the cylinder wall. Occasionally, such deep scores are produced that they break into the coolant jacket. When this happens, a thin-walled cast iron sleeve can be installed. The cylinder is bored oversize to a diameter to accept the sleeve. The sleeve is pressed in, then bored to the required cylinder diameter.

The cooling system may be plugged with deposits or, in unusual cases, may be miscast when a casting core was damaged. The water jacket should be thoroughly checked. Core plug openings should be checked for evidence of leakage.

In operation, the block is stressed mechanically and thermally. Mechanical stress comes from assembly bolt torques, combustion pressures, and dynamic loads. Thermal stress from combustion heat may cause the block to warp and take a set. The block must be checked for parting surface flatness, especially the head deck, and for shaft bore alignment. Misalignment of shaft bores can be recognized by the bearing distress difference between the bearing shells. Bearing bore alignment can be checked with a properly ground test arbor 0.001 in. (0.025 mm) smaller than the bearing bore that is bolted in place of the crankshaft. The block is aligned if the test arbor can be turned by hand with a 12-in. handle. Alignment may also be checked with a straightedge placed across three or more bearing saddles. A feeler gauge one half the bearing clearance should *not* go between the straightedge and saddle, as shown in Figure 20-60. If it does, warpage exists.

Cracks in the block will allow leaks or will not support engine loads. Some cracks are repairable and others are not. The location of the crack and cost of repair determine the technician's decision on whether to repair or replace the block. Cracks on the exterior portion of the coolant jacket are

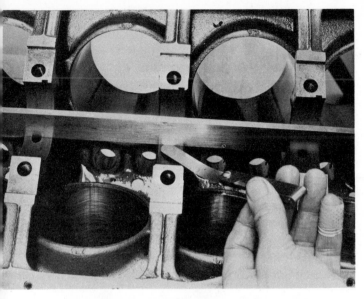

Fig. 20-60 Checking the main bearing saddle alignment with a straightedge.

usually repairable. Cracks in main bearing webs are not repairable.

20-10 BLOCK SERVICE

Blocks that have normal wear within specification limits may require no reconditioning. Many piston ring manufacturers recommend installing their rings on the worn glazed cylinder walls. The recommended procedures packaged with the new ring set should always be followed.

   Cylinder Walls. Some ring manufacturers recommend breaking the cylinder wall glaze with a hone, as shown in Figure 20–61, before installing new rings. When honing is not required, it eliminates the time needed for honing and for cleanup, and so reduces reconditioning cost.

   The cylinder wall should be honed to straighten the cylinder if the wall is wavy or scuffed. If honing is being done with the crankshaft in the block, the crankshaft should be protected to keep honing chips from getting on the shaft.

   Honing should be done with a clean lubricated cylinder hone, using 180 to 280 grit stones. The hone must be stroked fast enough to produce the proper crosshatch finish similar to the one shown in Figure 20–62.

   It is extremely important to thoroughly clean the cylinder wall after honing to remove all abrasive grit. If the crankshaft is in the block, cleaning is accomplished by thoroughly oiling the

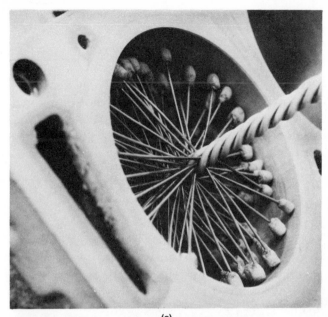

(a)

(b)

Fig. 20-61 Deglazing a cylinder bore. (a) Brush-type deglazer, (b) stone-type deglazer.

Fig. 20-62 Normal finish of a deglazed cylinder wall.

wall and wiping with a clean rag, and repeating this operation until a clean rag is not discolored by abrasives. If the block is bare, cleaning should be done by scrubbing the wall with a brush, using soap and water. Gasoline, kerosene, or commercial cleaners will remove the oil, but will allow abrasives to remain on the cylinder wall; therefore, they should *not* be used to clean the cylinder after honing.

Cylinder walls that are worn or scored beyond honing limits should be bored to the smallest standard oversize that will clean the cylinder walls. New oversize pistons are required to fit oversized cylinders.

Cylinders are bored perpendicular to the block deck. If there is any deck warpage, it must be ground or milled flat before boring cylinders. This usually is done in the same manner as heads, on a large table with a grinder or cutter work head that rotates in the center nearly flush with the surface. Passing the block back and forth across the work head takes small cuts until the surface is clean and smooth.

Cylinder boring is done with a piece of equipment especially designed for this process, usually called a *boring bar*. It consists of a power-driven cutting tool in a rigid arbor. The arbor is aligned on the cylinder center, near the bottom of the cylinder bore where the least wear has occurred. When centered, the boring machine is clamped in position, often on the block deck surface. The arbor is raised and fitted with a cutting tool. The cutting tool is adjusted to the diameter desired and the cylinder is then bored from the top down. Several passes, rough and fine, may be required to enlarge the cylinder to the required size. The bored finish appears as those in Figure 20–63. The size is determined by the new piston that is to be used. Pistons should be available before boring begins so the cylinder can be bored to an exact size required. The cylinder is bored to 0.0005 to 0.002 in. (0.0125 to 0.05 mm) less than required. Cylinder size and required wall finish are completed by honing. A typical wall finish is like Figure 20–64. This is followed by the thorough cylinder wall cleaning that is normally done after honing.

Cam Bearings. Cam bearings are replaced when servicing the block. The cam bearings are sleeve-bushing, steel-backed precision bearings. They are removed and installed using the same tool, either with a slide hammer or a long screw similar to the one shown in Figure 20–65. Some cam bearing tools use adapters installed in three bearings with an adapter shaft inserted in the adapters. A lock is placed on the shaft adjacent to the adapter in the bearing to be removed. The other two adapters act as guides to maintain alignment. The shaft is forced endwise, sliding the bearing from its bore. The new correct size and type bearing is installed on the adapter and turned so the oil holes will index. The bearing is carefully started squarely into the bore; then pulled to its normal position. This process is repeated on each

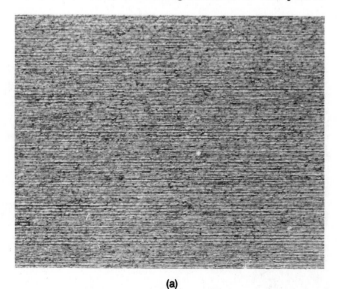

(a)

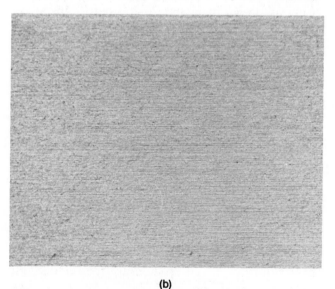

(b)

Fig. 20-63 Appearance of the cylinder wall after boring (Dana Corporation). (a) Rough boring, (b) finish boring.

camshaft bearing. An expansion plug is placed behind the rear cam bearing to seal the opening. Other cam bearing tools are designed to remove and install the cam bearing without the guide adapters.

If oil pump drive bushings are used, they can be replaced at this time when new bearings are needed. This usually requires pulling and installing equipment especially designed for this specific job.

Main Bearings. Main bearing bores in the block require no service if there is no sign of warpage. When warpage exists, the main bearing

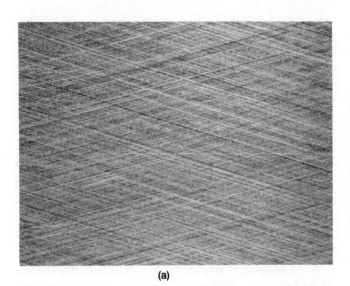

(a)

(b)

Fig. 20-64 Honed cylinder. (a) Desired crosshatch pattern (Dana Corporation), (b) hone in use.

Fig. 20-65 Tool to remove and install cam bearings (Buick Motor Division, General Motors Corporation).

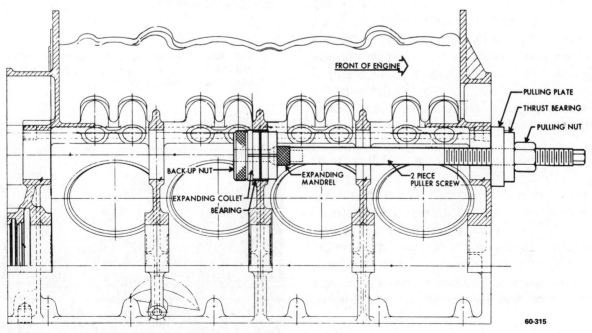

60-315

bores must be *align bored.* Before boring, 0.015 in. (0.4 mm) is removed from the main bearing cap parting surfaces; then the caps are installed on the block. The block is centered in an align boring machine. The cutting tool is set to the original bore diameter and then each crankcase bearing housing is bored on the same center.

Align boring may be done on the bearings rather than in the crankcase bearing housing. The block is fitted with 0.060 in. (1.5 mm) undersize bearings; these are bored to provide proper crankshaft main bearing oil clearance.

Oil Pump. Oil pumps are cleaned and inspected. They are checked for clearance between the gear and housing. The gears are checked for backlash. If the pump parts are worn or scored, the pump should be replaced. There is no recommended oil pump repair procedure.

Water Pump. Water pump problems usually result from rough bearings, leaking seals, or a damaged impeller. Present-day pumps are serviced as a unit, although parts can be specially ordered to rebuild the water pump. When a problem does exist, the pump is replaced with a new or factory rebuilt assembly. The pump is often replaced on an overhauled engine as a preventative maintenance item.

Covers. All parting surfaces should be flat and free from nicks or scratches. Cast covers can be smoothed by attaching abrasive paper to a flat surface; then passing the cover over the abrasive surface until the entire surface is clean. Stamped metal covers and pans can be straightened by placing the edge on a flat surface and tapping the high spots to flatten them.

Special Considerations. Engines that are to be used to provide maximum service life are reconditioned to provide minimum service clearances. Engines that are to be used for maximum performance, on the other hand, are reconditioned to provide maximum service clearances and minimum combustion chamber volumes. This technique is called *blue printing* the engine. It requires very careful fitting and balance of all components.

Blue printing takes special equipment and a lot of time, so it is a costly procedure. Special techniques will include cleaning and chamfering all threaded and oil hole openings, removing casting burrs with a hand grinder, honing lifter bores, priming the interior of the block with special paint, modifying the main bearing oil passages, balancing crankshaft and rod assemblies, hand grinding the combustion chambers to make their volumes equal, checking the valve-to-piston clearance, and many other fine details that reflect the individual engine rebuilder's touch.

20-11 ENGINE REASSEMBLY

The first step in engine reassembly is a final, thorough cleaning to remove any dust or dirt from the parts. Gasket sealing compound is put on the edge of the core plugs and they are seated in the block. All screw plugs are installed. The camshaft is liberally coated with the recommended lubricant, and carefully slipped into place, taking care not to score the cam bearings or to knock the plug from the rear of the camshaft bore. Some manufacturers have a special cam holding tool to keep this from happening and others depend on a thrust plate.

The rear main oil seal is installed before the crankshaft is replaced. Rope-type seals are packed into the seal groove as described in Chapter 6. The crankshaft and new main bearings are lubricated with SE motor oil. The crankshaft and bearing caps are installed, the thrust bearings aligned as shown in Figure 20–66, and the caps are torqued.

Fig. 20-66 Seating the thrust bearings before tightening the main bearing caps by moving the crankshaft endwise with a pry.

Fig. 20-67 Turning the crankshaft with a torque wrench as each bearing cap is tightened to immediately show any unusual tightness.

It is helpful to check crankshaft turning effort with a torque wrench after each cap is tightened (Figure 20-67). If the turning effort increases appreciably after one cap is tightened, remove that cap and determine the cause of binding. Use this procedure of measuring turning effort throughout engine assembly. Any tight spots or binding that exist will show up immediately, and therefore can be repaired before any further assembly is done. Care must be exercised to make sure all gaskets and seals around the rear main bearing cap are correctly installed, following any special instructions for that specific engine type.

Cam gears, sprockets, and chains are aligned and installed. Gear or chain backlash should be rechecked to see that it is within limits. A new oil seal is installed in the timing cover. If a slinger ring is used, it is installed on the crankshaft, followed by the timing cover with a new gasket. The gasket is usually coated with a nonhardening gasket compound. The crankshaft damper is installed before the timing cover is tightened. This allows the oil seal and timing cover to center themselves on the damper hub. The cover is then tightened to the correct torque.

Piston assemblies are installed in the manner previously described.

Oil pump gears are given a light coating of heavy oil or light grease to provide initial lubrication that will allow the pump to prime itself. The pump is installed with new gaskets and seals. In some engines, the oil pump drive rod must be installed as the pump is installed. Windage trays or baffles are installed where they are used.

Oil pan seals are carefully placed in position so they will seal properly. The pan is installed and the retaining bolts snugged up, then torqued.

This completes the assembly of the lower-engine. The heads, valve train, and manifolds are assembled and adjusted as described in Chapter 19. When the basic engine is completely assembled, the clutch and transmission are installed as described in Chapters 21 and 24.

The oil filter is put on the engine and the crankcase filled with the correct quantity and quality of motor oil. This is a good time to make sure the lubricating system is functioning before the engine is installed in the chassis and started. Oil pressure failure would ruin the new bearings and journals. The oil pump can be driven by hand using a properly fitting small socket, screwdriver, or hex rod, whichever is applicable. A socket speed handle is attached so it can be used to rotate the pump. Rotation using a drill motor can score the pump before oil pressure develops. This would lead to premature oil pump failure. Turning the pump by hand in the correct direction will fill the filter and develop oil pressure within 30 seconds. If pressure cannot be developed, this is a good time to find and correct the cause, while the engine is still out of the chassis.

It is considered to be a good practice to replace the engine mounts with new mounts before the engine is reinstalled. This is the most convenient time to replace the fatigued and worn out mounts. When the hoisting sling is installed, the engine is lowered into the chassis, transmission end first. The engine is aligned with the mounts and then the mounts are secured and the hoist is removed.

The underside of the installation is usually assembled first. This includes clutch and transmission controls, the speedometer cable, propeller shaft, steering linkages, and exhaust pipe.

On the top side of the engine, the radiator and air conditioner are installed. It is good practice to replace all coolant hoses and all belts to ensure maximum time before this service needs to be redone.

The carburetor, fuel pump, filter, and fuel lines are installed. All emission control units, instrument senders, and lines are properly connected. At this point, the technician will realize the time he has saved by putting tags on the parts as he disconnected them.

The starter and alternator are installed and the connecting wires secured. The fully charged battery should be installed so the engine can be cranked to aid in timing the ignition. The engine crankshaft is positioned at top center on the compression stroke of number one cylinder. The distributor is positioned to fire number one spark plug, then it is installed in the engine. Details of this basic timing procedure are given in Chapter 16.

All installation connections should be rechecked, the coolant system filled, and the hood replaced.

20-12 ENGINE BREAK-IN

If the engine overhaul and installation are done properly, the engine should crank and start on its own fully charged battery without the use of a fast charger or jumper. As soon as the engine starts and shows oil pressure, it should be brought up to a fast idle speed and kept there. This is necessary to make sure the engine gets proper lubrication. The fast turning oil pump develops full pressure and the fast turning crankshaft throws adequate oil on the cam and cylinder walls.

Just as soon as it can be assured that there are no serious leaks and the engine is running reasonably well, the automobile should be driven to a road with minimum traffic. Here, the automobile should be accelerated, full throttle, from 30 to 50 mph (48 to 80 kmph) and, with the throttle fully closed, the automobile should be allowed to return to 30 mph (48 kmph). This sequence should be repeated from 10 to 12 times. The acceleration sequence loads the piston rings to properly seat them against the cylinder walls. The piston rings are the only part of the modern engine that need to be broken in. Good ring seating is indicated by a dry white coating inside the tailpipe at the completion of the ring seating sequence.

The automobile is returned to the service area where the basic ignition timing and idle speeds are properly set. The engine is again checked for visible fluid leaks. If the engine is dry, it is ready to be turned over to the customer.

The customer should be instructed to drive the automobile in a normal fashion, neither babying it at slow speeds nor beating it at high speeds for the first 100 miles (160 km). The oil and filter should be changed at 500 miles (800 km) to remove any dirt that got into the engine during assembly and to remove the material that has worn from the surfaces during the break-in period.

A well-designed engine that has been correctly reconditioned and assembled using the techniques described should give reliable and durable service for many miles. Premature failure will result from problems that have been overlooked or from operational abuse.

REVIEW QUESTIONS

1. What is the difference between overhaul, rebuilding, and remanufacturing? [INTRODUCTION]

2. How can the technician know that an engine requires lower-end service? [INTRODUCTION]

3. What are the advantages and disadvantages of removing an engine from the chassis with the transmission remaining attached? [20-1]

4. List the items that must be disconnected to allow the engine to be removed. [20-1]

5. What should be done with the engine accessories while the engine is being overhauled? [20-1]

6. What should be checked first when the heads are removed? [20-2]

7. Why is it necessary to have the bearing caps marked? [20-2]

8. Why is ridge reaming required before the pistons are removed? [20-2]

9. What precautions should be observed while pushing the piston and rod assembly from the cylinder? [20-2]

10. What precautions should be observed while pulling the crankshaft damper? [20-2]

11. How is the camshaft removed? [20-2]

12. How is the piston removed from the rod? [20-2]

13. How are the pistons cleaned? [20-3]

14. How is rust prevented on the disassembled parts during overhaul? [20-4]

15. What two types of inspections are given to the engine parts? [20-4]

16. What should be done when a part is found to be faulty? [20-4]

17. Describe the method used to read a micrometer. [20-4]

18. How is run-out measured? [20-4]

19. When is Plastigauge used instead of a thickness gauge? [20-4]

20. How does Magniflux differ from Zyglo? [20-4]

21. What damage can excessive heat do to the piston and rings? [20-5]

22. What mechanical damage can be identified on a piston? [20-5]

23. How does airborn dirt affect pistons and rings? [20-5]

24. How can piston ring groove damage be specifically identified as being the result of a broken ring? [20-5]

25. Why are ring groove spacers installed above the top ring? [20-6]

26. How can the piston be resized? [20-6]

27. What is the result of either a loose or a tight piston pin fit in the piston? [20-6]

28. How are out-of-round connecting rod eyes repaired? [20-6]

29. Why is minimum piston ring gap so important? [20-6]

30. Why is the piston ring side clearance so important? [20-6]

31. What precautions should be observed when installing the pistons on the connecting rod? [20-6]

32. What precautions should be observed when installing the piston and rod assembly in the cylinder? [20-6]

33. What crankshaft condition should be looked for on a visual inspection? [20-7]

34. What crankshaft conditions should be checked with measuring equipment? [20-7]

35. When should a crankshaft be ground? [20-7]

36. What is the most common type of camshaft failure? [20-7]

37. When is a camshaft reground? [20-7]

38. Under what conditions would overlength push rods be required? [20-7]

39. What is the source of foreign particles that imbed in bearings? [20-7]

40. What causes the bearings to get too hot? [20-7]

41. Where does most of the cam bearing wear occur? [20-7]

42. How should the bearing journals be serviced? [20-8]

43. What is the most noticeable block wear condition? [20-9]

44. What can cause the block to warp? [20-9]

45. Describe the proper cylinder wall finish. [20-10]

---

46. How should the cylinder walls be cleaned after honing? [20-10]

47. When should the cylinder walls be rebored? [20-10]

48. When is the block align bored? [20-10]

49. What service is required on the pumps and covers? [20-10]

50. What is meant by blue printing an engine? [20-10]

51. How should parting surfaces and gaskets be prepared for assembly? [20-11]

52. What is the advantage of turning the crankshaft with a torque wrench during assembly? [20-11]

53. What part of the engine requires break-in? [20-12]

54. Describe the engine break-in procedure. [20-12]

propeller shafts and clutch

Engine power flows through the clutch and transmission to the final drive of the automobile. The final drive consists of a propeller shaft, a differential assembly, and a drive axle that transmits power to the drive wheels.

In order to remove any of the parts of the drive line ahead of the axles on a front-engine/rear-wheel-drive automobile, the drive line must be separated. This is done most easily by removing the propeller shaft. With the propeller shaft out of the automobile the differential can be serviced at the rear, and the transmission and clutch can be serviced in the front. The propeller shaft is discussed here because the technician will work on it before doing almost any other drive line work.

Drive line flexibility is required to allow for suspension movement and to provide a means of dampening vibration. The propeller shaft's universal joints and slip joint allow driving torque to be delivered through drive line angle changes and relative length changes as the suspension springs compress, or jounce, and rebound. Final drive vibration is isolated with elastomer mounts, flexible torsion drives, and torsional vibration dampers.

21-1 PROPELLER SHAFT

The propeller shaft, sometimes called the drive shaft, propels the vehicle by connecting the transmission output shaft to the differential input pinion. At least one universal joint must be used to provide continuous torque driving force as suspension movement produces changes in the relative position of the propeller shaft ends. This same movement

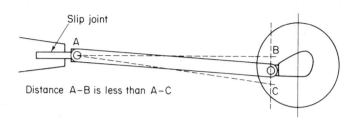

Slip joint

A

B

C

Distance A–B is less than A–C

Fig. 21-1 Changes in propeller shaft length as the rear axle moves up and down.

changes the distance between the ends so that the propeller shaft must include some type of slip joint, as shown in Figure 21-1.

Shaft. Driving torque and braking torque react against the chassis. At one time, the *torque-tube-type* propeller shaft absorbed these forces. A torque tube is a large diameter tube fastened securely to the rear axle housing and completely enclosing the propeller shaft. The torque tube is fitted into a spherical ball and socket surrounding one universal joint at the transmission end. These two units carry their respective loads while allowing suspension flexibility.

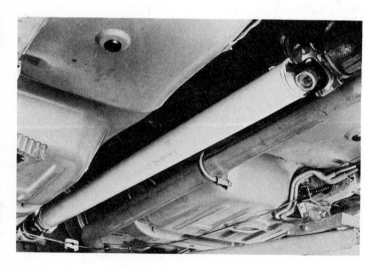

Fig. 21-2 Single-piece propeller shaft.

The torque-tube-type propeller shaft has been replaced by the Hotchkiss-type propeller shaft. Its essential difference is in the method used to absorb drive and braking torque. The Hotchkiss drive absorbs driving and braking torques through the front half of the rear leaf springs or through links and arms when used with coil-type springs. Details of these suspension systems are presented in Chapter 29.

The propeller shaft used with the Hotchkiss drive is essentially a steel tube with forged steel universal joints welded on each end. One is pictured in Figure 21-2. Its only function is to deliver transmission output torque to the differential input pinion. The shaft tube must be large enough to be strong enough to transfer output torque. Excess tube size increases the possibility of unbalance, is harder to straighten, tends to fan more air that may cause noise, requires more room under the floor pan, and is more expensive.

The propeller shaft, like any other rigid tube, has a natural frequency. If one end was held securely, it would vibrate at its own particular frequency when deflected and released. Its natural frequency occurs at its *critical speed*. Critical propeller shaft speed varies as the diameter of the tube changes and inversely as the square of the length. Diameters are as large as possible and shafts as short as possible to keep the critical speed frequency above the driving speed range. Propeller shafts over 60 in. (152.4 cm) between universal joints become a source for unbalance problems. Shaft lengths are minimized by using long transmission extension housings and center universal joints with two-piece propeller shafts as illustrated in Figure 21-3. When used, the center universal joint is supported by a center support bearing that must be insulated from the vehicle chassis.

Propeller shaft run-out or unbalance induces a phenomenon called *whirl*. Whirl is very similar to the action of a rope that is swung in an arc while being held at both ends. Once it has formed a bend, it keeps looping around as it rotates. Propeller shaft tubing is usually rolled from flat sheet

Fig. 21-3 Two-piece propeller shaft (Cadillac Motor Car Division, General Motors Corporation).

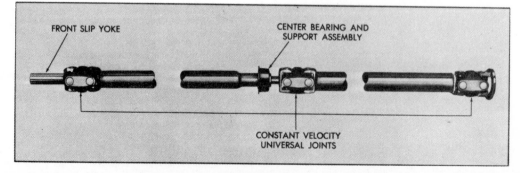

FRONT SLIP YOKE

CENTER BEARING AND SUPPORT ASSEMBLY

CONSTANT VELOCITY UNIVERSAL JOINTS

stock, straightened within 0.010 in. (0.25 mm) run-out and balanced within ¼ oz-inches. This keeps the center of mass very nearly on the longitudinal axis center to minimize whirl.

Universal Joint. Several types of universal joints are used in automobiles. The most common is the cross and yoke type. It is based upon principles invented independently by Cardan in Italy and Hooke in England. It is called either a *Cardan* universal joint and a *Hooke* universal joint. A second type of universal joint is formed from two cross and yoke joints and is called a *double Cardan* universal joint. Another type of universal joint was developed by Carl Weiss to give constant rotational speeds. It is built by Bendix and is called a *Bendix-Weiss* universal joint. A fourth type of universal joint used in passenger cars is a *ball and trunion* joint that acts as slip joint as well as a universal joint. A *Rzeppa* universal joint is a fifth type used in automobiles.

The propeller shaft in a Hotchkiss drive requires a universal joint at each end. The rear universal joint allows the shaft to drive as the rear axle housing nose twists up and down from driving and braking torque forces. The front universal joint allows the suspension to jounce and rebound while continuing to supply driving force.

Fig. 21-4 Single Cardan universal joint.

The cross and yoke type universal joint, shown in Figure 21-4, operating at an angle does not transfer uniform turning motion through the joint. With the input member turning at a uniform speed, the output side speeds up and slows down during two periods each revolution. The average speed or velocity of the input and output are the same. To say it another way, the output velocity is not constant. The reason for the change in motion is that the effective lever arm length varies continually at the motion transfer point. This action is difficult to visualize in a two-dimensional illustration. It can be plotted on a graph (Figure 21-5) to show the output velocity increase and decrease at each portion of the revolution.

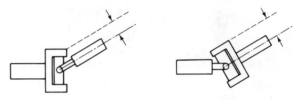

Turning radius changes as joint rotates

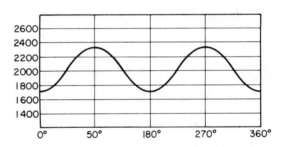

Fig. 21-5 Graph of a Cardan universal joint speed change with the joint operating through a 30° angle at 2000 rpm input.

This nonuniform velocity causes the propeller shaft to increase and decrease speed. In a two universal joint propeller shaft, this is partially corrected by reversing the action at the rear universal joint. It would be completely dampened if both universal joints always operated through the same angles.

A double Cardan universal joint, shown in Figure 21-6, consists of two closely spaced cross and yoke joints with a special link yoke. The two joints work to reverse the nonuniform action and thus provide constant velocity. Yoke centers are maintained by a ball and socket centering device so the joint working angle is the same in each joint half. This, then, forms a *constant velocity joint.* The output velocity is uniform when the input velocity is uniform, even though the joint center link has the typical velocity increase and decrease action.

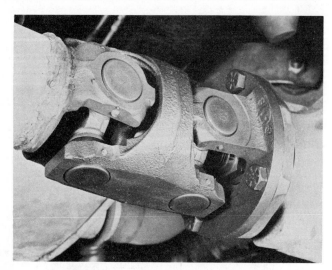

Fig. 21-6 Double Cardan constant velocity universal joint.

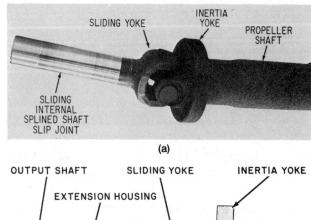

(a)

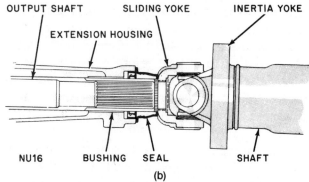

(b)

Fig. 21-7 Slip joint on the front of the propeller shaft. (a) Photograph of the parts, (b) drawing showing the cross section of the slip joint. (Chrysler Motors Corporation).

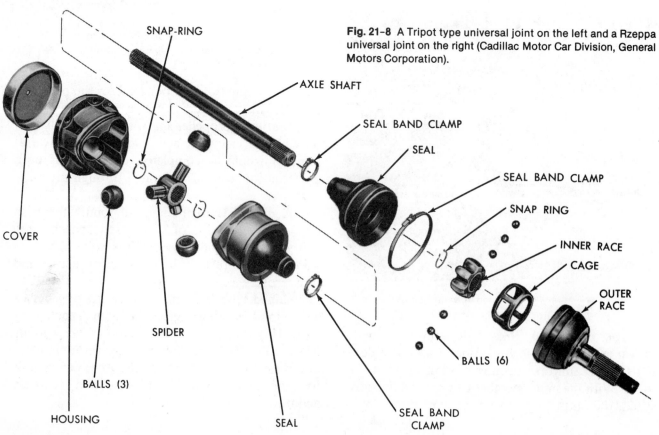

Fig. 21-8 A Tripot type universal joint on the left and a Rzeppa universal joint on the right (Cadillac Motor Car Division, General Motors Corporation).

Constant velocity universal joints are used as center joints on two-piece drive shafts. This can be seen in Figure 21-3. Two-piece shafts are used where drive shaft lengths would be excessive and where a low vehicle silhouette is desired. The center joint must be supported by a midship or center bearing.

Some cars use constant velocity universal joints exclusively. This is much more expensive, but it produces minimum noise and vibration. These premium qualities are demanded by the buyer of luxury vehicles, even at extra cost.

The cross and yoke universal joint requires a *slip joint* to allow for the effect of driving shaft length change as the rear axle housing moves up and down. The slip joint is located at the front joint of the rear propeller shaft section on either a one-piece (Figure 21-7) or a two-piece shaft. In this location, it is less apt to be damaged by stones thrown from the road by the tires. Most slip joints are involuted or square tooth splines on the transmission output shaft. Matching splines are located on the inner section of the front universal joint yoke. Some luxury cars use a recirculating ball-type slip joint. This operates with minimum noise and friction, but is expensive.

The Tripot universal joint, shown as the left joint in Figure 21-8, is a constant velocity joint that also acts as a slip joint. It consists of two *spiders,* each having three arms. Each spider arm is located between the adjacent arms of the second spider. Motion of one set of spider arms is transferred to the other spider arms by steel balls wedged in grooves that are cut at an angle so the balls will always operate in a plane that bisects the joint's operating angle. Thus, it will operate as a constant velocity joint. Tripot joints are usually used on front wheel drive vehicles, where steering is another universal joint requirement.

The Rzeppa universal joint, shown as the right joint in Figure 21-8, is a self-supported constant velocity joint. The drive is through caged balls that operate in curved races of the input and output components. The balls always operate in the center of the joint angle so all parts of the joint turn at a constant velocity. The Rzeppa-type joint is used on some front wheel drives.

The ball and triunion joint allows axial movement within the joint so no separate slip joint is necessary. The balls are mounted on a spider through needle bearings. Each ball fits into a partly

cylindrical housing bore that runs in the axial direction. This provides a means to drive through the joint in a radial direction and allows slip in the axial direction.

At one time a two-ball and trunion type was used. This type was replaced with the cross-and-yoke type joint because the cross-and-yoke joint transfers motion in the same way, is less expensive, and can operate through a greater joint angle. A three-ball and triunion joint has been developed. The use of three equally spaced balls causes the joint to transfer constant velocity motion to the output shaft. This type of joint is an ideal joint for the inside joint on front wheel drive vehicles, because it eliminates the slip joint and transfers constant velocity motion.

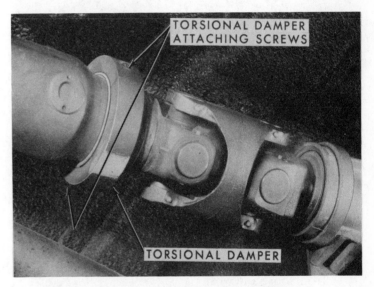

Fig. 21-9 Propeller shaft torsional damper [Cadillac Motor Car Division, General Motors Corporation).

Propeller shafts may use a heavy torsional damper ring to reduce vibration illustrated in Figure 21-9. It may be located either adjacent to the front universal joint or adjacent to the rear universal joint. Some propeller shafts also use an elastomer sleeve between an inner and outer drive shaft section. All torque in these shafts must be transmitted through the elastomer sleeve, shown in Figure 21-10, thus effectively isolating the running gear vibration from the transmission and dampening engine vibration.

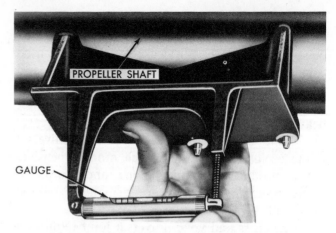

Fig. 21-11 Typical means of checking propeller shaft alignment (Chrysler Motors Corporation).

Fig. 21-10 Elastomer sleeve in the propeller shaft.

21-2 PROPELLER SHAFT SERVICE

Propeller shaft problems usually show up as noise and vibration. These may result from incorrect universal joint angles, from unbalanced parts, or from loose and worn parts.

When the drive line is suspected as being the source of vibration, it should be given a good visual inspection to check the physical appearance of the propeller shaft. Problems appear as loose universal joint parts, damaged propeller shaft tube, or material such as undercoating stuck to the tube to cause unbalance.

After the visual inspection, universal joint angles should be checked. Special alignment checking fixtures are available as special tools for each corporation's vehicles. They use spirit levels similar to the one being used in Figure 21-11 and plumb bobs with protractors to check the joint working angles. When checking the joint angles, the vehicle must be level and resting on its axles. The front

joint angle is changed by adding or removing shims from the transmission mount and the rear joint angle is changed by installing taper shims on leaf spring systems or by changing the suspension linkages on coil spring systems.

Propeller shaft run-out should also be checked with a dial gauge as shown in Figure 21-12. Run-out adjacent to the universal joint will give no problem if it is less than 0.010 in. (0.255 mm) while 0.015 in. (0.38 mm) run-out in the middle of the shaft will not produce noticeable vibration. A bent shaft is generally the result of an accident. It is usually expensive but more satisfactory to replace a bent propeller shaft than it is to try to straighten it.

Shaft unbalance causes drive line vibration. Unbalance can usually be corrected by properly

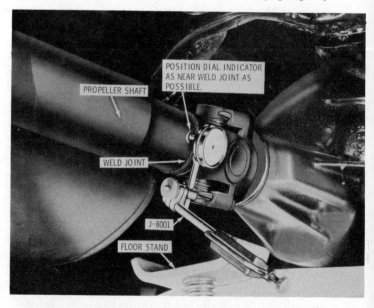

Fig. 21-12 Typical means of checking propeller shaft run out (Oldsmobile Division, General Motors Corporation).

positioning two worm-type Wittek hose clamps (Figure 21–13) adjacent to the welded balance weight at the rear of the propeller shaft. The vehicle is put on a hoist with the rear wheels removed and the lug nuts installed upside down to hold the brake drum in place. The drive line is run up to 60 miles per hour (100 kmph) and vibration speed noted. (Extended operation in this manner will cause engine overheating). With the drive line turning, gradually move a chalk or crayon toward the shaft near the rear universal joint until it just touches at the high point, then quickly remove it. This effectively marks the shaft heavy spot. The shaft is then marked at each 90° adjacent to the rear universal joint. The clamps are positioned with their tightening screws together opposite the heavy spot. The vehicle test is rerun and the vibration is again noted. The clamps are then slightly rotated in opposite directions by equal amounts, and the test rerun to check vibration. When the point of least vibration is found, the wheels should be reinstalled and the car road tested.

If a strobe-type wheel balancer is available, it can be used to quickly balance the propeller shaft. The wheel balancer pick-up is located on the carrier nose as close to the universal joint as possible. The clamps should be adjusted until the shaft falls within the normal balancing range of the balancer pick-up.

Excessive universal joint wear is the most common propeller shaft malfunction. The joint wear can be determined by lifting the automobile on a hoist and moving the joint by hand. Any movement in the joint bearings results from exces-

sive wear. Replacing the worn parts is the only way to repair the joint. When excessive wear becomes severe it will be perceived by the driver as a drive line noise or vibration most noticeable during acceleration. There will also be a heavy driveline clunk as the automobile is put into motion. Figure 21–14 shows a universal joint worn so badly that it fell apart.

Fig. 21–14 A worn out universal joint with missing needle bearings.

The propeller shaft must be removed to service universal joints. Before removal, each part of the shaft and companion flange should be marked so it can be reassembled in the same position. Single-piece shaft removal is accomplished by removing the rear universal joint from the differential drive pinion companion flange, with care being taken to keep the bearings in place. This can be done by wrapping tape around the joint bearings. The front end is removed by sliding the shaft from the slip joint. The oil seal portion of the slip joint yoke should immediately be covered to avoid damage that could cause the transmission rear seal to leak. Two-piece shafts require removal of the center or midship bearing as well as the rear universal joint companion flange before the shaft can be removed from the front slip joint.

The universal joint is disassembled when the shaft is on the bench (Figure 21–15). Each manufacturer has his own special tools to speed disassembly and reassembly while avoiding damage. The basic disassembly and reassembly procedures are the same, however. Disassembly is accomplished

Fig. 21–13 Wittek clamps used to balance a propeller shaft.

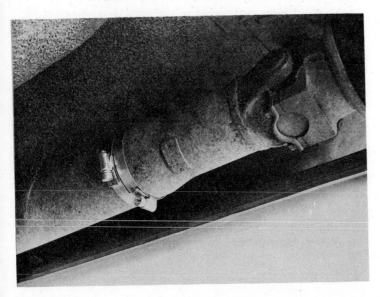

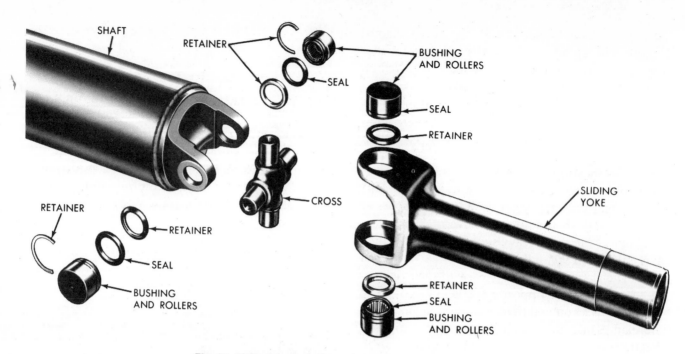

Fig. 21-15 Parts nomenclature of a typical Cardan universal joint (Chrysler Motors Corporation).

Fig. 21-16 Removing the retaining ring to start disassembly of the universal joint.

by first removing the bearing cap retaining clips (Figure 21-16). Some original equipment joint bearing caps are held in place by an injected nylon ring that can be seen in Figure 21-17. These nylon rings shear during disassembly and are replaced with a clip-type retainer. The yoke is supported around the lower bearing cap as the cross or spider is pushed down to force the lower cap from the yoke (Figures 21-18 and 21-19). The yoke is turned 180° to force the opposite cap from the yoke. With both bearing caps removed, the spider can be easily lifted out (Figure 21-20). Disassembled bearing caps, seals, and spacers are discarded and replaced with new parts.

A universal joint repair kit contains new bearing cups with needle bearings, new spacers, new seals, and new retainer clips. Most kits contain a new cross. Assembly of the joint requires care to keep the parts in alignment so the needle rollers stay in place and no binding occurs.

Fig. 21-17 Section view of a front Cardan universal joint showing a torsional damper ring and injected nylon ring cap retainers (Chevrolet Motor Division, General Motors Corporation).

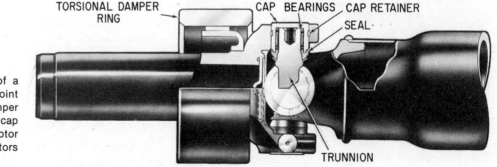

Fig. 21-18 One type of tool used to disassemble a universal joint (Buick Motor Division, General Motors Corporation).

Fig. 21-19 Pushing the lower bearing out by pushing the upper bearing in.

The cups are filled with specified grease, usually a number 2 consistency. The cross is placed in the yoke and allowed to extend through one opening as pictured in Figure 21-21. Spacers and seals are placed on the extended cross arm. These are followed by the bearing cup. It is then pressed into the yoke. Two methods are shown in Figure 21-22. The cross is carefully moved toward the other yoke opening where the second spacer, seals, and bearing cup are installed in the yoke. Clip retainers are installed and the yoke tapped to seat the retainer

Fig. 21-20 Removing the worn out cross from the yoke.

Fig. 21-21 Installing the new cross in the yoke (Oldsmobile Division, General Motors Corporation).

(a)   (b)

Fig. 21-22 Pressing the bearing in place in the yoke. (a) With a vice (Oldsmobile Division, General Motors Corporation), (b) with a press.

clips. Each yoke section is assembled in this same manner, taking care to assemble the parts in the correct order. If binding occurs, it may be that a needle roller has fallen to the bottom of the cap. The cap will have to be removed to check and realign the roller.

Double Cardan constant-velocity universal joints are disassembled in the same manner. They also have a ball stud in the center of the joint which must be carefully disassembled and re-assembled.

Two-piece propeller shafts have a slip joint just ahead of the center constant velocity joint. This slip joint is held together with a lock nut that can be seen in Figure 21-23. After the shaft is on

the bench, the lock nut is removed to separate the shaft in two sections. It is assembled in the reverse manner.

Center or midship bearings with their supports are usually replaced as an assembly. The assembly contains both the bearing and the insulating rubber mount. To replace this assembly, the propeller shaft will generally have to be removed from the vehicle and the two propeller shaft sections separated.

After the shaft is reassembled and installed, the universal joint angles should be rechecked for correct alignment.

21-3 CLUTCH

A clutch is a mechanism designed to disconnect and reconnect driving and driven members. The type of clutch discussed here is required in the drive line of a vehicle that uses a standard transmission. The engine must be disconnected from the drive line when starting to keep the vehicle from moving and to minimize engine load so the engine will start. The clutch connects the engine and drive line to power the vehicle. It disconnects to release the torque loads on the drive line so the transmission can be shifted from one gear ratio to another.

Fig. 21-23 Lock nut holding the slip joint at the center bearing of a two-piece propeller shaft.

The automobile clutch consists of a driving pressure plate and flywheel assembly attached to the engine and a driven clutch disc attached to the transmission. The clutch can be seen on the back of the engine in Figure 21-24. When the clutch disc is clamped between the pressure plate and flywheel by springs in the pressure plate, the clutch will carry engine driving force to the transmission and drive line. Maximum driving force or driving torque occurs just before the disc slips while it is clamped between the pressure plate and flywheel. This limits the maximum amount of engine driving torque the clutch can deliver to the drive train. When the pressure plate is forced away from the flywheel with clutch release levers, the clutch disc is free to turn independently from the pressure plate and flywheel assembly, so no torque is transferred between the engine and the drive line.

21-4 CLUTCH REQUIREMENTS

The clutch is designed to completely disengage the drive line using relatively light pedal pressures. The highly loaded release mechanism is pivoted on rolling surfaces or knife edges to minimize friction.

The release system has a mechanical leverage from 10:1 to 12:1 that will provide pedal pressures in a range of 20 to 30 pounds (9.07 to 13.6 kg) when using a 3-in. (76.2 mm) pedal travel. The linkage is often provided with an overcenter spring that helps hold the pedal in a released position. When the pedal is slightly depressed, the overcenter spring reverses its action and helps depress the pedal.

The clutch must provide smooth engagement without grabbing or chattering. This operation depends upon the coefficient of friction of the friction surfaces, along with the operation of cushion and damper spring action.

The clutch must have adequate *torque capacity* to handle the expected loads. It is usually designed to have a capacity of 125% to 150% of the maximum engine torque. Torque begins to be applied to the clutch as soon as the friction members touch. It will increase until the torque produced by the engine matches the load of the drive train. Clutch torque requirements are highest when the

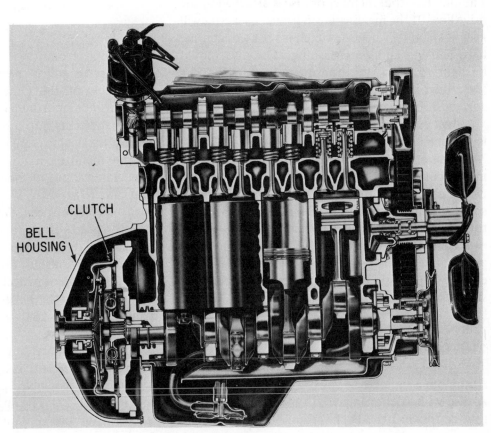

Fig. 21-24 Location of the clutch in the bell housing on the back of the engine.

input member, or engine, is turning and the output member, or drive line, is stationary. Slippage occurs during engagement. It continues until the input and output members are turning at the same speed. This slippage produces heat that must be absorbed by the clutch material and then dissipated into the air that surrounds the clutch. The amount of heat absorbed by the clutch is proportional to the time required to increase output speed to input speed. Clutch temperature is the major limiting factor in clutch capacity.

The clutch rotates with the engine and drive line. Centrifugal forces on the clutch increase as engine speed increases. The increase is at a ratio of four times the engine speed. When centrifugal forces become greater than the strength of the parts, the clutch will fly apart or *shatter*. Race cars have a scatter shield surrounding the clutch to protect the rest of the automobile if the clutch should break up at high engine speeds. Clutch "burst" speed is usually designed at twice the expected maximum engine speeds.

Inertia is another important clutch criterion. The clutch output member or disc is attached to the drive line. If the member is too heavy, its inertia will keep it spinning when the clutch is released, causing hard shifting and gear clashing. The disc should be light to allow the transmission synchronizers (described in Chapter 22) to bring the disc to the correct shifting speed.

Just as in all other automotive parts, the clutch is designed for easy manufacturing and low cost. Materials are adequate to meet their design requirements, but the clutch is not overbuilt. Larger capacity clutches are required as engine horsepower and speeds are increased. This, in turn, increases clutch torque capacity and clutch inertia.

Clutch maintenance is most important to the automotive technician. The clutch linkages are easy to adjust and clutch replacement is relatively simple.

21-5 CLUTCH DESIGN

Automotive clutches (Figure 21-25) operate dry. A disc with friction material on both sides is free to slide forward and backward on the splined shaft

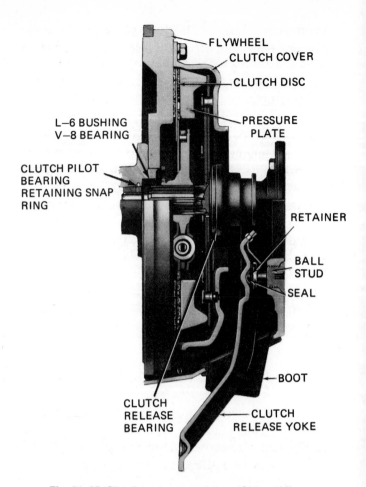

Fig. 21-25 Clutch part nomenclature (Oldsmobile Division, General Motors Corporation).

protruding from the front of the transmission. This shaft is called the transmission *clutch shaft.* The back of the clutch shaft is supported by the transmission front bearing. The front end of the clutch shaft fits into a *pilot bearing* located in the rear of the engine crankshaft. The *disc* is the clutch output member; it always runs at output speed. The clutch input members are the engine *flywheel* and *clutch pressure plate* assembly. They always turn at engine speed. When the input speed and output speed differ, there is slippage between the pressure plate and disc. The flywheel is bolted to the engine crankshaft and the pressure plate cover is bolted to the flywheel. In operation, the disc is clamped between the pressure plate and the flywheel (Figure 21-26).

Pressure Plate Assembly. Automotive clutch engagement pressure is applied by coil or Belleville springs. The assembled pressure plates are pictured in Figure 21-27. The springs are wedged between a cast iron pressure plate and a stamped steel cover plate. They provide the force to clamp the disc between the pressure plate and flywheel. High-tensile-strength gray iron is used for both flywheel and pressure plate. This is the best material to use with the asbestos-based friction facings used on the disc. In addition, the cast iron has sufficient mass to absorb the heat energy developed during engagement and it is sufficiently rigid to prevent distortion under operating loads.

Pressure plate assemblies using coil springs have spring pockets formed in the plate and in the stamped cover. A guide projects into the spring to control the spring during high inertia loads. The assembly is held together during storage and assembly by the location of release levers.

Coil spring pressure plates, as illustrated in Figures 21-28 and 21-29, are provided with three release lever tabs that are equally spaced around the back edge and to which the release lever struts attach. The release lever is pivoted on an eye bolt that protrudes through the cover. When assembled, the lever rests against the cover center opening and the lever fulcrum is pulled toward the cover with a nut on the tee pivot eye bolt. This causes the release lever strut to pull the pressure plate against the springs, holding the assembly together. Adjustment of the lever pivot eye bolt is used to correctly position the pressure plate and the release levers. When the pressure plate cover is attached to the flywheel, the pressure plate is pushed further

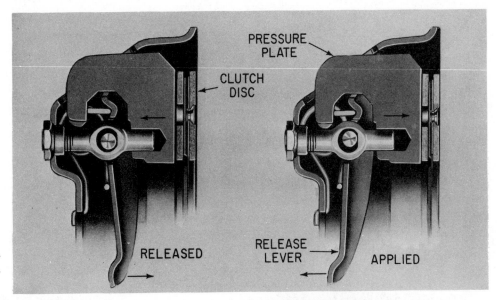

Fig. 21-26 Clutch release lever pivots (American Motors Corporation).

(a)

(b)

Fig. 21-27 Pressure plate. (a) Coil spring type, (b) Belleville spring type.

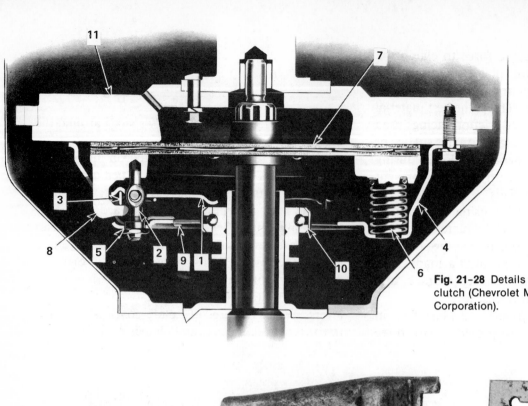

1. release lever
2. bolt
3. strut
4. pressure plate cover
5. adjusting nut
6. clutch spring
7. disc
8. pressure plate
9. damper spring
10. throw out bearing
11. engine flywheel

Fig. 21-28 Details of a coil spring pressure plate clutch (Chevrolet Motor Division, General Motors Corporation).

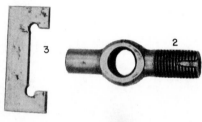

PIVOT PIN

(a)

(b)

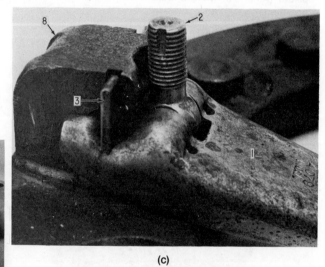

(c)

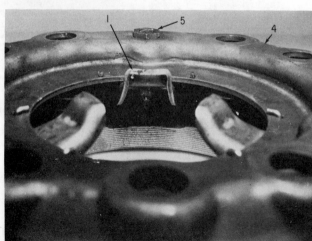

(d)

Fig. 21-29 Release levers on a coil spring type pressure plate. (a) Lever parts, (b) bolt in the plate, (c) lever attached, (d) cover installed. (See nomenclature above.)

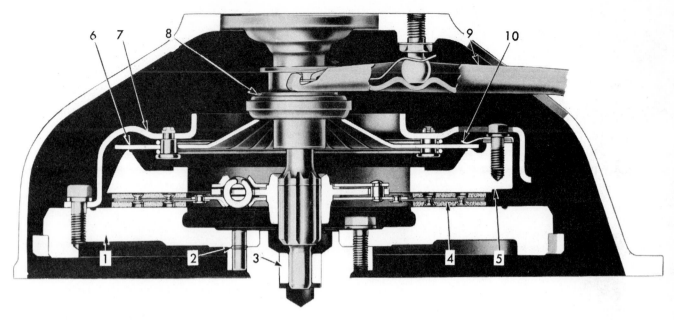

Fig. 21-30 Nomenclature of a Belleville diaphragm spring clutch (Chevrolet Motor Division, General Motors Corporation).

1. flywheel
2. alignment dowl between the crankshaft and flywheel.
3. pilot bearing
4. disc
5. pressure plate
6. diaphragm spring
7. cover
8. throw out bearing
9. release yoke
10. retaining clip

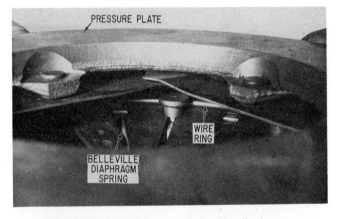

Fig. 21-31 Wire ring in a Belleville diaphragm spring pressure plate.

back against the springs, compressing them still more. This relaxes the release levers. *Anti-rattle springs* are connected to the release levers to prevent undesirable noise when the clutch is engaged. Friction of the release levers causes effective clutch plate pressure to be about 85% of the value expected by measuring spring force.

A number of different torque capacity pressure plates are possible using common plates, covers, and release levers. This is done by the selection of different coil spring lengths and spring rates. The springs may be long with low spring rates or short with high rates. In some cases, both types are used in the same assembly. The springs are usually color-coded for identification. Springs of the same color are equally spaced around the clutch plate. In some cases, the spring seats are provided with insulators to keep clutch heat from the spring.

The *diaphragm spring* or Belleville spring pressure plate assembly (Figure 21-30) has a different spring application and release operation. A Belleville spring is shaped like a nearly flat cone with an opening in the the center that resists flattening. Belleville springs are used in many applications where a constant controlled load is required. With a special diaphragm configuration, a Belleville spring is used as a pressure spring in many clutches.

The Belleville diaphragm spring has a solid outer rim. The inner portion is slotted into fingers that may be straight or bent. The diaphragm spring has a wire ring ahead and behind it where it is riveted to the cover. All bending force is applied on the edges of these two wire rings. The wire ring can be seen in Figure 21-31. The outer rim of the diaphragm pushes evenly against the pressure plate. The Belleville's natural arc pushes between the diaphragm and the wire ring at the cover rivets. Retraction spring clips are bolted over the outer edge of the diaphragm so they hold the plate to the spring for handling and storage. Coil springs follow Hook's Law. Their force is proportional to the amount of compression which is also called spring deflection. As the disc wears, the springs have less deflection and, therefore, will apply less force

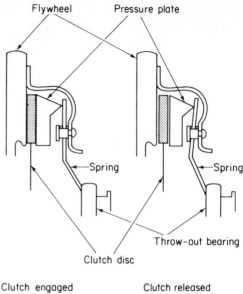

against the disc. The Belleville diaphragm spring, on the other hand, has a very interesting deflection curve illustrated in Figure 21-32. As the disc wears, pressure gradually increases, then decreases. At maximum disc wear, the spring pressure is nearly the equivalent of a new disc.

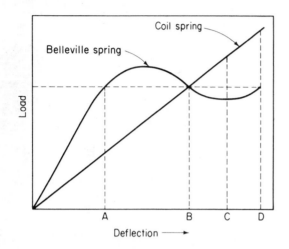

A. Engaged worn clutch
B. Engaged new clutch
C. Disengaged
D. Full pedal travel

Fig. 21-32 Deflection vs. load of a coil and Belleville spring pressure plate.

Compared to the coil spring-type, the diaphragm spring pressure plate has lower weight, fewer pieces, less operating friction, and lower pedal pressure.

More application force may be added to the pressure plate at high engine speeds by using centrifugal weights. One method is to have weights cast on the outer ends of the release levers in such a manner that their centrifugal force will apply additional loading on the plate. Another method uses centrifugal rollers that wedge between the pressure plate and cover. The use of these centrifugal systems allows the engineer to reduce pedal effort by using weaker pressure springs that provide only a 10% torque reserve.

The Belleville diaphragm spring clutch is released by applying pressure to the ends of the diaphragm fingers in the center of the diaphragm. This causes the cone to flatten, pulling the pressure plate from the disc with the retracting springs. The lever action is illustrated in Figure 21-33.

Fig. 21-33 Details of a Belleville diaphragm spring pressure plate engagement and release positions.

Throw-Out Bearing. The throw-out bearing is used to transfer pedal release pressure from the stationary linkage to the rotating clutch. A release yoke is attached inside the bell housing. The yoke fingers and throw-out bearing are both attached to the release collar. The collar slides on the front transmission bearing retainer extension as the clutch linkages move the yoke.

Disc. Clutch facings on each side of the disc transfer torque from the flywheel and pressure plate to the disc. Automotive disc linings are made from woven or random asbestos fibers that are bonded with organic resins. Sometimes, metallic chips or wire are included in the lining composition. The materials are compacted and molded to shape under high pressure and temperatures. Finished linings are riveted to the disc web.

Asbestos-based clutch facings must not operate above 450°F (332°C) or the binders will be driven out of the facing. This maximum temperature limits the clutch capacity. Another limit is maximum surface velocity at the time of engagement, which must not exceed 6000 ft/min (1828.8 m/min) at the mean radius. For maximum clutch disc life, the pressure plate force should not exceed 12 lb/in.^{2} (82.7 kPa) pressure against the linings. Clutch linings operating against cast iron have a coefficient of friction between 0.28 and 0.30. Coefficient of friction is the sliding force per square inch divided by the pressure applied.

Disc webs may be one piece or riveted from

Fig. 21-34 Clutch disc showing the wavy spring steel web between the disc facings.

several pieces. The portion of the web between the facings is wavy spring steel. This can be seen in Figure 21-34. Each facing is riveted to the high spot with brass rivets. This assembly method provides a cushion spring between the linings so the clutch will have a smooth engagement.

The cast iron disc hub is splined to fit the transmission clutch shaft. Springs are mounted circumferentially around the hub flange, spaced between the hub and disc web as pictured in Figure 21-35. These springs act as torsion dampers to isolate engine firing pulses from the drive line. These *torsion damper springs* are held in place in stamped disc pockets. The disc is held to the hub by rivets through the disc web on one side of the hub and a doubler plate on the other side. Friction drag or addition of friction washers between the hub and disc web provide a snubbing action as the damper springs recoil following an engine pulsation.

Torque capacity of a clutch can be calculated by the following formula, using the conventional measuring system:

$$T = NfPK \text{ lb/ft}$$

where T = Torque capacity
  N = Number of friction surfaces = two surfaces in automotive clutches
  f = Coefficient of friction = 0.3 for automotive clutches
  P = Total pressure on the linings
  K = disc mean radius $(r + R)/2$ (1.02) ft
  r = disc inner radius in ft
  R = disc outer radius in ft

For an automotive single disc clutch, the formula can be simplified to equal:

$$T = 0.294 \, P(r + R)$$

For example, what would be the torque

Fig. 21-35 Damper springs in the clutch hub.

capacity of a clutch with a pressure plate having nine springs each producing 130 lbs force pressing on a single disc clutch with a 7 in. inside diameter and an 11 in. outside diameter facing? The total force (P) of the 9 springs is 1170 lbs (9 × 130). The inner clutch disc facing radius (r) is 0.2916 ft (3.5/12) and the outer radius (R) is 0.4583 ft (5.5/12). Putting these values into the formula above to solve for torque capacity:

$$T = 0.306 \times 1170 \, (0.2916 + 0.4583)$$
$$= 268.48 \text{ lb-ft}$$

The torque capacity of any given clutch can be calculated by disassembling the pressure plate, measuring the spring pressures at their operating length, and then measuring the inside diameter and outside diameter of the disc facing.

21-6 CLUTCH SERVICE

Service on modern clutches is limited to linkage adjustment and replacement of components. Disc lining wear is a common cause of clutch failure. A weak pressure plate will allow excessive clutch slippage that builds heat and increases wear rates. Heat will sometimes be great enough to crack or burn the cast iron flywheel and pressure plate friction surfaces. Clutch wear will occur normally during vehicle starts. Automobiles used in city traffic will wear out a clutch in less mileage than an automobile driven on expressways. Clutch wear rate is aggravated by "riding the clutch" as the driver rests his foot on the clutch pedal. This reduces the effect of the pressure springs and reduces clutch capacity by allowing the clutch to slip.

Chatter or grabbing is another source of clutch failure. It results from oil on the clutch facing. Oil changes the coefficient of friction so the clutch does not apply smoothly. This problem can be corrected only by replacing the oil soaked disc and the rear crankshaft oil seal or clutch shaft seal so oil does not get on the new disc.

Maladjusted clutch linkages will cause clutch slippage when they do not completely move the throw-out bearing from contacting the release levers or fingers. The usual recommendation is to adjust clutch linkages to provide a 1-in. (25.4 mm) pedal free play before clutch release begins. Clutch release should be complete with the pedal at least 1 in. (25.4 mm) above the floor pan. Vehicle clutch adjustment procedures should be carefully followed.

If the clutch pedal action is sluggish or the pedal does not return properly, the overcenter spring (Figure 21-36) may be out of adjustment. Tightening the spring will reduce pedal effort and cause sluggish pedal return action. Loosening the overcenter spring provides a quick return but increases pedal effort.

When proper adjustment will not correct improper clutch operation, the clutch must be disassembled. The transmission must be removed before the clutch can be disassembled because the transmission clutch shaft goes through the center of the clutch components. The propeller shaft must be disconnected, the rear of the engine supported, and the rear transmission mount removed. Usually, the rear mount cross member must also be removed. The transmission linkages and speedometer cable have to be disconnected, and then four transmission bolts can be removed from the bell housing. The transmission is carefully moved straight back until the shaft is clear of the clutch. If the bottom half of the bell housing is not removable, the bell housing will have to be removed from the engine to get at the clutch. Bell housing types are shown in Figure 21-37. The pressure plate cover and flywheel should be punch marked

Fig. 21-36 Overcenter spring operation.

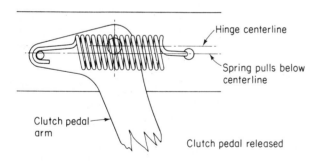

Hinge centerline

Spring pulls below centerline

Clutch pedal arm

Clutch pedal released

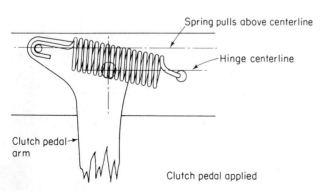

Spring pulls above centerline

Hinge centerline

Clutch pedal arm

Clutch pedal applied

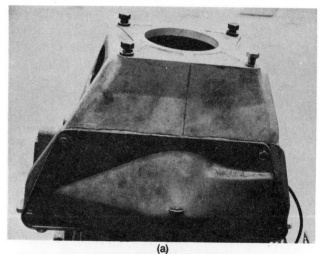

(a)

(b)

Fig. 21-37 Bell housing. (a) Removable lower section, (b) one piece housing.

Fig. 21-38 Clutch facing worn down to the rivets.

so these balanced parts can be reassembled in the same position if they are satisfactory for reuse. Evenly loosen the cover bolts from the flywheel and remove the clutch pressure plate and disc.

Examine the clutch for signs of wear, over-heating, contamination, and broken parts. This will aid in determining the cause of failure so it can be corrected before new parts are installed (Figure 21-38).

Because of the cost of labor in relation to parts, it is becoming a standard practice to replace all clutch parts, even if they show no signs of failure. Most shops do not have the gauging equipment to check spring tension and pressure plate adjustment. If one knows the history of the clutch being repaired, he may change only a few of the parts. Complete parts replacement includes a pilot bearing, disc, pressure plate, and throw-out bearing. If these are correctly installed as a set, there is little chance of a comeback.

Many discs and pressure plates can be exchanged for remanufactured units that have been completely reconditioned. They are as good as new.

During assembly, the clutch must be kept clean and dry. No lubricant is used, with the exception of a very thin coat on the transmission clutch shaft and inside the throw-out bearing release collar. The disc should be checked for a free sliding fit on the transmission clutch shaft. It is then held in place against the flywheel with a clutch pilot, while the pressure plate is being fastened to the flywheel. The clutch pilot is a special tool or an old clutch shaft. The rest of the assembly procedure is the reverse of the disassembly procedure. Linkages should be rechecked.

Proper clutch operation requires use of the correct parts. Discs and pressure plates may look alike, but they may have different facings, springs, lever action, etc. The incorrect application of a part will give unsatisfactory results. Follow the parts book recommendations.

If the vehicle is modified, it will most likely require a modified clutch. The information presented in this chapter will be helpful in selecting a clutch that will provide satisfactory service in a modified vehicle.

REVIEW QUESTIONS

1. Why are universal joints required on the propeller shaft? [INTRODUCTION]

2. What is a Hotchkiss drive? [21-1]

3. What limits the maximum and the minimum propeller shaft diameter? [21-1]

4. Why is the propeller shaft critical speed important? [21-1]

5. Name five types of universal joints used in passenger cars. [21-1]

6. What is a constant velocity universal joint? Why is it desirable? [21-1]

7. What type of universal joints do not require a slip joint? [21-1]

8. What propeller shaft features are designed to minimize the transmission of noise and vibration? [21-1]

9. What checks should be made when the propeller shaft causes vibration? [21-1]

10. What problems are caused by the propeller shaft? [21-2]

11. What is the most common propeller shaft malfunction? [21-2]

12. Describe the procedure used to remove the propeller shaft. [21-2]

13. Describe the procedure used to replace the universal joint cross and bearings. [21-2]

14. How does the repair of a constant velocity universal joint compare to a Cardan joint? [21-2]

15. Why is a clutch required in the drive line? [21-3]

16. When is the torque capacity of the clutch the greatest? [21-4]

17. What is the major factor limiting the clutch capacity? [21-4]

18. What causes a clutch to chatter? [21-4]

19. What parts of the clutch rotate with the engine? What parts rotate with the drive line? [21-5]

20. What materials are used for the pressure plate? [21-5]

21. Describe the release lever action. [21-5]

22. How does the diaphragm spring pressure plate differ from the coil spring pressure plate? [21-5]

23. What is connected to the throw-out bearing? [21-5]

24. Why is the type of clutch disc facing material important? [21-5]

25. What parts are assembled to form the clutch disc? [21-5]

26. What causes the clutch to slip? [21-6]

27. How is a clutch adjusted? [21-6]

28. How is a clutch disc removed? [21-6]

29. What parts are replaced in the clutch assembly when the clutch is replaced? [21-6]

standard transmissions

Each automobile engine produces a fixed amount of torque at any given speed and load. The low rpm engine torque is not great enough to move the automobile. Automobiles use transmissions to provide a means of increasing the driving torque available for starting, accelerating, and climbing slopes or hills. The transmission also provides the means to reverse the drive train so the automobile can be moved backward. In some driving situations the transmission is shifted into a lower gear ratio while the automobile is going down a steep grade. This forces the idling engine to act as a retarder to slow the automobile speed. Engine braking is especially useful while going down a long mountain grade because it keeps the speed under control. If the brakes were used they would overheat and tend to fade.

Standard transmissions are used in economy cars and in sport cars. Generally the economy cars use two gears below direct drive and sports cars use three to provide adequate driving torque. Figure 22-1 shows a standard transmission having five gear ratios.

The clutch is used to disconnect the engine from the drive line whenever a gear ratio change is to be made. This removes the torque load carried by the transmission. The unloaded transmission gears are synchronized at matching speeds before gear engagement is made in the new ratio. The clutch then reconnects the engine to the transmission in the new gear ratio.

22-1 TRANSMISSION REQUIREMENTS

The first gear of the transmission allows the engine to turn at a speed that will produce enough torque to move the automobile. This provides the torque needed to start and accelerate. The automobile can

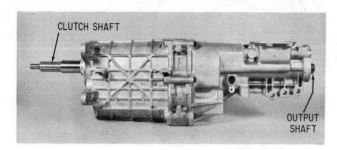

Fig. 22-1 A modern five-speed transmission (Warner Gear Division, Borg-Warner Corporation).

be accelerated whenever more torque is available than is being used. If more torque is required than the engine is producing, the automobile will slow to a stop unless the transmission is shifted into a lower gear. The lower gear will allow engine speed to increase to a speed at which it will produce more torque. Speed and torque are graphed in Figure 22-2.

Passenger car performance is based on acceleration, ability to go up a slope, top speed, fuel economy, noise level, and durability. Large domestic passenger car engines can produce enough power so most of their running is in direct drive. Small economy cars, on the other hand, usually have smaller engines and so they need to operate in gear reduction more of the time to provide adequate performance. The small economy cars, therefore, have relatively stronger transmissions than the large domestic passenger cars.

Transmission gearing is designed to provide maximum acceleration at low speed by holding the driving wheel torque output at the point of impending wheel spin. Acceleration becomes less than

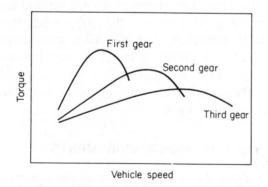

Fig. 22-2 Torque plotted against speed in each gear (not to scale.)

maximum when wheel spin occurs. On the other end of the gear design, fuel economy is maximum when the engine is developing 80% of its maximum torque as the automobile is moving at a constant speed. This gives 20% additional torque for acceleration.

The power required to drive an automobile increases as the cube of the speed. It takes eight times the horsepower to double the speed ($2 \times 2 \times 2$). When the power available matches the power required to push the vehicle, speed will be constant. Excess power is required for acceleration and hill climbing. Maximum speed is reached when there is no excess power remaining. The power available from the drive line and the power required to move the automobile at different speeds is plotted in Figures 22-3 and 22-4.

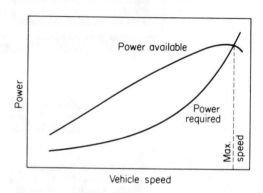

Fig. 22-3 Power available and power required curves (not to scale).

More gear ratios are required as the range of required torque speed from low to high increases. Trucks may have from 10 to 20 forward gear ratios. Three to four forward gear ratios are adequate for passenger cars.

The rear axle gear ratio affects vehicle performance in all transmission gear ratios. Because most of the driving is done with the transmission in direct drive, the rear axle ratio makes it possible to use the same engine-transmission combination in several different vehicle applications, thus reducing cost. Rear axle ratio used with a three-speed transmission is selected so the engine reaches maximum power before the vehicle reaches maximum speed. This provides excess power for acceleration and gradability even though it is more noisy, has poor economy, and has a top speed slightly lower than would be possible with other gearing. The rear axle gear ratio used with four-speed transmissions uses a ratio that will allow the vehicle to reach maximum speed at or slightly before the

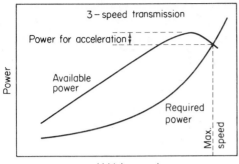

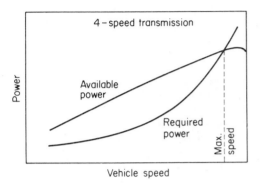

Fig. 22-4 Power available and power required of three-speed and four-speed transmissions.

engine reaches maximum horsepower. The third speed of the transmission can be used for acceleration and gradability. The first gear ratio in each type of transmission is selected to provide torque to pull the automobile up a 30% grade.

Economy became a major automobile consideration in 1975. Changing to a lower numerical rear axle ratio improved economy at the expense of performance. This brought back the overdrive idea that had been popular right after World War II. An overdrive is geared to turn the drive line 1.25 to 1.4 revolutions while the engine turns one revolution. This is the result of an overdrive ratio of 0.8 to 0.7. To accomplish this, an overdrive fourth gear is added to a standard three-speed transmission and an overdrive fifth gear is added to the standard four-speed transmission. A cut away of one of these five speed transmissions is pictured in Figure 22-5.

Full throttle engine power and torque are dependent on engine speed. Each gradually increases, peaks, and then decreases as engine speed increases from low to high speeds. Transmission gear ratios allow the engine to operate at its best speed while providing the desired drive shaft speed.

The clutch shaft, (Figure 22-6) which may be called by other names such as input shaft, main drive gear, and drive pinion; is the transmission

Fig. 22-5 Cut away five-speed standard transmission having the fifth speed ratio approximately 0.8 to provide an economical overdrive (Warner Gear Division, Borg-Warner Corporation).

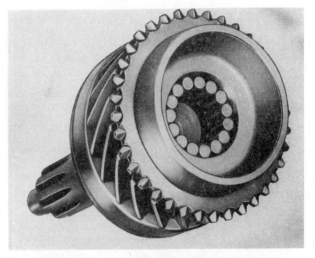

Fig. 22-6 Typical clutch shaft showing the main shaft roller bearings and synchronizer teeth (Oldsmobile Division, General Motors Corporation).

input shaft. It turns at engine speeds anytime the clutch is fully engaged. When this shaft is connected to the transmission main shaft, which is the output shaft, through a synchronizer, the main shaft and drive shaft also turn at engine speed. This is direct drive.

A gear on the back of the clutch input shaft gear engages the front gear on the counter gear cluster. The counter gear turns in a direction opposite to or counter to the input shaft gear. The front counter gear is usually larger and has more teeth than the input shaft gear. This allows the input gear to make *more* than one complete turn for each counter gear revolution. The torque increase is equivalent to the counter gear tooth number (driven) divided by the clutch shaft gear tooth number (driving). Small counter gears on the cluster turn larger second and first gears. The total torque increases can be determined by calculating the torque multiplication factor (TMF).

The torque multiplication factor is calculated for each gear set by multiplying the number of teeth on the driven gear by the number of teeth on the driving gear. In automotive transmissions the power flows through more than one gear set. The total TMF is calculated by multiplying the ratios of each separate gear set. A single idler gear or an idler gear with the same number of teeth on both input and output gears does not affect the total gear ratio.

In forward gears:

$$TMF = \frac{\text{Front counter gear}}{\text{Input shaft gear}} \times \frac{\text{Output shaft gear}}{\text{Last counter gear in use}}$$

In reverse gear:

$$TMF = \frac{\text{Front counter gear}}{\text{Input shaft gear}} \times \frac{\text{Reverse gear}}{\text{Reverse idler driving}}$$

$$\times \frac{\text{Reverse idler driven}}{\text{Reverse counter gear}}$$

A transmission having the following gear tooth combination is used to show how the above equations can be used to calculate torque multiplication factors.

Gear	Number of Teeth
clutch shaft gear	20
front counter gear	28
second counter gear	20
low-reverse counter gear	15
reverse idler driven	19
reverse idler driving	17
second gear	25
low gear	32
reverse gear	38

Using the equation above the torque multiplication factor for low gear is:

$$TMF = \frac{28}{20} \times \frac{32}{15}$$
$$= 1.4 \times 2.13 = 2.986$$

For reverse gear the torque multiplication factor is:

$$TMF = \frac{28}{20} \times \frac{19}{15} \times \frac{38}{17}$$
$$= 1.4 \times 1.266 \times 2.235 = 3.961$$

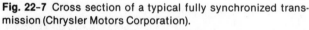

Fig. 22-7 Cross section of a typical fully synchronized transmission (Chrysler Motors Corporation).

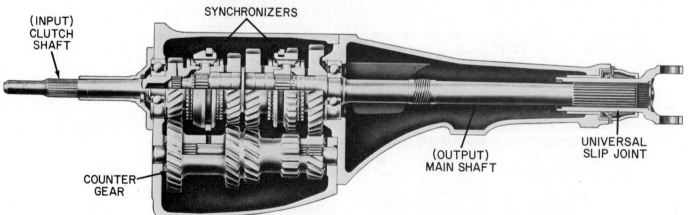

(INPUT) CLUTCH SHAFT

SYNCHRONIZERS

COUNTER GEAR

(OUTPUT) MAIN SHAFT

UNIVERSAL SLIP JOINT

The general designs of all three-speed domestic transmissions are very similar. There are more differences among the designs of four-speed and five-speed transmissions. All standard transmissions have a *reverted gear train*. In this gear train the input drive shaft and the output drive shaft are in the same centerline. An intermediate gear or *counter gear* is located directly below it. This can be seen in Figure 22-7. Input comes from the clutch disc into the transmission through the input shaft. In direct drive, the input shaft is coupled directly to the output or main shaft so it drives the propeller shaft like a one-piece shaft. In reduction, power goes to the counter gear and then reverts back to the main shaft located on the original input shaft centerline.

Transmission Shifting. Old transmission designs were shifted by moving some of the gears into mesh with other gears using shifting yokes. This method has been largely replaced with synchronizing engagement. Sliding gears are used in some transmissions for first and reverse gears because the vehicle is not moving when these gears are engaged. First gear may be synchronized in three-speed transmissions. It is always synchronized in four-speed transmissions. Reverse is synchronized in some late transmission designs. Speeds above first are synchronized in all current domestic standard transmissions.

Synchronizers, shown in an exploded view in Figure 22-8, allow the gear teeth to be in constant mesh, turning freely on their shafts. Driving torque is connected from the gear to the shaft through a synchronizer mechanism. A shifting yoke acting on a synchronizer sleeve is used to move the synchronizer into engagement.

Synchronizer. Shifting transmission gears is done with the clutch disengaged so that the only rotational drive speed comes into the transmission

from the rear wheels through the main shaft as the vehicle coasts. When the transmission is in neutral, the input shaft counter gear assembly will freewheel. The synchronizer speeds or slows this assembly to match main shaft speed. This makes it possible for an inexperienced driver to rapidly shift gears without clashing them.

Two types of synchronizers are used, the *pin-type* and the *plate-* or *strut-type*. Their designs are slightly different, but they operate in a very similar manner. The majority of transmissions use a plate-type synchronizer, so it will be used to describe synchronizer action.

The synchronizer consists of a hub, blocker ring, sleeve, and plates. The hub with external teeth, sometimes called a drum, is splined to the main shaft. All output power is transferred from the gear to the main shaft through the hub. It is surrounded by a sleeve that has internal teeth which mesh with the external hub teeth. Three plates or inserts with a ridge running across the middle are centered in the sleeve by a groove around the inside center of the sleeve. A circular wire insert spring on each side of the hub holds the insert outward so its ridge engages the sleeve internal groove, lightly holding the sleeve centered over the hub.

The outer edge of the synchronizer sleeve is provided with a groove in which the shifting yoke fits. Changing gears is accomplished by sliding the sleeve from its centered position on the drum until the internal sleeve teeth engage matching external teeth on the side of, and integral with, the driving gear. A brass blocking ring is fitted between the sleeve and the matching teeth to minimize coast time and to prevent engagement until speeds synchronize; then positive engagement can occur.

The internal surface of the blocking ring is the external portion of a cone-type clutch that can be seen in Figure 22-10. The blocking ring clutch

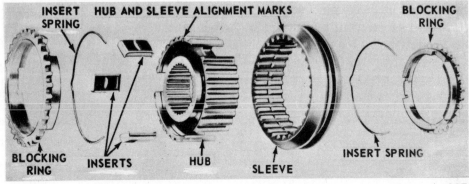

Fig. 22-8 Exploded view of a typical plate type synchronizer (Buick Motor Division, General Motors Corporation).

INSERT SPRING — HUB AND SLEEVE ALIGNMENT MARKS — BLOCKING RING

BLOCKING RING — INSERTS — HUB — SLEEVE — INSERT SPRING

(a)

(b)

Fig. 22-9 Synchronizer block ring. (a) In blocking position, (b) in the engaging position.

surface has fine grooves that cut through the oil film. It fits on a polished tapered cone that is integral with the gear. The exterior of the blocking ring has teeth that match the hub and are chamfered on the synchronizer side. The blocking ring is driven at synchronizer hub speed by the three inserts that fit into wide slots on the synchronizer end of the blocking ring. The slots are wide enough to allow the teeth to misalign by one-half a tooth in each direction. This can be seen in Figure 22-9.

During a gear shift, the drive clutch disengages the engine. A shifting yoke moves the synchronizer sleeve endwise toward the gear to be engaged. The insert ridge moves the insert endwise against the blocker ring as the sleeve moves. The insert exerts a 6- to 10-pound force against the blocker ring, engaging the cone clutch. This, in turn, pulls the

Fig. 22-10 Synchronizer blocking ring cone clutch.

blocking ring as far as the slots will allow in the direction of relative rotation, causing a mismatch of the teeth which effectively blocks engagement while a speed difference exists. When the speeds synchronize, the angle on the teeth causes a slight rotation that aligns the teeth and allows the sleeve

Fig. 22-11 Clutch side of blocking ring. (a) In blocking position, (b) in the engaging position.

(a)

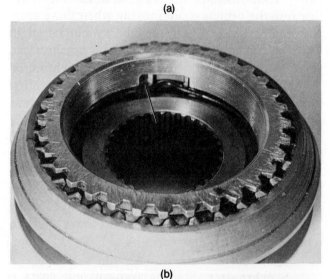

(b)

to engage the synchronizing teeth on the side of the drive gear. Blocker movement can be seen in Figure 22-11.

Any time the vehicle is moving, the drive shaft and the transmission main shaft rotate together. The synchronizer drums are splined to the main shaft so they also rotate. The drive train between the clutch plate and main shaft, previously called the input shaft counter gear assembly, is the section of the transmission that must accelerate or decelerate by the synchronizer cone clutch force to allow gear engagement. This drive train section includes the clutch disc, input shaft, counter gear, and all constant mesh gears. The lighter this assembly is, the quicker it will synchronize. Heavy clutch plates slow synchronization time.

Occasionally, a sliding reverse gear will have a half-synchronizer on one side. When the gear teeth are out of engagement, it can be used to synchronize first gear to the main shaft. When it is moved in the other direction, the gear teeth engage with the reverse idler to cause reverse mainshaft rotation. (Figure 22-12)

Synchronizers are always located between second and third on three-speed transmissions. Four-speed transmissions have all forward speeds synchronized. Many late model three-speed transmissions also have first gear synchronized. Syn-

chronizers on all forward speeds allow easy downshifting while the vehicle is is motion.

22-3 TRANSMISSION OPERATION

Engine power is transferred through the clutch to the transmission input shaft. The back of the input shaft has a gear that is part of the shaft. Behind this gear and also a part of the input shaft are located synchronizer teeth and cone. The input shaft gear is always in mesh with the front gear on the counter gear cluster. The cluster gear, in turn, is always in mesh with all of the synchronized gears. These members always rotate together. In neutral they are not connected to the main or output shaft. The following description refers to Figure 22-13.

First Gear. First gear may use a sliding gear or synchronizer. When a sliding gear is used, the gear is splined on the main shaft so it can move endwise but any rotational motion of the gear turns the main shaft. A shifter collar on the gear allows the

Fig. 22-12 Transmission gear train with a low-reverse sliding sleeve and gear (Oldsmobile Division, General Motors Corporation).

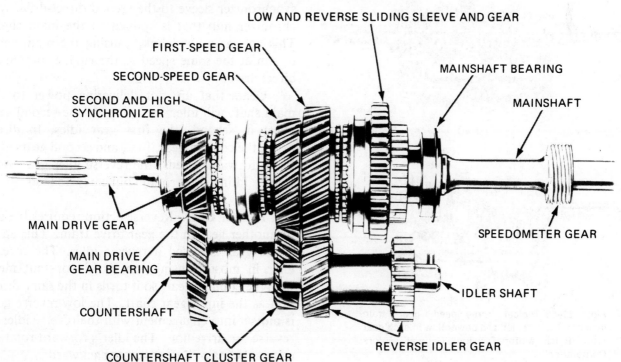

LOW AND REVERSE SLIDING SLEEVE AND GEAR

FIRST-SPEED GEAR

SECOND-SPEED GEAR

SECOND AND HIGH SYNCHRONIZER

MAINSHAFT BEARING

MAINSHAFT

MAIN DRIVE GEAR

MAIN DRIVE GEAR BEARING

COUNTERSHAFT

COUNTERSHAFT CLUSTER GEAR

SPEEDOMETER GEAR

IDLER SHAFT

REVERSE IDLER GEAR

NEUTRAL

FIRST

SECOND

THIRD

REVERSE

Fig. 22-13 Typical three-speed gear train synchronizer position and power flow in each gear ratio (Buick Motor Division, General Motors Corporation).

gear to be positioned by the shifter yoke. With the vehicle stopped, the shifting yoke moves the large low-reverse gear into engagement with the small low counter gear on the cluster. This connects the clutch shaft to the main shaft through the counter gear.

Synchronized first gears, as shown in Figure 22-13, are always in mesh with the low counter gear. The synchronized gear has a plain bearing that allows free rotation on the main shaft. The gear is connected to the main shaft by moving the synchronizer sleeve into engagement with the gear's synchronizer teeth. Power for the gear goes through the synchronizer sleeve to the hub that is splined to the main shaft.

Second Gear. Second speed is synchronized because the second gear is in constant engagement with the second counter gear. Like the synchronized first gear, the second gear has a plain bearing that rotates freely on the main shaft. The synchronizer sleeve connects the second gear to the main shaft for second speed operation.

The third gear of a four-speed transmission operates the same as the second gear synchronized gear change.

Direct Drive. The direct drive synchronizer sleeve moves into engagement with the synchronizer teeth located on the back of the input shaft. Engine power from the input shaft goes through the synchronizer sleeve to the second direct-drive synchronizer hub that is splined to the main shaft. This acts as a solid link, causing the main shaft to run at the same speed as the engine, providing direct drive.

Gears that are not delivering power to the main shaft will idle. In first gear, the second gear idles; in second, the first gear idles. In direct drive, the counter gear, first, and second gears idle. In all forward speeds, the reverse idler gear turns freely. Idling gears rotate, but carry no load.

Reverse Gear. Reverse action requires the use of another gear in the gear drive train. This additional gear is called a reverse idler. The reverse idler in most transmissions is in constant mesh with the counter gear, so it turns in the same direction as the input gear shaft. The low-reverse gear is moved into engagement with the reverse idler to reverse the drive line. The idler's forward rotation causes the main shaft to rotate backward.

Cast iron and aluminum transmission cases must be rigid enough to prevent distortion from tooth and thrust loads that tend to misalign the shafts and bearings. Gear teeth must have a tough, strong core to resist shock and a hard surface to resist pitting and abrasion. Tooth diameter and width determine the amount of torque the transmission gears can safely handle. Overloading is one of the most common causes of transmission failure. This usually occurs as the clutch is engaged when the engine is turning at high rpm.

The transmission has a mechanical efficiency above 90% in reduction gears and has an efficiency as high as 98% in direct drive. Ninety percent of driving is done in direct drive, so the transmission produces very little drive line friction.

The input shaft is supported by a ball bearing in the front of the transmission and by a pilot bearing in the back of the engine crankshaft. The main shaft is supported by a ball bearing in the back of the main transmission case and by roller bearings in the back end of the input shaft. A sleeve-type

Fig. 22-14 Section view of a four-speed transmission showing the location of bearings (Chevrolet Motor Division, General Motors Corporation).

1. bearing retainer
2. main drive gear
3. fourth speed synchronizing ring
4. third and fourth speed clutch assembly
5. third speed synchronizing ring
6. third speed gear
7. second speed gear
8. second speed synchronizing ring

9. first and second speed clutch assembly
10. first speed synchronizing ring
11. first speed gear
12. first speed gear sleeve
13. reverse gear
14. speedometer drive gear
15. mainshaft
16. reverse idler shaft roll pin

17. reverse idler gear (rear)
18. countergear bearing rollers
19. countergear
20. countershaft bearing roller spacer
21. countershaft bearing rollers
22. countershaft
23. oil slinger
24. reverse idler shaft
25. thrust washer
26. reverse idler gear (front)

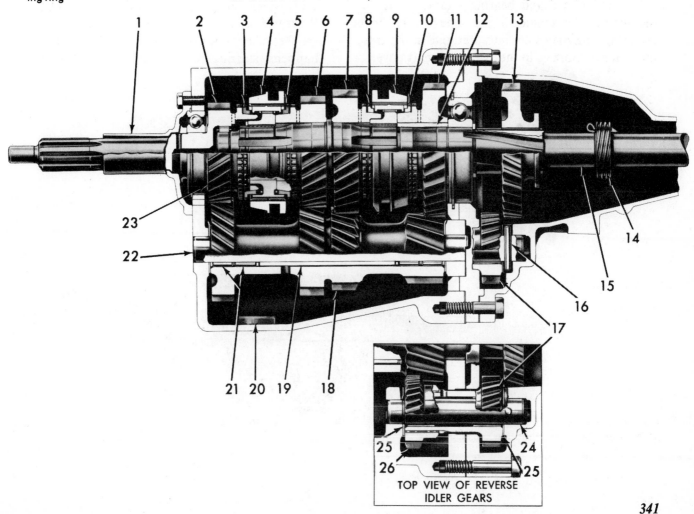

TOP VIEW OF REVERSE IDLER GEARS

bearing is located in the back of the extension housing to support the loads of the propeller shaft attachment to the main shaft. The bearing location can be seen in Figure 22-14 showing a four-speed transmission.

The counter gear cluster rotates on needle bearings. These, in turn, rotate on a counter shaft that is fit into reamed case holes. A short shaft supports the reverse idler gear. Input shaft and main shaft thrust is retained with ball bearings. Counter gear and reverse idler thrust is retained with thrust washers on each end of the gears. Washer thickness determines the thrust clearance. Drive gear teeth are cut on a helix angle, and so they are called *helical gears.* This type of gear provides quiet operation as the gears gradually mesh. The angle of the teeth induces a large part of the thrust that must be retained.

Input shaft and main shaft ball bearings are pressed on the shaft. They are held in the case with retaining rings. The front retaining ring is fastened between the case and bearing retainer. The rear bearing may be retained in the same manner or the retaining ring may snap into a groove in the transmission case bore or in the extension shaft bore.

A standard transmission should last the life of the vehicle without disassembly. Failure can result from maladjusted linkages, overloading, or from forcing a gear shift.

Linkages connect from the vehicle structure to the flexibly mounted engine-transmission assembly. When the linkages are not adjusted correctly, motion of the transmission may cause the transmission to slip out of gear. Maladjustment may also cause hard shifting. The shifting linkage is provided with a gate, detent cam, interlock, forcing the transmission to pass through neutral as shifts are made from one gear to the next. This also keeps the transmission from engaging two gears at the same time. A gate is usually located on the linkage system. Detent cams or an interlock are located within the transmission. One type of detent is shown in Figure 22-16.

Transmission overloading can result from sudden clutch engagement with the engine running at high speeds and the vehicle standing. The inertia of the crankshaft, flywheel, and clutch can put very high instantaneous torque loads on the transmission gears which can break the teeth and, in some cases, the transmission case. Forced shifting can damage synchronizer blocking rings and pins. When this happens, shifting becomes difficult and the trans-

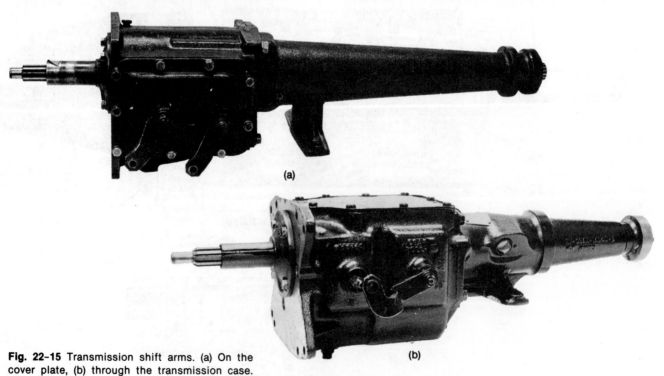

(a)

(b)

Fig. 22-15 Transmission shift arms. (a) On the cover plate, (b) through the transmission case.

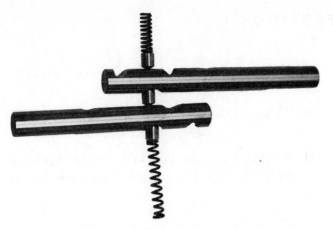

Fig. 22-16 Typical shift yoke rails with interlock

mission may slip out of gear when it is under load. These can only be repaired by completely disassembling the transmission.

Abnormal transmission noise usually indicates a problem that requires disassembly. It may be caused by excessive counter gear end play, loose synchronizer hub, damaged or worn gears, or rough or pitted bearings. Faulty parts must be replaced to correct the problem.

The general disassembly procedures are similar for all standard transmissions. Many details, however, are quite different. An applicable service manual should be followed when disassembling a transmission.

The transmission is removed by draining the lubricant, disconnecting the drive shaft, speedometer cable, and shifting rods. With the engine supported, the rear mount and cross member are removed and the four attachment bolts removed, freeing the transmission. The transmission must be carefully pulled straight back until the clutch shaft is free of the bell housing.

Transmission disassembly starts with the removal of the cover plate. One type of case cover plate contains the shifting fork yokes. These must be carefully removed from the yoke collars. Other transmission cover plates are stamped steel. These can be seen in Figure 22-15 (page 342). Their only purpose is to provide access to the transmission interior. On this type, the shifting yokes must be released and slid free of the yoke collars.

Most transmissions cannot be disassembled with the counter gear in place. The counter shaft locks are removed and the shaft pushed out of the case. If available, the shaft should be pushed out with a special dummy shaft of the same diameter as the counter shaft but only long enough to hold the thrust washers on both ends of the counter gear. This will help to keep all of the parts of the counter gear assembly together as a unit. The loosened counter gear is allowed to rest in the bottom of the case while the input shaft and main shaft are removed. These two shafts will separate at the main shaft front roller bearings located in the back of the clutch shaft. Gears and synchronizer drums are held on the main shaft with retaining rings so they will not fall off.

The extension shaft will come off from the main shaft before disassembly in some transmissions, and in others the extension shaft and main shaft are removed as a unit.

When the main and input shafts are out, the counter gear can be lifted from the case.

Gears, synchronizers, and bearings are removed from the main shaft by removing the retaining rings.

Generally, all needle bearings, thrust washers, gaskets, and seals are replaced with new parts. These come in a parts kit. Rough operating ball bearings are replaced. Also replace any gear or synchronizer with a chipped or damaged tooth.

Assembly is performed following a procedure that is the reverse of disassembly. All of the parts should be checked for condition and correct fit before reassembly. The parts should be thoroughly cleaned and lubricated with transmission lubricant during assembly in the case. After the transmission is installed it should be filled with the proper grade of transmission oil before it is operated.

REVIEW QUESTIONS

1. Why are transmissions needed in automobiles? [INTRODUCTION]

2. How does the transmission gear ratio affect the output torque and speed? [22-1]

3. How does the gear ratio of a small car differ from the ratio used in a large car? [22-1]

4. How much power is required to double the speed of the automobile? [22-1]

5. What is the advantage of having a large number of forward gear ratios? [22-1]

6. What is a reverted gear train? [22-2]

7. What is the advantage of synchronized gears? [22-2]

8. What part of a synchronizer is connected to the main shaft? [22-2]

9. Describe the operation of a synchronizer. [22-2]

10. What does the synchronizer blocker ring do? [22-2]

11. Describe the power flow in a three speed manual transmission in first, second, direct, and reverse. [22-3]

12. Where are the bearings located in a standard transmission? [22-4]

13. What type of operation indicates a problem in a standard transmission? [22-5]

14. What is the purpose of a shift yoke detent? [22-5]

15. In general terms, describe the overhaul of a standard transmission. [22-5]

23

automatic
transmission
fundamentals

The majority of domestic passenger cars are equipped with automatic transmissions. They have become popular with the motoring public because they are efficient, convenient, easy to operate, durable, and reliable. Over the years, automatic transmissions have been built in a number of different designs. Many fine features have disappeared from new transmission designs because they were relatively expensive to manufacture and to service. Some have returned because they increase the transmission efficiency. Current automatic transmission designs are lighter, smaller, less expensive to manufacture, and have superior operating characteristics when compared with some of the old designs.

It is beyond the scope of this book to discuss all of the automatic transmission design features. On the other hand, a detailed discussion of one type of transmission would not adequately cover the subject. Therefore, representative automatic transmission features will be used to describe current transmissions. Service manuals should be followed for details that apply to any specific automatic transmission.

Domestic automatic transmissions have a three-member torque converter driving through a two- or three-speed automatic shifting planetary gear train. This combination provides smooth torque characteristics from starting to the designed operating speed. A typical modern automatic transmission is shown in a cut-away view in Figure 23–1.

23-1 TORQUE CONVERTER

The torque converter was invented by Dr. Herman Föttinger in Europe for use on marine steam turbines. Its primary function is torque multiplication

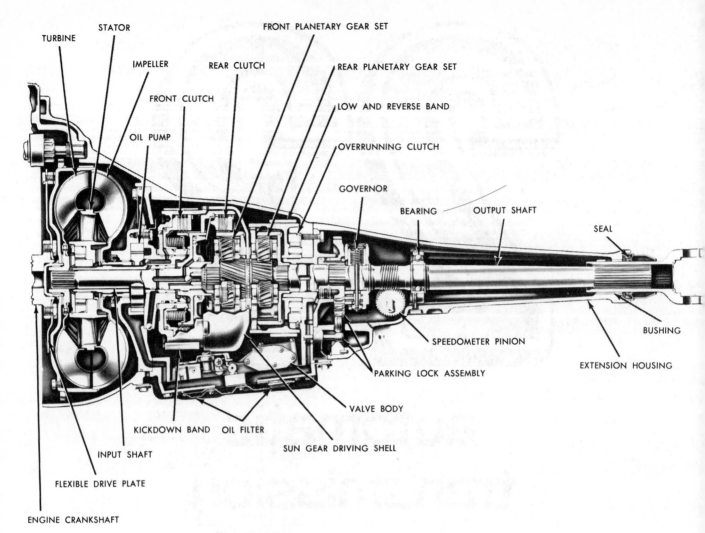

TURBINE
STATOR
IMPELLER
FRONT CLUTCH
OIL PUMP
REAR CLUTCH
FRONT PLANETARY GEAR SET
REAR PLANETARY GEAR SET
LOW AND REVERSE BAND
OVERRUNNING CLUTCH
GOVERNOR
BEARING
OUTPUT SHAFT
SEAL
SPEEDOMETER PINION
BUSHING
EXTENSION HOUSING
PARKING LOCK ASSEMBLY
VALVE BODY
SUN GEAR DRIVING SHELL
KICKDOWN BAND   OIL FILTER
INPUT SHAFT
FLEXIBLE DRIVE PLATE
ENGINE CRANKSHAFT

Fig. 23-1 Sectional view of a typical three-speed automatic transmission (Chrysler Motors Corporation).

Fig. 23-2 Edge view of a typical torque converter assembly with a welded housing.

through the force of hydrodynamic or fluid movement. It transmits power silently and smoothly, without shock, through speed and torque ratio changes. Its operation is completely automatic and reliable. All of its moving parts are submerged in lubricating oil and are practically immune to wear, so the coupling normally will last the life of the transmission without service.

Torque Converter Details. The torque converter is enclosed in a two-piece stamped steel shell or housing that is welded together. Figure 23-2 shows an external view of a typical torque converter. The front housing is connected to the engine crankshaft through a drive plate. A hub on the converter front cover fits into a counterbore in the back of the crankshaft to support the front of the converter. On the back of the converter, a rear hub is supported by a plain bearing located

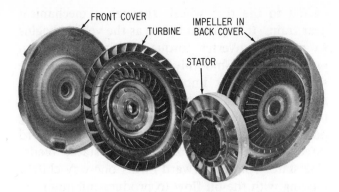

FRONT COVER
TURBINE
IMPELLER IN
BACK COVER
STATOR

Fig. 23-3 Torque converter parts from left to right: the front of the converter housing; the turbine; the stator and on the right is the impeller made as part of the back converter housing.

in the front of the transmission oil pump housing. The converter has three functional parts. The first is the *driving* member, or *impeller,* that is a part of the back shell of the converter housing. It rotates at engine speed with the housing. The second part is the *driven* member, or *turbine,* that drives into the planetary gear train. It is mounted on the transmission input shaft. The turbine hub is supported by and rotates in a bushing located inside the converter cover or it is supported by a bushing mounted just inside the stator shaft. The *stator* or *reactor* is the third member of the converter. It is connected to the transmission case through a one-way clutch mounted on an extension forward from the pump cover. This is called the *stator shaft.* The converter parts can be identified in Figure 23-3.

The converter housing rear hub performs an additional function, that of driving the transmission oil pump. The oil pump produces oil pressure for the transmission controls and pressure to keep the converter full of pressurized oil. Converter charge pressure is necessary when the housing rotates. Rotation causes the oil to build up centrifugal force that throws it toward the converter's outer edge. This tends to form air pockets near the converter center. When air pockets do form, the action is called *cavitation.* Cavitation is minimized by keeping the coupling under an oil charge pressure ranging from 30 to 180 psi (206.85 to 1241.1 kPa) between different transmission models.

Oil that leaves the converter flows through a cooler and transmission lubricating passages. From there, it drains to the transmission oil pan.

Converter Operation. The assembled converter housing is shaped like a tire. Its inner

diameter is approximately 1/3 of its outer diameter. Stamped steel blades are fastened to the inside of the rear housing shell in the back or transmission side using unequal spacing to minimize pulsation and noise. The blades, rotating at engine speed with the housing, form the impeller. When rotating, they throw converter oil outward, increasing its speed, to give the converter oil dynamic energy.

The converter is connected to the engine crankshaft so it rotates as the engine runs. Rotation of the impeller puts kinetic energy in the oil and flings it toward the outside of the housing. At the outer edge of the impeller the high energy oil leaves the impeller. It is thrown into the outer edge of the turbine. This high energy oil flow provides a force that tries to turn the turbine. The turbine is connected to the drive wheels through the transmission gears and drive line. When the force of the oil on the turbine is great enough as the engine speed is increased, it will cause the turbine to rotate and move the vehicle.

The turbine blade angle is curved to severely change the oil flow direction, so most of the oil's kinetic energy is removed. As the oil's energy is removed, the oil slows down and moves toward the housing center. Its flow is changed to a direction opposite that of impeller rotation. If the oil entered the impeller flowing in this backward direction, it would take a great deal of the input power to again accelerate the oil in the forward direction. The *stator* is a small curved bladed wheel located at the inner portion of the converter between the turbine and impeller. It is designed to redirect the backward oil flow as it leaves the turbine outlet.

Oil leaving the turbine in a backward direction hits the face of the stator blades. A free wheeling one-way clutch prevents stator backward rotation. The stator's curved blades redirect the oil with little energy loss, so it enters the impeller in the same direction as the impeller is turning. This oil flow is illustrated in Figure 23-4. In doing this, the stator in the torque converter-type hydrodynamic drive acts like a fulcrum in a lever system to increase torque transfer. When the stator is being used as a fulcrum it is said to be reacting.

Within the coupling, oil is flowing in two directions at once. It rotates in the direction the coupling turns, like a weight being swung on the

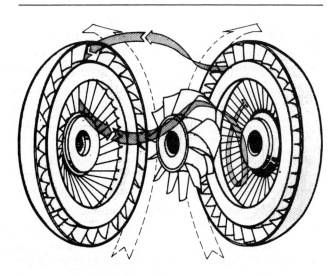

Fig. 23-4 Oil flow through the converter (American Motors Corporation).

end of a string. At the same time the oil is flowing around the torus core through the impeller-turbine-stator and back through the impeller. These two flows moving at the same time produce a very rapidly spiraling oil flow that is like a coil spring with its ends brought together. This type of flow is called a *vortex* flow. The vortex flow provides torque multiplication within the converter. As the turbine speed approaches the speed of the impeller, the amount of vortex flow is reduced. This is accompanied by a reduction in torque multiplication. Very little vortex flow occurs at the coupling point because all of the converter parts are rotating at nearly the same speed.

Some transmissions use a variable pitch stator. The blade angle can be changed from a high to a low angle. A low angle gives high torque conversion when there is a great difference between impeller and turbine speeds. A high angle gives less oil flow restriction as the turbine speed approaches impeller speed. A high angle will also be used at idle to minimize vehicle creep. The variable pitch stator is very efficient, but expensive to make.

The torque converter will have the greatest amount of vortex flow and torque multiplication when the turbine is stopped and the impeller is turning as fast as the engine will drive it. This is called *stall*. Maximum torque multiplication ratios at stall run from 2:1 to 2.6:1. The turbine is stopped when the vehicle is not moving because it is con-

nected to the rear wheels through a mechanical gear train. It begins to rotate as the vehicle begins to move. Converter torque multiplication ratio gradually and smoothly reduces as the turbine speed approaches impeller speed. The *coupling point* is reached when the turbine reaches 85% to 90% of the impeller speed. At the coupling point, the oil will leave the turbine in a forward direction, hitting the back of the stator blade. The stator rotates forward on its one-way clutch, moving with the oil flow to produce minimum oil flow resistance. Converter performance is graphed in Figure 23-5.

Maximum torque converter ratio at stall is built into the design by the converter size and blade angle. Stall speed of a converter is selected to prevent creep at idle and to be about 70% of the engine's maximum torque speed at *full throttle*. Operation at a high stall speed, which would provide high torque multiplication ratios, will cause excess heat to build up. A high stall speed would also produce excessive fuel consumption and noise. It would result in an excessively high coupling point that would allow the engine to race. This condition would make it impossible to fully use the engine's speed range. It is interesting to note that with the same input torque, converter stall speed is lowered at high altitude. This occurs when engine output is also lower at high altitude, so converter output torque is considerably lower.

During coasting, the turbine accelerates the oil, throwing it outward into the impeller. The impeller absorbs the oil's energy by trying to increase engine speed. The stator is forced to overrun. It is not efficient to operate the converter in this way, but it

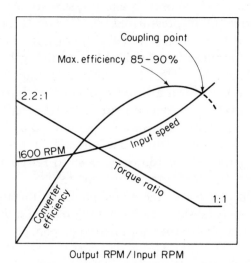

Fig. 23-5 Torque converter performance curves.

does help to slow the vehicle by transferring some of the vehicle's energy to the engine, forcing it to rotate faster than idle.

A clutch is used in a torque converter to minimize drive line loss on some transmissions. It engages as the converter coupling point is reached. Engagement connects the housing (which is bolted to the engine crankshaft) to the turbine (which is connected to the propeller shaft through the transmission gears) so no slippage can occur between the converter input and output members. In this way the vehicle uses the smooth torque multiplication of the torque converter during acceleration and lock-up to eliminate all slippage loss at road speeds.

Cooling. Oil flow through the converter must have a restricted outlet in order to maintain converter charge pressure. The transmission oil cooler and transmission gear train lubrication system provide this restriction. Two different systems are used. A series system sends all of the oil through the cooler, then on to the transmission lubrication system. The second system is a parellel system that sends part of the oil to the cooler and part to the transmission lubricating system. These cooling systems are illustrated in Figure 23-6.

Transmission oil is warmed as it flows across warm mechanical parts while lubricating and cooling them. Forced oil circulation in the converter also heats the oil rapidly, especially at low speeds. Serious heating problems are not encountered in turnpike driving, unless a heavy load is being pulled by the vehicle. Under severe operating conditions, oil temperatures may reach as high as 300°F (149°C); however, the normal maximum limit is near 275°F (135°C).

The transmission oil cooler is located in the radiator outlet tank where engine coolant temperature is lowest. This arrangement provides maximum transmission oil cooling. Some vehicles are equipped with an auxiliary, air cooled transmission oil cooler for more cooling capacity.

When transmission oil temperature is too low, the transmission will not function properly. By locating the cooler in the engine radiator, cold transmission oil is rapidly warmed to the engine operating temperature during cold weather operation. The desirable minimum operating temperature for automatic transmission oil is 190°F (88°C). Temperatures lower than this produce sluggish action.

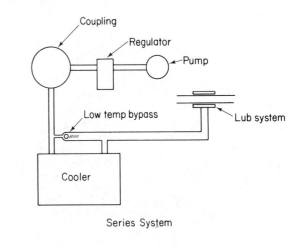

Series System

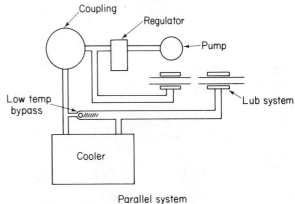

Parallel system

Fig. 23-6 Series and parallel transmission oil cooling system.

23-2 PLANETARY GEARS

The turbine shaft is the converter output shaft. It carries power from the torque converter to the gear train. Automatic transmission gear trains use planetary gear sets with input and output shafts located on the gear-set center line. The gear teeth are always in mesh, so gear ratio change is made by driving and holding different gear-set members. Most automatic transmissions use two planetary gear sets to obtain the required gear ratios.

Simple Planetary Gear Set. The planetary gear-set cross section looks somewhat like a caged roller bearing. The roller bearing has inner and outer races separated with rollers. If the contacting surfaces of the roller bearing had teeth to prevent slippage, it would act as a planetary gear set. This

member and the ring gear is held or the ring gear is the driving member and the sun gear is held (Figure 23-8). If the carrier does the driving, it will always produce an overdrive action on either the sun or ring gear, if the opposite member is held. When the carrier is held, the sun and ring gear will always turn in opposite directions to produce reverse. If the sun gear drives, it is reverse reduction and if the ring gear drives, it is reverse overdrive. When any two planet gear-set members are locked together, the complete set turns as a solid unit in

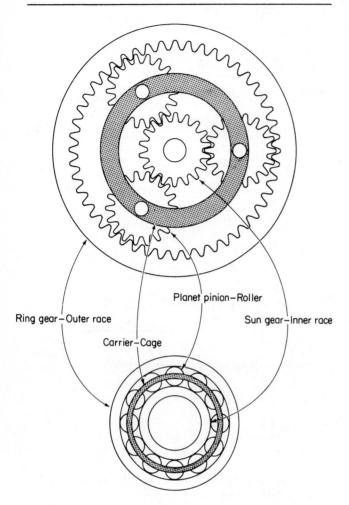

Fig. 23-7 Planetary gear set compared to parts of a roller bearing.

comparison is illustrated in Figure 23-7. The inner race is called a *sun gear*; the outer race is called a *ring, internal,* or *annulus* gear; and the rollers are called planet *pinions*.

In the bearing, roller spacing is maintained with a cage that turns around the inner race along with the roller centers. Planet gear sets have a similar cage called a planet pinion *carrier*.

In order to have a speed or torque ratio change, the planetary gear set must have a *driving* member, an *output* member, and a *reactor* or *held* member. These members are the sun gear, ring gear, and planet carrier. Any one of these members may be held, called *grounding,* as power is transferred between the other two. In a simple planetary gear set, the carrier is always the output member for forward reduction. Either the sun gear is the driving

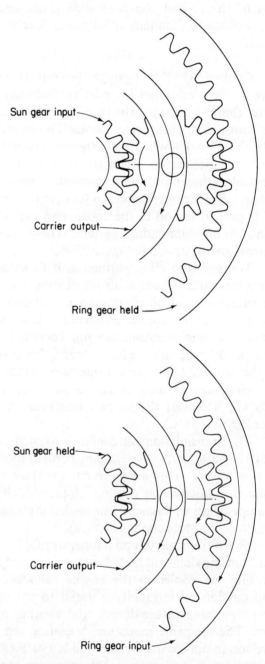

Fig. 23-8 Movement of the planetary members while transmitting torque.

direct drive. Power will not flow through the gear set if no member is held, and the gear train would be in neutral. Any time the holding member is suddenly released while power is being transferred through the gear set, the member just released will always spin backward. Because automatic transmissions use multiple planetary gear sets, output will be either from a carrier or from a ring gear.

Calculating Planetary Gear Ratios. Simple planetary gear speed reduction ratios may be calculated if the number of teeth on each member is known. Output torque increases at the same rate as the speed decreases, so the gear ratio calculation can be used for either. In reduction, the carrier output speed reduction ratio can be calculated by the formula:

$$\text{Speed reduction} = \frac{\text{Held member}}{\text{Driving member}} + 1$$

When the ring gear is held, the ratio is always greater than 2.5. If the sun gear is held, the ratio is always less than 1.66. This leaves a large gap in the ratio obtainable from planetary gear sets. This can be shown in an example using a planetary with a held, 66 tooth ring gear and a driving, 30 tooth sun gear. The speed reduction would be:

$$\text{Speed reduction} = \frac{66}{30} + 1 = 3.20$$

If the sun gear with 30 teeth were held and the ring gear with 66 teeth were driving the speed reduction would be:

$$\text{Speed reduction} = \frac{30}{66} + 1 = 1.45$$

The gap is filled by using two planetary gear sets in the transmission.

Overdrive ratios of a simple planetary gear set with the carrier driving can be calculated with a similar formula:

$$\text{Overdrive ratio} = \frac{\text{Output member}}{\text{Held member}} - 1$$

Using the same planetary, in overdrive the planet carrier drives, the 30 tooth sun gear is held and the

66 tooth ring gear is driven. The overdrive ratio would be:

$$\text{Overdrive ratio} = \frac{66}{30} - 1 = 1.2$$

In reverse, the carrier is held. Reverse gear ratios can be calculated by the formula:

$$\text{Reverse ratio} = \frac{\text{Output member}}{\text{Driving member}}$$

In reverse with the 30 tooth sun gear driving and the 66 tooth ring gear being the output member of the same planetary gear set, the reverse ratio would be:

$$\text{Reverse ratio} = \frac{66}{30} = 2.2$$

These formulas can be used in calculating automatic transmission reduction ratios when all the output of the first planetary is fed into one member of the second planetary.

23-3 TRANSMISSION GEAR TRAINS

Automatic transmission gear train members are connected together with clutches and held to the case, or grounded, for planetary reaction with either clutches or bands. These are engaged as needed by oil pressure directed to the operating

Fig. 23-9. Symbols used to identify planetary gear set parts.

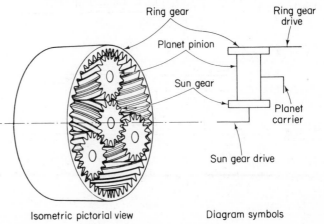

Ring gear

Ring gear drive

Planet pinion

Sun gear

Planet carrier

Sun gear drive

Isometric pictorial view

Diagram symbols

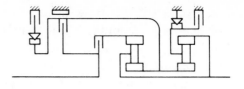

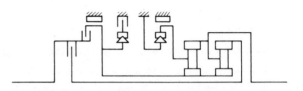

Fig. 23-11 Alternate designs using the Simpson gear train.

units by the hydraulic control system or by over-running free wheeling clutches.

Automotive automatic transmission designs have matured. In this process, two gear train arrangements have emerged as standards for the industry. One is the three-speed Simpson gear train and the other is the two-speed Ravingeau gear train. Symbols used to identify planetary gear set parts are shown in Figure 23–9.

Simpson Gear Train. The Simpson gear train uses two planetary gear sets, each having the same size gears with the same number of gear teeth. This reduces manufacturing costs. Three speeds provide high torque multiplication with relatively close speed ratios for smooth shifting. This gear train is used in automatic transmissions on high horse-

Fig. 23-10 Typical Simpson gear train operation in each gear.

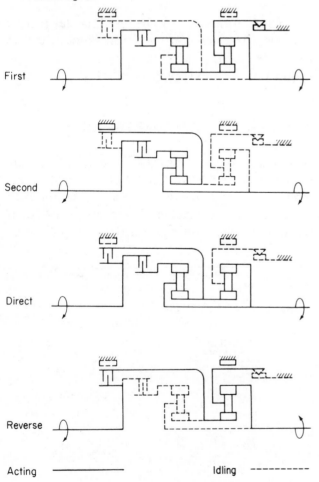

First

Second

Direct

Reverse

Acting ——————   Idling ----------

power engines and on many low horsepower engines to provide good performance with the available horsepower. A typical Simpson gear train is shown in Figure 23–10. It will be used as the reference for the following description. Figure 23–11 shows two alternate Simpson gear arrangements.

In first gear, the rear clutch engages the turbine shaft to drive the front ring gear in the same direction as the engine rotates. This direction of rotation is called *forward.* The front planetary carrier is connected to the rear wheels through the output shaft so it resists movement. Forward rotation of the front ring gear causes the front planetary gears to turn on their axis, acting as idler gears, so they rotate the front sun gear *backward,* which is opposite to engine rotation. The sun gear becomes the front planetary output. Both planetary sun gears are made in one piece, so the rear sun gear also turns backward to drive the rear planetary. The rear ring gear, as well as the front carrier, is connected to the output shaft so the rear sun gear rotating in the reverse direction tries to move rear planet carrier in a reverse direction. This is prevented because the rear carrier is held to the case by the free wheeling clutch in first gear. With the rear carrier held, the reverse rotating sun gear forces the rear ring gear forward producing maximum gear reduction in the Simpson gear train.

In second gear, the front ring gear is still driven, but the sun gear is held by the front band to prevent its reverse rotation. The ring gear pulls the outer edge of the pinion forward, causing the pinions to walk around the held sun gear. This pulls the carrier forward. The carrier is connected to the output shaft so the output shaft moves forward in

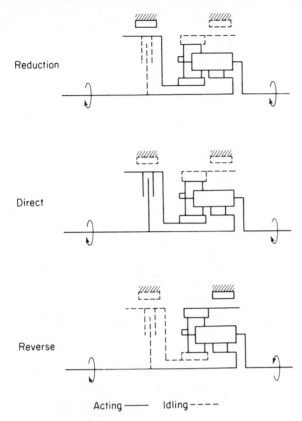

Reduction

Direct

Reverse

Acting ——— Idling - - - -

Fig. 23-12 Typical Ravingeau gear train operation in each gear.

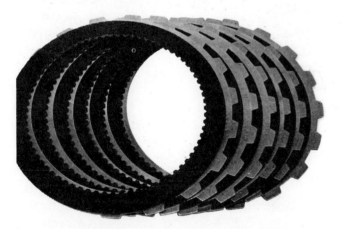

Fig. 23-13 Multiple disc clutch pack showing internal teeth on the discs and external teeth on the plates.

reduction through the front planetary. The rear carrier is released in second gear and the entire rear planetary idles forward, but does not enter into second gear reduction.

In direct drive, both clutches are applied to drive both the front planetary ring and sun gears at turbine speed. This eliminates pinion rotation and forces the carrier to rotate at turbine driving speed, along with the other planetary members. The carrier is connected to the output shaft so output

shaft speed equals driving speed. The rear planetary also idles at driving speed.

In reverse, the front clutch is applied to drive the front sun gear. The front ring gear is disengaged and allowed to idle while the rear carrier is held to the case with the rear band. The forward rotating rear planetary sun gear turns the pinion in a backward direction. Their reverse rotation forces the rear ring gear backward to carry the output shaft in a reverse direction.

When all clutches and bands are released, input power does not reach the planetaries. This provides a neutral position for the transmission when output power is not required.

Ravingeau Gear Train. The two-speed Ravingeau gear train (Figure 23-12) is at first glance somewhat more confusing than the Simpson gear train. It consists of two sun gears, two planet pinions, one carrier that carries intermeshed long and short planet pinions, and one ring gear. The carrier is permanently attached to the output shaft. The large rear sun gear is splined to the input shaft.

In first gear, power comes through the turbine, which is rotating the input shaft and the large sun gear in a forward direction. This rotates the long pinion backward. The long pinion is meshed with the short pinion so that the short pinion is turned forward. The short pinion also meshes with the small sun gear which is being held by the front band. The short forward rotating pinion gear walks forward around the stationary small sun gear, pulling the carrier and output shaft forward in rotation.

In direct drive, the clutch drives the small sun gear at turbine speed so both sun gears are driven at the same speed. This carries the entire planetary assembly at turbine speed because both sun gears and planet gears are interconnected.

In reverse, the ring gear is held. Power comes into the gear train through the large sun gear. It turns the long pinion backward. This, in turn, rotates the short pinion forward. Because the outer edge of the short pinion is engaged in the stationary ring gear, the short pinion walks around inside the ring gear in a reverse direction.

The Ravingeau gear train is in neutral when all holding devices are released.

Gear Ratios. Calculating gear ratios in planetary gear trains with two driving members is more complicated than using two simple planetaries. Solving these problems essentially involves breaking the problem into two parts. Each part is solved separately, then they are combined to calculate the total reduction. Details on these calculations are beyond the scope of this discussion.

23-4 DRIVING AND HOLDING DEVICES

Automatic transmissions use multiple disc clutches to connect driving members of the gear train. Multiple disc clutches are also used as holding devices in some transmission models. Bands and one-way clutches are used only as holding devices.

Multiple Disc Clutches. A multiple disc clutch consists of an alternating series of plates and discs. The plates are keyed on their outer edge and the discs on their inner edge. When disengaged, the discs rotate freely between the plates. These are shown in Figure 23–13.

The clutch is held in the disengagement position by springs. These springs may be coil springs, wave springs, or Belleville springs. Typical springs are pictured in Figure 23–14. The clutch is engaged with oil pressure applied to an open disc-shaped piston which has seals at both inner and outer diameters. Sufficient force is developed by the piston to compress the release spring and force the plates and discs together. Friction between their surfaces eliminates slippage. An exploded view of a typical automatic transmission clutch is shown in Figure 23–15.

Clutch plates have special compounded friction linings, usually paper based and bonded on both surfaces. Grooves on the surface provide passageways for the oil to flow from the clutch as the plates come together during application.

Friction materials and type of fluid affect the clutch friction. If the friction is too great, it may cause an objectionable bump or roughness as the clutch engages. If the friction is too low, excessive slippage will occur. Slippage will allow the engine to run away and the clutch to overheat.

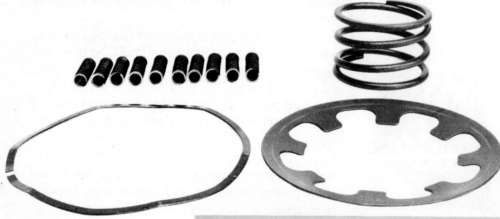

Fig. 23-14 Typical clutch release spring types.

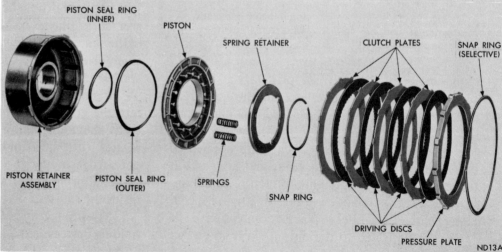

Fig. 23-15 Exploded view of a typical clutch assembly (Chrysler Motors Corporation).

Fig. 23-16 A variety of clutch facing groove designs.

The coefficient of friction changes with differences in surface speed between the plates and discs. If the friction increases as they approach the same speed during engagement, they may squawk or chatter. On the other hand, some clutches require this rise in friction to minimize slippage. The dynamic coefficient of friction for most automatic transmission clutches is approximately 0.12 when operating in automatic transmission fluid. Several clutch disc facing types are pictured in Figure 23-16.

The torque capacity of a clutch pack before slippage can be calculated using the following formula, using customary units of measurement:

$$T = \frac{NFC(D+d)}{4} \text{ lb-ft}$$

where　T = torque capacity (pound-feet)
　　　　N = number of plates in the clutch pack
　　　　F = force on the clutch pack (pounds)
　　　　C = coefficient of friction
　　　　D = outside diameter of the friction facing (feet)
　　　　d = inside diameter of the friction facing (feet)

For example, calculate the torque capacity of a 6 disc clutch pack having a 6-in. outside diameter and a 4-in. inside diameter when the force on the clutch pack is 1500 pounds.

$$T = \frac{6}{4} \text{ Plates} \times 1500 \text{ lb} \times 0.12 (0.5 \text{ ft} + 0.33 \text{ ft})$$
$$= 1.5 \times 1500 \text{ lb} \times 0.12 (0.83 \text{ ft})$$
$$= 240 \text{ lb ft}$$

Lining pressures operate between 50 and 400 pounds on each square inch of lining material during normal transmission operation.

(a)

(b)

Fig. 23-17 A band on a transmission drum. (a) Band on drum, (b) in transmission.

Bands. Transmission bands are wrapped around the outside of a rotating drum as pictured in Figure 23-17. One end of the band is attached to an anchor. Upon command from the control system a hydraulic piston, called a *servo,* is used to tighten the band to hold the drum. Typical servo pistons are shown in Figure 23-19. A spring built into the servo returns the piston to the release position when the servo is not pressurized. The servo may act directly on one end of the band or it may act through struts and links (Figure 23-20).

The band will be either a cast iron ring or a steel strap with friction lining material bonded to the inner surface. The lining may be grooved to allow the oil to escape as the band is applied. Typical bands are shown in Figure 23-18.

Band adjustment is required to make sure the

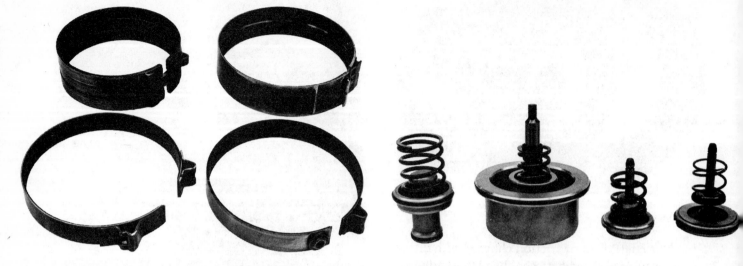

Fig. 23-18 Typical automatic transmission band designs.

Fig. 23-19 A number of different typical servo piston designs.

Fig. 23-20 Typical servo struts, links, and anchors.

band does not drag on the drum in the release position and to keep the servo from bottoming as it is applied to tighten the band. Some transmissions designs have no band adjustment because the band is not used during normal driving and therefore shows little wear. Bands that are used in the normal shift sequence have an adjustment either on the anchor end or on the servo end.

Band adjustment procedures usually involve tightening the band to zero clearance or against a gauging tool, then loosening the adjustment a specified number of turns. This is possible because the manufacturer has a known adjustment screw thread pitch. Each turn of the adjusting screw releases a specified clearance just as each turn of a micrometer opens the spacing a specified amount.

One-Way Clutches. Stators have always been mounted on one-way clutches to keep them from rotating backward during reaction and to allow them to rotate forward freely when reaction was no longer required. Because of its unique properties, the one-way clutch has found its way into the gear train as a reaction device to hold planetary gear set members. A one-way clutch has a large torque holding capacity, fits into a small space, is completely automatic, and applies no axial force when operating.

The one-way clutch is used in a fashion that causes it to be applied or to hold as the vehicle starts to move. When shifts occur, the one-way clutch very smoothly changes from a reaction member to an overrunning member as the direction of the torque force on the planetary gear set member changes.

The *cam and roller type clutch* (Figure 23–21) is used in many applications. The cam surfaces may be on either inner or outer race surface. The rollers are usually spring loaded in a direction to aid engagement. Rotation in one direction causes them to wedge between the two races, jamming the races together as they try to turn. When they turn in the opposite direction, the rollers move down the ramp against the spring to allow free movement between the races.

A second type of one-way clutch is a *Sprag clutch* (Figure 23–22). It operates between two smooth races. The engaging unit consists of a cam-shaped segment spaced in a cage between the races. Springs hold the segments against the races. The Sprag segments tip slightly to release the races so they turn freely. Figure 23–23 shows a comparison of both types of over-running clutches.

The one-way clutch cannot hold the planetary gear-set reaction member during coast because the coast force is applied in the one-way clutch in its release direction. Transmissions are provided with a multiple disc clutch or band that parellels the one-way clutch for use when the planetary member must be held, regardless of power flow direction. This can be seen in Figure 23–11.

In some applications, a one-way clutch is connected to the case through a multiple disc clutch. Application of this multiple disc clutch is used to bring the unit to stop for reaction while a one-way clutch releases the unit when reaction is no longer required.

23-5 DRIVE LINE FEATURES

Size and clearances in the automatic transmissions are very carefully controlled during manufacture.

Fig. 23-22 Typical one-way Sprag clutch.

Fig. 23-23 One-way clutch parts. Roller clutch on the left and a Sprag clutch on the right.

Fig. 23-21 Typical one-way cam and roller clutch installed in the transmission case.

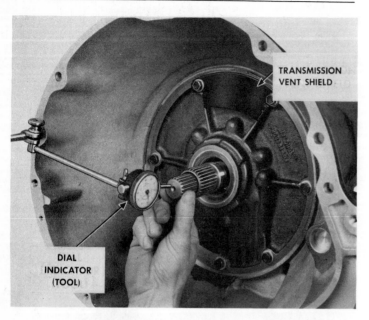

Fig. 23-24 Method of checking drive line axial clearance (Chrysler Motor Corporation).

Because of the buildup method, one part depends upon the accuracy of several other parts. For example, there are a number of shafts and thrust bearings in the transmission. Each is manufactured with its own tolerance. If a group of parts with minimum tolerance size should happen to be assembled together, excess clearance would exist. If, on the other hand, all maximum size pieces were put together, there would be hardly enough room to get them together. This is called *tolerance stack up*. The correct final axial movement or end clearance is controlled by a *selective fit* thrust spacer somewhere in the assembly. Proper end clearance is required for correct operation. It is usually checked before transmission disassembly and again after reassembly as shown in Figure 23-24.

All of the rotating parts must be supported on bushing-shaped bearings. Automatic transmissions usually use pressure lubricated bushing-type bearings on their main rotating parts. Most of these transmission bushings have babbitt or copper-lead bearing materials on a steel backing. Other materials are used where special demands require different bearing properties. All bushings are installed in bores located in either case or hub. The front of the gear train is supported on a hub extending back from the pump cover. Oil transfer rings are located on this hub to minimize leakage

as control oil transfers from the stationary hub to a rotating clutch drum. The rear of the gear train is supported by the rear of the transmission case. Shafts and drum hubs support one another on these two main support locations. Typical bearing locations can be identified in Figure 23-25.

The transmission input shaft is splined between the converter turbine and a front clutch hub. On the front, the turbine is supported in a bushing within the torque converter cover or inside the front of the stator shaft. The front clutch hub is mounted with a bushing on the rearward extension of the transmission pump cover (Figure 23-26). The front of the transmission output shaft rides on a bushing at the rear of the transmission case. The rear of the output shaft is supported by a bushing in the in the back of the transmission extension. In some transmissions, the output shaft extends almost to the input shaft while others use an intermediate shaft between them. The intermediate shaft will fit into pilot bores or bushings at the back of the input shaft and in front of the output shaft. These different details can be seen in Figures 23-1 and 23-25.

Planetary gear-set members, clutch hubs, and brake drums are splined to these shafts for driving and riding on bushings when they are required to be free turning. Nonrotating clutch and brake parts are supported by the transmission case to minimize the load that the shafts must support. In some transmissions, an oil transfer hub and seal rings are part of this nonrotating assembly.

The basic transmission disassembly procedure is to lift the torque converter from the input and stator shafts. Removal of the valve body assembly follows. The front pump assembly is removed to get to the gear train. Major gear train subassemblies can then be removed from the front of the transmission case.

Transmission rotating members are spaced with thrust bearings (Figure 23-27). Needle roller thrust bearings may be used where high loads are encountered. Babbitt on a steel backing is the standard thrust bearing material. Lightly loaded thrust bearings may be made of bronze, phenolic, or nylon to minimize cost.

Subassemblies are held together with snap rings and retaining rings (Figure 23-28). These must be removed to completely disassemble the transmission subassemblies. In clutches, the piston release spring is compressed against the retaining ring. When it is, the spring must be further com-

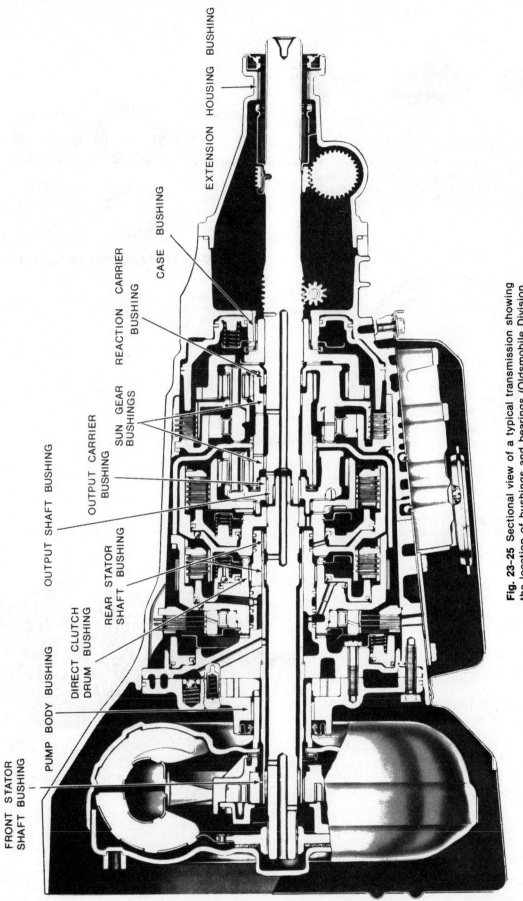

FRONT STATOR SHAFT BUSHING

PUMP BODY BUSHING

DIRECT CLUTCH DRUM BUSHING

OUTPUT SHAFT BUSHING

REAR STATOR SHAFT BUSHING

OUTPUT CARRIER BUSHING

SUN GEAR BUSHINGS

REACTION CARRIER BUSHING

CASE BUSHING

EXTENSION HOUSING BUSHING

Fig. 23-25 Sectional view of a typical transmission showing the location of bushings and bearings (Oldsmobile Division, General Motors Corporation).

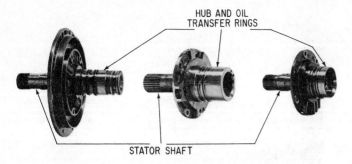

Fig. 23-26 Typical rear portion of pump covers with the stator shaft extending left and a clutch and bearing hub with oil transfer rings extending to the right.

Fig. 23-27 Typical thrust bearings and spacers.

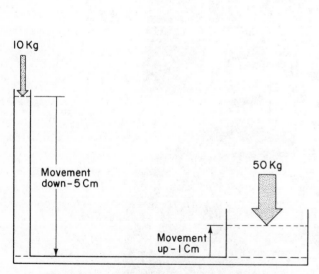

Fig. 23-28 Typical snap rings and retaining rings used to hold transmission parts in position.

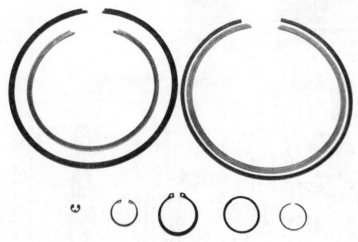

Fig. 23-29 Typical drive line subassemblies.

Fig. 23-30 Pressure remains equal but the moving distance and force change between two interconnected piston-in-cylinders of different sizes.

pressed to remove the ring. This usually requires the use of special tools.

Subassemblies that rotate together are connected with drive lugs at their outer edges. This method is inexpensive to make and easy to assemble. The major subassemblies are pictured in Figure 23-29.

23-6 TRANSMISSION SHIFT REQUIREMENTS

An automatic transmission gear ratio change is called a *shift*. Shifting requires the release of one planetary member and the application of a holding device of another. Release and application must be timed so the transmission keeps engine torque under control at all times.

The reaction member of the planetary gear set *always* tends to turn backward while the gear set is carrying a torque load. This reaction force is proportional to the torque being carried. As the torque load transfers from one planetary member to another, the load on the reaction member changes from reverse to forward direction. Ideally, the holding device should be applied or released at the instant torque reversal occurs.

During an upshift, the applied member must have a higher torque capacity than the released member. This is required because engine inertia momentarily increases torque as the engine is slowed to the new speed. This must be added to the torque being produced by the engine. When a holding or driving device becomes worn, it will first become apparent to the driver when it slips and fails to hold the required torque while it is being applied.

Shift quality or smoothness is primarily dependent upon the characteristic output torque which varies during the shift. If one member is released before the second member is applied, the transmission will momentarily be in neutral and the engine will tend to run away. On the other hand, if application occurs before release, the transmission will be momentarily locked in two gears, producing a bump. Either condition is unacceptable.

Good shift quality will transfer the load from one member to the next by allowing a slight amount of slippage to occur during application as the new member picks up the torque. This may take as long as 0.6 second. Longer application time will produce smoother shifts, but these will reduce the service life of the unit. The shift that is immediate

and positive will give the longest service life; however, it is unacceptable to the general motoring public.

During downshift, the engine speed must increase as the shift moves to a lower gear. Here again, the application force must gradually come on before the holding force is released to prevent engine run away. If it occurs too soon, a bump will be noticed, as it is during upshift.

23-7 HYDRAULIC FUNDAMENTALS

A review of hydraulic fundamentals is necessary in a discussion of the operation of a transmission hydraulic control system. Operation of the automatic transmission control system is based on Pascal's Law, which states that "pressure on a confined fluid is transmitted equally in all directions and acts with equal force on equal areas." Another way to say this, as it applies to hydraulic circuits in automobiles, is that the pressure in any one part of the fluid in an enclosed passage is equal to the pressure in any other part of the same passage.

The classic example used to illustrate Pascal's Law is to show two different size cylinders with pistons on fluid. A passage connects the fluid chambers of the two cylinders. A small weight on the small piston can balance a large weight on the large piston when the areas of the pistons are scaled properly. This is the same as balancing two weights on a mechanical lever system. Increasing the weight on the small piston provides a great increase in the weight that can be supported on the large piston. The force on the pistons is directly proportional to the ratio of the piston areas. If the small piston in Figure 23-30 has an area of one square centimeter and the large piston an area of five square centimeters, the weight on the large piston is five times the weight on the small piston when the system is in balance (large piston area/ small piston area = ratio of the force difference).

Nothing can be obtained free. In the hydraulic lever system just described, the movement of the large piston is less than the movement of the small piston. This is true of the mechanical lever system too. The amount of movement is the reciprocal of the force the piston produces (small piston area/

large piston area = ratio of the movement distance). When the one square centimeter piston moves down ten centimeters, the five square centimeter piston moves up two centimeters. The volume of the fluid displaced by each piston is equal when movement takes place. When one piston moves down, the fluid displaced by that piston is forced into the other cylinder to push the piston up. To summarize the operation of the hydraulic lever system: the force on the small piston times the distance it moves is equal to the force on the large piston times the distance it moves.

In both cases just described, when the pressure in one part of the system changes the pressure in all parts changes. The best example of this principle in automobiles is the brake system. In the brake system the fluid is trapped between the small area of the master cylinder piston and the large combined areas of all of the wheel cylinder pistons.

The power steering and the automatic transmission use hydraulic systems of a different type. Both use an oil pump to provide a volume of fluid under pressure. As piston movement takes place the oil pump continues to replace the pressurized fluid. A control system is located between the oil pump and piston to operate the units as required.

23-8 OIL PRESSURE

The automatic transmission uses oil pressure to apply the friction units, to transfer power through the torque converter, to lubricate bearings, and to cool internal parts. Some of the oil, called automatic transmission fluid (ATF), operates within the control valve assembly and acts as a signal to start or stop a shift sequence. The oil pump is the source of transmission oil pressure.

Oil Pump. The oil pump is driven by a hub on the back of the torque converter as shown in Figure 23-31. Its capacity must be large enough to provide pressure at all times. This is especially critical at low speeds with full throttle operation. On the other hand, the pump capacity must not be so large as to require excessive power to operate it. At highway speeds, automatic transmission pumps are capable of pumping up to 28 gallons

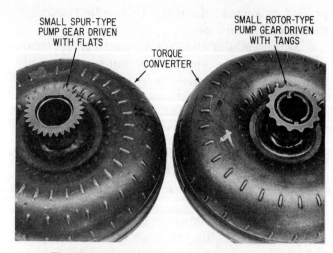

Fig. 23-31 Two typical oil pump drive methods. The small oil pump gear is driven by the torque converter housing rear hub.

per minute (106.94 liter per minute) at pressures up to 250 pounds per square inch (1723.75 kPa).

The automatic transmission oil pumps are classified as *internal-external* pumps, sometimes called IX pumps. The large gear with internal teeth is in mesh at one point with the small gear which has external teeth. The small gear is driven by the torque converter hub and the large gear idles around it. One side of the pump is connected to a passage from the oil screen or filter in the bottom of the oil pan. Oil is pulled into the pump inlet as the gear teeth come out of mesh as they rotate. The space between the separating gear teeth produces a partial vacuum that is filled by oil from the pan. As the gears continue to rotate, the teeth will again begin to mesh on the other side of the pump. A pressure passage is provided to allow the oil to be squeezed from between the teeth as they mesh. This provides a continuous oil supply as long as the engine is operating.

Two tooth forms are used in automatic transmission IX pumps. These are shown in Figure 23-32. One uses typical extended spur gear teeth. A crescent filler block is used between a portion of the pump where the gears are separated. This helps to separate the pump inlet from the pump outlet. The other pump is called a rotor-type pump. Its tooth form is designed so that the high points of the tooth form nearly contact at the open side of the gear set. This close operation helps to keep the inlet and outlet sides separated.

At one time, a second pump was used on the transmission output shaft. This rear pump was

Fig. 23-32 Typical automatic transmission oil pumps. (a) Extended spur gear tooth type, (b) rotor type pump.

valve opens a passage to allow excess oil to flow to the pump inlet, effectively limiting maximum pressure.

The second type of regulator valve is called a low flow valve. It is used to reduce pressures from line pressure to provide a lower regulated pressure. One application is a torque converter pressure regulator. It also operates on the principle of balancing a valve between oil pressure and a spring. The valve reaction area in this type is exposed to the valve's *outlet pressure*. When the outlet pressure reaches the required amount, the valve moves to restrict inlet flow to the valve. This effectively limits oil pressure.

Oil pressure that leaves the regulator is called *line pressure*. It is the highest pressure in the transmission. Other control pressures are reduced from it. Line pressure must be high enough to securely hold clutch pistons and band servos under the most severe loading conditions. This force may be excessive and require a lot of engine power under light loaded operating conditions. Some regulator valves are, therefore, designed to lower line pressure when less severe loads are being applied and raise them as the loads become greater. This is called *modulated line pressure*. Its function is to match line pressure to engine torque. This is done by using

discontinued to reduce expense and noise when front pump designs were improved to satisfactorily provide pressure under all operating conditions. Vehicles with transmissions that have no rear pump cannot be started by pushing the vehicle. Engine operation is needed to build up the required pressure to place the transmission in gear.

Uncontrolled pump pressure would change with engine speed. Oil from the pump flows directly from the pump to a regulator valve that limits pressure to the amount required.

Two methods are used to regulate oil pressure (Figure 23-33). The standard method is to have one end of the regulator valve, called a reaction area, exposed to *pump pressure*. A spring presses against the opposite end of the regulator valve. The increase in pump pressure applies a greater force on the regulator valve to move it toward the spring. When the required pressure is attained, the

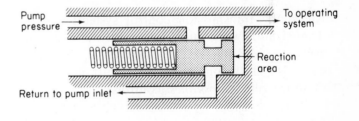

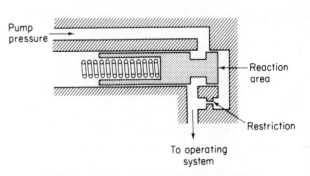

Fig. 23-33 Pressure regulator valve principles.

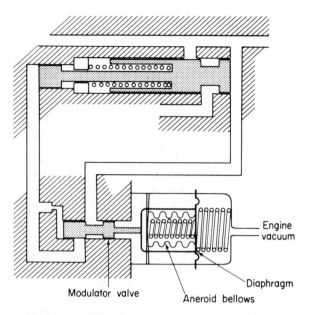

Fig. 23-34 Modulated pressure regulator principle.

an oil pressure that varies with the engine power to apply pressure on the regulator valve in the same direction as the spring force acts. This will raise line pressure at high engine power, as illustrated in Figure 23-34.

23-9 CONTROL SYSTEM

Automatic transmission control systems can be divided into two groups. One type will cause an event to take place. These are called *causative* controls. The second type affects shift quality and these are called *smoothness* controls.

Sliding spool-type control valves are used. Spool valves are illustrated in Figure 23-35. Porting of the oil is accomplished through passages that surround the entire spool. This balances the side forces on the spool so it can slide freely in

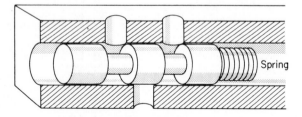

Fig. 23-35 Typical spool valve section showing pressure balance around the spool.

its bore. Most of the valves are held in one extreme position by a spring. Valving occurs when an oil pressure differential moves the valve toward the spring. Endwise movement aligns ports that allow oil to flow to or from the operating unit. The spool valves are accompanied with disc- or ball-

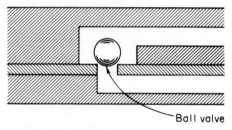

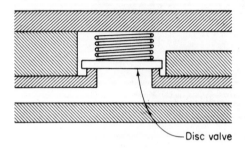

Fig. 23-36 Typical check valves.

Fig. 23-37 Oil passages in a typical transmission case.

check valves to control the transmission. Check valves, as shown in Figure 23–36, prevent flow until a specific pressure is reached or close passages to prevent back flow. Check valves are also used to do both of these operations.

Valves and operating units are connected through drilled passages and through ditches cast into the transmission case and valve body. These can be seen in Figure 23–37.

Causative Controls. Line pressure is directed to the manual valve which is connected to the driver operated selector. The manual valve directs oil pressure to operating valves used in the driving range selected (Figure 23–38). It fully applies the units required for neutral, reverse, and forward range. Automatic shifting only occurs during forward range operation.

In drive range, the selector valve directs oil to a shifter valve, a governor valve, and a throttle valve. When the shifter valve moves, it opens ports to allow line pressure to flow to the required clutch piston and band servo to produce a shift in gear ratios. Oil pressure from the governor provides the force to move the shifter valve, as can be seen in Figure 23–39.

The *governor,* as shown in Figure 23–40, is driven by the transmission output shaft and is sensitive to vehicle speed. Its pressure increases as vehicle speed increases. When the vehicle reaches the speed at which shifting should take place, the governor pressure is high enough to move the shifter valve against a spring to produce the shift. This system would be satisfactory if the loads and speeds were the same every time, but they aren't. This is why it is also necessary to have some means for the transmission to sense engine load.

The amount of power an engine produces is indicated by throttle position or by manifold vacuum (Figure 23–41). Automatic transmissions use either of these two methods to operate valves which will produce an oil pressure signal that is proportional to engine load. It may be TV pressure (*Throttle-Valve*) or modulator pressure. This oil pressure (called TV pressure for the rest of this discussion) is proportional to the vehicle load and is sent to the spring side of the shift valve to help the spring oppose governor pressure (Figure 23–39).

The shift valve is balanced between a spring load plus TV pressure on one end and governor pressure on the other end. Shifting occurs when the force produced by governor pressure is greater

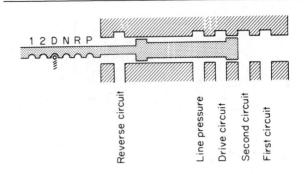
Fig. 23-38 Schematic of a typical manual selector valve.

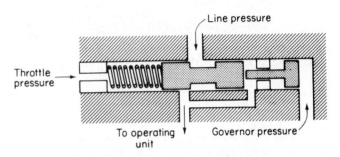
Fig. 23-39 Shift valve principle.

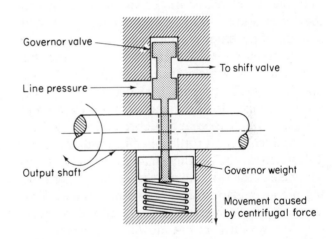

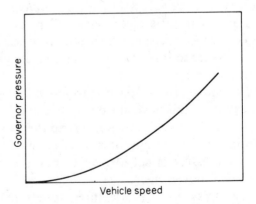
Fig. 23-40 Typical single-stage governor.

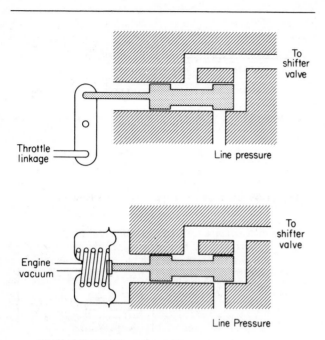

Fig. 23-41 Mechanical and vacuum operated throttle valve principles.

than the force created by the spring working with the TV pressure. At low throttle openings, a small amount of governor pressure is required to produce a shift because the TV pressure is low, so the shift occurs at low vehicle speeds. At higher throttle openings, the TV pressure is higher so the governor pressure must also be higher to produce a shift. The shift will then occur at higher vehicle speeds.

Sudden full throttle openings will raise the TV pressure much higher than governor pressure. This causes the shift valve to reverse itself, producing a transmission-forced downshift, called *kickdown*. Throttle pressure alone may not be sufficient to produce a fast downshift response. In these cases, a special valve (called a *detent*) that opens at full throttle gives detent oil pressure or boosted throttle pressure which is used in addition to TV pressure to force the shift valve back against governor pressure.

The shift valve is designed to move the spool to its extreme limit once movement begins. This is done by rerouting oil pressure to snap the valve to its limit. In the extreme position, either TV or governor pressure is cut off, depending upon the direction of movement.

Transmissions that use three speeds require two shift valves. Both operate in the same basic way just described. They differ in the amount of governor pressure required to make the shift. The 1-2 shift valve operates at a lower governor pressure than the 2-3 shift valve.

Two-stage governor weights are used. A large weight is used to produce adequate governor pressure at low speeds. This weight is blocked and a small governor weight takes over to increase the governor pressure that is required to operate the second shifter valve. The weights set governor valve position to allow proportional oil pressure to apply against the shifter valve pressure area. The two-stage governor is illustrated in Figure 23-42. The basic causative automatic transmission control system is shown in Figure 23-43.

Oil pressure from the shifter valve is often used to simultaneously release one reaction member and to apply another. This direct action is usually modified to give a rapid shift that will smoothly pick up the engine torque during the shift phasing. The controls that do this are called *smoothness controls*.

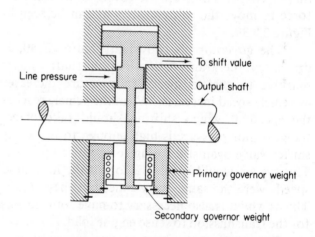

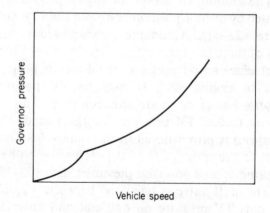

Fig. 23-42 Typical two-stage governor.

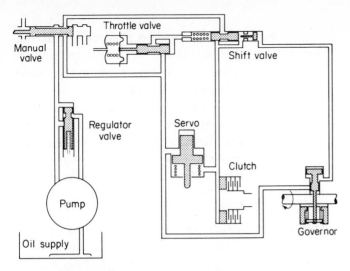

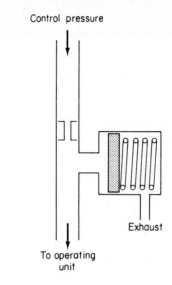

Fig. 23-43 Schematic of a basic causative automatic transmission control system.

Smoothness Controls. Smoothness controls are those control valves that help to time the application and the release of friction devices so the engine torque is always under control and that prevent two gear ratios from being applied at the same time. One of the most common smoothness controls is the *accumulator* illustrated in Figure 23–44. The accumulator is basically a spring loaded piston placed parallel to the passage to be controlled. Pressure will build up rapidly in the passage until the accumulator piston begins to compress the spring. The pressure is relatively constant for a

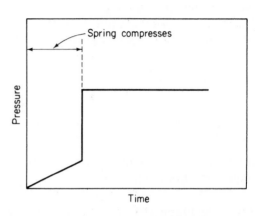

Fig. 23-44 Accumulator principles.

Fig. 23-45 Portions of a typical valve body, valves, and springs (Chrysler Motors Corporation).

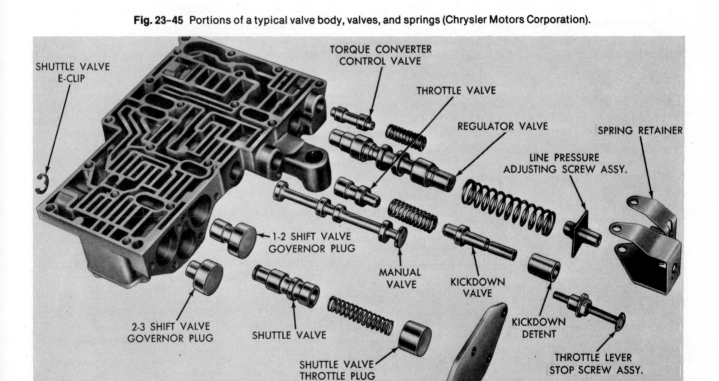

time as the accumulator fills. When it is full, the passage pressure again builds until it reaches full pressure. In this way, the accumulator controls the pressure for a time interval as the operating unit picks up the load, then it applies the full holding force. An accumulator may be designed into a servo or it may be a separate unit.

Other valves used to cushion the shift are called scheduling valves, shuttle valves, timing valves, etc. Even accurately drilled holes or orifices are used as an aid to cushion the shift. Their purpose is to help control the application and release of holding devices so they will have smooth shifts under any operating load and speed condition. Blocking

valves are sometimes used to prevent a shift that would cause damage if the shift were to occur at too great a speed. An exploded view of a valve body is pictured in Figure 23–45.

Each model automatic transmission is designed to be used in a number of vehicle-engine combinations. Each engine type in these vehicles has a different torque and power curve and each vehicle has a different weight. Therefore, they require different shift patterns and shift timing. To accommodate all of these combinations, the individual shift control valves are programmed to match their vehicle-engine application. This is usually done with minor changes in the valve porting and by using different control valve springs. In some cases, the drive line is modified by changing the number of clutch plates, changing the number of pinions, or by changing some of the materials used.

REVIEW QUESTIONS

1. In addition to torque multiplication, what does a torque convertor do? [23–1]

2. How is the torque converter driven by the engine? [23–1]

3. What part of the torque converter drives the transmission input shaft? [23–1]

4. What part of the torque converter drives the oil pump? [23–1]

5. During what operating condition is the stator providing its main function? [23–1]

6. Why is the stator mounted on a one-way clutch? [23–1]

7. What oil flow provides torque multiplication? [23–1]

8. Under what operating conditions does the torque converter have the greatest torque multiplication? [23–1]

9. What limits high torque multiplication ratios in a torque converter? [23–1]

10. What is the advantage of having the coupling point occur at low speed? [23–1]

11. Why is it necessary to have a restricted oil outlet on the converter? [23–1]

12. Where does the oil go when it leaves the torque converter? [23–1]

13. What are the advantages of having the oil cooler in the radiator? [23–1]

14. What must occur if power is transferred through a planetary gear set? [23–2]

15. What planetary gear member is driving, holding, and driven when the gear set is in reduction, overdrive, and reduction-reverse? [23–2]

16. What are the advantages of a Simpson gear train? [23–3]

17. How does the Ravingeau gear train differ from the Simpson gear train? [23–3]

18. What holds a multiple disc clutch in the disengaged position? [23–4]

19. What force applies the multiple disc clutch? [23–4]

20. What causes clutch chatter during engagement? [23–4]

21. What is the common clutch facing material? [23–4]

22. How do bands differ from clutches in design and operation? [23-4]

23. What does a servo do? [23-4]

24. Why is band adjustment important? [23-4]

25. When is a one-way clutch used? [23-4]

26. When is a one-way clutch ineffective as a holding device [23-4]

27. How is the correct turbine shaft axial movement controlled? [23-5]

28. From what materials are automatic transmission bearings made? [23-5]

29. What means are used to hold the automatic transmission parts together? [23-5]

30. How is a transmission shift made? [23-6]

31. Upon what does the shift quality depend? [23-6]

32. How do the large and small piston forces differ in a closed hydraulic system? [23-7]

33. How do the large and small piston pressures differ in a closed hydraulic system? [23-7]

34. How do the movements of the large and small pistons differ in a closed hydraulic system? [23-7]

35. Describe the operation of an IX pump. [23-8]

36. How is the maximum oil pressure limited? [23-8]

37. Where is oil pressure highest in a transmission? [23-8]

38. Why do some transmissions use a modulating oil pressure? [23-8]

39. What type of valves are used in automatic transmissions? [23-9]

40. List valves and holding devices that are causative controls. [23-9]

41. What oil pressure causes a shift to occur? [23-9]

42. What oil pressure delays the up-shift? [23-9]

43. What are the smoothness controls? [23-9]

44. What is the purpose of a two-stage governor? [23-9]

45. How does an accumulator function? [23-9]

automatic
transmission
service

Modern automatic transmissions require very little service unless they are abused. Abuse comes from operating at high temperatures and from forcibly changing gears with the engine operating at high rpm, especially between low and reverse. Damage may even result from towing the vehicle without removing the drive shaft, because there is no lubrication when the engine is not operating the transmission oil pump.

In nearly every case of automatic transmission failure, the failure is preceded by shift quality deterioration. This may result from maladjustment, debris in the hydraulic system, clogged screens and filters, worn parts, or internal leakage that reduces application pressures. When shift quality deteriorates, the wise driver will have the transmission serviced before a major and expensive failure occurs.

24-1 AUTOMATIC TRANSMISSION FLUID

The level and condition of the automatic transmission fluid should be checked periodically. It is the first thing to be checked when there is a question about the operating condition of the automatic transmission. Automatic transmission fluid will expand from 60°F (18°C) to the normal operating temperature of 240°F (118°C). This expansion is enough to raise the level on the dipstick from the add-mark to the full-mark. The transmission should be thoroughly warm for the fluid level to be accurately checked. The fluid level is then checked with the engine running and the transmission in neutral or park, depending upon the transmission type.

Automatic transmission fluid is required to perform four different jobs. It is used in the converter to transmit engine power from the impeller to the turbine. It also hydraulically operates the holding devices used to control planetary gear drives. While performing these tasks, the fluid lubricates the transmission bearings and carries heat from the hot transmission parts to a cooler, usually located in a radiator tank.

Automatic transmission fluids (ATF) are compounded to meet the variety of functions to which they are subjected. Matching the fluid to the transmission is essential for good clutch plate life and band durability as well as for smooth operation and elastomer seal life. For example, if paraffinic base oil is used for the fluid, it will tend to shrink oil seals, but if naphthenic oil is used, it will act as a swelling agent. ATF is made from 75% paraffinic-based and 25% naphthenic-based oil to control seal swelling.

Complex automatic transmission fluids are formulated for low temperature fluidity, oxidation resistance, anti-foaming, corrosion resistance, effect on seals, and effect on friction. Two types of fluids are used: M2C33, or *Type F,* developed by Ford for their products, and *Dexron II,* developed by General Motors and used in all vehicles except Ford. The greatest difference between these two fluids is the way they affect the clutch coefficient of friction. This is graphed in Figure 24-1.

At the start of application, the clutch plates and discs are turning at a great difference in speed. This can be measured in feet per minute. As the clutch applies, the difference in speed reduces as it picks up the load until the driving and driven members are turning at the same speed. As the clutch sliding speeds equalize, the coefficient of friction increases with Type F fluid to give a firm

aggressive shift. With Dexron fluid, the coefficient of friction reduces, which results in a soft, smooth shift. The correct fluid must be used in each transmission to minimize a squawk or bump as the discs and plates reach the same speed.

Red dye is added to automatic transmission fluids. This gives it an identification color that aids in determining the source of external leaks. Engine oil has a neutral color that can be differentiated from the red transmission fluid.

Automatic transmissions cause very few problems when used in standard passenger car operation. Routine service consists of an occasional oil level check. At the first sign of external leakage or abnormal shifting, transmissions should be given a thorough inspection and the required corrections made before serious damage occurs.

The automatic transmission fluid level should be checked at regular intervals. The best time to do this is at the same time the engine oil is being changed. Low fluid level is one of the first signs of a potential transmission problem.

Automatic transmission fluid deteriorates as it is used. In 25,000 miles (40,000 km) to 30,000 miles (48,000 km), the fluid reaches a stage where it will no longer function properly. The used fluid should then be replaced with the correct type of fresh ATF fluid. Deterioration results from the shearing action on the fluid as it moves through the pump, converter, and fluid passages. Temperature also contributes to fluid deterioration. The higher the operating temperature, the more rapidly the oil will break down. Heavy duty, commercial, and trailer-towing operation causes high transmission temperatures. The fluid change period is more frequent for transmissions used in these types of service. The main cause of fluid deterioration is the oxidation of the oil base and the breakdown and neutralization of the additives that make up about 10% of the fluid volume.

Fluid contamination is another reason for changing the fluid. Gradual wear occurs on the facings of the bands and clutch discs, as shown in Figure 24-2, as well as on the surface of bearings and bushings. Material worn from these parts is carried by the oil. A filter removes the larger particles, which fall to the bottom of the pan. The very small particles circulate with the fluid. Con-

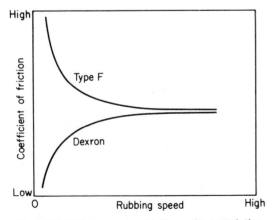

Fig. 24-1 Difference in friction characteristics between Type-F and Dexron automatic transmission fluids.

Fig. 24-2 Two discs from the same clutch pack. The upper disc is badly worn while the lower disc shows little wear.

tamination is removed when the transmission fluid is changed.

Changing the transmission fluid can best be done with the automobile raised on a hoist. Modern automatic transmissions do not have a drain plug the transmission pan so the fluid is removed as the transmission pan is removed. This can be a messy procedure if it is not done carefully. If the automobile has just come off the street the oil is hot, often above the temperature of boiling water. Extreme care should be taken to avoid the hot fluid.

The use of a drain pan larger than the transmission pan is necessary to catch the oil with

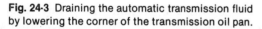
Fig. 24-3 Draining the automatic transmission fluid by lowering the corner of the transmission oil pan.

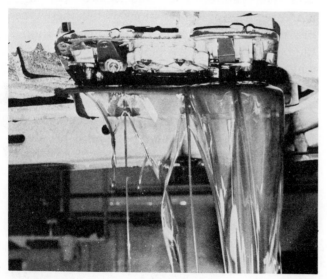

minimum splatter. This drain pan should be placed as close to the transmission as possible while the transmission pan is being removed. The transmission pan cap screws are loosened. The cap screws are removed at one corner and adjacent sides, leaving loosened cap screws on the opposite corner and sides. The pan is tapped on the flange to loosen the gasket. As the gasket breaks free, the loose corner will drop more than the opposite corner. This allows the fluid to flow from the low corner into the drain pan as pictured in Figure 24-3. Carefully remove the other screws to gradually lower the transmission pan. This will allow the remaining fluid to pour into the drain pan. The transmission pan can then be completely removed. Fluid will continue to drip from the bottom of the transmission, and so it is desirable to keep the drain pan under the transmission until the dripping stops.

Fig. 24-4 Normal amount of deposits found in the bottom of the automatic transmission oil pan after 33,000 miles of use.

The deposits in the bottom of the pan, such as those shown in Figure 24-4, should be examined to determine the source. The kind and quantity of deposits in the pan are a good indication of the amount of transmission wear and the location of that wear. The transmission pan should be thoroughly washed in cleaning fluid and then dried. The filter on the bottom of the valve body should be replaced with a new one. One type of filter is shown in Figure 24-5. The technician has a good chance to examine the visible internal parts of the transmission when the pan is off. Where required,

Fig. 24-5 An oil filter on the bottom of the transmission with the oil pan removed.

band adjustment should be made at this time. The pan is installed using a new gasket without sealer. The pan bolts are evenly tightened to the specified torque.

Some transmissions have a hex drain plug in the converter cover under a dust shield on the lower bell housing as shown in Figure 24–6. This plug is taken out to remove the contaminated fluid when the transmission fluid is changed. In other types of transmissions, the converter does not have a drain plug so the converter is only drained when the transmission has been removed. After the fluid is drained, the converter drain plug is installed securely and the dust shield replaced.

A small amount of the proper type of ATF fluid is poured in the transmission filler tube *before* the engine is started. The amount to be used is different with each transmission type. If the converter has been emptied, about six quarts (about 5 liters) of the proper type ATF fluid should be poured in. Most of this will be pumped into the converter when the engine is started. If the converter has not been drained only a quart (one liter) of fluid should be poured in. The engine is then started and the transmission shifted through all ranges to circulate the fluid throughout the transmission. Frequent checks of the fluid level should be made as the engine idles. Fluid should be added to keep the fluid at the *low* mark on the dipstick. When the fluid level stabilizes, the automobile should be driven to warm the fluid to its normal operating temperature. The fluid level should be rechecked and fluid added to bring the level to the full mark. Excess fluid should not be put in the transmission. This will cause foaming

and seal damage. Excess fluid should be removed when the transmission is accidentally overfilled. The transmission should be checked to be sure no external leaks exist. If any leaks are found, they should be repaired.

Fig. 24-6 An oil drain plug on the front of the converter.

24-2 TRANSMISSION SEALS

External leakage results in loss of transmission fluid and oil stains on the driveway where the automobile is parked. When too much fluid is lost, there will not be enough fluid remaining in the transmission to apply the holding devices so the transmission will slip and the rate of wear will be greatly increased.

Internal leakage affects the way the transmission shifts when the leak is great enough to use all of the pump capacity. When this happens, the transmission will no longer be able to build up sufficient pressure to securely hold the planetary gear member. Slippage can occur in only one gear as it is being applied or it can affect all gears if leakage occurs from a line pressure passage.

Gaskets, when used in transmissions, are used on the pan, oil pump, and extension housing to keep these joints from leaking. Figure 24–7 shows some typical gaskets. Transmission gaskets may be made of cork, paper, or composition, just as gaskets that are used in engines. They are either installed dry or they are coated with petroleum jelly before assembly, so they will seat smoothly without cracking or wrinkling.

Much of the internal sealing is accomplished

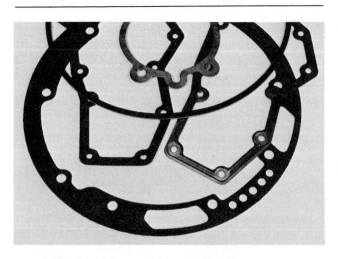

Fig. 24-7 Typical static seals used in an automatic transmission.

Fig. 24-8 Typical dynamic seals used in an automatic transmission.

Fig. 24-9 Hook seal joints on oil transfer rings.

by securely clamping flat stamped and machined surfaces with assembly cap screws. The clamping cap screws must be carefully torqued to seal these joints. Proper tightening keeps the high fluid pressure from bending the parts, which will cause leaks.

Seals are used to do the rest of the sealing job. Seals are divided into two divisions according to their function: *static seals* and *dynamic seals.* Static seals, like gaskets, seal a joint between two parts that have no relative motion between them. Dynamic seals prevent leakage from joints between two parts, one moving about or through the other. Dynamic seals that prevent external leakage are located at the torque converter hub and the propeller shaft. They are also used on the selector shaft and throttle shaft. Some of these seals are pictured in Figure 24–8. Leakage from any of these seals can be identified by a visual inspection of the external surface of the transmission. Dynamic seals are also used to prevent internal leakage at the clutch piston, band servos, and transfer rings. Damaged dynamic seals are the most likely source of internal leakage. In some locations, a small amount of leakage is designed into the transmissions to aid in cooling hot spots.

Dynamic seals are also classified by the material from which they are made and by their shape. Cast iron seals, shaped like small piston rings, are used as oil transfer rings between stationary and rotating members, and as seals on some servo pistons. Elastomer compounds, which are oil-resistant synthetic rubber-like materials such as Buna-N and Polyacrylic, are made in a number of shapes for specialized applications. Teflon seals have a self-lubricating property. They are used in place of cast iron when this property is necessary.

Cast iron rings do not seal completely so some leakage does occur. The ring gap is closely sized to control the amount of leakage. Where possible, the ring has a simple butt gap. In some locations, it is not possible to compress the ring during assembly so these rings are made with a hook joint gap that can be seen in Figure 24–9. Most of the iron rings have a phosphate coating that looks black. This coating helps to reduce wear.

Elastomer seals are made in three basic cross-section shapes: lathe-cut, O-ring, and lip, illustrated in Figure 24-10. Lathe-cut seals and O-ring seals are used for both static and dynamic sealing applications. Lip seals are only used for dynamic sealing. Lathe-cut seals have a rectangular cross-section similar to a cast iron ring. The O-ring has a round cross section. The lip seal has a number of cross-section shapes. They all have one similarity: the sealing lip. The sealing lip can be on the inside, on the outside, or on the side of the seal, depending on the sealing function. The seal shape opposite the lip is designed for a static seal on the supporting member.

Lathe-cut and O-ring seals fit loosely in their supporting groove. When assembled in the mating part the seal is squeezed from 0.012 in. to 0.025 in. (0.3 to 0.6 mm) to form the required seal. High pressure squeezes the seal against the opening clearance to form the required sealing function at that pressure.

Lip seals are more expensive than lathe-cut or O-ring seals so they are used only when the less expensive seals will not adequately function. The lip seal edge is deflected 0.030 in. to 0.050 in. (0.76 to 1.66 mm) when installed. This provides the required pressure to seal against the bore or shaft that forms the other sealing surface. When pressure is put against the open end of the seal, the lip is pushed tightly against the sealing surface to maintain its sealing function. Lip seals deflect or conform, as required, to seal on moderately out-of-round or eccentric surfaces.

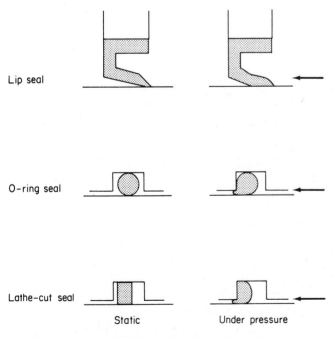

Lip seal

O-ring seal

Lathe-cut seal

Static   Under pressure

Fig. 24-10 Sealing principles.

Dirt is the biggest problem with reciprocating seals. It causes leak-producing scratches on the seal and the bore. As seals age, they harden and do not function properly. Seals are always replaced when removed, and scratched bores are polished. If the scratch remains after polishing, the part will have to be replaced to eliminate leakage.

24-3 PROBLEM DIAGNOSIS

There are only two types of service done on an automatic transmission. At a specified mileage, the transmission should be given routine service. This consists of an oil change, band adjustment, and visual inspection. Transmissions are also serviced when the operator recognizes that the transmission is not shifting or driving properly. The operator will bring the automobile to the service technician to diagnose and correct the problem.

For proper diagnosis, the technician must understand the operation of the transmission, especially the functioning of driving and holding devices in each gear range. The technician must also know which valves are controlling the holding devices. The operation of the gear train and holding devices of the common automatic transmission is shown in Chapter 23. It would also be helpful to use the manufacturer's applicable service manual to aid in diagnosis. Most of these manuals contain a detailed diagnosis guide giving the exact shift speeds and transmission fluid pressures to be expected in the transmission. Using the following diagnosis procedure, a technician who has a thorough understanding of the operating principles of a specific transmission should be able to identify the component causing the problem.

The first and most important part of diagnosis is to *listen* to the operator's complaint. The technician needs to know what the complaint is, how the operator knows there is a problem, when it occurs, and any other bits of information that might be useful. It may be necessary for the technician to ask the operator questions that would help pinpoint the cause of the problem.

Diagnosis should follow a regular procedure to eliminate every possible cause that can be corrected without removing the transmission. The first thing to check is the fluid. A transmission oil dipstick is shown in Figure 24–11. The fluid should have proper level with a red color. Fluid that has been subjected to heat over a period of time will oxidize and turn dark, but remain clear, in normal use. Sludge deposits on the transmission dipstick indicate foreign material in the oil. If the dipstick cannot be wiped clean, it is covered with a carbon-based material called *varnish.* If varnish is present on the dipstick, it can be expected to be on the valve pistons too. Varnish will cause valve pistons to stick, producing erratic shift timing. In severe cases, the valve may stick so tightly that it will not operate. If the varnish problem is not severe, a fluid change may be all that is required to correct the problem.

A road test with the operator is usually useful in determining the extent of the problem. The road test is run to check the severity of the problem and when it occurs. The transmission could be creeping in neutral, slipping in gear, upshifting early or late, or producing harsh shift or a downshift problem. Many of these problems can be caused by improper linkage adjustment.

All transmissions have a gear selector linkage. Some makes also have a throttle valve linkage while the others use an electric switch connected to the throttle to control forced downshift. The selector linkage should be adjusted so that the lever detent position in the transmission coincides with the driver's selector detent and position indicator. The starter should crank only with the selector in park and neutral. The throttle valve linkage should control the heavy acceleration shift point and cause full throttle downshift. These points are specified in the applicable service manual and they are determined on a road test. With the linkages properly set, diagnosis can be continued if the transmission problem remains. Typical automatic transmission linkages can be seen in Figure 24–12.

A pressure test will show if the correct fluid pressure exists at the proper time in the shift cycles. Pressure taps on the transmission case are

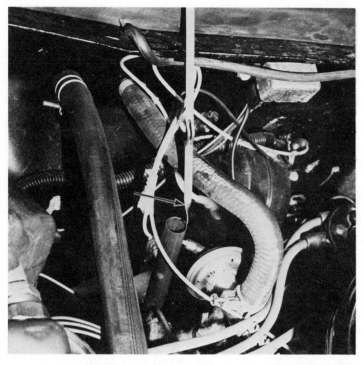

Fig. 24-11 Checking the transmission fluid level with a dip stick.

Fig. 24-12 Control linkages on the outside of the transmission.

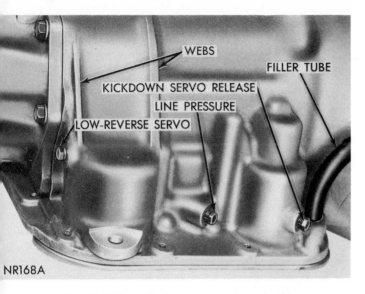

WEBS

FILLER TUBE

KICKDOWN SERVO RELEASE

LINE PRESSURE

LOW-REVERSE SERVO

NR168A

Fig. 24-13 Typical oil pressure test points (Chrysler Motors Corporation).

removed and pressure gauges installed. Typical pressure test point taps are shown in Figure 24–13. Special gauge sets are available with long hoses to make pressure testing convenient to use on a road test. Again, it is necessary to have the applicable service manual to determine the specified pressures for the transmission being tested. When the fluid level is correct, low pressure can be caused by leaking seals, a clogged filter, low pump output, or a faulty regulator valve. Pressure that builds up at the wrong time or to the wrong values is the result of leaking seals or sticking valves. Pressure testing should be the final step required in diagnosis. At this point, the technician should be able to determine the unit causing the problem and estimate the work that needs to be done.

24-4 MINOR TRANSMISSION SERVICE

All required repairs that can be done without removing the transmission should be done at this time. Late-model General Motors and Ford transmissions use a vacuum modulator to control line pressure. This unit can be replaced from the outside of the transmission when it is faulty. General Motors transmissions also have an access plate to remove the governor for service without disassembling the rest of the transmission.

The valve body is accessible by draining the transmission fluid and removing the transmission pan. With linkage controls disconnected the entire valve body can be removed from the transmission. If the spool control valves in the valve body are

faulty, they can be serviced with no further transmission disassembly. The band servos are also accessible with the valve body removed. They can be adjusted with no further transmission disassembly if improper adjustment is causing the problem. Ford, Chrysler, and American Motors transmissions have their governors in the rear transmission extension housing. In most automobile applications, this housing can be removed without pulling the transmission from the automobile. It is not considered a desirable procedure unless a simple specific fault can be corrected by removal in this way. It is advisable to thoroughly clean the underbody of the automobile and the transmission case to minimize the chance of getting dirt in the transmission. The propeller shaft is removed. The transmission must be supported and the rear mount removed. In some cases, it is necessary to remove the frame cross member. The extension housing flange bolts are removed and in some models an internal lock ring has to be released to free the case. The extension housing can then be slid back off the transmission output shaft. This exposes the governor and parking brake pawl. Repairs are made and a new seal installed with a new flange gasket between it and the transmission case.

If the problem is not in the valve body, servos, or extension housing, the transmission will have to be removed to repair the transmission.

24-5 TRANSMISSION REMOVAL

First, the battery ground is removed to prevent sparks that could occur from accidental shorts or grounding. Normally, the transmission fluid then is drained from the transmission before the transmission is removed from the automobile. (Working carefully, a technician can remove the transmission with the fluid remaining inside. It would then have to be drained when the transmission is on the bench, before the transmission could be disassembled.) After the fluid is drained, the selector linkage, throttle linkage, speedometer cable, vacuum hoses, and electrical wiring are disconnected from the transmission. It is always a good practice to mark each of these items with numbers on masking tape to aid in reassembly.

The propeller shaft is removed and the rear mount disconnected. The engine is supported by a fixture. These fixtures are available commercially, but they can be homemade. In any case, they must be adjustable so that the back of the engine can be raised or lowered as required. The frame cross member with the mount is removed from the automobile to provide access to the transmission.

In some cases, the exhaust system must be loosened and the starter is disconnected to clear the transmission. The splash plate is removed from the lower front of the transmission bell housing to expose the attaching bolts between the drive plate and the torque converter housing. The position of the drive plate and converter should be marked so they can be reassembled in the same position. The torque converter is disconnected from the drive plate (Figure 24–14). The engine support fixture is adjusted to lower the back of the transmission sufficiently to allow the technician to reach all of the

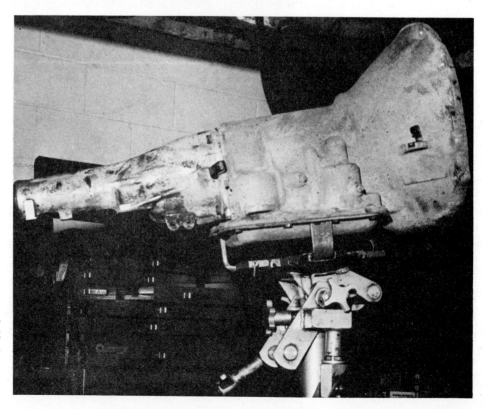

Fig. 24-14 Engine hanging without support with the transmission removed.

Fig. 24-15 Transmission handled with a transmission jack while removing and installing.

bell housing flange bolts. A transmission jack is necessary to handle and position the transmission during removal and installation. Transmission jacks may be of a low design that is used with the automobile on jack stands or it may be of a high design that is used with the automobile on a hoist. The transmission jack is positioned to take a little of the weight, then the bell housing flange bolts are removed. The bell housing is carefully separated slightly from the engine; then the torque converter is pushed away from the drive plate. The torque converter should be kept securely against the transmission to minimize damage that could occur if it were to fall. Often, technicians will fasten a clip on one of the lower bell housing bolt holes to retain the torque converter during removal and during installation. When the torque converter front hub is clear of the crankshaft pilot, the transmission can be carefully lowered from the automobile as shown in Figure 24-15. The transmission is placed on a bench for further service.

If front seal leakage is the problem, the torque converter is removed to expose the front seal in the transmission pump. The front seal will look similar to Figure 24-16. The seal can be removed with a special seal puller. A seal driver is used to install the new seal. If a leaking front seal is the only problem, the torque converter can be reinstalled. It should be turned as it is pushed toward the transmission. This will allow the turbine, stator, and pump drives to properly index and seat. The converter will slip on in three steps as each spline

indexes. The transmission can be reinstalled following a procedure that is the reverse of the removal procedure.

There is a lot of work involved in the removal of the transmission so it is the usual practice to disassemble, inspect, and replace worn parts and reseal the transmission while it is out of the automobile. This procedure is called a transmission overhaul.

24-6 TRANSMISSION OVERHAUL

A careful examination is very important when disassembling automatic transmissions. It is important to look for abnormal conditions that may have caused the original problem. All parts must be kept clean because it takes only one small particle to cause a valve to stick and this, in time, would cause the transmission to malfunction. Therefore, the exterior of the transmission should be thoroughly cleaned in a location away from the repair area before the transmission is disassembled. Disassembly should be done on a clean bench in a room free from dirt.

Before any disassembly is done, the end play of the turbine shaft should be measured with a dial gauge, as is being done in Figure 24-17. The

Fig. 24-16 The front oil seal located on the front of the oil pump.

Fig. 24-17 Checking the turbine shaft end play before disassembly.

Fig. 24-18 Removing the valve body.

Fig. 24-19 Removing a servo.

amount of end play should be noted for use when picking the correct selective washer thickness during assembly.

The general procedure used during transmission overhaul is to disassemble the transmission into its major subassemblies. The major subassemblies are then individually disassembled, cleaned, inspected, repaired, sealed, and reassembled. In this way, there are a minimum number of small parts to keep track of, and so there is less chance of improper reassembly. When all the subassemblies are overhauled, the transmission is reassembled.

Disassembly starts with the removal of the pan and the valve body (Figure 24–18), which is the first subassembly taken from the transmission. This is followed by the removal of accumulators,

Fig. 24-20 Removing the extension housing.

Fig. 24-21 Removing the pump with slide hammer pullers.

Fig. 24-22 The interior of an automatic transmission with the front pump removed. The turbine shaft and front drum are visible.

With the pump removed, the remaining shaft is the turbine shaft that is part of the front drum sub-assembly (Figure 24–22). This can be lifted from the transmission (Figure 24–23). Bands, clutches, discs, and drum assemblies are lifted from the transmission in the proper sequence and laid in order on a bench for service. The positions of thrust washers and lock rings should be noted and identified. This will help when the transmission is reassembled. The subassemblies are often slipped into plastic bags until they are to be worked on. The plastic bag retains the fluid that seeps from the subassembly and it keeps dust and dirt from the parts. If necessary, the bags can be marked for further identification.

Transmission overhaul continues with the overhaul of each subassembly. No specific order is better than any other. In general, clutch drums are overhauled one after another because they are similar. In all cases, each subassembly, in its turn, is completely disassembled and the parts thoroughly cleaned in cleaning solvents. The parts are dried with *clean* compressed air. They are then ready for a thorough visual inspection. Parts are examined for signs of excessive wear, scoring, overheating (as indicated by a change in color), chipping, or cracks. The part should be replaced if there is any question as to the serviceability of a part. Failure of a small part could completely ruin an overhauled transmission.

The normally used parts for automatic transmission overhaul are available in kits (Figure 24–24).

Fig. 24-23 Removing the front drum.

servos, and regulators, depending on the transmission type (Figure 24–19). Externally removable modulators and governors are then removed.

The extension housing is removed next (Figure 24–20). This will expose the speedometer drive gear, parking pawl, and governors on some transmissions. These are removed as a subassembly.

The transmission pump is unbolted and slide hammer pullers are inserted in special threaded holes in the pump case. The slide hammers are worked together to loosen the pump housing subassembly from the transmission case (Figure 24–21). The stator shaft is part of the pump housing.

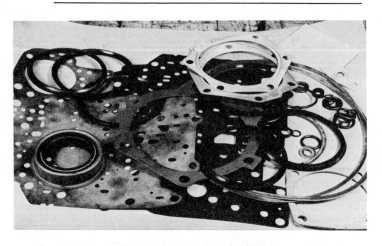

Fig. 24-24 Parts of an overhaul kit.

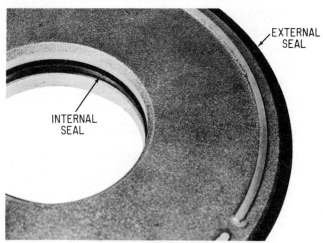

Fig. 24-26 Inner and outer piston seals.

Gaskets and seal kits are always used. Overhaul kits will also generally contain new clutch plates and discs along with new metal seal rings and new lock rings. Other parts are purchased on an individual basis.

Clutch packs form one of the common subassemblies. The clutch is held together with retaining rings. In many cases, it is necessary to slightly compress the clutch to free the retaining ring. The spring can be compressed in a press or by using a special screw compressor with adaptor plates (Figure 24-25). With the retaining ring removed, the spring pressure can be *gradually* released to free the clutch assembly. The springs,

Fig. 24-27 Universal bushing puller used to remove a transmission bushing.

discs, and plates are removed to free the clutch piston. The piston is removed to expose both inner and outer piston seals (Figure 24-26). The seals are always replaced on a transmission overhaul.

A plain bearing-type bushing is usually located in the clutch drum hub. This bearing, like engine bearings, will wear in use. The bushing should be replaced if it has excessive wear, or if it is scored or pitted. The bushing is removed and replaced with a properly fitting driver, similar to the way an engine cam bearing is replaced (Figure 24-27).

Scores on the cast parts can be polished out with crocus cloth. Steel clutch plates should be smooth and free from burned spots. The friction material on the disc should be in good condition (Figures 24-28 and 24-29).

The parts should be thoroughly cleaned before

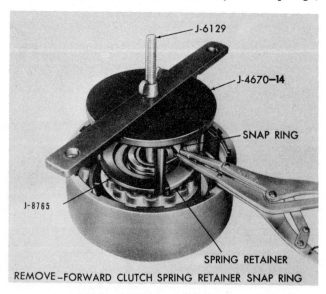

Fig. 24-25 Disassembly of a clutch while a press is used hold the release spring pressure (Oldsmobile Division, General Motors Corporation).

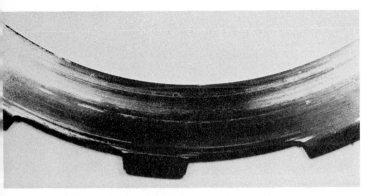

Fig. 24-28 Burned clutch plate.

Fig. 24-29 Burned clutch disc above a normally worn clutch disc.

reassembly. New inner and outer piston seals are installed, taking care to have the lip of the seal pointing away from the clutch pack when lip seals are used. The piston will slip into place more easily if the seals are coated with stick grease such as Door Ease, with petroleum jelly, or with transmission fluid. The return springs are installed and then compressed as the retaining ring is seated. The clutch pack is assembled in the drum and the retaining ring seated. Clutches require a specified clearance between the clutch pack and retaining ring when they are in the released position. It is checked by sliding a thickness gauge between the plates and disc, as shown in Figure 24–30. The clearance is adjusted by using retaining rings of different thicknesses. When the clutch drum subassembly is completely assembled, it can be placed in a plastic bag until it is required for assembly in the transmission case.

The fluid pump is another major subassembly used on all automatic transmissions. The pump cover is removed from the pump body to expose the pump gears, rotors, and, in some transmissions, valves. As with the clutch, the pump parts are cleaned and inspected for excessive wear and abnormal conditions (Figure 24–31). Worn stator shaft bushing-type bearings should be replaced. All seals are removed and new ones installed. The pump body contains the transmission front seal. It is most easily replaced while the pump is disassembled (Figure 24–32). It is considered standard procedure to replace check valves in the pump subassembly. Any part that is of questionable serviceability should be replaced. The pump parts are coated liberally with transmission fluid as they are assembled. The complete overhauled pump should be placed in a plastic bag.

The valve body consists of a number of passages, bores with free sliding spool valves, springs, and check balls. The spool valves have a

Fig. 24-30 Measuring the clearance on a clutch pack.

Fig. 24-31 Pump gears, bushing, and pump body.

Fig. 24-32 Driver used to install a new front pump oil seal.

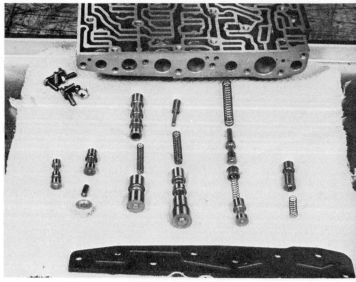

Fig. 24-33 Method of removing valve body parts for inspection and cleaning.

close fit in their bores and they may have similar shapes. Springs may look alike, but have different strengths and lengths. These parts and the check balls roll easily if placed on a bench. To avoid loss, damage, or mixing of parts, it is a good practice to disassemble the valve body over a pan or tray. A shop towel is often placed in the bottom of the tray, as pictured in Figure 24–33. If the valve body consists of more than one subassembly, only one should be disassembled at a time to minimize the chance of interchanging similar parts.

The parts are carefully removed from the valve body (Figure 24–34). All parts are thoroughly cleaned. A good carburetor cleaner works well to clean valve body parts that have varnish deposits on them. After being rinsed and blown dry, the parts should be examined for any abnormal appearance. The valve body should be free of cracks. The parting surfaces should be flat to minimize distortion and leakage when assembled (Figure 24–35). Springs should be square and the proper length. Each clean dry valve, in turn, should be placed in its bore. The valve body is then tipped from side to side to allow the spool valve to slide in its bore. It should slide by its own weight. If the valve does not move freely, it should be removed. Roll the valve to check for bending and examine its surfaces for burrs. Bent spool valves should be replaced. Burrs on spool valves should be carefully removed with crocus cloth on a flat plate, taking care to avoid rounding the sharp edges of the spool as demonstrated in Figure 24–36. When

Fig. 24-34 Dirty valve body.

Fig. 24-35 Checking the valve body flatness.

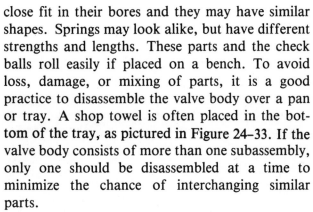

384

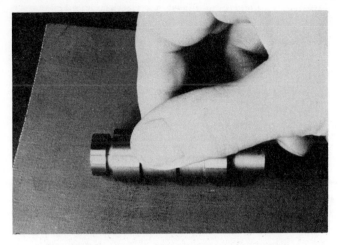

Fig. 24-36 Polishing a valve spool on crocus cloth.

all valves move freely, the valve body is recleaned and assembled. Service manuals have exploded views of the valve body and parts to aid the technician to properly assemble the valve body. The valve body parts should be thoroughly coated with transmission fluid as they are assembled. The assembled valve body can be placed in a plastic bag until it is required for installation in the transmission.

The governor is basically a small valve body. It is serviced as a subassembly using the same procedures that are used on the valve body.

Band servos and accumulators consist of pistons with seals in a bore. They are held in their static position with springs. Retaining rings keep them in the bore. The retaining rings are removed and the assembly pulled from the bore for cleaning. The condition of the piston and springs is checked in the same way as valve body parts. Metal seal rings may not require replacement but elastomer seals are always replaced.

The band, struts, levers, and anchors are checked for wear. The band should be replaced if the lining shows any excessive wear. In Figure 24–37 both band and drum are excessively worn.

The mechanical part of the transmission consists of the gear trains, overrunning clutches, and other types of subassembly. Gear teeth are examined for chips and signs of wear. The planet pinion gears should be checked for loose bearings. The carrier should have no cracks. Any abnormal parts should be replaced.

Overrunning clutches are checked to make sure that they function correctly and show no distortion. There should be no scoring of the operating surface. Some sprague clutch designs have to be replaced if the sprague has been overloaded so much that the sprague is reversed.

Thrust bearings should be checked for excessive wear. Any required change in the turbine shaft thrust clearance can be made by picking the selective-fit washer of the required thickness. The required washer thickness can be determined by the measured change in thrust washer thickness on the turbine shaft end plug.

Many technicians replace the small retaining rings on a routine basis. The small savings that might accompany the reuse of a used retaining ring is lost if it slips out of place while the transmission is in operation.

When all of the subassemblies are overhauled and all required parts are at hand, the transmission can be reassembled.

24-7 TRANSMISSION ASSEMBLY

Before the transmission is assembled, the case should be thoroughly cleaned and all passages blown out. All parts are coated with the proper type of automatic transmission fluid as they are being assembled. Bands should be soaked in the fluid for 20 minutes before they are installed.

Transmission installation is best done by supporting the transmission in the vertical position with the bell housing up. The weight of the parts will hold them in place and they will stay centered until the pump is secure in front of the case.

Fig. 24-37 Excessively worn and burned band and drum.

Carefully lower the parts into the case in the proper order, as shown in Figure 24–38, making sure that the clutch plates and band linkages are properly engaged. Thrust washers are thoroughly lubricated as they are installed. Sealing rings should be centered on their shafts so they will slide into their bores without breaking.

All assembly bolts should be coated with automatic transmission fluid to prevent galling and seizing, especially as they are turned into the threaded holes in the aluminum case. They should be tightened with a torque wrench. Proper torquing will make the joint secure without warping the part or damaging the threads.

The pump may require slight tapping with a soft mallet as the assembly screws are gradually snugged to help move the pump into place as the outer O-ring squeezes into the bore. When the pump is seated and the bolts fully torqued, the turbine shaft and the output shaft should turn freely. The turbine shaft end play should be rechecked. If it is incorrect, the transmission will have to be disassembled and the correct selective-fit washers installed. Where used, the linkages between the servos and bands are connected and the bands adjusted. The operation of the assembled components can be checked with air pressure. Figure 24–39 shows air being blown in the proper passages to operate the servos. Movement can

Fig. 24-38 Installing a clutch drum with the transmission in a vertical position.

Fig. 24-39 Checking the clutch and servo operation with air pressure before completing the assembly.

be observed. Clutch operation can be felt as a thud when the clutch is applied. If the passages have not been previously identified, the case passage openings are usually shown in the applicable service manuals.

The assembly of the transmission is completed with the installation of the governor, speedometer drive gear, rear extension housing, valve body, and pan. If the transmission fluid was clear before disassembly, the converter is most likely serviceable. If the fluid was contaminated, the cooler lines and converter should be flushed. This is best done with a specially designed piece of shop equipment. If the converter is faulty, it will have to be replaced. Converters can be repaired only at special rebuilding shops. The converter must be cut apart, overhauled, rewelded, and balanced.

The converter is put on the transmission over the turbine and stator shafts and rotated to seat the drive lugs, as previously described. It should be held in place against the pump. The transmission is ready for installation. It is placed on the transmission jack and carefully lined up on the dowel pins on the back of the engine. The bell housing bolts are secured and all other connections and fittings are reattached.

The transmission is filled with the correct type of automatic transmission fluid using the same procedure used when changing fluid. The transmission should be examined for leaks; then the automobile should be road tested to complete the transmission overhaul.

REVIEW QUESTIONS

1. How does a driver know that a problem exists in his automatic transmission? [INTRODUCTION]

2. What is the first thing to be checked when there is a question about the operation of the automatic transmission? [24-1]

3. What are the differences among automatic transmission fluids? [24-1]

4. What routine service is done on automatic transmissions? [24-1]

5. Why is fluid replaced in automatic transmissions? [24-1]

6. What precautions should be observed when changing the automatic transmission fluid? [24-1]

7. Describe the procedure to be used to refill the automatic transmission. [24-1]

8. What effect does internal fluid leakage have on an automatic transmission? [24-2]

9. What is the most likely cause of internal leakage? [24-2]

10. Why is leakage sometimes designed into a transmission? [24-2]

11. Describe three elastomer seal shapes used in automatic transmissions. [24-2]

12. When is a hook gap used on a cast iron seal? [24-2]

13. What is the biggest problem with reciprocating seals? [24-2]

14. What does the routine transmission service consist of? [24-3]

15. What is the first thing to do when diagnosing a transmission problem? [24-3]

16. Why is it important to follow a regular diagnosis procedure? [24-3]

17. What tests and adjustments are made before the transmission is removed from the automobile? [24-3]

18. What parts of the transmission can be serviced without removing the transmission? [24-4]

19. Why is the battery ground removed when removing a transmission? [24-5]

20. Why should the torque converter be held securely against the transmission during removal? [24-5]

21. What is a transmission overhaul? [24-6]

22. What is the general procedure used to overhaul an automatic transmission? [24-6]

23. What is the advantage of using plastic bags during overhaul? [24-6]

24. What parts are generally in a transmission overhaul kit? [24-6]

25. What holds the clutch packs together? [24-6]

26. What materials may be used to help ease the installation of the clutch piston? [24-6]

27. Why is it necessary to check the clutch pack clearance? [24-6]

28. How is the clutch pack clearance adjusted? [24-6]

29. What service is performed on the transmission pump? [24-6]

30. What service should be done on valve bodies? [24-6]

31. What is checked on the mechanical parts of the automatic transmission? [24-6]

32. What precautions should be observed as the transmission is assembled? [24-7]

33. How can the operation of the transmission be checked during assembly? [24-7]

34. What is done to the converter if the transmission was dirty when it was first disassembled? [24-7]

differential
and rear axle

Engine power is delivered to the transmission, where the power is divided to provide the required torque and speed. The transmission is designed to increase torque at the cost of reduced speed when moving the automobile from a dead stop. As the automobile speed increases, the need for high torque is reduced and so the transmission is shifted into a higher gear. The resulting torque and speed are sent through the propeller shaft to the rear axle assembly, which is the final drive.

The rear axle assembly includes a housing that encloses an axle to each drive wheel and a differential assembly with bearings and seals. Its purpose is to change the drive torque and speed direction 90° from the propeller shaft to the wheels. While doing this it provides the final speed reduction ratio, usually called the axle ratio. Using the differential, the driving torque splits, with an equal amount going to each drive wheel in standard differentials. Drive axles carry the power (speed and torque) from the differential to the drive wheels. The axle housing supports the vehicle on axle bearings, provides reaction for driving and braking torque, and resists side loads.

25-1 DIFFERENTIAL PRINCIPLES

A companion flange connects the propeller shaft to the differential drive pinion. Teeth on the side of the *drive pinion gear* mesh with teeth on the face of the *ring gear* to provide the final gear reduction and change the drive line rotation 90°. This can be seen in Figure 25-1. Modern vehicles use the *hypoid type* of gear mesh. The term hypoid is a contraction of the name of a geometrical

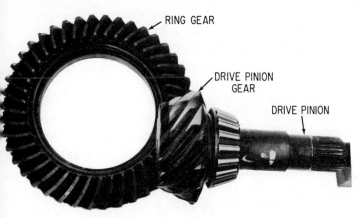

Fig. 25-1 Matching ring and pinion gear.

figure called a *hyperboloid of revolution*. In this design, the gears have a constant velocity ratio, even though the drive pinion and ring gear axis are nonintersecting and perpendicular to each other. The pinion axis is located well below the ring gear axis. The teeth slide into mesh with at least two pair of teeth in contact at all times. This provides quiet operation and high torque carrying capacity. The low axis of the pinion allows the vehicle to have a low floor pan and propeller shaft clearance tunnel.

Drive pinion size and ring gear size are largely determined by the maximum torque to be transmitted. Larger sizes are required for greater torque. The gear reduction ratio is not dependent on torque capacity, but is determined by the number of teeth in the pinion and ring gears. Reduction ratio can be calculated by the formula:

$$\text{Gear ratio} = \frac{\text{Number of teeth on the ring gear (output)}}{\text{Number of teeth on the drive pinion gear (input)}}$$

For example, the reduction ratio of a differential with 47 teeth on the ring gear and 16 teeth on the drive pinion would be 2.94:1 (47/16). Passenger car axle ratios run from approximately 2.3:1 to 4.25:1. Low numerical ratios help fuel economy while high numerical ratios help torque. The ratio used for any specific vehicle is a trade-off between economy and power to provide the required vehicle performance.

In operation, the ring gear is mechanically connected to the drive wheels. When the automobile is to be accelerated, the drive pinion forces the ring gear to turn forward. In doing this on

rear axle-type drives, the pinion tends to climb up the front of the ring gear, raising the carrier nose as illustrated in Figure 25-2. Front wheel-type drives would tend to move the carrier nose downward because the pinion is located behind the ring gear.

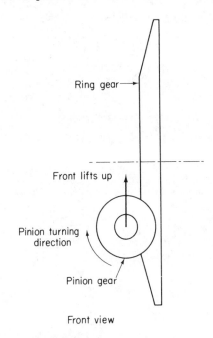

Fig. 25-2 Torque effect of the rotating pinion against a loaded ring gear.

Acceleration in reverse gear would cause the opposite effect. Control of carrier nose raising or lowering is accomplished by leaf springs, links, or arms. It is limited by a bumper shown in Figure 25-3. In independent drive suspensions, the drive torque is taken by the differential housing mount on the chassis.

A solid connection between standard passenger car drive wheels is not desirable because the wheels seldom turn at the same speed. This difference in wheel speeds results from bumps and dips in the road surface, from slightly different tire sizes, and from different turning radii for each wheel which causes the outside wheel to turn faster than the inside wheel.

A spur bevel *side gear* is splined to the inboard end of each rear axle. The teeth of at least two *differential pinion gears* engage these axle side gears as shown in Figure 25-5. The differential *case* encloses the gears and supports the side gears in plain bearings. The differential pinion gears are

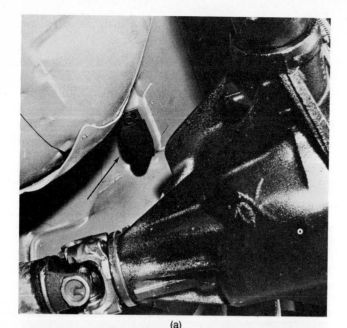
(a)

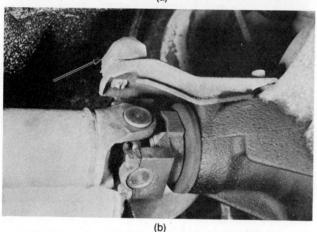
(b)

Fig. 25-3 Bumper located to contact under heavy torque loads. (a) Bumper on the body panel, (b) bumper on the carrier nose.

supported and turn freely on a differential pinion shaft between the side gears. Because of this arrangement, the side gears balance on each side of the differential pinion gears. The torque on one axle equals the torque on the other axle.

In operation, the ring gear is attached to the differential case so the case and ring gear rotate together. Because the differential pinion shaft is mounted in the case, it turns end-for-end with the case carrying the differential pinion gears around with it. The differential pinion gears, being in mesh with the axle mounted side gears, turn the axles at ring gear speed. This assembly is shown in Figure 25–6.

The differential acts as a speed averaging device. The case rotating speed is always equal to one half the sum of the axle speeds.

$$\text{Case speed} = \frac{\text{Right axle speed} + \text{ left axle speed}}{2}$$

For example, while making a right turn the right axle on the inside of the turn rotates 9 times and the left axle on the outside of the turn rotates 11 times. The differential case would rotate 10 times.

$$\text{Case speed} = \frac{9 + 11}{2} = 10$$

The differential also acts as a torque divider.

Fig. 25-5 Differential pinion gears assembled with two side gears.

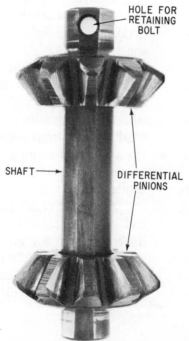

HOLE FOR RETAINING BOLT

SHAFT

DIFFERENTIAL PINIONS

Fig. 25-4 Differential pinion gears on a differential pinion shaft.

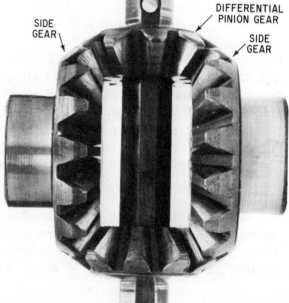

SIDE GEAR

DIFFERENTIAL PINION GEAR

SIDE GEAR

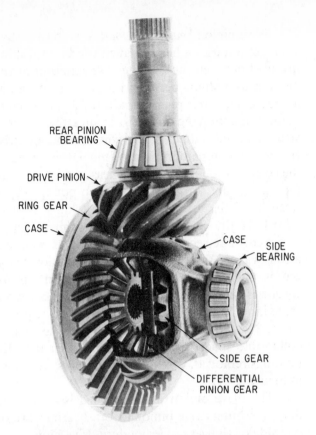

REAR PINION
BEARING

DRIVE PINION

RING GEAR

CASE

CASE

SIDE
BEARING

SIDE GEAR

DIFFERENTIAL
PINION GEAR

Fig. 25-6 Differential and side gears mounted in a case. The ring gear is attached to the case and meshes with the drive pinion.

Since the differential pinions are free to turn on their shafts, they cannot apply more torque to the teeth on one side gear than they can to the other side gear. Therefore, they act as a balance by dividing the input torque equally between the axle side gears, even when their speeds are different.

Current passenger cars use a semi-floating drive axle. The axle transmits driving torque from the side gears to the wheels. It also supports the vehicle weight through bearings located at the outer end of the axle housing. This can be seen in Figure 25-7. The wheel mounting is overhung; that is, it is mounted outside the bearing. The outer end of the axle is subjected to bending loads from road shock and from vehicle centrifugal loads as the vehicle goes around a curve.

25-2 DIFFERENTIAL DESIGN FEATURES

Most current passenger cars use rear end drives. Differential principles are the same in all of them. The rear axle assemblies are made in different ways,

Fig. 25-7 Section view of a typical unitized carrier rear axle assembly (Oldsmobile Division, General Motors Corporation).

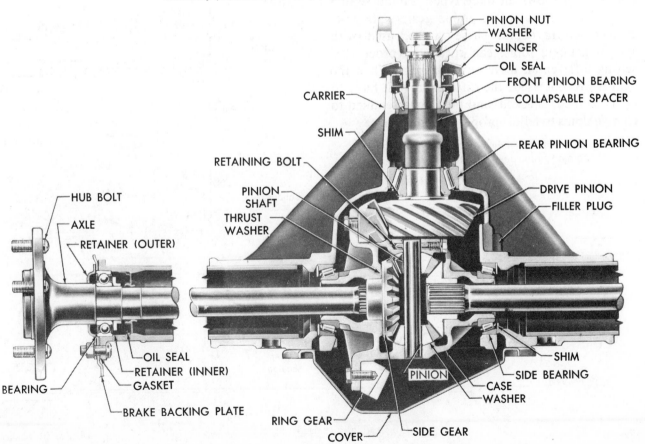

PINION NUT
WASHER
SLINGER
OIL SEAL
FRONT PINION BEARING
COLLAPSIBLE SPACER

CARRIER

SHIM

RETAINING BOLT

PINION
SHAFT

THRUST
WASHER

REAR PINION BEARING

DRIVE PINION
FILLER PLUG

HUB BOLT

AXLE

RETAINER (OUTER)

OIL SEAL
RETAINER (INNER)
GASKET

BEARING

BRAKE BACKING PLATE

PINION

SHIM
SIDE BEARING
CASE
WASHER

RING GEAR

COVER

SIDE GEAR

depending upon cost, torque requirements, and engineering preference.

The differential drive's pinion and ring gears are fitted and lapped together as a pair when they are manufactured so they will operate quietly. When installed in the carrier, they must be aligned in exactly the same relationship they had when they were lapped to provide quiet operation in the vehicle. Alignment is maintained by preloading the bearings so the parts cannot move out of their set position. Preloading involves adjusting the bearings so they have no clearance and then tightening an additional specified amount.

Drive Pinion Features. The drive pinion is mounted in bearings within the *carrier*. The bearings are taper roller bearings with the large end of the taper toward the pinion's ends. Bearing cups are mounted in carrier bearing bores. *Pinion depth position* in the ring gear is adjusted by placing or removing shims between the pinion gear and rear bearing on one type, by placing shims between the pinion retainer and carrier in a second type, and by placing shims between the carrier and rear bearing cup in a third type. The composite drawing Figure 25–8 shows all three types. Pinion setting is usually marked on the pinion gear to show its correct setting depth. These marks, used with special gauging tools, can speed the process of setting differential drive pinion depth. When the gauges are not used, the differential will have to be assembled, checked, and then disassembled to change shims to adjust proper pinion depth.

Fig. 25-8 Differential pinion composite illustration of alternate pinion depth adjustment shims.

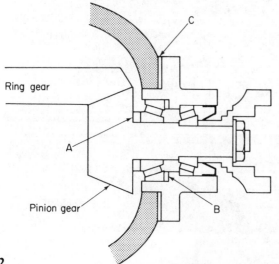

Drive pinion *bearing preload* is set in two ways. One method uses a heavy walled spacer with shims installed between the bearings. A variation of this method uses shims between the front bearing and a shoulder on the pinion shaft. Preload is set by adding or removing shims to change the effective spacing between the bearings when the pinion drive flange, or companion flange, nut is tightened to the correct torque. Preload is measured by checking pinion turning torque with an inch-pound torque wrench. If the torque is too high, shims must be added. If the torque is too low, shims must be removed. The second and most popular type uses a thin-wall crushable sleeve. The companion flange nut is tightened until the proper pinion turning torque is secured. The crushable sleeve keeps the front inner bearing race from turning on the pinion shaft. New crushable sleeves, sometimes called collapsible spacers, should be used each time the pinion is removed. Preload adjustments are shown in Figure 25–9.

The drive pinion just described is a standard duty overhung drive pinion. Both bearings are on one side of the gear. Heavy duty drive pinions are straddle mounted. They have a third supporting bearing, called a *pilot bearing,* on the other side of

Fig. 25-9 Three types of drive pinion bearing preload adjustment methods.

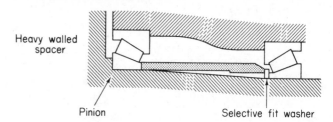

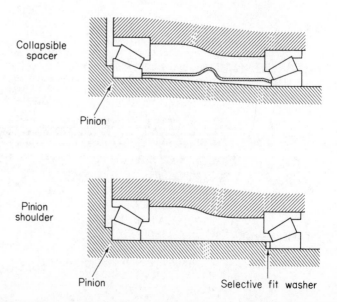

Fig. 25-10 Straddle mounted pinion.

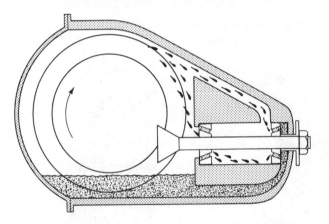

Fig. 25-11 Oil flow through the carrier housing passages.

the pinion gear. This reduces distortion under heavy torque loads. It can be seen in Figure 25-10.

Carrier bearings are lubricated by ring gear throw off. The ring gear picks up oil as it passes through the oil in the bottom of the housing. Oil is carried up and thrown forward. A cored or drilled passage in the upper carrier directs oil to pinion bearings. Oil return passages are provided in the carrier as illustrated in Figure 25-11.

An axle housing breather is required to allow air to flow into and out of the housing as barometric pressures and axle temperatures change to keep pressure equal on both sides of oil seals.

Carrier Features. The carrier supports the pinion and differential case. It is a one-piece unit cast from malleable cast iron, which is then machined. This type of construction keeps the drive pinion and ring gear in perfect alignment after they have been set. It will usually have stiffening ribs to increase its strength while still keeping it as light as possible.

The carrier may be designed to be removed from the axle housing. When it is, the housing is often called a banjo-type housing. The *SAE Handbook* calls it a *separable carrier* housing. If the

Fig. 25-12 Carrier types. (a) Separable carrier type, (b) unitized carrier type.

(a)

(b)

ADJUSTER NUT

FEELER GAUGE

BEARING CAP

INNER END OF
STRADDLE BEARING

Fig. 25-13 Differential side bearing adjustment with adjustment nut (Cadillac Motor Car Division, General Motors Corporation).

Fig. 25-14 Nomenclature of a rear axle assembly (Chevrolet Motor Division, General Motors Corporation).

1. companion flange
2. deflector
3. pinion oil seal
4. pinion front bearing
5. pinion bearing spacer
6. differential carrier
7. differential case
8. shim
9. gasket
10. differential bearing
11. "C" lock
12. pinion shaft lock bolt
13. cover
14. pinion shaft
15. ring gear
16. side gear
17. bearing cap
18. axle shaft
19. thrust washer
20. differential pinion
21. shim
22. pinion rear bearing
23. drive pinion

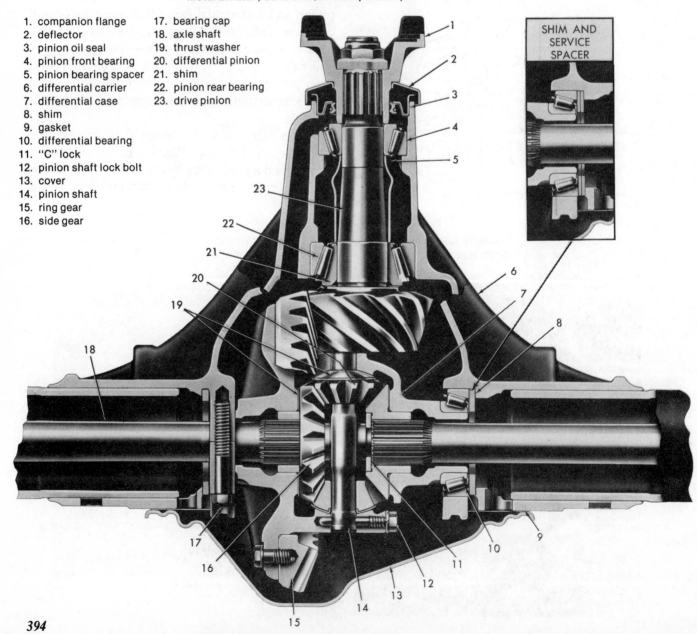

SHIM AND
SERVICE
SPACER

carrier has permanent housing tubes pressed and welded in its side, it may be called a *carrier-tube* or *Salisbury-type* housing. The SAE nonmenclature for this type of construction is a *unitized carrier* housing. Access to the differential in the unitized carrier housing is provided through a rear stamped cover. The majority of passenger cars use a unitized carrier-type housing. Both types are pictured in Figure 25-12.

Tapered roller bearings, called *differential side bearings,* support the case within the carrier housing. The small end of the bearing is pointed toward the wheels. The outer bearing cup is held to the carrier bearing saddle with a bearing cap. Positioning the case in its bearing also positions the ring gear, because the ring gear is attached to the case. Ring gear position and differential side gear preload are adjusted with adjusting nuts (Figure 25-13) in some carriers and, in others, they are adjusted with shims (Figure 25-14).

Axle Shaft Features. Axle shafts are hot forged or extruded steel. When used, integral flanges are impact extruded on one end. After machining, they are induction hardened and shot blasted for fatigue strength. Finally, they are finished by grinding to size.

The brake drum or disc is attached to the outer end of the axle shaft. The axle end may have a tapered end or a flange end. The flange end type is the most popular.

The outer axle bearing is located just inside the taper or flange that can be seen in Figure 25-15. The bearing may be a ball bearing, a roller bearing, or a taper roller bearing. Some manufacturers use different types in different size axles.

Rear axle bearings carry the vehicle weight which gives the bearing a radial load. It also absorbs vehicle cornering loads, called *thrust loads.*

Sealed and grease-lubricated radial ball bearings have been the most common type of rear axle bearings. They are quick and easy to assemble, needing no freeplay adjustment. They are, however, subject to early fatigue so their useful life is somewhat shorter than the other types. Differential oil-lubricated straight roller bearings roll directly on a ground surface of the axle shaft (Figure 25-15) or, in some cases, have an inner race. This provides an inexpensive, compact bearing that is easy to assemble. This type of axle bearing has become most popular. Thrust loads must, however, be absorbed by the differential gears and differential

pinion shaft, which may cause deflecting problems. Taper roller bearings have a longer life than other types, but they are more complicated to assemble and adjust, especially when used with a flanged axle shaft.

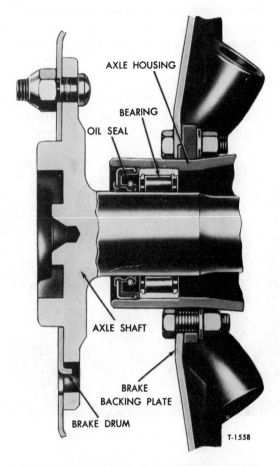

Fig. 25-15 Roller-type rear axle bearing operating directly on the axle shaft (Chevrolet Motor Division, General Motors Corporation).

Taper-type axle shafts usually use a taper roller bearing. The bearing cone is pressed against a shoulder on the shaft, with its small end outward. When being assembled, the axle shaft with the bearing is installed, followed by a retainer. Shims and gaskets between the retainer and bearings are used to provide correct taper roller bearing freeplay. A single unit hub and brake drum or only a hub flange may be installed on the taper shaft of the axle. A shaft key keeps the shaft from turning in the hub. This type of axle has limited use.

Most flange-type axles have their bearings pressed on from the inner end. The retainer is placed over the axle and is followed by the bearing. Bearings used with the flange axle may be ball, roller, or taper. A collar is pressed on after the ball or taper bearing to absorb axle end thrust. The retainer is bolted to the axle housing to hold the bearing and axle in place. When taper roller bearings are used with flange shafts, one retainer may be provided with an adjusting nut for adjusting freeplay. This can be seen in the left side of Figure 25–18. Other axles use shims between the retainer and axle housing for freeplay adjustment. Ball bearings have built-in freeplay so they require no adjustment. Roller bearings do not absorb

Fig. 25-16 "C" washer holding the axle in place.

shaft end thrust. Shaft end thrust of axles using roller bearings without inner races is absorbed at the inner end of the axle shaft with a *C-washer* retainer that keeps the axle from coming out of the housing. It is kept from going inward when it contacts the differential pinion shaft or a spacer block on the pinion shaft, as shown in Figures 25–14 and 25–16.

Bearing retainers contain an oil seal to keep grease and oil from getting into the brake. In some units, the outer oil seal is mounted in the housing. In others, the seal is located in the retainer. Bearings that are grease-lubricated have an inner seal as well as an outer seal to keep the differential oil separate from the wheel bearing grease. The inner seal is pressed in the housing before the axle is installed. Axles using only an outer seal have the bearing lubricated with differential oil. The seal and bearing types are illustrated in Figure 25–17.

25-3 LIMITED SLIP DIFFERENTIAL

The torque-equalizing feature of a standard differential does not adequately provide driving power when one or both drive wheels are on a slippery surface, during rapid acceleration, or when driving on rough roads. On slippery surfaces, driving torque to each wheel is no greater than the torque to the wheel with the smallest torque. On rough surfaces, the wheel will bounce free of the road and its speed will increase. When it lands on the road surface again, it will immediately have to re-

Fig. 25-17 Rear axle bearing types. (a) Ball bearing, (b) roller bearing, (c) taper roller bearing.

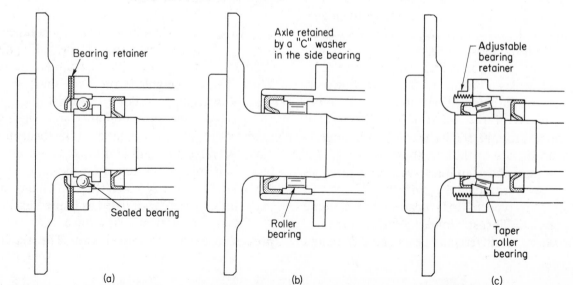

duce its speed to the vehicle speed. This gives the drive train a severe shock that could damage parts. Differentials have been designed to reduce or limit wheel slippage by transferring a portion of the unused torque from the slipping wheel to the wheel with traction.

In standard differentials the input power comes through the pinion and ring gear to the differential case. The differential case carries the differential pinion shaft and pinions to apply torque to the side gears and axle shafts. Assume that input torque remains constant when the right wheel loses traction as the vehicle starts to move. The left wheel, with good traction, will remain stationary, holding the left side gear stationary. The differential gears will then rotate on their pinion shafts as they go around the stationary left side gear. They force the freely moving right side gear forward at twice the case speed. Loss of motion, then, occurs between the case and the free moving

side gear. If these could be locked together, the wheel with traction would turn to move the vehicle.

Limited slip differentials provide this locking function. They have a clutch between the case and the side gear. Clutch engagement limits movement between the case and side gear so both axles will turn with the case. The axle with traction is turned so the vehicle will move.

Two types of clutches are used in automotive limited slip differentials. One type uses a *plate-type clutch* similar to the clutch plates used in automatic transmissions described in Chapter 23. Every other plate is attached to the axle shaft. The alternate plates are attached to the case. The clutch parts can be identified in Figure 25–18. Limited slip differentials may have one large diameter clutch

Fig. 25-18 An exploded view of a limited slip differential using two multiple disc clutches operated by torque differences in a unitized housing (Chrysler Motors Corporation).

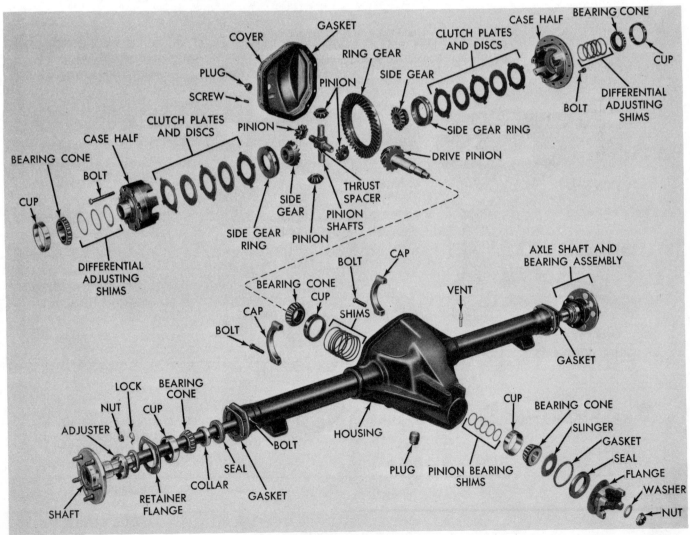

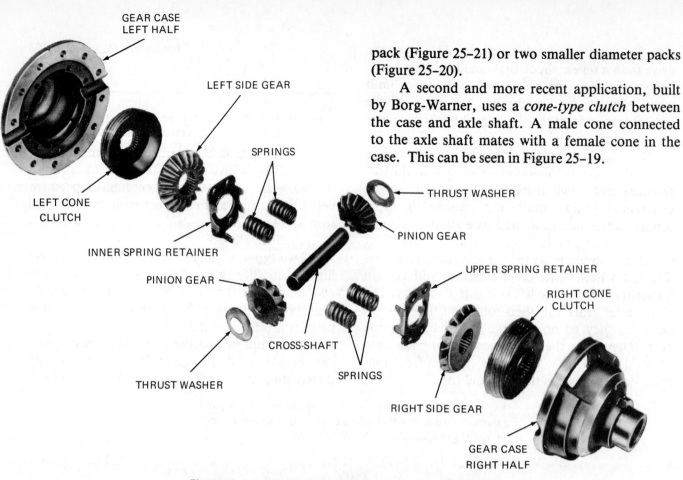

pack (Figure 25-21) or two smaller diameter packs (Figure 25-20).

A second and more recent application, built by Borg-Warner, uses a *cone-type clutch* between the case and axle shaft. A male cone connected to the axle shaft mates with a female cone in the case. This can be seen in Figure 25-19.

Fig. 25-19 An exploded view of a limited slip differential using two cone clutches with coil preload springs (Cadillac Motor Car Division, General Motors Corporation).

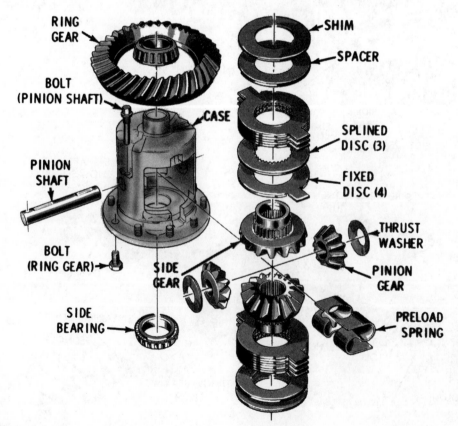

Fig. 25-20 An exploded view of a limited slip differential using two multiple disc clutches with a leaf spring preload (Oldsmobile Division, General Motors Corporation).

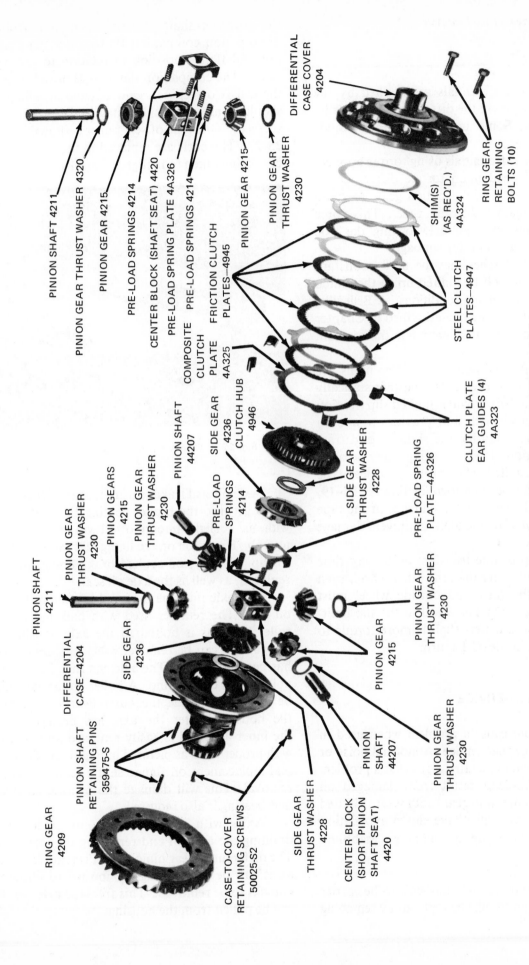

PINION SHAFT 4211

PINION GEAR THRUST WASHER 4320

PINION GEAR 4215

PRE-LOAD SPRINGS 4214

CENTER BLOCK (SHAFT SEAT) 4420

PRE-LOAD SPRING PLATE 4A326

PRE-LOAD SPRINGS 4214

COMPOSITE CLUTCH PLATE 4A325

FRICTION CLUTCH PLATES—4945

PINION GEAR 4215

PINION GEAR THRUST WASHER 4230

DIFFERENTIAL CASE COVER 4204

RING GEAR RETAINING BOLTS (10)

SHIM(S) (AS REQ'D.) 4A324

STEEL CLUTCH PLATES—4947

CLUTCH HUB 4946

CLUTCH PLATE EAR GUIDES (4) 4A323

PINION SHAFT 4211

PINION GEAR THRUST WASHER 4230

PINION GEARS 4215

PINION GEAR THRUST WASHER 4230

PINION SHAFT 44207

SIDE GEAR 4236

PRE-LOAD SPRINGS 4214

SIDE GEAR THRUST WASHER 4228

PRE-LOAD SPRING PLATE—4A326

RING GEAR 4209

DIFFERENTIAL CASE—4204

SIDE GEAR 4236

PINION SHAFT RETAINING PINS 359475-S

CASE-TO-COVER RETAINING SCREWS 50025-S2

SIDE GEAR THRUST WASHER 4228

CENTER BLOCK (SHORT PINION SHAFT SEAT) 4420

PINION SHAFT 44207

PINION GEAR THRUST WASHER 4230

PINION GEAR 4215

PINION GEAR THRUST WASHER 4230

Fig. 25-21 An exploded view of a limited slip differential using one multiple disc clutch and coil preload springs (Ford Division, Ford Marketing Corporation).

Limited slip differentials are applied by the difference in torque on the differential gears or by preload springs. Some units use both methods operating together.

Limited slip differentials using torque application methods depend upon torque difference on each side of the differential pinion gears to cause them to bear against the side gears. This force pushes the clutch into contact, locking the axle shafts to the case and limiting slippage.

Differential clutches may be under constant spring load. Load will be limited up to the clutch capacity under any driving conditions. A Belleville-type spring similar to the one described in Chapter 21 is used to provide clutch loading in the constant load type.

The majority of limited slip differentials are provided with a light preload spring that statically loads the clutch. This provides limited slip traction under light tractive loads and provides a smooth transition between limiting the slippage and tractive load operation. Preload springs may be a set of coil springs, a Belleville spring, or a leaf-type spring. They can be identified in Figures 25-19, 25-20 and 25-21. Differential clutches of the type described will slip if overloaded, to prevent damage from high loads.

Limited slip torque transfers occur any time one wheel rotates faster than the other wheel, even in a turn. In the turn, the outside wheel must rotate faster than the inner wheel so the slip limiting characteristic transfers slightly more torque to the wheel on the inside of the turn.

25-4 REAR AXLE SERVICE

Rear axles seldom cause a problem when used in standard passenger car service. Abnormal noise or fluid leaks are usually the first signs that a problem is occurring. Problems result from damaged oil seals, bearing failure, and gear tooth wear. Limited slip differentials may also have clutch application problems that show up as slipping, grabbing, or chattering.

Seals. Drive pinion oil seals leak at the carrier nose. This seal can usually be replaced by removing the propeller shaft rear universal joint from the drive pinion companion flange after marking the nut and flange position in relation to the pinion shaft. The companion flange is removed to expose the seal. Correct seal removing and installing tools should be used to avoid damaging the seal or sealing surfaces. One type of seal puller is shown in Figure 25-22. The parts are replaced in the reverse order, care being taken to realign the marks.

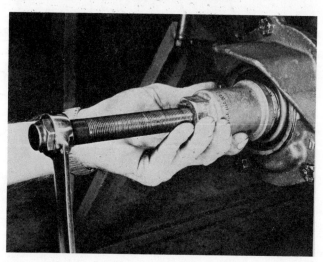

Fig. 25-22 Removing the pinion seal with a seal puller.

Axle oil seal leakage usually allows differential oil to get into the brake, coating the brake lining with oil. A slight amount of oil will cause the brake to grab. Excess oil on the lining will cause the brake to slip. Usually, oil soaked brake linings must be replaced, as well as the axle oil seal.

The axle must be removed to replace the axle oil seal. The retainer used with ball and tapered roller bearings is bolted to the axle housing end flange so it can be removed when the brake drum has been taken off. The axle can then be carefully pulled from the housing. A puller on the axle might be required to slide the outer bearing race from the housing. After the axle has been removed, the inner axle seal is easily removed and replaced with proper tools as pictured in Figure 25-23. Outer seal replacement on flange shafts requires bearing removal. This will damage the bearing so that a new bearing is also required.

Axles with roller bearings are removed by draining the axle oil and removing the rear cover. The differential gear pinion shaft is removed so the axles can be pushed slightly inward to allow the C-locks to be removed. This frees the axles so they can be pulled from the housing.

Fig. 25-23 Removing an axle shaft seal with a seal puller.

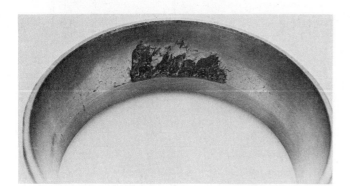

Fig. 25-24 Axle bearing damaged by fatigue.

Fig. 25-25 Method used to remove the bearing retainer collar (Chrysler Motors Corporation).

Fig. 25-26 Pressing a bearing on an axle shaft.

Bearings. Bearing failure usually shows up as a rumbling sound that is proportional to vehicle speed. The sound often becomes more distinct when the automobile is turning a corner in a direction that puts a load on the bearing. This is especially true with taper roller bearings. (Figure 25-24). In these, axle shaft end thrust is transferred through a thrust block on the differential pinion shaft between the two axles, so the thrust is taken by the bearing on the inside of the turn. This can be readily seen if one examines illustrations of the bearing installation method. (Figure 25-17). Each ball bearing absorbs thrust in both directions, so a thrust block is not required in axles using them.

Axle shafts using integral inner race roller bearings, taper roller bearings, or ball bearings are pressed onto the axle shaft. Special puller attachments are therefore used to remove them. The bearing retainer collar is removed first by partially cutting the collar with a chisel at 90° intervals or by drilling partly through it as shown in Figure 25-25. This expands the collar so it can be removed

easily. Some bearings have to be broken apart in order to attach pullers that will remove the inner race. While removing bearings, it is important to protect the oil seal surfaces on the axle shaft to prevent damage that could cause an oil leak.

After putting a new outer seal in the bearing retainer, the new well-lubricated bearing and bearing retainer collar are pressed on the axle shaft (Figure 25-26). They must be firmly seated against the axle shoulder so that end play can be properly adjusted.

With new seals in the housing, the axles are carefully installed through the inner oil seal and slipped into the side gear splines. When required, axle end play is adjusted with shims or adjusting nuts. A dial gauge is usually used to measure the end play as shown in Figure 25-27.

Fig. 25-27 Measuring axle shaft end play.

Differential Assembly. Ring and drive pinion gear problems are usually evidenced by a whine under both power and coast. Driving at the float point, under neither power nor coast, is usually quiet. Noise occurring only during a turn indicates a problem between the differential and side gears. In most cases, to correct abnormal differential noise, the differential must be disassembled.

Disassembly starts by draining the differential oil and removing axles as previously discussed. After the axles are removed the differential carrier can be removed from separable-carrier-type housings. Access to the carrier in a unitized-carrier-type housing that is integral with the housing is through the housing rear cover.

Case bearing looseness, ring gear run-out and

backlash, and obvious tooth wear are checked before removing the case from the housing. This check will be of help in determining the specific cause of any differential noise.

Differential carrier side bearing caps and adjusting nuts are punch marked to assure re-assembly in their same position. This is pictured in Figure 25-28. Adjusting nuts are loosened, when used, and the bearing caps are removed to free the case. If case adjustment is with shims, the housing must be slightly spread to release the case. This usually requires a special spreading tool and dial gauge to control the amount of spread as shown in Figure 25-29. The case can then be lifted from the carrier and examined for obvious defects.

Fig. 25-28 Side bearing caps punchmarked for identification before disassembly.

Fig. 25-29 A dial gauge is placed on the carrier when spreading to remove the case.

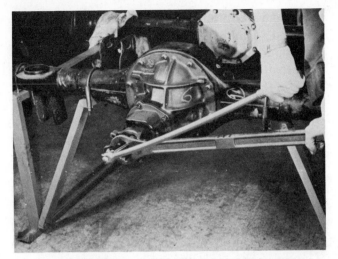

Fig. 25-30 Removing the companion flange nut.

The pinion nut is removed by holding the rear universal companion flange while loosening the drive pinion nut (Figure 25-30). The drive pinion can then be pushed out of the front bearing. Further disassembly can be accomplished by removing the ring gear, differential gears, and side gears.

An inspection of the parts should show evidence of the noise problem. Only bearings that show signs of abnormal wear need to be removed for replacement. Here again, special pullers are used to protect the pinion and case.

Before assembly, parts are thoroughly cleaned. As they are assembled, they are coated with differential oil. The side gears, differential gears, and ring gear are installed on the case. Bolts should be torqued to the correct specification to prevent warping the parts. Ring gear run-out must be within limits. The drive pinion is installed without an oil seal until correct pinion depth is established.

Pinion depth can be established with special tool gauges. These gauges differ greatly among manufacturers and among axle types. An example is shown in Figure 25-31. Service manuals give details that must be followed when using them.

Fig. 25-31 Typical pinion depth gauging tools.

Setting pinion depth without special tools is a time-consuming assembly operation that involves checking tooth contact pattern, removing to install corrective shims, then reinstalling and again checking tooth contact pattern. This has to be repeated until the correct tooth contact pattern is established.

Pinion depth can be increased by increasing shim thickness when shims are placed between the rear pinion bearing and the drive pinion gear or between the rear bearing outer race and carrier bore. On removable pinion retainer types, removing shims between the retainer and carrier will increase pinion depth. These locations can be seen in Figure 25-8.

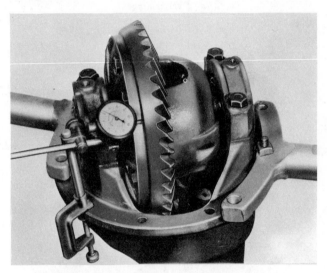

Fig. 25-32 Measuring ring gear run out (Chrysler Motors Corporation).

The carrier assembly is installed. Pinion depth must be coordinated with ring gear backlash. After the run-out is checked (Figure 25-32) backlash is reduced by moving the ring gear closer to the drive pinion gear, and increased by moving it away from the pinion gear (Figure 25-33).

Tooth contact can be observed by coating the ring gear with red lead. Turning the ring gear with tension held against pinion turning will wipe the red lead so that the tooth contact pattern can be observed, as illustrated in Figure 25-34. Pinion bearing preload must be set when the proper tooth contact pattern is established. Pinions with a solid spacer plus shims between the bearings have their preload adjusted by removing shims to increase preload. Preload is checked with no oil seal, the

Fig. 25-33 Adjusting ring gear backlash.

case removed, and the companion flange nut torqued. The drive pinion is then turned with an inch-pound torque wrench. After shims are selected to provide the correct turning torque, the companion flange is again removed and a front oil seal is installed, the companion flange is installed, and the nut is tightened to specified torque.

Preload on pinions using a compressed spacer between the bearings is adjusted by tightening the companion flange nut until the pinion turning torque (Figure 25–35) is correct with the oil seal in place. New spacers are always used.

Pinion preload is sufficient to eliminate any end play in the pinion shaft and still low enough to prevent bearing damage.

Differential side bearings must also be preloaded. This is done by tightening the adjusting

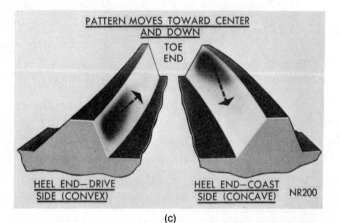

(a)

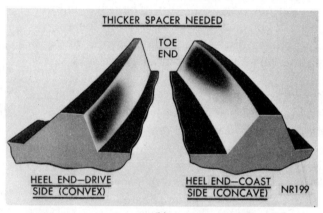

(b)

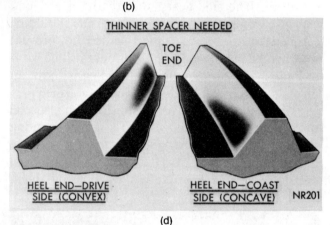

(c)

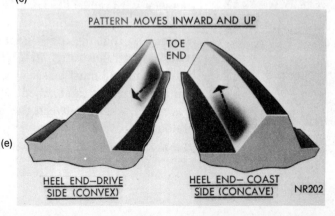

(d)

(e)

Fig. 25-34 Ring and pinion gear tooth pattern and corrections (Chrysler Motors Corporation).

Fig. 25-35 Measuring pinion preload (Oldsmobile Division, General Motors Corporation).

nuts on the adjustable type or by installing the correct thickness shims in the shim adjust type.

After final adjustments are made, the ring and pinion tooth contact pattern should be rechecked to see that it is still correct. If it is not, it will be necessary to disassemble the entire assembly and install corrective spacers and shims.

When final adjustments are complete, the rear axle can be reassembled using new gaskets, and then filled with new differential oil. With installation of the propeller shaft the automobile is ready for a road test.

Limited slip differentials are adjusted in the same manner as standard differentials. The clutch will require additional service. It is working cor-

rectly when one wheel is blocked and the other wheel has a minimum turning torque of about 30 foot-pounds (Figure 25-36).

Worn clutch disc and plates should be replaced. Wear may be determined by the space between the discs and plates as measured with a feeler gauge blade. Weak or warped clutch springs should also be replaced. Some manufacturers of conetype clutches recommend replacement of the cones and case as an assembly when they do not function properly.

Fig. 25-36 Measuring limited slip differential locking force.

REVIEW QUESTIONS

1. What is included in the rear axle assembly? [INTRODUCTION]

2. What is the advantage of hypoid-type ring and pinion gears? [25-1]

3. What is the reason for having different axle ratios? [25-1]

4. What causes the nose of a differential on the rear end to rise during acceleration? [25-1]

5. What causes a difference in wheel speeds? [25-1]

6. What is attached to the differential case? [25-1]

7. How do the differential pinion gears carry the driving torque from the ring gear to the drive axles? [25-1]

8. What is meant by a speed-averaging device and a torque divider as applied to a differential? [25-1]

9. What is meant by an overhung load on an axle? [25-1]

10. What is bearing preloading? [25-2]

11. What is the difference between the case and carrier? [25-2]

12. What method is used to adjust the pinion depth? [25-2]

13. How does a straddle-mounted pinion differ from an overhung pinion? [25-2]

14. How are the pinion bearings lubricated in a differential? [25-2]

15. Why is an axle housing breather required? [25-2]

16. What is the most popular type of differential carrier? [25-2]

17. What holds thrust loads on rear axles with a C-washer retainer? [25-2]

18. Why is an inner axle seal required on some axles and not on others? [25-2]

19. List the advantages of a limited slip differential. [25-3]

20. How does a limited slip differential transfer the torque to the wheel having traction? [25-3]

21. What problem will result from a leaking pinion seal? [25-4]

22. What problem will result from a leaking axle seal? [25-4]

23. How can a failed axle bearing be identified? [25-4]

24. How are pressed-on axle bearings replaced? [25-4]

25. What type of operation indicates a ring and pinion gear problem? [25-4]

26. What type of axle bearings require end-play adjustment? [25-4]

27. What items are checked before the carrier is disassembled? [25-4]

28. Why are the carrier side bearing caps punch-marked? [25-4]

29. Why are gauging tools useful during assembly? [25-4]

30. How is the pinion depth adjusted? [25-4]

31. How is the pinion preload set? [25-4]

32. What adjustment is made to change backlash? [25-4]

automotive brake systems

Automotive service brakes must be able to stop the car, prevent excess speed when coasting downhill, and hold the vehicle in position when stopped on grades. They are designed so that braking effort can be changed and controlled by the driver to keep the vehicle under control.

To reduce the wheel's rotating speed and slow the automobile, the service brake has a friction lining which presses against a moving cast iron surface that rotates with the wheel. The lining force against the moving surface is controlled by the driver through the use of mechanical and hydraulic mechanisms. Friction of the sliding brake surfaces converts the moving energy of the automobile into heat energy, which is dissipated into the air surrounding the brake parts. Braking effort increases as the driver increases force on the pedal to force the friction lining against the moving surface. Maximum braking effect occurs just before the wheel is stopped and the tire slides on the road. Maximum braking, therefore, depends upon good adhesion between the tire and the road surface. When the tire slides on the road, braking effort is reduced and vehicle directional control is lost.

26-1 BRAKE TYPES

Two types of mechanical devices are used in automotive service brakes. In one, a shoe with friction lining surface is expanded into the inside of a rotating drum. The other type of brake has friction pads that are pressed against each side of a rotating disc. The friction developed between the stationary friction element and rotating element is converted to heat, which is concentrated primarily in the rotating element.

407

Drum Brakes. The major difference among the various drum designs is the shoe attachment or *anchor* location and the location of the actuating mechanism or *wheel cylinder*. The shoes are attached and supported by a *backing plate* which is, in turn, attached to the vehicle steering knuckle on the front brakes and to the axle housing on the rear brakes.

Location of the shoe anchor in relation to forward wheel rotation is used to describe the type of shoe and its parts. The anchor end of the brake shoe is called the *heel*. Actuating force is applied to the toe end of the shoe. When the brake drum rotates from the shoe toe and toward the shoe heel, it is called a *leading shoe*. If the rotation is from the heel toward the toe end of the shoe, it is called a *trailing shoe*. Brake assemblies have been designed to use two leading shoes, two trailing shoes, and one of each brake shoe type. Details of the shoe types can be identified in Figure 26–1.

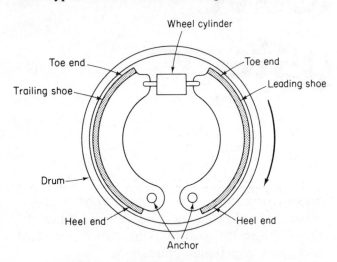

Fig. 26-1 Brake shoe type identification.

A leading shoe anchor allows the shoe to dig into the drum surface as it turns. This causes the shoe to *self-energize* and pull itself tighter into the drum, increasing friction and stopping the vehicle quicker with the same application effort. This action might be compared to a trailer that comes loose from a car and falls on its tongue, as illustrated in Figure 26–2. The tongue digs into the road surface, rapidly stopping the loose trailer. This type of self-energizing action in brakes is called *servo action.*

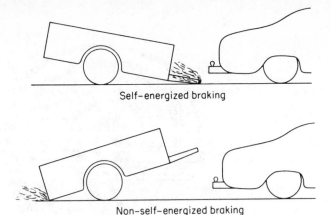

Fig. 26-2 Comparison of self-energizing and non-self-energizing braking.

The trailing shoe with the drum turning away from the anchor does not self-energize. Action between the shoe and the drum tends to push the friction lining away. If the trailer, in the previous example, had fallen onto its back end with the tongue in the air, it would easily drag or bounce over bumps, stopping much more slowly. This action can be compared to the trailing brake shoe's nonservo action.

The drum brake on most modern automobiles uses a dual servo brake shoe arrangement with two forward acting shoes. A typical self-adjusting automobile drum brake is pictured in Figure 26–3. One of these shoes is a *primary shoe* that transmits force to another shoe. The other shoe is a *secondary shoe* that receives force from the primary shoe. The primary shoe's heel end is attached through an adjustable link to the secondary shoe's toe end. The secondary shoe's heel fits against an anchor pin. In operation, the dual servo brake wheel cylinder actuates the brake by pushing the toe end of the primary shoe against the drum. The primary shoe has servo action because it is a self-energizing

Fig. 26-3 Drum brake part nomenclature (Oldsmobile Division, General Motors Corporation).

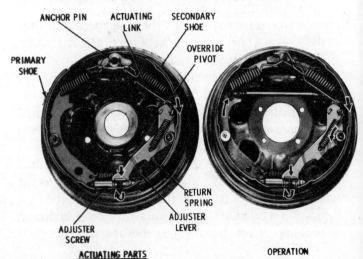

leading shoe. Its servo action pushes on the toe end of the secondary shoe with a force greater than that from the wheel cylinder alone. This, in turn, causes high self-energizing servo action of the secondary shoe. Dual servo action of both brake shoes may cause the secondary shoe to provide as much as 75% of the total braking effort. The dual servo brake was first patented by Bendix Corporation in 1928. They called it a Duo-Servo brake. The patents have expired and the basic

Bendix design is now used almost exclusively for automobile drum brakes.

Disc Brakes. Disc brakes absorb vehicle energy with friction pads or *shoes* that are forced against a rotating disc. Figure 26–4 is a sectional view of a

Fig. 26–4 Disc brake part nomenclature (Chrysler Motors Corporation).

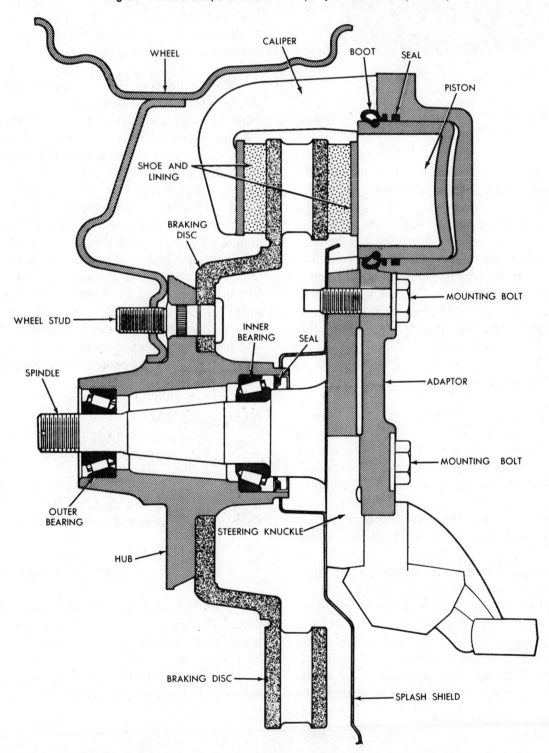

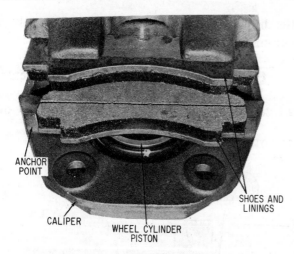

Fig. 26-5 Location of the anchor point in a typical disc brake caliper.

typical single piston disc brake. The shoes are held in a housing called a *caliper* that is supported on the steering knuckle or axle housing (Figure 26-5). The *disc* is attached to the wheel hub. Hydraulic pressure within the caliper cylinder pushes the shoe against the disc. Disc brakes have no servo action so they require four to five times more hydraulic pressure than is required by the dual servo brake. Most American passenger cars, therefore, use a power brake with disc brakes to provide this required extra pressure.

26-2 BRAKING REQUIREMENTS

The manufacturer's selection of the brake type is dependent upon the stopping force required, the kinds of friction material used, space available for the brakes, and the maximum driver effort expected.

It is desirable for a service technician to thoroughly understand brake system requirements to help him appreciate the physical demands on automobile brakes so that he will take proper care in making repairs. The brake requirements are more meaningful as a means of comparing automobile brake performance if the requirements are expressed in known values of time, pressure, distance, and energy. For this it is necessary to use several mathematical equations, just as the use of mathematical equations is needed when comparing engine performance. Mathematical expressions may be even more meaningful to a reader who wishes to build a modified vehicle to ensure satisfactory braking performance.

Horsepower in the customary measuring system is foot-pounds of work expended in a given period of time. The quicker a given number of foot-pounds of work can be done, the more horsepower is produced. This holds true of both engines and brakes. A vehicle that could be accelerated from a dead start to 60 mph in nine seconds may be required to stop from 60 mph in three seconds. The brakes are required to absorb three times the amount of engine horsepower energy in its heat equivalent form. Brakes must be and are capable of decelerating a vehicle at a faster rate than the engine is able to accelerate it.

Kinetic Energy. Heat of combustion is converted into mechanical energy by the engine to drive the vehicle. One BTU per second will produce 1.44 hp in the customary measuring system. The more horsepower the engine is able to produce, the faster a car can be accelerated. With equal power, a lighter car can accelerate faster than a heavy car. More horsepower is required to accelerate up to highway speeds than is required to maintain highway speed. Engine horsepower energy is converted to energy of motion, or *kinetic energy,* of the vehicle and is expressed in foot-pounds. Kinetic energy must be dissipated as heat by the brakes as the vehicle speed is reduced. This energy can be calculated using the following formula, which has been simplified to directly use vehicle gross weight in pounds and speed in miles per hour.

Vehicle kinetic energy = $0.334\ W\ [(V_1)^2 - (V_2)^2]$ ft-lb

Where: W = vehicle gross weight in pounds
V_1 = initial velocity in mph
V_2 = terminal velocity in mph

If a 4000 lb automobile (W) were brought from 60 mph (V_1) to a stop (V_2), the kinetic energy absorbed by the brakes would be 480,960 ft-lbs.

$$KE = 0.0334 \times 4000\ (60^2 - 0^2)\ \text{ft-lbs}$$
$$= 0.0334 \times 4000 \times 3600 = 480,960\ \text{ft-lbs}$$

Note that the kinetic energy doubles as the weight doubles, but it increases by four times as the speed is doubled.

Coefficient of Friction. Kinetic energy is the force that tends to keep the vehicle moving. Friction opposes this motion, consuming power and producing heat. Retarding friction can occur in the brakes or between a sliding tire and the road surface when the brakes lock wheel rotation. The vehicle's kinetic energy and its ability to stop is related to the coefficient of friction between the rubbing surfaces. The coefficient of friction is the force required to keep the vehicle moving at a constant velocity divided by the weight of the vehicle. Maximum usable coefficient of friction occurs between the tire and road surface, rather than in the brakes. The coefficient of friction, then, is dependent upon the type of materials that are sliding and not the weight. For example, if the weight of the vehicle is doubled, the force required to slide it is also doubled and the coefficient of friction remains the same. For dry concrete, the coefficient of friction is usually considered to be 0.6. Some specially compounded tires may have a coefficient of friction as high as 0.8 on dry concrete. If 600 lbs were required to keep a 1000-lb weight sliding on a one square inch surface at a constant speed, the coefficient of friction between these surfaces is 600/1000 or 0.6. This is the maximum available coefficient of friction under these conditions.

A free falling object accelerates at a rate of 32.2 feet per second^2 (ft/sec^2). To stop at this same rate would require a coefficient of friction of 1.0. With a coefficient of friction of 0.6, the maximum braking deceleration without sliding the wheels is approximately 20 ft/sec^2 (32.2 × 0.6 = 19.3). In actuality, this would be considered a panic stop. A 14 ft/sec^2 deceleration is a severe and uncomfortable stopping rate. Under 8 ft/sec^2 is a comfortable stopping rate. Maximum deceleration rates for passenger cars run as high as 19 ft/sec^2.

The shoe force against the drum or disc replaces the vehicle weight when calculating brake coefficient of friction. Passenger car brakes have a 0.3 to 0.5 coefficient of friction. The amount of energy the brakes are able to absorb is dependent upon the coefficient of friction of the brake materials, their diameter, their surface area, shoe geometry, and the pressure used to actuate them. Stopping a car quickly requires the vehicle motion energy to be converted into heat in a short time. This means that the total friction must be greater, resulting in high brake temperature.

Brake Balance. When the wheels are locked and skidding with the same tire and road conditions, the stopping distance is the same, regardless

of the weight, number of wheels, or vehicle load. Maximum braking power occurs when the wheels are braked just below the locking point, or point of *impending skid*. Nonskid brake systems are designed to operate at or below this point.

Changes in load on a wheel will change the point of impending skid. The load changes can occur as the vehicle leans while rounding a curve and as a result of weight transfer between front and rear wheels during braking.

The effective braking force of a vehicle occurs *at ground level*. Vehicle weight and kinetic energy of the vehicle effectively act through the vehicle center-of-gravity, which is *above ground level*. This causes the vehicle to tend to pitch forward as the brakes are applied. Figure 26–6 illustrates this action. Pitching forward effectively transfers some of the vehicle weight from the rear wheels to the front wheels. The front brakes, therefore, must absorb more kinetic energy than the rear brakes.

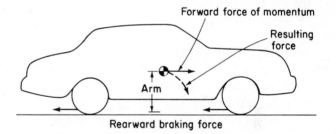

Fig. 26-6 Center of gravity arm causing forward weight transfer.

The maximum amount of weight transfer can be calculated by:

$$\text{Weight transferred (lbs.)} = \frac{\text{Coefficient of friction} \times \text{Height of CG (inches)} \times \text{VGW*}}{\text{Wheel base (in.)}}$$

*Vehicle gross weight

This weight transfer is subtracted from the static weight on the rear wheels and added to the static weight of the front wheels. The front wheel static weight is normally 55% of the vehicle weight.

For example, what is the amount of weight transfer during braking, on a 4000 lb vehicle with a 120 in. wheel base having a center of gravity 18 in.

above the road surface, when the coefficient of friction between the tire and road surface is 0.5?

$$\text{Weight transfer} = \frac{0.5 \times 18 \text{ in.} \times 4000 \text{ lb}}{120 \text{ in.}} = 300 \text{ lb.}$$

If the normal conditions placed 55% of the weight on the front wheels they would carry 2200 lbs and the rear wheels would carry 1800 lbs. The weight transfer of 300 lbs during braking would reduce the rear wheel braking weight to 1500 lbs and increase the front wheel braking weight to 2500 lbs.

Front brakes are designed to absorb this extra brake effort by selecting shoe-drum or shoe-disc combination types, brake size, lining coefficient of friction, wheel cylinder size, and differential hydraulic actuating pressures.

With full braking it is desirable to have the front brakes lock up slightly ahead of the rear brakes. This causes the car to go straight forward and not spin out.

Stopping Distance. Stopping distance is based on the deceleration rate. As shown, maximum deceleration occurs at approximately 20 ft/sec² or 0.6 times the force of gravity. Using this value as the deceleration rate (d ft/sec²) and the vehicle speed (V mph) in the following simplified equation, the stopping distance (S ft) can be calculated as:

$$S = 1.074 \times V^2/d \text{ ft.}$$

For example, if an automobile going 60 mph (V) stopped at a moderate deceleration rate (d) of 8 ft/sec² it would require 484 feet to stop from the time the brakes were applied.

$$S = 1.074 \times 60^2/8 = 1.074 \times 3600/8 = 484 \text{ ft}$$

The time (t sec) in seconds required to stop the vehicle from an initial speed (V mph) using the same deceleration rate (d ft/sec²) is expressed as:

$$t = 1.465 \frac{V}{d} \text{ seconds.}$$

It takes 11 seconds (t) to stop an automobile from 60 mph (V) at a deceleration rate of 8 ft/sec² (d):

$$t = 1.465 \times 60/8 = 11 \text{ sec}$$

The stopping distance is also affected by the tire deflection, air resistance, engine braking effects, and the inertia of the drive line. These additional stopping effects can be illustrated by having a car travel at 70 mph on a level road and placing it in neutral without braking. At the end of a mile, the car will still be going about 15 mph. Going uphill will reduce speed faster, whereas going down a slight grade will reduce the speed more slowly.

Brake Fade. Brake fade occurs after a number of severe stops or after holding the brakes on a long downhill grade. The brakes convert vehicle kinetic energy into heat. Brake lining material is a poor conductor of heat, so most of the heat goes into the brake drum or disc. If the drum or disc is heated by friction faster than it is cooled by the surrounding air, it will reach high temperatures. Under severe use, brake drums may reach 600°F (316°C). The coefficient of friction between the drum and lining is much lower at these high temperatures, so braking will require additional pedal pressure. A point is eventually reached when the coefficient of friction drops so low that little braking effect is available. This is called *brake fade.*

Drum brakes are more susceptible to fade than disc brakes. In drum brakes, the lining covers a large portion of the internal drum surface, allowing little cooling space. Disc shoes, on the other hand, cover only a small portion of the disc, so there is a lot of cooling time as the disc rotates. As the vehicle moves, cooling air is directed around the drum and disc to remove brake heat.

Another temperature factor that affects brake fade is drum and disc expansion. The drum brake diameter increases as the drum gets hot. The shoe arc will then no longer match the drum so the lining-to-drum contact surface becomes smaller as it contacts only the center of the shoe arc. The same stopping force requires higher pedal pressure and this in turn increases the temperature on the smaller brake contact surface. Continued braking compounds the problem until the braking becomes ineffective, regardless of the pedal force.

As the disc gets hot it too expands in diameter. This is not critical because the pads apply braking force on the side of the disc. The braking surface area remains constant so disc expansion has little effect on braking.

Leading shoes are more susceptible to fade than trailing shoes. This occurs because the self-actuating servo action force decreases as the coefficient of friction becomes less. Trailing shoes do not use servo action for their operation.

Dual servo drum brakes have outstandingly high output compared to the pedal input effort. However, they show large variations in brake coefficient of friction from wheel to wheel and are adversely affected by brake fade. Not only does the forward acting primary shoe lose its force, but it cannot actuate the forward acting secondary shoe. This type of brake is the most susceptible of all types of brakes to fade.

Fade-resistant drum brakes must limit brake shoe arc to 110° and the power absorption to 25 hp per square inch of lining. The horsepower absorbed by the brakes during a stop can be calculated by the formula:

$$hp = \frac{KE \text{ (ft-lb)}}{550 \text{ (ft-lb/sec/hp)} \times t}$$

The horsepower absorbed when stopping a 4,000 lb automobile in 11 seconds (t) can be calculated when using the kinetic energy of 480,960 ft-lbs determined using an earlier equation. Placing these values in the equation for horsepower above:

$$hp = \frac{480,960 \text{ ft-lb}}{550 \text{ ft-lb/sec/hp} \times 11 \text{ sec}} = 78.5$$

If 42.4 BTU is the heat equivalent of one horsepower then in one stop of this automobile from 60 mph, the brakes are required to absorb 3871 BTU of heat (78.5 × 42.4).

Brake Torque. When the brakes are applied, the drum or disc tries to twist the shoes or caliper anchors from their mountings. This twisting action is called *brake torque*. The amount of torque is determined by the effective axle height, which is the torque arm in feet, and the stopping force between the tire and road surface in pounds. This is illustrated in Figure 26–7. Torque is expressed in pound-feet.

Brake torque is absorbed on the front wheels by the knuckle and suspension control arms. In the rear, it is absorbed by the axle housing and the leaf spring or control arms. Braking torque

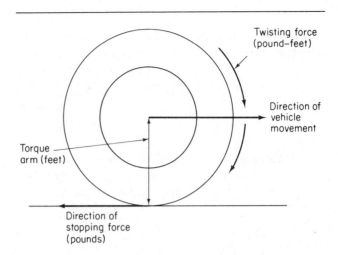

Fig. 26-7 Braking torque producing a twist on the brake anchor.

during a panic stop is much higher than accelerating torque at full throttle. Brake supporting and anchoring members must, therefore, have sufficient strength to withstand these high braking loads.

Brake Safety. Brake failure was a common problem with early automobiles. The federal government recognized this so it passed regulations requiring all automobiles and trucks to be equipped with an *emergency brake* that would operate independently from the service brakes. Service brakes in modern automobiles rarely fail, but the emergency brake is still required. It is usually set when the automobile is parked, and so it is commonly called a *parking brake.*

Safety standards require the parking brake to hold the automobile on a 30% slope (16.7°). The brake must hold on this slope with an application force of no more than 150 lbs (667 N)* for foot application or 100 lbs (445 N) for hand application. The system must hold indefinitely after the brake has been applied until the operator releases it.

The use of four-wheel disc brakes on high production volume passenger cars had been delayed due to the parking brake requirement. Engineers have developed parking brake systems for rear disc brakes, with automatic adjustment for pad

*The symbol N stands for the metric force unit called newton. It is derived from base SI units using the following equation: $m \times kq \times S - \pm$.

lining wear, that can be manufactured at a cost approaching drum brakes. Initially, four-wheel disc brakes were installed as options on premium automobiles in the same way that the first front wheel disc brakes appeared on domestic automobiles. A rear disc caliper with a parking brake is pictured in Figure 26–8.

Four-wheel disc brakes help to increase automobile safety. Disc brakes do not change their coefficient of friction and brake torque as drum brakes do. Disc brakes do not fade with heat or water and they are not contaminated by brake fluid seepage. Four-wheel disc brakes seldom lock up as disc/drum brakes do.

The antilock brake system is another brake safety item that is available as an option. These systems have sensors on the rear axles, wheels, or propeller shaft that send an electrical signal to an electronic control. The control senses the change in rear axle speed (Figure 26–9). When the rear wheels are about to stop rotating, the control reduces the hydraulic brake pressure to the rear brakes allowing the wheel speed to increase. The hydraulic pressure is increased as the wheel speeds up. This cycle of reducing and increasing hydraulic pressure repeats very rapidly to provide maximum stopping force while the wheel is kept from locking. When maximum braking is applied, the average wheel speed that results from the rapid cycling is about 85% of what the wheel speed would be with no slip. With maximum braking using the antilock brake system, the front wheels lock and the rear wheels rotate, and the automobile goes straight ahead. If the rear wheels were to lock and the front wheels to rotate, the rear of the automobile would generally start to slide. This would cause the automobile to swing around and spin out. Even though the front wheels would be capable of steering, they would have no effect as the automobile slid sidewise. If the antilock system fails, the brakes operate as standard service brakes.

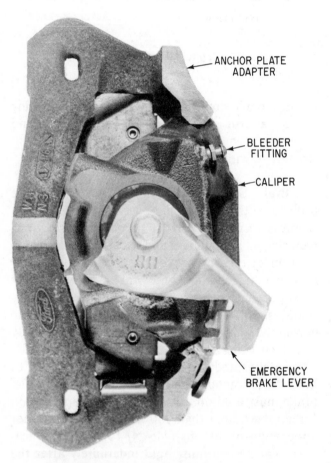

Fig. 26-8 A caliper with a parking brake for use on rear disc brakes.

ANCHOR PLATE ADAPTER

BLEEDER FITTING

CALIPER

EMERGENCY BRAKE LEVER

26-3 DUAL SERVO DRUM BRAKE DETAILS

The dual servo drum brake is supported by a *backing plate* which, in turn, is fastened to the *steering knuckle* in front or the *axle housing* in the rear. Brake torque is transferred from the *linings* and *shoes* through the *anchor* to the backing plate. The plate also serves as a dust and splash shield to keep contaminants from the brake. The upper ends of the shoes are held against the anchor with

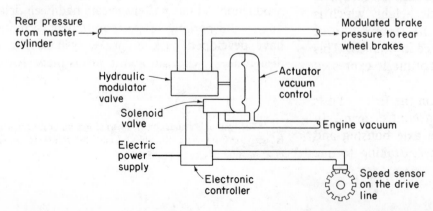

Rear pressure from master cylinder

Modulated brake pressure to rear wheel brakes

Hydraulic modulator valve

Actuator vacuum control

Solenoid valve

Engine vacuum

Electric power supply

Electronic controller

Speed sensor on the drive line

Fig. 26-9 Simplified drawing of an antilock brake system.

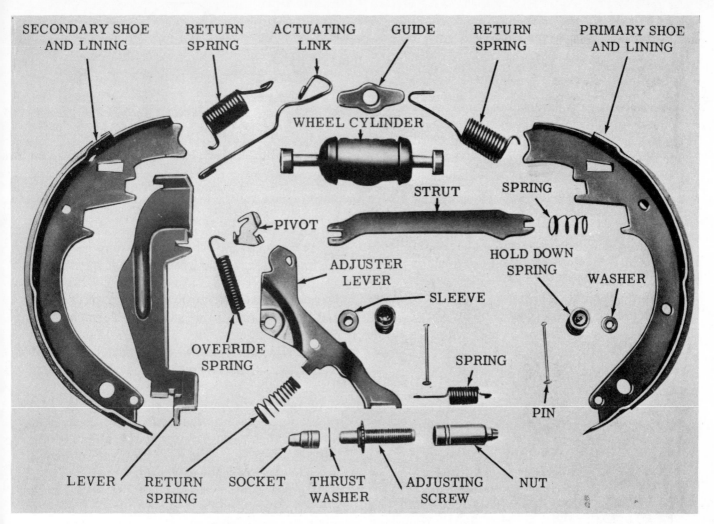

SECONDARY SHOE AND LINING — RETURN SPRING — ACTUATING LINK — GUIDE — RETURN SPRING — PRIMARY SHOE AND LINING

WHEEL CYLINDER

STRUT — SPRING

PIVOT

ADJUSTER LEVER

SLEEVE

HOLD DOWN SPRING — WASHER

OVERRIDE SPRING

SPRING

PIN

LEVER — RETURN SPRING — SOCKET — THRUST WASHER — ADJUSTING SCREW — NUT

Fig. 26-10 Right rear drum brake part identification (Oldsmobile Division, General Motors Corporation).

return springs. A short spring holds the lower ends against a *star wheel* adjusting screw. *Hold-down pins,* sometimes called *nails,* with springs and spring cups hold the shoes squarely against contact surfaces on the backing plate. Self-adjustment cables, levers, and springs are added to automatically turn the star wheel adjuster when shoe-to-drum clearance permits. Rear shoes are fitted with a cable operated *parking brake lever* and *strut* that can actuate the shoes. A *wheel cylinder* is located between the shoes directly under the anchor pin and guide. Wheel cylinder connecting links, sometimes called *push rods* or *actuator pins,* connect the wheel cylinder pistons to the brake shoes. This entire brake assembly is covered with a brake *drum* that is mounted on the axle. Parts of the brake can be identified in Figure 26–10.

Linings. Brake linings are made primarily from asbestos fibers, a material consisting chiefly of calcium and magnesium silicate. It is molded into the desired form with a high-temperature synthetic bonding agent. Other materials such as lead, zinc, brass, copper, graphite, and ceramics are added to give the lining the desired coefficient of friction and heat-resistance properties. These linings can withstand temperatures as high as 600°F (316°C). One stop from 60 mph (96 kmph) may raise the brake temperature to 450°F (232°C). Good quality brake linings maintain their friction characteristics at high temperatures and give long service life.

Sintered metal linings that can withstand higher temperatures without fade have been used where severe braking requirements are encountered. Sintered lining materials for drum brakes were dropped as a high performance material when disc brakes were adapted to these vehicles.

In a dual servo brake the secondary lining does about 75% of the braking. It is generally made longer than the primary lining, so the wear rate of the two linings will be nearly equal. Lining wear rate results from the amount of work required to stop the vehicle. Wear rate increases as the temperature increases. Passenger cars are provided

415

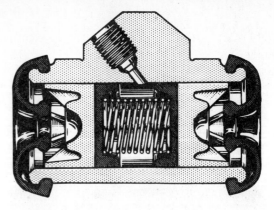

Fig. 26-12 Sectional view of a wheel cylinder (The Bendix Corporation).

with about one square inch of lining for each 25 pounds of vehicle gross weight (1cm² per 1.76 kg vehicle gross weight). A 4000-lb vehicle would use 160 square inches of lining.

Shoes. The linings are supported by brake shoes. Brake shoes form a metal backing for the lining and have a supporting web on which springs, actuators, and anchors attach. Linings are fastened to the shoes by rivets or a bonding cement as shown in Figure 26-11. Riveted linings usually provide a soft quiet brake. The bonded linings lend themselves to high volume, production line techniques.

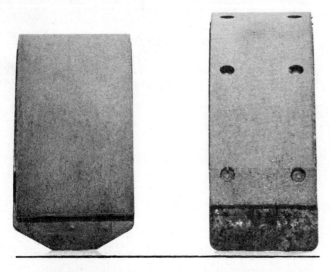

Fig. 26-11 Bonded brake lining (left) and riveted brake lining (right).

Brake shoe design and anchor location control the servo action that is developed by the shoe. Servo action increases as the anchor is moved toward the center of the brake. If the anchor were moved inward too far, the brake would lock like a Sprag one-way clutch. It would have to be turned backward to release the shoe. This, of course, would be unsatisfactory for service brakes. Service brake systems are designed so the wheel can be locked with no more than 100 pounds force on the brake pedal. When the wheel is locked all the braking friction occurs between the tire and road surface.

Wheel Cylinder. Brakes are actuated by hydraulic pressure in the wheel cylinder. The wheel cylinder has a piston on each end. Inside each

piston are two cup-type rubber seals that retain the brake fluid. Some wheel cylinders incorporate a spring between the brake cups. A rubber boot is fastened around the push rod or connecting link and over the end of the cylinder to keep contaminants out of the cylinder. Figure 26-12 is a cross-section view of a typical wheel cylinder.

When sufficient pressure is developed in the wheel cylinder to overcome return spring force, fluid pushes the pistons, connecting links, and shoes outward until they touch the drum. The linings in their release position are within 0.010 to 0.015 in. (0.25 to 0.38 mm) of the drum so there is actually very little shoe movement.

Brake return springs pull the shoes back away from the drum and against the anchor when fluid pressure is released. The returning shoes also force the wheel cylinder pistons back to their original released position. This returns fluid to the master cylinder.

Drums. Brake drums are designed to have adequate strength with minimum weight. They must be able to rapidly absorb and dissipate the heat that comes from friction. The braking surface must have good wear properties. It must fit within the wheel space available and be designed for low cost mass production. These requirements are satisfactorily met on production automobiles. Assembly details are shown in Figure 26-13.

The braking surface on brake drums is cast iron. Some brake drums are one-piece cast iron. Cast iron works very well as the drum friction surface, but cast iron tends to be too brittle for the drum back or disc. Composite drums were developed with stamped steel discs fastened to a cast iron hoop-shaped ring section braking surface. Another method used to make brake drums is to centrifugally cast an iron braking surface into a stamped steel drum (Figure 26-14). Centrifugal cast iron is **more**

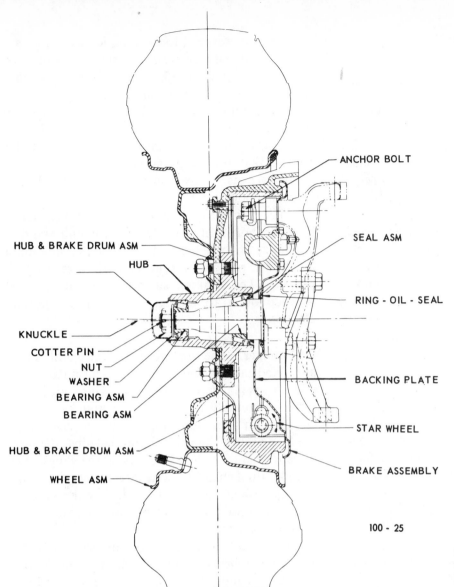

ANCHOR BOLT

HUB & BRAKE DRUM ASM

HUB

SEAL ASM

RING - OIL - SEAL

KNUCKLE

COTTER PIN

NUT

WASHER

BEARING ASM

BEARING ASM

BACKING PLATE

HUB & BRAKE DRUM ASM

STAR WHEEL

WHEEL ASM

BRAKE ASSEMBLY

100 - 25

Fig. 26-13 Drum brake fitting within the wheel (Buick Motor Division, General Motors Corporation).

(a)

(b)

Fig. 26-14 Drum construction. (a) Stamped disc with cast iron hoop braking surface, (b) steel drum with centrifugal cast iron braking surface.

dense than plain cast iron, which gives long service life. Sometimes, these drums use cast fins on their outer surface to aid in cooling, which will reduce brake fade. The most advanced brake drums are a bimetallic-finned aluminum casting with a braking surface of centrifugal cast iron bonded to the inner drum surface.

Brake drum size is limited by the space allowed behind the vehicle wheel. In the early 1960's, vehicle wheel sizes were made smaller to give the vehicle a lower silhouette. This limited brake size, so brake performance became critical. By the late 1960's, the wheel size was increased and larger brakes were installed to improve braking performance.

26-4 DISC BRAKE DETAILS

High performance and heavy passenger cars have overtaxed drum brake capacity. Disc brake development has provided the needed high capacity, fade resistant brake. Disc brakes have been used for years on lightweight European cars and on aircraft. The European brakes were too small to be used directly on domestic passenger cars. Aircraft disc brakes had time to cool after stopping the airplane before being used again and, therefore, they did not have the capacity, considering their size, that was required for passenger car applications.

Disc or Rotor. Most domestic passenger cars use a ventilated cast iron disc similar to the one pictured in Figure 26-15. The two solid outer disc surfaces are the braking surfaces. These are held apart in alignment with cast webs. Air flow through the disc cools it before fade can occur. Studies have shown that a solid disc would operate cooler on the first few stops because the added metal would act as a heat sink. The ventilated disc operates cooler after the first few stops.

The disc is attached to the hub or axle flange by wheel bolts. In some designs, the hub and disc are made in one piece. In each type, minimum lateral disc run-out must be maintained for smooth braking. The braking surfaces must be parallel to each other to minimize brake pedal pulsing effects.

Caliper. The first production disc brakes were of a fixed caliper, four-piston design similar to the one illustrated in Figure 26-16. The caliper was fastened securely to the steering knuckle or axle housing. In operation, two pistons on each side of the disc pushed the pads or shoes against the disc, thereby clamping the disc between the shoes. The cylinder fluid chambers were interconnected, so the pistons pushed with equal force. Friction between the shoes and disc converted the vehicle kinetic energy into heat.

One problem that developed in early disc brakes was boiling brake fluid. The heat from friction heated the caliper so hot that the fluid turned to a vapor, which could be compressed. Brakes require a solid fluid column to transfer the pedal force to the shoes. Heat insulators and a high boiling point brake fluid were developed for disc brake equipped vehicles. Only high-boiling-point brake fluid is suitable for use in disc-brake-equipped modern domestic passenger cars.

The four-piston fixed caliper required accurate

Fig. 26-16 Typical four-piston caliper assembly (Kelsey-Hays Company).

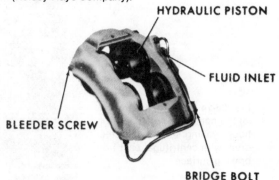

HYDRAULIC PISTON

FLUID INLET

BLEEDER SCREW

BRIDGE BOLT

Fig. 26-15 Typical front brake disc or rotor.

Fig. 26-17 Disc brake assembly showing how the caliper can squeeze the brake shoes against the rotor.

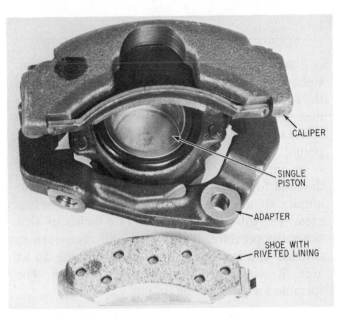

Fig. 26-18 Parts of a disc brake single-piston caliper.

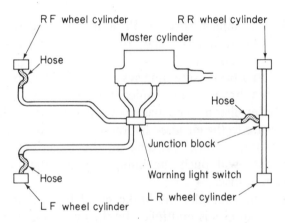

Fig. 26-19 Typical brake hydraulic system drawing.

centering so the shoes would not drag or the pistons come too far out of their bores. During overhaul, each caliper requires servicing all four cylinders. Interconnecting passages are subject to leaks and the caliper is expensive to manufacture.

A single-piston floating caliper has been developed for disc brakes. The inboard side of the caliper contains the piston and cylinder and holds the inboard shoe. This can be seen in Figure 26-17. The outboard side holds the outboard shoe. When the cylinder is pressurized, the piston pushes the shoe against the disc. Pressure in the cylinder fluid chamber moves the caliper along its anchor to force the outboard shoe against the disc. Single pistons are larger than any one of the pistons in a four-piston caliper, in order to do the same amount of work. The single piston can be seen in the Caliper shown in Figure 26-18.

Disc brakes have no servo action. All their force depends upon fluid pressure. Their shoes are much smaller than shoes used in drum brakes, so more pressure is required to get the same braking response. Compared to dual servo brakes, a disc brake requires from four to five times the cylinder area and twice the hydraulic pressure to provide the same braking.

26-5 BRAKE ACTUATION PRINCIPLES

Hydraulic brakes are applied by the driver through an actuating system using hydraulic principles to multiply brake pedal force. The science of hydraulics is based on Pascal's principle (discussed in Section 23-7) which states that pressure applied to any area of an enclosed fluid is transmitted undiminished in all directions to every interior surface of the vessel. In brake actuating systems, the enclosed vessel is a master cylinder and wheel cylinder with connecting lines and hoses. The system is illustrated in Figure 26-19. Any pressure applied to the master cylinder is transmitted undiminished to each wheel cylinder.

419

Brake System Forces. Hydraulic pressure multiplied by the area on which it acts determines the force produced. For example, using customary measuring units, if 100 psi pressure were applied on a one square-inch surface, the force would be 100 pounds. If, however, this same 100 psi pressure were applied against a 1½ inch square surface, the total force would be 150 pounds. This principle applies to any amount of pressure and surface area. The total force equals square inches of area times the pressure. This system can also work in reverse. If a mechanical force were pushing on an area, it would produce hydraulic pressure. The formula for this reaction is:

$$\text{Pressure} = \frac{\text{Force}}{\text{Area}}$$

If a mechanical force of 50 pounds pushed on an area of 0.75 square inches, the total pressure would be 66 psi (50 lb/0.75 in.²).

In a brake actuating system, the driver applies a force through a mechanical linkage to the master cylinder piston. The master cylinder piston applies pressure to the enclosed hydraulic brake fluid. This pressure, in turn, pressing on the wheel cylinder pistons, will push the linings against the brake drum or disc.

For example, the brake pedal force that the driver applies is multiplied by the mechanical linkage ratio to apply force on the master cylinder piston as illustrated in Figure 26-20. If the driver applies a 75-pound force through a 7:1 linkage ratio, the force applied to the master cylinder

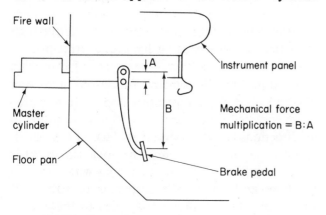

Fig. 26-20 Brake pedal mechanical force multiplication.

would be 525 pounds (75 × 7). This force divided by the master cylinder piston area will give the pressure in the hydraulic system. If the master cylinder bore diameter is one inch, its cross-sectional area is 0.785 square inches [π × (diameter/2)²] or (0.785 × diameter²). The hydraulic pressure, using the above mechanical force, is approximately 670 psi (525 lb/0.785 sq in.). Very often, the front and rear wheel cylinders are different sizes. If the front wheel cylinders in this example had a 1.125 in. diameter, their area would be 0.993 square in. (0.785 × 1.125²). The force pushing the front lining against the brake drum would be 665 pounds (670 psi × 0.993 sq in.).

If the rear brakes in the same example had a 0.875 inc. bore diameter, their piston area would be 0.600 square in. (0.785 × 0.875²). The force developed by the rear wheel cylinders to apply the rear shoes would be 402 pounds (670 psi × 0.600 sq in.).

If the vehicle in this example were equipped with front disc brakes instead of drum brakes, the wheel cylinders would be much larger. Using front wheel cylinders 2.5 in. in diameter, the cylinder area would be 4.90 square in. (0.785 × 2.5²). The force produced using the hydraulic pressure in the same example would be 3283 pounds (670 psi × 4.9 sq in.). Disc brakes require high forces such as this to apply the brakes. Power boosters are required to produce adequate braking force on heavy vehicles equipped with disc brakes.

In the above example, the driver's 75-pound force on the brake pedal resulted in a 665-pound force on the front linings with drum brakes and a 402-pound force on the rear linings. A higher force is usually required on the front brakes because they do a larger portion of the braking. Front disc brake force would be raised to 3283 pounds. The brake's hydraulic lines and hoses must be in good condition to withstand these pressures.

Force multiplication requires an equivalent increase in pedal travel. If the master cylinder had 1/2 the area of the wheel cylinder, the wheel cylinder output force would be twice the master cylinder input force, but the master cylinder piston travel would be twice as great as the wheel cylinder piston travel. Force is multiplied at the expense of pedal travel. This principle can be expressed as: output force × output travel = input force × input travel. This principle holds true only after the lining touches the drum or disc. The first part of the pedal travel is required to take up clearances in the linkage, cylinders, and lining-to-drum or lining-to-disc before pressure begins to be built up. This pedal movement is called *pedal free travel*. A high brake pedal indicates small clearances, while a low pedal indicates excess clearances. If the sum of the clearances becomes too large, the brakes will not apply on the first stroke, but will require "pumping" to get the shoes to touch the drum or disc. When the clearance is taken up, pressure can build up as described in the example above.

Brake Fluid. Water will transfer hydraulic force in an enclosed vessel. It would, however, be very unsatisfactory for brake fluid. Fluid used for brake systems is a specially compounded nonpetroleum liquid. It must remain as a liquid throughout the temperature extremes encountered. Its viscosity or thickness must change very little between the temperature limits encountered. Brake hydraulic systems use a number of different metals and rubbers. Brake fluid must not corrode the metal or attack the rubber. It must also be able to lubricate the moving parts in the master and wheel cylinders.

The brake fluid's most critical characteristic is its boiling point. Friction heat from stopping the vehicle raises the fluid's temperature. If the fluid temperature reaches the boiling point, it will turn to vapor. The brake pedal action would then become spongy, as it does with air in the line. Required pressures could not be developed and the brakes would become ineffective.

The Society of Automotive Engineers have specified 374°F (190°C) as the minimum brake fluid boiling point requirements in their handbook specification number J1703, which is a refinement of the older fluid specification 70R3. Most brake fluids exceed these minimum temperature specifications.

Brake fluids are manufactured by large chemical companies. They sell bulk fluid to other companies who, in turn, package it for the consumer under their own label. To ensure use of the correct brake fluid, most automobile manufacturer's package the required quality fluid and sell it by number through their own parts departments.

The minimum boiling point specifications of heavy-duty brake fluid must be at least 374°F (190°C). Brake fluid is also available with boiling points of 400°, 470°, 500°, and 550°F (204°, 243°, 260°, and 288°C). Disc brake fluid tends to get hotter than the drum brake fluid because the wheel cylinder is a bore right in the caliper body. Much heat is absorbed by the caliper and this heats the fluid. One automobile company recommends only the use of 550°F (288°C) boiling point fluid which they market through their own parts departments. The 550°F (288°C) fluid should be used on all disc brake systems. Use of any other heavy-duty brake fluid may allow the fluid to boil. For safety, the manufacturer's recommendations must be followed.

26-6 DETAILS OF BRAKE OPERATING COMPONENTS

The brake pedal mechanical linkages used to operate the master cylinder will differ between car models. The brake pedal is usually suspended from a channel bracketed between the steering column-to-dash attachment point and the fire wall. A push rod connects the pedal to the master cylinder piston. The location of the push rod pivot point between the pedal pivot and foot pad determines the mechanical force multiplication.

Master Cylinder. The master cylinder is a cast iron body containing a cylinder bore, a fluid reservoir, and fluid passages. Holes or ports are drilled between the reservoir and the cylinder bore to allow make-up fluid to enter the system or to allow expanded fluid to return to the reservoir.

A single master cylinder will be used to simplify the description of master cylinder operations. This can be followed in Figure 26-21. The master cylinder piston is a long piston with two lip-type cup seals, one close to each end. The inner seal, called a *primary cup*, is used to build up hydraulic pressure in the system. The outer seal, called a *secondary cup*, keeps fluid from leaking out of the master cylinder. An *inlet* or *breather port* between the cups allows any fluid that gets past the primary cup to return to the reservoir. The only pressure against the secondary cup is caused by the weight of the fluid in the reservoir. A piston spring holds the piston against the push rod coming from the pedal linkage. When the brake pedal is released, the piston is moved to its rest position at the push rod end of the cylinder bore. In this position, a small hole, called a *compensation port*, on the

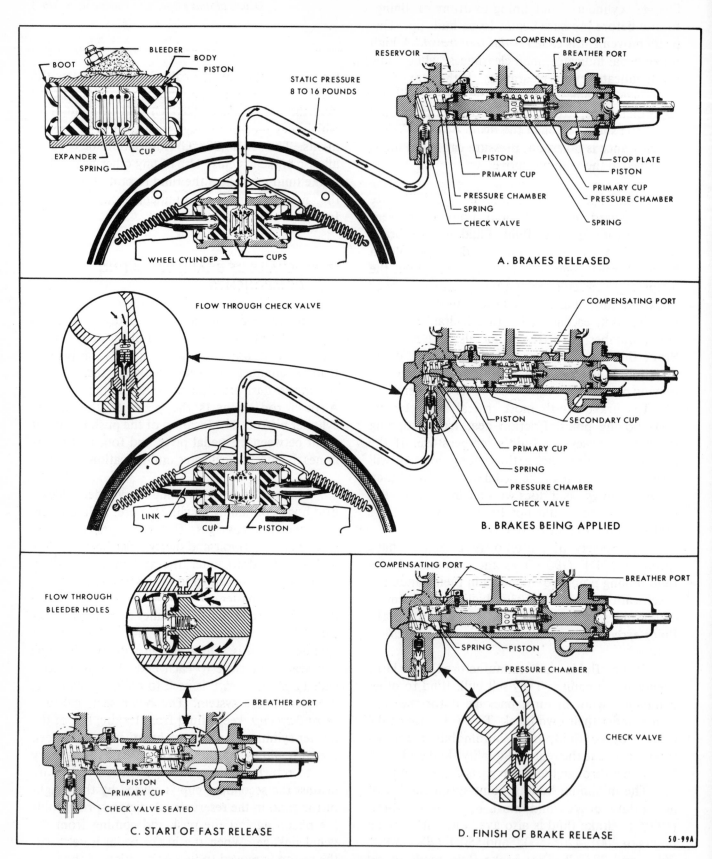

Fig. 26-21 Principle of the hydraulic brake system operation
(Buick Motor Division, General Motors Corporation).

spring side of the primary cup, is open between the cylinder bore and the reservoir. The lip of the primary piston must move across this compensating port before any fluid will be pushed into the lines or wheel cylinders. This movement or pedal *free travel* is part of the clearance or lash that must be taken up before brake pressure will build up.

Continued piston movement toward the outlet end of the cylinder opens a *check valve* that allows fluid to enter the brake lines. Check valves are used only with drum brakes. The lines and master cylinder are always full of fluid and free of air, so on application only sufficient fluid will enter the system to move the linings against the drum or disc. Additional force on the pedal increases pressure with no fluid flow.

When the brake pedal is released, the brake return springs pull the linings from the drum. This forces retraction of the wheel cylinder pistons. In disc brakes, the seal action retracts the piston. In both types, the piston movement returns a small amount of fluid to the master cylinder and the master cylinder piston is pushed back by the piston spring to its at-rest position. If the fluid is warm and expanded, excess fluid goes into the reservoir through the compensating port. When additional fluid is required in the system as the piston returns, fluid enters through the inlet port, goes through holes in the piston, then around the back side of the primary cup lip.

The residual check valve used with drum brakes holds from six to eighteen psi pressure in the hydraulic system. This pressure holds the parts under a slight force to minimize free play clearances in the system. This slight system pressure also prevents air leakage into the system. It is a positive means of keeping the system full of fluid and ready to operate each time the pedal is applied.

Master cylinders have been divided for safety

Fig. 26-22 Cross section of a typical drum brake master cylinder (The Bendix Corporation).

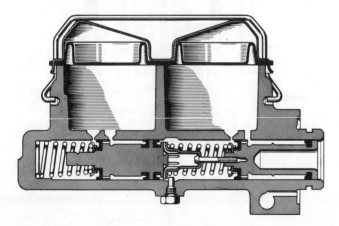

to form two separate hydraulic systems. Loss of pressure in one system does not cause complete loss of brakes as it does on single master cylinder systems. The pistons of the two systems are in the same cylinder bore, one behind the other, illustrated in Figure 26-22, so that pedal pressure is effective on both. This type of master cylinder is called a *dual* master cylinder or a *tandem* master cylinder.

Each section of the master cylinder operates the brakes on one axle, either front or rear. The piston closest to the push rod is called the *primary piston* and the piston furthest from the push rod is called the *secondary piston*. In some vehicles, the primary piston operates the rear wheel cylinders while in other systems, it operates the front wheel cylinders.

Hydraulically, each portion of the dual tandem master cylinder acts in the same manner as a single master cylinder. The difference is the way the secondary piston is moved. The primary piston is moved directly by the push rod. The pressure that is built up in the primary cylinder pushes on a reversed piston cup located on the primary end of the floating secondary piston. This force is transmitted through the secondary piston, sometimes called a *slave piston,* to the fluid behind the secondary piston. This method of moving the secondary piston equalizes the pressure in the two separate brake pressure systems. There is a piston spring between the pistons and a second spring behind the slave secondary piston. The primary spring between the pistons is stronger than the secondary spring. These springs help return the pistons to their at-rest position after brake pedal pressure is released.

Each piston has an extension on its lower end. If pressure is lost in the primary system, the projection on the primary piston bottoms against the secondary piston, moving it mechanically. If pressure is lost in the secondary system, the projection on the end of the secondary piston bottoms on the end of the cylinder. This allows pressure to be built up between the primary piston cup and the inverted secondary piston cup to pressurize the primary system.

Tandem master cylinders used with disc brakes omit the residual pressure check valve from the portion of the cylinder connected to the disc

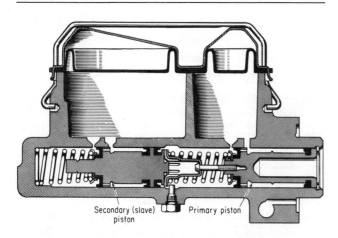

Fig. 26-23 Cross section of a typical disc brake master cylinder (The Bendix Corporation).

Secondary (slave) piston — Primary piston

brakes. Disc brake cylinders are larger than drum brake wheel cylinders, so the master cylinder has a larger reservoir for the front wheel portion. This can be seen in Figure 26–23.

Brake Warning Light or Distributor Switch. All automobiles that are provided with tandem brake master cylinders use a warning light to immediately indicate to the driver if one of the brake hydraulic systems is not functioning. The brake warning light switch takes the place of the tee fitting that would divide the flow of hydraulic fluid to the front and rear wheels on single master cylinder systems. The switch consists of a small two-headed piston that is centered by springs. This can be seen in Figure 26–24. Pressure from the primary piston is impressed against one head

of the piston and the secondary piston pressure against the other head. An insulated contact button is located between them. When one system fails, pressure in that system falls and the piston shifts toward the failed pressure, touching the insulated contact. This grounds to complete the electrical circuit of an instrument panel brake warning light. The centering springs are strong enough so slight variations in brake pressure that normally occur will not actuate the warning light.

Lines and Hoses. Brake pressures may approach 1500 psi when a strong person makes a panic stop in a car equipped with power-assisted brakes. Hydraulic brake pressure lines must have adequate strength to withstand these pressures. Manufacturers use steel tubing with double flared ends and inverted flare nut fittings. The double flaring procedure is pictured in Figures 26–25 and 26–26. Some of the lines are even double-walled steel. Special heavy-duty copper lines can be used, but they are much more expensive and are used only where corrosion resistance is required. Common copper lines have thin walls that will burst under high hydraulic brake pressures.

Metal tubing is used from the master cylinder to the bottom of the vehicle frame structure. A loop is provided between the master cylinder and frame to absorb any slight motion that might occur. One hose is used between the frame-mounted tubing and the rear axle fitting. Tubing runs along the rear axle housing from the fitting to the wheel cylinders. One hose is used on each front brake from the frame-mounted tubing to the wheel cylinder.

Brake hoses must be strong enough to retain

Fig. 26–24 Brake warning light switch (The Bendix Corporation).

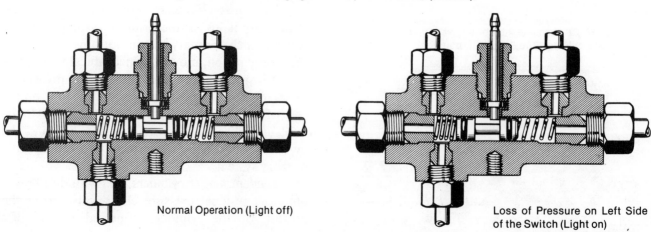

Normal Operation (Light off)

Loss of Pressure on Left Side of the Switch (Light on)

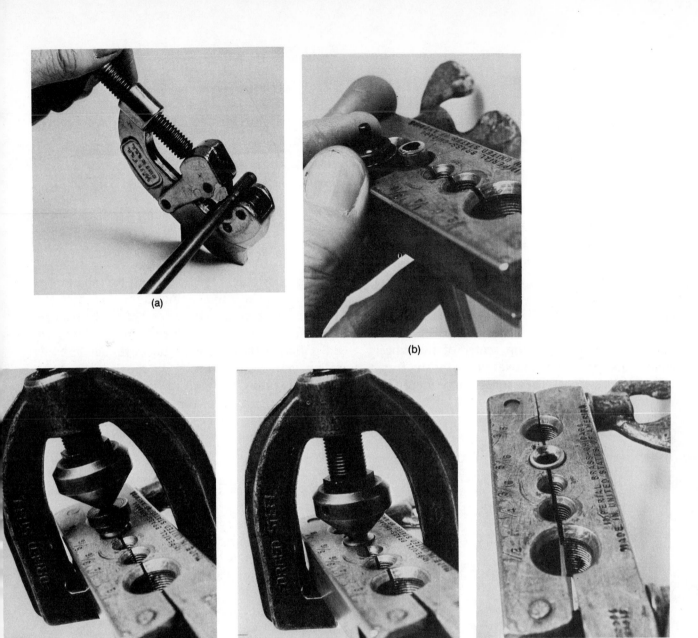

(a)

(b)

(c)

(d)

(e)

Fig. 26-25 Double flaring an end on metal brake tubing. (a) Cutting the tubing, (b) clamping the tubing at the correct length in the flaring tool, (c) upsetting the tubing end in the first operation, (d) finishing double flare in the second operation, (e) complete second flare operation.

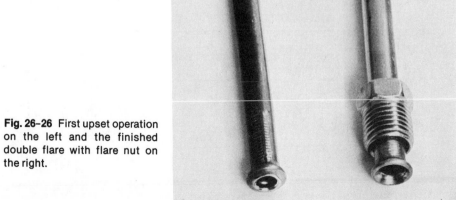

Fig. 26-26 First upset operation on the left and the finished double flare with flare nut on the right.

the hydraulic pressures encountered. Generally, they are as short as possible, but still long enough to avoid being stretched. They are routed across the suspension so they will not interfere with suspension motion.

Drum Brake Wheel Cylinders. Cast iron wheel cylinders are attached to the backing plate for firm support. A sealing gasket is used between them to keep contaminants out of the brake assembly. The brake hose or tubing is attached to the wheel cylinder fitting on the back side of the backing plate. The cylinder is provided with a bleeder screw fitting leading from the top center of the wheel cylinder bore to allow removal of all the air from the hydraulic system. These items can be identified in Figure 26-27.

Fig. 26-27 Brake line and bleeder fitting attached to the wheel cylinder located in the backing plate.

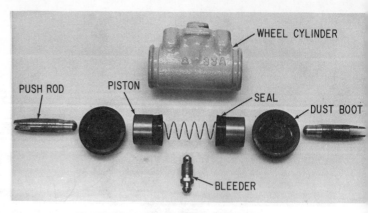

Fig. 26-28 Disassembled wheel cylinder.

Wheel cylinders are fitted with two aluminum pistons having an anodized finish, one on each end of the cylinder bore. The outer end of the pistons have a seat for the shoe push rod pin. The inboard end is flat to back up the wheel cylinder lip-type sealing cup. Some wheel cylinders have a light spring separating the cups to help keep lash from the brake system. A piston cup expander may be used on each end of the spring to hold the cup lip against the sides of the cylinder bore. Figure 26-28 is an exploded view of a typical wheel cylinder.

Dust boots are fitted over the cylinder end and around the push rod. This keeps the dust and moisture from the cylinder surface to help prevent sticking or corrosion.

The outer ends of the push rods are slotted to fit into notches on the brake shoe web.

Disc Brake Wheel Cylinders. Disc brake wheel cylinders are located in the calipers. The first disc brakes used on domestic passenger cars had four pistons in each caliper, two on the inside of the disc and two on the outside of the disc. The caliper had to be designed for disassembly in two halves in order to manufacture and service the cylinder bores. This can be seen in Figure 26-29. The pres-

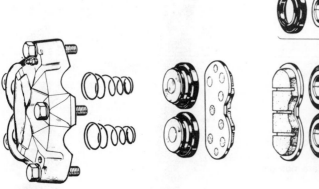
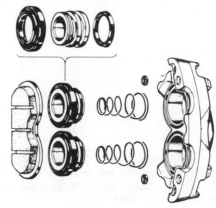

Fig. 26-29 Exploded view of a four-piston caliper (The Bendix Corporation).

sure areas of the two cylinder halves were interconnected with either internal passages or with external tubing to ensure equal pressure in all four pistons.

The pistons hold the linings close to the disc while at rest so little lost motion is present to cause excess pedal travel. Some early designs encountered a phenomenon called *knock back* as the disc hit the shoes while rotating. This would knock the pistons back into the bore and thus cause excess pedal travel on the next brake application. To compensate for knock back, a spring was installed behind the aluminum piston to give it a slight push toward the disc while still minimizing shoe to disc drag. The drag effects of this system used 0.8 hp at 100 mph, which is insignificant. This slight drag did not cause excessive wear.

The four-piston type *fixed caliper* uses a cast iron body securely attached to the steering knuckle through an adapter plate. Any variation in disc position or shoe wear is compensated for by the respective positions of the wheel pistons in their cylinder bore. This principle is illustrated in Figure 26-30. The fixed caliper has been replaced by a cast iron single-piston *floating caliper* on the majority of passenger cars. The single-piston caliper is one piece, so it is more rigid. Machining one bore uses less assembly time and is more economical.

A single-piston floating caliper works like a small hydraulic press. The portion of the caliper outside of the disc is like the press table, and the inside portion with the cylinder is like the press ram. If the press were turned on its side and supported on rods, it could move to center on the disc. The table would pull on one side as hard as the ram pushed on the other side. This principle is pictured in Figure 26–31.

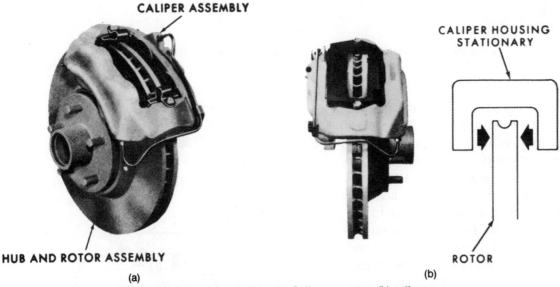

Fig. 26–30 Four-piston caliper. (a) Caliper on rotor, (b) caliper operation principle. (Kelsey-Hays Company).

Fig. 26–31 Single-piston caliper. (a) Caliper on rotor, (b) caliper operating principle. (Kelsey-Hays Company).

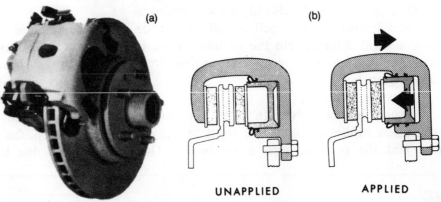

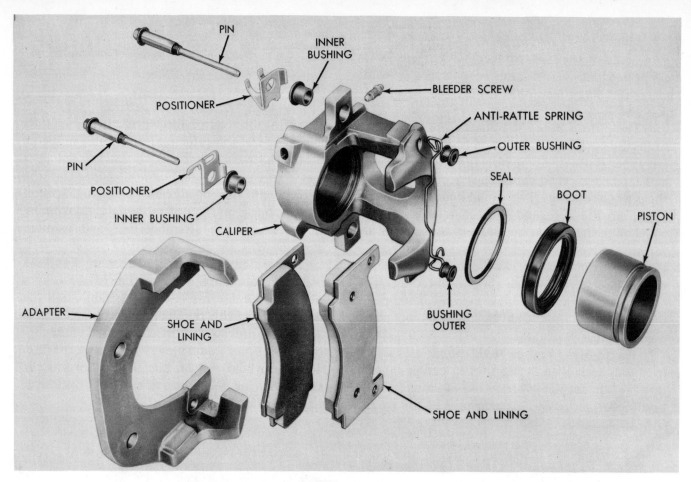

Fig. 26-32 Disassembled single piston caliper with part identification (Chrysler Motors Corporation).

The large single piston is formed of stamped steel, precision ground, and plated with nickel-chrome. The plating gives it a hard durable surface. A rectangular section seal fits into a groove in the wall of the cylinder and presses against the piston skirt. The open end of the piston contacts the lining. This design minimizes heat transfer to the fluid. Hydraulic pressure on the piston head pushes the piston toward the inner surface of the disc and the pressure in the cylinder head pulls the caliper toward the outer disc surface, applying the brake. Figure 26-32 shows an exploded view of a typical single piston caliper.

Movement of the piston and caliper distort the rectangular piston seal, as illustrated in Figure 26-33. When pressure is relieved, the seal returns to its normal position. This action pulls the piston back a slight distance into the cylinder. This, in turn, allows the shoe to move back to keep from dragging on the disc.

Proportioning Valves. In most applications where disc brakes are used, the front brakes are disc and the rear are dual servo brakes. Disc

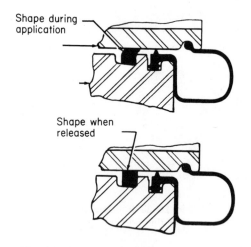

Fig. 26-33 Seal action to return caliper piston after application (The Bendix Corporation).

brakes require a higher pressure to get the same braking effort as the dual servo brakes, unless the disc brakes have large cylinders and use lining materials with a high coefficient of friction. Therefore, the front disc brakes and rear drum brakes require different pressures for proper braking. In a hard stop, the effective weight transfer increases the front disc brake requirements even more. If the brakes received equal pressure, the rear wheels would lock, causing rear end skid. A *proportioning valve* is used to provide a reduced pressure to the rear wheels in hard stops and to prevent skid.

The proportioning valve, located in the rear brake line, has a sliding core. Under light braking pressure, the fluid passes freely through the valve. On heavy applications, a pressure area causes the core to shift in the direction of fluid flow, blocking the outlet to the rear wheels. The outlet side of the sliding core senses outlet pressure on a large surface area. This balances the input pressure on a small pressure area. The output pressure increases as a percentage of the input pressure in proportion to the valve's balancing surface areas. Upon brake release, the input pressure drops, the proportioning valve opens, and the fluid freely returns to the master cylinder. This action can be followed on the drawings in Figure 26-34.

Metering Valve. On slippery or icy road conditions, light braking with the disc brakes may lock the front wheels. If this occurs, directional control

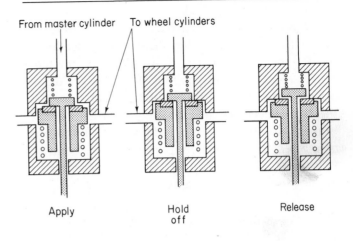

Fig. 26-35 Principle of the metering valve.

is lost. Some vehicles install a metering valve in the front wheel brake line to prevent front brake application during light braking. At pressures above 100 psi, the front brakes receive full master cylinder pressure.

In the metering valve, a spring holds a seal against master cylinder pressure. When the pressure is sufficient to move the valve against the spring, much like a pressure relief valve, the valve opens to allow the pressure to go to the front wheel cylinders. Upon release, a second valve allows free return of fluid to the master cylinder. These principles can be seen in Figure 26-35.

The metering valve is equipped with an external push rod that can be used to open the internal relief valve. The relief valve is held open for bleeding air from the hydraulic system.

Some vehicles are equipped with both a proportioning valve and a metering valve. Other vehicles may have either one or the other. Still other vehicles may not require either of these valves.

Fig. 26-34 Principle of the proportioning valve.

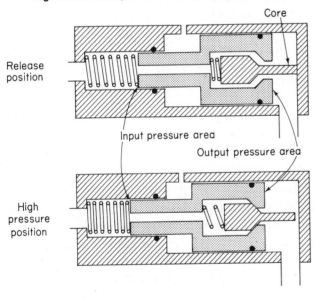

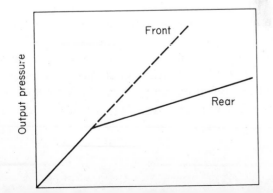

Parking Brakes. The parking brakes lock the rear wheels when set. They do this by either locking the propeller shaft or by applying the rear brakes. Modern automobiles using rear drum brakes have a mechanical linkage that bypasses the rear wheel cylinder to apply the rear service brakes. A cable from the parking brake linkage is connected to the driver's parking brake control. It is designed in a manner that will equalize the application force between both rear brakes.

When the parking brake is applied, the cable pulls on one end of the parking brake *lever* within the brake. The other end of the lever is attached near the heel end of the secondary shoe. A *strut* is hinged between the lever and the primary shoe. As the linkage expands the brake shoes, the secondary shoe lining touches the drum. Additional movement of the parking brake control will move the primary shoe lining into contact with the drum.

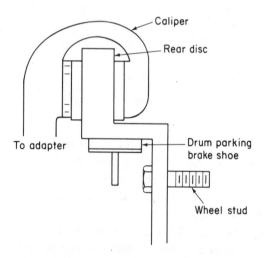

Fig. 26-36 Drum parking brake in a rear disc brake.

Fig. 26-37 Parking brake located in the rear caliper piston.

When both linings contact the drum, the rear brakes will lock. When the control is released, the brake shoe return springs pull the shoes from the drum to allow wheel rotation.

With four-wheel disc brakes, two different types of parking brakes are used. One uses a special small drum-type parking brake located within the brake disc, as shown in the illustration Figure 26-36. It operates in the same manner as the parking brake just discussed, using a cam—a somewhat different method of expanding the shoes. The second type of parking brake has a ball/ramp mechanism located within the wheel cylinder piston and caliper, pictured in Figure 26-37. Three balls are trapped between two ramps, a stationary one on the wheel cylinder piston end of the actuator and a rotating one on the caliper end. As the lever is pulled by the parking brake control cable, it rotates the caliper-end ramp, wedging the balls between the two ramps. This mechanically forces the piston from the caliper, which moves the linings against the disc to lock rear wheel rotation. The piston gradually has to move out of the caliper cylinder bore to maintain the normal lining-to-disc clearance as the brake linings wear during service brake use. An integral automatic adjuster is designed into the parking brake actuator assembly to reposition it to compensate for lining wear. The automatic adjuster is not repairable but is replaced as a complete unit when it malfunctions (Figure 26-37).

26-7 POWER BRAKES

Power brakes have been mentioned several times in this chapter. Their function is to provide the required hydraulic pressure while using much less pedal effort. In many cases, pedal travel has been reduced. This increases the power brake's force multiplication requirement.

Engine vacuum and atmospheric pressure are used as the power source to operate power brakes. Vacuum is applied to a chamber on one side of a diaphragm and atmospheric pressure to a chamber on the other side. This causes the diaphragm to tend to move toward the vacuum side. Diaphragm movement force is directed to the master cylinder piston through a push rod. The force on the master cylinder increases as the difference in pressure between the vacuum and atmospheric chambers increases. An assembly is shown in Figure 26-38.

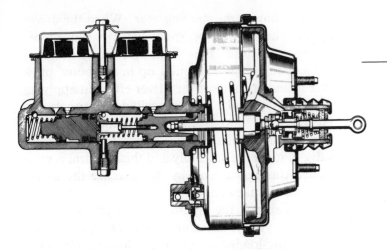

Fig. 26-28. Sectional view of a typical power brake unit (The Bendix Corporation).

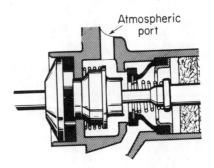

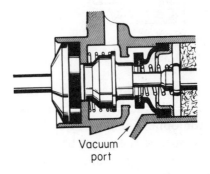

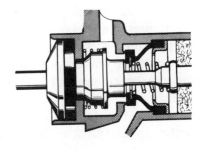

Fig. 26-39 Principle of the power brake control valve during apply, (atmospheric valve open), release (vacuum valve open), and hold (both valves closed).

In the at-rest position with the brake released, the pressure in both chambers is equal. When both chambers are under vacuum while at rest, the system is called a *vacuum suspended* power brake. If both chambers are under atmospheric pressure, it is called an *atmospheric suspended* power brake. For brake application, a control valve allows air to enter the back chamber of the vacuum suspended unit. The valve in the atmospheric suspended unit allows vacuum to be applied to the front chamber during application. On application, both units have atmospheric pressure in the rear chamber and vacuum in the front chamber.

An actuating push rod connects the pedal linkage to the control valve. The control valve housing or body is located in the diaphragm center. The control valve operation is shown in Figure 26–39. When the brakes are applied, the control valve moves forward, opening the required passages to unbalance the diaphragm chambers. Unbalancing causes the diaphragm to move forward, carrying the control valve housing forward with it. When the valve housing moves forward far enough, it catches up with the control valve, closing the valves so the diaphragm and valve body move forward to a new *hold* position. This type of action, which adds power effort to the mechanical input effort, is a form of servo action.

When the brake pedal is released, the control valve moves to the back of the body, opening the at-rest valving, equalizing the pressures in the two diaphragm chambers. A spring in the front chamber pushes the diaphragm back to its at-rest position. This diaphragm movement allows the master cylinder piston to return to its at-rest position.

Some power brakes require more assist than can be provided by a single diaphragm. These units use two diaphragms in tandem with a chamber-dividing support plate between them. This provides two atmospheric chambers and two vacuum chambers to double the power boost effect in the same diameter power brake unit. This can be seen in Figure 26–40.

Many trucks use air pressure to help the driver apply the brakes. Engine manifold vacuum has been the only source of power for assisting braking on passenger cars. It is the least expensive of all the assist methods. Unfortunately, the vacu-

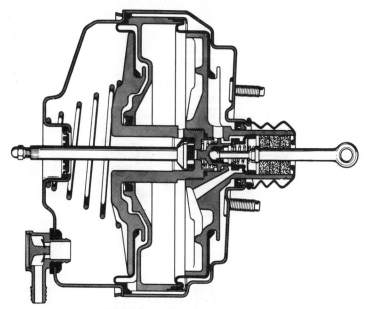

Fig. 26-40 Sectional view of a typical tandem diaphragm power brake booster (The Bendix Corporation).

um available on the domestic automobile has been reduced with the addition of emission controls. Some automobiles do not have enough vacuum to properly operate the power brakes. In 1975, the Ford Motor Company installed a hydraulic booster, called *Hydro-Boost,* rather than a large vacuum booster, to assist the application of the brakes on their luxury automobiles equipped with four-wheel disc brakes. It uses the power steering pump to provide the hydraulic pressure required to assist the driver to apply the brakes. A simplified drawing showing the operating parts of the Hydro-Boost is illustrated in Figure 26-41.

The power steering fluid is pumped through an open-center spool valve in the Hydro-Boost

before going to the steering gear. When the driver applies the brake, the spool valve is moved off center to close the fluid return port. This causes the pressure to build up in the boost pressure chamber to assist the driver effort in applying the normal brake master cylinder through the Hydro-Boost output rod. The amount of assist effort is controlled by the position of the spool valve in its sleeve assembly and this, in turn, is controlled through a lever by the distance the driver moves the brake pedal.

For safety, the Hydro-Boost is equipped with a reserve system, called an *accumulator,* consisting of a spring-loaded piston in a cylinder. When the system is in operation, the power steering fluid enters the accumulator. It pushes the piston against the spring. The spring holds the fluid under pressure. In the event of engine failure, the pressurized hydraulic fluid in the accumulator is used to assist the driver to bring the automobile to a normal stop. The accumulator holds enough fluid under pressure for two normal stops. When no hydraulic fluid pressure is available, the brakes will apply normally. This will require a high pedal force to move the master cylinder push rod. The brakes operate in a normal manner from the master cylinder. The Hydro-Boost used in 1975 had no service parts, so it had to be replaced as a complete unit when it malfunctioned.

Other variations of hydraulically operated brake systems are anticipated for use in future heavy automobiles. Lighter automobiles have lower braking requirements and can be stopped satisfactorily without power brakes.

Fig. 26-41 Simplified drawing of a hydro boost power brake unit operating off the power steering hydraulic system.

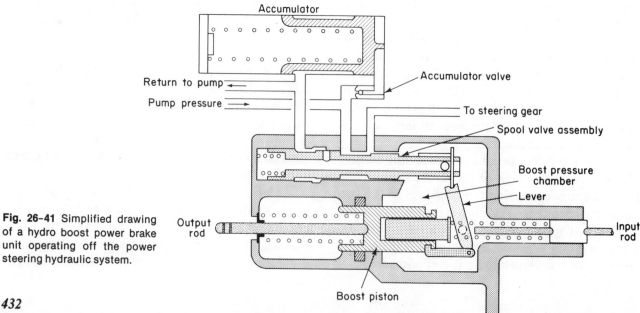

REVIEW QUESTIONS

1. What happens to the moving energy of the automobile as it is brought to a stop with the brakes? [INTRODUCTION]

2. When does the maximum braking effect occur? [INTRODUCTION]

3. What is servo-action in brakes? [26–1]

4. What is coefficient of friction and why is it important in brakes? [26–2]

5. What is the comfortable and maximum deceleration rate for passenger cars? [26–2]

6. Describe how the weight transfer occurs during braking. [26–2]

7. What affects the stopping distance when braking? [26–2]

8. What causes brake fade? [26–2]

9. What type of brake is most likely to fade and what type is least likely to fade? [26–2]

10. What suspension parts retain brake torque? [26–2]

11. What are the emergency brake requirements? [26–2]

12. Why are antilock brakes used on the rear rather than on the front wheels? [26–2]

13. What type of lining materials are used in drum brakes? [26–3]

14. Why is the secondary lining usually longer than the primary lining? [26–3]

15. How are linings fastened to the shoes? [26–3]

16. What forces the shoe and lining against the drum? [26–3]

17. What pulls the shoe and lining from the drum? [26–3]

18. What limits the maximum drum size? [26–3]

19. What part of the drum is cast and what part is stamped? [26–3]

20. What is the advantage of cooling fins in the disc? [26–3]

21. Why have single piston caliper designs replaced the four-piston caliper? [26–4]

22. What method is used to provide the front brake shoes with more applied force than the rear shoes? [26–5]

23. Why is it important to select the specified brake fluid? [26–5]

24. What is the purpose of the breather and compensating ports in a master cylinder? [26–6]

25. Why do drum brakes use a check valve on the master cylinder outlet? [26–6]

26. Why are master cylinders divided into two separate sections? [26–6]

27. Describe the action of a tandem master cylinder when the primary piston seal fails. [26–6]

28. How does the driver know when one part of the master cylinder has failed? [26–6]

29. From what types of materials are brake lines made? [26–6]

30. Why are double flare ends used on brake line tubing? [26–6]

31. Where are hoses used in the brake system? [26–6]

32. Where is the bleeder screw located in the wheel cylinder? [26–6]

33. How does a four-piston caliper compensate for shoe and disc wear? [26–6]

34. Besides the number of pistons what is the major difference between one-and four-piston calipers? [26–6]

35. What pulls the piston from the shoe on disc wheel cylinders? [26–6]

36. Why is a proportioning valve required on some automobiles? [26–6]

37. How does the function of a metering valve differ from a proportioning valve? [26–6]

38. What has delayed the application of four-wheel disc brakes on passenger cars? [26–6]

39. What is the function of the power brake? [26–7]

40. What is meant by vacuum suspended power brakes? [26–7]

41. How does the power brake apply the master cylinder? [26–7]

42. What happens to the control valve housing as the pedal moves downward? [26–7]

43. What is the advantage of a Hydro-Boost power brake? [26–7]

brake
system service

Brakes are serviced in a routine manner when a brake problem exists. The technician must understand the operation of all of the brake system components to do a fast, accurate diagnosis of braking problems. A preventive maintenance inspection of the brake system should be done at least once each year or each 10,000 miles (16,000 km), whichever occurs first. Brakes that are not equipped with automatic adjusters should be examined each time the brakes are adjusted. A routine brake inspection will usually show any abnormal conditions so they can be corrected before they cause a brake problem.

The driver notices brake problems during braking, either in the vehicle response to braking or in the brake pedal feel. A brake problem exists when one of the brakes controls more or less than the other brakes. This causes the automobile to pull toward the side with the most braking. A brake problem exists if the brakes either grab suddenly or fail to stop the automobile rapidly. Brake pedal response is noticed as excessive pedal travel, spongy pedal, hard pedal, fading pedal, and pulsing pedal. Unusual brake noise and chatter are indications of problems within the brake assembly.

Brake noise results from vibrating parts. During a stop, the lining may momentarily grab the drum, then release. This cycle may occur at a relatively fast rate. If the vibration frequency is within the audible range, it can be noisy. Most drum brakes are fitted with dampening or anti-rattle springs and retainers to reduce brake noise. Drums often have a spring around their outer edge to dampen drum vibrations. Excessive brake noise may be the result of failure of one of these parts.

It could also result from a hard or glazed brake lining and from drum hard spots.

27-1 BRAKE PROBLEMS

When the brakes are in the normal released position, the linings are positioned approximately 0.010 in. (0.25 mm) from the braking surface of the drum or just clear of the braking surface of the disc. As the brakes are applied, the first brake pedal movement will take up the lash in the pedal linkage called *free play*. Further movement will push the linings into contact with the braking surface. This movement is called pedal *free travel*. Braking begins to occur as additional force is applied to move the brake pedal further. The amount of vehicle braking depends on the force put on the pedal and the coefficient of friction between the lining and the braking surface. Anything that changes the pedal free play, the coefficient of friction, or the brake hydraulic actuating system will cause a braking problem.

As the linings wear, the lining-to-braking surface clearance will increase. This increases the pedal free play. If the brakes are not adjusted, the free play can be so severe that the pedal will have to be pumped several times to move the linings against the braking surface before braking can begin. Automatic adjusters in most modern automobiles prevent this problem when they are operating correctly. A *low* brake pedal usually indicates excess lining-to-braking surface clearance. An unusually *high* brake pedal position indicates insufficient clearance, and this is generally accompanied by dragging brakes. A high pedal could be the result of improper brake or linkage adjustment, malfunctioning of the return springs, or a problem in the hydraulic brake system components, such as a plugged master cylinder compensation port or check valve.

The brake coefficient of friction changes as the brake temperature increases. High-temperature brake linings have a low coefficient of friction, causing *fade*. At high temperatures, the drum diameter expands, so the linings have to move further to contact the drum. This tends to increase brake pedal travel as fade occurs. Discs also increase in diameter as they get hot. With the linings pushing on the side of the disc, expansion has no effect on the brake pedal position.

Lining contamination will affect brake coefficient of friction. Contamination comes from handling the lining or the drum with dirty hands, from thrown-off wheel bearing grease, from rear axle oil seal leakage, from wheel cylinder brake fluid leakage, from water, and from dust or dirt. Slight amounts of contaminants may increase the coefficient of friction while greater amounts of the same contaminant will reduce it. When brake pull occurs, all the brakes should be inspected to determine the exact cause. Contaminated linings should be replaced and the cause of contamination corrected.

Uneven vehicle braking response results from unequal coefficients of friction in the different brakes of the vehicle. If the braking surfaces, lining conditions, or return springs are different for brakes on the same axle, either front or rear, the vehicle will pull toward the brake that is giving the greatest braking effort. This can result from mismatched parts, from unequal wear, and from lining contamination. Contamination and wear can be determined by a visual inspection of the parts. Mismatched brake parts may not be obvious but should be checked. Brake return springs are color-coded for matching. If all conditions appear normal, the linings should be replaced with matched linings. This will usually correct brake pull.

Abnormal pedal action results from leakage out of the system, from internal fluid leakage, from improperly operating brake cylinders and valves, and from out-of-round or warped brake drums or discs. Low fluid level in the master cylinder reservoir indicates excessive wear or leakage from the system. Fluid can leak from cracked brake lines and hoses. It can leak past wheel cylinder seals and around master cylinder seals. When external leakage occurs, the leaking unit is either rebuilt or replaced.

No external leaks exist if the fluid level is normal. Internal leakage around seals will cause the pedal to gradually move toward the floorboard as the pedal is held down with a light continuous application force. This is called *pedal fade*. Air in the brake system makes a soft *spongy* pedal. This is corrected by bleeding the air from the system. A *hard* pedal is caused by an improperly operating master cylinder or power brake unit or by a low coefficient of friction between the linings and the braking surface. Front or rear wheel grabbing on disc/drum brake systems will occur when the proportioning valve or metering valve malfunctions or when one side of the master cylinder malfunctions. A pedal moving in and out or *pulsating* as the brakes are applied results from warped brake drums or discs. The only way to correct this type of problem is to recondition the braking surface of the drum or disc.

A road test and an inspection of the brakes will aid the technician in an analysis of the type of brake system problem. This can direct him to the item causing the problem so he can make a quick, accurate repair. Normally, the arrival of the first brake problem is an indication that the entire brake system needs to be reconditioned.

27–2 BRAKE SYSTEM INSPECTION

A routine brake system inspection starts with a visual inspection of exposed brake lines and hoses. Any sign of abrasion, rust, or cracks calls for a close examination. If the condition of any part is questionable, it should be replaced. The inspection includes a check of the fluid level in the master cylinder. The reservoir should be nearly full of clear fluid as pictured in Figure 27–1. Low fluid indicates excessive brake wear or an external fluid leak. If the cause of low fluid is brake wear, the master cylinder can be filled. If fluid is low because a leak exists, the leak should be repaired before brake fluid is added. If the fluid is dirty, it should be drained and the system flushed and refilled

Fig. 27-2 Measuring the brake pedal travel.

with the proper grade of brake fluid. Petroleum-based oils should not be used in automobile brakes because the oil will cause the rubber brake parts to swell. This will cause fluid leakage and loss of brakes.

The brake pedal should have ¼ to ½ in. (6 to 13 mm) free play and it should give full braking application with the pedal at least one in. (25 mm) above the floor pan. Brake application should operate the stop lights. The brake pedal position is measured as shown in Figure 27–2.

In automobiles with power brakes, the power brake unit operation can be checked after exhausting the vacuum reservoir by pumping the brake. While holding the brake pedal down, start the engine. The brake pedal will be felt to move slightly downward as the engine vacuum builds up immediately after the engine starts. The power brake unit is not functioning if such movement is not observed.

The brake inspection includes a visual check of at least one brake assembly. On drum brake systems, the right front brake is considered to be representative of all the brakes. The drum is pulled and the brake examined. On drum/disc brake systems, a rear drum is checked. All four brakes should be carefully checked when a brake problem exists.

A brake inspection of drum brakes requires the removal of the wheel and drum. To do this, the wheel cover is removed and the wheel nuts are loosened. The automobile is then jacked and sup-

Fig. 27-1 Checking the brake fluid level in the master cylinder reservoir.

ported on jack stands so that the wheel will be off the floor. With the automobile on *jack stands,* there is no danger of it falling. The wheel nuts are then removed and the wheel lifted off the hub. Front brake drums are removed by removing the dust cover, cotter pin, and hub retaining nut. Care must be exercised to keep dirt from the wheel bearings as the hub is removed. The rear hub may slide off the wheel studs. Some rear drums have sheet metal retaining nuts or cap screws that require removal before the drum can be lifted off the axle flange. Drums having excessive wear will have a ridge around the open side. On these drums, the brake shoes and the star wheel will have to be adjusted to provide maximum lining-to-drum clearance before the drum can be lifted off. Never use a puller on the edge of the drum because it will damage the brake assembly and usually warp the drum. Rear drums sometimes seize to the axle flange. Tapping on the drum near the flange will usually loosen it, and penetrating oil will help. In severe cases, the drum web will have to be heated. This causes the drum web to expand and the expansion loosens the drum from the flange. The heat may warp the drum so it is standard practice to recondition the drum after using heat for removal. Figure 27-3 shows a rear drum

Fig. 27-3 Checking the condition of the rear brake drum and brake assembly.

removed from a passenger car with 33,000 miles (52,800 km) of mixed city and highway driving.

With the drum removed, examine the drum braking surface condition. Maximum wear allowed before replacement is 0.090 in. (2.28 mm) over the original diameter. Domestic drum brakes are usually made in full inch sizes (8, 9, 10, 11, and 12 in.). Specifications should be checked before condemning the drum. The general condition of the brake drum is checked for cracks in the web at the bolt circle and along the outside edge of the axle flange. These cracks would cause rough brake operation or a chattering sound. The braking surface is also checked for scoring, enlargement of the open side (bell mouth), wear in the center (concave), wear on the edges (convex), high center, hard spots, heat checks, out-of-round, and warpage.

The open side of the drum has a heavy ridge and often includes a damper spring to help minimize brake noise. In spite of this, it is still the weakest side of the drum and so it may bell mouth, become out-of-round, or warp. Slight bell mouthing is not disastrous. Wear in the center or on the edges of the drum is caused by flexing of the brake shoe or contamination.

Hard spots in the braking surface are caused by localized hot spots. The heat produces a metallurgical change that causes a crystalline growth of cast iron grains. The growth is toward the lining, so that these areas become the only surface in contact with the lining. This causes them to heat still more as the brakes are applied. When the hard spots are allowed to remain on the drum, the crystalline structure will begin to break down to form fine cracks called heat checks. As heat checking continues, the drum will eventually crack. Drums with hard spots or heat checks should be replaced.

Brake linings should be more than 1/32 in. (0.8 mm) above the rivets or above the shoe metal on bonded linings. The linings should be scheduled for replacement if they are close to this minimum at the time of inspection. The lining thickness is measured as shown in Figure 27-4.

The brake springs must be in good condition and be properly installed. The operation of the automatic adjuster should be checked to determine that it is operating correctly.

The parking brake linkages are checked for proper installation; they should move freely. One of the most common parking brake problems in-

Fig. 27-4 Measuring the amount of lining remaining.

volves the operating cable that slides in a housing attached to the backing plate. The cable may show signs of excessive wear on automobiles that have their parking brakes used regularly. It may be sticky or frozen on automobiles that seldom have the parking brakes used. Some drivers do not use the parking brake but rather place the automatic transmission in park or the standard transmission in gear when parking the automobile. Sticking parking brake cables can often be loosened and lubricated so they will operate correctly. Excessively worn or frozen parking brake cables and their housings should be replaced. Parking brake cables should move freely and be adjusted to allow the shoes to fully return.

The wheel cylinders are checked for leakage and freedom of movement. This is done on some brake cylinder designs by lifting the edge of the wheel cylinder rubber dust boot, as pictured in Figure 27-5. If the inside surface of the boot is dry, the wheel cylinder is not leaking. Any sign of brake fluid indicates leakage that should be scheduled for repair. The cylinder should be checked if the cylinder bore is corroded.

If all parts of the brake being examined are in good condition and the brakes have been operating normally, the drum can be reinstalled. Before installation, all dust should be blown from the drum and brake assembly. Be sure that none of the dust is blown into the hub wheel bearings. This is usually a good time to repack the front wheel bearings. When this is done, the grease seal and inner wheel bearing are pushed from the hub. The bearings and hub are thoroughly cleaned in degreasing solvent and blown dry. The bearing should not be spun with air pressure. The high centrifugal forces

Fig. 27-5 Lifting the wheel cylinder dust boot to check for fluid leakage.

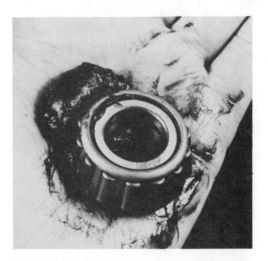

Fig. 27-6 Packing a wheel bearing with grease.

produced by spinning will damage the bearing. If the spinning bearing were to fly apart it could injure someone nearby. The clean bearing should be carefully inspected and packed full of wheel bearing grease using a grease packing fixture, or by hand (Figure 27-6) if one is not available. A coating of grease is placed in the hub. New grease seals are recommended to keep the grease from contaminating the brake linings.

The drum is carefully replaced. The sheet metal nuts or retaining cap screws are installed to

(a)

(b)

Fig. 27-7 Adjusting brake lining clearance with a brake spoon and wire to release the automatic adjuster. (a) Through an opening in the backing plate, (b) through an opening in the brake drum.

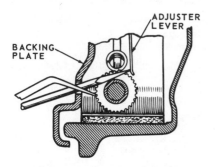
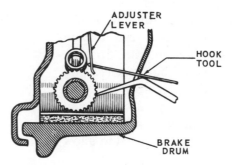

ADJUSTER LEVER

BACKING PLATE

BACKING OFF ON ADJUSTING SCREW
(Access Slot In Backing Plate)

ADJUSTER LEVER

HOOK TOOL

BRAKE DRUM

BACKING OFF ON ADJUSTING SCREW
(Access Slot In Brake Drum)

Fig. 27-8 Line drawing showing how the brake spoon and wire are used to move the star wheel adjuster screw (The Bendix Corporation).

Fig. 27-9 Checking the wear on the linings of a disc brake. These are new linings.

440

hold the rear drum in position. The outer bearing, keyed washer, and nut hold the front drum in place. The hub nut is tightened snugly as the drum is rotated. The nut is then loosened and retightened by hand to line up the tightest cotter pin slot. The cotter pin is installed and bent to lock the hub nut. Cotter pin installation should not interfere with static suppressors in the dust cover. The installation is completed when the hub dust cover is in place.

With the hub in place, the star wheel adjusters can be turned to provide a basic adjustment. When manual brake adjustment is required, it is done by turning the star wheel adjuster with a brake adjusting tool, often called a brake spoon. This can be done through an opening in the backing plate or drum as demonstrated in Figure 27-7. The brake is tightened by expanding the star wheel adjuster until the drum will not turn, then loosening the adjustment from 12 to 15 notches. This should allow the wheel to rotate freely. The adjuster lever has to be held away from the star wheel on brakes with automatic adjusters while the star wheel is being turned to loosen the brakes in the manner illustrated in Figure 27-8. The brake pedal should be checked to be sure it has a solid feel. The wheels can be installed and the jack stands removed. Automobiles with automatic adjusted brakes can be backed and stopped several times to allow the brakes to adjust properly.

An examination of a disc brake is much simpler. The brake disc, lining, and traces of seal leakage are visible with the wheel removed. This can be seen in Figure 27-9. It is not necessary to remove the caliper, wheel hub, or disc. The disc should be inspected on both sides for excessive wear and scoring. Scoring should be no deeper than 0.015 in. (0.375 mm). Some makes of disc brakes are manufactured with a groove around the disc face. Its purpose is to help keep the shoe in place and to reduce brake noise. The disc will not form hard spots as the drums do. Linings should be inspected around the edge. All sides of the lining should be at least as thick as the metal shoe to which it is attached. There should be no signs of fluid leakage. The caliper should be mounted correctly and the single piston caliper should not be binding on its mounting bolts or pins. If the parts show normal wear and service is not required, the wheel should be reinstalled. Disc brakes do not require adjustment. The brake pedal is pumped until it is hard. It will stay in this position.

27-3 COMPONENT REPAIR

Driver complaints, a road test, and a brake inspection taken together will indicate when the brakes require service. Service may include replacing the brake shoes with linings, resurfacing the drum and disc, and rebuilding or replacing the wheel cylinders. In some cases, the master cylinder is also rebuilt. The power brake unit and specialized valves in the brake system are rarely serviced unless they cause a braking problem. When they fail, they are usually exchanged for new or rebuilt units. Large service shops and specialized brake repair shops will have the necessary tools and equipment for power brake unit repair.

The most common brake repair is the replacement of the brake lining. Excessively worn linings are pictured in Figures 27-10 and 27-11. Replacement is usually done by removing the brake shoes and exchanging them for replacement shoes on both drum and disc brakes. It is a better practice to rebuild or replace the wheel cylinder while the shoes are removed. A new brake lining will reposition the shoe to push the wheel cylinder piston into its bore. This will place the piston seal on cylinder bore surfaces that have some rust and corrosion because no seal has been sliding on it. The seal operating on this rough surface will usually leak. If the brake fluid leaks out of the wheel cylinder and gets

Fig. 27-10 Excessively worn brake shoes from a drum brake. On the left the wear is into the rivets and on the right the lining is worn away completely so there is only metal-to-metal contact.

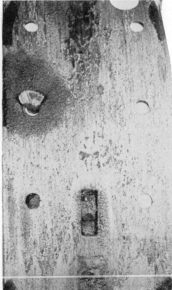

Fig. 27-11 Excessively worn bonded brake lining from drum brakes. The lining on the right is worn clear through the reinforcing mesh of the lining.

Fig. 27-12 A drum brake allowed to go until the shoe cut clear through the drum and there was complete loss of braking.

onto the new linings, it will contaminate and ruin them. It makes good sense to service the wheel cylinders when the linings are replaced. It also is desirable to recondition the drums and discs at this time. This is done by turning or grinding the braking surface to provide a true shape and a proper surface finish. Figure 27-12 shows a shoe that has had the lining completely worn off and the metal-to-metal contact has cut the drum in two.

Drum Brake Service. The drum is removed as described in the previous section of this chapter. Two special brake tools are required to remove the brake shoes from a dual servo brake. One is used to remove the return springs (Figure 27-13) and the other to remove the hold-down springs (Figure 27-14). It is a good practice for a beginner to finish the work on one brake assembly, except drums, before going to the next brake. In this way, one brake is always assembled so it can be used as a reference for assembly of the other brake.

Shoe removal starts by removing the return springs. Notice the order in which the springs are attached to the anchor pin and which holes in the shoes are used for the springs. Carefully check the position of the adjuster linkages and springs. They must be reassembled in the same order. Some of the automatic adjuster linkages may come off as the return springs are removed. The hold-down springs can be removed from the shoe after the return springs are disconnected from the anchor. Grasp one shoe in each hand and separate them

Fig. 27-13 Removing the brake springs with a brake spring tool.

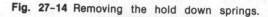

Fig. 27-14 Removing the hold down springs.

442

enough to disengage the wheel cylinder push rod and parking brake linkages on rear brakes, as demonstrated in Figure 27-15. The secondary shoe of the rear brake will be held by the parking brake cable. The two shoes with the adjuster and spring can be lifted off when they are clear of the anchor and backing plate. Overlapping the anchor ends of the shoes will release the adjuster and springs. The rear brake secondary shoe can then be disconnected from the parking brake cable. On some brake designs, this is done by compressing the cable spring and unhooking the cable from the parking brake link. On other brake designs, the parking brake lever is twisted to remove it from the shoe. The lever will remain on the cable. Be sure to notice which shoe has the long lining and which shoe has the short lining.

The wheel cylinder is the only brake system component remaining on the backing plate. If the master cylinder reservoir is kept over half full of brake fluid by frequent filling while the wheel cylinders are being serviced, one at a time, the system will stay full of fluid and little or no bleeding will be required after the brake job is completed. Fresh fluid seeping through the system by gravity will help flush the old contaminated fluid from the system.

It is wise to loosen the bleeder screw on the outside of the backing plate before working on the wheel cylinder. The bleeder screw should be carefully loosened with a *six*-point box or socket wrench so that it does not slip and damage the bleeder. The wheel cylinder will have to be replaced if the bleeder screw is stuck or damaged. It would serve no purpose to spend time reconditioning the old cylinder if the bleeder could not be used.

The wheel cylinder is reconditioned by removing the rubber dust boots and push rods, if so equipped, from both ends of the cylinder. It is helpful and in some cases necessary to free the wheel cylinder from the backing plate to service it. The brake line can remain attached to the cylinder. This will allow the cylinder to move enough to provide room to use the cylinder servicing tools. The pistons, seals, and springs can be pushed out of the wheel cylinder from either end. Fluid will continue to seep from the wheel cylinder if the master cylinder is kept more than half full. The fluid seepage is more help than hindrance. Wipe the interior of the wheel cylinder to check its condition for rust and pits. The wheel cylinder bore is cleaned and resurfaced with a brake hone driven by

an electric drill. The hone is stroked back and forth in the cylinder as it spins. The rotation of the hone must be stopped before it is pulled from the cylinder bore, or it will spread apart and catch on the backing plate (Figure 27-16). This will ruin the hone and it could injure the technician. The cylinder bore is wiped after honing. The seeping brake fluid will act as a honing oil and cleaning fluid. Wiping should continue until the rag comes out with only clean fluid. The honed diameter of the cylinder bore should not be more than 0.005 in. (0.125 mm) over the normal diameter. If honing

Fig. 27-15 Lifting the shoes from the backing plate after the springs have been removed.

Fig. 27-16 Honing a wheel cylinder.

has not removed the pits, the cylinder should be replaced. Many brake service technicians make it a practice to replace the wheel cylinders on each brake job rather than to spend time servicing them, only to find that they need replacement anyway. If honing has removed the rust and pits, the cylinder is ready for a new spring and rubber parts. The pistons should be thoroughly cleaned. It may be necessary to use a fine wet sandpaper on them to clean them completely. All abrasive matter should be removed. The rubber wheel cylinder cups should be coated with either a brake assembly fluid or with brake fluid. With the bleeder screw loosened, the springs, cups, and pistons are installed. The dust boots are put on the pushrods or over the raised portion of the piston, then placed on the ends of the wheel cylinder. The bleeder screw is left open to allow air to escape as the pistons are installed and to allow it to completely fill with fluid as the next wheel cylinder is serviced. When fluid begins to flow from the bleeder, the screw is closed and that portion of the brake hydraulic system is free of air if the master cylinder reservoir has been kept over half full.

Brake shoes can now be installed if the drums are not being reconditioned (Figure 27-17). This discussion assumes that the drums need to be turned. Brake shops and automotive machine shops have brake drum lathes especially designed for reconditioning the braking surface of the drum.

Fig. 27-18 Turning a brake drum to make the drum round and give it the proper surface finish. Drum has a damper attached while turning.

The brake drum diameter is checked to determine if it is serviceable. Rear drums are fitted on adapters that are mounted on the brake lathe arbor. Front drums are checked for looseness on the hub. When looseness is found, the wheel nuts are installed upside down and tightened. Front drums that are secure on their hubs are placed on adapters that fit against the bearing races in the hub. This whole assembly is placed on the arbor of the drum lathe. The lathe arbor is driven by an electric motor. A turning tool supported on the lathe in an adjustable tool holder is positioned so it can cut the drum braking surface, as shown in Figure 27-28.

The drum is shaped like a bell. It will ring if it is lightly hit while holding it at the center. The

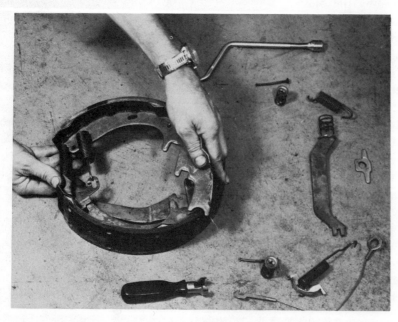

Fig. 27-17 Shoes are overlapped to release and reconnect the spring at the adjuster end.

sound is produced by vibration of the drum. If the lathe were cutting as the drum vibrated, it would cut a rough wavy finish. To prevent this rough finish, the drum is wrapped with a damper before being turned.

Drum lathes usually have two feeds, a coarse feed for fast metal removal and a fine feed to produce the proper finish. The lathe tool is adjusted to cut the braking surface, starting close to the web. The feed is out toward the open end. The first cut is a coarse cut, but not too deep. Deep cuts tend to follow drum irregularities. If the surface is not nearly clean with one coarse cut, a second coarse cut may be required. Cutting will make the drum round and parallel to the axle. The coarse cut is followed by a final cut using the fine feed. Unless otherwise specified, the drum should be turned no more than 0.060 in. (1.5 mm) over the standard inch diameter. This will allow 0.030 in. (0.75 mm) for additional wear before the drum must be replaced. The drum can be measured as shown in Figure 27-19. The generally accepted practice is to equally size both drums fitting one axle. This helps to keep brake balance. The refinished braking surface is usually sanded by hand, using #80 grit paper to remove any roughness and break up the machining pattern that remains. The drums should be handled very carefully. If they are dropped or banged against other material they will usually warp. This will be evident as a pulsating brake pedal after the brake job is completed. Drums that are worn beyond limits should be replaced. Front drums have to be pressed from the front hub for replacement. The new front drum is pressed on the hub and the lug bolt shoulders spread to lock the drum in place. It is usually considered to be a good practice to take a light cut across the braking surface of the new drum installed on the front hub to make sure no warpage exists.

After the drums are turned, they have a different arc so the linings do not fit exactly. If the brakes were assembled with this condition the drum would only contact a small part of the lining. High pedal forces required to stop the automobile using this small brake area would spring the shoe to give very high local pressures. This results in localized heating and possibly glazed lining in the area of high contact pressure. The springing shoe will give a spongy pedal feel, similar to when air is in the brake fluid lines. The lining fit would gradually improve with lining wear. To prevent this dangerous condition the lining arc is ground to

Fig. 27-19 Measuring the size of the turned drum.

Fig. 27-20 Grinding an arc on the brake lining to match the drum diameter.

match the drum. A brake shoe grinder is a standard piece of equipment for brake servicing. The shoe is mounted in a fixture that can be adjusted to the size of the drum radius. Figure 27-20 shows a shoe on a brake shoe grinder. Details of this adjustment differ among equipment manufacturers. The shoe is swung past a sanding drum that grinds the lining to fit the arc of the brake drum. The technician should take every precaution to keep the lining clean. Soil on the linings from handling can produce poor braking.

Brake Lining Selection. The technician usually purchases exchange brake shoes from his local parts store, where he will receive the set that is specified in the parts book. The technician will usually select the brand of brake parts that have given successful brake jobs in the past. He can be more selective if he observes lining codes stamped on the edge of the lining.

Brake lining codes are broken into three sections, separated with hyphens. The first section identifies the vendor by name, numbers, or letters. The second section of the code is the vendor's compound identification. The third section, which is more important to the technician, identifies the friction characteristic of the lining by letter, C through H. Code letter C indicates a coefficient of friction of less than 0.15. Each following letter indicates an additional coefficient range of 0.10; for example, D is 0.15 to 0.25, E is 0.25 to 0.35, etc. Unclassified linings are marked Z. Two letters indicating coefficient of friction are used in the third section of the brake lining code. The first letter indicates the *normal* coefficient of friction, while the second indicates the *hot* coefficient of friction. The minimum normal classification used on automobiles is the E class. Minimum hot codes used are the D class. Brake linings are required to meet SAE J998 specifications and Vehicle Equipment Safety Equipment Regulation V-3.

The primary lining can be the same as the secondary, but it is usually different. The same is true of disc linings. Metallic linings were used in drum brakes for fade resistance before disc brake systems were incorporated in domestic passenger cars. Some heavy-duty disc brake systems use an asbestos lining on one side of the disc and a metallic lining on the other side. This hybrid combination provides improved consistency of braking plus 20-25% better durability and 25-30% greater fade resistance. The asbestos lining helps dampen noise usually associated with metallic linings.

Brake Assembly. On dual servo brakes, assembly starts by checking the backing plate guide surfaces for roughness that could cause the shoes to catch or hang up. This should be smoothed out. A *light* coating of brake lubricant is put on all surfaces where the shoe contacts the backing plate and the anchor. The adjuster assembly is disassembled and all sliding parts are coated lightly with the same high-temperature brake lubricant.

The parking brake link on some models is attached to the secondary shoe on rear brakes. This subassembly is then attached to the parking brake cable because it is most readily accessible before other parts are attached. Be careful to avoid mixing left and right brake parts, and make sure to get the star wheel adjuster properly positioned to line up with the automatic adjuster lever or the access hole on brakes without automatic adjusters. To do this, the anchor ends of the shoes are overlapped. The adjuster is set at its smallest size. The adjuster and spring are placed in position between the shoes. This was shown in Figure 27-17. The free ends of the shoes are pulled apart so they no longer overlap. This shoe assembly is placed against the backing plate and anchor, while aligning the wheel cylinder push rods, and, on rear brakes, the parking brake strut is positioned in the correct shoe slots. Attach the hold-down pins and the springs to keep the shoes in position. Some hold-down springs are also used to secure the automatic adjuster. The guide is placed over the anchor to properly position the shoes. On other brake types, automatic adjuster parts are assembled as the return springs are installed. Specific details of the adjusters differ from manufacturer to manufacturer, from model to model, and from year to year. Use an appropriate service manual if all the brakes have been disassembled at once or if the assembly details have been overlooked.

This is a good time to adjust the brake shoes to size if a gauging tool, such as that shown in Figure 27-21, is available because the adjuster is still exposed for easy turning. If the gauging tool

Fig. 27-21 Adjusting the size of the assembled brakes to match the drum.

is not available, adjustment will have to be made through an access hole in the backing plate or drum. The drum can then be installed. On front drums, the wheel bearings should be packed with grease and new grease seals installed. With the drum on, the shoe-to-drum clearance can be adjusted as previously described. Properly adjust the hub nut and then secure it with a cotter pin and replace the dust cover. This completes the brake assembly service. The required parking brake adjustment should be done after *both* rear brakes have been serviced and adjusted. If the parking brake is dragging, it is possible to rotate the rear drums backward, but they will drag when rotated forward. Parking brakes should be fully loosened while the rear brakes are being adjusted. With the access hole covers and wheels installed, the brake job is ready for road testing.

Disc Brake Service. It is considered to be quicker and easier to service disc brakes than drum brakes. This is true when the components are not rusted and seized together. If they are, freeing them can often take a considerable amount of time. This will minimize the time difference compared to the time required to service drum brakes.

Disc brake service starts with the removal of the wheel. Be sure to have the automobile supported on solid stands or on a hoist so there is no chance of it falling. The caliper, disc, and lining edges can be seen with the wheel off. This is a good time to check the disc run-out. Fasten a dial gauge to the caliper or support bracket and adjust it so the dial gauge anvil is against the disc braking surface, as shown in Figure 27–22. Rotate the disc and observe the run-out on the dial gauge. Normal run-out should not exceed 0.0035 in. (0.09 mm). Excess run-out will cause knockback so there is a low pedal on the next application. The disc thickness should also be checked at twelve places around the disc. The thickness should not vary more than 0.0005 in. (0.013 mm) between the thinnest and the thickest measurements. A greater difference in thickness will cause a pedal pulsation while braking.

On disc brake systems, the caliper has to be removed from the steering knuckle or support bracket before the disc, or *rotor* as it is sometimes called, can be removed from the spindle. There are many variations of caliper designs and it is impossible to cover them all in this general discussion. If disassembly and assembly details are not obvious as the brake is being worked on,

Fig. 27-22 Checking the runout of a brake disc with a dial gauge.

service manuals covering the specific brake system should be consulted.

Two types of disc brake calipers will be found on domestic automobiles. Early disc brake systems and some imported automobiles use a four-piston caliper. These calipers are made in two halves that are separated for removal and service. A single-piston caliper was substituted in domestic automobiles for the four-piston caliper within a few years of the adoption of disc brakes. Disc brakes using a single-piston caliper have become a very popular option and are standard equipment on a large number of late model automobiles. The single-piston caliper is the most common type so it will be used in the following discussion of disc brake service. Much of this general discussion will also apply to the four-piston caliper.

The single-piston caliper must first have the piston pushed slightly back into the caliper cylinder to provide lining-to-disc clearance so the caliper can be removed. As the piston is pushed into the cylinder, it displaces brake fluid. This fluid is pushed back into the master cylinder reservoir. It is a good practice to remove about two-thirds of the fluid from the large side of the master cylinder reservoir to make room for the returning fluid so it does not overflow. The removed fluid should not be reused. The piston can be forced back slightly by prying between the edge of the

Fig. 27-23 Forcing the piston back into its bore slightly with a "C" clamp to free the caliper for removal.

Fig. 27-24 Worn disc brake lining. The upper lining got dirty as it was removed. The lower lining has been worn into the rivets.

caliper piston and the shoe. Avoid scratching the braking surface. If new linings are to be installed without disc reconditioning, the piston should be pushed all the way into the cylinder to provide space for the thick linings. This can be done using a C-clamp across the caliper, pushing on the outboard shoe as demonstrated in Figure 27-23. Remove the antirattle clips, retaining bolts, pins, retaining clips, and other hardware that hold the caliper to the steering knuckle. When the caliper mounting attachments are removed, the caliper can be lifted from the disc. The brake hose should remain attached to the caliper. Support the caliper so it does not hang on the brake hose. It is not necessary to remove the brake hose if only new shoes are to be installed.

Check the caliper for evidence of fluid leakage. If leakage is indicated, the caliper should be overhauled. The rubber dust boots should be properly mounted and free from cracks, cuts, or other damage. Just as in drum brake wheel cylinders, the caliper piston seal will be repositioned on an unused surface when new shoes are installed. This may produce a leak after the brake job is completed, even if there was no leakage before. It is, therefore, considered good practice to overhaul the caliper when the shoes are replaced.

The brake shoes are lifted from the caliper. In some cases, they are retained with antirattle clips

or hold-down pins in addition to those required for caliper removal. Shoes having a tight fit in the caliper may have to be pried free. Worn linings are shown in Figure 27-24. If the caliper or disc is not going to be serviced, new shoes are installed. Some new linings have retaining flanges that require bending to form a tight fit on the caliper anchor points to minimize noise. Specific instructions for this adjustment are supplied with the new brake shoes. The caliper is placed over the disc, and the attaching bolts, pins, bushings, and clips are installed. The master cylinder is maintained at least half full as the brake pedal is pushed several times to correctly position the linings. When the pedal becomes hard, the fluid level in the reservoir should be topped off.

The caliper will have to be removed from the automobile when it is to be overhauled. The brake line has to be disconnected to remove the caliper from the automobile. The hose is removed from the metal brake line on calipers that have the brake hose screwed into the caliper. On calipers having the brake hose attached to the caliper with a hollow bolt, the brake hose assembly is removed from the caliper by removing the bolt. This frees the caliper so it can be taken to the work bench. The brake line should be plugged to prevent fluid loss and to keep dirt out of the system.

The bleeder fitting should be loosened before

any additional work is done. In some areas of the country, salt is used on the roads in the winter to aid in ice removal. This causes corrosion that often seizes the bleeder fitting. In these areas, the bleeder fitting should be coated with good penetrating oil. A six-point box or socket wrench should be used to loosen the bleeder. The bleeder fitting is hollow so that excessive force will twist it off. If the bleeder fitting breaks, it must be removed like a broken stud.

If the piston has not been removed from the caliper, the bleeder screw is temporarily closed. Air pressure can be used to blow the piston from the caliper. Again, a shop towel is placed in the caliper to prevent damage to the piston. Another method of piston removal is to use a pair of special pry bars to mechanically pull the pistons from the cylinder, as shown in Figure 27-25. In severe cases, the piston can be drilled and the hole threaded. A screw turned into the hole will jack the piston out of the cylinder. A new piston will be required.

Fig. 27-25 Removing a piston from a caliper (Kelsey-Hays Company).

The rubber parts are removed from the piston and caliper. Take special pains to avoid scratching either the piston or cylinder bore. Where it is necessary to pry out rubber parts, it is desirable to use a wood or plastic pick that will not scratch.

Brake parts should be cleaned with either denatured alcohol or a special brake cleaner. The parts are then blown dry with clean filtered air. The air should contain no lubricant that will contaminate rubber brake parts.

The caliper mounting pins and bolts should

be inspected. If any wear or corrosion exists, the bolts should be replaced to minimize any chance of brake part failure. The pistons are checked for pitting, scoring, or badly worn plating. If damage is evident, the piston should be replaced. The cylinder bore should be polished with crocus cloth (Figure 27-26) or resurfaced with a special brake cylinder hone using brake fluid as a honing oil. Honing should not increase the bore over 0.002 in. (0.05 mm). If the bore does not clean up within this size, the caliper should be replaced. The cylinder should again be thoroughly cleaned.

Fig. 27-26 Cleaning a caliper wheel cylinder bore.

New rubber parts are coated with brake assembly fluid or clean brake fluid. Carefully insert the piston seal in the inner groove of the cylinder bore. Make sure the seal is not twisted, is evenly spaced, and is seated properly.

The cylinder dust boot on the Delco Moraine brake is placed in the groove on the piston before the piston is placed in the cylinder. On other brake systems, the boot is placed in the outer groove of the cylinder bore before the piston is installed. The piston is coated with assembly or brake fluid and carefully pushed into the cylinder through the piston seal, taking care to avoid unseating the seal. The dust boot is worked around the piston as it is pressed into the cylinder. Extreme care should be used to be sure the piston enters the bore straight to prevent scoring. Quite a bit of force is required to *push* the piston through the seal. When the piston is in place, the boot can be seated. The

Delco Moraine caliper requires a seating tool somewhat like a seal driver to seat the dust boot in the caliper. The boot on other brake types can be lifted into place around the piston by hand or with a wood or plastic strip (Figure 27–27). Installing the piston seal and boot is difficult at first. After it has been done a few times to develop the required technique, the seals will go right into place. The caliper is then ready to be installed.

Fig. 27-27 Pushing the piston through the dust boot.

Discs or rotors do not have to be resurfaced each time linings are replaced. They should be resurfaced if they are deeply scored or warped or if there is brake roughness. Some discs have intentional grooves to help keep the shoe in place and eliminate lift-out noise. The disc must have no more than 0.0035 in. (0.09 mm) run-out, and the thickness must not vary more than 0.0005 in. (0.013 mm). The surface should be in the 80/15 microinch range, which is a smooth finish.

A special brake lathe is required when the disc needs to be resurfaced. The lathe cuts both braking surfaces of the disc at the same time to minimize any chance of distortion, as shown in Figure 27–28. A damper is placed on the disc as it is turned. This eliminates surface roughness caused by vibration as the disc is being turned. In some cases, grinding is required after turning to give the correct surface finish. The surface should be cleaned with denatured alcohol to remove free carbon and other contaminants from the iron.

Fig. 27-28 Refinishing the braking surface of a disc. Both sides are turned at the same time to minimize the thickness variation.

As with drums, the disc is mounted on adapters that hold the disc properly on the lathe. Front disc adapters fit on the bearing races and hold the disc hub against a square shoulder. The disc run-out is again checked to make sure it is mounted properly before cutting is begun. The cutting tools are set to just contact the high spots on the disc and then they are adjusted to take only enough additional material to clean the surface. The machining pattern can be broken up using a #80 grit paper or it may be ground if a special grinding attachment is part of the drum lathe being used.

The wheel bearings are repacked, as previously described, and the disc installed, bearings adjusted, and the hub nut secured with a cotter pin. New linings are installed and secured in the caliper. To help minimize noise, one manufacturer puts contact cement on the piston and inner shoe to hold them together. The brake hose is attached and then the caliper is placed in position over the disc. New bushings are coated with high-temperature brake lubricant and installed where required. The retaining pins, bolts, and clips are then fastened. The brakes are then ready for fluid and bleeding.

Master Cylinder Service. The master cylinder does not need to be rebuilt each time the brakes are overhauled. Unlike wheel cylinders, the master cylinder always starts from the same at-rest position, regardless of the lining-to-braking surface clearance. Large clearances on worn brakes require a longer master cylinder stroke so the cylinder seals move across the same surface after the brakes are overhauled as they did before they were overhauled. Only two problems can be corrected by overhauling the master cylinder. One is internal leakage around the seals, indicated by a pedal that gradually moves to the floor as the driver holds it down. The other is visible external leakage from seals and gaskets. If these problems exist, the master cylinder will have to be removed from the automobile for overhaul. It is a good practice to obtain a parts repair kit before disassembly of the master cylinder is begun.

Three connections hold the master cylinder to the automobile: the brake lines, the pedal linkage, and the housing flange. First, the brake lines are removed from the master cylinder housing. The ends of the lines should be covered to prevent contamination. If a stop light switch is on the master cylinder, it should be disconnected. It is necessary to disconnect the master cylinder push rod from the pedal linkage in a large number of automobiles. This connection point is located under the instrument panel. After the lines and push rod are free, the housing flange can be unbolted from the engine side of the cowl panel or dash panel. In some power brake systems, the power brake booster must be removed with the master cylinder. Most master cylinders, however, are removed from the power brake booster. The booster will remain installed on the dash panel. The push rod is part of the booster on these units. Care must be taken to keep the hydraulic fluid from dropping on the automobile finish. Brake fluid will damage automobile paint.

The exterior of the master cylinder is thoroughly cleaned. Brake fluid remaining in the master cylinder is discarded in a waste container as the piston is pumped. This helps to get all the brake fluid out. The master cylinder can be taken to the work bench for disassembly and overhaul. If the push rod is still on the master cylinder, the dust boot will have to be pulled away from the master cylinder to expose the push rod retainer. This is released and the push rod and boot are removed.

The secondary piston stop bolt is removed. It may be located in the bottom of the reservoir or on the exterior bottom of the cylinder. The housing is placed in a vise with care to prevent distortion, and the retaining ring is removed from the groove in the cylinder bore. This will free the

pistons and spring so they can be removed from the master cylinder. Tapping the open end of the cylinder on a wooden block placed on the work bench will aid in removing the secondary piston. In stubborn cases, air pressure can be carefully used in the secondary outlet to blow the piston from the bore. Figure 27-29 shows the parts of a master cylinder. Some master cylinders require outlet tube seat replacement, while others do not. When removal is required, the old seats are drilled with a tap drill, then threaded. A washer is placed over the outlet. A screw is put through the washer and turned into the new threads. Tightening the screw will pull the outlet tube seat.

The position of all rubber parts, springs, and washers should be noted. All rubber parts are removed. In some master cylinders, the primary cup is not to be removed from the primary piston. A new primary piston assembly will be in the repair kit for these master cylinders. When the rubber parts are removed, they should be matched with the repair kit parts. Discard all used rubber parts that are to be replaced.

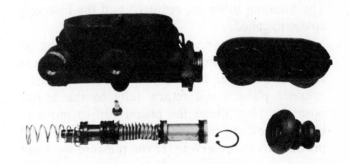

Fig. 27-29 Parts of a master cylinder.

When the master cylinder is disassembled, all parts are thoroughly cleaned with denatured alcohol or clean brake fluid. Avoid using any cleaning materials that may contain even a trace of mineral oil. The cylinder bore should be checked for scoring and corrosion. The bore is cleaned with crocus cloth or a good brake cylinder hone. Do not exceed honing size limits. Make sure the compensation and breather passages are clean after honing the cylinder.

Just before assembly, reclean all parts that will be used and coat them with brake or assembly fluid. Install the parts in the master cylinder in the proper order. The order is described in the instructions included in the parts kit and in applicable service manuals. Be sure to carefully work the piston cups into the bore to avoid damaging or twisting their edges. The lock ring is inserted to hold the parts in the cylinder. The secondary piston retaining screw and tube seats can then be installed. A spare brake line tube nut can be used to bottom the new tube seats. Where used, the push rod and boot should be installed to complete assembly of the master cylinder.

It is a good practice to bleed the master cylinder before it is installed on the automobile to reduce the time required to bleed the entire hydraulic brake system. This is done by connecting short lengths of brake tubing in the outlet openings, with the free ends bent to open in the bottom of the reservoir. Fill the reservoir with clean brake fluid. Using a wooden dowel, move the pistons slowly through their full stroke, as illustrated in Figure 27-30. This circulates the brake fluid throughout the master cylinder, allowing trapped air to escape as bubbles. The master cylinder is completely bled when bubbles no longer appear. The bleeding tubes are removed and the reservoir covers installed.

The master cylinder is now ready to mount on the vehicle. It is important that there be a slight amount of pedal free play, so that the master cylinder pistons will return fully to the at-rest position. This allows the piston cup to move in back of the compensating port to fully release fluid pressure to the reservoir. If the pressure were not

fully released, the pressure would cause the brakes to drag. The brake lines and push rod linkage are reconnected. If any other part of the hydraulic system has been opened, the system should be bled after reassembly.

Brake Lines. A brake hose is attached to each front wheel cylinder. A third hose is connected between the brake lines on the chassis and those on the rear axle. These hoses have permanently attached metal end fittings that are connected to the brake lines and cylinders. All other brake lines are steel.

If a brake hose shows signs of chafing or cracking, it should be replaced with a new hose of the correct length. The brake hose must be properly routed so it does not bind or stretch as the wheel turns and the suspension moves.

Metal brake line failure shows up as leaks. Leaks result from rust or cracks. Straight replacement steel brake lines with double flare ends and inverted flare fittings are available in standard lengths at automotive parts stores. They can be bent to the required shape to replace leaking brake lines. Sometimes it is necessary to make a special brake line length. To do this, the steel line is cut with a tubing cutter. It must be cut squarely and the sharp inner edge removed. The inverted flare nut is slipped over the tubing and the tube is clamped in a flaring tool keeping the specified length of tubing extended above the clamp. The first stage of the double flare upsets the tube so it bulges outward. The second stage pushes the open end into the bulged portion to complete the flare. When the flare is properly formed, the flaring tool is removed and the line is ready for use. Details were shown in Chapter 26.

Brake Bleeding. Brake bleeding is a process of removing trapped air from the hydraulic system. It is done by flowing brake fluid through the system to carry the air out. Fluid is pushed from the master cylinder toward the wheel cylinder. Fluid with air is allowed to flow from the wheel cylinder bleeder fitting, which is located at the top of the wheel cylinder bore, until all the air is removed.

Whenever the master cylinder cover is to be removed, it should be cleaned to keep dirt from getting into the hydraulic system. The master cylinder reservoir is kept over half full while the system is bled. The longest brake line in each system is bled before the short line. First, the bleeder fitting is wiped clean, then a bleeder hose is slipped

Fig. 27-30 Master cylinder bleeding method (The Bendix Corporation).

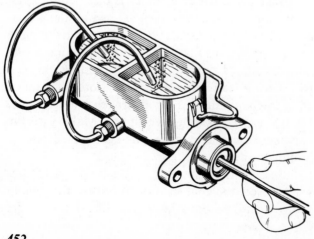

over the bleeder fitting. The free end of the bleeder hose is placed in a glass jar having some brake fluid in the bottom. As air comes from the system, it will show up as bubbles in the jar fluid. Air has been purged from the system when the bubbles stop forming.

Three methods can be used to bleed the brake system: pressure bleeding, gravity bleeding, and pedal bleeding. The brake system can be bled most rapidly using a pressure bleeder. The pressure bleeder is a tank with a diaphragm separating it into two parts. Brake fluid is placed on the lower side of the diaphragm and 35 psi air is put on the upper side. A line running from the fluid is attached to a special adapter cover that is fastened to the top of the master cylinder reservoir as shown in Figure 27-31. This keeps the master cylinder full of pressurized fluid. The wheel cylinder bleeder fitting is opened three-quarters of a turn with a properly fitting six-point box wrench. The pressurized fluid in the reservoir will force brake fluid containing air out of the bleeder hose. When bubbles stop forming, the bleeder fitting is closed and the process is repeated on the next brake. Disc/drum brake systems usually have a metering valve. This has to be held open manually while pressure bleeding. Some metering valves are held open with a clip that holds the valve stem out to keep it open. Other types have a rubber cover over the valve stem. This type must be held in by pushing on the rubber cover while pressure bleeding. When all four wheel cylinders are bled, the brake pedal should feel solid. If it is spongy, some air remains in the system and so bleeding must be redone.

The brake warning light switch should be checked when bleeding brakes. The electrical wire is first removed from the warning light switch and grounded. This should turn the warning light on when the ignition switch is on if the electrical circuit is operating satisfactorily. If the lamp bulb does not light, it should be replaced. When the electrical system is operating normally the wire is reattached to the brake warning light switch.

A bleeder hose is attached to one rear bleeder screw. The free end of the hose is placed in a container partly filled with brake fluid. While one person holds heavy pressure on the brake pedal a second person momentarily loosens the bleeder screw. This should turn the warning light on. The bleeder screw should be closed before the pedal pressure is released. The bleeder hose is moved to one front bleeder screw and the procedure is

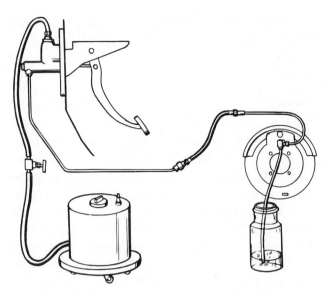

Fig. 27-31 Pressure bleeding a hydraulic brake system (The Bendix Corporation).

repeated to check the front brake system. The light should come on again. The brake system may contain the type of warning switch that will not self-center. This type of switch can be centered by again bleeding the rear brake with the pedal being pressed only hard enough to make that warning lamp go out. The bleeder screws are closed and the master cylinder fluid level is topped off.

The other two bleeding methods can be done without special equipment and without holding the metering valve open. Gravity bleeding is the least complex and may be the most satisfactory, but it usually takes the longest time. All that is necessary is to open the bleeder fitting with the bleeder hose placed in the jar. Keep the master cylinder over half full as the brake fluid containing air drains into the jar. Close the bleeder fitting when the bubbles stop forming. This process is repeated on each wheel.

The pedal bleeding method requires two people. One person uses the pedal to build up pressure that will force fluid containing air from the system. The other person opens the bleeder fitting as the pedal is pushed. The bleeder fitting is closed before the pedal is allowed to return to the released position. The master cylinder reservoir should not be allowed to become less than half full while pedal bleeding. The system is bled when no bubbles appear in the jar. The brake pedal should have a solid feel when bleeding is completed.

Power Brake Service. A faulty power brake will cause one of several driver complaints. It is faulty when there is a hard pedal and the brakes seem to be ineffective. It is also faulty when the brake action is severe as light pedal force is applied. The power brake is faulty when the system will not hold a vacuum for at least 10 minutes after the engine is turned off. In most cases, the faulty booster unit is exchanged for a new or rebuilt unit. The booster unit can be rebuilt when special tools, parts, and specific instructions are available.

The master cylinder is removed from the faulty booster as previously described. The power booster unit must have a vacuum line removed and the push rod linkage disconnected from the pedal linkage under the instrument panel. The booster unit can then be unbolted from the cowl and lifted from the engine compartment. If an exchange unit is to be used, it should be checked to make sure there is the proper amount of free-play on the master cylinder push rod. Insufficient free play will lead to dragging brakes. Excessive free play will give too much pedal travel.

The two halves of the power brake booster housing have to be separated when it is to be overhauled. The booster diaphragms are held between the two halves of the housing to make an air-tight seal. The housing halves are held together with a twist lock at their mating point.

Before disassembly, the mating edges of the housing should be marked so they can be reassembled in the same position. Special tools are required to push the two halves of the booster housing together, slightly compressing the edge of the diaphragms. This requires a great deal of pressure. While this pressure is being applied, one housing is held and the other is turned in a counterclockwise direction far enough to release the twist lock (Figure 27-32). The housings are then gradually separated to release the internal spring tension. If the housing does not freely separate, release the pressure slowly and tap the edge of the housing to break the seal. This will eliminate the possibility of the internal spring causing the housings to separate suddenly and unexpectedly, damaging parts. When the housing is separated, the internal components can be removed. Special tools are generally required to disassemble the power brake

Fig. 27-32 Tools used to separate a power brake booster.

control valve assembly. Specific details of the different types of power brake booster components are beyond the scope of this book. Required servicing details are usually packaged with the parts in the repair kit.

All components of the power brake booster repair kit are substituted for the used parts. The remaining used parts are checked for any indication of damage. Questionable parts should be replaced. The parts that are to be reused are cleaned with denatured alcohol. All passages are blown free with clean compressed air. Slight rust on parts should be removed with crocus cloth and the part washed clean.

During assembly, some of the rubber parts are coated with silicone lubricant; others require talcum powder. The control valve is assembled and gauged to make sure all tolerances are within specifications. New seals are installed using special seal drivers. The diaphragms, support plates, and springs can be assembled and placed in the housing. The marks are aligned, then the housing is compressed and turned clockwise to engage the twist locks. Before installation in the automobile, the master cylinder push rod length must be checked and adjusted to provide the proper free play.

Summary. Brakes are one of the most important automotive safety systems. The technician should use only the best materials and workmanship. Brakes are not difficult to learn to service and brake tools are designed so that they are simple to use. After service, brake problems usually result from a detail that is overlooked by the technician; therefore nothing less than the best possible service should be considered.

REVIEW QUESTIONS

1. What causes the automobile to pull to one side when braking? [INTRODUCTION]

2. What causes brake noise? [INTRODUCTION]

3. How does pedal free play differ from pedal free travel? [27-1]

4. What conditions make it necessary to pump the brake pedal to get a solid pedal? [27-1]

5. What does a low brake pedal usually indicate? [27-1]

6. Why does fade affect drum brakes more than disc brakes? [27-1]

7. How do the brake linings become contaminated? [27-2]

8. What problem is caused by air in the brake lines? [27-2]

9. What problem causes a pulsating pedal? [27-2]

10. List the items that should be checked on a brake system inspection. [27-2]

11. How is the operation of a vacuum power brake unit checked? [27-2]

12. What should be done to remove a brake drum when it rotates freely but seems to catch on the brake shoes? [27-2]

13. What items should be checked on a brake assembly after the drum is removed? [27-2]

14. What service should be performed as the drum is reinstalled? [27-2]

15. How is the initial brake adjustment made on drum brakes? [27-2]

16. Why do disc brakes need no adjustment? [27-2]

17. What is the most common brake repair? [27-3]

18. Describe the procedure used to remove brake shoes when the drum has been previously removed. [27-3]

19. What is the advantage of keeping the master cylinder reservoir at least half full while working on the wheel cylinders? [27-3]

20. When should a wheel cylinder be replaced rather than be overhauled? [27-3]

21. Why is it desirable to take light cuts with a brake drum lathe? [27-3]

22. Why are the new linings ground before being assembled on the backing plate? [27-3]

23. Describe the brake lining identification code. [27-3]

24. Why are asbestos and metallic linings mixed on some disc brakes? [27-3]

25. When is the parking brake adjusted? [27-3]

26. How does the removal of a four-piston caliper differ from the removal of a single-piston caliper? [27-3]

27. Why is it necessary to remove brake fluid from the master cylinder reservoir before removing the caliper? [27-3]

28. How are the shoe and the lining replaced on a single-piston-type caliper? [27-3]

29. How are the caliper piston seals replaced? [27-3]

30. What precautions must be observed when turning brake discs? [27-3]

31. Why is it often unnecessary to rebuild the master cylinder when doing a brake job? [27-3]

32. What two problems can be corrected by overhauling the master cylinder? [27-3]

33. What material is used to clean brake system parts? [27-3]

34. Describe the pedal bleeding process. [27-3]

35. What precautions should be taken when separating a power brake unit? [27-3]

tire design
and operation

Automobile control, acceleration, and braking occur through the tires and their footprint or contact patch on the road surface. Tire demands are low when the automobile is operated at low speed, with light loads on smooth, dry road surfaces. The requirements on them increase as speed, load, and handling demands increase.

Tires must be large enough and strong enough to support the load they are expected to carry. They must absorb or cushion, by deflecting, part of the shock from road irregularities. They must develop tractive forces for accelerating, cornering, and braking. While doing this, passenger car tires rotate approximately 800 revolutions for each mile traveled.

The force required to make the tire slip on its footprint, called traction, is the same in all directions while the tire tread is flat on the road surface,

whether it is accelerating, cornering, braking, or any combination of these. This is illustrated in Figure 28-1. The total available tractive force is not important until the automobile is near the tractive limit, where sliding or skidding will occur. Tractive force to control the automobile drops rapidly when a skid starts and control is lost.

28-1 TIRE CONSTRUCTION

A tire is made from rubberized fabric plies over a rubber liner. The edges of the plies are wrapped around a wire bead that holds the tire to the wheel rim. The fabric plies are covered with a rubber compound tread and a different rubber compound for the side walls. The tire is cured in a mold to vulcanize the parts into a single unit and form the

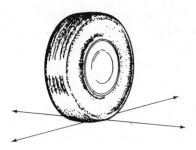

Fig. 28-1 Tractive force is equal in all directions.

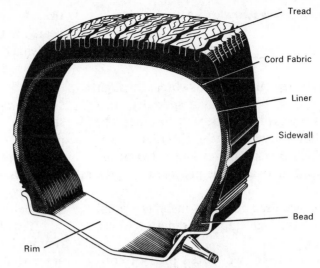

Fig. 28-2 Section of a tire showing the names of the parts (The Firestone Tire and Rubber Company).

tread design. The parts of a tire can be identified in Figure 28-2.

Plies. Several types of fabric cord materials are used in tire plies. Tire manufacturers and fabric producers are continually striving to improve their materials and develop new materials that will better meet tire requirements.

Rayon was introduced as a tire cord material to replace cotton in 1938, just before World War II. It was much more durable, produced a soft ride, was more resilient, and less expensive than cotton. Rayon's tensile strength, or the pulling force required to break it, is 94,000 lb per sq in. (648,110 kN/m²). After World War II, rayon became the major tire cord material. Since its first introduction, it has had several modifications to improve its characteristics and reduce its cost.

Two forms of nylon, another synthetic material, were introduced as tire cord material in 1947, soon after World War II. Its 122,000 lb per sq in. (841,160 kN/m²) tensile strength is about 30% greater than rayon, producing high impact strength. It is more heat resistant and water resistant than rayon. Nylon cord tires have less flexibility than rayon, and this feature helps to produce better vehicle handling. This same lack of flexibility, however, tends to produce a harsh ride. Nylon cord's major disadvantage is the characteristic that causes nylon cord tires to take a set while standing. This produces flat spots that produce a thump when the car first starts to roll. As the tires warm from rolling, the cords relax and the flat spot quickly disappears. Techniques have been developed

to stretch and temper nylon cord before it is used in a tire, to reduce the flat-spotting tendency. Nylon is expensive when purchased by the pound; however, smaller cord diameters, called *denier* in the English system and *tex* in the metric system, will be as strong as larger rayon cords. For this reason, the cost difference is not as great as the price per pound would indicate. Nylon cord has been improved over the years of use to enhance its characteristics for tires, as well as to reduce its cost.

In 1962, polyester cord was introduced for use in passsenger car tire fabrics. Its 104,000 lb per sq in. (717,050 kN/m²) tensile strength is between rayon and nylon. It produces a soft ride with no tendency to flat spot. It is less heat resistant than nylon and more heat resistant than rayon. Polyester cord tires have had increased use as original-equipment tires and appear to be becoming the dominant tire cord material.

Tire manufacturers give tire cord materials a trade name when the material is specially processed for their specific tire. Rayon has been called Dynacor and Tyrex. Nylon cord is usually followed by a number to designate the specific processing. Numbers 6 and 66 are the ones most often used for tire cords. Polyester has been called Vitacord, Dacron, and Kodel.

Strands of fiberglass show superior strength, 407,000 lb per sq in. (2,978,000 kN/m²) tensile strength, to other tire cord materials, but have a poor flexing resistance. In 1962, Owens-Corning perfected a technique to impregnate fiberglass yarn with a plastic material. This plastic separated the individual strands so they would not chafe against each other as they flexed. This breakthrough allowed fiberglass to be used as a specialty cord in tires. It is rarely used as a side wall cord because it has low flexibility strength. Fiberglass was initially used for a breaker ply or belt between the tire ply and tread in 1968. This provided a much longer tire life.

Steel cords are used for belts in many radial ply tires. They have high impact strength and are quite rigid.

Tires may use from two to ten plies of cord fabric. The cords in the plies may be large or small denier, and may have two or three twisted strands. The number of plies, in itself, does not indicate tire strength so a load rating scale has been developed by the Tire and Rim Association to classify and rate tires. Selected samples of this scale are given in Figure 28-7.

Tire Rubber. Rubber used in tires is an elastomer compound that blends natural and synthetic rubbers with additions of chemicals and filler compounds to produce the desired characteristics. Tire tread stock must be able to resist wear and abrasion while providing traction. Large amounts of carbon black are added to the tread rubber to increase wear and abrasion resistance. Traction results from tread rubber hardness, compounding, and tread design. Hard compounds provide good wear and poor traction. Soft compounds give good traction and poor wear. The tread compound is a selected compromise to provide the properties required for each tire application.

Side wall and ply impregnation rubber is a more flexible rubber compound than tread rubber. It gives the tire its required flexibility and strength properties. The side wall must be flexible enough to deflect as it passes the tire footprint on each revolution. It must also flex to absorb any shock that is produced by irregularities in the road surface. The side wall must have sufficient strength to transfer all the acceleration and braking torque between the wheel rim and tire tread. It also must withstand cornering forces that are applied to the automobile.

Tire rubber deteriorates with temperature and age. Rubber compounds are, therefore, varied to provide the expected service life requirements of the tire. A tractor tire may be expected to last twenty years, a truck tire 50,000 miles (80,467 km), a passenger car tire 30,000 miles (48,280 km), and a racing tire 500 miles (805 km).

Manufacturing Tires. Tire manufacturing starts with raw materials being processed in supplier plants. Natural rubber comes from plantations, while synthetic rubbers and the basic cord fiber materials come from the petrochemical industry. The cord material is made into a fabric in textile mills before it is sent to the tire manufacturer.

Tire fabric is primarily strands of tire cord running lengthwise in the fabric. Small cross strands are woven through the cords to hold them in place for handling during manufacture and have no function in the final tire.

Additional fabric processing is done by the tire manufacturer. The fabric is stretched and heated to give it uniform mechanical properties, then coated with an adhesive. Adhesive is required as a bonding agent between the cord and rubber compound. The treated fabric then goes to large steel rollers, called *calendars,* that squeeze the uncured rubber into the cord fabric to produce a sheet. This rubberized sheet is cut into strips at an angle or *bias,* then reassembled into a long strip with the cords running at the required bias angle for bias-ply tires. The cords remain straight for radial tires. The rubberized cord fabric is now ready to be used in tire construction.

Tread rubber and side wall rubber compounds are extruded into the required shape and cut to length at an angle to provide a long tapered joint.

Wire for the tire bead is rubber coated and rolled into the required size bundle or bead, two per tire.

The bias-ply tire is made on an expandable drum. One bead is slid over the drum to be in position when needed. The drum rotates as the tire is built in layers. The first layer consists of a rubber sheet that takes the place of an innertube to seal the air. This is followed by two or more plies of rubberized cord fabric. The fabric is carefully cut to length parallel to its cords, then lapped over the other end of the ply with the required overlap joint, to produce an enclosed cylinder shape. Adjacent plies have their bias in alternate directions to give the tire strength, much like the grain in plywood. The plies are followed by belts or breakers when required. The beads are placed over the edges of the ply. The ply is then wrapped over the bead back onto itself, locking the bead bundle into place.

A tread and side wall rubber strip is wrapped around the plies. White or colored rubber used for tire identification and trim is molded within the side wall strip. The entire assembly is pressed together by a process called stitching.

At this point, bias-ply tire construction is completed. The tire looks like an open ended barrel. It is inspected and, if deviations are noted, the tire can be repaired because it is still *green* or uncured rubber.

The manufacture of the radial-ply tire is somewhat different from that of the bias-ply tire. The radial tire is built on a drum that forms the green tire in nearly the same shape as the finished tire.

After the green tire passes inspection, it is sent to the mold to be cured. The green tire slides over a bladder that expands as the hot mold closes around the tire. This bladder forces the tread surface outward into the mold. The tread pattern and identification data for the tire are cut into the mold surface. Small holes in the mold allow air to escape as the rubber fills the mold. These holes also produce the small rubber projections often seen on new tires. The rubber composition determines the mold temperature, about 320°F (160°C), and time needed for curing, around twenty minutes.

The tire is trimmed and inspected when it comes from the mold. Side walls are cut or ground to expose tire-striping rubber. The tire is now ready to be packaged and sent to the customer.

28-2 TIRE DESIGN FEATURES

Tires of the same size can differ in their tread design, trim stripes, and name or identification data. The greatest difference in tires, however, is in the cord material and the way it is put into the tire.

Tire Body. Most original-equipment tires have the cord running at an angle or bias. This provides a cross-cord side wall to give the required strength to transfer acceleration and braking torque. The cross-bias cord angle runs from 30 to 40°.

Original-equipment tires and the majority of replacement tires have gone from four-ply to two-ply construction. Two-ply tires run cooler, are more flexible to absorb shock from road irregularities, and apply greater self-aligning torque to the steering system after a turn. Two-ply tires are as strong as four-ply tires, because the tire cord denier is larger than that used in four-ply tires. The strength of the ply is the result of the weight of the cord rather than the number of plies. Service experience has shown fewer failures with two-ply tires than with four-ply tires. This is primarily the result of lower temperature operation and their ability to flex over road hazards rather than resisting a hazard that would break the cord.

Bias-ply tires allow the tire to squirm as it goes through the tire footprint, as illustrated in Figure 28–3. The tread is pushed together as it goes into the footprint. This stores energy in the rubber. As it comes out of the footprint, the tire rapidly expands and goes beyond the neutral point into a stretched position. The tread then contracts, causing an oscillation. At high speeds, this tread squirm is evidenced as a standing wave on the back side of the tire as it comes up from the tire contact patch or footprint. The standby wave is pictured in Figure 28–4. Closing and opening of the tread as it goes through the contact patch is one of the major causes of normal tire wear.

Tread stability and reduction of squirm in belted tires results in up to 100% improvement in tire mileage compared to bias-ply tires. By hold-

Fig. 28-3 Tire flexing through the tire contact patch.

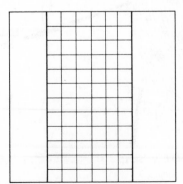

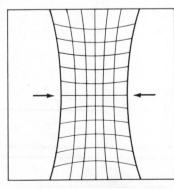

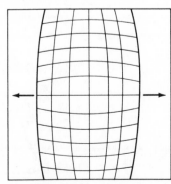

Normal tread ahead of contact patch   Contracted tread in contact patch   Expanded tread behind contact patch

Fig. 28-4 Belted tire on the left with minimum squirm. Bias tire on the right shows excessive squirm (The Goodyear Tire and Rubber Company).

ing the tread shape, belted tires run cooler, improve fuel mileage, improve traction, and double blow-out resistance when compared to bias-ply tires.

Belted tires do not flex as easily as bias-cord tires, so they transfer more road shock into the wheels and suspension system. Because of this, the wheel spindles, knuckles, and suspension system need to be stronger. Vehicle springing is modified to reduce road shock transfer to the passenger compartment when the vehicle is designed to use the bias belted tires.

Radial-ply belted tires have been built in Europe for a number of years on special tire building equipment. The radial ply cord angles run from 88 to 90° and the belt cords run from 12 to 20°. The radial cord provides a soft side wall that will produce a softer ride than belted bias tires. The belt (steel wires, fiberglass, or rayon) around the radial cords holds the tread shape through the contact patch or footprint. Radial belted tires provide more cornering power and less wear than bias belted tires as a result of a lower slip angle. Low slip angle helps the tire hold the road under nearly 10% higher side load forces. With the radial belted tires, loss of tire-to-road adhesion occurs suddenly, with little warning, especially on wet surfaces. Ultimate adhesion of belted tires is the

Fig. 28-5 Tire construction details. (a) Bias angle construction, (b) bias belted construction, (c) radial construction (Uniroyal Incorporated).

(a)

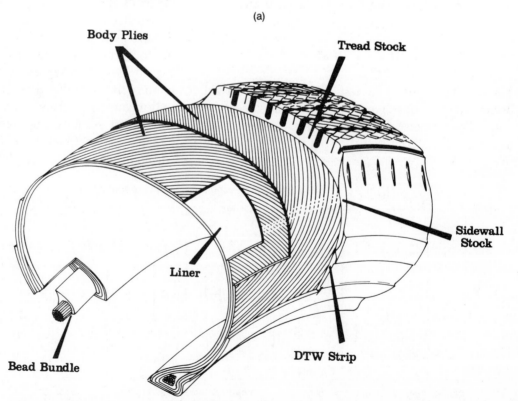

Body Plies

Tread Stock

Sidewall Stock

Liner

Bead Bundle

DTW Strip

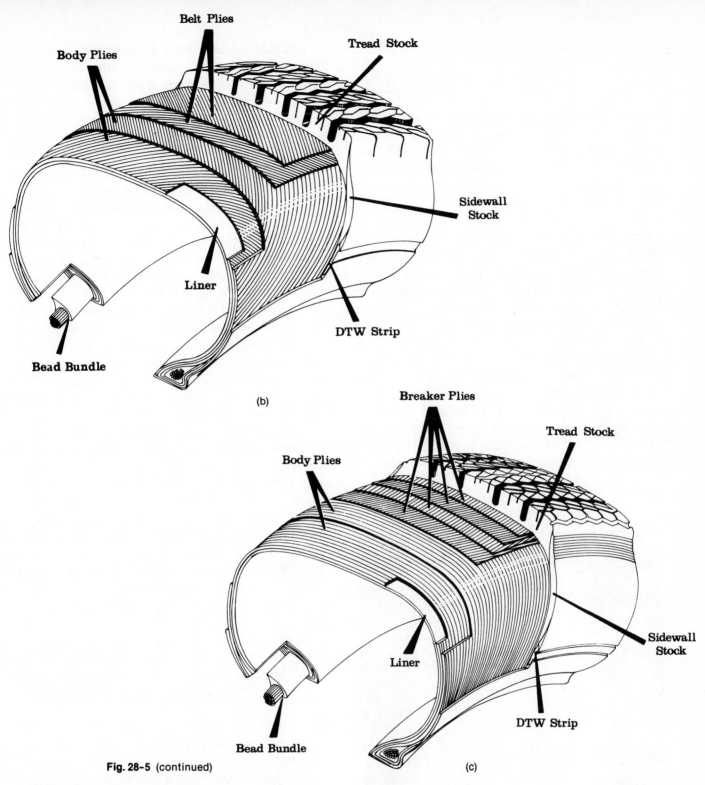

Body Plies

Belt Plies

Tread Stock

Sidewall Stock

Liner

DTW Strip

Bead Bundle

(b)

Breaker Plies

Tread Stock

Body Plies

Liner

Sidewall Stock

DTW Strip

Bead Bundle

(c)

Fig. 28-5 (continued)

same as the bias and bias belted tire. This sudden loss of adhesion may come too rapidly for the average driver to make a compensating adjustment and control will be lost. Radial belted tires produce a harsh ride at low speeds, require a high steering effort, especially when parking, and are expensive. The steel-belted radial tire has less tread flexing, so it rolls easier, thereby improving gasoline mileage. Tire construction is shown in Figure 28-5.

Tire Tread. Tire tread design is not necessary for a tire running on dry pavement. The best example of this is the racing "slicks" that are designed to have maximum possible tire-to-road adhesion on dry hard surfaces. Tire tread design becomes important when the automobile is operated on gravel, sand, snow, or wet surfaces. Tire treads that are satisfactory for a trailer may not be satisfactory for use on the steering wheels. Still another tread design may be better for the driving wheels. When the wheels are required to both drive and steer, such as in front wheel drives, the best tire design becomes more complex. Original-equipment tire tread designs are a compromise among normal steering, driving, and braking requirements, modified by cost considerations. Premium tires have a much finer tread pattern than original-equipment tires. Some of the premium tires have small cuts across the tread surface that are called *blades* or *sipes.* They act as many edges to grip the road surface and as fins to dissipate heat. The blades are cut in an unequal pattern to break up the harmonic noise that would result from equal spacing.

The average tread depth on new tires is 3/8 in. Tread can be safely worn down to 1/16 in. Tires have a *wear indicator* that shows as a flat streak across the tread when the tire tread is worn to 1/16 in. deep. When the indicator appears as it has on the tire in Figure 28–6, the tire should be replaced.

Fig. 28–6 Tire worn until the tread wear indicator shows. This tire should be replaced.

Economy tires have a coarse tread pattern, compared to original-equipment tires. Specialized tire treads for snow, rain, sand, etc., are available where special tire-to-road traction requirements exist.

Tire-to-road adhesion is much less when the road becomes wet. The water must squeeze from the contact patch on the road surface in order for the tire to contact the road surface to give adhesion. Water on the road surface is displaced by the tire as it rolls so the water must be moved. Water displacement can be seen by the splash from a tire traveling through water. It is also evident by the relatively dry tracks left behind a car traveling on a wet surface. The noticeable splash comes from the side of the tire; however, a large portion of the water will squirt endwise through the tread grooves and this is not easily seen on a rolling tire. Grooves forming the tread design provide a place for the water to flow from the tire contact patch. The groove in a worn tread is small, and so the water moves slowly from the contact patch.

Water has mass and requires time to displace. A tire moving at high speeds through 1/8 in. of surface water may actually climb up on the top of the water and hydroplane. This occurs because the water cannot find a rapid path to escape from the contact patch, especially on worn tires. A hydroplaning tire cannot drive, steer, or brake, so it provides no control of the automobile. Large straight tread grooves provide the best tire adhesion on a wet surface. As a tire wears, the groove depth reduces and its wet adhesion depreciates. A nearly smooth tire will have poor wet adhesion. "Slicks" will obviously have very poor adhesion on a wet surface. This is the reason that it is a good practice for a driver to slow down when driving on a wet road, especially with worn tires.

Tire Size. Tire sizes are based upon the size of wheel rim, the load range, the capacity, and the tire series.

Wheel diameter and width between rim flanges are measured at the wheel bead diameter. Larger wheel diameters require larger tires which, in turn, will support more weight. Under-fender clearance limits the maximum tire size that can be used on an automobile. Oversize tires usually require wheels with wider rim widths, because the rim width must also match the tire size and tire design. Automobile or tire manufacturer's specifications should be consulted.

Tire size			Cold inflation pressure		Load rating B →					Load rating C →		Load rating D →	
78 Series	70 Series	60 Series	20	22	24	26	28	30	32	34	36	38	40
A78-13			810	860	900	940	980	1020		1090	1130	1160	1200
B78-14			870	910	960	1000	1050	1090	1130	1170	1200	1240	1280
C78-14			950	1000	1050	1100	1140	1190	1230	1270	1320	1360	1400
D78-14	D70-14		1010	1070	1120	1170	1220	1270	1320	1360	1410	1450	1490
E78-14 E78-15	E70-14 E70-15	E60-15	1070	1130	1190	1240	1300	1350	1400	1440	1490	1540	1580
F78-14 F78-15	F70-14 F70-15	F60-15	1160	1220	1280	1340	1400	1450	1500	1550	1610	1650	1700
G78-14 G78-15	G70-14 G70-15	G60-15	1250	1310	1380	1440	1500	1560	1620	1680	1730	1780	1830
H78-14 H78-15	H70-14 H70-15	H60-15	1360	1440	1510	1580	1650	1710	1770	1830	1890	1950	2010

Maximum pound load limit per tire

Fig. 28-7 Selected sample of tire sizes and load limits.

Tire sizes use a letter preceding a number to designate tire capacity. The letter is independent of the rim size or load range. As the letters advance from A, the capacity becomes greater. This can be seen in Figure 28-7.

The tire industry has replaced the ply rating with another letter to indicate the tire load range. B load range is used in standard automotive applications. The D load range may be used on vehicles that carry heavy loads or tow trailers. As the load range increases the tire can be inflated to a higher pressure (up to a maximum) to support the higher load. A sample tire size designation would be G78-15 load range B.

Series. The series number indicates the approximate ratio of the tire section height to the section width. If the height of the tire is 78% of the width, the tire is a 78 series. If the tire section has the same height, but is wider, the ratio of height to width changes. For example, this wider tire's height could be 70% of the width to make a 70 series tire. This ratio of height to width is called tire *aspect ratio*. Passenger car tires' aspect ratios may run from 95% to 60%, the smaller number indicating a relatively wide tire. Racing tires may have an aspect ratio as low as 35% to 45%. Tires above 80% have bias-ply construction. Below 80%, they may be bias; however, they are usually belted bias and belted radial (Figure 28-8).

The trend is to use low profile belted radial-ply tires with low aspect ratios. These tires improve vehicle handling and give a performance styling look to the vehicle.

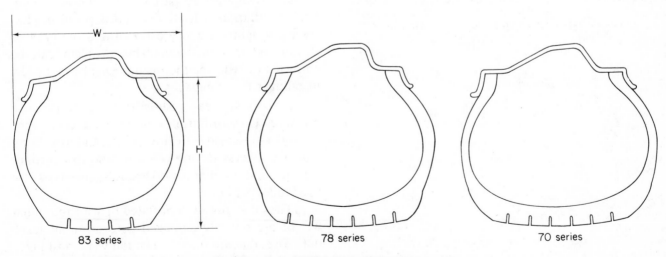

83 series   78 series   70 series

Fig. 28-8 Cross section of tire series proportions.

Tire Size Designation. The series number designation is placed on the tire directly behind the letter that indicates tire capacity. This, in turn, is followed by the rim diameter. The complete designation for the tire size is, for example, E78-14 or H70-15. Radial-ply tires of 70 series have an R immediately after the capacity letter—for example, GR 70-14 or FR 70-15—to indicate the tire size and capacity. Most passenger car tires are available in load ranges B, C, and D.

Tire size and type should not be mixed on vehicles. The slip angle of each tire type is different. Mixing tire types results in unpredictable control at highway speeds; thus the vehicle could be dangerous to drive.

28-3 TIRE OPERATION

The width of the wheel rim in relation to the size of the tires is important. If the rim width nearly matches the tread width, the side wall will be approximately straight up and down. This allows very little flexing and produces a harsh ride. Passenger car rims are narrower than the tread and the side wall curves inward to produce a softer ride. Some racing wheel rims are wider than the tread, allowing the side wall to lean outward. The tire is designed to match the rim to keep a tight air seal which keeps air pressure in the tire. This tire bead-to-rim match serves another function that is often overlooked. Engine acceleration torque tries to turn the rim inside of the tire. The only

Fig. 28-9 Tire deflection caused by a side force.

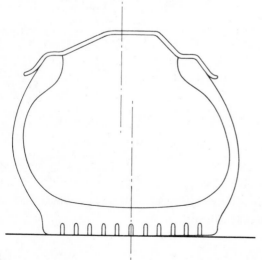

thing that keeps this from happening is the friction between the bead and rim. This type of force also occurs during braking, but in the reverse direction.

During a turn, the tire is deflected sidewise as illustrated in Figure 28-9. This force tends to loosen the bead from the rim on one side of the tire. The tire bead must be secure enough to maintain rim contact.

At high vehicle speeds, centrifugal force increases the tire diameter. This force tries to throw the bead from the rim. The bead wire holds the bead diameter so it will remain in contact with the rim. Belted tires keep the tread from expanding at high speeds, thus stabilizing the tread and minimizing heat build-up.

Tires flex as they rotate while carrying vehicle load. This flexing distorts the tire, especially when the tire assumes a side load while going around a curve. Distortion is a natural reaction of a tire. It allows the tire to absorb road shock and to flex through the contact patch without skidding as the vehicle makes a turn.

Natural tire flexing causes heat build-up in the tire. Heat in a normal tire operated within its load range will stabilize at a safe temperature. Excessive heat is a tire's worst enemy. Temperatures above 250°F (121°C) result in the loss of tire strength, the rubber-to-cord bond separates, and the air escapes, often as a blowout. In some cases, tires become so hot they start to burn.

Tire heat can be reduced by reducing the factors that produce heat. The simplest method is to slow the vehicle speed. This results in less flexing per minute and provides more cooling time between flexing. Excess heat can be the result of underinflation, which allows the sidewalls to flex excessively as they go past the tire contact patch. Proper inflation will eliminate this problem. Excessive weight on a tire causes the same type of flexing as underinflation. This problem can be corrected by reducing the weight being carried or by installing a larger capacity tire.

Abnormal wear results from improper tire pressure. Underinflation causes tread edge wear as well as excessive flexing, heat, and tire body damage. Excess flexing will also lead to improper vehicle handling that is noticeable at speeds as low as 35 miles per hour.

Tires that run underinflated or with too much weight are severely damaged before the air leaks out. Tires that are ruined when flat were most likely damaged well before the air pressure escaped.

Overinflation prevents flexing. It usually causes wear on the center of the tire tread. The reduction in flexing produces a harsh ride and the tire is vulnerable to impact that could puncture the tire rather than allowing the tire to flex over the obstacle.

28-4 TIRE SELECTION

Tire selection is based upon the wheel rim size and the kind of operation expected from the vehicle. Operating considerations include the type of driving, the type and condition of the road surface, the weight to be carried, the miles driven per year, and the length of time the vehicle is to be used.

Original-equipment tires are called 100 level tires. Tires of less quality will cost less and tires of better quality will cost more. Each tire manufacturer has a large selection of tire brand names and styles in their inexpensive tires below the 100 level quality. These are usually competitively priced and are satisfactory only for low speed, lightly loaded service. Each manufacturer will usually have only one or two tire styles in their premium classification.

In summary a stiffer tire will provide better handling and a harsh ride; belted radial tires give more tire mileage, along with a ride more harsh than bias-ply tires; wide treads have more style and are more difficult to steer, especially while parking; and tires with hard rubber in their treads wear longer, but provide less tire-to-road adhesion. No one tire is best for all types of vehicle operation. Vehicle and tire manufacturer recommendations should be followed for the most satisfactory results.

28-5 TIRE SERVICE

Tire service starts with a visual inspection for abnormalities that may exist. Abnormal wear is the most obvious. Tread wear shows the result of abnormal inflation, abnormal suspension alignment or condition, and cornering wear. These conditions are illustrated in Figure 28-10. The tread rubber should be checked for cracks in the grooves and for cuts or tears from hitting objects. Side walls should be checked for abrasion and cuts from operating at low pressure or from hitting objects. Any bulges on the tire indicate separation of plies,

tread rubber, or side wall rubber. Internal damage may exist that does not show up on the outside of the tire. The tire should be removed from the rim for inspection anytime the tire has gone flat or if there is any reason to suspect possible tire body damage.

Punctures should be patched on the inside of the tire following approved plugging and patching techniques. Emergency repairs of small punctures may be made from the outside of the tire. These should be permanently repaired on the inside at the earliest possible opportunity.

Normal tire tread wear is rated at 60 miles per hour (96.5 kmph). Lower speeds improve tire mileage while higher speeds reduce it. The 55 mph (88.5 kmph) speed limit improves tire life. Tire mileage on a set of tires may be extended by rotating the tire and wheel position each 5,000 miles (8,000 km). This can be doubled for radial tires. Experience has shown that the most even wear will result when the tires and wheels are rotated as shown in Figure 28-11. Some vehicles use different tire pressures on front and rear so the tire pressure should be checked and adjusted after tire rotation.

Wheel and tire balance is another of the service operations that will extend tire mileage and suspension life while producing a smooth riding vehicle. Wheel unbalance sets up vibrations in the suspension system that shake the vehicle.

To roll smoothly, the tire must not only be balanced, but must be round. Out-of-roundness can come from tire and wheel tolerance stack up. The wheel is centered on the attaching bolt holes. Figure 28-12 illustrates how run-out is measured. When mounted on the hub, the tire bead surface must not run-out beyond the limit specification. These limits are approximately 0.035 in. (0.89 mm) radial run-out and 0.045 in. (1.12 mm) lateral run-out. The tire is also made with tolerances, but these are difficult to check when the tire is not mounted on a wheel. Total wheel-tire radial run-out is usually limited to 0.090 in. (2.286 mm) and lateral run-out to 0.125 in. (3.18 mm). Some manufacturers may recommend slightly different limits.

When tire-wheel run-out is excessive, it can be corrected by repositioning the tire on the wheel or by removing tread rubber from the high side on special tire-truing equipment. Truing the tire, along

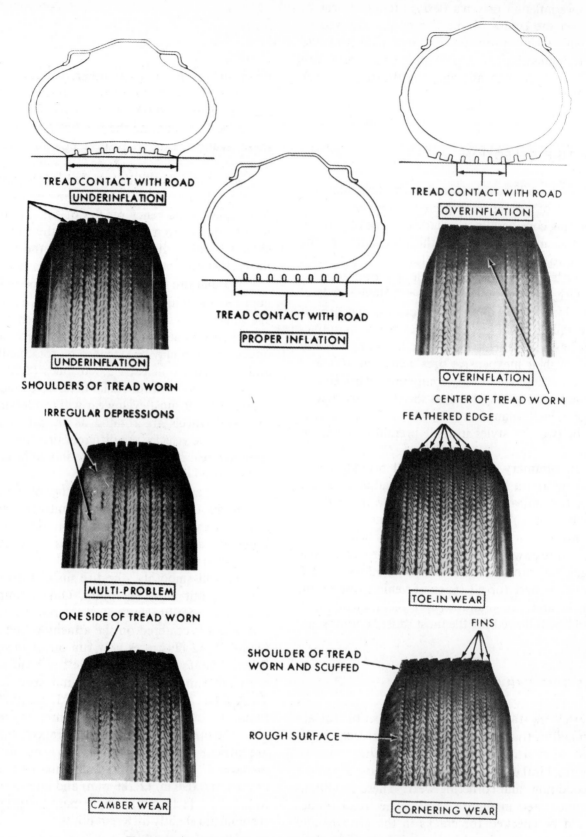

TREAD CONTACT WITH ROAD
UNDERINFLATION

UNDERINFLATION

SHOULDERS OF TREAD WORN

TREAD CONTACT WITH ROAD

PROPER INFLATION

TREAD CONTACT WITH ROAD
OVERINFLATION

OVERINFLATION

CENTER OF TREAD WORN

IRREGULAR DEPRESSIONS

FEATHERED EDGE

MULTI-PROBLEM

TOE-IN WEAR

ONE SIDE OF TREAD WORN

FINS

SHOULDER OF TREAD
WORN AND SCUFFED

ROUGH SURFACE

CAMBER WEAR

CORNERING WEAR

Fig. 28–10 Tire wear indications (Cadillac Motor Car Division,
General Motors Corporation).

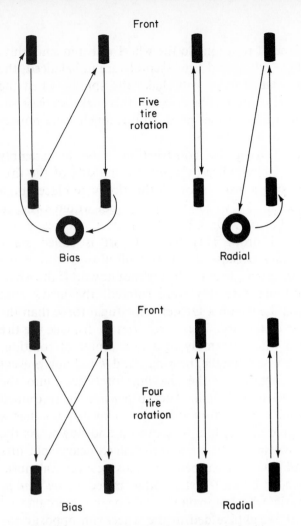

Fig. 28-11 Normal tire rotation sequence for bias and radial tires.

with balancing, will give the tire smooth rolling operation and maximum mileage, when the tire has uniform tire stiffness.

Steel-belted tires, especially belted radial tires, have produced some operating characteristics not found in bias tires. If the belt is straight but slightly off center the tire will lead in one direction. This problem is only evident when the tire is on the front wheel. If the belt is not perfectly straight within the tire, the tire will cause the automobile to shake sideways. This action is called *waddle*. Waddle is most evident at speeds below 30 mph (48 kmph). The only correction for waddle is to replace the faulty tire.

A problem tire is usually located by switching the tire and wheel to a different location on the automobile or by replacing the suspected wheel and tire by one known to be satisfactory. The faulty tire can be more easily and positively found using a piece of shop equipment called a *Tire Problem Detector*, illustrated in Figure 28-13. It consists of a motor-driven drum placed under the tire. A dial indicator is connected to a pointer that measures the movement of the wheel center as the tire and

Fig. 28-12 Tire run-out. (a) Radial run out (b) lateral run out (American Motors Corporation)

(a)

(b)

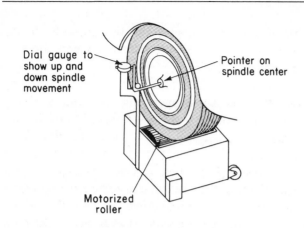

Fig. 28-13 Tire problem detector.

wheel turn. A perfectly true tire and wheel combination will have no spindle or axle movement as the tire and wheel rotate. If there is movement, the tire is marked and the dial gauge adjusted to measure rim movement. It is often possible to reposition the tire on the wheel rim to minimize spindle movement.

If an object is spun in space, all forces tend to balance each other. Spinning action is in a plane of rotation around the center of gravity, regardless of the object shape. If an odd-shaped object is thrown, it spins in a plane of rotation around its center of gravity. A round solid ball has its center of gravity in the geometric center. Some plastic "funny balls" are made with heavy sides. When thrown, they appear to wobble, but they are actually spinning in a plane around their center of gravity and not their geometric center. A wheel and tire would react in the same way if allowed to spin freely, but they are attached to a spindle. This can be seen in Figure 28-14. If the wheel and tire are in perfect balance, the spindle is located at the center of gravity and the tread centerline is on the

plane of rotation, so the wheel will spin smoothly. If the wheel and tire assembly are unbalanced, the unbalance force will shake the spindle when the wheel is spun. The effect of this shake increases as the square of the speed, so it is much more noticeable at high speeds.

During tire construction, random assembly may place splice overlaps on one side of the tire, causing a heavy spot. If this tire were placed on a free-turning wheel, the heavy spot would swing to the bottom. On a bubble balancer, the heavy side would drop. This type of test is called *static balance* because the wheel will always stop at the same point, with the heavy spot down. If the wheel and tire assembly were rotated, the heavy spot would develop a greater centrifugal force than the rest of the tire. This force tries to displace the tire and wheel assembly to a new center of rotation. The wheel spindle, bearings, and wheel hub prevent this action, so the shaking force goes into the suspension system. The suspension is restrained from moving forward and backward, but has a degree of freedom to move up and down. As the wheel spins, the static unbalanced heavy spot lifts and lowers the suspension, causing a vertical vibration or bounce that is often called *wheel tramp*. Static wheel unbalance can be counterbalanced with weights added to the wheel rim opposite the heavy point. A static balanced wheel will cause no tramp and will stay level on a bubble wheel balancer.

During tire manufacture, the ply splices may be concentrated on one edge of the tire tread or the tread rubber may be more dense on one side of the tread centerline than it is on the other. This tire could have perfect static balance, but when it is spun on a spindle, the tire force will try to establish a new plane of rotation, as shown in Figure 28-15. The top and bottom ends of the suspension knuckle are retained by the ball joints and front suspension, but the system has a degree of freedom to

Fig. 28-14 Wheel static unbalance.

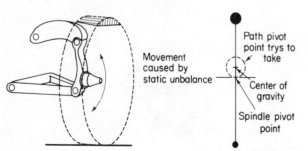

Fig. 28-15 Wheel dynamic unbalance.

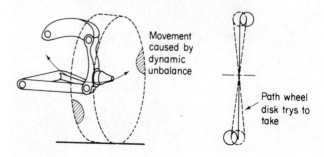

shake the front and rear of the tire-wheel assembly, turning the wheel inward and outward causing a *shimmy* condition. This type of unbalance can only be detected while the tire-wheel assembly is spinning. The test for this condition is, therefore, called *dynamic balance*. Dynamic unbalance can be counterbalanced by placing two equal weights on the light portion of the wheel rim 180° apart and on opposite sides of the wheel. The use of two weights corrects dynamic unbalance, while maintaining static balance as illustrated in Figure 28–16.

Many times, the correct placement of static balance weights can also be used to counterbalance dynamic unbalance. Balancing equipment instructions must be followed for satisfactory wheel balance.

Wheel balancing can eliminate about 75% of highway-speed vibration. The remaining vibration can be caused by tire and wheel run-out. It can also be caused by the variations in tire stiffness. These are readily located and identified with the Tire Problem Detector. Tire stiffness can be most

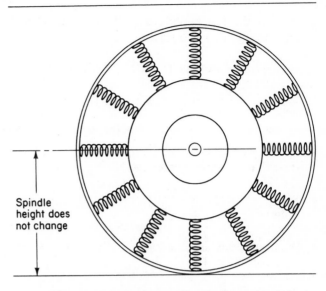

Fig. 28-17 Tire forces act as if springs were located between the rim and the belt.

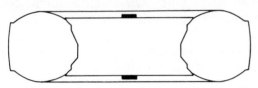

Location of static balance weights at the tire light point

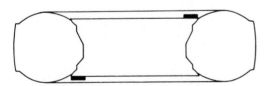

Location of dynamic balance weights to counter balance tire heavy section

Fig. 28-16 Location of balance weights.

easily understood if one thinks of a tire as a series of springs between the rim and belt, as illustrated in Figure 28–17. If the springs do not have equal strength, the spindle will go up and down as the tire operates, even when the tire is perfectly balanced statically and dynamically. Tire stiffness can be corrected with a special grinder synchronized with the Tire Problem Detector. It grinds the edge of the tread at the proper location to equalize tire stiffness.

Maximum tire mileage and maximum customer satisfaction occur when an accurately aligned vehicle in good condition is fitted with the correct tires, properly inflated and properly balanced. Tires should be rotated and inspected at recommended intervals.

REVIEW QUESTIONS

1. Why is the tire important to the control of the automobile? [INTRODUCTION]

2. What is a tire ply? [28-1]

3. What types of materials are used for tire cords? [28-1]

4. How does the manufacture of radial tires differ from that of bias-ply tires? [28-1]

5. What is the greatest difference in tires of the same size? [28-1]

6. What are the advantages and disadvantages of radial tires? [28-1]

7. Why are the sipes in the tread cut at unequal lengths? [28-2]

8. What causes a tire to hydroplane? [28-2]

9. What limits maximum tire size that can be used on an automobile? [28-2]

10. How are the sizes of tires designated? [28-2]

11. Why should all four wheels have the same type of tire construction? [28-3]

12. What functions does the rim-to-bead contact serve? [28-3]

13. What is the result of natural flexing of the tire as it operates? [28-3]

14. What is a tire's worst enemy? [28-3]

15. How can tire heating be minimized? [28-3]

16. What is the basis for tire selection? [28-4]

17. How should tire punctures be repaired? [28-5]

18. How does the steel belt affect tire operation? [28-5]

19. How does static balance differ from dynamic balance [28-5]

20. What is tire stiffness? [28-5]

suspension
and handling

High production domestic passenger cars are designed for drivers who may be poorly equipped physically and mentally to drive, even though these drivers actually feel that they are very good drivers. Passenger car suspensions and steering are designed so that poorly equipped drivers will be able to sense impending loss of control in sufficient time to safely take corrective action. This slow driver-handling response may be contrasted to a quick, sensitive handling response right up to the point that control is lost, that is found in race cars. The race driver must have trained senses to enable him to drive his race car at its maximum handling limit while he maintains control of the car.

Vehicle handling characteristics depend upon the chassis and suspension design. At one extreme is the suspension designed to give a soft boulevard ride of the type found on domestic luxury automobiles. At the other extreme is the suspension designed to give a stiff firm ride, such as the suspension of a racing car. The great majority of domestic automobiles have suspensions that provide a ride that is a compromise between these extremes.

An improperly operating suspension is usually most noticeable to the driver as the vehicle handling characteristics change. These characteristics may change so slowly that he is not aware of the change until it has become dangerous. The suspension should be checked anytime there is any suspension noise or a sign that the vehicle is handling improperly.

29-1 HANDLING REQUIREMENTS

All forces affecting automobile handling must pass through the interaction of the tire and road. Almost all automobile ride and handling characteristics are related directly to the properties of the tires being used. Changes in tire types, design, and condition will usually cause a drastic change in a vehicle's ride and handling reactions. Therefore, replacing the tires with new ones having the desired properties is often the best solution to a handling complaint.

Ride and handling are subjective values. They are terms that relate to the passenger and driver *feel*. No objective values have been devised that will satisfy everyone; however, passenger car manufacturers have run studies using large numbers of persons to determine driver feel characteristics that are acceptable to the majority of drivers for each vehicle type. For this reason, driver feel is different in a luxury passenger car, a sports car, and performance car.

Driver feel includes sensations created by changes in the vehicle direction, tire squeal, and body roll. Forces proportional to the road condition and the amount of tire slippage are felt in the steering wheel to warn the driver that the vehicle is approaching a skidding condition. This is less detectable with radial tires. A vehicle becomes uncontrollable in a skid.

The vehicle suspension, along with the tires and steering linkages, is designed to provide the driver with safe positive vehicle control and to be free of irritating vibrations. Its design will produce minimum wear on the tires and other parts of the suspension system.

29-2 SUSPENSION REQUIREMENTS

Suspension systems may be designed to give a soft or firm ride. A soft ride, usually found on luxury passenger cars, results from large vehicle deflections using soft springs and mild shock absorber dampening that allows the deflection energy to be absorbed over a longer period of time. Sudden changes in the road, wind gusts, or steering positions will cause a sidewise body roll or fore and aft pitch. This, in turn, may produce difficult handling control. Conditions like this seldom occur on modern highways. As the amount of suspension deflection is reduced, the ride becomes harsh and vehicle control improves. Automobile suspension designs are a compromise between ride softness and handling ability, depending upon the manufacturer's design objective.

Maximum automobile control exists when all four tires are in equal contact with the road surface. Control depends upon the friction between the tires and the road. The amount of friction results from the type and surface condition of both tire and road, as well as from the weight on the tire. Acceleration forces, braking forces, and steering forces are *dynamic forces* that depend upon this tire-to-road friction. The automobile suspension and weight distribution are designed to keep the wheels in maximum contact with the road to maintain desirable control. Control is lost on any wheel if the dynamic load exceeds the tire-to-road friction, because the tire will slip or skid.

Tires encounter both large and small bumps as they roll over the road surface. Deflections from small bumps are absorbed by the tires. As the bumps become larger, the tires can no longer absorb the shock so the vertical deflection is sent through the wheels, drums, and bearings to the vehicle suspension system. Suspensions with large deflections can absorb these bumps and allow the vehicle body to ride smoothly. Suspensions with limited deflection bounce the vehicle body.

Bumps tend to bounce the tire from the road, thereby reducing tire-to-road friction when the effective weight becomes less at the high side of the bounce. Vehicle control is lost when the tire loses contact with the road. The suspension system must not only absorb shock, but it must keep the tire in contact with the road to ensure vehicle control.

Suspension systems must support the automobile weight while being flexible enough to absorb road shock. At the same time, the suspension must keep the tires in proper contact with the road surface. Automobile load is supported by a flexible coil, leaf, or torsion spring. As a car goes over a bump, the spring is compressed. This motion is called *jounce*. Jounce stores energy in the spring. The stored energy forces the spring to return to its original shape. As it returns, it overruns the neutral position into the expanded or ex-

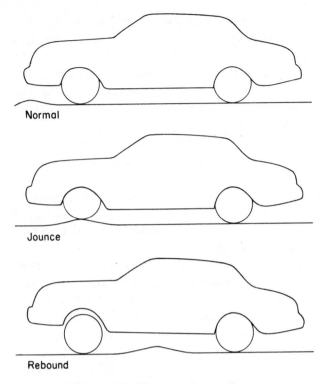

Fig. 29-1 Front wheel position in normal, jounce, and rebound positions.

tended position. This motion is called *rebound*. Figure 29-1 illustrates jounce and rebound. The spring oscillates back and forth from jounce to rebound at a rate of 60 to 80 cycles per minute. Each cycle, jounce and rebound become smaller and smaller, due to friction of the spring's molecular structure and the suspension pivot joints. A shock absorber is added to each suspension to rapidly dampen and stop spring oscillation. Maximum jounce is limited by a rubber bumper and maximum rebound is limited by a bumper or by the extended limit of the shock absorber.

Tire position is controlled during jounce by the spring itself or by linkages, levers, and arms. One end of the linkage is connected to the movable portion of the suspension and the other end is attached to the vehicle structure. As the suspension moves into jounce or rebound, the movable end of the linkage swings in an arc. It is necessary to understand the characteristics of linkages swinging through an arc in order to understand the suspension reaction on an automobile.

The vertical and horizontal distances between the stationary end and the movable end of a link change as the link rotates through an arc. There is a variable distance between the vehicle structure when the hinge point of the suspension is on the

stationary vehicle structure and the movable point is connected to the spindle, wheel, and tire. This action forms the basis for suspension and steering geometry.

In Figure 29-2, the vertical distance (A) is called displacement when it is applied to automotive suspensions. For a given displacement, a long linkage (1) will give less horizontal change (B) than a short linkage (2). Linkage length and hinge points (P) are designed to maintain the best possible tire-to-road contact during all vehicle maneuvers while staying within the limits of lever length and available space in the vehicle.

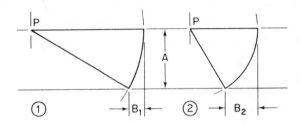

Fig. 29-2 Vertical and horizontal distance moved by an arc.

29-3 REAR SUSPENSION DESIGN

The simplest example of lever system principles on automobiles is the leaf-type rear spring suspension. The front portion of the leaf spring is attached to a spring hanger on the automobile frame member. The rear axle housing is fastened near the middle of the spring. At rest in a static position or curb position, the section of the spring in front of the axle housing is nearly horizontal with the ground. During jounce and rebound, the axle will be at its maximum aft position when the spring hanger center and the axle center are the same distance above the ground. The axle will move forward from this position during all other positions of jounce and rebound. Forward movement increases, for the same amount of spring deflection, when a short spring section is used in front of the axle. This can be seen in Figure 29-3.

The leaf spring also serves as a lever to absorb rear axle torque that occurs during acceleration and braking. Torque tends to twist the axle housing which, in turn, attempts to twist the spring, as

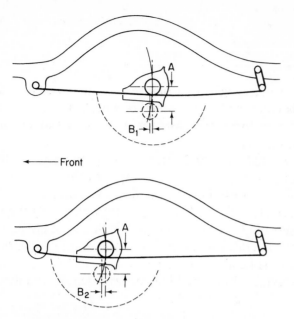

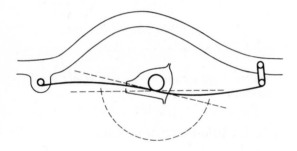

Fig. 29-3 Vertical distance (A) compared to horizontal distance (B) on different rear suspension geometry.

Fig. 29-4 Differential twist on acceleration.

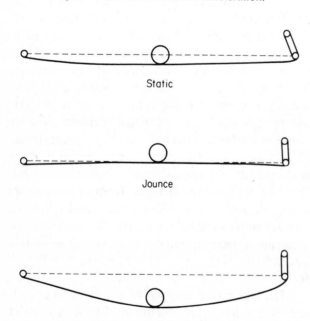

Static

Jounce

Rebound

Fig. 29-5 Spring shackle movement as the leaf spring arc changes.

illustrated in Figure 29-4. This action is often called *wind-up*. The effect of wind-up is reduced with a short stiff forward spring section. Automotive leaf spring designs compromise the torque absorbing properties of the spring with the rear suspension geometry to produce the desired effects.

The rear portion of the leaf spring does not control torque but merely helps to support vehicle weight and control *side sway* which occurs when the rear of the car moves sideways. Spring shackles are attached between the rear end of the spring and automobile frame. The shackle provides a flexible link that will compensate for spring length changes as the spring flexes. The spring shortens as it curves and lengthens when it straightens. This can be seen in Figure 29-5. The weight in pounds necessary to deflect the spring one inch is called *spring rate*. The higher the spring rate, the stiffer the spring will be and the heavier the load it can support. The rear suspension spring rate is about 120% of the front suspension spring rate. Increasing spring rate will decrease spring flexibility and increase ride harshness. Shock absorbers are added to dampen oscillation, and they are often placed at an angle to help control side sway.

Coil springs can support weight. They require linkages to maintain tire-to-road alignment and to transfer braking torque and acceleration torque to the frame. Figure 29-4 illustrates the typical linkages used with coil springs. One or two links near each end of the rear axle housing hold the axle in the correct fore and aft position. These links are also used to transfer braking and acceleration torque to the frame. Side sway is controlled by linkages near the center of the axle. The axle end of each of these links swings through an arc. This changes the relative position of the body and tires during jounce and rebound.

Ideally, the tires should contact the ground squarely and should roll without any sidewise force or side thrust. This, of course, is not possible on a moving automobile encountering road irregularities, wind gusts, required directional control, changes in weight, acceleration, and braking, and having movable suspension systems to absorb shock.

Rear wheel torque, produced by the engine, pushes the forward part of the driving tires downward. This, in turn, lifts the front of the driving axle housing, producing *rearward weight transfer*. The upward force on the axle housing is transferred to the chassis through the rear suspension.

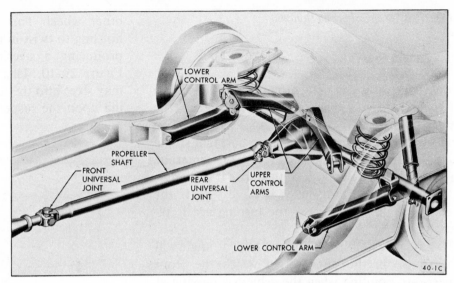

Fig. 29-6 Typical rear suspension using coil springs (Buick Motor Division, General Motors Corporation).

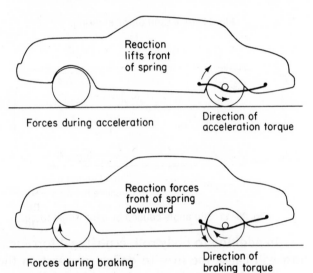

Reaction lifts front of spring

Forces during acceleration

Direction of acceleration torque

Reaction forces front of spring downward

Forces during braking

Direction of braking torque

Fig. 29-7 Rear wheel torque forces on the automobile.

This tends to lift the vehicle's front tires from the ground, reducing front tire-to-road friction, which will reduce steering control. Some specialized drag racing cars have so much torque delivered to the rear wheels that the front tires leave the ground and steering control is completely lost. Rearward weight transfer moves the rear suspension into jounce and the front suspension into rebound. On vehicles with a straight rear axle, the tire remains straight while the front tire changes its angularity in relation to the road surface as a result of front suspension geometry.

During braking, the axles are forced in the direction that the wheels are turning. The rear suspension absorbs this torque and transfers it into the frame and body. Braking torque will force the front suspension into jounce as it accepts greater

effective weight when the rear suspension goes into the rebound position. This action produces a *forward weight transfer* that reduces rear brake effect while increasing the load on the front brakes. Weight transfer is illustrated in Figure 29-7.

The drive wheels push against the suspension to accelerate the automobile mass; braking action holds back against the suspension member to slow the automobile mass. This fact is ofter overlooked when discussing automobile suspension.

29-4 VEHICLE DYNAMICS

A side load is put on the suspension system whenever the vehicle is turned from the straight-ahead direction. When the front wheels are slightly turned, they move in a track that is at an angle to the direction that the vehicle is traveling. This angle is called the *steering angle,* described in Figure 29-8. Turned wheels produce a side load on the

Fig. 29-8 Steering angle.

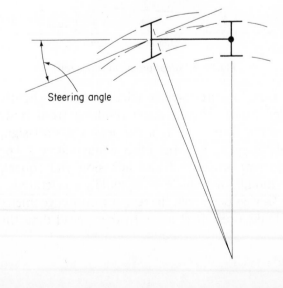

Steering angle

475

front suspension that moves the front of the vehicle in the direction the wheels are pointing. If the driver holds the wheels at this angle, the relative angle between the tire and the car is constant so the car will continue to turn in an arc and the centerline of each tire will be tangent to that arc. If this angle is reduced, the arc diameter is increased. If the steering angle is increased, the turning arc is reduced.

A vehicle holding a constant steering angle will only move in the direction in which the front wheels are pointing when the vehicle is moving at very low speeds. As vehicle speed increases, centrifugal action on the vehicle mass will tend to cause the vehicle body to roll outward.

The centrifugal force acts through the vehicle's center of gravity. The center of gravity is the point that has an equal amount of weight on every side of it. The center of gravity in automobiles is always above ground level. The centrifugal force will tend to tip or roll the vehicle body toward the outside of the turning arc as shown in Figure 29-9. *Body roll* causes a sidewise weight transfer that forces the outside suspension to go into jounce and the inside suspension to go into rebound. Sidewise weight transfer places a great deal of weight on the outside wheels and lightens the load on the inside wheels.

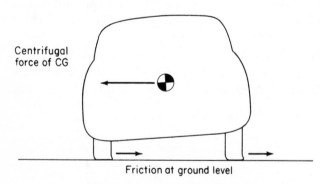

Fig. 29-9 Forces producing body roll.

Loss of tire-to-road friction on the lightly loaded inside driving wheel resulting from body roll often shows up as a car leaves a stop sign, accelerating as it turns onto a busy street. The inside rear wheel will lose adhesion and squeal, even though the vehicle is only mildly accelerated.

During body roll, the rear suspension geometry will make one wheel move further ahead than the

other wheel. This causes the straight rear axle housing to twist in relation to the body center line producing a steering tendency as illustrated in Figure 29-10. This is called *roll steer*. Roll steer may steer into the turn or out of the turn, depending upon the suspension linkage length and pivot position.

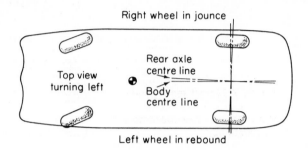

Fig. 29-10 Result of roll steering.

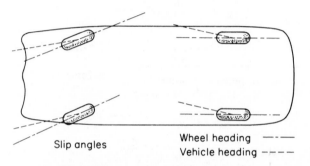

Fig. 29-11 Slip angle caused by centrifugal force.

In addition to body roll, centrifugal force in a turn will cause the tires to deflect or twist so the actual path or angle that the vehicle follows is somewhat less than the steering angle. The difference in these two angles is called *slip angle,* even though the tire is only deformed within the tire-to-road contact patch area. Slip angle can be seen in Figure 29-11.

Centrifugal force increases as the vehicle speed increases in a turn, while a constant steering angle is held. When the centrifugal force exceeds the force of tire-to-road friction, the tires begin to slide and the vehicle skids, resulting in loss of vehicle control.

Engine torque is applied down the driveshaft, twisting it in a counterclockwise direction as viewed from the driver position. During heavy acceleration, this driveshaft torque pushes downward on the left rear wheel and lifts the right wheel. This causes the left rear suspension to go into rebound and the right suspension to go into jounce, which produces a roll steer effect. It also reduces the effective weight on the right rear tire so it loses its tire-to-road friction before the more highly loaded left wheel does; therefore, the right wheel will spin free before the left wheel when the vehicle is under high acceleration. This can be seen in Figure 29-12.

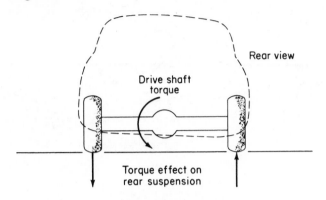

Fig. 29-12 Engine torque effect on the rear suspension tire loading.

29-5 FRONT SUSPENSION DESIGN

Front suspension geometry is much more complex than rear suspension geometry. Each side of the front suspension of modern passenger cars has independent springing. It must provide a method for steering the front tires while controlling deflection loads, side loads, and braking loads.

Two types of springs are used in automobile front suspensions; coil springs and torsion bars. If one were to study a one-inch section of each of these springs during jounce and rebound, it would be obvious that each section would be twisted in the same manner. A torsion bar is basically a stretched out or unwound coil spring. To say it another way, a coil spring is a coiled torsion bar. Their main difference lies in the method of attaching one end to the frame and the other end to the suspension linkage system.

The front wheel hub or drum is placed on bearings that are supported by a spindle which is part of the steering knuckle. A brake backing plate or caliper is bolted to the knuckle behind the wheel drum or disc. The inboard end of the wheel knuckle has two attachment points with ball joints used to support the spindle while allowing rotation for steering. A typical front suspension is illustrated in Figure 29-13.

The upper and lower ball joints are held to the frame with control arms. The length of these arms and the placement of the inner pivot points control tire position during jounce and rebound. This

can be observed in Figure 29-14. The upper control arm is shorter than the lower control arm. With a given suspension deflection in jounce, the upper arm goes through a larger portion of its arc than the lower arm. If the arms were parallel while in the static position, the change during jounce would cause the upper ball joint to move inward a greater amount than the lower joint. This, in turn, would move the top of the tire inward more than the bottom. This produces a tire angle called *negative camber*.

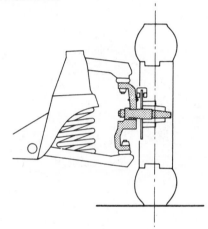

Fig. 29-13 Typical front suspension configuration.

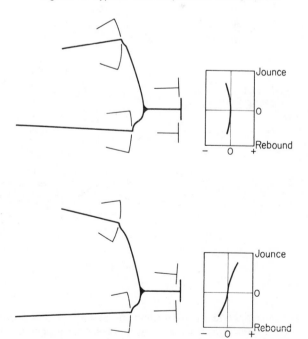

Fig. 29-14 Typical front suspension geometry change produced by repositioning the support arms.

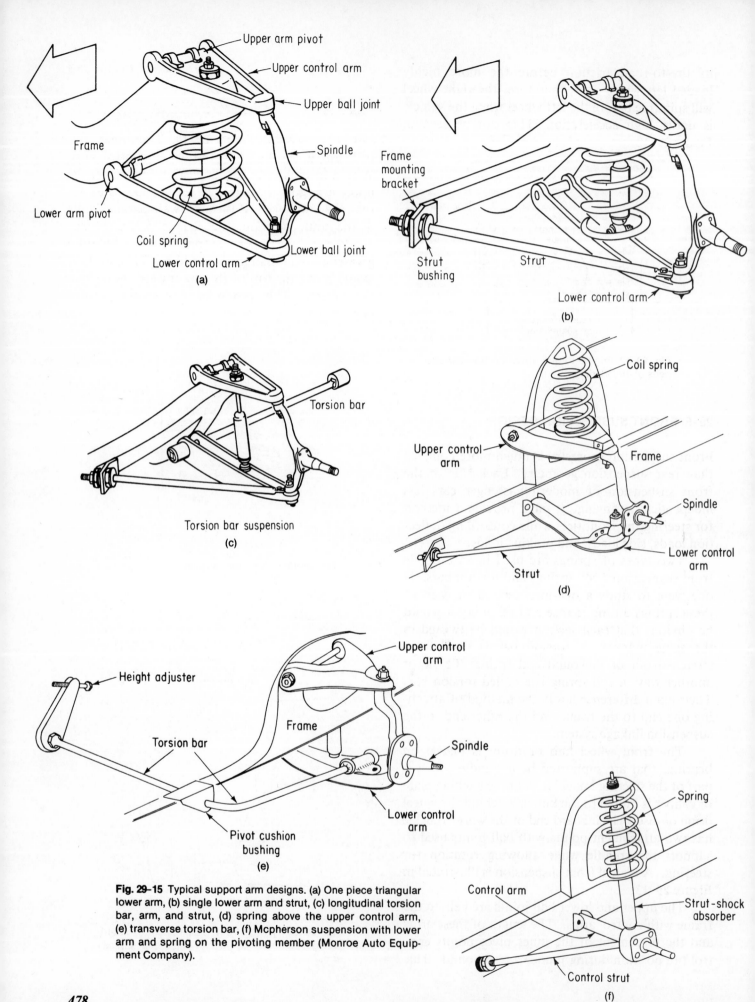

Fig. 29-15 Typical support arm designs. (a) One piece triangular lower arm, (b) single lower arm and strut, (c) longitudinal torsion bar, arm, and strut, (d) spring above the upper control arm, (e) transverse torsion bar, (f) Mcpherson suspension with lower arm and spring on the pivoting member (Monroe Auto Equipment Company).

If the control arm pivot points were widely separated so the control arms moved in a different portion of the arc, the top of the tire could move outward during jounce. This tire angle is called *positive chamber*. A number of front suspensions are illustrated in Figure 29–15.

The upper control arm is a stamped steel triangularly shaped member. The upper ball joint is attached to one point of the triangle. The other two points of the triangle are attached to the vehicle frame through rubber insulation bushings.

Two types of lower control arms are used. The one that has been used for the longest time is similar to the upper control arm, being a stamped, riveted, or welded steel triangular member with the lower ball joint at one point, the other two points being connected to the frame through insulation bushings. The second type of lower control arm is made of two pieces. The main arm is a stamped steel channel with the lower ball joint at the outboard end and an insulation bushing at the inboard end. A rod or strut extends forward from a point just inboard of the ball joint to a point on the front section of the frame. This second lower control arm type allows more space for engine and brakes, as well as reducing tooling costs when compared to the one-piece type of lower control arm.

The hub of the front wheel and the spindle are located near the bottom of the knuckle, so the fore-and-aft road shock is transmitted primarily to the lower control arm. The inboard portion of the lower control arm is, therefore, widely spaced. Wide spacing gives the insulating bushings and supporting members the large leverage that is necessary to reduce the forces they must retain. The upper control arm stabilizes the upper end of the knuckle; thus, front suspension geometry is controlled by the position of the control arms.

Front coil springs may be located either between the center of the lower control arm and the frame, or between the center of the upper control arm and a frame spring tower under the front fender, as shown in Figure 29–16. In each case, the vehicle weight is supported through the spring, control arm, knuckle, spindle, hub, wheel, and tire.

The front suspension of a vehicle equipped with front torsion bars absorbs the load through the lower control arms. The torsion bar in some models is connected from the inboard end of the lower control arm pivot to the vehicle frame at a point parallel with the rear engine mount. In other models it is connected between the outer end of the

lower control arm and the front cross member. A torsion bar is pictured in Figure 29–17.

The ball joint on either the upper or lower end of the spring-loaded control arm is called the *weight-carrying* ball joint. When this ball joint fastens to the knuckle above the control arm, it is called a *tension ball joint* because the automobile weight tends to pull the ball joint from the knuckle. When the control arm is located above the ball joint, it pushes the ball joint into the spindle and is, therefore, called a *compression ball joint*.

The ball within the ball joint that is located on the unloaded control arm is not held in its socket by automobile weight so it is preloaded with an elastomer disc or metal spring. It is, therefore, called a *preloaded ball joint*, a *friction ball joint*,

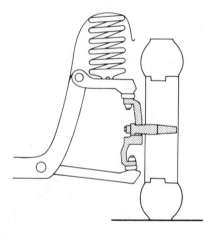

Fig. 29-16 Front suspension with the spring above the upper arm.

Fig. 29-17 Torsion bar attachment points.

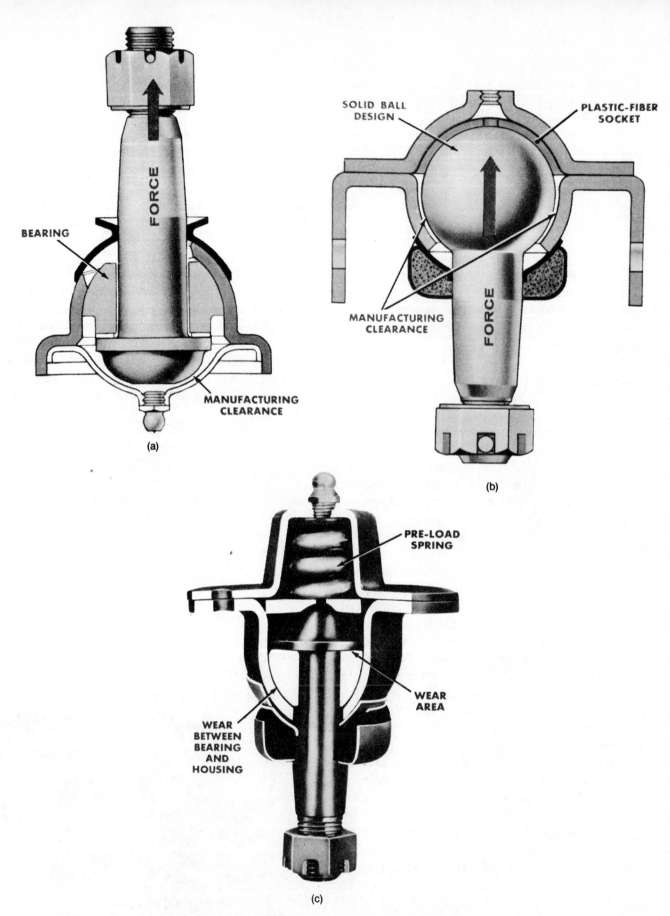

Fig. 29-18 Typical ball joint types. (a) Tension-type ball joint, (b) compression-type ball joint, (c) preloaded ball joint (TRW Replacement Division).

or a *follower ball joint*. The preload must be sufficient to keep the ball seated during various automobile loads, road irregularities, cornering, and panic brake stops. Ball joint types are illustrated in Figure 29-18.

The inboard pivot point axis of the upper control arm is angled upward at the front to minimize vehicle *brake dive*, that is, the lowering of the front of the vehicle during braking as a result of forward weight transfer. During braking, the brake tries to force the spindle to rotate in the direction the wheels are rotating. This means that the upper part of the spindle tries to move forward. This forces the outer end of this upper control arm forward. The outer end of this control arm is below the front inner pivot so the forward force tries to go under the front pivot point. This force, as shown in Figure 29-19, attempts to lift the front of the vehicle. The diving force will be balanced by the lifting force when the pivot point axis has the correct upward angle.

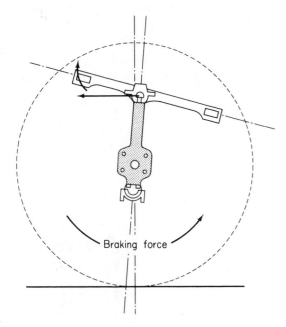

Fig. 29-19 Upper control arm position to reduce brake dive.

29-6 SUSPENSION CONTROL DEVICES

Rubber bushings are used between the control arms, hangers, and shackles to help absorb road shock, provide deflection, and reduce the transmission of noise to the passenger compartment. Bushing rubber type and hardness are carefully selected to provide correct physical and durability properties required for each application. The use

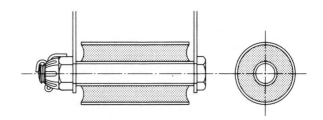

Fig. 29-20 Cross section of a typical rubber suspension bushing.

of rubber bushings provides a better suspension system and, at the same time, minimizes the number of lubrication points and allows for slight assembly misalignment, both of which reduce vehicle cost by allowing larger manufacturing tolerances.

Rubber bushings are usually constructed with a metal outer shell and a metal inner bushing. During assembly, the bushing is pressed or screwed into a sized hole in the control arm or spring eye and then fastened to the frame bracket with a bolt. The bracket is tightened against the inner bushing, as illustrated in Figure 29-20. All movement occurs within the rubber deflections and the metal-to-metal contact does not move. This type of bushing, therefore, has no need of lubrication, not even rubber lube. It is important during suspension assembly that the vehicle be in the neutral position before the bushing bracket bolt is tightened. This prevents preloading the bushing rubber in a position that would lead to unnatural loads and short bushing life.

A sway bar, or stabilizer bar, is used on the front suspension of some vehicles. It is also used on some rear suspensions. The stabilizer bar is a U-shaped rod whose center is attached to the frame through rubber insulator bushings with one end attached to each control arm, as pictured in Figure 29-21. As both wheels go into jounce, the stabilizer bar merely rotates in its insulator bushings. This will not affect a soft ride. It is a different matter when one wheel goes into jounce. The stabilizer bar twists, just like a torsion bar, to lift the frame and the opposite suspension arm. This action reduces the vehicle roll tendency. Excessively heavy stabilizer bars usually cause the vehicle to wander by overcorrecting.

The automobile weight resting on a spring will oscillate up and down when its static equilibrium is

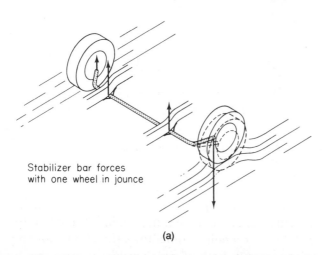

Stabilizer bar forces
with one wheel in jounce

(a)

(b)

Fig. 29-21 Stabilizer bar. (a) Forces produced by deflection, (b) typical stabilizer bar installation.

disturbed, such as by driving over a bump. The amplitude of the oscillations is gradually diminished by friction in the suspension system. Suspension system friction is in the pivot bushings and in the spring molecular structure. Coil springs, single leaf springs, and torsion bars develop very little friction. Multileaf springs develop friction as the leaves rub together on insulating spacers and so they dampen or stop the oscillation more rapidly.

An oscillating automobile is very difficult to control. It is dangerous to drive, because the effective weight on the tires keeps changing. This type of oscillation could allow the tires to bounce clear of the road so all control would be lost. It would also allow the body to roll steer, making directional control difficult. Shock absorbers are installed on

a suspension system to rapidly dampen the natural vehicle spring oscillation and thus improve ride, vehicle controllability, and vehicle handling.

The spring supports the weight and the shock absorber controls the spring oscillation. Contrary to many people's ideas, the shock absorbers do not support weight. Some shock absorbers have accessories added to them to absorb weight, such as external springs or a compressed air chamber. New standard shock absorbers cannot lift a sagging suspension system.

A shock absorber (Figure 29-22) is basically a cylinder with a piston moving in it. Both sides of the piston are fitted with valves and sized openings or orifices that allow fluid to flow through the piston at controlled rates as the piston moves back and forth in the cylinder. The cylinder is surrounded by a fluid reservoir tube. A valve between the cylinder and reservoir chamber controls the flow of fluid between them. The bottom of the shock absorber housing is mounted on the suspension through rubber bushings. A rod extending from the piston is connected to the vehicle frame through rubber bushings. The piston is forced downward in the cylinder during jounce and upward in the cylinder during rebound. Different valve and

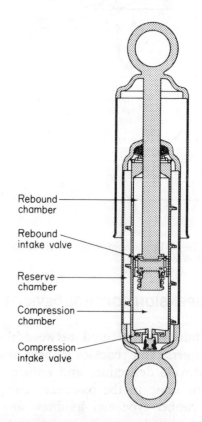

Rebound
chamber

Rebound
intake valve

Reserve
chamber

Compression
chamber

Compression
intake valve

Fig. 29-22 Cross section of a typical shock absorber (Monroe Auto Equipment Company).

orifice designs control resistance to piston movement.

The energy absorbed by the shock absorber is converted into heat. The heat warms the fluid and dissipates it through the housing into the surrounding air. When the shock absorber is larger, it can absorb more heat and can, therefore, absorb more energy than small-diameter shock absorbers.

Rear axle shock absorbers are connected between the spring seat on the rear axle housing and the frame. The shock absorber may be mounted vertically or it may be canted inward and slightly forward in a "sea leg" type mounting, to add control to body roll, handling, and roadability. The mounting methods are shown in Figure 29-23.

Front shock absorbers are mounted inside the spring when coil springs are used. This location provides good mounting attachments, uses otherwise wasted space, and provides protection from damage. The shock absorber is mounted in the same location between the lower control arm and frame when using coil springs above the upper arm

and torsion bar springs, as it is when using a coil spring mounted on the lower control arm.

Many shock absorbers look identical. Their difference lies in their internal valving, which is designed to match the vehicle suspension dynamics. Shock absorbers of the correct part number must be installed to produce satisfactory ride and handling performance.

Shock absorbers are designed to rapidly dampen suspension oscillation. Standard passenger car shock absorbers are usually designed to provide greater control on extension as the vehicle rebounds than it is on compression during jounce. These shock absorbers would be specified as 20-80 (20% control during compression to 80% control during rebound), 30-70, etc., as percentages of the shock absorber's full control capacity. The ratio is entirely dependent upon the vehicle design, ride

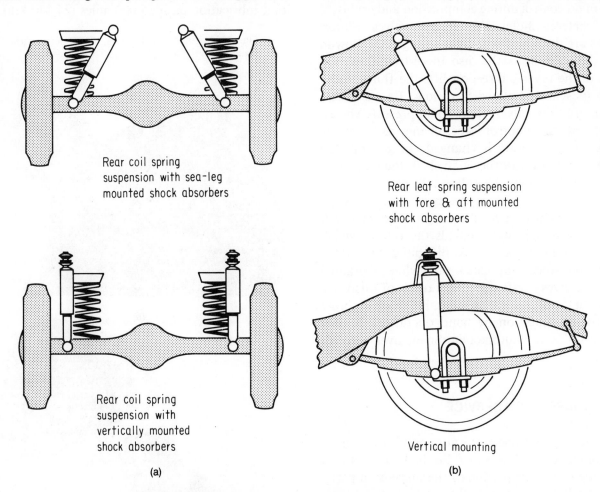

Rear coil spring suspension with sea-leg mounted shock absorbers

Rear leaf spring suspension with fore & aft mounted shock absorbers

Rear coil spring suspension with vertically mounted shock absorbers

Vertical mounting

(a)

(b)

Fig. 29-23 Typical rear shock absorber mountings. (a) Front view, (b) side view (Monroe Auto Equipment Company).

requirements, handling needs, and driving conditions. In general, racing cars have heavier control than passenger cars, but they also have a harsh ride, reduced driver comfort, and less vehicle durability.

During shock absorber extension, the oil trapped above the piston in the rebound chamber meters through the piston to the lower compression chamber below the piston. The piston rod displaces fluid in the upper rebound chamber and there is no rod in the lower compression chamber. Because of this, during extension some fluid must also flow from the reservoir into the lower compression chamber to make up for the fluid displaced by the piston rod. During rebound, fluid is, therefore, flowing through both piston valves and reservoir valves. During compression, a reverse fluid flow occurs to both chambers.

Fluid control during compression and extension uses metered holes and flutter valves. Flutter valves are discs held with light springs. Oil flow in one direction seats the disc to restrict flow. Oil flow in the reverse direction lifts the flutter valve from its seat and allows free flow. Because these valves are flow valves, rather than pressure valves, shock absorber control forces change as the shock absorber stroke rate is changed. In general, the faster the shock absorber is stroked, the more control force it applies. This allows the vehicle to have a soft, easy ride and, at the same time, provides heavy control over sudden severe jounce or rebound. The valve design also controls the rate at which control build-up occurs. Rapid build-up gives a solid and somewhat harsh ride while a gradual build-up gives a soft ride. As a result of this valve action, it is not possible to determine shock absorber control or condition by hand operation. It only shows up as the automobile moves over a rough road.

29-7 SUSPENSION SERVICE

Routine maintenance of the automobile suspension is limited to lubrication of the ball joints and a thorough visual inspection of the suspension parts. Steering linkages are usually checked at the same time. Front suspensions are always inspected as part of the wheel alignment procedure. Suspension parts seldom break without first becoming worn and cracked. When a suspension part requires repair, the faulty part is replaced. The technician must learn to identify abnormal conditions, pinpoint the cause of the faulty condition, and make repairs.

Suspension problems normally encountered will include failed shock absorbers, sagging springs, worn out suspension bushings, and worn ball joints (Figure 29-24). The tie rod ends wear and become loose. In extreme cases, they fall apart. If these are not repaired, the part will usually fail when the automobile is in use. This will be inconvenient to the driver and it may cause an accident. Preventive maintenance is the best insurance against suspension breakdown on the road.

Ball joint lubrication is required on some automobiles each 4,000 miles (6437 km). Other automobiles have ball joints that are sealed for life and these cannot be lubricated. Most automobiles are between these extremes. Some require ball joint lubrication each 15,000 miles (24,140 km) or

Fig. 29-24 Faulty ball joints, (a) Cracked, (b) separated.

(a)

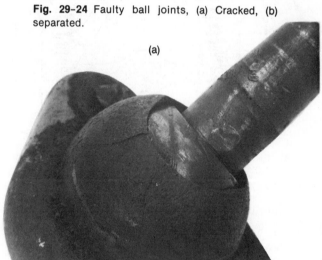

(b)

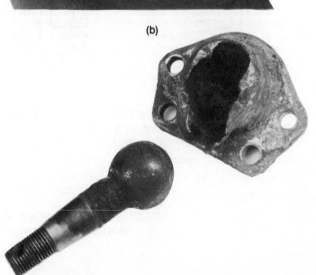

Fig. 29-25 Greasing a ball joint.

each year. Others specify 30,000 miles (48,280 km) or every other year. It is a common practice to lubricate the steering linkage at the same time that the ball joints are lubricated. The same procedures are used to lubricate both (Figure 29-25).

A grease fitting that requires periodic lubrication is installed in the ball joint if it does not have one. If it has a fitting, it is cleaned so that dirt doesn't get into the joint bearing with the grease. A hand grease-gun is recommended so that the joint can be filled slowly to prevent damage to the joint seal. Grease should be put into the joint until the seal swells slightly. Excess grease will break the seal and allow water and dirt to enter. This will shorten the joint life.

Inspection of the suspension starts with a visual inspection of the way the automobile stands on a level surface. Sagging, as pictured in Figure 29-26, indicates spring weakness. Service manuals provide specifications for the location and distance to be used in measuring the suspension height. A typical measuring method is illustrated in Figure 29-27. In most torsion bar systems, the height can be adjusted at one end of the torsion bar. Coil and leaf springs are not adjustable. The recommended procedure is to replace the weak spring, preferably replacing them on both sides of the automobile at the same time. Shims are on the market to go between the coil spring and the spring seat. These are patch-up devices that will correct the static height, but they limit jounce travel when the coils bottom or bind as they come together before the suspension reaches full jounce. Suspension height

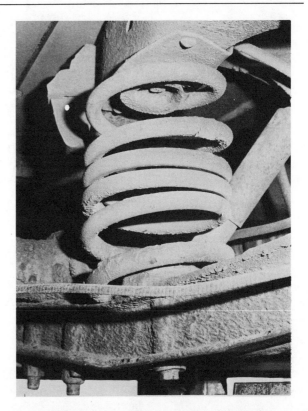

Fig. 29-26 A coil spring that has sagged as the center coils weakened.

Fig. 29-27 Measuring the suspension height at the front suspension (Chrysler Motors Corporation).

can also be positioned using helper springs, which are often placed around the shock absorbers, or shock absorbers that can be inflated with air pressure. Suspension height is checked and corrected before the front wheels are aligned.

Ball joints gradually wear as they are used. When their wear becomes excessive, they must be replaced. Starting with some 1974 automobiles, the load-carrying ball joint has a wear indicator that must not show beyond the surface of the ball

Fig. 29-28 Checking ball joint looseness (Chrysler Motors Corporation).

Fig. 29-29 Ball joint indicator protrudes through the opening adjacent to the grease fitting when the ball joint is not worn excessively.

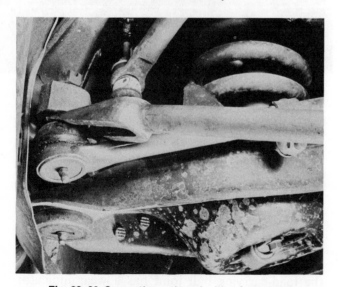

Fig. 29-30 Separating a tie rod with a forked tool made for this operation.

joint. The location is identified in Figure 29-29. Excessive wear exists when this indicator shows. Joints without the indicator are checked by jacking the suspension in a manner that removes all the load from the load-carrying ball joint. There will always be some movement in this joint. Excessive movement can be measured by clamping a dial gauge on the suspension with the gauge anvil on the joint as shown in Figure 29-28. The wheel and tire are then lifted to measure the amount of joint looseness as shown on the dial gauge. The looseness is compared to the specifications to determine if replacement is required. There should be no free play in the preloaded joint.

It is necessary to separate the suspension control arm from the steering knuckle if either the ball joint or front spring needs to be replaced. Figure 29-30 shows a spreader in use. With jack stands under the frame, the brake assembly is removed and secured to the automobile frame so no weight is placed on the brake hose. The shock absorber is removed when coil spring or control arm bushing work is needed. The load is removed from the load-carrying lower ball joint when it requires replacement by placing a garage-type floor jack under the lower control arm. Allowing the suspension to come to rest at its fully extended position on automobiles with the load-carrying ball joint on the upper control arm will usually allow removal of this ball joint. If the spring is to be removed, the spring must be compressed with a special compressing tool. If the automobile is equipped with torsion bars, they are loosened to free the load from the ball joint.

With the spring supported, the ball nut is loosened about three turns. If the stud end of the ball joint is between the support arms, the stud can be removed by pushing with a spreader tool. This

Fig. 29-31 Spreading the ball joint with a forked tool.

Fig. 29-32 Loosening a ball joint by hitting the fastening with a hammer.

Fig. 29-33 Coil spring compressed for removal.

Fig. 29-34 A rubber suspension bushing with deteriorated rubber.

is shown in Figure 29-31. If the stud nut is outside the support arms, the stud can be loosened by hitting the joint boss of the steering knuckle with a heavy hammer as another heavy hammer is held on the other side of the knuckle boss as demonstrated in Figure 29-32. The jarring will loosen the stud. When the stud is free, the nut is removed.

The compressed spring (Figure 29-33) can be lifted from the suspension member if removal is required. It is important to realize that a coil spring is highly preloaded while compressed, so it should be handled with extreme care. When a floor jack is used, it must be swung perpendicular to the side of the automobile so that it can follow the suspension as the control arm is gradually lowered. With the spring removed, the suspension can be disassembled and repaired as required. Repairs may include the replacement of the suspension bushings as well as the ball joints. Figure 29-34 shows a bushing that is worn out.

When the repairs are made, all of the suspension is assembled except the loaded ball joint. The spring is compressed and seated on the control arm as the lower support arm is moved into position. The stud is inserted in the steering knuckle boss and secured with the nut. The fasteners are torqued after the weight of the automobile is on the suspension. All castle nuts are locked with cotter pins. The shock absorber and brake are reinstalled to complete the suspension repair. The front suspension should be aligned after it is reassembled.

One of the more common repair procedures on the suspension is the replacement of the shock absorbers. Shock absorber replacement does not affect alignment except in suspensions using the shock absorber as an integral part of the suspension system. Shock absorber failure, other than breakage, is noted by oil leaking from the shock absorber and by continued oscillation after the automobile is bounced and released. Shock absorber replacement is a simple job. All that is required is to remove nuts from each end of the shock absorber to release it. New bushings and nuts are installed with the new shock absorber. The problem comes when the assembly nuts are frozen to their threaded stud. This is the normal condition in some parts of the country. Often the only way to remove the shock absorber is to crack the rusted nut to break it from the threads. New nuts are packaged with the new shock absorbers.

The rear suspension will be either a coil spring or a leaf spring. The automobile frame is supported ahead of the rear suspension when a rear spring is to be removed. A garage-type floor jack is used under the rear axle housing to lift and lower the housing as required. This repair can also be done on a garage hoist. The hoist must be accompanied by a stand to support the axle housing.

When coil springs are used, the axle is supported with the floor jack and the rear shock absorbers are removed from the housing. The rear axle housing is gradually lowered with the floor jack until the coil springs are free. In some cases, it may be necessary to loosen some of the control arms. New springs are properly seated and the axle housing is jacked up until the shocks and control arms are connected. The control arm nuts are tightened securely after the full weight of the automobile is supported by the spring.

When leaf springs are to be replaced, the shock absorber may not have to be removed. The axle housing is supported by the floor jack and the U-bolts over the axle housing are loosened, then removed. The spring shackle at the rear of the spring is removed, and then the front hanger bolt is removed to free the spring. The replacement spring should have new bushings. It is also a good practice to replace the upper shackle bushing. The spring is installed in the reverse order. The spring hanger and shackle bolts should not be tightened until the full weight of the automobile is on them.

After the rear springs are installed, the propeller shaft universal joint angles should be checked and adjusted if necessary. Some coil spring rear axles have eccentric washers on their control arms to twist the axle nose up and down to set the correct universal joint angle. Leaf springs can be shimmed with taper shims between the axle housing and the spring to set the universal joint angle.

Any repair of the suspension that affects the height of the automobile above the floor or any replacement of suspension bushings should be followed by a front end alignment. The details of this procedure are covered in the next chapter.

REVIEW QUESTIONS

1. How do tires affect the automobile handling? [29–1]

2. What is drive feel? [29–1]

3. How does suspension deflection affect the ride? [29–2]

4. Under what condition does maximum automobile control exist? [29–2]

5. When is control lost on a wheel? [29–2]

6. What is the purpose of the shock absorber? [29–2]

7. Describe the change in horizontal movements when the arc radius length changes as the steering linkage arm is rotated 45°. [29–2]

8. On a leaf rear spring how does the action of the front portion differ from the rear portion? [29–3]

9. What is spring rate? [29–3]

10. How does the rear spring rate differ from the front spring rate? [29–3]

11. How do the functions of a rear coil and a rear leaf spring differ? [29–3]

12. How do the drive wheels produce rearward weight transfer? [29–3]

13. When is a side load put on the suspension system? [29–4]

14. What causes a sidewise weight transfer in turns? [29–4]

15. How does sidewise weight transfer on the rear suspension affect steering? [29–4]

16. Where does the slip angle take place? [29–4]

17. What happens to produce a skid? [29-4]

18. In what way are torsion bars and coil springs similar? [29-5]

19. What is the purpose of ball joints? [29-5]

20. How is camber controlled during jounce and rebound? [29-5]

21. What is the advantage of having the spindle located near the bottom of the knuckle? [29-5]

22. How do the weight carrying ball joints differ from preloaded ball joints? [29-5]

23. What causes brake dive? [29-5]

24. What precautions should be taken when assembling chassis parts with rubber bushings? [29-6]

25. How does a stabilizer function? [29-6]

26. In what way does the shock absorber help a spring? [29-6]

27. Why does the automobile ride "stiffer" when it is cold than when it has been driven for a few miles? [29-6]

28. Why does a shock absorber provide more control for rapid movement than for slow movement? [29-6]

29. When should ball joints be lubricated in normal use? [29-7]

30. How is suspension height checked? [29-7]

31. How is excessive ball joint wear determined? [29-7]

steering and wheel alignment

The paramount requirement of the automotive steering system is *safety*. Parts are made from special alloy steels that are often heat treated to develop the strength properties required. The entire suspension system and steering geometry are designed with a neutral directional sense so the automobile will naturally go straight ahead. They are also designed to allow the driver to safely guide the automobile on a selected path with minimum effort. It should do this with minimum tire wear.

Maximum tire mileage and maximum tire-to-road friction for control occurs when the tire is rolling straight in an upright position. The wheel-tire position is maintained by the suspension and steering linkage design. Adjustment devices that are provided within the suspension system are used to compensate for manufacturing tolerances and for service wear conditions.

The specifications for alignment may not position the tire upright or straight ahead when the automobile is standing at a curb or on an alignment rack. In operation, the suspension system is under dynamic forces. These forces take up linkage slack and slightly deflect the suspension system members. The alignment angle specifications used to set the adjustments when the automobile is stationary on the alignment rack are such that the tires will run straight most of the time, when the automobile is moving and dynamic forces are acting on the tires.

Dynamic forces and their reactions on suspension and steering are interrelated to produce the required ride and handling characteristics. When discussing the effects of suspension geometry, it is necessary to discuss each suspension property and its effect on the function of the entire suspension system.

Camber is the angle measured in degrees between the tire tread centerline and a line perpendicular to the road surface. If the top of the tire leans slightly outward, the suspension has *positive camber*. If the top of the tire leans slightly inward, the suspension has *negative camber*. Suspension linkages cause the camber to change as the suspension goes to jounce or to rebound. Camber is illustrated in Figure 30-1.

Some suspensions are designed to have negative camber during both jounce and rebound in order to keep the tire tread centerline following a straight path down the road. Other suspensions are designed to have positive camber during jounce and negative camber during rebound. This will keep the tire tread surface flat on the road when going over bumps and dips that cause body roll. During a turn, high negative camber on the outside tire helps provide cornering power as the tire deflects under the high side loads that result from the centrifugal force on the automobile. This same high negative camber will also cause rapid tire wear. The final suspension camber is a compromise of these factors to produce the desired handling results. Normal camber on automobiles is small, usually within $+1°$ to $-1°$, with a tolerance of $\pm\frac{1}{2}°$ with the automobile standing.

Camber on any automobile is the result of the designer's objectives and of the front end geometry. Incorrect camber usually is noted by abnormal tire wear along one half of the tread. This can be seen in Figure 30-15.

Camber is adjustable by changing the position of one end of the steering knuckle. Some automobiles have adjustments at the upper control arm pivots and others at the upper ball joint. Still others adjust the lower control arm pivot. Each method provides a means to move the knuckle end inward or outward to adjust camber.

30-2 STEERING AXIS INCLINATION

The steering axis is an extension of the ball joint pivot centerline to the road surface when looking at the front of the automobile. The steering axis is inclined outward at the bottom and inward at the top. The angle of the axis compared to a line perpendicular to the road surface is measured in degrees, and is called the *Steering Axis Inclination* (SAI) as shown in Figure 30-2.

If the steering axis centerline is extended to the road surface it would contact the road surface near the tire tread centerline. The distance between these two lines at the point they intersect the road surface is called the *scrub radius*. A small scrub radius is desirable because it minimizes steering wheel shock from road irregularities and reduces steering effort.

Dynamic forces on the front tire tend to push the tire backward. These forces tend to concentrate at the tire tread centerline. If the steering axis centerline contacts the road surface inside the tire tread centerline, the natural tendency of the scrub radius will cause the tire to be turned outward as it goes down the road. The scrub radius in this example, shown in Figure 30-3, would be positive. The turning tendency would be inward if the

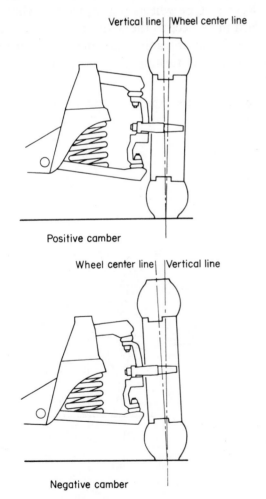

Vertical line | Wheel center line

Positive camber

Wheel center line | Vertical line

Negative camber

Fig. 30-1 Camber illustrated.

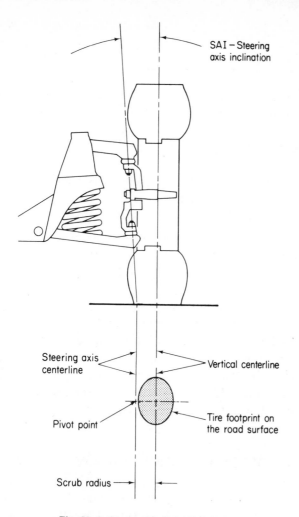

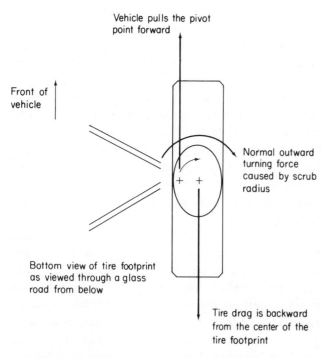

steering axis centerline contact point is designed to contact the road surface outside the tire centerline. In this case, the scrub radius is negative.

The effect of unequal brake force on the front wheels increases when the scrub radius is large, as illustrated in Figure 30-4. This would contribute to poor vehicle control by making the vehicle pull sideways as the brakes are applied. The wheel with the highest braking force will pull outward on a suspension with a positive scrub radius.

Air pressure in the tire also affects vehicle directional pull. A vehicle with a positive scrub radius tends to pull outward or toward the side which has a tire with low pressure. The scrub radius is designed into the knuckle and spindle. It will remain correct as long as the knuckle is not bent. If the knuckle is damaged so the scrub radius is incorrect, the knuckle must be replaced. This damage can be detected by measuring both camber and steering axis inclination. If steering axis inclination does not fall within specifications when camber is correct, the knuckle is bent.

Reverse-type wheels that move the wheel rim outward in respect to the wheel center disc greatly increase the scrub radius, causing a large increase in the outward turning tendency, hard steering,

Fig. 30-2 Steering axis inclination.

Fig. 30-4 Reverse-type wheel increases the scrub radius.

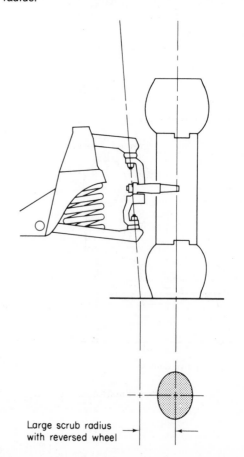

Fig. 30-3 Forces in the tire footprint producing a scrub radius.

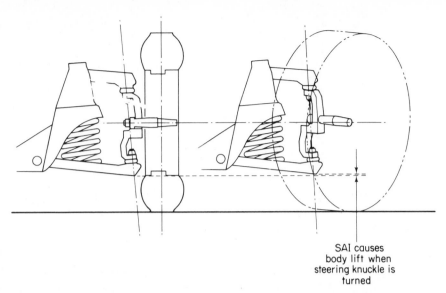

Fig. 30–5 Vehicle lift produced by steering axis inclination in a turn.

SAI causes
body lift when
steering knuckle is
turned

and steering wheel shock. The stated purpose of reverse wheels is to provide widely spaced tires that make a wide wheel tread for stability and good appearance. Its purpose is not to improve steering or handling. The location of the tire centerline of these wheels is out beyond the spindle so there are large overhung loads on the wheel bearings that overload the outer small wheel bearings and reduce bearing life.

When the wheels are in the straight-ahead position, steering axis inclination positions the automobile body as low as possible. As the wheels are turned in either direction, the tip of the spindle tries to move downward; however, it cannot move downward because the spindle is in the center of the wheel and the wheel is in contact with the ground. Therefore, as the spindle pivots in the ball joints, it must lift the vehicle. This is illustrated in Figure 30–5. The weight of the automobile will, therefore, produce a strong tendency to return the wheels to a straight-ahead position after the turn has been completed. This force is great enough to provide excellent directional stability so the vehicle has a natural tendency to run straight ahead.

The *steering axis inclination* angle is selected as a compromise between steering effort, neutral returning force, and wheel pull sensitivity. In passengers cars, it is inclined from 4° to 8°. The final steering axis inclination is dictated by vehicle design and handling requirements.

30-3 CASTER

Caster is the tendency of a steerable wheel to follow the lead of the *point,* where an extension of the

pivot axis contacts the road surface. The weight of the automobile causes the tire to flatten slightly to form a contact patch where it rests on the road surface. The effective weight of the automobile can be considered to be concentrated at the contact patch center point, directly under the center of the spindle. This contact patch center point tends to follow the pivot axis center point. The pivot point always moves in the direction that the vehicle is moving. This action can be observed in Figure 30–6.

This is most familiar on the front wheel of a bicycle. The extension of the fork pivot centerline contacts the road ahead of the tire contact patch center. This positive caster gives the bicycle a natural tendency to steer straight ahead, the contact patch center following the pivot center point. This caster tendency allows the bicycle rider to ride without holding on to the handle bars.

Backward tilt of the pivot axis tends to aid directional steering. The angle produced by the axis tilt with respect to vertical is called the *caster angle.* The caster angle is *positive* when the top tilts backward and *negative* when the top tilts forward. No steering force is exerted when the pivot point axis extension contacts the center of the tire patch. Positive directional steering force occurs when the pivot point is in front of the contact patch center, leaving a large portion of the contact patch behind the pivot point. This causes the tire to swing behind the pivot point to produce a positive caster effect. If the pivot point is behind the center of the contact patch, the large portion of tire contact patch is ahead of the pivot point. The normal tendency of the large area is to move around behind the pivot point. When the large area is in

493

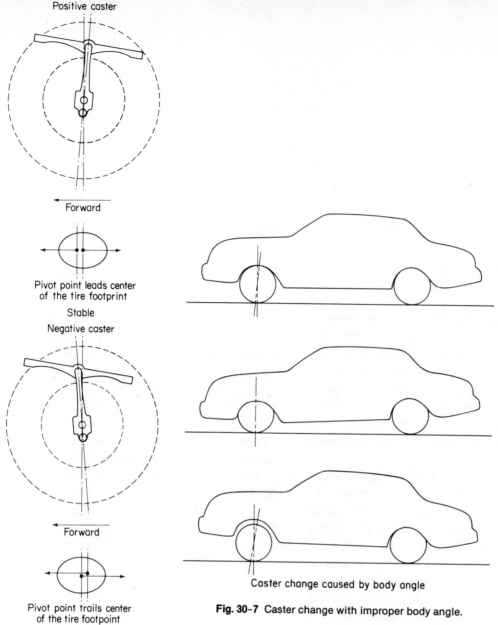

Positive caster

Forward

Pivot point leads center
of the tire footprint

Stable

Negative caster

Forward

Pivot point trails center
of the tire footpoint

Unstable

Fig. 30-6 Caster illustrated.

Caster change caused by body angle

Fig. 30-7 Caster change with improper body angle.

front, it results in a continual force to turn from the straight-ahead position, producing a negative caster effect.

Sag from weak springs or overloading will affect caster because steering axis changes with vehicle body angle. This is shown in Figure 30-7. A low rear body tends to increase caster directional stability and steering effort. A high vehicle rear end reduces caster and reduces directional stability resulting in poor vehicle control. It is important for the automobile to have correct spring height and body angle for proper vehicle handling and control.

Caster angle can be designed to add to or sub-

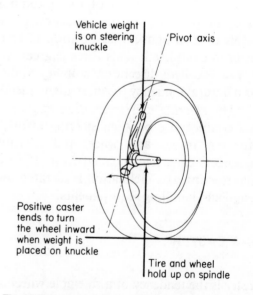

Vehicle weight
is on steering
knuckle

Pivot axis

Positive caster
tends to turn
the wheel inward
when weight is
placed on knuckle

Tire and wheel
hold up on spindle

Fig. 30-8 Inward turning tendency caused by caster.

tract from the tendency of the front wheels to return to the straight-ahead position resulting from steering axis inclination. Normal caster on passenger cars falls between $+2°$ to $-2\frac{1}{2}°$ with a tolerance range of $\pm 1°$.

Caster, like steering axis inclination, tends to change vehicle height when it is not set at zero. This can be observed in Figure 30-8. The weight of the automobile having positive caster tends to turn a wheel inward to allow the body to lower. Negative caster causes an outward turning effect. The greater the caster angle, the greater the turning effect on the automobile. Caster angle is adjustable and, therefore, may be changed to correct for directional pull or drift tendencies.

Caster adjustments can be made on most automobiles by repositioning the inner pivots of the upper control arm to move the upper ball joint forward or backward. Some suspensions are designed to move the lower ball joint forward or backward by adjusting the lower control arm strut at the frame-attaching pivot.

30-4 TOE

Zero toe exists when the tires are running parallel. If they are closer together at the front than at the rear, they have *toe-in*. Toe-in causes the tires to slide or scuff sidewise, from the outside. *Toe-out* occurs when the wheels are further apart at the front than at the rear. This results in a scuff across the tread from the inside. Toe is shown in Figure 30-9.

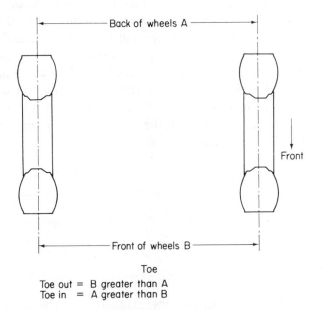

Toe out = B greater than A
Toe in = A greater than B

Fig. 30-9 Toe illustrated.

The wheels are set with a slight amount of toe-in while at rest on an alignment rack. Static toe-in specifications on passenger cars run from 0 to 5/16 in. Toe-in returns to zero as the dynamic forces develop as the automobile is moving down the road, to deflect steering linkages and take up slight clearances. Excessive steering linkage looseness will, of course, allow the wheels to toe-out under dynamic loads.

Toe-in and toe-out cause excessive tire wear. Toe wears the edge of the tire grooves to a sharp edge or feather on their insides with toe-in and on the outside with toe-out. Toe-out also may contribute to road wander as the wheels deflect back and forth when the tire hits road irregularities, compressing and releasing the steering linkages.

Toe is adjusted with threaded sleeves on linkage members called *tie rods*. Both sides must be adjusted to keep the steering wheel centered as the automobile goes straight down the road. This is required because the steering gear mechanism has a high spot or tight spot in the center to reduce steering mechanism looseness. Steering mechanism tightness is not required in a turn, because all of the dynamic loads are in one direction and tend to return the wheel to the center position.

30-5 STEERING LINKAGES

Steering linkages are designed not only to hold the front wheels parallel as they go straight down the road, but also to turn the wheels the correct amount as they move the vehicle smoothly through a turn. Both of the rear wheels are on the same axle so the rear tire centerlines remain parallel during a turn. The front wheels are on independent spindles. During a turn, the inside wheel turns in a smaller radius arc than the outside wheel. Each tire tread centerline is tangent to the arc of the turn and the spindle is on the radius of the arc. This was illustrated in Figure 29-8. The steering angle of either wheel in a steady turn is equal to the wheel base of the vehicle divided by the radius of the turn. A steering linkage that allows the wheels to track correctly through the turn is also known as the *Ackerman layout*. It is illustrated in Figure 30-10.

The Ackerman layout uses the previously

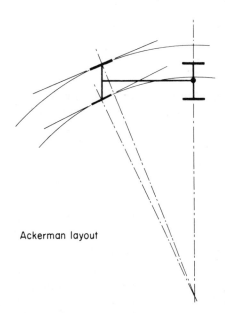

Fig. 30-10 Ackerman steering layout requiring toe out on turns.

discussed principle of levers moving through different portions of an arc to produce the required reaction as shown in Figure 30–11. Steering arms attached to the spindles angle inward in the general

Fig. 30-11 Typical domestic passenger car parallel steering linkage layout.

Parallel steering linkages

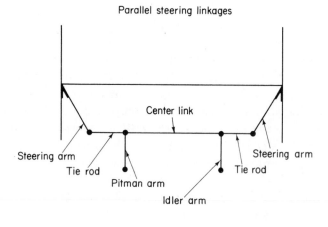

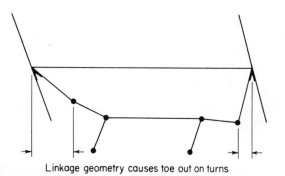

Linkage geometry causes toe out on turns

direction of the rear axle midpoint. In a turn, the linkages push the outside wheel steering arm through the portion of an arc that produces little angular rotation. This same linkage travel moves the inside wheel steering arm through the portion of an arc that creates large angular rotation. The angularity difference makes the wheels *toe-out on turns* to follow the correct path for each wheel. The length and direction of the steering arms are made to match the vehicle tread and wheelbase.

A parallelogram-type steering linkage is used on most domestic passenger cars. A straight center link connects between the steering gear lever, or *Pitman arm* on the left, and an idler arm mounted on the right frame member. A short tie rod connects each steering arm to the center link at a point near the lower suspension control arm pivots. This minimizes toe changes or roll steering effects during suspension jounce and rebound. Steering linkages are not altogether geometrically perfect, but are compromises made necessary by other vehicle features and by the dynamic action of the steering linkages, suspension, and vehicle mass.

30-6 SLIP ANGLE

Centrifugal force causes more side load to be applied to the tires as the speed through a turn increases or as the turn sharpens. This force causes both front and rear tires to deflect. First, the tire tends to roll inward. Second, the contact patch or footprint twists. If the tire contact patch could be viewed from the bottom through a glass road, it would be seen to twist in relation to the rest of the tire. This twist allows the automobile to actually travel in a direction slightly different from the direction in which the tires are headed. The angle between the heading and the actual direction of travel is really an *apparent* slip angle, but it is called *slip angle,* even though the tire is distorting (Figure 30–12) rather than slipping.

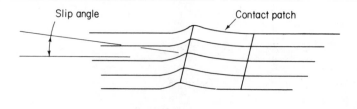

Twist in tire contact patch

Fig. 30-12 Tire twist in the tire patch to match the slip angle.

Equally loaded tires on a vehicle develop greater cornering ability at a given slip angle than unequally loaded tires. Tire size, stiffness, and type of construction will affect the slip angle. Overloading decreases cornering ability and increases slip angle. As ultimate cornering force is approached, the slip angle rapidly increases with little additional lateral load. The driver can sense this change and make corrections before the tires start to slide, causing loss of control. Ninety percent of all handling considerations involve cornering loads and vertical loads resulting from weight.

If the cornering load produces equal slip angles (Figure 30–13) at the front and rear tires, the automobile will follow a turning arc at an angle to the original heading. This reaction is called *neutral steer*. If the slip angle is greater on the front tires than on the rear, the front tends to reduce its turning arc, producing *understeer*. If the rear tire slip angle is greater than that of the front tire, the rear end of the vehicle tends to increase the turning arc as the back end slips outward. This turns the vehicle into the corner by *oversteering* (Figure 30–14).

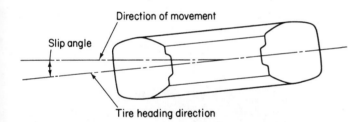

Fig. 30-13 Slip angle compared to tire heading.

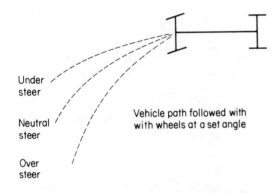

Fig. 30-14 Understeer is less than neutral and oversteer is greater than neutral.

Automobiles with large amounts of weight on the front tires generally tend to understeer while those with large amounts of weight on the rear tires tend to oversteer. Understeer is indicated when larger steering wheel turning angles are needed at highway speeds as compared to the turning angle required at near-zero speed. Low tire pressure and heavy weights will increase the slip angle. The front and rear slip angle, not weight distribution, determine how a vehicle can negotiate a corner.

An understeering automobile is directionally stable. It is necessary to hold the steering wheel into the turn to continue the turn. Upon release of the steering wheel, the vehicle will tend to go straight. Understeer reduces vehicle responsiveness and is good for the average driver. An oversteering automobile is unstable. It will negotiate a turn with small steering wheel angles and, in some cases, will require reverse steering wheel position. An oversteering automobile is very responsive, but will spin out if pushed too hard into turns.

A strong crosswind has an effect on slip angle. As the wind blows against the side of the car, all of the side force can be considered to react through the center of pressure, the point around which all of the air pressure forces are balanced. The center of pressure is usually behind the center of gravity. Slip angle caused by the wind is compounded by the understeer tendency to correct the line of vehicle travel. The worst possible condition would exist in a crosswind with a normally oversteering, heavily loaded station wagon or van. Wind gusts on the large rear section would exaggerate the oversteer condition, resulting in rapid loss of control.

Roll steer characteristics, as discussed in Chapter 29, are useful in designing a stable car. With properly designed suspension and steering linkages, body roll will move the wheels to compensate for slip angles by changing camber and toe. Generally, a large rear roll steer increases understeer and stability.

30-7 WHEEL ALIGNMENT

The suspension and steering linkage alignment is usually checked when abnormal tire wear exists, when the automobile handles improperly, when the suspension has been repaired, or when making a normal preventative maintenance check. It is helpful for the technician to know the reason for an alignment, so abnormalities can be carefully examined.

A number of preliminary checks must be made

before aligning the front suspension and steering systems. The suspension pivots and ball joints must be in good condition, the spring height must be correct, the shock absorbers should be in good condition, and the tires must be inflated to the correct pressure. Faulty parts should be replaced, as described in Chapter 29, to ensure satisfactory operation after alignment is completed.

Tires should be "read" to see if they indicate any specific alignment problem. Tire wear on one side of the tread usually indicates improper camber on that wheel. Smooth tire wear on both sides of both front tires suggests excessive slippage when negotiating corners at high speeds. Wear on the edges of only one tire generally indicates underinflation of that tire. Wear of the center portion of the tire tread results from tire overinflation. Feather edge tread indicates improper toe. Cupping around the tire edge may be caused by underinflation or by suspension mechanical irregularities. Tire wear caused by alignment problems is shown in Figure 30-15.

Alignment machines are either portable or permanent installations, as shown in Figure 30-16. Some of the alignment adjustments are made from under the car as the car weight rests on its wheels, so some means must be provided to allow the technician to get under the car to make these adjustments. Portable wheel stands to support the car are used with portable alignment heads. Alignment racks are either above the floor or extended over a pit in which the technician can work. In all cases, the alignment rack or set of wheel stands must be level so that alignment angles can be compared to vertical lines. Turntables are located under the front tires to allow the wheels to be turned left or right any desired degree.

Fig. 30-15 Tire wear indications. (a) Toe, (b) camber, (c) cupping caused by multi-problems.

(a)

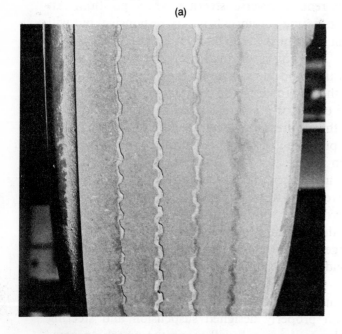

(b)

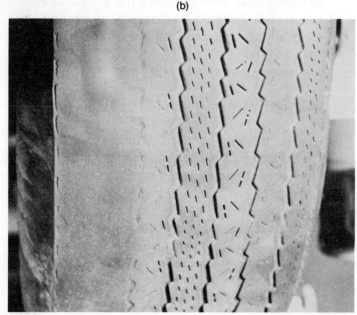

(c)

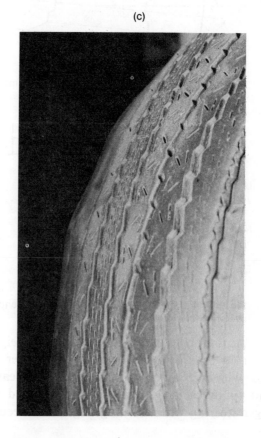

(a)

(b)

Fig. 30-16 Wheel alignment machines. (a) Portable, (b) permanent installation.

Alignment gauges use some method of sensing a vertical position. One form uses a bubble level to set the gauges and read the angles. Other gauges use a swing weight to sense the vertical position. The position of the swinging weight may be amplified or expanded with electricity or a light beam and displayed on a visual screen for easy reading. These two systems are pictured in Figure 30–17.

Instrument heads are attached to the front wheels or to the spindle end as shown in Figure 30–18. If they are attached to the wheel rim, it is necessary to check the adaptor run-out so that wheel and adaptor clamping variations do not affect the readings. Direct readings may be made from the adapters attached directly to the spindle.

Camber is read directly from the instrument head or screen after the instrument head has been leveled.

Fig. 30-17 Alignment readout. (a) Bubble, (b) screen.

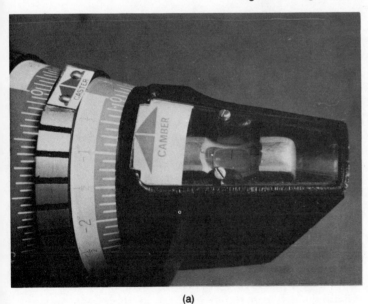

(a)

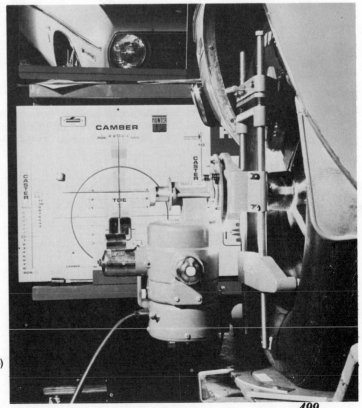

(b)

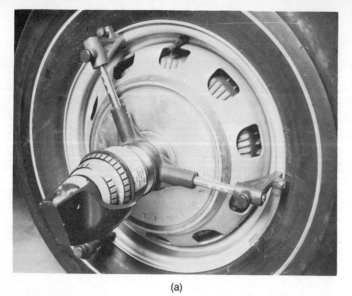

Fig. 30-18 Instrument attachments. (a) Clamp on, (b) spindle adapter.

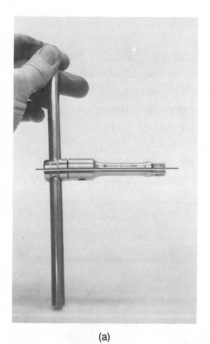
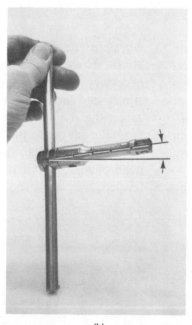
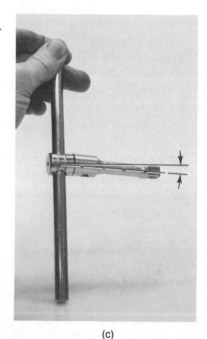

(a)   (b)   (c)

Fig. 30-19 Example of how positive caster is measured. A level would be attached to the socket extension. (a) Level straight ahead, (b) raised when turned inward, (c) lowered when turned outward.

Caster is measured as it affects camber angle during a turn. This is demonstrated in Figure 30-19. Basically, the change in camber of the wheel that exists as the wheel is turned from 20° inward to 20° outward, with the brake applied, will indicate caster. If caster is zero, there is no change in camber as the wheels are turned. Camber change as the wheel turns 40° will increase as caster increases. Caster is read on a special scale that converts the camber change into a caster reading.

Steering axis inclination is measured in a manner similar to caster, as illustrated in Figure 30-20. However, it uses a change in caster during the same 40° wheel turn instead of camber change. This requires the use of a repositioned scale or a different scale for readout.

Toe is checked by measuring the difference in distance between the front tires at their rear and at their front. This can be done by rotating the wheel to scribe a line on the surface of the tire. Some alignment equipment measures between the wheel rim at the front, then the car is rolled forward

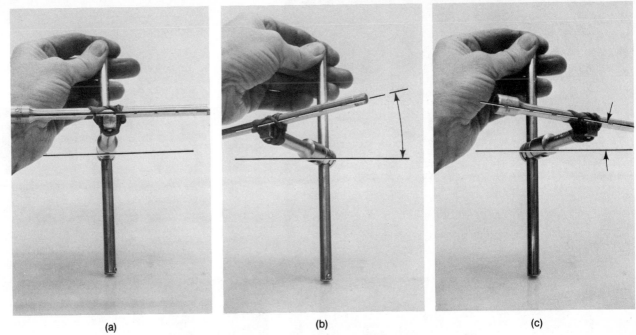

Fig. 30-20 Example of how steering axis inclination is measured. A level would be attached to the socket extension. (a) Level straight ahead, (b) tipped forward when turned inward, (c) tipped backward when turned outward.

to remeasure the wheel at the same point when it is in the rear. Some alignment equipment racks have reference points built onto them so that toe can be read directly. Others use a light beam for toe adjustment.

Detailed instructions describing specific alignment procedures are supplied with each wheel alignment unit. These instructions must be followed for correct alignment angle readout.

Alignment readings are compared to the specifications that apply. If the readings fall within specifications on a routine maintenance inspection and the vehicle drives properly, no further work is needed. Tire wear or handling complaints may be corrected by adjusting the suspension geometry within the specification range.

30-8 ALIGNMENT ADJUSTMENT

Means are provided on the front suspension to adjust camber and caster. Many automobiles use the same adjustment devices to adjust both camber and caster. Some vehicles provide separate adjustment means. The most common of these are pictured in Figures 30–22 and 30–23.

The majority of domestic automobiles provide a means to adjust both upper control arm pivot

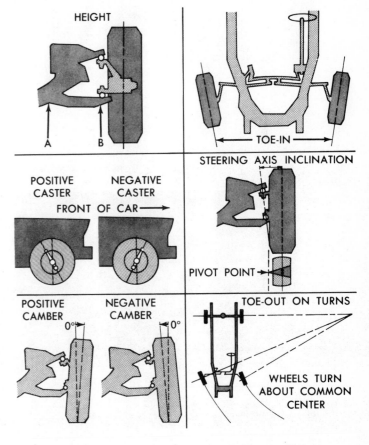

Fig. 30-21 Alignment items to be checked (Chrysler Motors Corporation).

(a)

(c)

Fig. 30-22 Caster-camber adjustment methods. (a) Shims, (b) cam adjust, (c) slot adjust.

(b)

Fig. 30-23 (a) Strut caster adjustment (Cadillac Motor Car Division, General Motors Corporation), (b) eccentric camber adjustment at the upper ball joint.

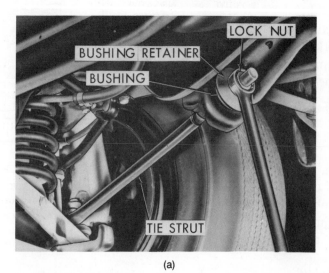

BUSHING RETAINER

LOCK NUT

BUSHING

TIE STRUT

(a)

(b)

points. This may be by shims, cams, or slots. Both pivots are moved outward or inward the same amount to adjust camber. One is moved outward and the other inward by the same amount to change caster. If both caster and camber need to be changed, it may be possible to make the entire correction at only one of the pivot points.

Some automobiles provide an eccentric adjustment around the upper ball joint to adjust camber. Others use a cam at the lower control arm pivot. Both methods control camber by changing the relative position of the steering knuckle, spindle, wheel, and tire.

Some models adjust caster by lengthening or shortening the lower control arm strut. Adjustment nuts are provided at the front strut-to-frame attachment. This moves the lower end of the knuckle forward or backward to change caster.

Toe is always adjusted by adjusting sleeves on the tie rods. These are shown in Figure 30–24. One end of the sleeve has left-hand threads; the other end has right-hand threads. Turning the sleeve will lengthen or shorten the tie rod to obtain correct toe. It is usually necessary to adjust both of the tie rods to keep the steering wheel centered.

Steering axis inclination cannot be adjusted separately from camber but is used only to check for a bent steering knuckle. When both camber and steering axis inclination do not fall into their respective specification range, the knuckle is bent.

Alignment adjustments should always be followed by a road test to see that the car tracks straight and handles properly. Slight changes in caster, within the specification range, will usually correct tracking problems if the suspension is in normal condition.

(a)

(b)

Fig. 30–24 Tie rod adjustments. (a) Tie rod location, (b) adjustment location.

REVIEW QUESTIONS

1. How does positive camber differ from negative camber? [30–1]

2. How does camber change during jounce and rebound? [30–1]

3. Where is camber adjustment made on the suspension? [30–1]

4. How would a change in steering axis inclination affect the scrub radius? [30–2]

5. Why is a small scrub radius desirable? [30–2]

6. When is the scrub radius positive? [30–2]

7. How do the reverse-type wheels affect the scrub radius? [30–2]

8. What happens to the suspension height as a result of SAI change when the wheels are turned? [30-2]

9. How does SAI help to provide directional stability? [30-2]

10. Describe caster in terms of the center of the contact patch and the point where an extension of the pivot axis contacts the road surface. [30-3]

11. How would a suspension, modified to raise the rear of the automobile, affect directional stability? [30-3]

12. How is caster adjusted? [30-3]

13. Why are the wheels set for toe-in when they are aligned? [30-4]

14. What are the results of excessive toe? [30-4]

15. How is toe adjusted? [30-4]

16. Why is toe set when the wheels are pointing straight ahead? [30-4]

17. Why is it necessary to have toe-out on turns? [30-5]

18. How does tire deflection affect the automobile control in a turn? [30-6]

19. What conditions affect the slip angle? [30-6]

20. How does the slip angle help the driver control the automobile? [30-6]

21. What reaction is felt by the driver of an understeering automobile? [30-6]

22. How can body roll be used to help to compensate for slip angle? [30-6]

23. When are the suspension and the steering linkages alignments checked? [30-7]

24. What methods are used to sense the neutral steer position during wheel alignment? [30-7]

25. How is camber change used to measure caster? [30-8]

26. How can the upper support arm be moved to change camber? [30-8]

27. How can the upper support arm be moved to change caster? [30-8]

28. What is adjusted to change toe? [30-8]

29. How is the steering axis inclination changed? [30-8]

steering gears and columns

The driver controls the direction of the front wheels of the automobile with the steering gear. The modern steering gear is made up of two major units, a gear unit and a steering column. The gear unit multiplies the driver's steering effort to provide adequate force for steering control. The steering column is primarily a supported shaft that connects the driver's steering wheel to the gear unit.

The power steering gear is similar to the standard steering gear but it has surfaces upon which hydraulic pressure is applied to aid the driver's control of the front wheels. Power for the steering gear is provided by an engine-driven pump. The pump forces fluid through a system controlled by a valve that is sensitive to the driver's steering effort to put fluid pressure against the pressure surfaces to assist the driver.

The steering column in the modern automobile

is a complex mechanism. It is designed to collapse in a collision to protect the driver. In some installations it may be tilted and telescoped to place it at a convenient angle for the driver. To reduce the chance of theft, it contains steering gear and transmission locks. Because it is easily accessible to the driver the steering column carries the transmission shift control, turn signal switch, and flasher switch. It must, therefore, be thoroughly understood so that it can be properly serviced.

31-1 STANDARD STEERING GEAR

The standard steering gear unit consists of two gears, a *worm gear* and a section or sector of a *spur gear*. A rack and pinion is finding popularity in small automobiles. The steering gear is normally designed to swing the front wheels through a 60° arc, from lock to lock. Turning effort on the steering wheel is multiplied through the steering gears to turn the front wheels, even when the vehicle is not moving. If a steering wheel requires five full turns from lock to lock to swing the wheels 60°, the steering ratio is 30:1. This is because each full turn of the steering wheel is 360°. In five turns, the steering wheel turns 1800°. Eighteen hundred degrees of steering wheel turn divided by 60° wheel steering turn equals the 30:1 steering ratio.

Steering gears are based on the action between a worm gear and a spur gear section or a pinion and rack to give the required mechanical advantage. Therefore, the driver can easily control the front wheels and the front wheel road shock will not twist the steering wheel from his hands.

Friction between the worm and sector in standard gears is usually quite large. This friction was reduced as steering gear designs improved, by replacing the sector with a roller (Figure 31-1), and

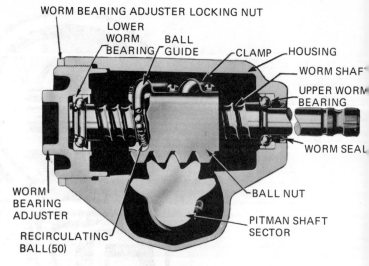

Fig. 31-2 Typical worm and recirculating ball nut-type steering gear (Buick Motor Division, General Motors Corporation).

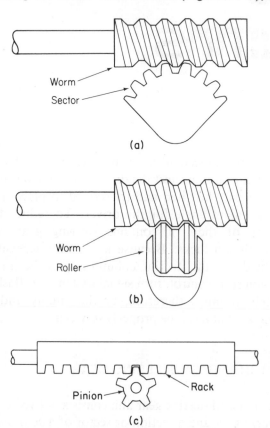

Fig. 31-1 Worm-sector, worm-roller, and rack-and-pinion type steering gears.

then further reduced by placing a nut with exterior teeth over the worm as pictured in Figure 31-2. The threads between the nut and worm are modified into grooves that will take ball bearings. Selective fit balls, very close to the same size, are placed between the nut and worm so the turning action is as free rolling as a ball bearing. The ball groove may be cut for either right-or left-hand thread directions.

The balls are fed into what is the equivalent of two separate ball races. These races are on an angle so the balls move endwise as the worm turns. The balls are redirected by a guide from the end of each slot back to the entrance across the outside of the nut. The guide can be identified in Figure 31-3.

The ball nut gear teeth engage with the sector that, in turn, is part of the cross or Pitman shaft. This whole assembly is enclosed in a case that can be attached to the chassis frame. A *Pitman arm* connects the Pitman shaft to the steering linkage.

Each end of the worm is supported in ball bearings. A worm lash adjustment provides a bearing preload that holds the worm securely in position. On some steering gears, the worm shaft bearing preload adjustment is on the lower end of the gear case, while others have the adjustment on the upper end of the case.

Needle bearings or bushings support the Pitman shaft. Both may be located on the Pitman arm side of the sector or one may be on each side of the sector. The ball nut gear teeth and the sector teeth are cut at an angle. Moving the sector gear into close mesh with the ball nut teeth reduces

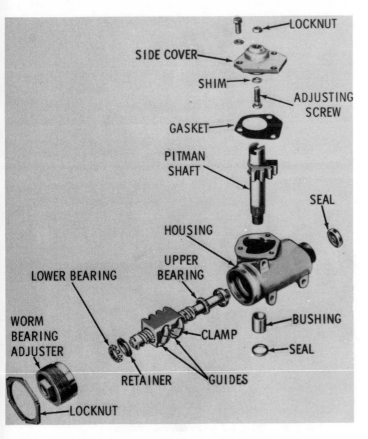

Fig. 31-3 Exploded view of a typical worm-ball nut steering gear (Oldsmobile Division, General Motors Corporation).

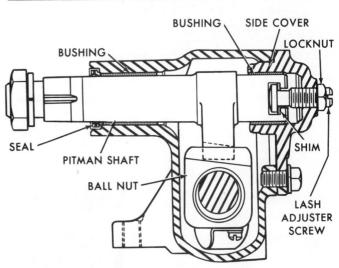

Fig. 31-4 Cross section of a typical worm-ball nut type steering gear showing angled teeth that allow lash adjustment (Chevrolet Motor Division, General Motors Corporation).

backlash. This adjustment is made in the cover on the upper end of the cross shaft. This adjustment can be observed in Figure 31-4.

The steering gear teeth are cut to provide a closer fit at the center teeth than at the end teeth as illustrated in Figure 31-5. This reduces gear backlash at the center position where most of the driving occurs and, at the same time, allows sufficient cost-reducing gear tolerance at the off-center positions where the close fits are not needed. Sector backlash adjustments must be made at the normally tight center position.

The standard steering gear case is partly filled with a specified lubricant, usually the same lubricant that is used in the differential. An oil seal is installed at the lower end of the Pitman shaft to keep the oil from leaking out the bottom of the gear case. In most standard steering gears, there is no seal on the upper end of the worm shaft because it is usually above the lubricant level, where only a dust seal is required.

A *rack and pinion* steering gear (Figure 31-6) is used on a number of small automobiles. Its design is simple, light, and responsive and is uses

minimum linkage parts. It does, however, feed back road shock to the driver and it requires more steering effort than a recirculating ball type steering gear.

The rack and pinion steering gear takes the place of the center steering linkage. The steering gear housing is fastened to the front frame member through rubber type insulators. The rack ends, under a rubber boot, fasten to the tie rods with ball

Fig. 31-5 Typical steering gear sector-to-ball nut tooth contact (Buick Motor Division, General Motors Corporation).

Fig. 31-6 Rack and pinion steering gear.

Fig. 31-7 Pinion removed to show the rack.

type ends. A pinion, controlled by the steering wheel, has teeth that engage with the teeth of the rack. These can be seen in Figure 31-7. A yoke bearing puts a preload on the rack directly across from the pinion.

When the rack and pinion is a power steering gear, the control valve is a part of the pinion and the power piston is a part of the rack, sliding in the housing.

31-2 POWER STEERING GEAR

A power steering gear is basically a power-assisted standard steering gear. The driver supplies part of the steering effort and the power assist portion of the unit supplies the remaining effort required. This reduction in driver steering effort allows the power steering gear ratio to be about ⅔ of the standard steering ratio. Power steering, therefore, provides much faster steering response than standard steering.

The power steering system consists of an engine-driven oil pump with reservoir, a control valve, and pressure surfaces that are used to assist steering effort. The power steering system is illustrated in Figure 31-8. The pump is usually belt-driven and

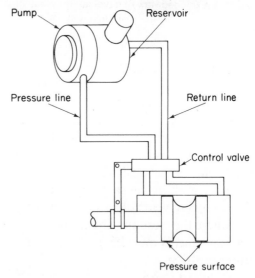

Fig. 31-8 Schematic of a typical power steering gear.

located on the front of the engine. In some applications it is mounted at the front of the crankshaft. Pressure surfaces in most power steering systems are located in the steering gear case. This type of power steering gear is called an *integral type*. A few power steering pressure surfaces are located in an exterior power cylinder connected between the steering linkages and vehicle frame. These are called *link-type* power steering gears. A power rack and pinion is similar to a link-type power steering gear.

Control Valve. All the time the engine is running, power steering fluid keeps flowing through the system from the pump to the control valve, then back to the reservoir. Both pressure surfaces are exposed to the same system pressure. When the wheels are straight ahead, the fluid flows freely through this circuit. This can be seen in Figure 31-9. When steering effort is applied to the steering wheel, the control valve shifts. This directs fluid to one pressure surface and increases the size of the return passage opening from the opposite pressure surface to the reservoir. The amount of valve shift is proportional to the effort applied to the steering wheel. The amount that the control valve shifts provides the proportional amount of pressure to give the required power assist.

The power steering control valve is either located inside or is attached to the exterior of the integral-type power steering gear. The link-type power steering may have the control valve built into the end of the power cylinder or it may be a separate unit, depending upon its design.

The control valve is balanced between the mechanical input force applied by the steering

wheel, and the mechanical-hydraulic resistive force of the steering linkage and tires on the road while the steering wheel is centered. As the steering wheel is turned, its mechanical input force moves the control valve toward the linkage resistive force. In this position, the control valve restricts the pressure area outlet flow to cause a pressure buildup on the pressure surface in a direction that assists the steering wheel input force to move against the steering linkage resistance. During steering wheel movement, the input force always leads by first moving the control valve. The hydraulic assist force is always trying to catch up with the control valve position by helping to move the steering linkage. When the steering wheel arrives at the desired position, it is held steady and the linkage finally catches up, centering the control valve to terminate assist.

The control valve is provided with some type of natural centering device, usually springs. When no effort is being applied to the system, the centering springs center the spool position to balance pressures on both pressure surfaces, holding the steering linkage in place.

If the steering wheel is held in position when the front tires hit an object that tries to deflect them, the control valve directs pressure to the pressure surface that opposes the upsetting force. This allows the driver to maintain vehicle control.

Two types of control valves are used, sliding spools and rotating spools. The sliding spool valve may be located between the Pitman arm and steering linkage in the link-type units, mounted concentric with the worm shaft, or placed parallel in a housing outside the steering gear case in integral types. When a rotary spool-type valve is used, it is always mounted concentric with the worm shaft. In any of these types of power steering gears, control action is the same.

The sliding spool valve in the integral steering gear is controlled by either of two actuating methods. One movement is actuated by a slight endwise movement of the worm shaft or steering linkage. The front wheels and steering linkages hold the sector so it resists movement. The worm shaft is pushed endwise against one of its bearings as the ball nut tries to move the sector. This slight movement is transmitted to the parallel spool valve with a pivot lever. This type is shown in Figure 31-10.

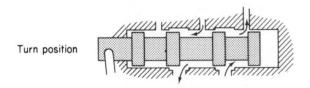

Turn position

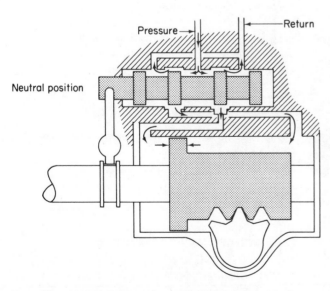

Neutral position

Fig. 31-9 Principle of a power steering control valve in neutral and during a turn.

The concentric spool valve endwise movement is actuated by a torsion bar. The worm shaft is turned through a torsion bar, so the upper end turns slightly more than the lower end. The maximum amount of torsion bar flex is limited by a loose fitting spline between the input shaft and worm shaft. A short length helical spline around the input shaft engages an actuator. The other end of the actuator is splined to the worm shaft.

The steering wheel input effort twists the torsion bar. This twist changes the relative position of the worm shaft actuator assembly in relation to the input shaft position to move the actuator endwise on the helical splines. This can be observed in Figure 31-11.

The spool valve is held in position on the actuator with snap rings so any actuator endwise movement also moves the spool valve endwise.

Endwise movement of the spool valve fully opens the fluid return from one pressure surface. At the same time, pressure is built up on the other pressure surface to provide steering effort assist.

The rotary spool control valve, shown in Figure

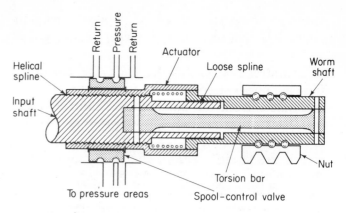

Fig. 31-11 Sectional view of a torsion bar actuated sliding control valve.

31-12, is also operated with a torsion bar. The spool valve body surrounds the control valve. It is attached to the worm shaft. The valve spool is attached to the input shaft. Steering effort on the input shaft twists the torsion bar. This makes a relative difference between the valve body attached to the worm shaft and the valve spool attached to the input shaft. Repositioning the valve spool within the valve body opens a return passage to one of the pressure areas and directs fluid under pressure to the opposite pressure area.

Fig. 31-10 Sectional view of a sliding spool control valve (Chrysler Motor Corporation).

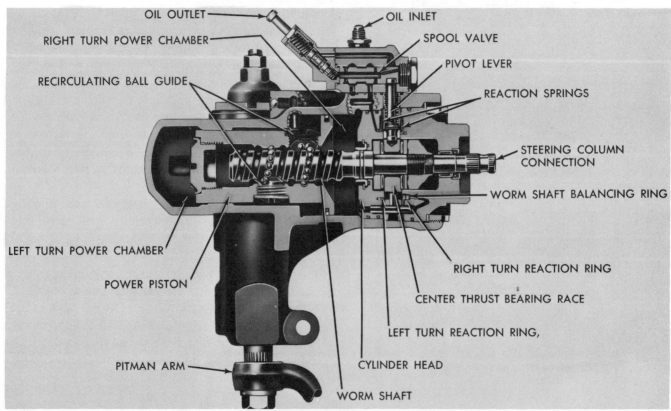

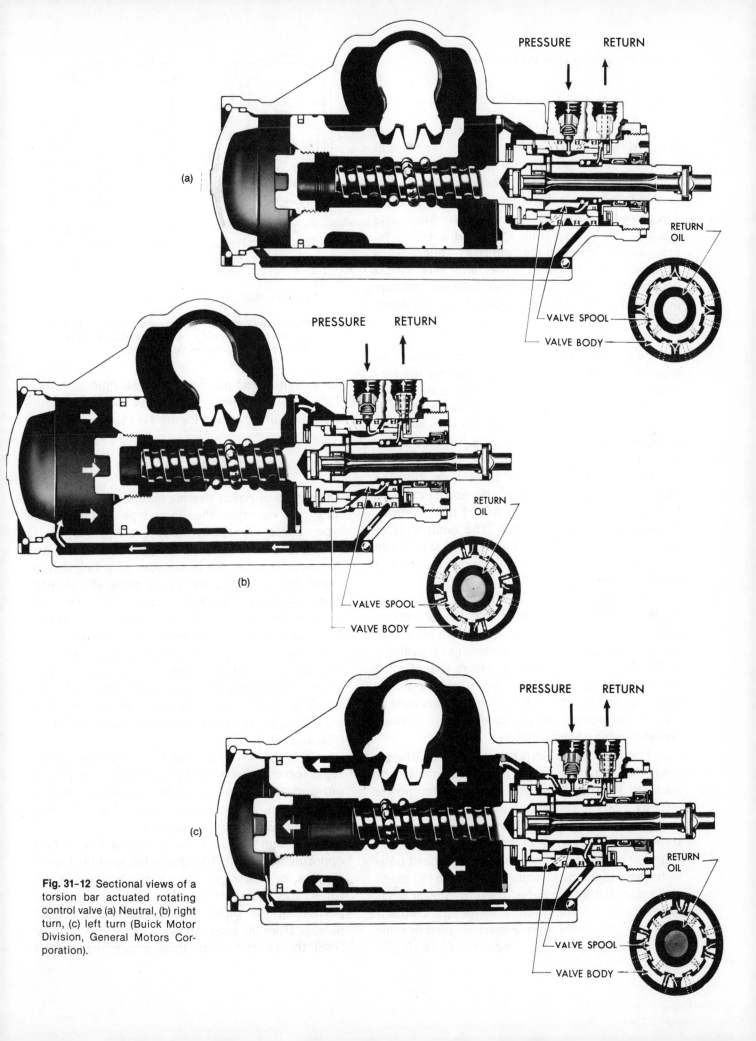

PRESSURE   RETURN

(a)

RETURN
OIL

VALVE SPOOL
VALVE BODY

PRESSURE   RETURN

(b)

RETURN
OIL

VALVE SPOOL
VALVE BODY

PRESSURE   RETURN

(c)

RETURN
OIL

VALVE SPOOL
VALVE BODY

Fig. 31-12 Sectional views of a torsion bar actuated rotating control valve (a) Neutral, (b) right turn, (c) left turn (Buick Motor Division, General Motors Corporation).

Reaction Control. Power steering gears are designed to give the driver some feel of the amount of effort he is putting into the steering system. This driver feel is called *reaction control.* The torsion bars provide driver feel when they are used. The pivot-lever-actuated type of control valve gives driver feel with centering springs and with fluid pressure developed on reaction rings while assist is occurring. The link-type power unit may have a reaction valve that is proportional to the pressure developed in the steering system to provide driver feel.

Power Chambers. The pressure surfaces or areas of the link-type power steering are the surfaces on either side of the piston within the power cylinder. As pressure rises, the chamber fluid is pressurized and fluid is forced into the chamber. At the same time, fluid is returned from the opposite side of the piston.

In integral power steering gear designs, the ball-nut exterior acts as a piston and is called a *ball-nut power piston.* Each side of this piston is, therefore, a power chamber. The control valve directs fluid pressure to the side of the piston which will assist the ball-nut in moving the sector in the desired direction.

The ball-nut piston seal ring may be above or below the rack teeth. In either case, the oil pressure can go between the worm shaft and ball-nut to pressurize the interior when the ball-nut is assisting in the downward direction. Pressure is applied to the ball-nut end and piston flange when assisting in the upward direction. Reaction areas are used to balance the worm shaft and control valve in some power steering applications.

The ball-nut power piston has a rack of gear teeth that rotate a sector in the same way the standard steering does. Steering ratios for power steering gears are usually numerically lower than the standard steering gears, so they have a quicker response to steering wheel movement. A very fast response is not desirable in the straight-ahead position where slight movements would make too much correction, but it is desirable in a turn. Power steering gears are a compromise when using a constant ratio. Variable-ratio steering gears are used in some automobiles to give a slow ratio when steering in

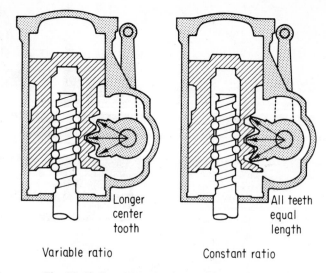

Fig. 31-13 Constant steering ratio compared to a variable steering ratio steering gear (Buick Motor Division, General Motors Corporation).

the straight-ahead position and a fast ratio on turns. This is done primarily by the way the sector teeth are cut, as illustrated in Figure 31-13.

31-3 POWER STEERING PUMPS

Three types of power steering pumps are in common usage: the vane type, the slipper type, and the roller type. These are shown in Figure 31-14. Their principles of operation and design are very similar. A power steering pump consists of a belt-driven rotor that is turned within an eliptically shaped cam insert ring. Vanes, slippers, or rollers are installed in the rotor slots, grooves, or cavities. Pressure thrust plates on each side of the rotor and cam seal the pump. This assembly is placed in a housing that contains rotor bearings and oil passages. The pump housing is usually surrounded by an oil reservoir. The pump and reservoir are sealed with O-rings for easily assembled oil-tight joints (Figure 31-15).

In operation, the rotor spins, causing centrifugal force to throw the vanes, slippers, or rollers outward so their outer surface maintains contact with the cam. Slippers usually have a backup spring to aid in maintaining cam contact.

The cam fits the rotor closely at one or two opposing locations. The spaces between the vanes, slippers, or rollers gradually move outward as the rotor turns them past the close fitting point. This portion of the pump is connected to the inlet passage from the reservoir, so pump fluid will flow from the reservoir into these expanding spaces.

(a)

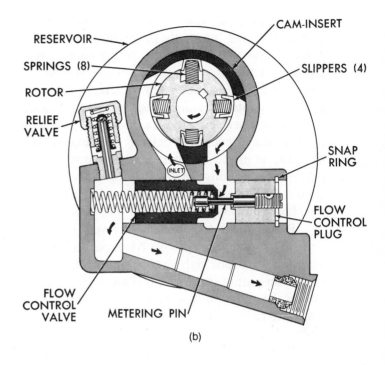

RESERVOIR

CAM-INSERT

SPRINGS (8)

SLIPPERS (4)

ROTOR

RELIEF VALVE

INLET

SNAP RING

FLOW CONTROL PLUG

FLOW CONTROL VALVE

METERING PIN

(b)

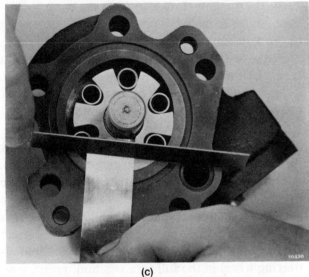

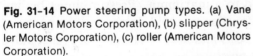

(c)

Fig. 31-14 Power steering pump types. (a) Vane (American Motors Corporation), (b) slipper (Chrysler Motors Corporation), (c) roller (American Motors Corporation).

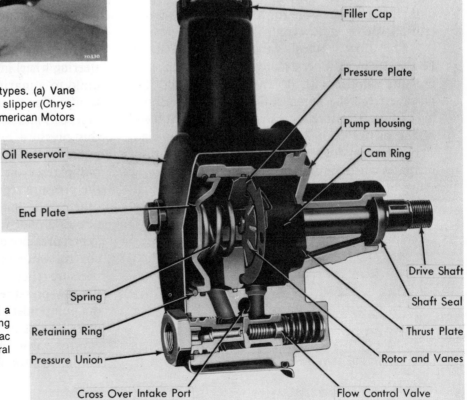

Filler Cap

Pressure Plate

Pump Housing

Cam Ring

Oil Reservoir

End Plate

Drive Shaft

Shaft Seal

Thrust Plate

Rotor and Vanes

Flow Control Valve

Spring

Retaining Ring

Pressure Union

Cross Over Intake Port

Fig. 31-15 Sectional view of a typical vane power steering pump and valves (Cadillac Motor Car Division, General Motors Corporation).

As the vanes, slippers, or rollers reach the widest part of the cam insert, they pass the inlet passage from the reservoir and contact the pressure passage. Continued turning now decreases the volume between the vane, slippers, or rollers, forcing the pump fluid into the pump pressure outlet passage.

Power steering pumps are positive displacement pumps. Each revolution delivers the same amount of fluid, no matter at what speed it is turning. The pump capacity must be large enough to supply the required fluid volume and pressure required for parking while the engine is idling.

Power assist requirements are very low when driving at highway speeds. At these speeds, the pump will produce high volume and pressure unless the pump output is modified. This is done by providing the pump with a flow control valve and a pressure relief valve.

Flow Control Valve. The greatest amount of steering effort is required as the wheels are turned with the vehicle not moving or while parking. This is the operating condition that requires most assist. Unfortunately, the engine is idling during this time, so the engine-driven power steering assist pump is also running slowly. Pump speeds are fast at highway speeds, when little or no power assist is required. To compensate for high pump volumes at cruising speeds, a flow control valve is used.

The flow control valve, as illustrated in Figure 31-16, is operated by small differences in pressure along with a calibrated spring. The passage from the pump outlet contains a restricting orifice. Pressure is greater on the upstream end of the orifice than it is on the downstream end. The pressure drop difference across the orifice increases when the oil flow increases.

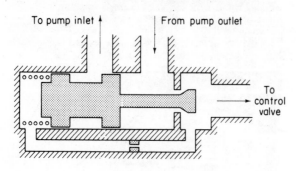

Fig. 31-16 Flow valve principle.

High oil pressure from the upstream side of the orifice is directed at one end of the flow control valve. Low oil pressure from the downstream side of the orifice is directed at the other end of the flow control valve. A calibrated spring also is located on the low pressure side of the flow control valve.

Flow Control Valve Operation. As the engine speed increases from idle, the pump flow and pressure increase, causing a pressure drop across the orifice. When flow increases to the maximum required flow, the flow control valve moves toward its low pressure end. This movement opens a passage between the pump outlet and pump inlet, bypassing a portion of the fluid back to the pump inlet. The opening gets larger as the pump speed increases, thus keeping the flow at the maximum required rate. Recirculating the oil back through the pump reduces the pump power requirement and keeps the oil temperature low. Some control valves have a tapered metering pin that moves in the orifice to provide a variable orifice which reduces the effective orifice size at high pump speeds. Another type of flow control valve does this by restricting a passage that parallels the orifice. These both provide close flow control operation.

Pressure Relief Valve. The flow control valve just described operates when there is little restriction in the power steering system. Flow is restricted by the control valve when it sends fluid to one of the power chambers causing the pressure to rise. If the driver turns the wheels against the steering linkage turning stops and continues to hold the steering wheel in the full turn position, pressure will build to a maximum. Pressure must be limited to a safe value to avoid damage to the power steering unit seals and hoses. The pressure relief valve limits this pressure by opening a passage between the pump outlet chamber and the pump inlet or the pump reservoir. In some power steering pumps, the pressure regulator is a separate valve, while in others, it is built into the flow control valve and acts as a pilot valve as illustrated in Figure 31-17. When pressure on the low pressure side of the flow control valve reaches a predetermined point, the pressure relief valve opens to allow oil to flow from the low pressure side of the flow control valve to the pump inlet. This drops the pressure in the low pressure side of the flow control valve so the flow control valve will snap open to allow the pump output to flow freely into the inlet, thus lowering

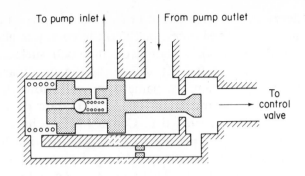

Fig. 31-17 Pressure regulator principle.

Fig. 31-18 Power steering test valve and gauge (Cadillac Motor Car Division, General Motors Corporation).

the pressure. Pressure will balance the valve at the pressure for which it is set.

The power steering pump is connected to the power steering gear control valve with one high pressure hose and one low pressure return hose. The high pressure hose is frequently made in two sizes that will dampen oil pulsations to reduce noise. The ends have screw-type tubing fittings to hold the high pressure. The low pressure hose, on the other hand, is attached to the steering gear and reservoir with less expensive hose clamps.

31-4 POWER STEERING SERVICE

Power steering problems are either external fluid leaks or operating problems. External fluid leaks are the result of damaged oil seals, damaged O-rings, cracked hoses, or cracks in the metal parts. These can be readily seen and corrected by replacing the damaged items.

The first thing to do in any power steering test is to see that there is adequate fluid in the reservoir and that the drive belt has correct tension. Operational problems involving hard steering or lack of assist will involve the pump assembly, the steering gear assembly, or the steering linkage. The steering linkage should be checked for binding before accusing the pump or steering gear of being at fault. A pump pressure test will indicate the problem location. The pressure test unit consists of a valve with a gauge on the high pressure side. This unit is installed between the pump and the steering gear high pressure hose, as pictured in Figure 31-18. The pressure should rise when the steering gear is turned to the extreme position. If it does not, the valve is closed. If the pressure does increase, then the pump is functioning satisfactorily, so the problem is in the steering gear. If, on the other hand, the pressure still does not rise when the valve is closed, the pump is causing the problem.

The most likely cause of pump failure is either the flow control or the pressure valve sticking open. These can be removed, cleaned, and polished with crocus cloth. Care must be taken to avoid rounding the edges of these valves. If this does not correct the problem the pump is usually replaced.

Self-steering or unequal assist are other problems encountered. This usually results from an improperly centering control valve. Self-steering of the parallel sliding type control valve housing can usually be corrected from the outside by adjustment. Gears using the concentric-type control valve will have to be disassembled and inspected to correct the problem. Unequal assist may also result from internal fluid leaks in the steering gear. The steering gear will have to be disassembled to make either of these repairs.

Before disassembly, be sure to have the service manual that applies to the gear being serviced. Usually, special tools are required for alignment and installing seals without damage. These are required for satisfactory servicing. To avoid damage, the disassembly instructions must be carefully followed and all precautions observed.

The gear should be thoroughly cleaned externally to avoid contaminating the interior during disassembly. Fluid is drained and the gear is carefully disassembled, with the technician noting the condition of parts, and making the required checks as the parts are removed. The parts should be thoroughly cleaned after disassembly, then inspected for looseness, binding, scoring, wear, etc., as described in the applicable service manual.

Any required repairs are made; replacement parts, including all new seals, are obtained; and the parts are lubricated with power steering fluid or other specified lubricant as they are assembled. All domestic passenger car manufacturers specify a special power steering fluid for use in their automobiles. This fluid is essentially a clear fluid with properties similar to automatic transmission fluid. Some manufacturers package their fluid as a combination power steering and automatic transmission fluid. Assembly instructions must be followed carefully to be sure that all parts are put in their proper place with the correct adjustments. After assembly, the steering gear unit should be tested before installation in the vehicle by connecting it to the power steering hoses. With fluid in the system and the engine running, the gear may be operated throughout its range to purge air from the system. Details for each gear type are given in the applicable service manual.

Power steering gear worm preload is set as part of the assembly procedure. The Pitman shaft adjustment is done in the same way as it is done on standard steering gears.

31-5 STEERING COLUMN

Automobile safety engineering has brought a focus on the steering wheel and steering column as a potential safety hazard. Engineers have concentrated a lot of effort on steering column design to make it collapse as it absorbs impact energy in collisions. In 1956, the first deep-dish steering wheel designs were installed on cars to move the actual column away from the driver. In 1967, a collapsible column was designed that would crush on impact. In 1969, a steering column that increased protection from theft was introduced. It has since been improved. The ignition switch, located on the column, locks the steering wheel position and locks the transmission shift linkage in park when the switch is turned off.

Braking a vehicle to a stop absorbs the vehicle

energy by converting it to heat in the brakes. In a panic stop, the brakes lock and the energy is absorbed by the tires sliding on the road surface, stopping at about 20 ft/sec², using the customary measuring system. A panic stop will slow the vehicle at the maximum deceleration rate of 20 ft/sec² (d) as discussed in Chapter 26. Using the given equation: $t = 1.465\ V/d$, the required time to stop a vehicle from 20 mph (V) is 1.5 seconds [$t = (1.465 \times 20/20$ sec]. This panic stop tends to lift the passengers from their seats. If the car stopped in a still shorter time, it would stop faster than the driver and passengers within the car. The driver's and passengers' energy would carry them into the front of the passenger compartment, unless they were secured with seat and shoulder belts.

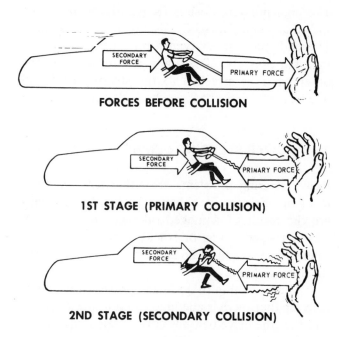

FORCES BEFORE COLLISION

1ST STAGE (PRIMARY COLLISION)

2ND STAGE (SECONDARY COLLISION)

Fig. 31-19 Stages of vehicle crash forces (Chevrolet Motor Division, General Motors Corporation).

In a head-on collision, two collisions actually occur. The first is the vehicle's collision with the object and the second is the occupants' collision with the instrument panel and windshield in the front of the passenger compartment (Figure 31-19). The modern passenger car front end is designed to crush approximately 1 in./mph (15.5 mm/km) on collision, in order to decelerate the passenger compartment in the longest possible time period and, thereby, reduce the severity of the secondary collision of the occupants.

In a head-on collision, the driver is thrown against the steering wheel about one one-hundredth of a second after the front of the vehicle begins to crush. The old-style steering column was often pushed into the driver as the front of the vehicle collapsed. Impact-absorbing steering columns are designed to have their lower section collapse, rather than having it pushed back into the driver. The upper end of these columns is also designed to absorb the secondary impact of the driver hitting the wheel by collapsing as the driver is thrown into it. As an extra precaution, wedges located at the upper attaching point cause the column to be pushed downward while absorbing impact loads.

The steering column must be strong enough and rigid enough to support normal driving loads and yet collapse at a controllable rate when collision loads are applied. Extreme care must be taken when removing or installing the column so the collapsing components are not damaged. It should not be hammered in any way to remove or assemble parts. Instead, special puller tools should be used. The column must be carefully aligned and fastened through break-away attachments with the correct length bolts properly torqued. Carelessness or abuse will cause permanent failure or improper crushing action in case of impact collision. If the column is damaged, it must be entirely replaced. It is not repairable.

Column Construction Features. The steering column consists of three major components: a steering shaft, a shift tube, and a column or mast jacket. The steering shaft connects the steering wheel through a universal-joint-type coupling to the steering gear unit. In some of the old steering gears, the steering shaft was an extension of the steering gear worm shaft. A shift tube surrounds the steering shaft. The upper end is connected to the shift selector lever and the lower end has a bell crank that attaches to the shift linkages. The shift tube is enclosed in the mast jacket that provides the supporting shaft bearings, the mounting brackets, and column trim.

The mast jacket is held in the vehicle by a floor plate retainer at the lower end and a break-away bracket just below the instrument panel. Attachments are designed to allow the column to move downward in a collision and prevent any upward movement.

The first impact absorbing mast jackets had a section with diamond perforation cutouts. In a collision, these perforation sections bulge outward, allowing the jacket to shorten. The perforation folds collapse quite easily after they start to fold.

A second generation impact absorbing mast jacket is made of two tubes. The upper tube section is sized to just slip over the lower section. Steel balls in an injected plastic sleeve are wedged between the two tubes, jamming them together to make a secure mast jacket. Upon impact collision, the two sections of the mast jacket telescope together. The steel balls extrude grooves in the tubes as they are forced together and, thus, gradually slow the secondary driver impact at a controlled rate. Typical impact absorbing mast jackets are shown in Figure 31-20.

Another collapsible design uses a large diameter crushable can just below the steering wheel. The secondary collision will collapse the can to minimize personal injury.

An adapter is placed in each end of the mast jacket to serve as either a bearing or a bearing support for the shift tube and steering shaft.

The shift tube is made of two or three short pieces of tubing, one fitted inside the other. Rectangular and round holes are cut in the tubes at the joints. These joints are then injected with plastic to hold their position. In a collision, the plastic inserts in the holes will shear, allowing the shift tubes to telescope together. The shift tube is in all steering columns to provide rigidity, even though the vehicle may be equipped with a floor-mounted gear shift lever.

The steering shaft has a solid rod upper section that fits into a hollow lower section. Two external flats on the upper section mate with internal flats in the lower section to transmit steering effort. Plastic inserts are injected into holes in the lower section and around grooves in the upper section just under the holes. This injected plastic locks the two steering shafts together. An impact will shear the plastic to allow the steering shaft to telescope and become shorter.

The upper end of the steering column has become quite complex on the modern automobile. There are a number of items in addition to the upper steering shaft bearing and steering wheel that are installed on the upper end of the steering column. These items include the transmission selector lever, turn signal switch, emergency flasher switch, ignition switch, shift and steering lock mechanisms, speed control, steering wheel tilt

(a)

(c)

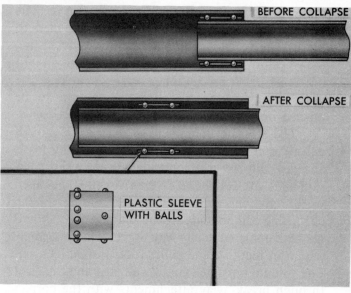

BEFORE COLLAPSE

AFTER COLLAPSE

PLASTIC SLEEVE
WITH BALLS

(b)

(d)

Fig. 31-20 Collapsible steering gear jacket types. (a) Diamond-shaped jacket perforation type, (b) steel balls between jacket sections type (Chevrolet Motor Division, General Motors Corporation), (c) bellows jacket type, (d) corrugated can type.

mechanism, and a means to allow the wheel to travel in and out. It is very important to follow the manufacturer's service manual when working on these units to make sure the great number of pieces are removed, installed, and adjusted in the correct order, using the correct special tools.

The transmission selector lever is connected to the shift tube. It has a gate that restricts shifter movement between neutral and drive unless the shift lever is lifted as it is moved. This prevents accidental movement into a lower gear, reverse, or park, which could cause transmission damage. Standard transmission gates are designed so the

shift linkage goes through neutral before a new gear can be selected. The selector lever fits through a housing or hub that trims the upper end of the steering column.

The turn signal switch is located directly under the steering wheel. A protrusion on the bottom of the steering wheel cancels the signal switch after a turn is completed.

A horn contact touches a slip ring on the steering wheel. When the horn is actuated, contact is made between the slip ring and the steering column metal. This completes the horn circuit to ground, blowing the horn.

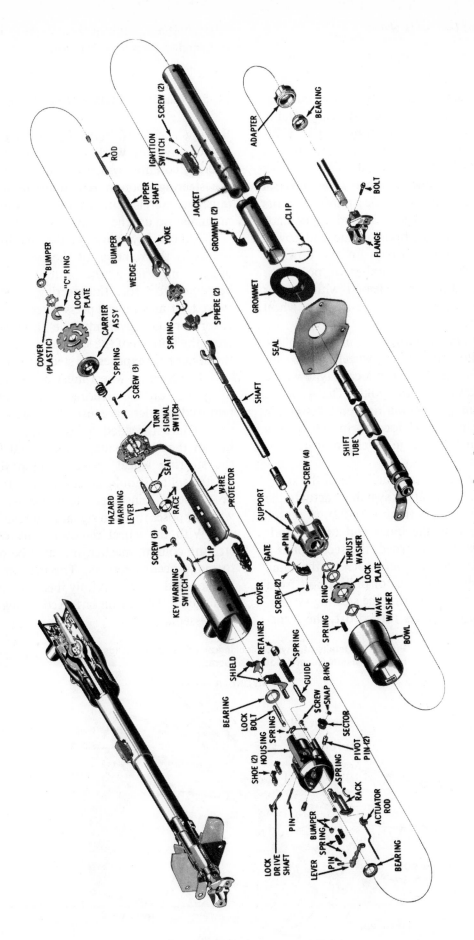

Fig. 31-21 Exploded view of a typical tilt and travel collapsible steering column (Oldsmobile Division, General Motors Corporation).

mission shaft actuator and steering lock bolt are returned to their lock position.

Tilting and telescope traveling steering columns have a much more complex upper steering column end. An exploded view is shown in Figure 31–21. The upper end of the steering shaft is fitted with a yoke that is part of a universal joint. A short upper shaft is also fitted with a yoke. The universal joint is completed with a plastic sphere that fits between the two yokes. The yoke and upper shaft are enclosed in a support housing and end cover. The upper shaft support swivels up and down in the housing, locking in a number of positions. Position locking shoes are released with a lever when the driver wishes to tilt the steering wheel to a new position.

The hollow upper shaft slides into the hollow upper yoke to allow the steering wheel to travel in-and out. It is held in place with a cam-type wedge locking into a keyway in the yoke. The wedge is locked by tightening a locking ring on the steering wheel. This pushes a rod located in the hollow upper shaft against the wedge which, in turn, locks the sliding action.

A rod extends from the back side of the steering-column-mounted ignition switch to actuate the steering and shifting locks (Figure 31–22). A plastic sector is mounted on the inner end of this rod. When the ignition key is turned, the sector pulls a rack that releases the shift actuator. At the same time, the other side of the sector pulls a bolt from the steering lock plate, releasing the steering system. When the ignition switch is turned off, the trans-

31-6 STEERING COLUMN SERVICE

Barring accidents, most of the steering column service involves work on the upper end of the steering column. Much of this can be done with the steering column remaining in the car. Care must be exercised to follow the applicable shop manuals and use the required special tools.

Almost any work on the steering column is begun by the removal of the steering wheel. The upper trim, often a horn button, bar, or ring must be removed before the steering wheel can be removed. It may have a press-fit cover, a twist-lock-cover, or the cover may be fastened by screws from the bottom of the steering wheel. Removal of the upper trim exposes the steering wheel nut.

The steering wheel must be pulled from a set of splines on the steering shaft after the nut is removed. Pullers are usually attached to screws turned into threaded holes in the steering wheel hub or they have padded hooks that loop around the steering wheel spokes. The position of the master spline should be checked so the wheel can be properly reinstalled. Removal of the steering wheel exposes the turn signal switch mechanism.

With the wheel removed, any of the upper steering column mechanisms may be disassembled to make needed repairs. The mechanisms should be handled very carefully because they can be damaged if they are hit or forced during disassembly or reassembly.

Fig. 31-22 Details of a typical locking steering column (Oldsmobile Division, General Motors Corporation).

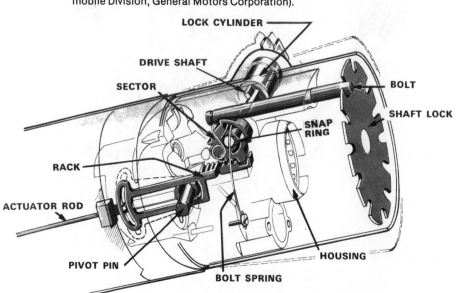

REVIEW QUESTIONS

1. How is the steering ratio determined? [31-1]

2. How was friction reduced in standard steering gears? [31-1]

3. How is the steering gear worm shaft preload adjusted? [31-1]

4. How is the sector back lash adjusted? [31-1]

5. What are the advantages and disadvantages of the rack and pinion steering gear? [31-1]

6. Name the parts of a power steering gear. [31-2]

7. Name three types of power steering gears. [31-2]

8. When the steering gear is turned what happens to the power steering fluid pressure? [31-2]

9. What balances the power steering control valve when the steering wheel is centered? [31-2]

10. During a turn, what centers the position of the power steering control valve? [31-2]

11. How does the power steering gear help the driver control the automobile on rough roads? [31-2]

12. What two types of control valves are used? [31-2]

13. What is the purpose of a torsion bar in a control valve? [31-2]

14. Why is reaction control important in a power steering gear? [31-2]

15. What forms the pressure surfaces in an integral power steering gear? [31-2]

16. How does the power steering ratio affect steering response? [31-2]

17. What types of power steering pumps are in common usage? [31-3]

18. What is a positive displacement pump? [31-3]

19. When are power assist requirements the highest? [31-3]

20. Why is a flow control valve used in a power steering control? [31-3]

21. How does the operation of the pressure relief valve differ from the flow control valve? [31-3]

22. How can a problem in a power steering gear be positively identified with a pressure test unit? [31-4]

23. What types of problems require the disassembly of the power steering gear? [31-4]

24. Why is a collapsible steering column used? [31-5]

25. How does the steering column collapse? [31-5]

26. Why are special pullers and assembly tools required for working on steering columns? [31-5]

27. What are the three major parts of the steering column? [31-5]

28. What is done with the shift tube when the automobile has a floor shift? [31-5]

29. Why is a gate used in the transmission selector? [31-5]

30. How is the steering wheel removed? [31-6]

instruments
and accessories

Light, instrument, and accessory systems are often neglected in a study of the automobile. This is most evident in automobile repair shops where technicians often find it difficult to pinpoint the cause of malfunctions in these areas. Service manuals have trouble shooting charts and give specific test procedures that should be followed. In new car dealerships, these charts are accompanied by service bulletins. The technician often overlooks this valuable information, and will change parts until the faulty system functions properly. Even though each car type and model is different, they all have a number of common elements. An understanding of these elements will be a great aid in helping a technician follow specific servicing procedures provided by the manufacturer.

To properly service electrical accessories, the technician must have an understanding of the principles upon which the accessories operate and the technician needs to develop a systematic testing procedure to pinpoint the cause of any accessory malfunction. When both of these are accomplished the technician will be able to rapidly diagnose, repair, and adjust lights, instruments, and accessories.

32-1 ELECTRICAL CIRCUITS

Wiring diagrams of an automobile's electrical system are very confusing at first glance. This can be seen in the simplified drawing of a wiring diagram in Figure 32-1. They are different for each manufacturer, model, and body style. When the variety of electrical accessories available is added to wiring diagrams, it is not surprising to see why the technician ignores them!

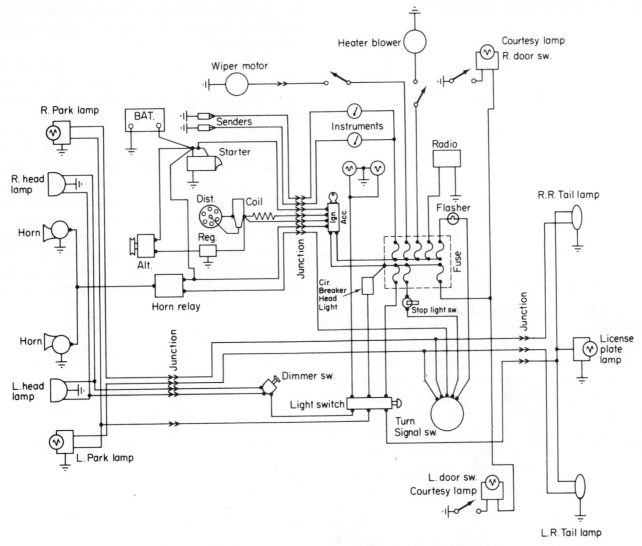

Fig. 32-1 A simplified automotive electrical system schematic drawing.

Wiring Diagram. Wiring diagrams are not difficult when one understands the basic automobile electrical circuit requirements and the symbols used to identify individual parts.

Electricity and electrical circuits required for engine operation have already been covered in Chapters 13 through 16. The rest of the automobile electrical system connects into the engine system to make use of the electrical energy from the battery and charging system. Electricity is conducted through wires and switches to the operating units, and through the *vehicle body metal* to complete the circuit with the battery and charging systems.

Electrical units must have a complete circuit supplying them with adequate current in order to function. Wiring diagrams use lines to show the insulated circuit connections. In general terms using electron theory, electrical power flows from the negative battery post to the body sheet metal. Electricity goes through operating units and into the insulated circuit. The circuit is connected through a switch to a fuse block that is part of a junction block where many circuits combine. The electricity completes its circuit to the positive battery post from the junction block.

Each operating unit on the wiring diagram is represented by a symbol, either a simple line drawing picture or an electrical schematic drawing. The wiring diagram is essentially a road map between two or more of these electrical units. It includes a means to identify each wire, each junction, each switch, and each safety device. A simple means of avoiding confusion while following one circuit is to lay a thin paper over the wiring diagram, then trace the desired circuit on the paper. Some service manuals have separate circuit drawings as individual illustrations.

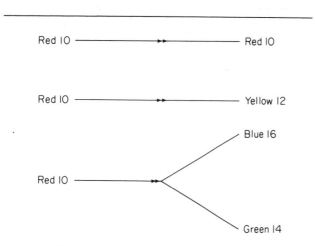

Fig. 32-2 Typical connector arrangement.

All lines on the wiring diagram that represent wires are given a color code. In general, the color follows from the fuse to the operating unit; however, in some cases, it will change color from one side of a junction to the other side as shown in Figure 32-2. There are even cases where two different colored wires come from the far side of a junction. The color codes used in the diagram are the same colors as those used on the vehicle's wires.

This makes it easy to follow the circuit in the wiring diagram and then to find the same circuit wire in the automobile.

Automobile wiring is made of several wiring harnesses. One end of each harness is connected to a junction block or connector block. The major junction blocks are located at the fire wall. The other end of the harness wire is attached to the operating units. The junction block end of the wire has a terminal that snaps into the block. This allows the terminals to make electrical contact when the two halves of the junction block are assembled. The terminal must be partly compressed to remove it from the block. Many types are used, so the service manual should be consulted for the specific terminal removal method when removal is necessary. The front end horn and lighting harness

Fig. 32-3 Typical wiring harness in an automobile body.

Fig. 32-4 Typical wiring harness behind an instrument panel (Oldsmobile Division, General Motors Corporation).

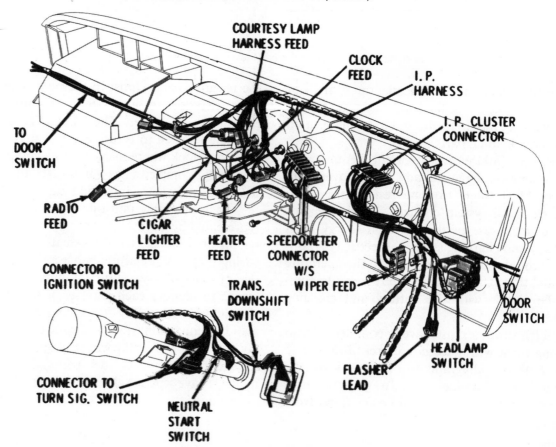

is routed along the fire wall and front fenders. The body wiring usually runs from behind the dash along the left lower sill to the rear of the car with branches running to interior lights. This is shown in Figure 32–3. A number of smaller harness assemblies are usually attached to the main harness, such as the one shown in Figure 32–4.

Wiring Requirements. The engineer designs automobile wiring to provide safe and efficient operation at a minimum cost. It is installed in the automobile so that it is accessible for assembly and for service. In most cases, the junction connectors are designed in a manner that prevents accidental incorrect connection.

Wires must be large enough to carry the current required with minimum voltage loss. If resistance is high, the wire temperature will increase. Wire and connector temperature rise must be less than 225 °F (108 °C) above the surrounding air temperature. If the wires are larger than necessary, they will increase vehicle weight, take additional space, and increase vehicle cost. Generally, Number 16 is the smallest size used in body wiring and Number 10 is the largest. Most wire sizes fall between these two extremes.

Wiring used for automobile lights, instruments, and accessories is called primary wiring. The wire is covered with a molded plastic insulation. Different colors are used to identify the circuit. Many types of plastic compounds are used. Their main differences are in their insulating properties and their melting points. The one that will meet the operational requirements at least cost is the one that is used.

Terminals are attached to the ends of the wires to connect to an operating unit or junction. Many of the original equipment terminals are attached to the wire, then covered with molded plastic insulation. Other terminals are attached by crimping, swaging, welding, or soldering. All of these methods are satisfactory if they make a good electrical bond that is mechanically strong. Each wire terminal is exposed, even though a number of wires are held, together with a fabric braid, plastic shield, or tape to form a wiring harness. In some cases, a soldered joint may be located inside a harness.

Instrument panels use printed circuits. These consist of thin conductor ribbons on an insulator that can be seen in Figure 32–5. If the printed circuit is damaged, the entire circuit board will require replacement.

Wiring Service. When an electrical operating unit fails to function, the unit should be checked. If there is no apparent problem with the unit, the wiring may be at fault. Wiring can break to cause an *open,* two wires can contact each other to cause a *short,* or a wire can contact the frame, causing a *ground.* Each of these can be partial or intermittent, which increases the difficulty in locating the problem point.

When a malfunction exists in a circuit, the first thing to do is to see that voltage is available at the operating end. These checks can be made with a test light or a voltmeter. The test light usually

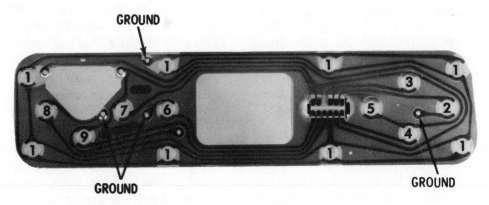

1. ILLUMINATION LAMPS	4. BRAKE LAMP	7. AMP LAMP
2. LEFT TURN SIGNAL	5. COLD LAMP	8. RIGHT TURN SIGNAL
3. HOT LAMP	6. CENTER LAMP	9. OIL LAMP

Fig. 32–5 Typical printed instrument panel circuit (Oldsmobile Division, General Motors Corporation).

has a pointed prod to get into the circuits. It will draw some current and is easy to use. A voltmeter will show if adequate voltage is available. Each method has its own advantage.

If voltage is available to the circuit but it doesn't arrive at the operating unit, the circuit is open and its section must be checked to pinpoint the problem. The connectors at the fuses, junction blocks, and switch terminals make convenient points to check for voltage. Move the insulated voltmeter lead from terminal to terminal down the circuit until the specific wire causing the problem is identified. This principle is illustrated in Figure 32-6. This part of the harness should be loosened from its attachments and thoroughly inspected. If the problem point is not visible, the harness will have to be opened at intervals and the test prod forced through the insulation of the problem wire until it touches the metal. Several prod points are made until the exact problem point is located. It can usually be repaired by soldering the wire with rosin core solder, then taping the repair and all prod openings.

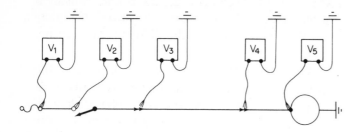

Fig. 32-6 Voltage tests to determine system opens.

Grounds allow current to bleed to the automobile sheet metal. They will usually draw enough current to open one of the safety devices that are installed in the circuit to protect the wiring from overheating. Junctions should be disconnected to locate the specific wire that is grounded. Grounds may be located by lifting the harness away from the sheet metal and giving it a thorough inspection. Ground and short finders are available. They consist of a circuit breaker that can be installed in place of the circuit's safety device. These allow current to flow and then break before the circuit wiring is overheated. When the breaker cools, it again closes the circuit. This provides the circuit with a pulsing direct current. When current flows,

it induces a surrounding magnetism which can be sensed with a magnetism indicator. The indicator is moved along the conductor. When it reaches the short, it will no longer indicate a magnetic field. This can be used to quickly pinpoint the ground or a short.

Shorts between wires usually put electrical power into adjacent circuits. For example, a short between filaments in a tail light bulb could cause the instrument panel lights to flash as the turn signal flashes. Shorts are difficult to locate. The best procedure is to follow both circuits on the wiring diagram to see where they might possibly be shorted together. The system should be separated at the junctions to locate the specific wires that are shorting. The actual short can usually be seen.

When electrical circuit problems are encountered, the technician should check the safety device, the operating unit, and the wiring diagram. Consider the possible cause of the problem and then proceed with a systematic check of the system causing the problem.

Safety Devices. All electrical circuits, other than engine circuits, are protected with safety devices. The safety device opens the circuit when high current flows so the wiring, insulation, or surrounding structure is not damaged. Safety devices used in automobiles take three forms: fuses, circuit breakers, and fusible links.

A *fuse* is a small metal strip in a glass tube that burns out to break the circuit when high current flows. Fuses are usually grouped together in a fuse block under the dash. Figure 32-7 pictures a typical fuse block. Sometimes they are mounted separately in a circuit. A fuse will carry a 10% overload and will burn out immediately with a 35% overload. This protects the wiring and operating units. Fuses are used in low amperage light and accessory circuits. Circuits that draw high current usually use circuit breakers.

A *circuit breaker* is a set of contact points mounted on a bimetal arm as illustrated in Figure 32-8. As excess current flows, the bimetal arm heats. Heat causes the arm to bend, breaking the point contact which stops current flow in the circuit. When the arm cools, the points close to reestablish a complete electrical circuit. Circuit breakers are used as a safety feature in the headlight circuit. In case of a short, the lights do not stay out, but will flash on and off to give the driver a chance to safely stop the automobile. Circuit

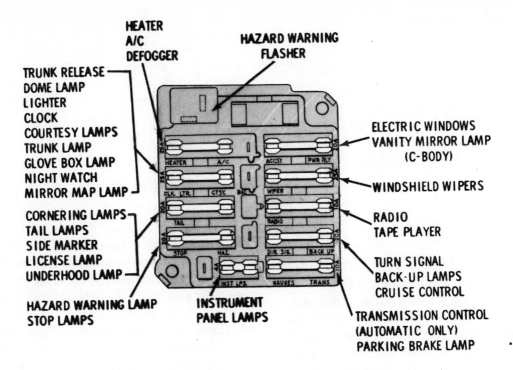

HEATER
A/C
DEFOGGER

HAZARD WARNING
FLASHER

TRUNK RELEASE —
DOME LAMP
LIGHTER
CLOCK
COURTESY LAMPS
TRUNK LAMP
GLOVE BOX LAMP
NIGHT WATCH
MIRROR MAP LAMP

CORNERING LAMPS
TAIL LAMPS
SIDE MARKER
LICENSE LAMP
UNDERHOOD LAMP

HAZARD WARNING LAMP
STOP LAMPS

INSTRUMENT
PANEL LAMPS

ELECTRIC WINDOWS
VANITY MIRROR LAMP
(C-BODY)

WINDSHIELD WIPERS

RADIO
TAPE PLAYER

TURN SIGNAL
BACK-UP LAMPS
CRUISE CONTROL

TRANSMISSION CONTROL
(AUTOMATIC ONLY)
PARKING BRAKE LAMP

Fig. 32-7 Typical fuse block (Oldsmobile Division, General Motors Corporation).

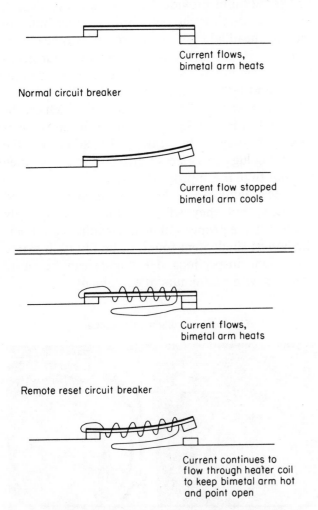

Current flows,
bimetal arm heats

Normal circuit breaker

Current flow stopped
bimetal arm cools

Current flows,
bimetal arm heats

Remote reset circuit breaker

Current continues to
flow through heater coil
to keep bimetal arm hot
and point open

Fig. 32-8 Principles of typical circuit breakers.

breakers are also used on high-current-drawing units like power windows and power seats. The breaker may be located under the dash or adjacent to the operating unit.

Some circuit breakers do not automatically reset, so the circuit remains open until repairs are made. They may be reset manually after being tripped. A remote reset breaker has been developed to reset the breaker at will. It has a resistance wire coiled around the bimetal spring and connected across the points. When the points are closed, no current will flow through the coil. When excess current causes the bimetal spring points to open, current flows through the resistance coil and the coil gets hot. Coil heat holds the points open. The circuit breaker will automatically close when the switch is turned off or when the battery is disconnected.

Many circuits are further protected with a *fusible link,* even though they have a fuse or a circuit breaker. Fusible links will protect the circuit if someone accidentally shorts out one of the other safety devices. A fusible link is a short piece of wire four sizes smaller than the circuit wire it is designed to protect. For example, the #10 wire in the charging circuit is protected by a #14 fusible link and a #16 light wire is protected by a #20 fusible link. The fusible link is covered with thick Hypalon plastic insulation that will not burn. Its exterior size suggests that is a large wire. When the link fails, the grounded point that caused the failure must be repaired before a new link is installed. In some cases, the link is connected with terminals, and in other cases it is soldered in the circuit as an integral part of the circuit.

32-2 LIGHTS

Exterior lights are a safety factory any time visibility is poor. Under these conditions, many states require their use. Lights inside the automobile are a convenience that helps to reduce driver strain and, thus, leads to safety. Any time a light does not function, it becomes a factor contributing to an unsafe vehicle.

In most cases, light failure results from a burned out filament in the bulb. This is easily corrected by bulb replacement. Bulb failure can also be caused by the wiring, terminals, or bulb socket. When a whole set of lights fail, it is often caused by an open system safety device.

The light bulb must be of the correct type. It must have a base to match the bulb socket and it must have the correct filament. Filament size and design control bulb brightness. The bulb must be bright enough to give the necessary light, but not so bright that it uses excess current or is blinding bright.

Headlights. The most critical lights on the automobile are the headlights. They must be bright enough so the driver can see the road ahead but not so bright that they will blind the oncoming driver. Many state laws have limited the headlight brightness to a maximum of 75,000 candle power.

With candle power limited, headlight engineers have designed headlights that will concentrate the available light onto the road and avoid blinding the oncoming driver. This is done by making prisms and asymmetric left flutes in the bulb lens interior to widen the beam and minimize glare as illustrated in Figure 32-9. Careful filament placement and a tilted reflector aims the light beam to the road.

Automobiles are equipped with high beam and low beam lights. Most of the driving in cities and on busy highways is done using low beams.

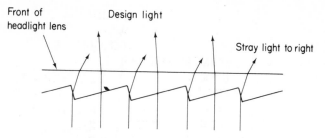

Fig. 32-9 Headlight lens design.

High beam only is used when there is no oncoming traffic.

Two types of headlights are used to meet driving needs. Type-1 headlights have one filament aimed to give maximum light on the road. They are used as the inboard or lower lights in the four-headlight system. Type-2 headlights have two filaments. The main filament is located to provide maximum light on low beam. These were brought onto the market as more cars made traffic heavier, so that more of the driving was being done with low beam than with high beam. The second filament in Type-2 bulbs provides high beam light. Type-2 lights are used for the outboard or upper bulbs in the four-headlight system and for all two-headlight systems. Headlight bulbs used in the four-headlight system are 5-¾ in. in diameter or are rectangular, and bulbs used in the two-headlight system are 7 in. diameter. The type number, which can be observed in Figure 32-10, is embossed on the lens face for easy identification. In addition, the mounting lugs are offset at different angles so they will not fit in the improper location.

Headlights can be designed and manufactured correctly, but they will function correctly only when they are properly aimed. Headlight aiming is the largest single item found to be faulty in safety check lane inspections. Headlights can be easily adjusted with a minimum of equipment.

Fig. 32-10 Headlight bulb number.

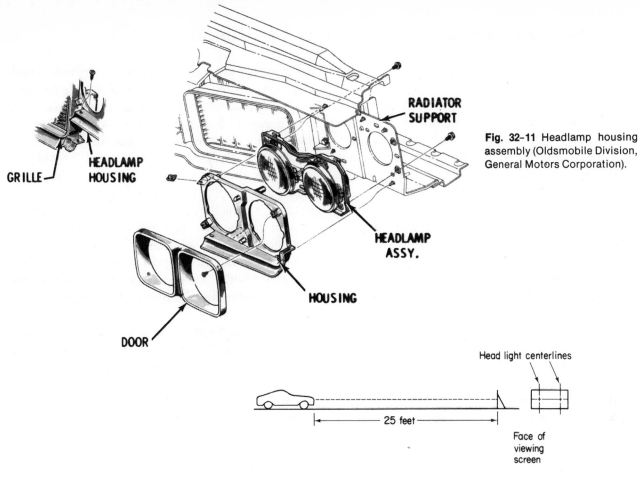

GRILLE — HEADLAMP HOUSING

RADIATOR SUPPORT

HEADLAMP ASSY.

HOUSING

DOOR

Fig. 32-11 Headlamp housing assembly (Oldsmobile Division, General Motors Corporation).

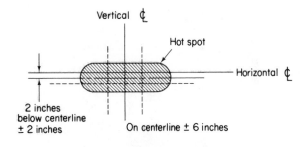

Head light centerlines

25 feet

Face of viewing screen

Fig. 32-12 Headlight aiming principle.

The headlight bulb is fastened in a metal adjuster ring. The adjuster ring has one screw that controls horizontal movement and another that controls vertical movement. These are used to place the light beam hot spot in the correct position so it will provide the driver with maximum road lighting.

Headlight aiming is based on a distance of 25 feet between the front of the headlight bulb and a viewing screen, which may be a wall as illustrated in Figure 32-12. The center of the vertical lines should be directly in front of the automobile headlights and the horizontal line should be at the same height as the center of the headlight bulbs. Before the headlights are aimed, the automobile should have a full tank of fuel, the spare tire should be in its normal location, all tires should be inflated correctly, and any other regularly carried materials should be loaded. The hot spot should be located as shown in Figure 32-13. Adjusting screws are used to correctly position the hot spot. Type-1 bulbs are aimed with high beam turned on, while Type-2 bulbs are aimed with low beam turned on. When the bulbs are rectangular they are called Type-1A and Type-2A.

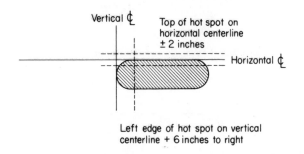

Vertical ℄

Hot spot

Horizontal ℄

2 inches below centerline ± 2 inches

On centerline ± 6 inches

Type 1 headlight

Vertical ℄

Top of hot spot on horizontal centerline ± 2 inches

Horizontal ℄

Left edge of hot spot on vertical centerline + 6 inches to right

Type 2 headlight

Fig. 32-13 Viewing screen patterns of the headlight hot spot aiming area.

Light-beam aiming requires a relatively dark area. Mechanical aimers have been devised for use in full daylight. They are built with mathematical corrections to aim the light bulbs as accurately as with the light beam method. Mechanical aimers are seated against three reference locating lugs provided on the bulb, as described in Figure 32-14. Specific operating details differ between aimers. In general, they use spirit levels, strings, and reflecting mirrors with split images to align headlight pairs. Some aimers used in daylight use the headlight beam with optics so the pattern in the aimer appears the same as it would be on the viewing screen.

No matter what method is used, headlights should be accurately aimed for proper night visibility. At today's driving speeds, any light less than the maximum possible does not give the driver sufficient reaction time in case there is an unexpected change in the road ahead.

Instruments are used to indicate many automobile operating conditions. All automobiles are equipped with a speedometer and odometer to show speed and distance. Some means is provided to indicate low engine oil pressure, high coolant temperature, and battery discharge. A fuel gauge is provided to show the amount of fuel remaining in the tank. Each automobile has an indicator to show the operation of high-beam headlights and turn signals.

In addition to these basic instruments, many automobiles have additional instruments to give the driver more information about the operation of the automobile. These would include instruments such as a tachometer, clock, and compass.

Indicator Lights. Many operating conditions are shown by indicator lights. These are frequently referred to as "idiot lights" by those who do not recognize their value. A driver's attention is immediately called to a light signal that indicates a problem, even though he is concentrating on driving. It is interesting to note that the aerospace industry

Fig. 32-14 Mechanical headlamp aiming (Cadillac Motor Car Division, General Motors Corporation).

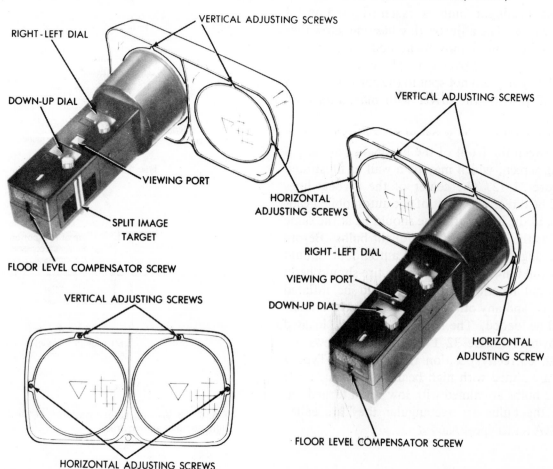

uses lights to indicate abnormal operating conditions to alert the pilot to the problem; there may also be a gauge to check the actual operating value.

Indicator lights pick up their power at the engine or tank sending unit. The circuit goes through to the indicator light bulb, then on to the ignition switch, where it is attached to a junction block to complete the circuit as shown in Figure 32–15. It should be noted that these indicator bulbs are some of the few in the vehicle that are not grounded at the bulb. The engine and tank units are electrical switches that connect the circuit to ground to turn the indicator light on.

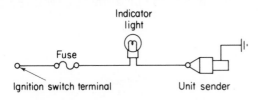

Fig. 32–15 Typical indicator light circuit.

A diaphragm in the oil pressure unit opens contact points when sufficient oil pressure exists. When the pressure drops dangerously low, the points close to turn on the indicator light. Points on a bimetal arm are used in the temperature sender unit. When engine temperature is excessive, the heat bends the bimetal arm in the engine unit so the points close to complete the circuit and turn on the red warning light. In some cases, the temperature unit is equipped with a second set of points to indicate low temperature. These points are normally closed to keep the green cold light on. As the engine warms, the bimetal arm bends enough to separate the points which turn out the cold signal light.

Charging system discharge lights operate in a different manner. Mechanical regulators use a light relay, usually located within the regulator. When the generator is charging, the relay is energized to open the points. When the system is not charging, the points close, completing the indicator circuit and the warning light comes on. Solid-state regulators use electronic circuits to turn on the charge indicator.

A number of other warning lights may be used, such as parking brake signal, low fuel level, seat belt fastening, door ajar, etc. Each helps to improve safety and convenience, while adding to the original and maintenance costs.

A relatively new indicating method makes use of fiber optic conductors, consisting of a bundle of plastic filaments that transmit light. They are used to show the driver if lights are on or off. One end of the bundle is at the light source and the other is visible to the driver.

Gauges. Instrument gauges are used where it is important to know values, such as vehicle speed and remaining fuel. Oil pressure, engine temperature, and charging rate values are also used to indicate impending failure before it occurs. Gauges are generally more expensive than indicating lights, and the majority of drivers would not notice or recognize an incorrect reading anyway, so lights are usually used. Gauges are standard equipment on certain sport and performance model cars and optional equipment on many other cars.

The speedometer is a mechanical device, making use of induction between a rotating magnet and a cup. The cup position is retained by a hair spring. As the magnet rotates, it pulls the cup against the hair spring an amount proportional to the magnet's rotating speed. The cup is connected to an indicator needle to show speed. The rotating magnet is driven by a flexible shaft which, in turn, is driven by a gear in the transmission output shaft or by a gear on the left front wheel.

Most of the other gauges are electrically operated. In one type of gauge, a coil of resistance wire is wound around a bimetal arm. The more current that flows through the coil, the more it heats and bends the bimetal arm. The movable end of the arm is connected by a linkage to an indicator needle. Different scale panels are placed behind the needle to show the correct value. This is illustrated in Figure 32–16.

Fig. 32–16 Typical instrument circuit using thermostatic heating.

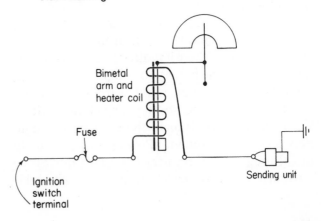

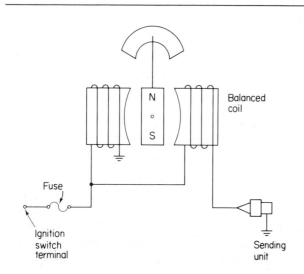

Fig. 32-17 Typical instrument circuit using balanced coils.

Another method used to operate instruments uses a balanced-coil principle as shown in Figure 32-17. A series coil carries full instrument current. The current then splits, part going to a variable resistance in the sending unit and the rest going to the shunt coil. Current flowing through the sending unit changes as its resistance changes and this weakens and strengthens the shunt coil. High resistance in the sending unit increases the shunt coil magnetic strength and a low resistance weakens the shunt coil magnetic strength. The indicator needle is deflected by the difference in the magnetic strength of the sensing and shunt coils.

Because the instrument gauge mechanism is sensitive to current flow, it is important to have a constant voltage source for accuracy. In most cases, these instruments are supplied from a vibrating point voltage regulator that keeps the voltage at a constant value, usually five volts. The instrument voltage regulator may be a separate unit or part of the fuel level gauge.

The gauge sender, which is a tank or engine unit, actually connects the instrument electrical system to ground where it indirectly connects to the negative side of the battery to complete the circuit. In the fuel gauge sending unit, variable resistance rheostat is connected to the hinged tank float. When the fuel level is high, the gauge circuit connects directly to ground, allowing full current to flow through the instrument coil. This moves the instrument needle to the top of the scale. As fuel is

used, the float drops. This causes the instrument circuit current to flow through part of the variable resistance, adding resistance that reduces current flow. On thermal instruments this reduces instrument coil temperature so the gauge reading lowers. The gauge reading is, therefore, proportional to the tank fuel level.

Electric oil pressure and temperature gauges work in a similar manner, as illustrated in Figure 32-18. Design of the engine unit is their only difference. Oil pressure gauge senders have a spring loaded diaphragm. Diaphragm movement caused by the oil pushing the diaphragm toward the spring changes the instrument circuit resistance

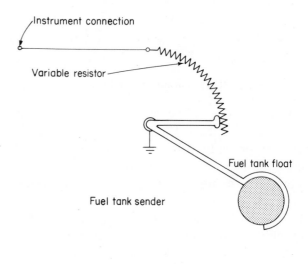

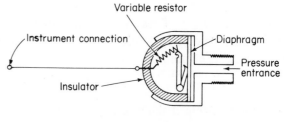

Fig. 32-18 Typical instrument tank and engine unit principles.

proportional to the diaphragm movement. Resistance is low when oil pressure is high, giving a high instrument reading. The temperature gauge sending unit has a bimetal spring that changes resistance proportional to engine heat. The free end of the bimetal spring is attached to a variable resistance so the instrument circuit resistance is changed proportionately to the engine temperature. When the engine is hot, the engine unit resistance is low, which will give a high instrument reading.

If the sending unit end of the wire is grounded, the normal reading will always be high. If no current flows, the reading will always be zero. Some service manuals give resistance values that can be temporarily inserted in the circuit to check gauge accuracy. They are also helpful in troubleshooting a gauge problem.

The ammeter is connected in the part of the charging circuit that leads to the battery. Its purpose is to indicate the amount of current being put into or taken from the battery. It does not indicate generator output. Ammeter wiring circuits are, therefore, made from large wire sizes. The ammeter itself must also have heavy construction to carry high current. Several ammeter movement types are used. All basically use an application of induction. As current flows, it forms a magnetic field that is deflected by a permanent magnet in the instrument. High current flow causes high magnetic field deflection. The moving portion of the gauge is connected to an indicator needle. The needle's normal position is upright. The needle would move to the right when the current is flowing to charge the battery and to the left when discharging current flows from the battery.

Trouble shooting becomes routine when the technician understands the basic operating principles of these instruments and when the service manual instructions are followed. The biggest problem encountered in instrument trouble shooting in some vehicle models is to get to the instrument leads to check them, especially in a car equipped with air conditioning and a center console.

32-4 ACCESSORIES

Accessories are items added to the basic vehicle for additional safety, comfort, or appearance. Vehicle operation is not impaired if they fail; however, their failure is a great source of annoyance to the driver or his passengers.

Radio. A radio is one of the most common accessories. It may be merely an AM radio or a complex AM/FM stereo with a tape deck. The automotive technician's only responsibility is to properly install or remove it, see that it is supplied with electrical power, trim the antenna, and adjust the push buttons. If additional service is required, the radio will have to be removed and repaired by a specialist.

In most cases, the radio is connected to the ignition accessory terminal and is fused in the connecting wire. In some cases, the fuse is built into the radio chassis.

Trimming the antenna is a means of balancing the radio and antenna with a trimmer screw located on the back or bottom of the radio chassis. The radio is turned to a weak station around 1600 KC and the trimmer screw adjusted to get the strongest signal.

Push buttons are pulled outward to release them. The station is tuned in with the dial. When the push button is pushed in, it will lock the station to the button. In most cases, the driver will adjust the push buttons to the station himself.

Motors. Many accessories operate with small electric motors. Examples of some of these small motors are shown in Figure 32-19. In some cases,

Fig. 32-19 Small electric motors used in automobiles.

they are reversible motors. Electric motors used for accessories make use of the same motor principles as starters, described in Chapter 14. The motor has a rotating armature within a field. Current is transferred to the armature through commutator brushes. The armature is supported in bearings within the housing.

Reversible motors are equipped with two fields. One field is used when the motor runs clockwise and the other field is used when the motor runs counterclockwise.

Motors are used as fan drives in the heater, air conditioner, and defogger. They are used for power to operate power windows, power seats, power antennas, hydraulic pumps for power tops, windshield wipers, windshield washers, electric fuel pumps, and many other units.

If a motor does not operate, the first thing to do is check to see that electrical power is available at the motor lead. If it isn't, the circuit should be checked as previously described. If power is available, the motor should be removed for service. Many of these motors are low cost, high production units that are not repairable but must be replaced. Motors that are repairable should be disassembled.

Motor repair follows the same procedures used for servicing starters. The parts are wiped clean and then inspected for grounds or opens. The commutator can be turned and new brushes installed. Bearings and gear housings should be properly lubricated as the motor is assembled. After assembly, it should be checked for correct operation before installing it in the vehicle.

Buzzer. Buzzers are used to call the driver's attention to an unusual condition, such as the key left in the ignition when the door is opened. The buzzer principle is also used for vehicle horns. In horns, the vibrating armature is connected to a metal diaphragm that is vibrated to produce the sound.

In the buzzer, current flows through a coil, then on to spring-loaded, normally closed points, as shown in Figure 32–20. Coil magnetism pulls the armature to open the points, which breaks the coil's electrical circuit, so the coil loses its magnetism. The spring will then close the points and the

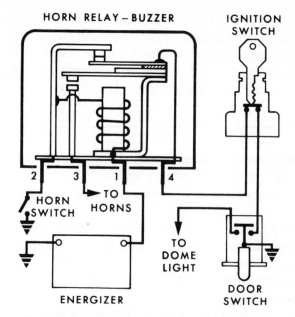

Fig. 32-20 Typical horn and safety buzzer circuit (Chevrolet Motor Division, General Motors Corporation).

cycle repeats. Cycling speed or frequency is based on the balance between the spring force, coil strength, air gap, and armature weight. Different cycling frequencies produce different horn pitches. Most horns have an adjusting screw to change spring tension for tuning the horn pitch.

Solenoid. A solenoid provides a pull force. Solenoid details in Chapter 14 explain its use to engage the starter drive. It is also used as a remote control to operate items such as door locking, trunk opening, and applying the air conditioning compressor clutch. A movable core is attached to the mechanism. When current flows through a coil, the core is pulled toward the coil center to operate the mechanism.

Relay. A relay is a remote switch. It is usually used where heavy current is required and voltage losses would be too great if the entire circuit ran to the driver's control switch. A horn relay or a starter relay are examples of this requirement. The normally open relay points on the relay armature are heavy enough to carry the required current. One end of a fine wire coil is connected to the relay power input and the other end lead is connected to a switch on the dash. When the driver closes the switch, current flows through the coil to close the relay points. This supplies current to the required units. Upon release of the switch, the relay opens to break the circuit and the current stops.

Vacuum Controls. Some accessories are vacuum operated, rather than electric. Engine manifold vacuum is the vacuum source. Small vacuum hoses and valves are connected together in a manner very similar to the electrical wiring to connect the vacuum source to the operating unit.

Vacuum is used for a pull motion. It is usually used to position heater, air conditioning, and ventilation doors. It may be used in some applications in the place of solenoids on door locks, trunk locks, and headlight covers.

Vacuum actuators may also be called vacuum motors. They consist of a rod extending from a spring-loaded diaphragm. Vacuum on the spring side of the diaphragm moves the diaphragm to pull the rod. This action can be observed in Figure 32-21.

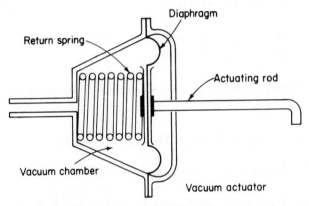

Fig. 32-21 Sectional view of a typical vacuum actuator.

Trouble shooting vacuum systems is similar to electrical trouble shooting. The line may be plugged (like an electrical open) or the hose may have a leak (like an electrical ground). Valves or vacuum switches may be faulty and the vacuum actuator diaphragm may be perforated. Vacuum systems may be equipped with a reservoir to provide a limited vacuum source when the engine is not operating.

Speed Control. A speed control is an accessory to reduce driver fatigue. The driver can lock it at almost any desired speed. It will hold the automobile speed constant within the engine power range. The driver can override the control with the throttle and release it with a slight touch of the brake pedal.

Speed is sensed by a regulator. The regulator is a mechanical governor driven by the speedometer cable. The governor opens and closes contact points. Electrical current is sent across the points when the driver energizes the system. This current flows through an electrical solenoid that controls a vacuum valve. A vacuum bellows assembly is used to position the throttle. Opening and closing governor points controls the average position of the bellows vacuum valve so that the bellows position will match the control speed. Underspeed opens the throttle and overspeed closes it. Details can be seen in the simplified drawing in Figure 32-22.

Many other accessories are used and many new ones will be developed. If the technician can master the basic concepts, he can easily adapt to the new and varied units as he has occasion to work on them.

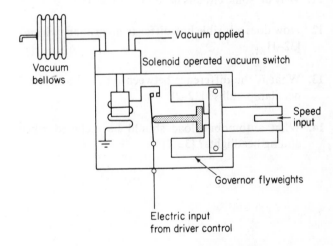

Fig. 32-22 Schematic of a typical speed control.

REVIEW QUESTIONS

1. Why is an electrical circuit drawing compared to a road map? [32-1]

2. How do the color codes on the wiring diagram compare to the actual colors of the wires in the automobile? [32-1]

3. How does the wiring harness run through an automobile body? [32-1]

4. What limits the wire size in automobiles? [32-1]

5. What is primary wiring? [32-1]

6. Where is a printed circuit used? [32-1]

7. What electrical problems can cause an electrical unit to fail? [32-1]

8. What is the first check to make when an electrical unit doesn't function? [32-1]

9. How are junctions used to locate a wiring problem? [32-1]

10. How does a short finder work? [32-1]

11. Why do some circuits have fuses? [32-1]

12. How does a fusible link differ from primary wiring? [32-1]

13. What is the difference between type-1 and type-2 headlamp bulbs? [32-2]

14. What automobile load should be included when aiming headlights? [32-2]

15. What is the advantage of mechanical headlight aimers? [32-2]

16. What instruments do all automobiles have? [32-3]

17. Why are the indicator lights not grounded to the body metal? [32-3]

18. List the circuits that could have warning indicators. [32-3]

19. When are gauges used rather than warning lights? [32-3]

20. What two gauge operating methods are described in this chapter? [32-3]

21. What happens to the gauge reading when the sender is grounded? [32-3]

22. What radio work would a technician be expected to do? [32-4]

23. How are radio antennas trimmed? [32-4]

24. How are radio push buttons set? [32-4]

25. What is the first thing to be checked if a small motor doesn't operate? [32-4]

26. How does a horn operate? [32-4]

27. What is a vacuum motor? [32-4]

28. What is the speed sensing regulator in a speed control? [32-4]

automotive air conditioning

Air conditioning has become a very important optional accessory in the northern United States and a necessity in the South. The air conditioner, operating in conjunction with the heater, provides control of the passenger compartment temperature, humidity, and air cleanliness to provide a quiet, clean, comfortable environment for the occupants. Safety is improved because the driver does not become fatigued as quickly as he does without air conditioning.

Air is conditioned by directing an air flow across a cool metal surface called an *evaporator*. This cools the air and causes moisture in the air to condense, much as the moisture will condense on the outside of a glass that contains a cool drink. Condensed moisture traps dust and pollen to help clean the air. The dirty condensed water is drained from the system through a hose.

Automobile air conditioning is divided into two distinct systems—the air distribution system and the refrigeration system. Both must function correctly to provide adequate air conditioning.

33-1 AIR DISTRIBUTION SYSTEM

The air distribution system consists of blower fans to move the air, ducts to carry the air, and valves to control the air flow direction. Electric motors drive the fans; air valves are positioned by vacuum adjusters or mechanical controls.

Air distribution systems differ among automobile manufacturers, models, and air conditioner types. Their details are described in the applicable service manual; however, they fall into three basic air conditioning system types.

The simplest type is the self-contained air conditioner. Its air distribution system is completely separate from the automobile heater system. Air flow is controlled by fan speed and by louvers that control the air flow direction.

In the second type, most factory-installed air conditioners are built to combine their air distribution system with the heater air distribution system as shown in Figure 33–1. All of the air to be cooled flows across the evaporator. If this cools the air too much, some or all of the cool air is then directed across the heater core to be reheated to the desired temperature. A combination of cooling, which removes moisture and dirt, followed by sufficient reheating, provides ideal air conditioning.

The most complex type of air conditioning is factory installed air conditioning systems have fully automatic air distribution controls. The driver can set the temperature desired and the controls will cool or heat the air and set the blower speed as necessary to maintain that temperature within maximum cooling to maximum heating limits.

The air distribution system is basically a mechanical system. Its service involves mechanical adjustments that move air distribution valves in the position required for each range selected. If a valve doesn't operate, it may be the result of an inoperative vacuum control or binding valve mechanism. Specific test procedures as described in the service manual may be required to locate the cause of problems in automatic control type systems.

33-2 REFRIGERATION SYSTEM

In simplified terms, the air conditioner refrigeration system is similar to an engine cooling system. The engine coolant is forced to circulate by a pump. It picks up engine heat and carries it to the radiator, where the heat is transferred to the outside air. Heat is always transferred from the highest temperature to the lowest temperature. The coolant then recirculates back through the engine to remove more heat.

In the air conditioner's refrigeration system, refrigerant picks up heat from the passenger compartment, is pumped to the condenser where it gives up its heat to the outside air, and then flows back through the system to pick up more heat. This is illustrated in Figure 33–2. Refrigerant is recycled in a closed system as is engine coolant.

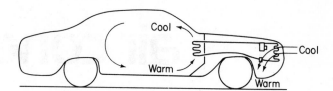

Fig. 33-2 Heat movement from the passenger compartment through the refrigeration system to the outside air.

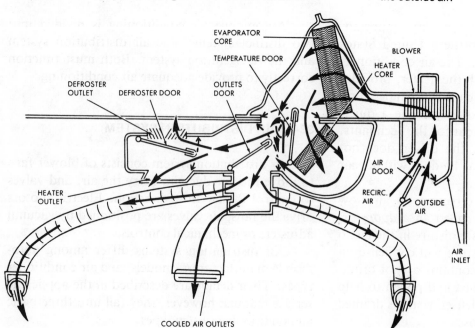

Fig. 33-1 Typical air distribution system (Chevrolet Motor Division, General Motors Corporation).

Freon-12 is used as the heat transfer medium in automotive air conditioner refrigeration systems. It is usually called Refrigerant 12, F-12, or R-12. This refrigerant provides good heat transfer in the required temperature range and does not deteriorate system components.

In operation, the refrigerant continually changes from a liquid to a gas, then back to a liquid again. A great amount of heat is required to boil the refrigerant in the evaporator while turning it into a vapor. Heat to boil, the refrigerant is taken from the passenger compartment air, thus cooling the air.

The refrigerant boiling point is dependent upon its pressure just as the engine cooling system boiling point can be changed by means of a pressure cap. High pressure raises the boiling point and low pressure reduced it. Atmospheric pressure Freon-12 boils at –21°F (–30°C). Refrigerant in the closed system is allowed to evaporate or boil in the evaporator under controlled pressures, which, in turn, controls evaporator temperature.

It is a well-known physical principle that it requires a great deal more heat to change a liquid to a gas at the same temperature than it does to raise the temperature of a liquid. The refrigeration cycle makes use of this principle. Liquid refrigerant enters the evaporator at a controlled rate. Heat from the passenger compartment air warms the refrigerant in the evaporator and thus cools the air. This heat causes the refrigerant to boil as it changes from a liquid to a vapor. The vapor is then pumped from the evaporator by the compressor, compress-

ing the vapors to increase pressure in the same way a compressor would compress air. These high-pressure, high-temperature vapors are run through a condenser where they are cooled with outside air. Cooling at high pressure causes the vapors to condense back to the liquid state to be reused in the evaporator. This forms a continuous cycle to carry heat from the evaporator in the passenger compartment to the condenser where it is given up to outside air. The cycle is illustrated in Figure 33–3.

33-3 AIR CONDITIONING REQUIREMENTS

Automobile air conditioning requirements are based upon a number of factors. Heat comes into the automobile from the temperature of outside air, from the sun radiation heat, from engine heat that filters in and from occupants' body heat. The amount of heat absorbed is modified by the automobile insulation, position and intensity of the sun, variations of light and shadow, vehicle color, tinted glass, vehicle speed, and wind direction and velocity. An automobile air conditioner must be capable of removing all the heat input in addition to reducing the temperature of a vehicle that has been standing in the sun.

Heat load on the air conditioner (in customary units) may be as high as 15,000 BTU per hour. This is equivalent to 1.5 tons of air conditioning. About half of this heat is conducted through the body metal and glass. The remainder comes from air leaks, warm parts within the automobile, and occupants' body heat. The air conditioner can transfer only about one-third of this heat at engine idle, so full cooling cannot occur until engine speed increases.

Temperature is only one comfort factor. Humidity, in many cases, is an even more important factor. Removing excess humidity, therefore, is one of the most important air conditioning requirements. This is especially true in the humid climates, which include areas in the North that have satisfactory temperatures, but high humidity. The factory-installed, reheat-type air conditioner can be adjusted by the operator to remove humidity without lowering temperature to provide occupant comfort in these climates.

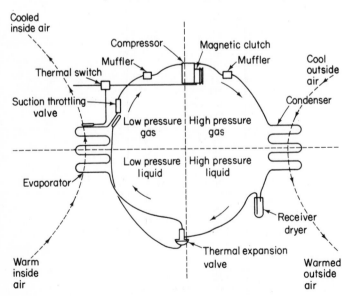

Fig. 33-3 Schematic composite diagram of an automotive air conditioning refrigeration system.

Condensed moisture that accumulates on the evaporator core will fall to a drip pan to be drained from the system. When the air conditioner is not used for some time, a fungus may form on these wet surfaces and produce a stale odor when the air conditioner is restarted.

33-4 REFRIGERATION CONTROLS

Refrigeration controls use the principle that the refrigerant boiling temperature depends upon its pressure. An *expansion valve* is used to control the refrigerant flow into the evaporator.

Expansion Valve. Maximum cooling occurs when all of the liquid refrigerant is turned to a vapor as it rises through the evaporator. If insufficient refrigerant is allowed to flow into the evaporator, the system will be starved. No cooling occurs after the liquid has vaporized. When too much liquid refrigerant is allowed to enter the evaporator, there is not enough room for vapor to form, so the system is flooded and inefficient. The expansion valve controls this refrigerant quantity. It is controlled by temperature and pressure at the evaporator outlet. At idle, the temperature will be about 55°F (13°C), while at highway speed, the temperature will go down to about 35°F (2 °C) and sometimes slightly lower.

The expansion valve changes the medium-temperature, high-pressure liquid refrigerant from the condenser to a low-temperature, low-pressure liquid to feed the evaporator. The temperature control portion of the expansion valve opens the valve when the evaporator outlet temperature rises 10 to 15°F (5.5 to 8.3°C) above the refrigerant boiling point and closes the valve when the temperature lowers to 10 to 15°F (5.5 to 8.3°C) below the refrigerant boiling point.

The amount of heat picked up by the evaporator will control the evaporator temperature. When the heat load is greatest, a large quantity of refrigerant is converted to vapor. When the vehicle cools and the heat load is less, it will vaporize less refrigerant, so the expansion valve reduces refrigerant flow, keeping the evaporator outlet temperature nearly constant.

Freeze-Up Control. The expansion control does not satisfactorily control minimum temperature throughout the wide speed range of engine driven compressors found on automobiles. Additional control is required to keep the temperature as low as possible, but still above the freezing point of water. If evaporator temperature goes below freezing, the condensed moisture would freeze, plugging the air flow passage. This blockage would prevent air flow, so the air would not be cooled.

Self-contained air conditioners and some factory installed units use a thermostatic switch that senses evaporator temperature. When the temperature approaches freezing, the thermostatic switch disengages the compressor clutch to stop the refrigerant cycle. When evaporator temperatures increase, the compressor is again engaged to start the cycle. It is normal to have rapid compressor clutch cycling when the system is under a high heat load. In some of these units, the thermostatic switch is manually adjustable, so it can be used to control air conditioning temperature above minimum temperature. This system is the least expensive type of automotive air conditioning and is usually used in add-on units. It does produce temperature variations as it cycles and is reported to be hard on compressor drive belts in some installations.

Temp °F	PSI
0	9.2
5	11.7
10	14.6
15	17.7
20	21.0
25	24.6
30	28.5
35	32.6
40	37.0
45	41.7
50	46.7
55	52.5
60	57.7
65	63.8
70	70.2
75	77.0
80	84.2
85	91.8
90	99.8
95	108.3
100	117.2
105	126.6
110	136.4
115	146.8
120	157.7
125	169.1
130	181.0

Fig. 33-4 Table of Freon 12 pressure at a range of temperatures.

A second method of preventing freeze-up is to keep evaporator pressure above 28.5 psi. At this pressure, as shown in Figure 33-4, refrigerant-12 boils at 30°F (−1°C), which is slightly below the freezing point of water. The rate at which heat is removed from the air keeps the evaporator from freezing with the refrigerant at this temperature. Minimum evaporator pressure is maintained with a valve located between the evaporator and compressor. It will be located either on the evaporator outlet or within the compressor inlet. It goes under names such as *Suction Throttling Valve* (STV), *Pressure Operated Absolute* (POA), and *Evaporative Pressure Regulator* (EPR). It is open wide under high heat loads and automatically reduces the opening as the heat load reduces.

The suction throttling valve may be adjusted on some systems to control evaporator temperature and, thus, control the amount of air conditioned cooling. When used in this way, the suction throttling valve has a thermal element to sense temperature. The temperature is converted into an electrical or vacuum signal to adjust the valve. In some cases, the valve is moved mechanically to give the operator direct control of the desired cooling temperature.

Valves used with the factory-installed, reheat air distribution system are completely automatic. They are factory set for maximum cooling. If the evaporator gives too much cooling, part of the air is passed through the heater core to provide an air mixture of the desired temperature.

A receiver dryer is located in the system between the condenser and expansion valve. It serves as a refrigerant reservoir with an element for absorbing small amounts of moisture that may have become trapped in the closed refrigeration system. A sight glass is usually located on or adjacent to the receiver dryer outlet. Its purpose is to allow the service technician to observe refrigerant flow. Flow should be in a liquid form. Bubbles or foam in the sight glass usually indicate a loss of refrigerant. The evaporation valve and suction throttling valve are built into the receiver dryer in some air conditioning systems.

33-5 COMPRESSOR

Four types of compressors are used in automotive air conditioners. One is a two-cylinder in-line unit. A second is a 90° vee design. The third is a four-cylinder radial design. These three operate with typical piston, connecting rod, and crankshaft combinations. The fourth type is an axial compressor. It has three double-ended pistons lying parallel to the drive shaft. A wobble plate on the drive shaft produces piston endwise movement to pump refrigerant.

(a)

(b)

(c)

Fig. 33-5 Air conditioning compressors. (a) Two-cylinder inline, (b) two-cylinder V, (c) three-cylinder axial.

The entire compressor, including the crankcase, is sealed into the closed refrigeration system. Some of the compressor lubricant oil will flow with the refrigerant, but it is not lost because it returns with the refrigerant as it completes the cycle through the air conditioning system. In some cases, oil return lines and passages are provided from pockets where the oil can separate from the refrigerant.

Compressors are belt-driven through an electromagnetic clutch. Magnetism formed by an electric current engages the clutch. When not operating, the drive pulley rotates freely on bearings. When the clutch magnet is energized, it pulls the clutch into engagement to drive the compressor. Clutch drive wear is a direct function of the number of clutch applications. This is especially critical on

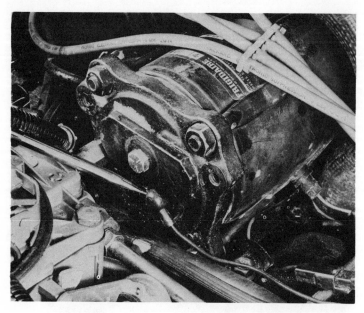

Fig. 33-6 Superheat switch on an axial compressor.

the systems that engage and disengage the clutch to control evaporator temperature. Many systems are fitted with inlet and outlet mufflers to reduce the pulsing noise produced by the pumping action of the compressor.

Some compressors are fitted with a superheat switch to detect high inlet temperatures. Vapors coming to the compressor have a temperature above normal when the refrigerant flow rate to the compressor is low. Low refrigerant flow is the result of loss of refrigerant or malfunctioning valves.

The superheat switch is located on the suction side of the compressor as shown in Figure 33-6. The switch controls a thermal fuse in the compressor clutch circuit. The superheat switch contacts close when the inlet temperature is too high. This puts an electrical current through a resistance type heater. The heater melts the fuse link that is in series with the clutch to open the compressor clutch circuit. This stops the air conditioner compressor before it is damaged.

33-6 SERVICE

When there is a complaint about insufficient cooling the technician should first check the temperature of the air coming from the cooling duct when the air conditioner is set on full cold and the engine is operating at fast idle. The duct air temperature

should be between 35° and 40°F (2° and 4°C) with high air flow. Low air flow at this setting can be caused by an improperly operating blower and by restricted or leaking air ducts. The technician should be able to correct air flow problems using techniques discussed in Chapter 32. The air flow will also be low if the evaporator pressure is low so the temperature drops below freezing. When this happens ice is formed on the evaporator any time moisture is present. Low-temperature problems and most high-temperature problems are corrected by servicing the refrigeration system.

There are a number of preliminary checks that must be made when checking the refrigeration system. The drive belt must have proper tension and be in good condition. The air conditioning clutch must be functioning properly. The thermal fuse should not be overlooked. All air conditioning components should be mounted securely. The condenser that is mounted ahead of the radiator should be externally clean. The air conditioner hoses and lines must be in good condition and properly supported. There should be no trace of oil leaks on the hoses or connections.

One of the most common causes of inadequate cooling is the loss of refrigerant. The refrigeration system is a sealed system and it is always under pressure. In normal operation the refrigerant will gradually seep through the hoses and fittings so that the refrigerant will have to be replenished in three or four years of normal service. More rapid loss results from leakage. The leak should be located and repaired and then the system will have to be recharged with refrigerant.

There is a sight glass in the line between the condenser and expansion valve. This is usually a part of the receiver dryer as pictured in Figure 33-7. The sight glass will appear clear when the air conditioner is operating and a solid flow of liquid refrigerant is passing. When the quantity of refrigerant is low some of the refrigerant will vaporize and form bubbles in the flow. These bubbles of vaporized refrigerant can be seen as they flow past the sight glass. Bubbles usually indicate that the refrigerant level is low. Bubbles can also occur if the suction throttling valve is not functioning or if there is a restriction between the sight glass and condenser.

Before the system is recharged it should be checked for leaks. Two types of leak detectors are in common use. One is an electronic detector that produces an audible signal or meter movement in the presence of refrigerant. The other is a special

Fig. 33-7 Bubbles in a sight gauge indicating low fluid.

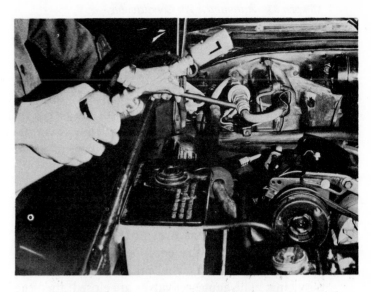

Fig. 33-8 Refrigeration system leak detector.

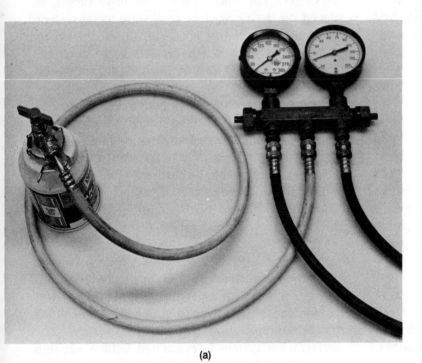

(a)

Fig. 33-9 Refrigeration charging equipment. (a) Gauge set and refrigerant can, (b) charging station.

(b)

purpose propane torch, shown in Figure 33-8. The torch flame will change color in the presence of refrigerant. Refrigerant is heavier than air so it settles. The leak detector pick-up is passed immediately below all refrigerant lines, hoses, and fittings. The low pressure side is checked before the compressor is started so it will have high pressure. The high pressure side is checked as the air conditioner is operated at maximum cooling with the engine running at fast idle. Any leaks will have to be corrected for satisfactory repair of the air conditioner.

The refrigeration system is discharged and recharged through a gauge set. The simple gauge set consists of a common center hose on a passage connecting between a low pressure valve, gauge, and hose; and a high pressure valve, gauge, and hose. Technicians doing a lot of air conditioning work will use a portable air conditioning service station that includes a vacuum pump, charging cylinder, and gauge set. The charging equipment is pictured in Figure 33-9.

Refrigerant evaporates very rapidly. As it

evaporates it absorbs heat. If the expanding refrigerant gets on one's body it will freeze the skin immediately. Whenever working on the refrigeration system, wear safety glasses that fully cover the eyes. Normal precautions must be taken to avoid touching the refrigerant or its vapors.

There is a suction valve fitting on the evaporator side of the compressor and a pressure valve fitting on the condenser side. Some air conditioning systems have service valves at these fittings. The other valve fittings are equipped with a Schrader valve and dust cap. The caps are removed for servicing. The gauge set valves are closed; then the hoses of the gauge set are connected to the system valve fittings. The high pressure hose is connected to the condenser side and the low pressure hose is connected to the evaporator side. The service valves on the compressor can then be opened, if the system is equipped with them. Air must be removed from the gauge set and hoses. The process of removing the air is called *purging*. First open the low pressure valve slightly until refrigerant begins to come out of the center hose; then close the valve. Next just crack the high pressure valve until refrigerant comes out then close it. This will purge the gauge set. If either valve is opened too much some of the refrigeration oil used for compressor lubrication will come out with the refrigerant. The gauge valve must be closed down if this occurs.

Performance Testing. With the test gauges in place, the refrigeration system performance can be checked. Different automobile makes and models have different procedures and specifications. In general, to check performance the air conditioner is set on full cold with the automobile windows open to provide a high heat load and the engine running at fast idle to operate the compressor. The engine is run for fifteen minutes to stabilize the system. The outlet duct air temperature and the compressor inlet and outlet pressures are read. In some cases the wet bulb temperature is also required when measuring the air conditioner performance. These readings are compared to the specifications that apply to the specific automobile being tested.

Excessively high pressure is the result of an overheated condenser, restricted refrigerant flow, flooded evaporator, or too much refrigerant in the system. When the refrigerant charge quantity is too low the high pressure gauge will indicate low pressure. If both gauges show nearly the same pressure the compressor is not pumping properly. A faulty suction throttling valve or starved evaporator will give very low inlet pressures. The inlet pressure must stay above 22 pounds to keep the evaporator temperature above the freezing point of moisture. This can be seen in Figure 33–4.

Discharging. When leaks or faulty components are found in the refrigeration system, the system must be discharged before the repair work is accomplished. With the gauge set in place, the high pressure valve is opened slightly to allow the refrigerant to escape through the center hose of the gauge set. The open end of the hose should be placed on the floor close to a shop exhaust vent. The refrigerant charge is allowed to escape *slowly* so no oil is lost. When the charge is gone the refrigeration system can be opened and the necessary repairs made. The repairs generally consist of replacing the faulty components. Whenever the system is opened the opening should be immediately plugged to minimize the chance of getting moisture or dirt in the system. The refrigerant oil level in the compressor should be checked while the system is discharged. Refrigerant oil should be added as required. It is even better to drain the used oil and replace it with fresh oil.

Evacuating. The evacuation process removes all of the air and moisture from the system. This prevents moisture from freezing inside the system. Ice will cause the valves to stick and it will block the refrigerant flow through the system. The refrigeration system is evacuated with a vacuum pump. At low pressures that exist in a vacuum any moisture that is in the refrigeration system will evaporate. It will be pumped from the system through the vacuum pump. The center of the gauge set is attached to the vacuum pump, keeping both valves closed. With the vacuum pump operating, service valves and both gauge valves are opened slowly so no refrigerant oil will be forced from the system. Vacuum is built up on both sides of the refrigeration system. If the system is leak-free it will pump to 26 to 28 in. (660 to 711 mm) of vacuum, depending on the atmospheric pressure and altitude at which the work is done. The vacuum pump should run thirty minutes at maximum vacuum to remove the maximum amount of moisture. With the vacuum pump still operating, both gauge valves and the service valves, when used, are closed. The vacuum pump can then be turned off. Vacuum should hold for ten minutes if there is no leak in the system. If a leak exists, about one pound of refrigerant should be put in the system and the leak detector used to locate the leak.

Charging. If the system has just been evacuated the center hose of the gauge set is removed from the vacuum pump and connected to the refrigerant supply tank. The supply is turned on and the center hose loosened at the gauge set to purge air from the hose. If the system has not been evacuated but needs additional refrigerant the low and high pressure hoses are attached to the pressure and suction fittings. The center hose of the gauge set is connected to the refrigerant supply. Each valve is opened for a few seconds as the hose is loosened on the supply tank to purge the air from the hoses.

The high pressure valve is fully opened to allow the refrigerant to flow into the evacuated refrigerant system. The amount of refrigerant that is required is measured by volume on some portable service stations. In others the amount of refrigerant is weighed. Service garages that only occasionally charge air conditioning systems can obtain refrigerant in one-pound cans. If the refrigerant is taken from the bottom of the supply tank, a fast-filling liquid charge can be accomplished. This can be done by inverting the supply tank.

If liquid filling does not fully charge the

system, the supply tank should be heated to 125 °F (55 °C), using a water bath for small supply cans or an electric heater built into the portable service station. If the system still does not take a full charge the high pressure valve is closed and the tank turned so the supply is taken from the top as a vapor. The engine and compressor are started and run at idle. The low pressure valve should be opened so the vaporized refrigerant is pulled in by the compressor. When the correct amount of refrigerant is in the system the gauge and service valves are closed.

The system should be rechecked for leaks before the gauge set is removed. If there are no leaks and the air conditioning system performs normally the gauge set can be removed. A cloth should be placed around the high pressure gauge fitting before loosening it to prevent injury if some of the high-pressure refrigerant escapes.

Additional Service. Replacing air conditioning components, stopping leaks, checking refrigerant oil level, charging the refrigeration system, and servicing the air controls can be done in the service garage. Special tools, instructions, parts, and technical skill are required to overhaul the repairable refrigeration system components. This work is usually done in a shop specializing in air conditioning repair. The details of these service procedures are beyond the scope of this chapter.

REVIEW QUESTIONS

1. Into what two systems is the automobile air conditioning divided? [INTRODUCTION]

2. What are the three basic air conditioner system types? [33–1]

3. In simple terms, describe the refrigeration cycle in terms of high and low pressures; liquid and gasses; and high and low temperatures. [33–2]

4. What factors control the amount of heat to be removed from the passenger compartment? [33–3]

5. How does the air conditioning system help remove humidity? [33–3]

6. Upon what principle does the boiling temperature of R-12 depend? [33–4]

7. When is a refrigerant evaporator starved? [33–4]

8. What controls the quantity of refrigerant flowing into the evaporator? [33–4]

9. What controls the high pressure liquid, allowing it to become a low pressure liquid? [33–4]

10. How is the minimum evaporator temperature controlled? [33–4]

11. What is controlled by suction throttling an automobile air conditioner? [33–4]

12. How does a superheat switch protect the compressor? [33–5]

13. What can cause low flow from an air conditioner air duct? [33–6]

14. What is one of the most common causes of inadequate cooling? [33–6]

15. What do bubbles in a sight gauge indicate? [33–6]

16. How are refrigerant leaks located? [33–6]

17. Describe the gauge set. [33–6]

18. What safety precautions should be taken when working on refrigeration systems? [33–6]

19. Why is it necessary to purge the gauge set and hoses? [33–6]

20. What causes excessively high pressures? [33–6]

21. What causes excessively low pressures? [33–6]

22. What is indicated when both gauges indicate the same pressure? [33–6]

23. Describe the procedure used to discharge the refrigerant system. [33–6]

24. Describe the procedure used to evacuate the refrigeration system. [33–6]

25. Describe the procedure used to charge the refrigeration system. [33–6]

appendix

METRIC UNIT PREFIXES

Multiplication Factor	Prefix	Symbol
$1000 = 10^3$	kilo	k
$100 = 10^2$	hecto	h
$10 = 10$	deka	da
$0.1 = 10^{-1}$	deci	d
$0.01 = 10^{-2}$	centi	c
$0.001 = 10^{-3}$	milli	m
$0.0001 = 10^{-4}$	micro	μ

METRIC CONVERSION FACTORS

Quantity	Multiply	By	To Get Equivalent Number of
length	inch (in.)	25.4	millimeters (mm)
	mile (mi)	1.609	kilometers (km)
area	square inch (in.²)	645.2	square millimeters (mm²)
volume	cubic inch (in.³)	16.387	cubic centimeters (cm³)
	quart (qt)	0.946	liters (1)
	gallon (gal)	3.785	liters (l)
mass	pound (lb)	0.455	kilogram (kg)
force	ounce (oz)	0.278	newtons (N)
	pound (lb)	4.448	newtons (N)
temperature	degrees Fahrenheit (F) $[(T° - 32) \times 0.556)]$		degrees Celsius (C)
acceleration	feet per second² (ft/sec²)	0.3048	newton per second² (N/s²)
velocity	miles per hour (mph)	1.609	kilometers per hour (km/h)
torque	pound-inch (lb-in.)	0.113	newton-meters (Nm)
	pound-foot (lb-ft)	1.356	newton-meters (Nm)
power	horsepower (hp)	0.746	kilowatts (kW)
pressure or stress	inches of water (in.)	0.249	kilopascals (kPa)
	pounds per square inch (psi or lb/in.²)	6.895	kilopascals (kPa)
energy or work	British thermal unit (BTU)	1055	joules (J)
	foot-pound (ft-lb)	1.356	joules (J)
fuel performance	miles per gallon (mpg)	0.425	kilometers per liter (km/1)

SAMPLE USES OF METRIC CONVERSION FACTORS

Length:	Engine bore 4 in. $\times$ 25.4 = 101.6 mm or 10.16 cm Miles driven 75 mi $\times$ 1.609 = 120.68 km
Area:	Area of a wheel cylinder 1.75 in.^{2} $\times$ 645.2 = 1129 mm^2 or 11.29 cm^2
Volume:	Engine displacement 250 CID $\times$ 16.387 = 4096.75 cm^3 Engine oil capacity 5 qt $\times$ 0.946 = 4.73 l Gasoline tank capacity 21 gal $\times$ 3.785 = 79.485 l
Mass:	Automobile weight 3100 lb $\times$ 0.455 = 1410.5 kg
Force:	Breaker point spring tension 21 oz $\times$ 0.278 = 5.838 N Valve spring force 60 lb $\times$ 4.448 = 266.88 N
Temperature:	Engine thermostat setting 180°F $-$ 32 = 148 $\times$ 0.556 = 82.29 °C
Acceleration:	Vehicle acceleration of 10 ft/sec^2 $\times$ 0.3048 = 5.79 N/s^2
Velocity:	Legal speed 55 mph $\times$ 1.609 = 88.5 km/h
Torque:	Pan bolt torque 25 lb-in. $\times$ 0.113 = 2825 N-m Engine head bolt torque 60 lb-ft $\times$ 1.356 = N-m
Power:	Rated horsepower 150 hp $\times$ 0.746 = 11.9 kW
Pressure:	Carburetor pressure signal 15 in. water $\times$ 0.249 = 3.735 kPa Engine oil pressure 40 psi $\times$ 6.895 = 275.8 kPa
Energy or Work:	Energy equivalent of one horsepower 42.4 BTU $\times$ 1055 = 57.5 J Work used to install a 50 lb tire on an axle one foot above its normal position 50 ft-lb $\times$ 1.356 = 67.8 J
Fuel Performance:	Fuel consumption of 20 mpg $\times$ 0.425 = 8.5 km/l

glossary

A

ACCELERATION: A change in speed in a given period of time such as one second or one minute.

ACKERMAN: Steering geometry that turns the inner and outer wheels at different angles to minimize scuff during a turn.

ADDITIVE: A product added to a material that will improve a certain characteristic of the material.

ADHESION: The characteristic that causes one material to stick to or cling to another material.

AEROSOL: Very small particles that float in the air.

AFTERBURNER: A device attached in place of the exhaust manifold that holds the exhaust gases at high temperature to aid in oxidizing unburned hydrocarbons.

AFTERBURNING: Luminous products remaining in the gases after combustion.

AFTERMARKET: The sales market designed for the consumer after he purchases a product from the dealer.

AIR/FUEL RATIO: A mixture of air and fuel by weight. Pounds of air per pound of fuel.

ALTERNATOR: The name given to a diode-rectified automotive generator.

AMBIENT: The temperature of the surrounding air.

AMMETER: An instrument connected in series in an electrical circuit to measure current flow.

AMPERE: A measure of the rate of electrical current flow.

AMPLITUDE: The extent or size limits of vibrating motion.

ANCHOR: The stationary terminal at one end of a brake shoe or band.

ANNULUS: An outer ring.

ANODIZE: An electrochemical process that hardens the surface of aluminum.

ANTI-PERCOLATOR: A device used in carburetors to vent fuel vapors from the manifold when the engine is not running.

API: American Petroleum Institute.

ARMATURE: A rotating conductor within a magnetic field.

AROMATIC: A hydrocarbon with a benzene ring form that has a natural high octane number.

ASPECT RATIO: The ratio of width to length, also the ratio of tire cross section width to cross section height.

ASYMMETRIC: Unequal surfaces or sizes.

ATOMIZATION: Breaking into very fine particles, such as fuel delivery by a discharge nozzle.

AVAILABLE VOLTAGE: Maximum voltage an ignition system is capable of producing.

AXIAL: Having the same direction or being parallel to the axis of rotation.

B

BACK FIRE: Ignition of the air/fuel mixture in the intake manifold producing a flame from the carburetor bore.

BACK FLUSH: A procedure used to clean a system by forcing reverse flow from an external source.

BALANCE: Having equal weight on each side of a supporting point. No change in the position of the center of gravity when a part is in motion.

BALL AND TRUNION JOINT: A universal joint with pivoting spherical rollers that transfer motion between a pin and a housing that has partial cylindrical bores.

BALL JOINT: A suspension attachment connecting the knuckle to the control arms allowing movement upward and downward as well as rotation.

BALL NUT: A casting with internal threads used in a steering gear. Ball bearings roll in the threads to move the casting along the worm to rotate a sector which in turn moves a Pitman arm.

BAND: A strip of metal with friction lining that is used as a brake to stop and hold drum rotation in an automatic transmission.

BANK: The portion of a V-block containing four inline cylinders.

BARREL: The opening in the carburetor through which air/fuel mixture enters the manifold.

BASE CIRCLE: The part of the cam with the smallest diameter from the camshaft center.

BDC: Bottom dead center. The lowest position of the piston.

BEAD: A reinforcing ridge. The wire reinforcing around a tire opening where it fits the wheel rim.

BEARING: The surface that supports a load. In vehicles it supports a moving load with minimum drag.

BEARING TANG: A notch or lip on a bearing shell used to correctly locate the bearing during assembly.

BELL CRANK: A moving arm that pivots near the middle. It is used to change the direction of motion.

BENDIX-WEISS JOINT: One type of constant velocity universal joint using two yokes to drive through inter-meshed balls.

BEST AIR/FUEL RATIO: The air/fuel ratio that will produce the most engine power.

BEST TIMING: Ignition timing that produces the highest engine torque at the running speed.

BEVEL: Angled. Usually gears cut on an angle to change the direction of rotation.

BIAS: Lines running at an angle. Refers to the cord angle in tire plys.

BI-METALLIC SPRING: A coil spring made of a double strip of two different metals. When it is heated it will either wind tighter or unwind, depending on the metals and spring design.

BLADES: Sharp edges, often used to describe windshield wiper edges and the edges of tire grooves.

BLOCKING RING: A ring that blocks tooth engagement until equal speeds are reached.

BLOW-BY: Combustion chamber gases that slip past the piston and rings to get into the crankcase.

BLOW-DOWN: Release of combustion pressure immediately after the exhaust valve opens.

BMEP: Brake mean effective pressure. The average pressure within a cylinder during the power stroke that would produce the horsepower determined on a dynamometer.

BOG: An expression used to describe an engine misfiring condition that may occur as the throttle is opened, and which causes engine power to drop rather than increase.

BORDERLINE: The line between satisfactory operation and failure.

BORDERLINE LUBRICATION: A term that may be used in place of boundary lubrication. Minimum lubrication that occurs when the oil film can't quite support the load and high spots touch.

BORE: (1) A process of enlarging a hole with a cutting tool. (2) The diameter of a hole, especially the cylinder.

BOSS: A heavy cast section that is used for support, such as the heavy section around a bearing.

BOUNDARY: The line between normal and unsatisfactory

operation. For example, boundary lubrication that occurs when the oil film breaks down and the parts start to contact.

BRAKE: A device used to slow, stop, or hold a moving member.

BRAKE DIVE: The tendency of the front of the vehicle to lower during braking as a result of forward weight transfer.

BRAKE FADE: The loss of braking power due to excess heat from previous brake applications.

BREAKER POINTS: Cam-operated contacts in the distributor that connect and separate the primary circuit.

BREATHING: Air flow into an engine during operation.

BRIDGING: A build-up of current carrying crystals through the battery separator.

BROACH: A machining operation that is completed in one pass of a tool having a large number of cutting edges.

BULKHEAD: A strengthening partition separating compartments, such as the firewall or engine main bearing webs.

BURNISHING: A sizing process that pushes metal to size by pressure.

BUSHING: A spacing device, usually a sleeve. In engine applications it often has a bearing surface on its inside surface.

BUTT: Square ends used on a piston ring.

BYPASS: Go around some restriction such as a valve, switch, circuit, etc.

C

CAM ANGLE: The number of degrees of cam rotation while the breaker points are closed between each cam lobe.

CAMBER: The angle of the vertical wheel center line to absolute vertical.

CAM FOLLOWER: A device that follows the cam contour as it rotates, usually a lifter or tappet.

CAMSHAFT: A long shaft on which lobes and bearing journals are located. It is usually used to open the valves.

CANISTER: A container filled with activated charcoal to absorb evaporative emissions.

CANTED: Angled away from another object or from vertical.

CAPACITIVE DISCHARGE: An ignition system that stores a high voltage charge in a condenser. When the distributor is in position the charge is released through the spark plug to ignite the mixture.

CAPACITOR: A device consisting of two metal plates in close proximity to each other with an insulator between. Electrons readily collect at one plate and holes collect at the other.

CARBON PILE: A variable resistance made of carbon discs or plates that can carry high currents.

CARBURETOR: A device that mixes air and fuel in the correct proportions for engine operating conditions.

CARBURETOR THROAT: The portion of a carburetor between the venturi and intake manifold where the throttle plate is located.

CARDAN JOINT: A cross and yoke universal joint. Also called a Hooke joint.

CARRIER: A part that carries other parts. Usually referring to the part of a differential or a planetary gear set that carries the pinions.

CAST: A part made by pouring melted metal into a mold where it cools to the shape of the mold.

CASTER: The tendency of a wheel to line up in the direction of its pivot point movement.

CASTING: The process of making a cast part.

CATALYST: A product that increases the speed of a reaction but does not enter into the reaction.

CATALYTIC CONVERTER: A chamber in the exhaust system that contains a catalyst which aids in oxidizing exhaust gases to reduce the amount of unburned hydrocarbons in the exhaust gases.

CAVITATION: A space created at the center of a rotating pump when it does not fill as fast as the fluid is pumped out.

CEMF: Counter electromotive force. Electrical pressure within a device that opposes external electrical pressure.

CENTER OF GRAVITY: A point around which all weights balance.

CENTER OF PRESSURE: A point around which all pressures balance.

CENTRIFUGAL: A force in a direction away from the turning center of an object moving in a curved path.

CHAMFER: An angle cut across the corner of an otherwise sharp edge.

CHARGE: A process of replacing the material in an expended container. For example, charge a battery to store electrical energy or charge an air conditioner system so it has sufficient refrigerant to operate.

CHASSIS: The vehicle frame, suspension and running gear.

CHECK VALVE: A valve that will allow flow in one direction and will stop flow in the opposite direction.

CHOKE: A variable restriction in the carburetor air inlet to produce a rich mixture for starting.

CHOKE STOVE: A pocket or tube that heats choke air by the exhaust heat so the choke's bi-metallic spring can sense engine temperature.

CIRCUIT BREAKER: An electrical device that protects the circuit from overload by opening the circuit. It can be reset to again close the circuit.

CLUSTER GEAR: A group of gears made on a common casting. Used in a standard transmission to connect the clutch shaft to the first, second, and reverse idler gears.

CLUTCH: A device to connect and disconnect members that are rotating at different speeds.

CLUTCH SHAFT: The shaft coming out of the front of the transmission that goes through the center of the clutch.

COEFFICIENT OF FRICTION: An expression that relates the force to move an object to the weight or load produced by the object. Coefficient of friction = force/load.

COLOR CODE: Color marking on lines and wires to identify the circuit.

COMBUSTIBLE MIXTURE: A mixture of air and gasoline vapors in a ratio that will burn.

COMBUSTION: A rapid chemical reaction between air and fuel that releases heat.

COMMUTATOR: A number of bars connected to armature windings that transfers current to the brushes and rectifies the current.

COMPENSATION SYSTEM: A portion of the carburetor circuit that prevents overenriching the air/fuel ratio as air velocities increase.

COMPRESSION IGNITION: A term applied to the diesel engine operating principle. Heat to initiate combustion is produced by compression.

COMPRESSION RATIO: A ratio between the volume above the piston when it is at bottom center to the volume above the piston when it is at top center.

COMPRESSION TEST: A test using a pressure gauge to measure maximum pressure in the cylinder while cranking the engine with the starter.

CONCENTRIC: Located evenly around a common center.

CONDUCTOR: A material that will carry electrical current.

CONE CLUTCH: A clutch made of an inner and outer cone. When the outer cone is forced over the inner cone a wedging action occurs that locks them together while they remain under the force.

CONTACT PATCH: The part of the tire that contacts the road surface.

CONTROL ARM: A suspension member mounted nearly horizontal with one end attached to the frame and the other end to the knuckle or axle housing.

CORE: The central portion, usually a part used in casting to form an opening in the finished part when the core is removed after casting.

CORROSION: A combination of a metal and oxygen or water that causes the surface of the metal to disappear.

COUNTER BORE: A concentric machined surface around a hole opening.

COUNTER GEAR: A gear that rotates backward. The cluster gear in a standard transmission.

CRANK ANGLE: The number of degrees the crankshaft has turned past top center.

CRANK PIN: The portion of the crankshaft upon which the connecting rod fastens.

CRANKSHAFT: The part of an engine that changes the reciprocating motion of the pistons into rotating motion.

CROCUS CLOTH: An extremely fine abrasive cloth that is used for polishing.

CROSS OVER: An opening through the intake manifold below the carburetor that connects the two exhaust manifolds.

CROSS SHAFT: The Pitman shaft in a steering gear.

CRUSH: A slight distortion of the bearing shell that holds it in place as the engine operates.

CUBIC INCH DISPLACEMENT: The volume displaced by all of the pistons as the crankshaft makes one revolution.

CYCLE: A complete circle back to the beginning. In engines, a series of events; intake, compression, power and exhaust.

D

DAMPEN: To slow or reduce oscillations or movement.

DASHPOT: A variable displacement chamber that has a restriction. It is used to slow or dampen movement.

DEAD CENTER: Refers to the maximum upper or lower piston position when all movement in one direction stops before it reverses direction.

DECARBONIZING: The process of removing carbon from parts during overhaul.

DECK: The flat upper surface of the engine block where the head mounts.

DEFLECTION: Bending or moving to a new position as the result of an external force.

DEGREASING: The process of removing grease from parts.

DEGREE WHEEL: A disc divided in 360 equal parts that can be attached to a shaft to measure angle of rotation.

DENIER: The size of a strand that makes up tire cord.

DETONATION: Engine knock produced by rapid chemical reaction of the gases ahead of the combustion flame front.

DIAPHRAGM: A flexible membrane on one side of an enclosed chamber.

DIECAST: A casting process for light metals using permanent forms and pressure to accurately form a part.

DIESEL: A fuel-injected charge ignited by temperature resulting from high compression.

DIFFERENTIAL: The part of a rear axle that allows the rear wheels to rotate at different speeds.

DIFFERENTIAL PRESSURE: Differences in pressure that cause flow from the highest pressure to the lowest pressure.

DIODE: A solid-state electrical check valve.

DISC: The plate shaped part of the brake or clutch that rotates as the vehicle moves.

DISC BRAKE: A brake type having a disc plate that rotates with the wheel. Pads or shoes press against the disc to slow or stop the vehicle.

DISH: A depression in the top of a piston.

DISPLACEMENT: The volume displaced by the pistons during one crankshaft revolution.

DISTILLATE: A low volatility fuel used in diesel and turbine engines.

DISTILLATION: The process of separating hydrocarbons by their boiling temperatures.

DIVERGENT ANGLES: Lines that are further apart at one end than at the other end.

DOWN SHIFTING: Shifting to a higher numerical ratio that is usually associated with lower speed, high-torque operation.

DRAW FILE: Smoothing a surface with a file moved sidewise.

DRIFT: A gradual random movement.

DRIVE LINE: The power carrying part of a vehicle from the engine to the drive wheels.

DRIVE LUGS: Projections on a plate or disc that interlock in slots on a hub or in a drum.

DRUM: A hoop shape with a web or plate across one side of the opening.

DRUM BRAKE: A ring-shaped drum surface that rotates with the wheel. Brake shoes slow and stop rotation by pressure against the inside of the drum.

DWELL: The number of degrees the cam turns while the breaker points are closed between cam lobes.

DYNAMIC: Moving parts.

DYNAMOMETER: A device that is used to measure loads, engine torque, and driving forces.

E

ECCENTRIC: Two or more circles, one surrounding the other and each having a different center.

ECONOMY: The lowest cost for the same result.

EDDY CURRENT: Localized induced currents in parts that are rotating in a magnetic field. These currents produce heat and absorb power.

EFFECTIVE PRESSURE: The pressure that does work. Usually the mean or average pressure in the combustion chamber during the power stroke.

EFFICIENCY: Obtaining the highest possible output for a given input.

ELASTOMER: A rubber-like plastic or synthetic material.

ELECTRO-CHEMICAL: A reaction between chemicals that produces a current or a current that produces a chemical reaction.

ELECTROLYTE: The acid solution in battery cell.

ELECTRON: The smallest, negative charged particle. It is part of an atom. Its movement to adjacent atoms forms electricity.

ELEMENT: The smallest distinct variety of matter. Also the combined plates and separators of a battery cell.

END GASES: The combustion gases ahead of the flame front after ignition.

ENERGIZED: Charged or full of energy. Ready to be operated.

ENGINE: A prime power source.

ENGINE LOAD: The vehicle resistance applied to the engine crankshaft.

ENGINE SPEED: Crankshaft revolutions per minute.

ERODE: Wear away by high velocity abrasive particles.

EXPAND: Increase in volume.

EXPANSION PLUGS: Hole plugs that can be expanded to securely close a hole.

F

FADE: Loss of braking effect when brakes get hot.

FATIGUE: A breakdown of material through a large number of loading and unloading cycles. The first signs are cracks followed shortly by breaks.

FIELD: The area of magnetic force surrounding a magnet, either permanent or electromagnet.

FIELD STRENGTH: A measurement of the effective size of a magnetic field.

FILAMENT: A wire in a light bulb that glows when current passes through it to produce light.

FILLER: Material added to produce bulk. It may add special properties to the product.

FILLET: A rounded joint between two surfaces.

FIN: A thin metal surface usually used to transfer heat between metal and air.

FIRE WALL: The metal surface separating the passenger compartment from the engine compartment.

FLANGE: A small surface at an angle to the major surface used to position, reinforce, or fasten the major surface in place.

FLANK CIRCLE: The part of a cam that has constant diameter. No lift is produced from the flank circle.

FLOAT: (1) Device supported by fluid, as a carburetor float, to sense fluid levels. (2) Float can occur when the valve train is tossed from the cam and the parts float on air until control is regained.

FLOAT BOWL: The carburetor compartment that houses the float.

FLOOR PAN: The metal surface that forms the base of the passenger compartment.

FLUTE: Angular grooves in the face of a headlight bulb used to deflect light.

FLUTTER VALVE: A spring-loaded valve that moves to allow flow in only one direction.

FLUX: The force of magnetism. Also a substance applied during soldering or welding to free oxides.

FLYWHEEL: A weighted disc on a crankshaft that provides inertia to carry the crankshaft between power pulses.

FOOT PAD: A surface on a pedal upon which to push with one's foot to produce pedal movement.

FOOT PRINT: The area on the road in contact with the tire.

FORGED: A part made by forging.

FORGING: A process of hammering or compressing a red hot metal part to form it into the desired shape.

FOUR-STROKE CYCLE: An engine cycle consisting of a downward intake stroke, and an upward compression stroke, a downward power stroke, and an upward exhaust stroke. The cycle then repeats on the next four strokes.

FRAME: The base structure upon which the rest of the structure is mounted or attached.

FREE PLAY: Looseness in a linkage between the start of application and the actual movement of the device.

FREQUENCY: The number of cycles or vibrations per second.

FRICTION: The resistance to slipping or skidding.

FUEL DROP OUT: Liquid gasoline separating from an air/fuel mixture.

FUEL MIXTURE: A mixture of air and gasoline. The gasoline must be in a vapor state to burn.

FULCRUM: The hinge point of a lever.

FUSE: A soft wire in a holding device that melts when a circuit is overloaded.

FUSIBLE LINK: A small diameter wire section of a circuit that will melt before any of the rest of the circuit is damaged by overheating.

G

GALLERY: A large passage in the engine block that forms a reservoir for engine oil under pressure.

GASSING: Formation of bubbles in the battery electrolyte during charging.

GENERATOR: An electromechanical device to supply electrical power by changing mechanical energy to electrical energy.

GRADABILITY: The ability of a vehicle to climb slopes.

GROUND: To connect an electric circuit to the vehicle frame or structure.

GROUP: A number of battery plates welded to a connector.

H

HEAVY DUTY: Applications more severe than passenger car service.

HEEL: The anchor end of a brake shoe.

HELICAL GEARS: Gears cut on an angle so that at least two pairs of gear teeth are in contact at all times.

HELIX ANGLE: The angle produced by a spiral form around a round part.

HOOK JOINT: A universal joint formed by a cross and two trunions.

HORSEPOWER: A value calculated from engine torque and rotating speed. One horsepower equals 33,000 ft-lbs per min.

HOT SOAK: A part warming to the surrounding temperature.

HYDRAULICS: A study of fluids.

HYDROCARBONS: Molecules made from hydrogen and carbon atoms.

HYDRODYNAMIC: A study of fluid in motion.

HYDRODYNAMIC LUBRICATION: A lubricating film generated in a fluid by relative motion between two surfaces.

HYDROMETER: A floating device that measures specific gravity of a fluid by the depth the float sinks into the fluid.

I

IDLE: Running freely with no power or load being transferred.

IDLING GEARS: Rotating gears that are not transferring a load.

IMPENDING SKID: The tire traction point at which any increase in load will produce a tire skid.

IMPINGE: Hit against the surface.

IMEP: Indicated mean effective pressure. The average indicated pressure in the combustion chamber during the power stroke as measured on a pressure-volume indicator card graph.

IMPELLER: A rotating part that increases the moving speed or velocity of a fluid.

INDUCTANCE: The process of an electromagnetic force being produced in a conductor located in a moving magnetic field.

INERTIA: The tendency of a body at rest to stay at rest or when moving, to keep moving.

INERTIA TORQUE: Twisting force produced by the inertia of a rotating body.

INLINE ENGINE: Cylinders located one next to the other with parallel bore centerlines.

INSULATOR: A material that will not conduct. It may not conduct heat or electricity.

INTEGRAL: Part of or contained within a larger major part.

INVOLUTE: A curve traced by a point on a thread as it is wound on a drum.

ION: An atom having excess electrons (negative ion) or lacking electrons (positive ion).

J

JET: A carefully sized opening in a carburetor passage to measure the flow of either gasoline or air.

JOUNCE: The condition of the suspension which will cause spring compression.

JOURNAL: The surface on which a bearing operates.

JUNCTION: An electrical connection.

K

KEEPER: The split lock that holds the valve spring retainer in position on the valve stem.

KEYED: Prevented from rotating with a small metal device called a key.

KICK DOWN: A forced downshift on an automatic transmission.

KNOCK: The sound produced in the combustion chamber as a result of abnormal combustion, usually detonation.

KNUCKLE: The part of the front suspension that connects to the control arms and supports the wheel spindle.

KNURL: A roughened surface caused by a sharp wheel that displaces metal outward as its sharp edges push into the metal surface.

L

LAMINAR FLOW: Flowing in smooth layers, not turbulent.

LAMP: A light bulb.

LANDS: The large diameter portions between piston ring grooves.

LASH: Looseness in linkages that must be absorbed before movement can begin.

LEACH: To dissolve one material out of another.

LEADING SHOE: A brake shoe that has the drum rotate from the toe toward the heel.

LIFTER: The part that rides against the cam to transfer motion to the rest of the valve train.

LIFTER VALLEY; The chamber between the cylinder banks on a V-block engine.

LOAD: The part of the system that absorbs energy.

LOAD—ELECTRICAL: An electrical device that draws current.

LOCK: A device to easily connect or disconnect two parts.

LUG: To operate an engine with high loads at low speeds.

LUGS: Heavy fastening flanges on parts.

M

MAGNETIC LINES OF FORCE: Lines that form when iron filings are sprinkled on a surface over a magnet.

MAGNITUDE: Size.

MANIFOLD: Cast passages that connect openings from each cylinder to a common opening.

MANIFOLD RUNNER: A single passage in a manifold from one cylinder to the major manifold opening.

MASS: The amount of material in a part. Often equated to weight for easy understanding.

MASTER CYLINDER: The cylinder in a brake system that converts mechanical force to hydraulic force.

MEAN EFFECTIVE PRESSURE: The calculated average pressure in the combustion chamber during the power stroke.

MEAN RADIUS: A radius that has equal surfaces on each side.

MECHANICAL EFFICIENCY: Calculated as brake horsepower divided by indicated horsepower.

MENISCUS: The curved upper surface of a liquid in a chamber.

MIDSHIP: An engine location immediately ahead of the rear axle.

MODULE: A small compact complete unit. The whole unit can be replaced as a unit, but not in parts.

N

NAILS: A common name given to brake shoe hold-down pins.

NEUTRON: A neutral charged particle that makes up part of most atom nuclei.

NODE: A point in a vibrating body that is relatively free of movement.

NOMINAL: Normal position, size, or operating condition.

NOSE CIRCLE: The high curved portion of a cam that produces maximum lift.

NUCLEUS: The central part of an atom that contains most of the atom's weight.

O

OCTANE NUMBER; A number that indicates a gasoline's resistance to detonation knock.

OCTANE REQUIREMENT: The lowest octane number fuel on which an engine can operate knock free.

OFFSET: A part having parallel centerlines on different planes.

OHM: A unit of electrical resistance.

OHM'S LAW: A constant relationship between resistance (R), voltage (E), and current (I). $R = E/I$.

OIL SEAL: A device to keep oil from leaking out of a compartment. It usually refers to a dynamic seal around a rotating shaft.

OLEFIN: An unsaturated hydrocarbon molecule with a double carbon bond.

ONE-WAY CLUTCH: A clutch that will allow free rotation in one direction but locks when reversed.

OPEN: In an electrical circuit the circuit is broken so a gap exists and no current can flow.

ORIFICE: A carefully sized opening that controls a fluid flow.

OSCILLATION: A vibration back and forth or up and down.

OSCILLOSCOPE: A device that displays a trace on the face of a picture tube proportional to input voltages.

OVERHUNG: A load outside of a bearing.

OVER RUNNING CLUTCH: A clutch that will run freely in one direction but locks when turned in the opposite direction.

OXIDIZE: A combination with oxygen causing a change in the molecule. Generally, it reduces the value of the oxidized material.

P

PAD: Flat surfaces on castings upon which parts are mounted.

PANIC STOP: A stop with maximum brake pedal pressure, usually locking the wheels and causing the tires to skid.

PARALLEL: Straight lines that are the same distance apart from end to end.

PARAMETER: The maximum limit in a direction.

PEAK PRESSURE: The highest pressure in the combustion chamber that occurs during the early part of the power stroke.

PEENED: Upset surfaces by pounding.

PERFORMANCE: Effectively operating at the maximum designed specification.

PHOTOCHEMICAL: A process requiring light and a chemical.

PIEZOELECTRIC CRYSTAL: A crystal that produces a voltage proportional to the pressure applied to the crystal.

PILOT BEARING: The bearing in the back of the crankshaft that supports the front of the clutch shaft.

PINION GEAR: A gear that rotates with a carrier to transfer loads between the carrier and two intermeshing gears.

PISTON HEAD: The top or crown of a piston.

PISTON PIN: The connecting pin that attaches the piston to the connecting rod.

PISTON SLAP: A sound made by a piston with excess skirt clearance as the crankshaft goes across top center.

PITMAN ARM: The arm that connects the steering gear to the steering linkages.

PIVOT: A point around which an item turns.

PLANETARY: A type of gear train having pinion gears rotating around a central gear.

PLASTIC: A material capable of being deformed without rupturing. Generally a synthetic material.

PLASTIGAUGE: A small-sized plastic thread for measuring clearances. It is smashed as parts are assembled, then disassembled to check the width of the smashed gauge.

PLATE: A thin flat surface.

PLOTTING: Locating points on a graph.

PLYS: Layers assembled together. Usually the grain direction is alternated between adjacent layers.

POLE SHOES: Extended core material of an electromagnet.

PONTOON: A container or block that will float on a liquid to support an object.

POPPET VALVE: A valve that moves perpendicularly to and from its seat.

POP UP: A raised portion of a piston head.

PORT: An opening through which liquids or gases flow.

PORTING: A process of enlarging the intake and exhaust passages of the head.

PREFLAME REACTION: Chemical reactions that occur in the gases before the flame front reaches them.

PREIGNITION: Ignition of the combustion charge before the spark forms across the sparkplug electrodes.

PRELOAD: Mechanically loading bearings to prevent end play.

PREVENTATIVE MAINTENANCE: Service procedures that are done before a malfunction occurs to prevent failure.

PRESSURE DEPRESSION: A term describing less than atmospheric pressure or vacuum.

PRESSURE HEAD: The height of a column of fluid that produces pressure by the weight of the fluid.

PRESSURE PLATE: A heavy plate with back up springs or hydraulic pressure to lock it against a clutch disc.

PRIMARY SHOE: A brake shoe actuated by a wheel cylinder.

PROPAGATION: Self sustaining and spreading or expanding.

PROPELLER SHAFT: The shaft that connects the transmission to the rear axle to propel or drive the vehicle.

PROPRIETARY: A product sold to the public with a formula owned by the manufacturer.

PROTON: A positively charged particle of an atom nucleus containing most of the atom's weight.

P-T CURVE: Pressure-time curve that shows the change in pressure in the combustion chamber as combustion progresses.

PUMP GRADES: Gasoline available at service stations.

PUMPING LOSS: Engine power required to move the piston during the intake, compression, and exhaust strokes.

PUSH ROD: The rod between the lifter and rocker arm that pushes the rocker arm to open the valve.

P-V CURVE: Pressure-volume curve that shows the pressure in the combustion chamber at each piston position.

Q

QUENCH: Cool to the temperature at which the flame will go out.

R

RACE: The part of a bearing on which the rollers or balls roll.

RADIAL: Moving straight out from the center.

RADIATOR: A thin metal heat transfer device that lowers the temperature of the engine coolant by air flow.

RAM: Air pressure produced by air velocity.

RAMP: A gradual slope or incline on a cam to take up lash clearance.

RANKIN: An absolute temperature scale that uses the same temperature divisions as Fahrenheit. $°R = 459.6 + °F$.

REACH: The length of the threaded portion of a spark plug.

REACTION: The result of an action.

REACTOR: A device that acts to produce a reaction, such as a stator in a torque converter.

REAM: To size a hole to exact dimensions with a cutting tool called a reamer.

REAR AXLE: The drive between the differential side gear and the wheel.

REBOUND: An expansion of a suspension spring after it has been compressed as the result of jounce.

RECIPROCATE: Move back and forth.

RECTIFY: To straighten out. To convert an A-C current to a D-C current.

RELAY: A remote control switch that carries a large current.

RELIEVING: Grinding restrictions from around valves and seats.

REQUIRED VOLTAGE: Ignition voltage high enough to form an arc across the spark plug electrodes.

RESISTOR: A unit installed in an electrical circuit to provide the required resistance.

RETAINER: A device to hold parts together.

REVERTED GEAR TRAIN: A gear train that drives to the side and then returns to the original centerline.

RHEOSTAT: A device to provide variable resistance. It is sometimes called a pot.

RIDE: The characteristic feel as one rides in a vehicle.

RING GEAR: A hollow gear that has a ring shape.

ROCKER ARM: A lever that converts the upward movement of the push rod to the downward movement required to open a valve.

ROLL: Movement around the center of gravity.

ROLL STEER: The steering effect as a result of body lean during a turn.

ROTOR: A rotating drive mechanism. Also a brake disc.

RUMBLE: A characteristic low frequency vibration that results from surface ignition.

RUN OUT: The amount a shaft rotates out of true.

S

SADDLE: The upper main bearing seat.

SADDLE MOUNTING: A bearing on each side of a gear.

SAE: Society of Automotive Engineers.

SAG: Engine power loss during acceleration as the result of improper air/fuel ratios.

SAYBOLT: An obsolete method used to measure oil viscosity.

SCAVENGE: Clean out or remove either exhaust gas or sump oil.

SCROLL: A curved passage that gets larger and has a larger radius toward the outer edge.

SCRUB RADIUS: The distance on the road surface under the front tire between an extension of the pivot point and the center of weight.

SCUFFING: Sliding a tire on the road surface.

SEALS—DYNAMIC: An item that prevents leakage around a rotating shaft or sliding member.

SEALS—STATIC: An item that prevents leakage between two stationary parts. It is usually called a gasket.

SECONDARY SHOE: A brake shoe that is actuated by a primary shoe.

SECTOR: A section of a gear.

SEMICONDUCTOR: An electronic component that allows current to flow under special conditions.

SEPARATION: A porous insulator sheet between battery plates.

SERIES: A single path through a number of items, one after the other.

SERVICE MARKET: The people who need service work done on their cars.

SERVO: A device that can control a large force by being remotely operated with a small force.

SERVO ACTION: A large action that results from a small input action.

SET: Repositioning of a spring as the result of loading for long periods of time.

SHEDDING: Active material loosening from battery plates.

SHIMMY: A violent front wheel shake caused by over-corrective action.

SHOE: The brake part that supports the lining.

SHORT: An electrical path that goes back to the battery without going through the complete circuit.

SHROUD: A cover between the edges of the radiator and fan tip used to increase the fan's efficiency.

SHUNT: An electrical device connected in parallel to bypass some of the current.

SIAMESED PORTS: An intake or exhaust port that serves two cylinders.

SIDESWAY: A force causing a lean one way then the other.

SIGNALS: Changing pressures in a carburetor or automatic transmission that controls fluid flow.

SINTER: A process of pressing and heating powdered metal which will fuse to form the desired part.

SIPES: Slits in the tire tread to produce more blade surface for traction.

SKID: A tire sliding on the road surface.

SLAVE PISTON: A piston that moves as a result of the movement of a primary piston.

SLINGER: A ring on a shaft that throws oil from the shaft before it gets to the oil seal.

SLIP ANGLE: The angle between the tire heading and the actual direction of movement.

SLIPPER SKIRT: A piston with a lower surface on the thrust surfaces only.

SOFT PLUGS: Expandable plugs used to securely close machined holes in metal parts.

SOLENOID: A remote controlled electrical device that produces mechanical movement.

SPARK IGNITED: The combustion started by an arc across the spark plug electrodes.

SPARK PLUG: An electrical unit with two electrodes and an air gap between them that fits into the head. A spark across the gap ignites the combustion charge.

SPEED: Distance or revolutions in a given period of time.

SPENT GAS: Hot gases remaining in the combustion chamber after combustion.

SPIDER: A name often given to the cross in a universal joint.

SPINDLE: The part of the front suspension that supports the wheel bearings.

SPLINED: Sized grooves on a shaft and in a hole that match to prevent torque slippage.

SPRAG: A special form of over running clutch that has smooth races and cam shaped segments between them.

SPREAD: Wider than normal.

SPRING: An elastic part that recovers its original shape after being distorted and released.

SPRING RATE: The weight required to deform a spring one inch.

SPUR: A pointed projecting part.

SPUR GEAR: The simplest form of toothed wheel with radial teeth parallel to its axis.

SQUIRM: The twist of the tire rubber in the foot print.

SQUISH AREA: An area in the combustion chamber where the piston approaches very close to the head.

STALL: Operating the engine at full throttle on a torque converter equipped car placed in gear while the car is held with the brakes.

STAMPING: A process of forming sheetmetal by forcing it between shaped dies.

STANDING WAVE: A wave in a flexible body that continues to stay when the vibrating frequencies match the wave frequencies.

STAR WHEEL: An adjustable link between a primary and secondary brake shoe.

STATIC: Stationary.

STATOR: A part of a torque converter that stands still as torque is being multiplied, then rotates as the turbine approaches the impeller speed.

STEADY STATE: Constant conditions with no variation.

STEERING: A means to control the direction of a vehicle.

STEERING AXIS INCLINATION: The inward tilt of the front wheel pivot axis.

STITCHING: A method of pressing the green tire parts tightly together before curing.

STOICHIOMETRIC: A chemically balanced air/fuel mixture.

STOVE: A pocket or passage where heat is picked up to send to the choke bi-metal spring.

STROBOSCOPIC LIGHT: A high-intensity, short-duration light that has a controlled flash time.

STROKE: Piston movement in one direction, from one extreme to the other.

STUB FRAME: A short frame on the front of a unitized body that carries the engine, front suspension, and front sheet metal.

SULPHATION: Hardening of the sulfur crystals in the battery plates while the battery has a low state of charge.

SUMP: The lowest part of the oil pan.

SUN GEAR: The central gear in a planetary gear set.

SUPERCHARGER: Device which forces the charge into the combustion chamber with a pressure greater than atmospheric pressure.

SURFACE IGNITION: Ignition caused by some hot spot other than the arc across the sparkplug electrodes.

SURFACE-TO-VOLUME RATIO: The ratio of all of the combustion chamber surfaces to its contained volume. The surface-to-volume ratio reduces as the shape approaches a sphere.

SURGE: Increasing and decreasing engine speed while holding a steady throttle position.

SUSPENSION: The springs, shock absorbers, and linkages that support the vehicle.

SYNCHRONIZER: A device in a standard transmission that gets two parts operating at the same speed before engagement.

SYNCHRONIZER HUB: The part of the synchronizer attached to the shaft.

SYNCHRONIZER SLEEVE: The engaging part of the synchronizer that slides on the outside of the hub.

SYPHON: A means to allow liquid to flow to a lower level over an intermediate elevation.

T

TANDEM: One directly in front of the other and working together.

TANG: A lip on the end of a plain bearing used to align the bearing during assembly.

TAPPET: Transfers the cam position to the push rod. Usually referred to as a lifter.

TAPPET VALLEY: The chamber in the block that contains tappets or lifters.

TDC: Top dead center. The highest a piston can move.

TEX: The same as denier but in the metric system.

THERMAL EFFICIENCY: The equivalent heat energy of the brake horsepower produced divided by the total heat energy in the fuel used.

THERMOSTATIC VALVE: A valve that is controlled by heat.

THERMODYNAMICS: A study of heat transfer in gases.

THROATING: Removing metal from the narrowest part of the valve seat with a high angle stone to raise the seat.

THROW ANGLES: The angle in degrees between crankshaft throws.

THROW-OUT BEARING: The bearing between the clutch fork and the pressure plate release fingers.

THRUST WASHERS: Washers with bearing surfaces that are designed to retain end thrust.

TIMING: An event occurring in relation to the angle of crankshaft rotation.

TOE: (1) The leading edge of a brake shoe. (2) The angle between the center lines of the front tires.

TOPPING: Removing metal from the widest part of the valve seat with a low angle stone to lower the seat.

TORQUE: The twisting force on a shaft in lb-ft.

TORQUE ARM: The length of the turning arm from the center.

TORQUE CAPACITY: The maximum twisting force a clutch or brake can hold before slipping or breaking.

TORQUE CONVERTER: A hydromechanical device that will multiply torque through a fluid.

TORQUE MULTIPLICATION FACTOR: The total torque multiplication of a standard transmission.

TORSIONAL MOTION: Motion around the turning center.

TORSIONAL VIBRATION: Back and forth motion around the turning center.

TRACE: A line appearing on the face of an oscilloscope.

TRAILING SHOE: A brake shoe with the anchor at the toe end.

TRANSISTOR: A semiconductor used as a solid-state electrical switch.

TRANSMISSION: A device to multiply torque and to provide reverse gearing.

TREEING: A build-up of current carrying crystals through the battery separator.

TURBINE: A finned disc that is made to rotate by the force of a high velocity fluid stream.

TURBINE WHEEL: A wheel-shaped turbine.

U

UMBRELLA: An oil deflector placed near the valve tip to throw oil from the valve stem area.

UNDERCUT: A machined groove below the normal surface.

UNITIZED FRAME: A chassis frame built as an integral part of the body.

UNIVERSAL GAS CONSTANT: A gas pressure times its volume divided by its temperature will always equal the same number for a given gas when absolute values are used. This number is its universal gas constant.

UNIVERSAL JOINT: A coupling that allows power to be transferred through an angle.

UNLOADER: A lever device on a carburetor that slightly opens the choke when the throttle is fully opened.

UPSET: Bent over.

V

VACUUM: Less than atmospheric pressure, approaching zero pressure.

VALVE: A device that will open or seal an opening.

VALVE CLEARANCE: Looseness designed into the valve train so the valve will positively seat.

VALVE FLOAT: A valve train that cannot keep up with the cam so excess clearance is temporarily allowed to occur.

VALVE GUIDE: A sized hole in the head to hold the valve in position.

VALVE LIFT: The maximum distance a poppet valve will open.

VALVE LOCK: A device that connects the valve spring retainer to the valve stem.

VALVE OVERLAP: The number of crankshaft degrees the exhaust valve opens before the intake valve closes.

VALVE SEAT: The surface of the head on which the valve rests when the port is closed off.

VALVE SPRING SURGE: A natural vibration in a valve spring that may allow a valve to open at the wrong time.

VAPOR: The gaseous form of a liquid.

VAPOR LOCK: Vapors forming on the inlet side of the fuel pump that stops fuel flow.

VAPOR PRESSURE: Pressure produced by the evaporation of the portion of the fluid.

VARIABLE DISPLACEMENT: A chamber whose effective volume changes as it operates.

VEHICLE: A self-propelled controllable conveyance.

VELOCITY: The distance traveled in a given time.

VENTURI: A smooth flowing restriction in the carburetor that increases air velocity to lower its pressure.

VIBRATION: A very rapid back and forth movement.

VISCOSITY: The thickness or fluid body of a liquid.

VISCOSITY INDEX: A comparison of the change in a fluid's viscosity, as temperature changes, with a standard fluid.

VOLATILITY: The tendency to evaporate.

VOLT: A measurement of electrical pressure.

VOLUMETRIC EFFICIENCY: The actual air consumed by an engine compared to the cubic displacement of the engine.

VULCANIZE: The process of bonding and curing rubber with heat and pressure.

W

WEB: A supporting structure across a cavity.

WELL: A deep chamber.

WHEEL CYLINDER: A device in the brake that converts hydraulic force to mechanical force to apply the brakes.

WHIRL: Rapid rotation of a shaft with slight bend in it.

WILD PING: An occasional knock in an engine caused by deposit ignition. When the deposit is consumed the ping stops.

WINDAGE: Air movement around a spinning object.

WORM GEAR: A gear built with a spiral thread.

WRIST PIN: A piston pin.

Y

YAW: Move or turn sideways.

YOKE: A link connecting two driving points to produce movement at a center connection.

Z

ZENER: A diode that will allow reverse current flow at the designed voltage.

index

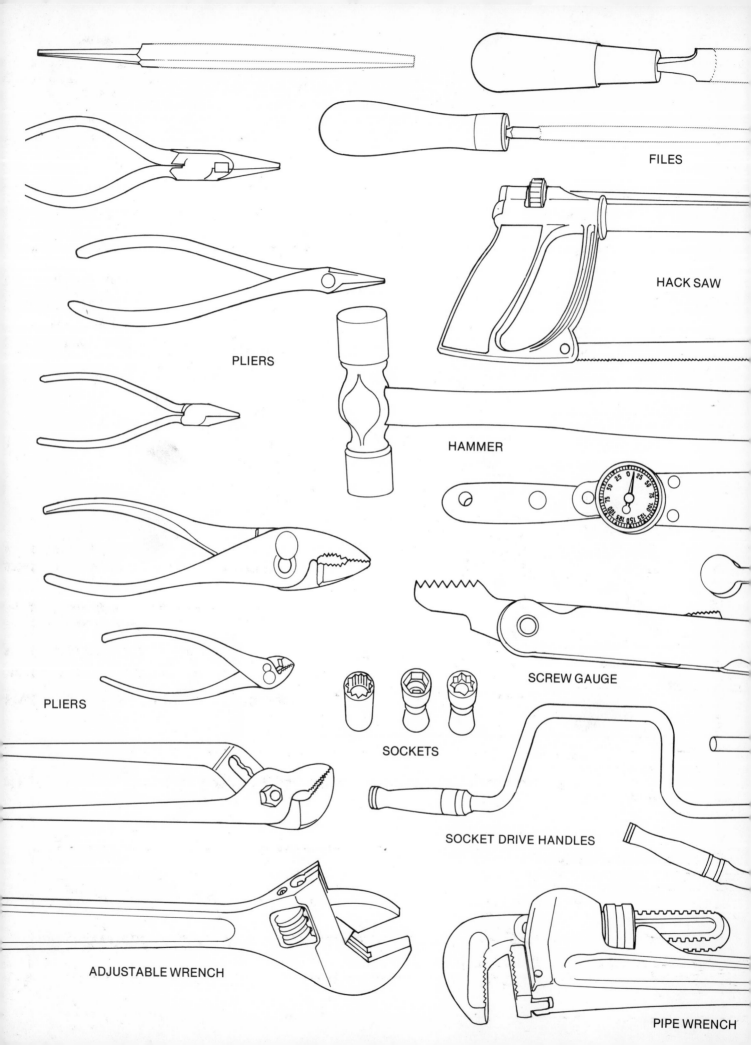

FILES

PLIERS

HACK SAW

HAMMER

PLIERS

SCREW GAUGE

SOCKETS

PLIERS

SOCKET DRIVE HANDLES

ADJUSTABLE WRENCH

PIPE WRENCH